The Editor

Claudia L. Johnson is Professor of English at Princeton University. She is the author of *Jane Austen: Women, Politics, and the Novel; Equivocal Beings: Politics, Gender, and Sentimentality in the 1790s;* and many articles on eighteenth- and nineteenth-century literature. She is editor of the Norton Critical Edition of Jane Austen's *Mansfield Park.*

W. W. NORTON & COMPANY, INC.
Also Publishes

ENGLISH RENAISSANCE DRAMA: A NORTON ANTHOLOGY
edited by David Bevington et al.

THE NORTON ANTHOLOGY OF AFRICAN AMERICAN LITERATURE
edited by Henry Louis Gates Jr. and Nellie Y. McKay et al.

THE NORTON ANTHOLOGY OF AMERICAN LITERATURE
edited by Nina Baym et al.

THE NORTON ANTHOLOGY OF CHILDREN'S LITERATURE
edited by Jack Zipes et al.

THE NORTON ANTHOLOGY OF ENGLISH LITERATURE
edited by M. H. Abrams and Stephen Greenblatt et al.

THE NORTON ANTHOLOGY OF LITERATURE BY WOMEN
edited by Sandra M. Gilbert and Susan Gubar

THE NORTON ANTHOLOGY OF MODERN AND CONTEMPORARY POETRY
edited by Jahan Ramazani, Richard Ellmann, and Robert O'Clair

THE NORTON ANTHOLOGY OF POETRY
edited by Margaret Ferguson, Mary Jo Salter, and Jon Stallworthy

THE NORTON ANTHOLOGY OF SHORT FICTION
edited by R. V. Cassill and Richard Bausch

THE NORTON ANTHOLOGY OF THEORY AND CRITICISM
edited by Vincent B. Leitch et al.

THE NORTON ANTHOLOGY OF WORLD LITERATURE
edited by Sarah Lawall et al.

THE NORTON FACSIMILE OF THE FIRST FOLIO OF SHAKESPEARE
prepared by Charlton Hinman

THE NORTON INTRODUCTION TO LITERATURE
edited by Alison Booth, J. Paul Hunter, and Kelly J. Mays

THE NORTON INTRODUCTION TO THE SHORT NOVEL
edited by Jerome Beaty

THE NORTON READER
edited by Linda H. Peterson and John C. Brereton

THE NORTON SAMPLER
edited by Thomas Cooley

THE NORTON SHAKESPEARE, BASED ON THE OXFORD EDITION
edited by Stephen Greenblatt et al.

For a complete list of Norton Critical Editions, visit
wwnorton.com/college/English/nce_home.htm

A NORTON CRITICAL EDITION

Jane Austen
SENSE AND SENSIBILITY

AUTHORITATIVE TEXT
CONTEXTS
CRITICISM

Edited by

CLAUDIA L. JOHNSON

PRINCETON UNIVERSITY

W • W • NORTON & COMPANY • *New York* • *London*

This title is printed on permanent paper containing 30 percent
post-consumer waste recycled fiber.

Copyright © 2002 by W. W. Norton & Company, Inc.

All rights reserved.
Printed in the United States of America.
First Edition.

The text of this book is composed in Fairfield Medium
with the display set in Bernhard Modern.
Composition by PennSet, Inc.
Manufacturing by the Maple-Vail Book Manufacturing Group.
Book design by Antonina Krass.

Library of Congress Cataloging-in-Publication Data

Austen, Jane, 1775–1817.
    Sense and sensibility : authoritative text, contexts, criticism / Jane Austen ;
    edited by Claudia L. Johnson.
        p. cm.—(Norton critical edition)
    Includes bibliographical references.

    ISBN 0-393-97751-X (pbk.)

    1. Austen, Jane, 1775–1817. Sense and sensibility. 2. Young women—
Fiction. 3. Sisters—Fiction. 4. England—Fiction. I. Johnson, Claudia L.
II. Title.

PR4034.S4 2001b
23'.7—dc21   2001042709

W. W. Norton & Company, Inc., 500 Fifth Avenue, New York, N.Y. 10110
www.wwnorton.com

W. W. Norton & Company Ltd., Castle House, 75/76 Wells Street,
London W1T 3QT

3 4 5 6 7 8 9 0

Contents

Acknowledgments

Sense and Sensibility was the first novel by Jane Austen that I read, and for years it was a secret attachment. Reviewing each word has inspired me to declare openly that I can feel no sentiment of approbation inferior to love.

Many people have helped me to prepare this edition. Gene Ruoff, Susan Wolfson, Jonathan Lamb, and Anne Mellor advised me about background texts, and Jessica Richard's contributions were particularly authoritative and timely. Edward Copeland was enormously helpful not only with suggestions about the *Lady's Magazine* but also with vital information about domestic economy. Simon Eliot kindly shared his expertise on economy and material culture, and Brian Stewart was a splendidly generous resource regarding the picturesque and cover design.

Special thanks go to the Department of Rare Books and Special Collections at Princeton University for letting me examine its copies of the first and second editions of *Sense and Sensibility*. I am incalculably grateful once again to Jan Fergus for her erudition as well as for her kindness in lending me her personal copy of the second edition, on which this text is based.

Norton Critical Editions are teaching texts, and students enrolled in my Spring 2000 graduate class on Austen and Edgeworth—Timothy Aubry, Jasmin Darznik, Marah Gubar, James Moyer, Alexandra Neel, Kimberly Oldenburg, Robin Schore, Natasha Tessone, and Amanda Wilkins—provided me with wonderful advice regarding the kinds of information likely to help diverse students. Julie Park, Paul Kelleher, and Roger Schwartz were exceptionally helpful.

My deepest thanks go to Carol Bemis of W. W. Norton and Company for her patience and assistance, and to Sarah M. Anderson for her uncompromising scholarship and her unstinting encouragement.

Introduction

Sense and Sensibility was Jane Austen's first published novel, and until recently it has been the least appreciated. To the general public, as well as to a good number of literary critics, *Pride and Prejudice* was the model for what a novel by Jane Austen ought to be, and, set against that model, *Sense and Sensibility* came up short. With all the wishfulness and mercy of high comedy, the loss of affluence and status remains for the Bennet women no more than a remote threat, thanks to the improbably fabulous marriages of the eldest daughters. The worthy Dashwood women aren't so lucky, for *Sense and Sensibility* begins with their abrupt fall down the social ladder, and the injustice with which that fall is strongly marked shadows the entire novel. Nor, taking second place to the sister-sister and mother-daughter relationships, is the conventional love plot in *Sense and Sensibility* permitted to be as idealized, much less as freighted with social and ethical significance as it is in *Pride and Prejudice*. No wealthy, handsome, effectual, and (eventually) accomodating equivalent of Darcy here. One of the good guys is painfully shy—well-intentioned to be sure, but idle and rather weak; and if the other, older hero seems more promising as a romantic lead by virtue of being rich, reserved, and brooding, his bouts of rheumatism keep us from getting too carried away. For most of the novel, the men whom the heroines love are offstage, doing the heroines know not what, and when the couples *are* brought together, their repartee is marked not by the combination of wit and passion that proves so thrilling in *Pride and Prejudice*, but by a misunderstandability and at times even a dullness that baffle the heroines themselves. And the double marriage at the end, which customarily augments and multiplies a sense of pleasure, here produces a decidedly underwhelming felicity that is defined solely in negative terms: "among the merits and the happiness of Elinor and Marianne," the narrator writes, "let it not be ranked as the least considerable, that though sisters, and living almost within sight of each other, they could live without disagreement between themselves, or producing coolness between their husbands" (269).

Clearly, *Sense and Sensibility* is a far cry from the "light & bright & sparkling" work that many—wrongly—assume is quintessentially

Austenian.[1] Laboring under this uninspired and uninspiring assumption, critics up to the 1970s tended to produce somewhat schematic readings. Rather like Austen's own niece—who, not in the secret of Austen's authorship, came across the novel at the Alton circulating library and exclaimed, "Oh that must be rubbish I am sure from the title"[2]—generations of critics have based their readings of the novel on a misapprehension of the title, and, as if the titular conjunction were (as Margaret Doody has observed) "versus" rather than "and," have held that the purpose of this novel is to depreciate "sensibility" and recommend "sense," rather than to explore their shared vulnerabilities.[3] More recently, the critical fortunes of the novel have improved. As historicist and feminist criticism suggested new and more complex readings of the novel, and as the appearance in 1995 of Ang Lee's feature-length motion picture of it, based on an excellent screenplay by Emma Thompson, showed the general public how gripping, funny, and unsettling it was, *Sense and Sensibility* has for perhaps the first time ever been accorded the dignity it deserves in Austen's canon.

Begun reportedly as an epistolary novel as early as 1795 under the title "Elinor and Marianne," *Sense and Sensibility* has a complex developmental history about which we shall probably never know as much as we wish.[4] In 1797, it was recast as a third-person narrative, and the dating of several allusions proves that Austen revised again, perhaps at the turn of the century, and certainly between 1805 and 1810. In 1811 it was published at her own expense by Thomas Egerton. Like most new authors, Austen was fondly absorbed in preparing it for publication—"I am never too busy to think of S&S," she wrote her sister, "I can no more forget it, than a mother can forget her sucking child"[5]—and in doing so she was coming of age. *Sense and Sensibility* thus encompasses a large portion of Austen's career, and its roots are in her earliest work. It has several affinities with *Love and Freindship* (1790), for example, one of Austen's most polished juvenile pieces, a raucous and high-spirited satire on sentimental fiction that pokes fun at some of the conventional features of heroic love and sentiment that Marianne

1. This is how Austen's description of *Pride and Prejudice* is often quoted. In fact, Austen's description is somewhat more critical, for in full it reads, "too light & bright & sparkling." See *Jane Austen's Letters*, ed. Deirdre Le Faye (Oxford: Oxford UP, 1995), February 4, 1813, p. 203. Subsequent references to Le Faye's edition of the *Letters* will include the dates alone.
2. This story is recounted in William Austen-Leigh and Richard Arthur Austen-Leigh, *Jane Austen: A Family Record*, revised and enlarged by Deirdre Le Faye (London: British Library, 1989), p. 171.
3. See Margaret A. Doody's splendid Introduction to *Sense and Sensibility* (Oxford: Oxford World Classics, 1990), especially pp. xiii-xx and xxxiii–xxxviii.
4. For a detailed discussion of the probable composition of *Sense and Sensibility*, see B. C. Southam, *Jane Austen's Literary MSS* (Oxford: Clarendon, 1964), pp. 55–57.
5. Letter to Cassandra, April 25, 1811.

Dashwood cherishes, such as love at first sight, love-madness, and a somewhat shortsighted (if not hollow) contempt for worldly riches. In the novel's several discussions of money, and even more forcibly in places like volume I, chapter 9—where Marianne's high-falutin faith in the joys of nature is followed fast by a driving rain set full in her face—we can discern the youthful Austen's penchant for undercutting her heroine's adherence to the heroic codes of sensibility.

But while *Sense and Sensibility* is indeed a youthful work, it is not a juvenile one, and to read it as a mockery of sentiment a la *Love and Friendship* would be to misread both works. What *Sense and Sensibility* shares with the very early work is the irreverence, the exuberance, and at times even the delicious blatancy of its satire—delicacy, nuance, and irony, after all, are the qualities readers are more likely to associate with Austen than vigor and excess, and some of the revisions Austen introduced in the second edition suggest an attempt to rein in these qualities. The mordant description of the poverty of the Middletons' domestic life—"Sir John was a sportsman, Lady Middleton a mother. He hunted and shot, and she humoured her children; and these were their only resources" (26)—is clearly akin to the devastating elan of Austen's earlier understatement, "Our neighborhood was small, for it consisted only of your mother."[6] The differences are equally striking, however. As Austen grew up and turned from parody—which exposes the valences of literary forms—to social criticism—which exposes the interests of social forms—the stakes get higher, and the zany shades into the sardonic. We can afford first to enjoy and then to forget Austen's description of Miss Simpson—who "was pleasing in her person, in her manners, and in her disposition; an unbounded ambition was her only fault"[7]—because her ruthlessness is frankly unreal. But the comparable trenchancy of her characterization of John Dashwood—"He was not an ill-disposed young man, unless to be rather cold-hearted, and rather selfish, is to be ill-disposed" (7)—is more unnerving because we're not in the world of parody any longer, but in a far more referential work where John Dashwood does harm.

Set against the artistry Austen achieved when she was hitting her stride—say in *Emma*, where the narrative voice is almost completely effaced—*Sense and Sensibility* seems to give us exceptionally generous access to authorial voice. In the narrator's remarks on ill-behaved children and the fatuity of their indulgent parents, for ex-

---

6. *Love and Freindship*, Letter 4th in *Catharine and Other Writings*, ed. Margaret A. Doody (Oxford: Oxford World Classics, 1993), p. 77.
7. "Jack and Alice," in *Catharine and Other Writings*, p. 11.

ample, we have the impression that Austen is inviting us into her own mind, and that hers is a mind impatient with the vapid and the vulgar, as opinionated and as superior to the commonplace as Marianne's (though more bemused than pained by it, perhaps), a mind that looks upon the worldlings around her in much the same way as Elinor looks upon Robert Ferrars's "sterling insignificance" (156). When we read that the bland and excruciatingly proper Lady Middleton does not like Elinor and Marianne Dashwood because they "were fond of reading"—and on these grounds, "she fancied them satirical: perhaps without exactly knowing what it was to be satirical; but that did not signify. It was censure in common use, and easily given" (174)—we can be forgiven for wondering whether at least some of her family and acquaintance felt the same way about Austen herself. Perhaps implicated in the same process of social climbing as Lady Middleton, Austen's earliest biographers— her brother, and then her nephew—were eager to assure the public that Austen was uniformly sweet and denied the obvious fact that her work is patently, though not exclusively, "satirical." The same qualities of intelligence, penetration, and judgment and the same capacities for sarcasm and ridicule that endear the Dashwood sisters to us are evident in the narrator of *Sense and Sensibility* as well.

The satire that drives *Sense and Sensibility* emerges from the so-cial criticism of the 1790s, when the novel was first drafted and revised. Like characters in the political fiction of the time, char-acters here are conscious of how ideology—an only apparently nat-ural system of priorities, practices, and attitudes—conditions not only our social behavior, but also our means and methods of ac-quiring knowledge (or what we take for knowledge) about each other, and the novel exposes how dominant ideology privileges— that is, gives more authority, standing, money, status to—the greedy, mean-spirited, and pedestrian. Whereas didactic, conser-vative novels in the 1790s teach young women the social codes they must adopt if they are to live as good Christians and as good wives and daughters, integrated into their communities, this novel makes those codes and those communities the subject of its interrogation. What kinds of public status and what sorts of behavior give a man or woman credibility? What is important to know, what kinds of "evidence" do we consult when we form judgments about people? Do we consider their tastes, their status in the neighborhood, the source of their income, the extent of their property, their words, their conduct, their hunting dogs?

The question is not academic, for the world as Elinor and Mar-ianne encounter it is more opaque than either of them has any reason to suspect, and collective judgments are as fallible as private ones, for Edward and Willoughby both, as it turns out, have secrets. Like the terms "pride" and "prejudice," the titular abstractions of "sense" and "sensibility" can start a conversation about the novel, but not finish one, for the novel highlights not an opposition between reason and feeling (or between the inevitable binaries of public and private, disciplined and undisciplined, good and bad that have all too predictably followed from them). Rather the novel is organized around epistemological problems—problems of knowing and assenting—that baffle Elinor and Marianne equally. The characters sometimes formulate this problem explicitly. When Elinor argues with her mother about Willoughby's sudden departure and the possible ill it forebodes for Marianne, Mrs. Dashwood, asks indignantly, "Are no probabilities to be accepted, merely because they are not certainties?" (59). Terms like "doubt," "belief," "conjecture," "certainty," and "probability" recur on every page, and characters are always making the wrong inferences. Accepting probabilities as certainties can be a dangerous business, and what is at stake finally is not propriety, but something more like survival.

Marianne believes the world and people in it are transparent, and if Willoughby encourages her belief in him, that very belief almost makes him believe in himself as well. And these beliefs are shared: all onlookers know or think they know the honor of his intentions, and count on that knowledge as certain. By contrast, Elinor hesitates to equate hope and knowledge; she wants formal proof—and not surprisingly so, in a novel that opens with a solemn but private, oral promise that a man who passes for respectable in the world never keeps—and her skepticism is derived not from an allegiance to doctrines of propriety, but from a need to protect herself from wishing, dreaming about, and finally depending upon what may never be. But one of the deepest ironies of the novel is that, with the prominent exception of her doctrine about second attachments, most of Marianne's convictions—after seeming silly, credulous, naive—are vindicated. She has been right to think that Edward behaves inappropriately for a suitor, right to believe that Willoughby really loves her, and right to infer that he did not write that cruel letter. And, on her side, Elinor's skepticism has not saved her from erroneous conjectures, nor has her self-control preserved her from heartbreaking dependency. *Sense and Sensibility* is the only novel Austen wrote in which the heroine almost dies. In a world driven by wealth and status, where even gentlemen of wealth and status do not consider themselves independent or free, where people often do not honor their trusts, what almost kills Marianne is the intensity—even the obsessiveness—of her desire for, belief in, and dependency on Willoughby, a sort of raw and helpless need that the cagier, almost hypercautious Elinor resists.

This is a dark and disenchanted novel that exposes how those sacred and supposedly benevolizing institutions of order—property, marriage, and family—can enforce avarice, selfishness, and mediocrity. If it is sometimes scathing in its exposure of calculation and triteness, it is sometimes wonderfully tolerant as well, as a character like Mrs. Jennings (first dismissed as vulgar by Marianne and by Elinor as well) ultimately surprises us by a warmth and genuineness which, like so much else in the novel, we could not have predicted. Once the force of *Sense and Sensibility* is acknowledged, Austen's canon looks entirely different. The sobriety of *Mansfield Park* no longer seems odd. The venturesomeness of *Persuasion*, with its disdain of prudence and its impatience with the world of status-seeking and manor houses, will look more like a continuation rather than a reversal. And Austen's most popular novel, *Pride and Prejudice*, will seem exceptional among the novels in the harmony and felicity it accomplishes. *Sense and Sensibility* promises no such concord. It is only by recourse to incalculable acts of chance that Austen gets her heroines happily married at last, and that happiness is marked by a refusal of moral compromises. Marianne changes her opinions about second attachments, but she is never obliged to surrender to the "commonplace," and in permitting her to inhabit a world where her sensitivity will be protected rather than harmed, *Sense and Sensibility* grants her the highest happiness it can imagine.

Because *Sense and Sensibility* is so richly implicated in the literature of the late eighteenth and early nineteenth centuries, the opportunity to select backgrounds is rewarding as well as risky, and the very wealth of secondary material can overwhelm the novel itself. In selecting the background texts, I have attempted to broaden as well as to complicate the inevitable subject of sensibility, and to contextualize issues such as sense, judgment, self-control, family, inheritance, second attachments, and characterization. Space restrictions prevented the inclusion of excerpts from Austen's *Love and Friendship*, Jane West's *A Gossip's Story*, Mary Brunton's *Self-Control*, to say nothing of works by William Gilpin. It is hoped that the extensive selection of critical essays can compensate for these lacunae. *Sense and Sensibility* has been well-served by recent criticism, which has uncovered social and political contexts, re-examined Austen's relations to her publishers and to her own writing, and de-centered the titular terms in favor of issues such as plotting, desire, and inwardness. In order to include as many selections as possible, I have kept the critical essays fairly brief. The footnotes to these essays have been edited and renumbered where necessary. A bibliography is provided at the end of this volume to point interested readers toward material that regrettably could not be included here and to supplement the sometimes abbreviated bibliographical material mentioned in the critical essays.

The Text of *Sense and Sensibility*

Jane Austen's autograph manuscript of *Sense and Sensibility* is not extant. The first edition of *Sense and Sensibility* (hereafter called *A*) was published in November 1811 by Thomas Egerton at Austen's expense. After it sold out, a second edition (hereafter called *B*) was printed in November 1813, at Egerton's suggestion. *B* corrects as well as revises *A*, and because it incorporates Austen's latest revisions, it has been the basis of virtually all editions of *Sense and Sensibility*. It is adopted here as well.[8] Nevertheless, *B* introduces errors of its own, and while there is nothing uncommon in this, these errors, along with those *A* and *B* share, have prompted the speculation that *B* was printed from a copy of *A* that Austen corrected by hand and was not corrected by her later in page proof as well.[9] In a letter dated April 25, 1811, Austen does mention correcting proofs of *A*; and though she announces the plan to print a second edition in a letter of September 25, 1813, she does not mention correcting proofs for it.[1] Clearly, *A* is the text to consult where *B* errs.

With only two versions to collate, establishing the text of *Sense and Sensibility* is straightforward. Still, *Sense and Sensibility* shares with *Mansfield Park* the distinction of being one of the two novels Austen revised for a second edition, and because Austen is a writer whom scholars and students read very closely, it is worth describing the differences between *A* and *B* in some detail. While the vast majority of the differences between *A* and *B* consist of variations and errors that Austen described in another context quaintly and dismissively as "Typical,"[2] some are substantive. *Sense and Sensibility* was Austen's first published novel, after all, and Austen's satisfaction was probably the keener given her previous lack of success in publishing early versions of *Northanger Abbey* and *Pride and Prej-*

8. One exception is the Penguin edition of *Sense and Sensibility*, edited by Ros Ballaster with the textual advice of Claire Lamont, published in 1995, which is based on *A*. Although it is certainly intriguing and valuable to be able to see Austen's earlier version in full, it is hard to imagine a text critical reason for preferring *A* over *B* given the significant revisions Austen made in the second edition.
9. See for example James Kinsley's "Note on the Text" in the Oxford World Classics edition of *Sense and Sensibility*, first published in 1980, p. xlvii.
1. For a complete discussion of the circumstances surrounding the publication of the first and second editions of *Sense and Sensibility*, see Jan Fergus's *Jane Austen: A Literary Life* (New York: St. Martin's Press, 1991), pp. 129–36, 141, excerpted below on p. 325.
2. January 29, 1813.

udice. Tracking Austen's revisions can help us think about how she may have read and responded to seeing her work in print for the first time.

The changes of most interest to literature students are those that can be attributed to Austen herself. Austen revised *A* in several contained but significant respects. In two separate places—both occurring in the first volume—she cuts whole sentences and in the process mollifies the pointedness of her satire, a quality that typifies her early work. Further, whereas most of the substantive changes to *Mansfield Park* are confined to one chapter in the third volume, in each of the three volumes of *Sense and Sensibility*, she makes a number of smaller revisions, mostly in the form of one-word changes or deletions here and there in the interests of precision, emphasis, and control (e.g., replacing *division of* with *charge on*, *scarcely* with *certainly not*, *Mr. Edward Ferrars* with *Mr. Ferrars*). At the very outset of the sixth chapter of volume III, she goes so far as to tidy an entire clause. R. W. Chapman has asserted that the "changes" to *Sense and Sensibility* "made by the author" are "less interesting" than the changes she made to *Mansfield Park*,[3] but I cannot agree. In the later novel, Austen's revisions concentrate mostly on the accuracy of nautical and marine terminology. By contrast, the revisions to *Sense and Sensibility* afford us a glimpse of more general aspects of Austen's compositional process, and cumulatively they suggest how and where she considered exactitude, modulation, and the control of suspense important. In all instances where authorial revision is at stake, the present text will print *B* and note the readings from *A*.

Sometimes the differences between *A* and *B* are equivocal, however, consisting either of minor authorial alterations or of printer's interventions that produce intelligible readings (e.g., replacing *affections* with *affection*; *suspicion of its nature* with *suspicion*; *their* with *her*; *round to her* with *round her*). Such differences must be eyed carefully. Where cases in *B* can almost certainly be attributed to the inadvertent errors introduced when the text was set, *A* will be preferred; in cases where Austen may be fine-tuning her prose, particularly with respect to maintaining parallel structure, *B* will stand. Equivocal variants of these kinds will be noted.

A further class of equivocal differences consists of the addition or deletion of particles (e.g., *to persuade* for *persuade*), conjunctions introducing relative clauses (e.g., *told him* for *told him that*), articles (e.g., *time of the year* for *time of year*), and prepositions (e.g., *give* for *give to*). In all probability, printers are responsible for such

---

3. "Introductory Note to *Sense and Sensibility*" in *The Novels of Jane Austen*, 3rd ed. (London: Oxford UP, 1933) I: xiv.

changes, in *A* and *B* alike, but because authorial revision cannot be ruled out, *B* will be followed and the reading from *A* will be noted. Most of the minor differences between *A* and *B* are corrections of outright printing errors in *A*. *B* corrects *A*'s numerous slips regarding plural possessives, misplaced or missing quotation marks, failures to indent for dialogue, as well as its occasionally wrong pronouns and omitted words or letters. In all such instances where *B* is clearly correcting *A*, *B* will be followed without note. As stated above, in the process of resetting the text, *B* introduces errors of its own, such as misspellings (e.g., *sooth* for *soothe*, *Davis* for *Davies*), wrong pronouns (e.g., *he* for *her*, *her* for *their*), dropped letters and spaces (e.g., *ever* for *every*, *unpremidated* for *unpremeditated*, *Thset* for *This set*), missed or misplaced quotation marks or apostrophes for plural possessives, and failures to indent for dialogue. I will adopt *A* silently to correct clear errors in *B*.

In several places, errors in *A* have been carried over into *B*, unnoticed and uncorrected by Austen as well as by the printers of *B*. Where *A* and *B* agree in blatant error—regarding, for example, the misnumbering of volume I, chapter 22, or the mishandling of quotation marks and indentations—I correct silently. In the single instance where the correction of both *A* and *B* involves inserting a word, I supply a note.

It is worth noting that *A* and *B* differ on matters of spelling and punctuation. Like most novelists of the time, Austen left such matters to the printers, as printers' manuals advised, on the grounds that printers have by "constant practice" acquired "a uniform mode of punctuation."[4] Since this edition is for students of novels, rather than for students of early-nineteenth-century printing, I will not note punctuation differences between *A* and *B* unless they impinge on sense. Most of these differences consist of variations in the use of a dash after an endstop (e.g., .— or ;—); in the treatment of commas, semicolons, and colons; and in the printing of compound words (e.g., *good breeding/good-breeding, piano forté/piano-forté/pianoforté, every body/everybody*). Nor will I note or regularize spelling variants between and within volumes of *A* and *B* (e.g., *stile/style, inquiry/enquiry, entreat/intreat*), or differences regarding capitalization (e.g., *Gentleman/gentleman, Park/park*). Finally, in resetting the text for the Norton Critical Edition, I have retained the hyphens in compound words that fall at linebreaks in *B* in cases where such words are usually hyphenated elsewhere in *B* (e.g., *head-ache; house-keeping*). Although it is safe to say that *B* hyphenates com-

---

4. C. Stower, *The Printer's Grammar; or, Introduction to the Art of Printing* (London, 1808), p. 80. Stower's claim notwithstanding, pointing and spelling are less than uniform even within volumes set by the same printer.

pound words somewhat more heavily than A, the practice of type-setters in both texts does not appear to be systematic or consistent. But because eliminating hyphens at linebreaks would introduce an entire class of emendations that would be invisible to readers, I have elected not to do so.

Until quite recently, the undisputed authority on the texts of Austen's novels was R. W. Chapman, whose *The Novels of Jane Austen* first appeared in 1923, revised slightly by Mary Lascelles in subsequent editions. Chapman's edition was the first full-scale scholarly edition not only of Austen's novels, but of any set of novels in English, and it deserves its status as a landmark. But although Chapman's editorial principles are sound, and his judgments always worth consideration, some of his editorial decisions seem questionable. It is hoped that the editorial style of the present edition is more conservative and less prone to overcorrection.

The Text of
SENSE AND SENSIBILITY

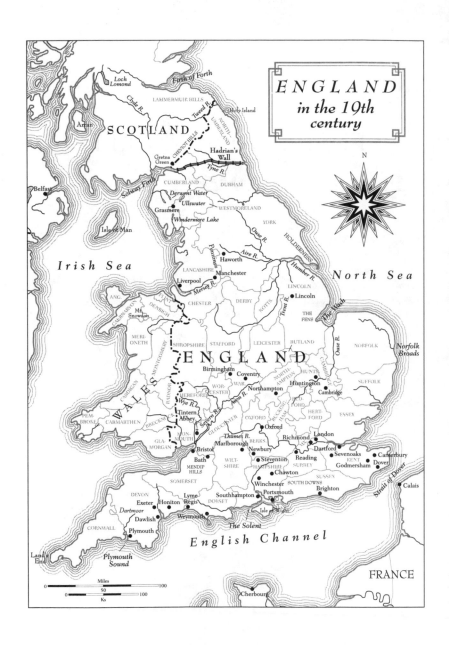

ENGLAND
in the 19th
century

SENSE

AND

SENSIBILITY:

A NOVEL.

IN THREE VOLUMES.

BY THE

AUTHOR OF "PRIDE AND PREJUDICE."

THE SECOND EDITION.

VOL. I.

London:

PRINTED FOR THE AUTHOR,

By C. Roworth, Bell-yard, Temple-bar,

AND PUBLISHED BY T. EGERTON, WHITEHALL.

1813.

By kind permission of Jan Fergus. The first edition of *Sense and Sensibility*, published in 1811, was said to be "By a Lady." This was the only time Austen was so described on a title page.

Volume I

Chapter I.

The family of Dashwood had been long settled in Sussex. Their estate was large, and their residence was at Norland Park, in the centre of their property, where, for many generations, they had lived in so respectable a manner, as to engage the general good opinion of their surrounding acquaintance. The late owner* of this estate was a single man, who lived to a very advanced age, and who for many years of his life, had a constant companion and housekeeper in his sister. But her death, which happened ten years before his own, produced a great alteration in his home; for to supply her loss, he invited and received into his house the family of his nephew Mr. Henry Dashwood, the legal inheritor of the Norland estate, and the person to whom he intended to bequeath it. In the society of his nephew and niece, and their children, the old Gentleman's days were comfortably spent. His attachment to them all increased. The constant attention of Mr. and Mrs. Henry Dashwood to his wishes, which proceeded not merely from interest, but from goodness of heart, gave him every degree of solid comfort which his age could receive, and the cheerfulness of the children added a relish to his existence.

By a former marriage, Mr. Henry Dashwood had one son: by his present lady, three daughters. The son, a steady respectable young man, was amply provided for by the fortune of his mother, which had been large, and half of which devolved on him on his coming of age. By his own marriage, likewise, which happened soon afterwards, he added to his wealth.** To him therefore the succession[1] to the Norland estate was not so really important as to his sisters; for their fortune, independent of what might arise to them from

---

* late owner] last owner but one A. *Austen's revision makes it clearer that the novel opens when Mr. Henry Dashwood, the father of the heroines, is still alive.*
** wealth.] *Here* A *continues*: His wife had something considerable at present, and something still more to expect hereafter from her mother, her only surviving parent, who had much to give. *It is likely that Austen revised because she thought the economic claims and needs of the Dashwood daughters were clear enough.*
1. That is, his acquisition of the Norland estate through patrilineal descent, as was customary.

their father's inheriting that property, could be but small. Their mother had nothing, and their father only seven thousand pounds in his own disposal; for the remaining moiety of his first wife's fortune was also secured to her child, and he had only a life interest[2] in it.

The old Gentleman died; his will was read, and like almost every other will, gave as much disappointment as pleasure. He was neither so unjust, nor so ungrateful, as to leave his estate from his nephew;—but he left it to him on such terms as destroyed half the value of the bequest. Mr. Dashwood had wished for it more for the sake of his wife and daughters than for himself or his son:—but to his son, and his son's son, a child of four years old, it was secured, in such a way, as to leave to himself no power of providing for those who were most dear to him, and who most needed a provision, by any charge on* the estate, or by any sale of its valuable woods. The whole was tied up for the benefit of this child, who, in occasional visits with his father and mother at Norland, had so far gained on the affections of his uncle, by such attractions as are by no means unusual in children of two or three years old; an imperfect articulation, an earnest desire of having his own way, many cunning tricks, and a great deal of noise, as to outweigh all the value of all the attention which, for years, he had received from his niece and her daughters. He meant not to be unkind however, and, as a mark of his affection** for the three girls, he left them a thousand pounds a-piece.

Mr. Dashwood's disappointment was, at first, severe; but his temper was cheerful and sanguine, and he might reasonably hope to live many years, and by living economically, lay by a considerable sum from the produce of an estate already large, and capable of almost immediate improvement. But the fortune, which had been so tardy in coming, was his only one twelvemonth. He survived his uncle no longer; and ten thousand pounds, including the late legacies, was all that remained for his widow and daughters.

His son was sent for, as soon as his danger was known, and to him Mr. Dashwood recommended, with all the strength and ur-

---

2. A claim to the property during his lifetime only. Mr. Henry Dashwood has a right to Norland and the income it can generate until his own death, after which time it becomes the property of his son, Mr. John Dashwood. *Sense and Sensibility* carefully represents different notions of *interest*.

* charge on] division of A. *In A, Mr. Henry Dashwood wants to provide for his daughters by giving part of his estate to them and is prevented from doing so by the terms of the Old Gentleman's will. R. W. Chapman suggests that Austen emended to* charge *(a payment from the estate) because her brother advised her that no sensible man would consider dividing the estate to begin with.*

** affection] affections A.

gency which illness could command, the interest of his mother-in-law[3] and sisters.

Mr. John Dashwood had not the strong feelings of the rest of the family; but he was affected by a recommendation of such a nature at such a time, and he promised to do every thing in his power to make them comfortable. His father was rendered easy by such an assurance, and Mr. John Dashwood had then leisure to consider how much there might prudently be in his power to do for them.

He was not an ill-disposed young man, unless to be rather cold hearted, and rather selfish, is to be ill-disposed: but he was, in general, well respected; for he conducted himself with propriety in the discharge of his ordinary duties. Had he married a more amiable woman, he might have been made still more respectable than he was:—he might even have been made amiable himself; for he was very young when he married, and very fond of his wife. But Mrs. John Dashwood was a strong caricature of himself;—more narrow-minded and selfish.

When he gave his promise to his father, he meditated within himself to increase the fortunes of his sisters by the present of a thousand pounds a-piece. He then really thought himself equal to it. The prospect of four thousand a-year, in addition to his present income, besides the remaining half of his own mother's fortune, warmed his heart and made him feel capable of generosity.—"Yes, he would give them three thousand pounds: it would be liberal and handsome! It would be enough to make them completely easy. Three thousand pounds! he could spare so considerable a sum with little inconvenience."—He thought of it all day long, and for many days successively, and he did not repent.

No sooner was his father's funeral over, than Mrs. John Dashwood, without sending any notice of her intention to her mother-in-law, arrived with her child and their attendants. No one could dispute her right to come; the house was her husband's from the moment of his father's decease; but the indelicacy of her conduct was so much the greater, and to a woman in Mrs. Dashwood's situation, with only common feelings, must have been highly unpleasing;—but in *her* mind there was a sense of honour so keen, a generosity so romantic,[4] that any offence of the kind, by whomsoever given or received, was to her a source of immoveable disgust. Mrs. John Dashwood had never been a favourite with any of her husband's family; but she had had no opportunity, till the present,

---

3. Here, stepmother.
4. Appealing to the imagination and feeling, and of an idealistic and fervent character. Used pejoratively, *romantic* suggests extravagant and impractical ideals.

of shewing them with how little attention to the comfort of other people she could act when occasion required it.

So acutely did Mrs. Dashwood feel this ungracious behaviour, and so earnestly did she despise her daughter-in-law for it, that, on the arrival of the latter, she would have quitted the house for ever, had not the entreaty of her eldest girl induced her first to reflect on the propriety of going, and her own tender love for all her three children determined her afterwards to stay, and for their sakes avoid a breach with their brother.

Elinor, this eldest daughter whose advice was so effectual, possessed a strength of understanding, and coolness of judgment, which qualified her, though only nineteen, to be the counsellor of her mother, and enabled her frequently to counteract, to the advantage of them all, that eagerness of mind in Mrs. Dashwood which must generally have led to imprudence. She had an excellent heart;—her disposition was affectionate, and her feelings were strong; but she knew how to govern them: it was a knowledge which her mother had yet to learn, and which one of her sisters had resolved never to be taught.

Marianne's abilities were, in many respects, quite equal to Elinor's. She was sensible and clever; but eager in every thing; her sorrows, her joys, could have no moderation. She was generous, amiable, interesting: she was every thing but prudent. The resemblance between her and her mother was strikingly great.

Elinor saw, with concern, the excess of her sister's sensibility; but by Mrs. Dashwood it was valued and cherished. They encouraged each other now in the violence of their affliction. The agony of grief which overpowered them at first, was voluntarily renewed, was sought for, was created again and again. They gave themselves up wholly to their sorrow, seeking increase of wretchedness in every reflection that could afford it, and resolved against ever admitting consolation in future. Elinor, too, was deeply afflicted; but still she could struggle, she could exert herself. She could consult with her brother, could receive her sister-in-law on her arrival, and treat her with proper* attention; and could strive to rouse her mother to similar exertion, and encourage her to similar forbearance.

Margaret, the other sister, was a good-humoured well-disposed girl; but as she had already imbibed a good deal of Marianne's romance, without having much of her sense, she did not, at thirteen, bid fair to equal her sisters at a more advanced period of life.

---

* with proper] with every proper A.

Chapter II.

Mrs. John Dashwood now installed herself mistress of Norland; and her mother and sisters-in-law were degraded to the condition of visitors. As such, however, they were treated by her with quiet civility; and by her husband with as much kindness as he could feel towards any body beyond himself, his wife, and their child. He really pressed them, with some earnestness, to consider Norland as their home; and, as no plan appeared so eligible to Mrs. Dashwood as remaining there till she could accommodate herself with a house in the neighbourhood, his invitation was accepted.

A continuance in a place where every thing reminded her of former delight, was exactly what suited her mind. In seasons of cheerfulness, no temper could be more cheerful than hers, or possess, in a greater degree, that sanguine expectation of happiness which is happiness itself. But in sorrow she must be equally carried away by her fancy, and as far beyond consolation as in pleasure she was beyond alloy.

Mrs. John Dashwood did not at all approve of what her husband intended to do for his sisters. To take three thousand pounds from the fortune of their dear little boy, would be impoverishing him to the most dreadful degree. She begged him to think again on the subject. How could he answer it to himself to rob his child, and his only child too, of so large a sum? And what possible claim could the Miss Dashwoods, who were related to him only by half blood, which she considered as no relationship at all, have on his generosity to so large an amount. It was very well known that no affection was ever supposed to exist between the children of any man by different marriages; and why was he to ruin himself, and their poor little Harry, by giving away all his money to his half sisters?

"It was my father's last request to me," replied her husband, "that I should assist his widow and daughters."

"He did not know what he was talking of, I dare say; ten to one but he was light-headed at the time. Had he been in his right senses, he could not have thought of such a thing as begging you to give away half your fortune from your own child."

"He did not stipulate for any particular sum, my dear Fanny; he only requested me, in general terms, to assist them, and make their situation more comfortable than it was in his power to do. Perhaps it would have been as well if he had left it wholly to myself. He could hardly suppose I should neglect them. But as he required the promise, I could not do less than give it: at least I thought so at the time. The promise, therefore, was given, and must be performed. Something must be done for them whenever they leave Norland and settle in a new home."

"Well, then, *let* something be done for them; but *that* something need not be three thousand pounds. Consider," she added, "that when the money is once parted with, it never can return. Your sisters will marry, and it will be gone for ever. If, indeed, it could ever be restored to our poor little boy—"

"Why, to be sure," said her husband, very gravely, "that would make a great difference. The time may come when Harry will regret that so large a sum was parted with. If he should have a numerous family, for instance, it would be a very convenient addition."

"To be sure it would."

"Perhaps, then, it would be better for all parties if the sum were diminished one half.—Five hundred pounds would be a prodigious increase to their fortunes!"

"Oh! beyond any thing great! What brother on earth would do half so much for his sisters, even if *really* his sisters! And as it is— only half blood!—But you have such a generous spirit!"

"I would not wish to do any thing mean," he replied. "One had rather, on such occasions, do too much than too little. No one, at least, can think I have not done enough for them: even themselves, they can hardly expect more."

"There is no knowing what *they* may expect," said the lady, "but we are not to think of their expectations: the question is, what you can afford to do."

"Certainly—and I think I may afford to give them five hundred pounds a-piece. As it is, without any addition of mine, they will each have above three thousand pounds on their mother's death— a very comfortable fortune for any young woman."

"To be sure it is: and, indeed, it strikes me that they can want no addition at all. They will have ten thousand pounds divided amongst them. If they marry, they will be sure of doing well, and if they do not, they may all live very comfortably together on the interest of ten thousand pounds."

"That is very true, and, therefore, I do not know whether, upon the whole, it would not be more advisable to do something for their mother while she lives rather than for them—something of the an-nuity kind I mean.—My sisters would feel the good effects of it as well as herself. A hundred a year would make them all perfectly comfortable."

His wife hesitated a little, however, in giving her consent to this plan.

"To be sure," said she, "it is better than parting with fifteen hun-dred pounds at once. But then if Mrs. Dashwood should live fifteen years, we shall be completely taken in."

"Fifteen years! my dear Fanny;* her life cannot be worth half that purchase."

"Certainly not; but if you observe, people always live for ever when there is any annuity to be paid them; and she is very stout and healthy, and hardly forty. An annuity is a very serious business; it comes over and over every year, and there is no getting rid of it. You are not aware of what you are doing. I have known a great deal of the trouble of annuities; for my mother was clogged with the payment of three to old superannuated servants by my father's will, and it is amazing how disagreeable she found it. Twice every year these annuities were to be paid; and then there was the trouble of getting it to them; and then one of them was said to have died, and afterwards it turned out to be no such thing. My mother was quite sick of it. Her income was not her own, she said, with such perpetual claims on it; and it was the more unkind in my father, because, otherwise, the money would have been entirely at my mother's disposal, without any restriction whatever. It has given me such an abhorrence of annuities, that I am sure I would not pin myself down to the payment of one for all the world."

"It is certainly an unpleasant thing," replied Mr. Dashwood, "to have those kind of yearly drains on one's income. One's fortune, as your mother justly says, is *not* one's own. To be tied down to the regular payment of such a sum, on every rent day, is by no means desirable: it takes away one's independence."

"Undoubtedly; and after all you have no thanks for it. They think themselves secure, you do no more than what is expected, and it raises no gratitude at all. If I were you, whatever I did should be done at my own discretion entirely. I would not bind myself to allow them any thing yearly. It may be very inconvenient some years to spare a hundred, or even fifty pounds from our own expences."

"I believe you are right, my love; it will be better that there should be no annuity in the case; whatever I may give them occasionally will be of far greater assistance than a yearly allowance, because they would only enlarge their style of living if they felt sure of a larger income, and would not be sixpence the richer for it at the end of the year. It will certainly be much the best way. A present of fifty pounds, now and then, will prevent their ever being distressed for money, and will, I think, be amply discharging my promise to my father."

"To be sure it will. Indeed, to say the truth, I am convinced within myself that your father had no idea of your giving them any money at all. The assistance he thought of, I dare say, was only such as

---

* my dear Fanny;] My dear Fanny, A.

might be reasonably expected of you; for instance, such as looking out for a comfortable small house for them, helping them to move their things, and sending them presents of fish and game, and so forth, whenever they are in season. I'll lay my life that he meant nothing farther; indeed, it would be very strange and unreasonable if he did. Do but consider, my dear Mr. Dashwood, how excessively comfortable your mother-in-law and her daughters may live on the interest of seven thousand pounds, besides the thousand pounds belonging to each of the girls, which brings them in fifty pounds a-year a-piece, and, of course, they will pay their mother for their board out of it. Altogether, they will have five hundred a-year amongst them, and what on earth can four women want for more than that?—They will live so cheap! Their house-keeping will be nothing at all. They will have no carriage, no horses, and hardly any servants; they will keep no company, and can have no expences of any kind! Only conceive how comfortable they will be! Five hundred a-year! I am sure I cannot imagine how they will spend half of it; and as to your giving them more, it is quite absurd to think of it. They will be much more able to give *you* something."

"Upon my word," said Mr. Dashwood, "I believe you are perfectly right. My father certainly could mean nothing more by his request to me than what you say. I clearly understand it now, and I will strictly fulfil my engagement by such acts of assistance and kindness to them as you have described. When my mother removes into another house my services shall be readily given to accommodate her as far as I can. Some little present of furniture too may be acceptable then."

"Certainly," returned Mrs. John Dashwood. "But, however, *one* thing must be considered. When your father and mother moved to Norland, though the furniture of Stanhill was sold, all the china, plate, and linen was saved, and is now left to your mother. Her house will therefore be almost completely fitted up as soon as she takes it."

"That is a material consideration undoubtedly. A valuable legacy indeed! And yet some of the plate would have been a very pleasant addition to our own stock here."

"Yes; and the set of breakfast china is twice as handsome as what belongs to this house. A great deal too handsome, in my opinion, for any place *they* can ever afford to live in. But, however, so it is. Your father thought only of *them*. And I must say this: that you owe no particular gratitude to him, nor attention to his wishes, for we very well know that if he could, he would have left almost every thing in the world to *them*."

This argument was irresistible. It gave to his intentions whatever of decision was wanting before; and he finally resolved, that it would be absolutely unnecessary, if not highly indecorous, to do more for the widow and children of his father, than such kind of neighbourly acts as his own wife pointed out.

Chapter III.

Mrs. Dashwood remained at Norland several months; not from any disinclination to move when the sight of every well known spot ceased to raise the violent emotion which it produced for a while; for when her spirits began to revive, and her mind became capable of some other exertion than that of heightening its affliction by melancholy remembrances, she was impatient to be gone, and indefatigable in her inquiries for a suitable dwelling in the neighbourhood of Norland; for to remove far from that beloved spot was impossible. But she could hear of no situation that at once answered her notions of comfort and ease, and suited the prudence of her eldest daughter, whose steadier judgment rejected several houses as too large for their income, which her mother would have approved.

Mrs. Dashwood had been informed by her husband of the solemn promise on the part of his son in their favour, which gave comfort to his last earthly reflections. She doubted the sincerity of this assurance no more than he had doubted it himself, and she thought of it for her daughters' sake with satisfaction, though as for herself she was persuaded that a much smaller provision than 7000l, would support her in affluence. For their brother's sake too, for the sake of his own heart she rejoiced; and she reproached herself for being unjust to his merit before, in believing him incapable of generosity. His attentive behaviour to herself and his sisters convinced her that their welfare was dear to him, and, for a long time, she firmly relied on the liberality of his intentions.

The contempt which she had, very early in their acquaintance, felt for her daughter-in-law, was very much increased by the farther knowledge of her character, which half a year's residence in her family afforded; and perhaps in spite of every consideration of politeness or maternal affection on the side of the former, the two ladies might have found it impossible to have lived together so long, had not a particular circumstance occurred to give still greater eligibility, according to the opinions of Mrs. Dashwood, to her daughters' continuance at Norland.

This circumstance was a growing attachment between her eldest girl and the brother of Mrs. John Dashwood, a gentlemanlike and pleasing young man, who was introduced to their acquaintance soon after his sister's establishment at Norland, and who had since spent the greatest part of his time there.

Some mothers might have encouraged the intimacy from motives of interest, for Edward Ferrars was the eldest son of a man who had died very rich; and some might have repressed it from motives of prudence, for, except a trifling sum, the whole of his fortune depended on the will of his mother. But Mrs. Dashwood was alike uninfluenced by either consideration. It was enough for her that he appeared to be amiable, that he loved her daughter, and that Elinor returned the partiality. It was contrary to every doctrine of her's that difference of fortune should keep any couple asunder who were attracted by resemblance of disposition; and that Elinor's merit should not be acknowledged by every one who knew her, was to her comprehension impossible.

Edward Ferrars was not recommended to their good opinion by any peculiar graces of person or address. He was not handsome, and his manners required intimacy to make them pleasing. He was too diffident to do justice to himself; but when his natural shyness was overcome, his behaviour gave every indication of an open affectionate heart. His understanding was good, and his education had given it solid improvement. But he was neither fitted by abilities nor disposition to answer the wishes of his mother and sister, who longed to see him distinguished—as—they hardly knew what. They wanted him to make a fine figure in the world in some manner or other. His mother wished to interest him in political concerns, to get him into parliament, or to see him connected with some of the great men of the day. Mrs. John Dashwood wished it likewise; but in the mean while, till one of these superior blessings could be attained, it would have quieted her ambition to see him driving a barouche.[1] But Edward had no turn for great men or barouches. All his wishes centered in domestic comfort and the quiet of private life. Fortunately he had a younger brother who was more promising.

Edward had been staying several weeks in the house before he engaged much of Mrs. Dashwood's attention; for she was, at that time, in such affliction as rendered her careless of surrounding objects. She saw only that he was quiet and unobtrusive, and she liked him for it. He did not disturb the wretchedness of her mind by ill-timed conversation. She was first called to observe and approve him farther, by a reflection which Elinor chanced one day to make on the difference between him and his sister. It was a contrast which recommended him most forcibly to her mother.

"It is enough," said she; "to say that he is unlike Fanny is enough. It implies every thing amiable. I love him already."

---

1. Defined in the *OED* as a four-wheeled carriage with a hood which can be raised or let down at pleasure, having a seat in front for the driver, and seats inside for two couples to sit facing each other.

"I think you will like him," said Elinor, "when you know more of him."

"Like him!" replied her mother with a smile. "I can feel no sentiment of approbation inferior to love."

"You may esteem him."

"I have never yet known what it was to separate esteem and love."

Mrs. Dashwood now took pains to get acquainted with him. Her manners were attaching and soon banished his reserve. She speedily comprehended all his merits; the persuasion of his regard for Elinor perhaps assisted her penetration; but she really felt assured of his worth: and even that quietness of manner which militated against all her established ideas of what a young man's address ought to be, was no longer uninteresting when she knew his heart to be warm and his temper affectionate.

No sooner did she perceive any symptom of love in his behaviour to Elinor, than she considered their serious attachment as certain, and looked forward to their marriage as rapidly approaching.

"In a few months, my dear Marianne," said she, "Elinor will in all probability be settled for life. We shall miss her; but *she* will be happy."

"Oh! mama, how shall we do without her?"

"My love, it will be scarcely a separation. We shall live within a few miles of each other, and shall meet every day of our lives. You will gain a brother, a real, affectionate brother. I have the highest opinion in the world of Edward's heart. But you look grave, Marianne; do you disapprove your sister's choice?"

"Perhaps," said Marianne, "I may consider it with some surprise. Edward is very amiable, and I love him tenderly. But yet—he is not the kind of young man—there is a something wanting²—his figure is not striking; it has none of that grace which I should expect in the man who could seriously attach my sister. His eyes want all that spirit, that fire, which at once announce virtue and intelligence. And besides all this, I am afraid, mama, he has no real taste. Music seems scarcely to attract him, and though he admires Elinor's drawings very much, it is not the admiration of a person who can understand their worth. It is evident, in spite of his frequent attention to her while she draws, that in fact he knows nothing of the matter. He admires as a lover, not as a connoisseur. To satisfy me, those characters must be united. I could not be happy with a man whose taste did not in every point coincide with my own. He must enter into all my feelings; the same books, the same music must charm us both. Oh! mama, how spiritless, how tame was Edward's manner in reading to us last night! I felt for my sister most severely. Yet she

2. Needing; lacking.

bore it with so much composure; she seemed scarcely to notice it. I could hardly keep my seat. To hear those beautiful lines which have frequently almost driven me wild, pronounced with such impenetrable calmness, such dreadful indifference!"—

"He would certainly have done more justice to simple and elegant prose. I thought so at the time; but you *would* give him Cowper."[3]

"Nay, mama, if he is not to be animated by Cowper!—but we must allow for difference of taste. Elinor has not my feelings, and therefore she may overlook it, and be happy with him. But it would have broke *my* heart had I loved him, to hear him read with so little sensibility. Mama, the more I know of the world, the more am I convinced that I shall never see a man whom I can really love. I require so much! He must have all Edward's virtues, and his person and manners must ornament his goodness with every possible charm."

"Remember, my love, that you are not seventeen. It is yet too early in life to despair of such an happiness. Why should you be less fortunate than your mother? In one circumstance only, my Marianne, may your destiny be different from her's!"

Chapter IV.

"What a pity it is, Elinor," said Marianne, "that Edward should have no taste for drawing."

"No taste for drawing," replied Elinor; "why should you think so? He does not draw himself, indeed, but he has great pleasure in seeing the performances of other people, and I assure you he is by no means deficient in natural taste, though he has not had opportunities of improving it. Had he ever been in the way of learning, I think he would have drawn very well. He distrusts his own judgment in such matters so much, that he is always unwilling to give his opinion on any picture; but he has an innate propriety and simplicity of taste, which in general direct him perfectly right."

Marianne was afraid of offending, and said no more on the subject; but the kind of approbation which Elinor described as excited in him by the drawings of other people, was very far from that rapturous delight, which, in her opinion, could alone be called taste. Yet, though smiling within herself at the mistake, she hon-

---

3. Perhaps the most admired poet of Austen's day, William Cowper (1731–1800) was best known for his long poem *The Task* (1785). Although he was revered for his celebrations of the tranquil pleasures of rural life and for the sometimes bemused and sometimes deeply melancholy sensibility that animates them, many of his poems were biting criticisms of contemporary life, such as "Tirocinium," an attack on public schools, and "The Negro's Complaint," an attack on the slave trade. Cowper was one of Austen's favorite writers.

oured her sister for that blind partiality to Edward which produced it.

"I hope, Marianne," continued Elinor, "you do not consider him as deficient in general taste. Indeed, I think I may say that you cannot, for your behaviour to him is perfectly cordial, and if *that* were your opinion, I am sure you could never be civil to him." Marianne hardly knew what to say. She would not wound the feelings of her sister on any account, and yet to say what she did not believe was impossible. At length she replied:

"Do not be offended, Elinor, if my praise of him is not in every thing equal to your sense of his merits. I have not had so many opportunities of estimating the minuter propensities of his mind, his inclinations and tastes as you have; but I have the highest opinion in the world of his goodness and sense. I think him every thing that is worthy and amiable."

"I am sure," replied Elinor with a smile, "that his dearest friends could not be dissatisfied with such commendation as that. I do not perceive how you could express yourself more warmly."

Marianne was rejoiced to find her sister so easily pleased.

"Of his sense and his goodness," continued Elinor, "no one can, I think, be in doubt, who has seen him often enough to engage him in unreserved conversation. The excellence of his understanding and his principles can be concealed only by that shyness which too often keeps him silent. You know enough of him to do justice to his solid worth. But of his minuter propensities as you call them, you have from peculiar circumstances been kept more ignorant than myself. He and I have been at times thrown a good deal together, while you have been wholly engrossed on the most affectionate principle by my mother. I have seen a great deal of him, have studied his sentiments and heard his opinion on subjects of literature and taste; and, upon the whole, I venture to pronounce that his mind is well-informed, his enjoyment of books exceedingly great, his imagination lively, his observation just and correct, and his taste delicate and pure. His abilities in every respect improve as much upon acquaintance as his manners and person. At first sight, his address is certainly not striking; and his person can hardly be called handsome, till the expression of his eyes, which are uncommonly good, and the general sweetness of his countenance, is perceived. At present, I know him so well, that I think him really handsome; or, at least, almost so. What say you, Marianne?"

"I shall very soon think him handsome, Elinor, if I do not now. When you tell me to love him as a brother, I shall no more see imperfection in his face, than I now do in his heart."

Elinor started at this declaration, and was sorry for the warmth she had been betrayed into, in speaking of him. She felt that Edward stood very high in her opinion. She believed the regard to be mutual; but she required greater certainty of it to make Marianne's conviction of their attachment agreeable to her. She knew that what Marianne and her mother conjectured one moment, they believed the next—that with them, to wish was to hope, and to hope was to expect. She tried to explain the real state of the case to her sister.

"I do not attempt to deny," said she, "that I think very highly of him—that I greatly esteem, that I like him."

Marianne here burst forth with indignation—

"Esteem him! Like him! Cold-hearted Elinor! Oh! worse than cold-hearted! Ashamed of being otherwise. Use those words again and I will leave the room this moment."

Elinor could not help laughing. "Excuse me," said she, "and be assured that I meant no offence to you, by speaking, in so quiet a way, of my own feelings. Believe them to be stronger than I have declared; believe them, in short, to be such as his merit, and the suspicion—the hope of his affection for me may warrant, without imprudence or folly. But farther than this you must *not* believe. I am by no means assured of his regard for me. There are moments when the extent of it seems doubtful; and till his sentiments are fully known, you cannot wonder at my wishing to avoid any encouragement of my own partiality, by believing or calling it more than it is. In my heart I feel little—scarcely any doubt of his preference. But there are other points to be considered besides his inclination. He is very far from being independent. What his mother really is we cannot know; but, from Fanny's occasional mention of her conduct and opinions, we have never been disposed to think her amiable; and I am very much mistaken if Edward is not himself aware that there would be many difficulties in his way, if he were wish to marry a woman who had not either a great fortune or high rank."

Marianne was astonished to find how much the imagination of her mother and herself had outstripped the truth.

"And you really are not engaged to him!" said she. "Yet it certainly soon will happen. But two advantages will proceed from this delay. *I* shall not lose you so soon, and Edward will have greater opportunity of improving that natural taste for your favourite pursuit which must be so indispensably necessary to your future felicity. Oh! if he should be so far stimulated by your genius as to learn to draw himself, how delightful it would be!"

Elinor had given her real opinion to her sister. She could not consider her partiality for Edward in so prosperous a state as Marianne had believed it. There was, at times, a want of spirits about him which, if it did not denote indifference, spoke a something almost as unpromising. A doubt of her regard, supposing him to feel it, need not give him more than inquietude. It would not be likely to produce that dejection of mind which frequently attended him. A more reasonable cause might be found in the dependent situation which forbad the indulgence of his affection. She knew that his mother neither behaved to him so as to make his home comfortable at present, nor to give him any assurance that he might form a home for himself, without strictly attending to her views for his aggrandizement. With such a knowledge as this, it was impossible for Elinor to feel easy on the subject. She was far from depending on that result of his preference of her, which her mother and sister still considered as certain. Nay, the longer they were together the more doubtful seemed the nature of his regard; and sometimes, for a few painful minutes, she believed it to be no more than friendship.

But, whatever might really be its limits, it was enough, when perceived by his sister, to make her uneasy; and at the same time, (which was still more common,) to make her uncivil. She took the first opportunity of affronting her mother-in-law on the occasion, talking to her so expressively of her brother's great expectations, of Mrs. Ferrars's resolution that both her sons should marry well, and of the danger attending any young woman who attempted to *draw him in*; that Mrs. Dashwood could neither pretend to be unconscious, nor endeavour to be calm. She gave her an answer which marked her contempt, and instantly left the room, resolving that, whatever might be the inconvenience or expense of so sudden a removal, her beloved Elinor should not be exposed another week to such insinuations.

In this state of her spirits, a letter was delivered to her from the post, which contained a proposal particularly well timed. It was the offer of a small house, on very easy terms, belonging to a relation of her own, a gentleman of consequence and property in Devonshire. The letter was from this gentleman himself, and written in the true spirit of friendly accommodation. He understood that she was in need of a dwelling, and though the house he now offered her was merely a cottage, he assured her that every thing should be done to it which she might think necessary, if the situation pleased her. He earnestly pressed her, after giving the particulars of the house and garden, to come with her daughters to Barton Park, the place of his own residence, from whence she might judge, herself, whether Barton Cottage, for the houses were in the same parish, could, by any alteration, be made comfortable to her. He seemed really anxious to accommodate them, and the whole of his letter was written in so friendly a style as could not fail of giving pleasure to his cousin;[1] more especially at a moment when she was suffering under the cold and unfeeling behaviour of her nearer connections. She needed no time for deliberation or inquiry. Her resolution was formed as she read. The situation of Barton, in a county so far distant from Sussex as Devonshire, which, but a few hours before, would have been a sufficient objection to outweigh every possible advantage belonging to the place, was now its first recommendation. To quit the neighbourhood of Norland was no longer an evil; it was an object of desire; it was a blessing, in comparison of the misery of continuing her daughter-in-law's guest: and to remove for ever from that beloved place would be less painful than to inhabit or visit it while such a woman was its mistress. She instantly wrote Sir John Middleton her acknowledgment of his kindness, and her acceptance of his proposal; and then hastened to shew both letters to her daughters, that she might be secure of their approbation before her answer were sent.

Elinor had always thought it would be more prudent for them to settle at some distance from Norland than immediately amongst their present acquaintance. On *that* head, therefore, it was not for her to oppose her mother's intention of removing into Devonshire. The house, too, as described by Sir John, was on so simple a scale, and the rent so uncommonly moderate, as to leave her no right of objection on either point; and, therefore, though it was not a plan which brought any charm to her fancy, though it was a removal from the vicinity of Norland beyond her wishes, she made no attempt to dissuade her mother from sending her letter of acquiescence.

Chapter V.

No sooner was her answer dispatched, than Mrs. Dashwood indulged herself in the pleasure of announcing to her son-in-law and his wife that she was provided with an house, and should incommode them no longer than till every thing were ready for her inhabiting it. They heard her with surprise. Mrs. John Dashwood said nothing; but her husband civilly hoped that she would not be settled far from Norland. She had great satisfaction in replying that she was going into Devonshire.—Edward turned hastily towards her, on hearing this, and, in a voice of surprise and concern, which required no explanation to her, repeated, "Devonshire! Are you, indeed, going there? So far from hence! And to what part of it?" She explained the situation. It was within four miles northward of Exeter.

1. A kinsman or kinswoman; a relative.

"It is but a cottage," she continued, "but I hope to see many of my friends in it. A room or two can easily be added; and if my friends find no difficulty in travelling so far to see me, I am sure I will find none in accommodating them." She concluded with a very kind invitation to Mr. and Mrs. John Dashwood to visit her at Barton; and to Edward she gave one with still greater affection. Though her late conversation with her daughter-in-law had made her resolve on remaining at Norland no longer than was unavoidable, it had not produced the smallest effect on her in that point to which it principally tended. To separate Edward and Elinor was as far from being her object as ever; and she wished to shew Mrs. John Dashwood by this pointed invitation to her brother, how totally she disregarded her disapprobation of the match.

Mr. John Dashwood told his mother again and again how exceedingly sorry he was that she had taken an house at such a distance from Norland as to prevent his being of any service to her in removing her furniture. He really felt conscientiously vexed on the occasion; for the very exertion to which he had limited the performance of his promise to his father was by this arrangement rendered impracticable.—The furniture was all sent round by water. It chiefly consisted of household linen, plate, china, and books, with an handsome pianoforte of Marianne's. Mrs. John Dashwood saw the packages depart with a sigh: she could not help feeling it hard that as Mrs. Dashwood's income would be so trifling in comparison with their own, she should have any handsome article of furniture.

Mrs. Dashwood took the house for a twelvemonth; it was ready furnished, and she might have immediate possession. No difficulty arose on either side in the agreement; and she waited only for the disposal of her effects at Norland, and to determine her future household, before she set off for the west; and this, as she was exceedingly rapid in the performance of every thing that interested her, was soon done.—The horses which were left her by her husband, had been sold soon after his death, and an opportunity now offering of disposing of her carriage,[1] she agreed to sell that likewise at the earnest advice of her eldest daughter. For the comfort of her children, had she consulted only her own wishes, she would have kept it; but the discretion of Elinor prevailed. *Her* wisdom too limited the number of their servants to three;[2] two maids and a man,

---

1. Maintaining horses and a carriage was a matter of considerable expense, and also a sign of status, hence Mrs. Dashwood's reluctance to part with them. Austen's father found them difficult to maintain on £700 a year. The collective income of the Dashwood women is £500.
2. Domestic economists of the time would support Elinor's judgment that an annual income of £500 was sufficient for only three domestic servants.

with whom they were speedily provided from amongst those who had formed their establishment at Norland.

The man and one of the maids were sent off immediately into Devonshire, to prepare the house for their mistress's arrival; for as Lady Middleton was entirely unknown to Mrs. Dashwood, she preferred going directly to the cottage to being a visitor at Barton Park; and she relied so undoubtingly on Sir John's description of the house, as to feel no curiosity to examine it herself till she entered it as her own. Her eagerness to be gone from Norland was preserved from diminution by the evident satisfaction of her daughter-in-law in the prospect of her removal; a satisfaction which was but feebly attempted to be concealed under a cold invitation to her to defer her departure. Now was the time when her son-in-law's promise to his father might with particular propriety be fulfilled. Since he had neglected to do it on first coming to the estate, their quitting his house might be looked on as the most suitable period for its accomplishment. But Mrs. Dashwood began shortly to give over every hope of the kind, and to be convinced, from the general drift of his discourse, that his assistance extended no farther than their maintenance for six months at Norland. He so frequently talked of the increasing expenses of housekeeping,[3] and of the perpetual demands upon his purse, which a man of any consequence in the world was beyond calculation exposed to, that he seemed rather to stand in need of more money himself than to have any design of giving money away.

In a very few weeks from the day which brought Sir John Middleton's first letter to Norland, every thing was so far settled in their future abode as to enable Mrs. Dashwood and her daughters to begin their journey.

Many were the tears shed by them in their last adieus to a place so much beloved. "Dear, dear Norland!" said Marianne, as she wandered alone before the house, on the last evening of their being there; "when shall I cease to regret you!—when learn to feel a home elsewhere!—Oh! happy house, could you know what I suffer in now viewing you from this spot, from whence perhaps I may view you no more!—And you, ye well-known trees!—but you will continue the same.—No leaf will decay because we are removed, nor any branch become motionless although we can observe you no longer!—No; you will continue the same; unconscious of the pleasure or the regret you occasion, and insensible of any change in those who walk under your shade!—But who will remain to enjoy you?"

3. Expenses required to maintain a house and estate, and all its business and affairs.

Chapter VI.

The first part of their journey was performed in too melancholy a disposition to be otherwise than tedious and unpleasant. But as they drew towards the end of it, their interest in the appearance of a country which they were to inhabit overcame their dejection, and a view of Barton Valley as they entered it gave them cheerfulness. It was a pleasant fertile spot, well wooded, and rich in pasture. After winding along it for more than a mile, they reached their own house. A small green court was the whole of its demesne in front; and a neat wicket gate admitted them into it.

As a house, Barton Cottage, though small, was comfortable and compact; but as a cottage it was defective,[1] for the building was regular, the roof was tiled, the window shutters were not painted green, nor were the walls covered with honeysuckles. A narrow passage led directly through the house into the garden behind. On each side of the entrance was a sitting room, about sixteen feet square; and beyond them were the offices[2] and the stairs. Four bed-rooms and two garrets formed the rest of the house. It had not been built many years and was in good repair. In comparison of Norland, it was poor and small indeed!—but the tears which recollection called forth as they entered the house were soon dried away. They were cheered by the joy of the servants on their arrival, and each for the sake of the others resolved to appear happy. It was very early in September; the season was fine, and from first seeing the place under the advantage of good weather, they received an impression in its favour which was of material service in recommending it to their lasting approbation.

The situation of the house was good. High hills rose immediately behind, and at no great distance on each side; some of which were open downs, the others cultivated and woody. The village of Barton was chiefly on one of these hills, and formed a pleasant view from the cottage windows. The prospect in front was more extensive; it commanded the whole of the valley, and reached into the country beyond. The hills which surrounded the cottage terminated the val-

1. Defined in Samuel Johnson's *Dictionary* (1755) as "a mean habitation," the cottage later in the eighteenth century was increasingly glamorized and sentimentalized, seen no longer as a laborer's dwelling but as a site of rustic simplicity and retirement from the debasing pleasures of the city. Tiled rather than thatched, tidily symmetrical rather than irregular, yet a far cry from the affluence of Norland Park, Barton Cottage is not the elegantly quaint abode then becoming fashionable. *Sense and Sensibility* stages competing attitudes toward cottages and different ideals of rural retirement. See also p. 177, n. 6.
2. The parts of a house devoted to household work or service, i.e., the kitchen, pantry, scullery, etc.

ley in that direction; under another name, and in another course, it branched out again between two of the steepest of them.

With the size and furniture of the house Mrs. Dashwood was upon the whole well satisfied; for though her former style of life rendered many additions to the latter indispensable, yet to add and improve was a delight to her; and she had at this time ready money enough to supply all that was wanted of greater elegance to the apartments. "As for the house itself, to be sure," said she, "it is too small for our family, but we will make ourselves tolerably comfortable for the present as it is too late in the year for improvements. Perhaps in the spring, if I have plenty of money, as I dare say I shall, we may think about building. These parlours are both too small for such parties of our friends as I hope to see often collected here; and I have some thoughts of throwing the passage into one of them with perhaps a part of the other, and so leave the remainder of that other for an entrance; this, with a new drawing-room which may be easily added, and a bed-chamber and garret above, will make it a very snug little cottage. I could wish the stairs were handsome. But one must not expect every thing; though I suppose it would be no difficult matter to widen them. I shall see how much I am before-hand with the world in the spring, and we will plan our improvements accordingly."

In the mean time, till all these alterations could be made from the savings of an income of five hundred a-year by a woman who never saved in her life, they were wise enough to be contented with the house as it was; and each of them was busy in arranging their particular concerns, and endeavouring, by placing around them their books and other possessions, to form themselves a home. Marianne's pianoforte was unpacked and properly disposed of; and Elinor's drawings were affixed to the walls of their sitting room.

In such employments as these they were interrupted soon after breakfast the next day by the entrance of their landlord, who called to welcome them to Barton, and to offer them every accommodation from his own house and garden in which their's might at present be deficient. Sir John Middleton was a good looking man about forty. He had formerly visited at Stanhill, but it was too long ago for his young cousins to remember him. His countenance was thoroughly good-humoured; and his manners were as friendly as the style of his letter. Their arrival seemed to afford him real satisfaction, and their comfort to be an object of real solicitude to him. He said much of his earnest desire of their living in the most sociable terms with his family, and pressed them so cordially to dine at Barton Park every day till they were better settled at home, that, though his entreaties were carried to a point of perseverance beyond civility, they could not give offence. His kindness was not confined to words; for within an hour after he left them, a large basket full of garden stuff[3] and fruit arrived from the park, which was followed before the end of the day by a present of game. He insisted moreover on conveying all their letters to and from the post for them, and would not be denied the satisfaction of sending them his newspaper[4] every day.

Lady Middleton had sent a very civil message by him, denoting her intention of waiting on Mrs. Dashwood as soon as she could be assured that her visit would be no inconvenience; and as this message was answered by an invitation equally polite, her ladyship was introduced to them the next day.

They were of course very anxious to see a person on whom so much of their comfort at Barton must depend; and the elegance of her appearance was favourable to their wishes. Lady Middleton was not more than six or seven and twenty; her face was handsome, her figure tall and striking, and her address graceful. Her manners had all the elegance which her husband's wanted. But they would have been improved by some share of his frankness and warmth; and her visit was long enough to detract something from their first admiration, by shewing that though perfectly well-bred, she was reserved, cold, and had nothing to say for herself beyond the most common-place inquiry or remark.

Conversation however was not wanted, for Sir John was very chatty, and Lady Middleton had taken the wise precaution of bringing with her their eldest child, a fine little boy about six years old, by which means there was one subject always to be recurred to by the ladies in case of extremity, for they had to inquire his name and age, admire his beauty, and ask him questions which his mother answered for him, while he hung about her and held down his head, to the great surprise of her ladyship, who wondered at his being so shy before company as he could make noise enough at home. On every formal visit a child ought to be of the party, by way of provision for discourse. In the present case it took up ten minutes to determine whether the boy were most like his father or mother, and in what particular he resembled either, for of course every body differed, and every body was astonished at the opinion of the others.*

An opportunity was soon to be given to the Dashwoods of de-

---

3. Vegetables for the table.
4. R. W. Chapman notes the two newspapers published in Exeter at the time: *Trewman's Exeter Flying Post or Plymouth and Cornish Advertiser*, and *The Devon and Exeter Daily Gazette*. Because newspapers were relatively expensive, neighbors commonly shared them.
* at the opinion of the others.] at each other's opinions. A.

bating on the rest of the children, as Sir John would not leave the house without securing their promise of dining at the park the next day.

Chapter VII.

Barton Park was about half a mile from the cottage. The ladies had passed near it in their way along the valley, but it was screened from their view at home by the projection of an hill. The house was large and handsome; and the Middletons lived in a style of equal hospitality and elegance. The former was for Sir John's gratification, the latter for that of his lady. They were scarcely ever without some friends staying with them in the house, and they kept more company of every kind than any other family in the neighbourhood. It was necessary to the happiness of both; for however dissimilar in temper and outward behaviour, they strongly resembled each other in that total want of talent and taste which confined their employments, unconnected with such as society produced, within a very narrow compass. Sir John was a sportsman,[1] Lady Middleton a mother. He hunted and shot, and she humoured her children; and these were their only resources. Lady Middleton had the advantage of being able to spoil her children all the year round, while Sir John's independent employments were in existence only half the time. Continual engagements at home and abroad, however, supplied all the deficiencies of nature and education; supported the good spirits of Sir John, and gave exercise to the good-breeding of his wife.

Lady Middleton piqued herself upon the elegance of her table, and of all her domestic arrangements; and from this kind of vanity was her greatest enjoyment in any of their parties. But Sir John's satisfaction in society was much more real; he delighted in collecting about him more young people than his house would hold, and the noisier they were the better was he pleased. He was a blessing to all the juvenile part of the neighbourhood, for in summer he was for ever forming parties to eat cold ham and chicken out of doors, and in winter his private balls were numerous enough for any young lady who was not suffering under the insatiable appetite of fifteen.

The arrival of a new family in the country was always a matter of joy to him, and in every point of view he was charmed with the inhabitants he had now procured for his cottage at Barton. The Miss Dashwoods were young, pretty, and unaffected. It was enough to secure his good opinion; for to be unaffected was all that a pretty

---

1. One who hunts or shoots wild animals or game for pleasure.

girl could want to make her mind as captivating as her person. The friendliness of his disposition made him happy in accommodating those, whose situation might be considered, in comparison with the past, as unfortunate. In shewing kindness to his cousins therefore he had the real satisfaction of a good heart; and in settling a family of females only in his cottage, he had all the satisfaction of a sportsman; for a sportsman, though he esteems only those of his sex who are sportsmen likewise, is not often desirous of encouraging their taste by admitting them to a residence within his own manor.

Mrs. Dashwood and her daughters were met at the door of the house by Sir John, who welcomed them to Barton Park with unaffected sincerity; and as he attended them to the drawing room repeated to the young ladies the concern which the same subject had drawn from him the day before, at being unable to get any smart young men to meet them. They would see, he said, only one gentleman there besides himself; a particular friend who was staying at the park, but who was neither very young nor very gay. He hoped they would all excuse the smallness of the party, and could assure them it should never happen so again. He had been to several families that morning in hopes of procuring some addition to their number, but it was moonlight² and every body was full of engagements. Luckily Lady Middleton's mother had arrived at Barton within the last hour, and as she was a very cheerful agreeable woman, he hoped the young ladies would not find it so very dull as they might imagine. The young ladies as well as their mother, were perfectly satisfied with having two entire strangers of the party, and wished for no more.

Mrs. Jennings, Lady Middleton's mother, was a good-humoured, merry, fat, elderly woman, who talked a great deal, seemed very happy, and rather vulgar. She was full of jokes and laughter, and before dinner was over had said many witty things on the subject of lovers and husbands; hoped they had not left their hearts behind them in Sussex, and pretended to see them blush whether they did or not. Marianne was vexed at it for her sister's sake, and turned her eyes towards Elinor to see how she bore these attacks, with an earnestness which gave Elinor far more pain than could arise from such common-place raillery as Mrs. Jennings's.

Colonel Brandon, the friend of Sir John, seemed no more adapted by resemblance of manner to be his friend, than Lady Middleton was to be his wife, or Mrs. Jennings to be Lady Middleton's mother. He was silent and grave. His appearance however was not unpleas-

---

2. Because the light afforded by lanterns was not very good, people preferred to schedule their evening social engagements for moonlit nights, and as a result, Sir John's attempt to gather a party on short notice fails.

ing, in spite of his being in the opinion of Marianne and Margaret an absolute old bachelor, for he was on the wrong side of five and thirty; but though his face was not handsome his countenance was sensible, and his address was particularly gentlemanlike.

There was nothing in any of the party which could recommend them as companions to the Dashwoods; but the cold insipidity of Lady Middleton was so particularly repulsive, that in comparison of it the gravity of Colonel Brandon, and even the boisterous mirth of Sir John and his mother-in-law was interesting. Lady Middleton seemed to be roused to enjoyment only by the entrance of her four noisy children after dinner, who pulled her about, tore her clothes, and put an end to every kind of discourse except what related to themselves.

In the evening, as Marianne was discovered to be musical, she was invited to play. The instrument was unlocked, every body prepared to be charmed, and Marianne, who sang very well, at their request went through the chief of the songs which Lady Middleton had brought into the family on her marriage, and which perhaps had lain ever since in the same position on the pianoforté, for her ladyship had celebrated that event by giving up music, although by her mother's account she had played extremely well, and by her own was very fond of it.

Marianne's performance was highly applauded. Sir John was loud in his admiration at the end of every song, and as loud in his conversation with the others while every song lasted. Lady Middleton frequently called him to order, wondered how any one's attention could be diverted from music for a moment, and asked Marianne to sing a particular song which Marianne had just finished. Colonel Brandon alone, of all the party, heard her without being in raptures. He paid her only the compliment of attention; and she felt a respect for him on the occasion, which the others had reasonably forfeited by their shameless want of taste. His pleasure in music, though it amounted not to that extatic delight which alone could sympathize with her own, was estimable when contrasted against the horrible insensibility of the others; and she was reasonable enough to allow that a man of five and thirty might well have outlived all acuteness of feeling and every exquisite power of enjoyment. She was perfectly disposed to make every allowance for the colonel's advanced state of life which humanity required.

Chapter VIII.

Mrs. Jennings was a widow, with an ample jointure.[1] She had only two daughters, both of whom she had lived to see respectably married, and she had now therefore nothing to do but to marry all the rest of the world. In the promotion of this object she was zealously active, as far as her ability reached; and missed no opportunity of projecting weddings among all the young people of her acquaintance. She was remarkably quick in the discovery of attachments, and had enjoyed the advantage of raising the blushes and the vanity of many a young lady by insinuations of her power over such a young man; and this kind of discernment enabled her soon after her arrival at Barton decisively to pronounce that Colonel Brandon was very much in love with Marianne Dashwood. She rather suspected it to be so, on the very first evening of their being together, from his listening so attentively while she sang to them; and when the visit was returned by the Middletons' dining at the cottage, the fact was ascertained by his listening to her again. It must be so. She was perfectly convinced of it. It would be an excellent match, for *he* was rich and *she* was handsome. Mrs. Jennings had been anxious to see Colonel Brandon well married, ever since her connection with Sir John first brought him to her knowledge; and she was always anxious to get a good husband for every pretty girl.

The immediate advantage to herself was by no means inconsiderable, for it supplied her with endless jokes against them both. At the park she laughed at the colonel, and in the cottage at Marianne. To the former her raillery was probably, as far as it regarded only himself, perfectly indifferent; but to the latter it was at first incomprehensible; and when its object was understood, she hardly knew whether most to laugh at its absurdity, or censure its impertinence, for she considered it as an unfeeling reflection on the colonel's advanced years, and on his forlorn condition as an old bachelor.

Mrs. Dashwood, who could not think a man five years younger than herself, so exceedingly ancient as he appeared to the youthful fancy of her daughter, ventured to clear Mrs. Jennings from the probability of wishing to throw ridicule on his age.

"But at least, mama, you cannot deny the absurdity of the accusation, though you may not think it intentionally ill-natured. Colonel Brandon is certainly younger than Mrs. Jennings, but he is old enough to be *my* father; and if he were ever animated enough to be in love, must have long outlived every sensation of the kind.

---

1. A financial settlement providing for a wife after her husband's death.

It is too ridiculous! When is a man to be safe from such wit, if age and infirmity will not protect him?"

"Infirmity!" said Elinor, "do you call Colonel Brandon infirm? I can easily suppose that his age may appear much greater to you than to my mother; but you can hardly deceive yourself as to his having the use of his limbs!"

"Did not you hear him complain of the rheumatism? and is not that the commonest infirmity of declining life?"

"My dearest child," said her mother laughing, "at this rate you must be in continual terror of *my* decay; and it must seem to you a miracle that my life has been extended to the advanced age of forty."

"Mama, you are not doing me justice. I know very well that Colonel Brandon is not old enough to make his friends yet apprehensive of losing him in the course of nature. He may live twenty years longer. But thirty-five has nothing to do with matrimony."

"Perhaps," said Elinor, "thirty-five and seventeen had better not have any thing to do with matrimony together. But if there should by any chance happen to be a woman who is single at seven and twenty, I should not think Colonel Brandon's being thirty-five any objection to his marrying *her*."

"A woman of seven and twenty," said Marianne, after pausing a moment, "can never hope to feel or inspire affection again, and if her home be uncomfortable, or her fortune small, I can suppose that she might bring herself to submit to the offices of a nurse, for the sake of the provision and security of a wife. In his marrying such a woman therefore there would be nothing unsuitable. It would be a compact of convenience, and the world would be satisfied. In my eyes it would be no marriage at all, but that would be nothing. To me it would seem only a commercial exchange, in which each wished to be benefited at the expense of the other."

"It would be impossible, I know," replied Elinor, "to convince you that a woman of seven and twenty could feel for a man of thirty-five any thing near enough to love, to make him a desirable companion to her. But I must object to your dooming Colonel Brandon and his wife to the constant confinement of a sick chamber, merely because he chanced to complain yesterday (a very cold damp day) of a slight rheumatic feel in one of his shoulders."

"But he talked of flannel waistcoats," said Marianne; "and with me a flannel waistcoat is invariably connected with aches, cramps, rheumatisms, and every species of ailment that can afflict the old and the feeble."

"Had he been only in a violent fever, you would not have despised him half so much. Confess, Marianne, is not there something interesting to you in the flushed cheek, hollow eye, and quick pulse of a fever?"

Soon after this, upon Elinor's leaving the room, "Mama," said Marianne, "I have an alarm on the subject of illness, which I cannot conceal from you. I am sure Edward Ferrars is not well. We have now been here almost a fortnight, and yet he does not come. Nothing but real indisposition could occasion this extraordinary delay. What else can detain him at Norland?"

"Had you any idea of his coming so soon?" said Mrs. Dashwood. "*I* had none. On the contrary, if I have felt any anxiety at all on the subject, it has been in recollecting that he sometimes shewed a want of pleasure and readiness in accepting my invitation, when I talked of his coming to Barton. Does Elinor expect him already?"

"I have never mentioned it to her, but of course she must."

"I rather think you are mistaken, for when I was talking to her yesterday of getting a new grate for the spare bedchamber, she observed that there was no immediate hurry for it, as it was not likely that the room would be wanted for some time."

"How strange this is! what can be the meaning of it! But the whole of their behaviour to each other has been unaccountable! How cold, how composed were their last adieus! How languid their conversation the last evening of their being together! In Edward's farewell there was no distinction between Elinor and me: it was the good wishes of an affectionate brother to both. Twice did I leave them purposely together in the course of the last morning, and each time did he most unaccountably follow me out of the room. And Elinor, in quitting Norland and Edward, cried not as I did. Even now her self-command is invariable. When is she dejected or melancholy? When does she try to avoid society, or appear restless and dissatisfied in it?"

Chapter IX.

The Dashwoods were now settled at Barton with tolerable comfort to themselves. The house and the garden, with all the objects surrounding them, were now become familiar, and the ordinary pursuits which had given to Norland half its charms, were engaged in again with far greater enjoyment than Norland had been able to afford, since the loss of their father. Sir John Middleton, who called on them every day for the first fortnight, and who was not in the habit of seeing much occupation at home, could not conceal his amazement on finding them always employed.

Their visitors, except those from Barton Park, were not many;

for, in spite of Sir John's urgent entreaties that they would mix more in the neighbourhood, and repeated assurances of his carriage being always at their service, the independence of Mrs. Dashwood's spirit overcame the wish of society for her children; and she was resolute in declining to visit any family beyond the distance of a walk. There were but few who could be so classed; and it was not all of them that were attainable. About a mile and a half from the cottage, along the narrow winding valley of Allenham, which issued from that of Barton, as formerly described, the girls had, in one of their earliest walks, discovered an ancient respectable looking mansion, which, by reminding them a little of Norland, interested their imagination and made them wish to be better acquainted with it. But they learnt, on inquiry, that its possessor, an elderly lady of very good character, was unfortunately too infirm to mix with the world, and never stirred from home.

The whole country about them abounded in beautiful walks. The high downs which invited them from almost every window of the cottage to seek the exquisite enjoyment of air on their summits, were an happy alternative when the dirt of the valleys beneath shut up their superior beauties; and towards one of these hills did Marianne and Margaret one memorable morning direct their steps, attracted by the partial sunshine of a showery sky, and unable longer to bear the confinement which the settled rain of the two preceding days had occasioned. The weather was not tempting enough to draw the two others from their pencil and their book, in spite of Marianne's declaration that the day would be lastingly fair, and that every threatening cloud would be drawn off from their hills; and the two girls set off together.

They gaily ascended the downs, rejoicing in their own penetration at every glimpse of blue sky; and when they caught in their faces the animating gales of an high south-westerly wind, they pitied the fears which had prevented their mother and Elinor from sharing such delightful sensations.

"Is there a felicity in the world," said Marianne, "superior to this?—Margaret, we will walk here at least two hours."

Margaret agreed, and they pursued their way against the wind, resisting it with laughing delight for about twenty minutes longer, when suddenly the clouds united over their heads, and a driving rain set full in their face.—Chagrined and surprised, they were obliged, though unwillingly, to turn back, for no shelter was nearer than their own house. One consolation however remained for them, to which the exigence of the moment gave more than usual propriety; it was that of running with all possible speed down the steep side of the hill which led immediately to their garden gate.

They set off. Marianne had at first the advantage, but a false step brought her suddenly to the ground, and Margaret, unable to stop herself to assist her, was involuntarily hurried along, and reached the bottom in safety.

A gentleman carrying a gun, with two pointers playing round him, was passing up the hill and within a few yards of Marianne, when her accident happened. He put down his gun and ran to her assistance. She had raised herself from the ground, but her foot had been twisted in the fall, and she was scarcely able to stand. The gentleman offered his services, and perceiving that her modesty declined what her situation rendered necessary, took her up in his arms without farther delay, and carried her down the hill. Then passing through the garden, the gate of which had been left open by Margaret, he bore her directly into the house, whither Margaret was just arrived, and quitted not his hold till he had seated her in a chair in the parlour.

Elinor and her mother rose up in amazement at their entrance, and while the eyes of both were fixed on him with an evident wonder and a secret admiration which equally sprung from his appearance, he apologized for his intrusion by relating its cause, in a manner so frank and so graceful, that his person, which was uncommonly handsome, received additional charms from his voice and expression. Had he been even old, ugly, and vulgar, the gratitude and kindness of Mrs. Dashwood would have been secured by any act of attention to her child; but the influence of youth, beauty, and elegance, gave an interest to the action which came home to her feelings.

She thanked him again and again; and with a sweetness of address which always attended her, invited him to be seated. But this he declined, as he was dirty and wet. Mrs. Dashwood then begged to know to whom she was obliged. His name, he replied, was Willoughby and his present home was at Allenham, from whence he hoped she would allow him the honour of calling to-morrow to inquire after Miss Dashwood. The honour was readily granted, and he then departed, to make himself still more interesting, in the midst of an heavy rain.

His manly beauty and more than common gracefulness were instantly the theme of general admiration, and the laugh which his gallantry raised against Marianne, received particular spirit from his exterior attractions.—Marianne herself had seen less of his person than the rest, for the confusion which crimsoned over her face, on his lifting her up, had robbed her of the power of regarding him after their entering the house. But she had seen enough of him to join in all the admiration of the others, and with an energy which always adorned her praise. His person and air were equal to what her fancy had ever drawn for the hero of a favourite story; and in his carrying her into the house with so little previous formality, there was a rapidity of thought which particularly recommended the action to her. Every circumstance belonging to him was interesting. His name was good, his residence was in their favourite village, and she soon found out that of all manly dresses a shooting-jacket was the most becoming. Her imagination was busy, her reflections were pleasant, and the pain of a sprained ancle was disregarded.

Sir John called on them as soon as the next interval of fair weather that morning allowed him to get out of doors; and Marianne's accident being related to him, he was eagerly asked whether he knew any gentleman of the name of Willoughby at Allenham.

"Willoughby!" cried Sir John; "what, is *he* in the country? That is good news however; I will ride over to-morrow, and ask him to dinner on Thursday."

"You know him then," said Mrs. Dashwood.

"Know him! to be sure I do. Why, he is down here every year."

"And what sort of a young man is he?"

"As good a kind of fellow as ever lived, I assure you. A very decent shot, and there is not a bolder rider in England."

"And is *that* all you can say for him?" cried Marianne, indignantly. "But what are his manners on more intimate acquaintance? What his pursuits, his talents and genius?"

Sir John was rather puzzled.

"Upon my soul," said he, "I do not know much about him as to all *that*. But he is a pleasant, good humoured fellow, and has got the nicest little black bitch of a pointer I ever saw. Was she out with him to-day?"

But Marianne could no more satisfy him as to the colour of Mr. Willoughby's pointer, than he could describe to her the shades of his mind.

"But who is he?" said Elinor. "Where does he come from? Has he a house at Allenham?"

On this point Sir John could give more certain intelligence; and he told them that Mr. Willoughby had no property of his own in the country; that he resided there only while he was visiting the old lady at Allenham Court, to whom he was related, and whose possessions he was to inherit; adding, "Yes, yes, he is very well worth catching, I can tell you, Miss Dashwood; he has a pretty little estate of his own in Somersetshire besides; and if I were you, I would not give him up to my younger sister in spite of all this tumbling down hills. Miss Marianne must not expect to have all the men to herself. Brandon will be jealous, if she does not take care."

"I do not believe," said Mrs. Dashwood, with a good humoured smile, "that Mr. Willoughby will be incommoded by the attempts of either of *my* daughters towards what you call *catching him.* It is not an employment to which they have been brought up. Men are very safe with us, let them be ever so rich. I am glad to find, however, from what you say, that he is a respectable young man, and one whose acquaintance will not be ineligible."

"He is as good a sort of fellow, I believe, as ever lived," repeated Sir John. "I remember last Christmas, at a little hop at the park, he danced from eight o'clock till four, without once sitting down."

"Did he indeed?" cried Marianne, with sparkling eyes, "and with elegance, with spirit?"

"Yes; and he was up again at eight to ride to covert."[1]

"That is what I like; that is what a young man ought to be. Whatever be his pursuits, his eagerness in them should know no moderation, and leave him no sense of fatigue."

"Aye, aye, I see how it will be," said Sir John, "I see how it will be. You will be setting your cap[2] at him now, and never think of poor Brandon."

"That is an expression, Sir John," said Marianne, warmly, "which I particularly dislike. I abhor every common-place phrase by which wit is intended; and 'setting one's cap at a man,' or 'making a conquest,' are the most odious of all. Their tendency is gross and illiberal; and if their construction could ever be deemed clever, time has long ago destroyed all its ingenuity."

Sir John did not much understand this reproof; but he laughed as heartily as if he did, and then replied,

"Aye, you will make conquests enough, I dare say, one way or other. Poor Brandon! he is quite smitten already, and he is very well worth setting your cap at, I can tell you, in spite of all this tumbling about and spraining of ancles."

Chapter X.

Marianne's preserver, as Margaret, with more elegance than precision, stiled Willoughby, called at the cottage early the next morning to make his personal inquiries. He was received by Mrs. Dashwood with more than politeness; with a kindness which Sir John's account of him and her own gratitude prompted; and every thing that passed during the visit, tended to assure him of the sense,

1. Defined in Johnson's *Dictionary* as a "thicket or hiding place." Because game takes shelter in coverts, hunters seek it there.
2. According to the *OED*, said of a woman who decides to gain the affections of a man.

elegance, mutual affection, and domestic comfort of the family to whom accident had now introduced him. Of their personal charms he had not required a second interview to be convinced. Miss Dashwood had a delicate complexion, regular features, and a remarkably pretty figure. Marianne was still handsomer. Her form, though not so correct as her sister's, in having the advantage of height, was more striking; and her face was so lovely, that when in the common cant of praise she was called a beautiful girl, truth was less violently outraged than usually happens. Her skin was very brown, but from its transparency, her complexion was uncommonly brilliant; her features were all good; her smile was sweet and attractive, and in her eyes, which were very dark, there was a life, a spirit, an eagerness which could hardly be seen without delight. From Willoughby their expression was at first held back, by the embarrassment which the remembrance of his assistance created. But when this passed away, when her spirits became collected, when she saw that to the perfect good-breeding of the gentleman, he united frankness and vivacity, and above all, when she heard him declare that of music and dancing he was passionately fond, she gave him such a look of approbation as secured the largest share of his discourse to herself for the rest of his stay.

It was only necessary to mention any favourite amusement to engage her to talk. She could not be silent when such points were introduced, and she had neither shyness nor reserve in their discussion. They speedily discovered that their enjoyment of dancing and music was mutual, and that it arose from a general conformity of judgment in all that related to either. Encouraged by this to a further examination of his opinions, she proceeded to question him on the subject of books; her favourite authors were brought forward and dwelt upon with so rapturous a delight, that any young man of five and twenty must have been insensible indeed, not to become an immediate convert to the excellence of such works, however disregarded before. Their taste was strikingly alike. The same books, the same passages were idolized by each—or if any difference appeared, any objection arose, it lasted no longer than till the force of her arguments and the brightness of her eyes could be displayed. He acquiesced in all her decisions, caught all her enthusiasm; and long before his visit concluded, they conversed with the familiarity of a long-established acquaintance.

"Well, Marianne," said Elinor, as soon as he had left them, "for *one* morning I think you have done pretty well. You have already ascertained Mr. Willoughby's opinion in almost every matter of importance. You know what he thinks of Cowper and Scott; you are certain of his estimating their beauties as he ought, and you have received every assurance of his admiring Pope[1] no more than is proper. But how is your acquaintance to be long supported, under such extraordinary dispatch of every subject for discourse? You will soon have exhausted each favourite topic. Another meeting will suffice to explain his sentiments on picturesque[2] beauty, and second marriages,[3] and then you can have nothing farther to ask."—

"Elinor," cried Marianne, "is this fair? is this just? are my ideas so scanty? But I see what you mean. I have been too much at my ease, too happy, too frank. I have erred against every common-place notion of decorum; I have been open and sincere where I ought to have been reserved, spiritless, dull, and deceitful:—had I talked only of the weather and the roads, and had I spoken only once in ten minutes, this reproach would have been spared."

"My love," said her mother, "you must not be offended with Elinor—she was only in jest. I should scold her myself, if she were capable of wishing to check the delight of your conversation with our new friend."—Marianne was softened in a moment.

Willoughby, on his side, gave every proof of his pleasure in their acquaintance, which an evident wish of improving it could offer. He came to them every day. To inquire after Marianne was at first his excuse; but the encouragement of his reception, to which every day gave greater kindness, made such an excuse unnecessary before it had ceased to be possible, by Marianne's perfect recovery. She was confined for some days to the house; but never had any confinement been less irksome. Willoughby was a young man of good abilities, quick imagination, lively spirits, and open, affectionate manners. He was exactly formed to engage Marianne's heart, for with all this, he joined not only a captivating person, but a natural ardour of mind which was now roused and increased by the example of her own, and which recommended him to her affection beyond every thing else.

1. Marianne prefers contemporary—i.e., Romantic—poetry, with its interest in intense feeling, to the wittier and more detached poetry of Augustans such as Alexander Pope (1688–1744). Marianne's fondness for Sir Walter Scott (1771–1832)—as distinct from Cowper—could not have appeared in the early drafts of *Sense and Sensibility*, for Scott's first popular poem, *The Lay of the Last Minstrel*, appeared in 1805. This suggests that Austen was at pains to show Marianne's literary interests to be contemporary. Although Austen shared Marianne's fondness for Scott and Cowper, she also admired Pope, averring in one of her letters, "There has been one infallible Pope in the world" (26 October 1813), and subsequent episodes of *Sense and Sensibility* possibly allude to his *Rape of the Lock*.
2. A term used to describe a kind of natural scene that lends itself to representation in painting. As distinct from the *beautiful* (which can look dull or flat when painted), the picturesque is marked by irregularity, by rugged textures, and by a variety of light and shade. The picturesque in painting and landscape gardening was in vogue in the late eighteenth and early nineteenth century.
3. The romantic notion that the sensitive soul in general, and the sensitive woman in particular, loves truly only once had much currency at this time. See Contexts, p. 306.

His society became gradually her most exquisite enjoyment. They read, they talked, they sang together; his musical talents were considerable; and he read with all the sensibility and spirit which Edward had unfortunately wanted. In Mrs. Dashwood's estimation, he was as faultless as in Marianne's; and Elinor saw nothing to censure in him but a propensity, in which he strongly resembled and peculiarly delighted her sister, of saying too much what he thought on every occasion, without attention to persons or circumstances. In hastily forming and giving his opinion of other people, in sacrificing general politeness to the enjoyment of undivided attention where his heart was engaged, and in slighting too easily the forms of worldly propriety, he displayed a want of caution which Elinor could not approve, in spite of all that he and Marianne could say in its support.

Marianne began now to perceive that the desperation which had seized her at sixteen and a half, of ever seeing a man who could satisfy her ideas of perfection, had been rash and unjustifiable. Willoughby was all that her fancy had delineated in that unhappy hour and in every brighter period, as capable of attaching her and his behaviour declared his wishes to be in that respect as earnest, as his abilities were* strong.

Her mother too, in whose mind not one speculative thought of their marriage had been raised, by his prospect of riches, was led before the end of a week to hope and expect it; and secretly to congratulate herself on having gained two such sons-in-law as Edward and Willoughby.

Colonel Brandon's partiality for Marianne, which had so early been discovered[4] by his friends, now first became perceptible to Elinor, when it ceased to be noticed by them. Their attention and wit were drawn off to his more fortunate rival; and the raillery which the other had incurred before any partiality arose, was removed when his feelings began really to call for the ridicule so justly annexed to sensibility. Elinor was obliged, though unwillingly, to believe that the sentiments which Mrs. Jennings had assigned him for her own satisfaction, were now actually excited by her sister; and that however a general resemblance of disposition between the parties might forward the affection of Mr. Willoughby, an equally striking opposition of character was no hindrance to the regard of Colonel Brandon. She saw it with concern; for what could a silent man of five and thirty hope, when opposed by a very lively one of five and twenty? and as she could not even wish him

---

* abilities were] ability was A.
4. Disclosed or revealed; this sense is now rare.

successful, she heartily wished him indifferent. She liked him—in spite of his gravity and reserve, she beheld in him an object of interest. His manners, though serious, were mild; and his reserve appeared rather the result of some oppression of spirits, than of any natural gloominess of temper. Sir John had dropt hints of past injuries and disappointments, which justified her belief of his being an unfortunate man, and she regarded him with respect and compassion.

Perhaps she pitied and esteemed him the more because he was slighted by Willoughby and Marianne, who, prejudiced against him for being neither lively nor young, seemed resolved to undervalue his merits.

"Brandon is just the kind of man," said Willoughby one day, when they were talking of him together, "whom every body speaks well of, and nobody cares about; whom all are delighted to see, and nobody remembers to talk to."

"That is exactly what I think of him," cried Marianne.

"Do not boast of it, however," said Elinor, "for it is injustice in both of you. He is highly esteemed by all the family at the park, and I never see him myself without taking pains to converse with him."

"That he is patronized by *you*," replied Willoughby, "is certainly in his favour; but as for the esteem of the others, it is a reproach in itself. Who would submit to the indignity of being approved by such women as Lady Middleton and Mrs. Jennings, that could command the indifference of any body else?"

"But perhaps the abuse of such people as yourself and Marianne, will make amends for the regard of Lady Middleton and her mother. If their praise is censure, your censure may be praise, for they are not more undiscerning, than you are prejudiced and unjust."

"In defence of your protegé you can even be saucy."

"My protegé, as you call him, is a sensible man; and sense will always have attractions for me. Yes, Marianne, even in a man between thirty and forty. He has seen a great deal of the world; has been abroad; has read, and has a thinking mind. I have found him capable of giving me much information on various subjects, and he has always answered my inquiries with the readiness of good-breeding and good nature."

"That is to say," cried Marianne contemptuously, "he has told you that in the East Indies the climate is hot, and the mosquitoes are troublesome."

"He *would* have told me so, I doubt not, had I made any such inquiries, but they happened to be points on which I had been previously informed."

"Perhaps," said Willoughby, "his observations may have extended to the existence of nabobs, gold mohrs, and palanquins."[5]

"I may venture to say that *his* observations have stretched much farther than *your* candour.[6] But why should you dislike him?"

"I do not dislike him. I consider him, on the contrary, as a very respectable man, who has every body's good word and nobody's notice; who has more money than he can spend, more time than he knows how to employ, and two new coats every year."

"Add to which," cried Marianne, "that he has neither genius, taste, nor spirit. That his understanding has no brilliancy, his feelings no ardour, and his voice no expression."

"You decide on his imperfections so much in the mass," replied Elinor, "and so much on the strength of your own imagination, that the commendation *I* am able to give of him is comparatively cold and insipid. I can only pronounce him to be a sensible man, well-bred, well-informed, of gentle address, and I believe possessing an amiable heart."

"Miss Dashwood," cried Willoughby, "you are now using me unkindly. You are endeavouring to disarm me by reason, and to convince me against my will. But it will not do. You shall find me as stubborn as you can be artful. I have three unanswerable reasons for disliking Colonel Brandon: he has threatened me with rain when I wanted it to be fine; he has found fault with the hanging of my curricle,[7] and I cannot persuade him to buy my brown mare. If it will be any satisfaction to you, however, to be told, that I believe his character to be in other respects irreproachable, I am ready to confess it. And in return for an acknowledgment, which must give me some pain, you cannot deny me the privilege of disliking him as much as ever."

Chapter XI.

Little had Mrs. Dashwood or her daughters imagined, when they first came into Devonshire, that so many engagements would arise to occupy their time as shortly presented themselves, or that they

---

5. *Nabobs*: Muslim officials, who acted as deputy governors of provinces or districts in the Mogul Empire. By extension, a person of high rank or great wealth, especially one who returned from India with a large fortune acquired there; a newly rich and luxurious person. *Gold mohrs*: coins used in British India. *Palanquins*: covered litters or conveyances, usually for one person, used in India, and usually carried by four men by poles projecting in front and behind

6. Defined in the *OED* as openness of mind, fairness, impartiality, justice; and in Johnson's *Dictionary* as free from malice, not desirous to find faults.

7. A *curricle* is a lightweight, two-wheeled carriage, drawn by two horses. *Hanging* generally refers to the manner in which the seat is suspended between the wheels, a matter of fashion as well as convenience.

should have such frequent invitations and such constant visitors as to leave them little leisure for serious employment. Yet such was the case. When Marianne was recovered, the schemes of amusement at home and abroad, which Sir John had been previously forming, were put in execution. The private balls at the park then began; and parties on the water were made and accomplished as often as a showery October would allow. In every meeting of the kind Willoughby was included; and the ease and familiarity which naturally attended these parties were exactly calculated to give increasing intimacy to his acquaintance with the Dashwoods, to afford him opportunity of witnessing the excellencies of Marianne, of marking his animated admiration of her, and of receiving, in her behaviour to himself, the most pointed assurance of her affection.

Elinor could not be surprised at their attachment. She only wished that it were less openly shewn; and once or twice did venture to suggest the propriety of some self-command to Marianne. But Marianne abhorred all concealment where no real disgrace could attend unreserve;[1] and to aim at the restraint of sentiments which were not in themselves illaudable, appeared to her not merely an unnecessary effort, but a disgraceful subjection of reason to common-place and mistaken notions. Willoughby thought the same; and their behaviour, at all times, was an illustration of their opinions.

When he was present she had no eyes for any one else. Every thing he did, was right. Every thing he said was clever. If their evenings at the park were concluded with cards, he cheated himself and all the rest of the party to get her a good hand. If dancing formed the amusement of the night, they were partners for half the time; and when obliged to separate for a couple of dances, were careful to stand together and scarcely spoke a word to any body else. Such conduct made them of course most exceedingly laughed at; but ridicule could not shame, and seemed hardly to provoke them.

Mrs. Dashwood entered into all their feelings with a warmth which left her no inclination for checking this excessive display of them. To her it was but the natural consequence of a strong affection in a young and ardent mind.

This was the season of happiness to Marianne. Her heart was devoted to Willoughby, and the fond attachment to Norland, which

---

1. The extent to which women could with propriety reveal their attachments to men prior to a formal engagement was intensely and acrimoniously debated during the 1790s. Marianne's readiness to oppose reigning standards of female manners aligns her with the protofeminist in Frances Burney's *The Wanderer* (1814), who avows her love for a man by declaring: "How paltry is shame where there can be disgrace—I disdain it!— disclaim it!—and am ready to avow to the whole world that I dare speak and act, as well as think and feel for myself!" (Chapter 16).

she brought with her from Sussex, was more likely to be softened than she had thought it possible before, by the charms which his society bestowed on her present home. Elinor's happiness was not so great. Her heart was not so much at ease, nor her satisfaction in their amusements so pure. They afforded her no companion that could make amends for what she had left behind, nor that could teach her to think of Norland with less regret than ever. Neither Lady Middleton nor Mrs. Jennings could supply to her the conversation she missed; although the latter was an everlasting talker, and from the first had regarded her with a kindness which ensured her a large share of her discourse. She had already repeated her own history to Elinor three or four times; and had Elinor's memory been equal to her means of improvement, she might have known very early in their* acquaintance, all the particulars of Mr. Jennings's last illness, and what he said to his wife a few minutes before he died. Lady Middleton was more agreeable than her mother, only in being more silent. Elinor needed little observation to perceive that her reserve was a mere calmness of manner with which sense had nothing to do. Towards her husband and mother she was the same as to them; and intimacy was therefore neither to be looked for nor desired. She had nothing to say one day that she had not said the day before. Her insipidity was invariable, for even her spirits were always the same; and though she did not oppose the parties arranged by her husband, provided every thing were conducted in style and her two eldest children attended her, she never appeared to receive more enjoyment from them, than she might have experienced in sitting at home;—and so little did her presence add to the pleasure of the others, by any share in their conversation, that they were sometimes only reminded of her being amongst them by her solicitude about her troublesome boys.

In Colonel Brandon alone, of all her new acquaintance, did Elinor find a person who could in any degree claim the respect of abilities, excite the interest of friendship, or give pleasure as a companion. Willoughby was out of the question. Her admiration and regard, even her sisterly regard, was all his own; but he was a lover; his attentions were wholly Marianne's, and a far less agreeable man might have been more generally pleasing. Colonel Brandon, unfortunately for himself, had no such encouragement to think only of Marianne, and in conversing with Elinor he found the greatest consolation for the total indifference of her sister.

Elinor's compassion for him increased, as she had reason to suspect that the misery of disappointed love had already been known

---

* their] A; her B.

by him. This suspicion was given by some words which accidentally dropt from him one evening at the park, when they were sitting down together by mutual consent, while the others were dancing. His eyes were fixed on Marianne, and, after a silence of some minutes, he said with a faint smile, "Your sister, I understand, does not approve of second attachments."

"No," replied Elinor, "her opinions are all romantic."

"Or rather, as I believe, she considers them impossible to exist."

"I believe she does. But how she contrives it without reflecting on the character of her own father, who had himself two wives, I know not. A few years however will settle her opinions on the reasonable basis of common sense and observation; and then they may be more easy to define and to justify than they now are, by any body but herself."

"This will probably be the case," he replied; "and yet there is something so amiable in the prejudices of a young mind, that one is sorry to see them give way to the reception of more general opinions."

"I cannot agree with you there," said Elinor. "There are inconveniences attending such feelings as Marianne's, which all the charms of enthusiasm and ignorance of the world cannot atone for. Her systems have all the unfortunate tendency of setting propriety at nought; and a better acquaintance with the world is what I look forward to as her greatest possible advantage."

After a short pause he resumed the conversation by saying—

"Does your sister make no distinction in her objections against a second attachment? or is it equally criminal in every body? Are those who have been disappointed in their first choice, whether from the inconstancy of its object, or the perverseness of circumstances, to be equally indifferent during the rest of their lives?"

"Upon my word, I am not acquainted with the minutia of her principles. I only know that I never yet heard her admit any instance of a second attachment's being pardonable."

"This," said he, "cannot hold; but a change, a total change of sentiments—No, no, do not desire it,—for when the romantic refinements of a young mind are obliged to give way, how frequently are they succeeded by such opinions as are but too common, and too dangerous! I speak from experience. I once knew a lady who in temper and mind greatly resembled your sister, who thought and judged like her, but who from an inforced change—from a series of unfortunate circumstances"——Here he stopt suddenly; appeared to think that he had said too much, and by his countenance gave rise to conjectures, which might not otherwise have entered Elinor's head. The lady would probably have passed without suspicion, had he not convinced Miss Dashwood that what concerned her ought not to escape his lips. As it was, it required but a slight effort of fancy to connect his emotion with the tender recollection of past* regard. Elinor attempted no more. But Marianne, in her place, would not have done so little. The whole story would have been speedily formed under her active imagination; and every thing established in the most melancholy order of disastrous love.

Chapter XII.

As Elinor and Marianne were walking together the next morning the latter communicated a piece of news to her sister, which in spite of all that she knew before of Marianne's imprudence and want of thought, surprised her by its extravagant testimony of both. Marianne told her, with the greatest delight, that Willoughby had given her a horse, one that he had bred himself on his estate in Somersetshire, and which was exactly calculated to carry a woman. Without considering that it was not in her mother's plan to keep any horse,[1] that if she were to alter her resolution in favour of this gift, she must buy another for the servant, and keep a servant to ride it, and after all, build a stable to receive them, she had accepted the present without hesitation, and told her sister of it in raptures.

"He intends to send his groom into Somersetshire immediately for it," she added, "and when it arrives, we will ride every day. You shall share its use with me. Imagine to yourself, my dear Elinor, the delight of a gallop on some of these downs."

Most unwilling was she to awaken from such a dream of felicity, to comprehend all the unhappy truths which attended the affair; and for some time she refused to submit to them. As to an additional servant, the expence would be a trifle; mama she was sure would never object to it; and any horse would do for *him*; he might always get one at the park; as to a stable, the merest shed would be sufficient. Elinor then ventured to doubt the propriety of her receiving such a present from a man so little, or at least so lately known to her. This was too much.

"You are mistaken, Elinor," said she warmly, "in supposing I know very** little of Willoughby. I have not known him long indeed, but I am much better acquainted with him, than I am with any other creature in the world, except yourself and mama. It is not

---

* past] passed A.
1. According to John Trusler, a domestic economist of the time, the cost of feeding and maintaining horses doubled during the Napoleonic Wars, rising to about £40 per year, which would be a huge portion of Mrs. Dashwood's annual budget. I am grateful to Edward Copeland for this information.
** very] but A.

time or opportunity that is to determine intimacy;—it is disposition alone. Seven years would be insufficient to make some people acquainted with each other, and seven days are more than enough for others. I should hold myself guilty of greater impropriety in accepting a horse from my brother, than from Willoughby. Of John I know very little, though we have lived together for years; but of Willoughby my judgment has long been formed."

Elinor thought it wisest to touch that point no more. She knew her sister's temper. Opposition on so tender a subject would only attach her the more to her own opinion. But by an appeal to her affection for her mother, by representing the inconveniences which that indulgent mother must draw on herself, if (as would probably be the case) she consented to this increase of establishment,[2] Marianne was shortly subdued; and she promised not to tempt her mother to such imprudent kindness by mentioning the offer, and to tell Willoughby when she saw him next, that it must be declined.

She was faithful to her word; and when Willoughby called at the cottage, the same day, Elinor heard her express her disappointment to him in a low voice, on being obliged to forego the acceptance of his present. The reasons for this alteration were at the same time related, and they were such as to make further entreaty on his side impossible. His concern however was very apparent; and after expressing it with earnestness, he added in the same low voice—"But, Marianne, the horse is still yours, though you cannot use it now. I shall keep it only till you can claim it. When you leave Barton to form your own establishment in a more lasting home, Queen Mab[3] shall receive you."

This was all overheard by Miss Dashwood; and in the whole of the sentence, in his manner of pronouncing it, and in his addressing her sister by her christian name alone,[4] she instantly saw an intimacy so decided, a meaning so direct, as marked a perfect agreement between them. From that moment she doubted not of their being engaged to each other; and the belief of it created no other surprise, than that she, or any of their friends, should be left by tempers so frank, to discover it by accident.

Margaret related something to her the next day, which placed

---

2. A staff of employees and servants.
3. A fairy queen, described by Mercutio in Shakespeare's *Romeo and Juliet* (1.4) as one who inspires dreams. This fanciful and initially charming allusion grows more ominous, since Mercutio associates Mab with "dreams" that are begotten "of nothing but vain fantasy" and that are "more inconstant than the wind." Like the Dashwood family (which reads *Hamlet*) and the Bertrams in *Mansfield Park*, Austen read widely in Shakespeare's plays as a matter of course.
4. Strict rules regulated forms of address, and because the use of Christian names (without the customary "Miss" and/or surname) signified an intimate relationship, gentlemen would not address young ladies by their Christian names unless they were engaged.

this matter in a still clearer light. Willoughby had spent the preceding evening with them, and Margaret, by being left some time in the parlour with only him and Marianne, had had opportunity for observations, which, with a most important face, she communicated to her eldest sister, when they were next by themselves.

"Oh! Elinor," she cried, "I have such a secret to tell you about Marianne. I am sure she will be married to Mr. Willoughby very soon."

"You have said so," replied Elinor, "almost every day since they first met on High-church Down; and they had not known each other a week, I believe, before you were certain that Marianne wore his picture round her neck; but it turned out to be only the miniature of our great uncle."

"But indeed this is quite another thing. I am sure they will be married very soon, for he has got a lock of her hair."

"Take care, Margaret. It may be only the hair of some great uncle of *his*."

"But indeed, Elinor, it is Marianne's. I am almost sure it is, for I saw him cut it off. Last night after tea, when you and mama went out of the room, they were whispering and talking together as fast as could be, and he seemed to be begging something of her, and presently he took up her scissars and cut off a long lock of her hair, for it was all tumbled down her back; and he kissed it, and folded it up in a piece of white paper, and put it into his pocket-book."

From such particulars, stated on such authority, Elinor could not withhold her credit: nor was she disposed to it, for the circumstance was in perfect unison with what she had heard and seen herself.

Margaret's sagacity was not always displayed in a way so satisfactory to her sister. When Mrs. Jennings attacked her one evening at the park, to give the name of the young man who was Elinor's particular favourite, which had been long a matter of great curiosity to her, Margaret answered by looking at her sister, and saying, "I must not tell, may I, Elinor?"

This of course made every body laugh; and Elinor tried to laugh too. But the effort was painful. She was convinced that Margaret had fixed on a person, whose name she could not bear with composure to become a standing joke with Mrs. Jennings.

Marianne felt for her most sincerely; but she did more harm than good to the cause, by turning very red, and saying in an angry manner to Margaret,

"Remember that whatever your conjectures may be, you have no right to repeat them."

"I never had any conjectures about it," replied Margaret; "it was you who told me of it yourself."

This increased the mirth of the company, and Margaret was eagerly pressed to say something more.

"Oh! pray, Miss Margaret, let us know all about it," said Mrs. Jennings. "What is the gentleman's name?"

"I must not tell, ma'am. But I know very well what it is; and I know where he is too."

"Yes, yes, we can guess where he is; at his own house at Norland to be sure. He is the curate of the parish I dare say."

"No, *that* he is not. He is of no profession at all."

"Margaret," said Marianne with great warmth, "you know that all this is an invention of your own, and that there is no such person in existence."

"Well then he is lately dead, Marianne, for I am sure there was such a man once, and his name begins with an F."

Most grateful did Elinor feel to Lady Middleton for observing at this moment, "that it rained very hard," though she believed the interruption to proceed less from any attention to her, than from her ladyship's great dislike of all such inelegant subjects of raillery as delighted her husband and mother. The idea however started by her, was immediately pursued by Colonel Brandon, who was on every occasion mindful of the feelings of others; and much was said on the subject of rain by both of them. Willoughby opened the piano-forte, and asked Marianne to sit down to it; and thus amidst the various endeavours of different people to quit the topic, it fell to the ground. But not so easily did Elinor recover from the alarm into which it had thrown her.

A party was formed this evening for going on the following day to see a very fine place about twelve miles from Barton, belonging to a brother-in-law of Colonel Brandon, without whose interest it could not be seen, as the proprietor, who was then abroad, had left strict orders on that head. The grounds were declared to be highly beautiful, and Sir John, who was particularly warm in their praise, might be allowed to be a tolerable judge, for he had formed parties to visit them, at least, twice every summer for the last ten years. They contained a noble piece of water; a sail on which was to form a great part of the morning's amusement; cold provisions were to be taken, open carriages only to be employed, and every thing conducted in the usual style of a complete party of pleasure.

To some few of the company, it appeared rather a bold undertaking, considering the time of year, and that it had rained every day for the last fortnight;—and Mrs. Dashwood, who had already a cold, was persuaded by Elinor to stay at home.

Chapter XIII.

Their intended excursion to Whitwell turned out very differently from what Elinor had expected. She was prepared to be wet through, fatigued, and frightened; but the event was still more unfortunate, for they did not go at all. By ten o'clock the whole party were assembled at the park, where they were to breakfast. The morning was rather favourable, though it had rained all night, as the clouds were then dispersing across the sky, and the sun frequently appeared.—They were all in high spirits and good humour, eager to be happy, and determined to submit to the greatest inconveniences and hardships rather than be otherwise.

While they were at breakfast the letters were brought in. Among the rest there was one for Colonel Brandon;—he took it, looked at the direction, changed colour, and immediately left the room.

"What is the matter with Brandon?" said Sir John.

Nobody could tell.

"I hope he has had no bad news," said Lady Middleton. "It must be something extraordinary that could make Colonel Brandon leave my breakfast table so suddenly."

In about five minutes he returned.

"No bad news, Colonel, I hope;" said Mrs. Jennings, as soon as he entered the room.

"None at all, ma'am, I thank you."

"Was it from Avignon? I hope it is not to say that your sister is worse."

"No, ma'am. It came from town, and is merely a letter of business."

"But how came the hand to discompose you so much, if it was only a letter of business? Come, come, this wo'nt do, Colonel; so let us hear the truth of it."

"My dear Madam," said Lady Middleton, "recollect what you are saying."

"Perhaps it is to tell you that your cousin Fanny is married?" said Mrs. Jennings, without attending to her daughter's reproof.

"No, indeed, it is not."

"Well, then, I know who it is from, Colonel. And I hope she is well."

"Whom do you mean, ma'am?" said he, colouring a little.

"Oh! you know who I mean."

"I am particularly sorry, ma'am," said he, addressing Lady Middleton, "that I should receive this letter today, for it is on business which requires my immediate attendance in town."

"In town!" cried Mrs. Jennings. "What can you have to do in town at this time of year?"

"My own loss is great," he continued, "in being obliged to leave so agreeable a party; but I am the more concerned, as I fear my presence is necessary to gain your admittance at Whitwell."

What a blow upon them all was this!

"But if you write a note to the housekeeper, Mr. Brandon," said Marianne eagerly, "will it not be sufficient?"

He shook his head.

"We must go," said Sir John.—"It shall not be put off when we are so near it. You cannot go to town till to-morrow, Brandon, that is all."

"I wish it could be so easily settled. But it is not in my power to delay my journey for one day!"

"If you would but let us know what your business is," said Mrs. Jennings, "we might see whether it could be put off or not."

"You would not be six hours later," said Willoughby, "if you were to defer your journey till our return."

"I cannot afford to lose *one* hour."—

Elinor then heard Willoughby say in a low voice to Marianne, "There are some people who cannot bear a party of pleasure. Brandon is one of them. He was afraid of catching cold I dare say, and invented this trick for getting out of it. I would lay fifty guineas the letter was of his own writing."

"I have no doubt of it," replied Marianne.

"There is no persuading you to change your mind, Brandon, I know of old," said Sir John, "when once you are determined on any thing. But, however, I hope you will think better of it. Consider, here are the two Miss Careys come over from Newton, the three Miss Dashwoods walked up from the cottage, and Mr. Willoughby got up two hours before his usual time, on purpose to go to Whitwell."

Colonel Brandon again repeated his sorrow at being the cause of disappointing the party; but at the same time declared it to be unavoidable.

"Well then, when will you come back again?"

"I hope we shall see you at Barton," added her ladyship, "as soon as you can conveniently leave town; and we must put off the party to Whitwell till you return."

"You are very obliging. But it is so uncertain, when I may have it in my power to return, that I dare not engage for it at all."

"Oh! he must and shall come back," cried Sir John. "If he is not here by the end of the week, I shall go after him."

"Aye, so do, Sir John," cried Mrs. Jennings, "and then perhaps you may find out what his business is."

"I do not want to pry into other men's concerns. I suppose it is something he is ashamed of."

Colonel Brandon's horses were announced.

"You do not go to town on horseback, do you?" added Sir John.

"No. Only to Honiton. I shall then go post."[1]

"Well, as you are resolved to go, I wish you a good journey. But you had better change your mind."

"I assure you it is not in my power."

He then took leave of the whole party.

"Is there no chance of my seeing you and your sisters in town this winter, Miss Dashwood?"

"I am afraid, none at all."

"Then I must bid you farewell for longer time than I should wish to do."

To Marianne, he merely bowed and said nothing.

"Come, Colonel," said Mrs. Jennings, "before you go, do let us know what you are going about."

He wished her a good morning, and attended by Sir John, left the room.

The complaints and lamentations which politeness had hitherto restrained, now burst forth universally; and they all agreed again and again how provoking it was to be so disappointed.

"I can guess what his business is, however," said Mrs. Jennings exultingly.

"Can you, ma'am?" said almost every body.

"Yes; it is about Miss Williams. I am sure."

"And who is Miss Williams?" asked Marianne.

"What! do not you know who Miss Williams is? I am sure you must have heard of her before. She is a relation of the Colonel's, my dear; a very near relation. We will not say how near, for fear of shocking the young ladies." Then lowering her voice a little, she said to Elinor, "She is his natural[2] daughter."

"Indeed!"

"Oh! yes; and as like him as she can stare. I dare say the Colonel will leave her all his fortune."*

When Sir John returned, he joined most heartily in the general

---

1. The post-chaise was a four-wheeled carriage drawn by up to six horses, which would typically be changed at posting stations. It was the quickest and most expensive form of transportation.
2. Illegitimate.
* fortune."] Here A continues: Lady Middleton's delicacy was shocked; and in order to banish so improper a subject as the mention of a natural daughter, she actually took the trouble of saying something about the weather. *Austen's decision to delete this sentence has occasioned misunderstanding, largely because Chapman claimed she did so "in the interests of propriety." This is not quite right, because Austen actually retains the scandalous phrase. It might be apter to say that Austen curbed the irreverence of her satire on propriety.*

regret on so unfortunate an event; concluding however by observing, that as they were all got together, they must do something by way of being happy; and after some consultation it was agreed, that although happiness could only be enjoyed at Whitwell, they might procure a tolerable composure of mind by driving about the country. The carriages were then ordered; Willoughby's was first, and Marianne never looked happier than when she got into it. He drove through the park very fast, and they were soon out of sight; and nothing more of them was seen till their return, which did not happen till after the return of all the rest. They both seemed delighted with their drive, but said only in general terms that they had kept in the lanes, while the others went on the downs.

It was settled that there should be a dance in the evening, and that every body should be extremely merry all day long. Some more of the Careys came to dinner, and they had the pleasure of sitting down nearly twenty to table, which Sir John observed with great contentment. Willoughby took his usual place between the two elder Miss Dashwoods. Mrs. Jennings sat on Elinor's right hand; and they had not been long seated, before she leant behind her and Willoughby, and said to Marianne; loud enough for them both to hear, "I have found you out in spite of all your tricks. I know where you spent the morning."

Marianne coloured, and replied very hastily, "Where, pray?"—

"Did not you know," said Willoughby, "that we had been out in my curricle?"

"Yes, yes, Mr. Impudence, I know that very well, and I was determined to find out *where* you had been to.—I hope you like your house, Miss Marianne. It is a very large one I know, and when I come to see you, I hope you will have new-furnished it, for it wanted it very much, when I was there six years ago."

Marianne turned away in great confusion. Mrs. Jennings laughed heartily; and Elinor found that in her resolution to know where they had been, she had actually made her own woman enquire of Mr. Willoughby's groom, and that she had by that method been informed that they had gone to Allenham, and spent a considerable time there in walking about the garden and going all over the house.

Elinor could hardly believe this to be true, as it seemed very unlikely that Willoughby should propose, or Marianne consent, to enter the house while Mrs. Smith was in it, with whom Marianne had not the smallest acquaintance.

As soon as they left the dining-room, Elinor enquired of her about it; and great was her surprise when she found that every circumstance related by Mrs. Jennings was perfectly true. Marianne was quite angry with her for doubting it.

"Why should you imagine, Elinor, that we did not go there, or
that we did not see the house? Is not it what you have often wished
to do yourself?"

"Yes, Marianne, but I would not go while Mrs. Smith was there,
and with no other companion than Mr. Willoughby."

"Mr. Willoughby however is the only person who can have a right
to shew that house; and as we* went in an open carriage, it was
impossible to have any other companion. I never spent a pleasanter
morning in my life."

"I am afraid," replied Elinor, "that the pleasantness of an employment does not always evince its propriety."

"On the contrary, nothing can be a stronger proof of it, Elinor;
for if there had been any real impropriety in what I did, I should
have been sensible of it at the time, for we always know when we
are acting wrong, and with such a conviction I could have had no
pleasure."

"But, my dear Marianne, as it has already exposed you to some
very impertinent remarks, do you not now begin to doubt the discretion of your own conduct?"

"If the impertinent remarks of Mrs. Jennings are to be the proof
of impropriety in conduct, we are all offending every moment of all
our lives. I value not her censure any more than I should do her
commendation. I am not sensible of having done any thing wrong
in walking over Mrs. Smith's grounds, or in seeing her house. They
will one day be Mr. Willoughby's, and" . . . . .

"If they were one day to be your own, Marianne, you would not
be justified in what you have done."

She blushed at this hint; but it was even visibly gratifying to her;
and after a ten minutes' interval of earnest thought, she came to
her sister again, and said with great good humour, "Perhaps, Elinor,
it *was* rather ill-judged in me to go to Allenham; but Mr. Willoughby
wanted particularly to shew me the place; and it is a charming
house I assure you.—There is one remarkably pretty sitting room
up stairs; of a nice comfortable size for constant use, and with
modern furniture it would be delightful. It is a corner room, and
has windows on two sides. On one side you look across the bowling-
green, behind the house, to a beautiful hanging wood,³ and on the
other you have a view of the church and village, and, beyond them,
of those fine bold hills that we have so often admired. I did not see
it to advantage, for nothing could be more forlorn than the
furniture,—but if it were newly fitted up——a couple of hundred

* we] A; he B. *Certainly a printer's error.*
3. Forests on a slope or hillside.

pounds, Willoughby says, would make it one of the pleasantest summer-rooms in England."

Could Elinor have listened to her without interruption from the others, she would have described every room in the house with equal delight.

Chapter XIV.

The sudden termination of Colonel Brandon's visit at the park, with his steadiness in concealing its cause, filled the mind and raised the wonder of Mrs. Jennings for two or three days; she was a great wonderer, as every one must be who takes a very lively interest in all the comings and goings of all their acquaintance. She wondered with little intermission what could be the reason of it; was sure there must be some bad news, and thought over every kind of distress that could have befallen him, with a fixed determination that he should not escape them all.

"Something very melancholy must be the matter, I am sure," said she. "I could see it in his face. Poor man! I am afraid his circumstances may be bad. The estate at Delaford was never reckoned more than two thousand a year, and his brother left every thing sadly involved. I do think he must have been sent for about money matters, for what else can it be? I wonder whether it is so. I would give any thing to know the truth of it. Perhaps it is about Miss Williams—and, by the bye, I dare say it is, because he looked so conscious when I mentioned her. May be she is ill in town; nothing in the world more likely, for I have a notion she is always rather sickly. I would lay any wager it is about Miss Williams. It is not so very likely he should be distressed in his circumstances *now*, for he is a very prudent man, and to be sure must have cleared the estate by this time. I wonder what it can be! May be his sister is worse at Avignon, and has sent for him over. His setting off in such a hurry seems very like it. Well, I wish him out of all his trouble with all my heart, and a good wife into the bargain."

So wondered, so talked Mrs. Jennings. Her* opinion varying with every fresh conjecture, and all seeming equally probable as they arose. Elinor, though she felt really interested in the welfare of Colonel Brandon, could not bestow all the wonder on his going so suddenly away, which Mrs. Jennings was desirous of her feeling;

---

* Mrs. Jennings. Her] AB. *Evidently uncomfortable with the grammar of this construction, R. W. Chapman and other editors emend to* Mrs. Jennings, her *For another site in* Sense and Sensibility *where Austen appears content with a sentence fragment, see pp.* 200–201.

for besides that the circumstance did not in her opinion justify such lasting amazement or variety of speculation, her wonder was otherwise disposed of. It was engrossed by the extraordinary silence of her sister and Willoughby on the subject, which they must know to be peculiarly interesting to them all. As this silence continued, every day made it appear more strange and more incompatible with the disposition of both. Why they should not openly acknowledge to her mother and herself, what their constant behaviour to each other declared to have taken place, Elinor could not imagine.

She could easily conceive that marriage might not be immediately in their power; for though Willoughby was independent, there was no reason to believe him rich. His estate had been rated by Sir John at about six or seven hundred a year; but he lived at an expense to which that income could hardly be equal, and he had himself often complained of his poverty. But for this strange kind of secrecy maintained by them relative to their engagement, which in fact concealed nothing at all, she could not account; and it was so wholly contradictory to their general opinions and practice, that a doubt sometimes entered her mind of their being really engaged, and this doubt was enough to prevent her making any inquiry of Marianne.

Nothing could be more expressive of attachment to them all, than Willoughby's behaviour. To Marianne it had all the distinguishing tenderness which a lover's heart could give, and to the rest of the family it was the affectionate attention of a son and a brother. The cottage seemed to be considered and loved by him as his home; many more of his hours were spent there than at Allenham; and if no general engagement collected them at the park, the exercise which called him out in the morning was almost certain of ending there, where the rest of the day was spent by himself at the side of Marianne, and by his favourite pointer at her feet.

One evening in particular, about a week after Colonel Brandon had left the country, his heart seemed more than usually open to every feeling of attachment to the objects around him; and on Mrs. Dashwood's happening to mention her design of improving the cottage in the spring, he warmly opposed every alteration of a place which affection had established as perfect with him.

"What!" he exclaimed—"Improve this dear cottage! No. *That* I will never consent to. Not a stone must be added to its walls, not an inch to its size, if my feelings are regarded."

"Do not be alarmed," said Miss Dashwood, "nothing of the kind will be done; for my mother will never have money enough to attempt it."

"I am heartily glad of it," he cried. "May she always be poor, if she can employ her riches no better."

"Thank you, Willoughby. But you may be assured that I would

not sacrifice one sentiment of local attachment of yours, or of any one whom I loved, for all the improvements in the world. Depend upon it that whatever unemployed sum may remain, when I make up my accounts in the spring, I would even rather lay it uselessly by than dispose of it in a manner so painful to you. But are you really so attached to this place as to see no defect in it?"

"I am," said he. "To me it is faultless. Nay, more, I consider it as the only form of building in which happiness is attainable, and were I rich enough, I would instantly pull Combe down, and build it up again in the exact plan of this cottage."

"With dark narrow stairs, and a kitchen that smokes, I suppose," said Elinor.

"Yes," cried he in the same eager tone, "with all and every thing belonging to it;—in no one convenience or *in*convenience about it, should the least variation be perceptible. Then, and then only, under such a roof, I might perhaps be as happy at Combe as I have been at Barton."

"I flatter myself," replied Elinor, "that even under the disadvantage of better rooms and a broader staircase, you will hereafter find your own house as faultless as you now do this."

"There certainly are circumstances," said Willoughby, "which might greatly endear it to me; but this place will always have one claim on my affection, which no other can possibly share."

Mrs. Dashwood looked with pleasure at Marianne, whose fine eyes were fixed so expressively on Willoughby, as plainly denoted how well she understood him.

"How often did I wish," added he, "when I was at Allenham this time twelvemonth, that Barton cottage were inhabited! I never passed within view of it without admiring its situation, and grieving that no one should live in it. How little did I then think that the very first news I should hear from Mrs. Smith, when I next came into the country, would be that Barton cottage was taken: and I felt an immediate satisfaction and interest in the event, which nothing but a kind of prescience of what happiness I should experience from it, can account for. Must it not have been so, Marianne?" speaking to her in a lowered voice. Then continuing his former tone, he said, "And yet this house you would spoil, Mrs. Dashwood? You would rob it of its simplicity by imaginary improvement! and this dear parlour, in which our acquaintance first began, and in which so many happy hours have been since spent by us together, you would degrade to the condition of a common entrance, and every body would be eager to pass through the room which has hitherto contained within itself, more real accommodation and comfort than any other apartment of the handsomest dimensions in the world could possibly afford."

Mrs. Dashwood again assured him that no alteration of the kind should be attempted.

"You are a good woman," he warmly replied. "Your promise makes me easy. Extend it a little farther, and it will make me happy. Tell me that not only your house will remain the same, but that I shall ever find you and yours as unchanged as your dwelling; and that you will always consider me with the kindness which has made every thing belonging to you so dear to me."

The promise was readily given, and Willoughby's behaviour during the whole of the evening declared at once his affection and happiness.

"Shall we see you to-morrow to dinner?" said Mrs. Dashwood when he was leaving them. "I do not ask you to come in the morning, for we must walk to the park, to call on Lady Middleton."

He engaged to be with them by four o'clock.

Chapter XV.

Mrs. Dashwood's visit to Lady Middleton took place the next day, and two of her daughters went with her; but Marianne excused herself from being of the party under some trifling pretext of employment; and her mother, who concluded that a promise had been made by Willoughby the night before of calling on her while they were absent, was perfectly satisfied with her remaining at home.

On their return from the park they found Willoughby's curricle and servant in waiting at the cottage, and Mrs. Dashwood was convinced that her conjecture had been just. So far it was all as she had foreseen; but on entering the house she beheld what no foresight had taught her to expect. They were no sooner in the passage than Marianne came hastily out of the parlour apparently in violent affliction, with her handkerchief at her eyes; and without noticing them ran up stairs. Surprised and alarmed they proceeded directly into the room she had just quitted, where they found only Willoughby, who was leaning against the mantle-piece with his back towards them. He turned round on their coming in, and his countenance shewed that he strongly partook of the emotion which overpowered Marianne.

"Is any thing the matter with her?" cried Mrs. Dashwood as she entered—"is she ill?"

"I hope not," he replied, trying to look cheerful; and with a forced smile presently added, "It is I who may rather expect to be ill—for I am now suffering under a very heavy disappointment!"

"Disappointment!"

"Yes, for I am unable to keep my engagement with you. Mrs.

Smith has this morning exercised the privilege of riches upon a poor dependant cousin, by sending me on business to London. I have just received my dispatches, and taken my farewel of Allenham; and by way of exhilaration I am now come to take my farewel of you."

"To London!—and are you going this morning?"

"Almost this moment."

"This is very unfortunate. But Mrs. Smith must be obliged;—and her business will not detain you from us long I hope."

He coloured as he replied, "You are very kind, but I have no idea of returning into Devonshire immediately. My visits to Mrs. Smith are never repeated within the twelvemonth."

"And is Mrs. Smith your only friend? Is Allenham the only house in the neighbourhood to which you will be welcome? For shame, Willoughby. Can you wait for an invitation here?"

His colour increased; and with his eyes fixed on the ground he only replied, "You are too good."

Mrs. Dashwood looked at Elinor with surprise. Elinor felt equal amazement. For a few moments every one was silent. Mrs. Dashwood first spoke.

"I have only to add, my dear Willoughby, that at Barton cottage you will always be welcome; for I will not press you to return here immediately, because you only can judge how far *that* might be pleasing to Mrs. Smith; and on this head I shall be no more disposed to question your judgment than to doubt your inclination."

"My engagements at present," replied Willoughby confusedly, "are of such a nature—that—I dare not flatter myself"—

He stopt. Mrs. Dashwood was too much astonished to speak, and another pause succeeded. This was broken by Willoughby, who said with a faint smile, "It is folly to linger in this manner. I will not torment myself any longer by remaining among friends whose society it is impossible for me now to enjoy."

He then hastily took leave of them all and left the room. They saw him step into his carriage, and in a minute it was out of sight.

Mrs. Dashwood felt too much for speech, and instantly quitted the parlour to give way in solitude to the concern and alarm which this sudden departure occasioned.

Elinor's uneasiness was at least equal to her mother's. She thought of what had just passed with anxiety and distrust. Willoughby's behaviour in taking leave of them, his embarrassment, and affectation of cheerfulness and, above all, his unwillingness to accept her mother's invitation, a backwardness so unlike a lover, so unlike himself, greatly disturbed her. One moment she feared that no serious design had ever been formed on his side; and the next that some unfortunate quarrel had taken place between him and her sister;—the distress in which Marianne had quitted the room was such as a serious quarrel could most reasonably account for, though when she considered what Marianne's love for him was, a quarrel seemed almost impossible.

But whatever might be the particulars of their separation, her sister's affliction was indubitable; and she thought with the tenderest compassion of that violent sorrow which Marianne was in all probability not merely giving way to as a relief, but feeding and encouraging as a duty.

In about half an hour her mother returned, and though her eyes were red, her countenance was not uncheerful.

"Our dear Willoughby is now some miles from Barton, Elinor," said she, as she sat down to work,[1] "and with how heavy a heart does he travel?"

"It is all very strange. So suddenly to be gone! It seems but the work of a moment. And last night he was with us so happy, so cheerful, so affectionate? And now after only ten minutes notice—Gone too without intending to return!—Something more than what he owned to us must have happened. He did not speak, he did not behave like himself. You must have seen the difference as well as I. What can it be? Can they have quarrelled? Why else should he have shewn such unwillingness to accept your invitation here?"—

"It was not inclination that he wanted, Elinor; I could plainly see *that*. He had not the power of accepting it. I have thought it all over I assure you, and I can perfectly account for every thing that at first seemed strange to me as well as to you."

"Can you indeed?"

"Yes. I have explained it to myself in the most satisfactory way; —but you, Elinor, who love to doubt where you can——It will not satisfy *you*, I know; but you shall not talk *me* out of my trust in it. I am persuaded that Mrs. Smith suspects his regard for Marianne, disapproves of it, (perhaps because she has other views for him,) and on that account is eager to get him away;—and that the business which she sends him off to transact, is invented as an excuse to dismiss him. This is what I believe to have happened. He is moreover aware that she *does* disapprove the connection, he dares not therefore at present confess to her his engagement with Marianne, and he feels himself obliged, from his dependent situation, to give into her schemes, and absent himself from Devonshire for a while. You will tell me, I know, that this may, or may *not* have happened; but I will listen to no cavil, unless you can point out any other method of understanding the affair as satisfactory as this. And now, Elinor, what have you to say?"

"Nothing, for you have anticipated my answer."

---

1. To do needlework or embroidery.

"Then you would have told me, that it might or might not have happened. Oh! Elinor, how incomprehensible are your feelings! You had rather take evil upon credit than good. You had rather look out for misery for Marianne and guilt for poor Willoughby, than an apology² for the latter. You are resolved to think him blameable, because he took leave of us with less affection than his usual behaviour has shewn. And is no allowance to be made for inadvertence, or for spirits depressed by recent disappointment? Are no probabilities to be accepted, merely because they are not certainties? Is nothing due to the man whom we have all so much reason to love, and no reason in the world to think ill of? To the possibility of motives unanswerable in themselves, though unavoidably secret for a while? And, after all, what is it you suspect him of?"

"I can hardly tell you myself.—But suspicion of something unpleasant is the inevitable consequence of such an alteration as we have just witnessed in him. There is great truth, however, in what you have now urged of the allowances which ought to be made for him, and it is my wish to be candid in my judgment of every body. Willoughby may undoubtedly have very sufficient reasons for his conduct, and I will hope that he has. But it would have been more like Willoughby to acknowledge them at once. Secrecy may be advisable; but still I cannot help wondering at its being practised by him."

"Do not blame him, however, for departing from his character, where the deviation is necessary. But you really do admit the justice of what I have said in his defence?—I am happy—and he is acquitted."

"Not entirely. It may be proper to conceal their engagement (if they *are* engaged) from Mrs. Smith—and if that is the case, it must be highly expedient for Willoughby to be but little in Devonshire at present. But this is no excuse for their concealing it from us."

"Concealing it from us! my dear child, do you accuse Willoughby and Marianne of concealment? This is strange indeed, when your eyes have been reproaching them every day for incautiousness."

"I want no proof of their affection," said Elinor; "but of their engagement I do."

"I am perfectly satisfied of both."

"Yet not a syllable has been said to you on the subject, by either of them."

"I have not wanted syllables where actions have spoken so plainly. Has not his behaviour to Marianne and to all of us, for at least the last fortnight, declared that he loved and considered her as his future wife, and that he felt for us the attachment of the nearest

2. Defense.

relation? Have we not perfectly understood each other? Has not my consent been daily asked by his looks, his manner, his attentive and affectionate respect? My Elinor, is it possible to doubt their engagement? How could such a thought occur to you? How is it to be supposed that Willoughby, persuaded as he must be of your sister's love, should leave her, and leave her perhaps for months, without telling her of his affection;—that they should part without a mutual exchange of confidence?"

"I confess," replied Elinor, "that every circumstance except *one* in favour of their engagement; but that *one* is the total silence of both on the subject, and with me it almost outweighs every other."

"How strange this is! You must think wretchedly indeed of Willoughby, if after all that has openly passed between them, you can doubt the nature of the terms on which they are together. Has he been acting a part in his behaviour to your sister all this time? Do you suppose him really indifferent to her?"

"No, I cannot think that. He must and does love her I am sure."

"But with a strange kind of tenderness, if he can leave her with such indifference, such carelessness of the future, as you attribute to him."

"You must remember, my dear mother, that I have never considered this matter as certain. I have had my doubts, I confess; but they are fainter than they were, and they may soon be entirely done away. If we find they correspond,[3] every fear of mine will be removed."

"A mighty concession indeed! If you were to see them at the altar, you would suppose they were going to be married. Ungracious girl! But *I* require no such proof. Nothing in my opinion has ever passed to justify doubt; no secrecy has been attempted; all has been uniformly open and unreserved. You cannot doubt your sister's wishes. It must be Willoughby therefore whom you suspect. But why? Is he not a man of honour and feeling? Has there been any inconsistency on his side to create alarm? can he be deceitful?"

"I hope not, I believe not," cried Elinor. "I love Willoughby, sincerely love him; and suspicion of his integrity cannot be more painful to yourself than to me. It has been involuntary, and I will not encourage it. I was startled, I confess, by the alteration in his manners this morning;—he did not speak like himself, and did not return your kindness with any cordiality. But all this may be explained by such a situation of his affairs as you have supposed. He had just parted from my sister, had seen her leave him in the greatest af-

---

3. Because marriageable men and women customarily wrote letters to each other only if they were engaged, Elinor is looking for an exchange of letters here in order to determine the nature of her sister's relationship with Willoughby.

fliction; and if he felt obliged, from a fear of offending Mrs. Smith, to resist the temptation of returning here soon, and yet aware that by declining your invitation, by saying that he was going away for some time, he should seem to act an ungenerous, a suspicious part by our family, he might well be embarrassed and disturbed. In such a case, a plain and open avowal of his difficulties would have been more to his honour I think, as well as more consistent with his general character;—but I will not raise objectious against any one's conduct on so illiberal a foundation, as a difference in judgment from myself, or a deviation from what I may think right and consistent."

"You speak very properly. Willoughby certainly does not deserve to be suspected. Though we have not known him long, he is no stranger in this part of the world; and who has ever spoken to his disadvantage? Had he been in a situation to act independently and marry immediately, it might have been odd that he should leave us without acknowledging every thing to me at once: but this is not the case. It is an engagement in some respects not prosperously begun, for their marriage must be at a very uncertain distance; and even secrecy, as far as it can be observed, may now be very advisable."

They were interrupted by the entrance of Margaret; and Elinor was then at liberty to think over the representations of her mother, to acknowledge the probability of many, and hope for the justice of all.

They saw nothing of Marianne till dinner time, when she entered the room and took her place at the table without saying a word. Her eyes were red and swollen; and it seemed as if her tears were even then restrained with difficulty. She avoided the looks of them all, could neither eat nor speak, and after some time, on her mother's silently pressing her hand with tender compassion, her small degree of fortitude was quite overcome, she burst into tears and left the room.

This violent oppression of spirits continued the whole evening. She was without any power, because she was without any desire of command over herself. The slightest mention of any thing relative to Willoughby overpowered her in an instant; and though her family were most anxiously attentive to her comfort, it was impossible for them, if they spoke at all, to keep clear of every subject which her feelings connected with him.

Chapter XVI.

Marianne would have thought herself very inexcusable had she been able to sleep at all the first night after parting from Willoughby. She would have been ashamed to look her family in the face the next morning, had she not risen from her bed in more need of repose than when she lay down in it. But the feelings which made such composure a disgrace, left her in no danger of incurring it. She was awake the whole night, and she wept the greatest part of it. She got up with an headache, was unable to talk, and unwilling to take any nourishment; giving pain every moment to her mother and sisters, and forbidding all attempt at consolation from either. Her sensibility was potent enough!

When breakfast was over she walked out by herself, and wandered about the village of Allenham, indulging the recollection of past enjoyment and crying over the present reverse for the chief of the morning.

The evening passed off in the equal indulgence of feeling. She played over every favourite song that she had been used to play to Willoughby, every air in which their voices had been oftenest joined, and sat at the instrument gazing on every line of music that he had written out for her, till her heart was so heavy that no farther sadness could be gained; and this nourishment of grief was every day applied. She spent whole hours at the piano-forte alternately singing and crying; her voice often totally suspended by her tears. In books too, as well as in music, she courted the misery which a contrast between the past and present was certain of giving. She read nothing but what they had been used to read together.

Such violence of affliction indeed could not be supported for ever; it sunk within a few days into a calmer melancholy; but these employments, to which she daily recurred, her solitary walks and silent meditations, still produced occasional effusions of sorrow as lively as ever.

No letter from Willoughby came; and none seemed expected by Marianne. Her mother was surprised, and Elinor again became uneasy. But Mrs. Dashwood could find explanations whenever she wanted them, which at least satisfied herself.

"Remember, Elinor," said she, "how very often Sir John fetches our letters himself from the post, and carries them to it. We have already agreed that secrecy may be necessary, and we must acknowledge that it could not be maintained if their correspondence were to pass through Sir John's hands."

Elinor could not deny the truth of this, and she tried to find in it a motive sufficient for their silence. But there was one method so direct, so simple, and in her opinion so eligible of knowing the real state of the affair, and of instantly removing all mystery, that she could not help suggesting it to her mother.

"Why do you not ask Marianne at once," said she, "whether she is or is not engaged to Willoughby? From you, her mother, and so kind, so indulgent a mother, the question could not give offence. It would be the natural result of your affection for her. She used to be all unreserve, and to you more especially."

"I would not ask such a question for the world. Supposing it possible that they are not engaged, what distress would not such an inquiry inflict! At any rate it would be most ungenerous. I should never deserve her confidence again, after forcing from her a confession of what is meant at present to be unacknowledged to any one. I know Marianne's heart: I know that she dearly loves me, and that I shall not be the last to whom the affair is made known, when circumstances make the revealment of it eligible. I would not attempt to force the confidence of any one; of a child much less; because a sense of duty would prevent the denial which her wishes might direct."

Elinor thought this generosity overstrained, considering her sister's youth, and urged the matter farther, but in vain; common sense, common care, common prudence, were all sunk in Mrs. Dashwood's romantic delicacy.

It was several days before Willoughby's name was mentioned before Marianne by any of her family; Sir John and Mrs. Jennings, indeed, were not so nice; their witticisms added pain to many a painful hour;—but one evening, Mrs. Dashwood, accidentally taking up a volume of Shakespeare, exclaimed,

"We have never finished Hamlet, Marianne; our dear Willoughby went away before we could get through it. We will put it by, that when he comes again . . . . . But it may be months, perhaps, before *that* happens."

"Months!" cried Marianne, with strong surprise. "No—nor many weeks."

Mrs. Dashwood was sorry for what she had said; but it gave Elinor pleasure, as it produced a reply from Marianne so expressive of confidence in Willoughby and knowledge of his intentions.

One morning, about a week after his leaving the country, Marianne was prevailed on to join her sisters in their usual walk, instead of wandering away by herself. Hitherto she had carefully avoided every companion in her rambles. If her sisters intended to walk on the downs, she directly stole away towards the lanes; if they talked of the valley, she was as speedy in climbing the hills, and could never be found when the others set off. But at length she was secured by the exertions of Elinor, who greatly disapproved such continual seclusion. They walked along the road through the valley, and chiefly in silence, for Marianne's *mind* could not be controuled, and Elinor, satisfied with gaining one point, would not then attempt more. Beyond the entrance of the valley, where the country, though still rich, was less wild and more open, a long stretch of the road which they had travelled on first coming to Barton, lay before them; and on reaching that point, they stopped to look around them, and examine a prospect which formed the distance of their view from the cottage, from a spot which they had never happened to reach in any of their walks before.

Amongst the objects in the scene, they soon discovered an animated one; it was a man on horseback riding towards them. In a few minutes they could distinguish him to be a gentleman; and in a moment afterwards Marianne rapturously exclaimed,

"It is he; it is indeed;—I know it is!"—And was hastening to meet him, when Elinor cried out,

"Indeed, Marianne, I think you are mistaken. It is not Willoughby. The person is not tall enough for him, and has not his air."

"He has, he has," cried Marianne, "I am sure he has. His air, his coat, his horse. I knew how soon he would come."

She walked eagerly on as she spoke; and Elinor, to screen Marianne from particularity, as she felt almost certain of its not being Willoughby, quickened her pace and kept up with her. They were soon within thirty yards of the gentleman. Marianne looked again; her heart sunk within her; and abruptly turning round, she was hurrying back, when the voices of both her sisters were raised to detain her, a third, almost as well known as Willoughby's, joined them in begging her to stop, and she turned round with surprise to see and welcome Edward Ferrars.

He was the only person in the world who could at that moment be forgiven for not being Willoughby; the only one who could have gained a smile from her; but she dispersed her tears to smile on *him*, and in her sister's happiness forgot for a time her own disappointment.

He dismounted, and giving his horse to his servant, walked back with them to Barton, whither he was purposely coming to visit them.

He was welcomed by them all with great cordiality, but especially by Marianne, who shewed more warmth of regard in her reception of him than even Elinor herself. To Marianne, indeed, the meeting between Edward and her sister was but a continuation of that unaccountable coldness which she had often observed at Norland in their mutual behaviour. On Edward's side, more particularly, there was a deficiency of all that a lover ought to look and say on such an occasion. He was confused, seemed scarcely sensible of pleasure in seeing them, looked neither rapturous nor gay, said little but what was forced from him by questions, and distinguished Elinor by no mark of affection. Marianne saw and listened with increasing surprise. She began almost to feel a dislike of Edward; and it ended, as every feeling must end with her, by carrying back her thoughts to Willoughby, whose manners formed a contrast sufficiently striking to those of his brother elect.

After a short silence which succeeded the first surprise and inquiries of meeting, Marianne asked Edward if he came directly from London. No, he had been in Devonshire a fortnight.

"A fortnight!" she repeated, surprised at his being so long in the same country with Elinor without seeing her before.

He looked rather distressed as he added, that he had been staying with some friends near Plymouth.

"Have you been lately in Sussex?" said Elinor.

"I was at Norland about a month ago."

"And how does dear, dear Norland look?" cried Marianne.

"Dear, dear Norland," said Elinor, "probably looks much as it always does at this time of year. The woods and walks thickly covered with dead leaves."

"Oh!" cried Marianne, "with what transporting sensations have I formerly seen them fall! How have I delighted, as I walked, to see them driven in showers about me by the wind! What feelings have they, the season, the air altogether inspired! Now there is no one to regard them. They are seen only as a nuisance, swept hastily off, and driven as much as possible from the sight."

"It is not every one," said Elinor, "who has your passion for dead leaves."

"No; my feelings are not often shared, not often understood. But *sometimes* they are."—As she said this, she sunk into a reverie for a few moments;—but rousing herself again, "Now, Edward," said she, calling his attention to the prospect, "here is Barton valley. Look up it, and be tranquil if you can. Look at those hills! Did you ever see their equals? To the left is Barton park, amongst those woods and plantations.[1] You may see one end of the house. And there, beneath that farthest hill, which rises with such grandeur, is our cottage."

"It is a beautiful country," he replied; "but these bottoms[2] must be dirty in winter."

"How can you think of dirt, with such objects before you?"

"Because," replied he, smiling, "among the rest of the objects before me, I see a very dirty lane."

"How strange!" said Marianne to herself as she walked on.

"Have you an agreeable neighbourhood here? Are the Middletons pleasant people?"

1. Here, areas where trees are planted.
2. Low lands, valleys.

"No, not at all,"* answered Marianne, "we could not be more unfortunately situated."

"Marianne," cried her sister, "how can you say so? How can you be so unjust? They are a very respectable family, Mr. Ferrars; and towards us have behaved in the friendliest manner. Have you forgot, Marianne, how many pleasant days we have owed to them?"

"No," said Marianne in a low voice, "nor how many painful moments."

Elinor took no notice of this, and directing her attention to their visitor, endeavoured to support something like discourse with him by talking of their present residence, its conveniences, &c. extorting from him occasional questions and remarks. His coldness and reserve mortified her severely; she was vexed and half angry; but resolving to regulate her behaviour to him by the past rather than the present, she avoided every appearance of resentment or displeasure, and treated him as she thought he ought to be treated from the family connection.

Chapter XVII.

Mrs. Dashwood was surprised only for a moment at seeing him; for his coming to Barton was, in her opinion, of all things the most natural. Her joy and expressions of regard long outlived her wonder. He received the kindest welcome from her; and shyness, coldness, reserve could not stand against such a reception. They had begun to fail him before he entered the house, and they were quite overcome by the captivating manners of Mrs. Dashwood. Indeed a man could not very well be in love with either of her daughters, without extending the passion to her; and Elinor had the satisfaction of seeing him soon become more like himself. His affections seemed to reanimate towards them all, and his interest in their welfare again became perceptible. He was not in spirits however; he praised their house, admired its prospect, was attentive, and kind; but still he was not in spirits. The whole family perceived it, and Mrs. Dashwood, attributing it to some want of liberality in his mother, sat down to table indignant against all selfish parents.

"What are Mrs. Ferrars's views for you at present, Edward?" said she, when dinner was over and they had drawn round the fire; "are you still to be a great orator in spite of yourself?"

"No. I hope my mother is now convinced that I have no more talents than inclination for a public life!"

"But how is your fame to be established? for famous you must be to satisfy all your family; and with no inclination for expense, no affection for strangers, no profession, and no assurance, you may find it a difficult matter."

"I shall not attempt it. I have no wish to be distinguished; and I have every reason to hope I never shall. Thank Heaven! I cannot be forced into genius and eloquence."

"You have no ambition, I well know. Your wishes are all moderate."

"As moderate as those of the rest of the world, I believe. I wish as well as every body else to be perfectly happy; but like every body else it must be in my own way. Greatness will not make me so."

"Strange if it would!" cried Marianne. "What have wealth or grandeur to do with happiness?"

"Grandeur has but little," said Elinor, "but wealth has much to do with it."

"Elinor, for shame!" said Marianne; "money can only give happiness where there is nothing else to give it. Beyond a competence,[1] it can afford no real satisfaction, as far as mere self is concerned."

"Perhaps," said Elinor, smiling, "we may come to the same point. *Your* competence and *my* wealth are very much alike, I dare say; and without them, as the world goes now, we shall both agree that every kind of external comfort must be wanting. Your ideas are only more noble than mine. Come, what is your competence?"

"About eighteen hundred or two thousand a-year; not more than *that*."

Elinor laughed. "*Two* thousand a-year! *One* is my wealth! I guessed how it would end."

"And yet two thousand a-year is a very moderate income," said Marianne. "A family[2] cannot well be maintained on a smaller. I am sure I am not extravagant in my demands. A proper establishment of servants, a carriage, perhaps two, and hunters,[3] cannot be supported on less."

Elinor smiled again, to hear her sister describing so accurately their future expenses at Combe Magna.

"Hunters!" repeated Edward—"But why must you have hunters? Every body does not hunt."

---

1. Defined in Johnson's *Dictionary* as "Such a fortune as, without exuberance, is equal to the necessities of life." As the ensuing conversation indicates, the precise income that might constitute a "competence" varies according to what one deems minimally necessary to sustain one's rank and status. Many commentators regarded £200–£300 as the minimum annual income necessary to support genteel status, although this amount is regarded as very little in this novel. After her father's death, Jane Austen lived with her mother and sister on an annual income of £460.
2. Here, a household; the persons who live in one house, including parents, children, servants, etc.
3. Spirited horses, adapted for use especially in fox hunting, and trained for speed, endurance, and jumping. They were known as expensive horses to keep.

Marianne coloured as she replied, "But most people do."

"I wish," said Margaret, striking out a novel thought, "that some-body would give us all a large fortune apiece!"

"Oh that they would!" cried Marianne, her eyes sparkling with animation, and her cheeks glowing with the delight of such imaginary happiness.

"We are all unanimous in that wish, I suppose," said Elinor, "in spite of the insufficiency of wealth."

"Oh dear!" cried Margaret, "how happy I should be! I wonder what I should do with it!"

Marianne looked as if she had no doubt on that point.

"I should be puzzled to spend a large fortune myself," said Mrs. Dashwood, "if my children were all to be rich without my help."

"You must begin your improvements on this house," observed Elinor, "and your difficulties will soon vanish."

"What magnificent orders would travel from this family to London" said Edward, "in such an event! What a happy day for book-sellers, music-sellers, and print-shops! You, Miss Dashwood, would give a general commission for every new print of merit to be sent you—and as for Marianne, I know her greatness of soul, there would not be music enough in London to content her. And books!— Thomson,[4] Cowper, Scott—she would buy them all over and over again; she would buy up every copy, I believe, to prevent their falling into unworthy hands; and she would have every book that tells her how to admire an old twisted tree. Should not you, Marianne? Forgive me, if I am very saucy. But I was willing to shew you that I had not forgot our old disputes."

"I love to be reminded of the past, Edward—whether it be melancholy or gay, I love to recall it—and you will never offend me by talking of former times. You are very right in supposing how my money would be spent—some of it, at least—my loose cash would certainly be employed in improving my collection of music and books."

"And the bulk of your fortune would be laid out in annuities on the authors or their heirs."

"No, Edward, I should have something else to do with it."

"Perhaps then you would bestow it as a reward on that person who wrote the ablest defence of your favorite maxim, that no one can ever be in love more than once in their life—for your opinion on that point is unchanged, I presume?"

"Undoubtedly. At my time of life opinions are tolerably fixed. It is not likely that I should now see or hear anything to change them."

4. James Thomson (1700–1748), poet whose long poem in blank verse, *The Seasons* (1726–30), celebrates an unmediated relation to nature and, by standing in such contrast to the wittier art of Pope, has been seen to anticipate Romantic poetry.

"Marianne is as stedfast as ever, you see," said Elinor, "she is not at all altered."

"She is only grown a little more grave than she was."

"Nay, Edward," said Marianne, "*you* need not reproach me. You are not very gay yourself."

"Why should you think so!" replied he, with a sigh. "But gaiety never was a part of *my* character."

"Nor do I think it a part of Marianne's," said Elinor; "I should hardly call her a lively girl—she is very earnest, very eager in all she does—sometimes talks a great deal and always with animation—but she is not often really merry."

"I believe you are right," he replied, "and yet I have always set her down as a lively girl."

"I have frequently detected myself in such kind of mistakes," said Elinor, "in a total misapprehension of character in some point or other: fancying people so much more gay or grave, or ingenious or stupid than they really are, and I can hardly tell why, or in what the deception originated. Sometimes one is guided by what they say of themselves, and very frequently by what other people say of them, without giving oneself time to deliberate and judge."

"But I thought it was right, Elinor," said Marianne, "to be guided wholly by the opinion of other people. I thought our judgments were given us merely to be subservient to those of our neighbours. This has always been your doctrine, I am sure."

"No, Marianne, never. My doctrine has never aimed at the subjection of the understanding. All I have ever attempted to influence has been the behaviour. You must not confound my meaning. I am guilty, I confess, of having often wished you to treat our acquaintance in general with greater attention; but when have I advised you to adopt their sentiments or conform to their judgment in serious matters?"

"You have not been able then to bring your sister over to your plan of general civility," said Edward to Elinor. "Do you gain no ground?"

"Quite the contrary," replied Elinor, looking expressively at Marianne.

"My judgment," he returned, "is all on your side of the question; but I am afraid my practice is much more on your sister's. I never wish to offend, but I am so foolishly shy, that I often seem negligent, when I am only kept back by my natural aukwardness. I have frequently thought that I must have been intended by nature to be fond of low company, I am so little at my ease among strangers of gentility!"

"Marianne has not shyness to excuse any inattention of hers," said Elinor.

"She knows her own worth too well for false shame," replied

Edward. "Shyness is only the effect of a sense of inferiority in some way or other. If I could persuade myself that my manners were perfectly easy and graceful, I should not be shy."

"But you would still be reserved," said Marianne, "and that is worse."

Edward stared—"Reserved! Am I reserved, Marianne?"

"Yes, very."

"I do not understand you," replied he, colouring. "Reserved!— how, in what manner? What am I to tell you? What can you suppose?"

Elinor looked surprised at his emotion, but trying to laugh off the subject, she said to him, "Do not you know my sister well enough to understand what she means? Do not you know* she calls every one reserved who does not talk as fast, and admire what she admires as rapturously as herself?"

Edward made no answer. His gravity and thoughtfulness returned on him in their fullest extent—and he sat for some time silent and dull.

Chapter XVIII.

Elinor saw, with great uneasiness, the low spirits of her friend. His visit afforded her but a very partial satisfaction, while his own enjoyment in it appeared so imperfect. It was evident that he was unhappy; she wished it were equally evident that he still distinguished her by the same affection which once she had felt no doubt of inspiring; but hitherto the continuance of his preference seemed very uncertain; and the reservedness of his manner towards her contradicted one moment what a more animated look had intimated the preceding one.

He joined her and Marianne in the breakfast-room the next morning before the others were down; and Marianne, who was always eager to promote their happiness as far as she could, soon left them to themselves. But before she was half way up stairs she heard the parlour door open, and, turning round, was astonished to see Edward himself come out.

"I am going into the village to see my horses," said he, "as you are not yet ready for breakfast; I shall be back again presently."

Edward returned to them with fresh admiration of the surrounding country; in his walk to the village, he had seen many parts of

---

* know] know that A.

the valley to advantage; and the village itself, in a much higher situation than the cottage, afforded; a general view of the whole, which had exceedingly pleased him. This was a subject which ensured Marianne's attention, and she was beginning to describe her own admiration of these scenes, and to question him more minutely on the objects that had particularly struck him, when Edward interrupted her by saying, "You must not inquire too far, Marianne —remember I have no knowledge in the picturesque, and I shall offend you by my ignorance and want of taste if we come to particulars. I shall call hills steep, which ought to be bold; surfaces strange and uncouth, which ought to be irregular and rugged; and distant objects out of sight, which ought only to be indistinct through the soft medium of a hazy atmosphere. You must be satisfied with such admiration as I can honestly give. I call it a very fine country—the hills are steep, the woods seem full of fine timber, and the valley looks comfortable and snug—with rich meadows and several neat farm houses scattered here and there. It exactly answers my idea of a fine country because it unites beauty with utility—and I dare say it is a picturesque one too, because you admire it; I can easily believe it to be full of rocks and promontories, grey moss and brush wood, but these are all lost on me. I know nothing of the picturesque."

"I am afraid it is but too true," said Marianne; "but why should you boast of it?"

"I suspect," said Elinor, "that to avoid one kind of affectation, Edward here falls into another. Because he believes many people pretend to more admiration of the beauties of nature than they really feel, and is disgusted with such pretensions, he affects greater indifference and less discrimination in viewing them himself than he possesses. He is fastidious and will have an affectation of his own."

"It is very true," said Marianne, "that admiration of landscape scenery is become a mere jargon. Every body pretends to feel and tries to describe with the taste and elegance of him who first defined what picturesque beauty was.[1] I detest jargon of every kind, and sometimes I have kept my feelings to myself, because I could find no language to describe them in but what was worn and hackneyed out of all sense and meaning."

"I am convinced," said Edward, "that you really feel all the delight

---

1. William Gilpin (1724–1804), whose well-known *Remarks on Forest Scenery* (1791), *Three Essays: On Picturesque Beauty* (1792), and illustrated series of tours throughout the British Isles began the vogue for the picturesque. Other writers who helped define "what picturesque beauty was" include Uvedale Price (1747–1829), William Payne Knight (1750–1824), and the landscape gardener Humphry Repton (1752–1818), who figures in *Mansfield Park*. Austen admired Gilpin's work and knew it thoroughly.

in a fine prospect which you profess to feel. But, in return, your sister must allow me to feel no more than I profess. I like a fine prospect, but not on picturesque principles. I do not like crooked, twisted, blasted trees. I admire them much more if they are tall, straight and flourishing. I do not like ruined, tattered cottages. I am not fond of nettles, or thistles, or heath blossoms. I have more pleasure in a snug farm-house than a watch-tower—and a troop of tidy, happy villagers please me better than the finest banditti in the world."

Marianne looked with amazement at Edward, with compassion at her sister. Elinor only laughed.

The subject was continued no farther; and Marianne remained thoughtfully silent, till a new object suddenly engaged her attention. She was sitting by Edward, and in taking his tea from Mrs. Dashwood, his hand passed so directly before her, as to make a ring, with a plait of hair in the centre, very conspicuous on one of his fingers.

"I never saw you wear a ring before, Edward," she cried. "Is that Fanny's hair? I remember her promising to give you some. But I should have thought her hair had been darker."

Marianne spoke inconsiderately what she really felt—but when she saw how much she had pained Edward, her own vexation at her want of thought could not be surpassed by his. He coloured very deeply, and giving a momentary glance at Elinor, replied, "Yes; it is my sister's hair. The setting always casts a different shade on it you know."

Elinor had met his eye, and looked conscious likewise. That the hair was her own, she instantaneously felt as well satisfied as Marianne; the only difference in their conclusions was, that what Marianne considered as a free gift from her sister, Elinor was conscious must have been procured by some theft or contrivance unknown to herself. She was not in a humour, however, to regard it as an affront, and affecting to take no notice of what passed, by instantly talking of something else, she internally resolved henceforward to catch every opportunity of eyeing the hair and of satisfying herself, beyond all doubt, that it was exactly the shade of her own.

Edward's embarrassment lasted some time, and it ended in an absence of mind still more settled. He was particularly grave the whole morning. Marianne severely censured herself for what she had said; but her own forgiveness might have been more speedy, had she known how little offence it had given her sister.

Before the middle of the day, they were visited by Sir John and Mrs. Jennings, who, having heard of the arrival of a gentleman at the cottage, came to take a survey of the guest. With the assistance of his mother-in-law, Sir John was not long in discovering that the name of Ferrars began with an F. and this prepared a future mine of raillery against the devoted Elinor, which nothing but the newness of their acquaintance with Edward could have prevented from being immediately sprung. But, as it was, she only learned from some very significant looks, how far their penetration, founded on Margaret's instructions, extended.

Sir John never came to the Dashwoods without either inviting them to dine at the park the next day, or to drink tea with them that evening. On the present occasion, for the better entertainment of their visitor, towards whose amusement he felt himself bound to contribute, he wished to engage them for both.

"You *must* drink tea with us to night," said he, "for we shall be quite alone—and to-morrow you must absolutely dine with us, for we shall be a large party."

Mrs. Jennings enforced the necessity. "And who knows but you may raise a dance," said she. "And that will tempt *you*, Miss Marianne."

"A dance!" cried Marianne. "Impossible! Who is to dance?"

"Who! why yourselves, and the Careys, and Whitakers to be sure.—What! you thought nobody could dance because a certain person that shall be nameless is gone!"

"I wish with all my soul," cried Sir John, "that Willoughby were among us again."

This, and Marianne's blushing, gave new suspicions to Edward. "And who is Willoughby?" said he, in a low voice, to Miss Dashwood, by whom he was sitting.

She gave him a brief reply. Marianne's countenance was more communicative. Edward saw enough to comprehend, not only the meaning of others, but such of Marianne's expressions as had puzzled him before; and when their visitors left them, he went immediately round to* her and said, in a whisper, "I have been guessing. Shall I tell you my guess?"

"What do you mean?"

"Shall I tell you?"

"Certainly."

"Well then; I guess that Mr. Willoughby hunts."

Marianne was surprised and confused, yet she could not help smiling at the quiet archness of his manner, and, after a moment's silence, said,

"Oh! Edward! How can you—But the time will come I hope. . . . I am sure you will like him."

"I do not doubt it," replied he, rather astonished at her earnestness and warmth; for had he not imagined it to be a joke for the

---

* round to] A; round B.

good of her acquaintance in general, founded only on a something or a nothing between Mr. Willoughby and herself, he would not have ventured to mention it.

Chapter XIX.

Edward remained a week at the cottage; he was earnestly pressed by Mrs. Dashwood to stay longer; but as if he were bent only on self-mortification, he seemed resolved to be gone when his enjoyment among his friends was at the height. His spirits, during the last two or three days, though still very unequal, were greatly improved—he grew more and more partial to the house and environs—never spoke of going away without a sigh—declared his time to be wholly disengaged—even doubted to what place he should go when he left them—but still, go he must. Never had any week passed so quickly—he could hardly believe it to be gone. He said so repeatedly; other things he said too, which marked the turn of his feelings and gave the lie to his actions. He had no pleasure at Norland; he detested being in town; but either to Norland or London, he must go. He valued their kindness beyond any thing, and his greatest happiness was in being with them. Yet he must leave them at the end of a week, in spite of their wishes and his own, and without any restraint on his time.

Elinor placed all that was astonishing in this way of acting to his mother's account; and it was happy for her that he had a mother whose character was so imperfectly known to her, as to be the general excuse for every thing strange on the part of her son. Disappointed, however, and vexed as she was, and sometimes displeased with his uncertain behaviour to herself, she was very well disposed on the whole to regard his actions with all the candid allowances and generous qualifications, which had been rather more painfully extorted from her, for Willoughby's service, by her mother. His want of spirits, of openness, and of consistency, were most usually attributed to his want of independence, and his better knowledge of Mrs. Ferrars's disposition* and designs. The shortness of his visit, the steadiness of his purpose in leaving them, originated in the same fettered inclination, the same inevitable necessity of temporising with his mother. The old, well established grievance of duty against will, parent against child, was the cause of all. She would have been glad to know when these difficulties were to cease, this opposition was to yield,—when Mrs. Ferrars would be re-

* disposition] A; dispositions B. *The typesetter of B probably anticipates the plural noun* designs.

formed, and her son be at liberty to be happy. But from such vain wishes, she was forced to turn for comfort to the renewal of her confidence in Edward's affection, to the remembrance of every mark of regard in look or word which fell from him while at Barton, and above all to that flattering proof of it which he constantly wore round his finger.

"I think, Edward," said Mrs. Dashwood, as they were at breakfast the last morning, "you would be a happier man if you had any profession to engage your time and give an interest to your plans and actions. Some inconvenience to your friends, indeed, might result from it—you would not be able to give them so much of your time. But (with a smile) you would be materially benefited in one particular at least—you would know where to go when you left them."

"I do assure you," he replied, "that I have long thought on this point, as you think now. It has been, and is, and probably will always be a heavy misfortune to me, that I have had no necessary business to engage me, no profession to give me employment, or afford me any thing like independence. But unfortunately my own nicety, and the nicety of my friends, have made me what I am, an idle, helpless being. We never could agree in our choice of a profession. I always preferred the church, as I still do. But that was not smart enough for my family. They recommended the army. That was a great deal too smart for me. The law was allowed to be genteel enough; many young men, who had chambers in the Temple,[1] made a very good appearance in the first circles, and drove about town in very knowing gigs.[2] But I had no inclination for the law, even in this less abstruse study of it, which my family approved. As for the navy,[3] it had fashion on its side, but I was too old when the subject was first started to enter it—and, at length, as there was no necessity for my having any profession at all, as I might be as dashing and expensive without a red coat on my back as with one, idleness was pronounced on the whole to be the most advantageous and honourable, and a young man of eighteen is not in general so earnestly bent on being busy as to resist the solicitations of his friends to do nothing. I was therefore entered at Oxford and have been properly idle ever since."

"The consequence of which, I suppose, will be," said Mrs. Dashwood, "since leisure has not promoted your own happiness, that

1. The site of property once the seat of the Knights Templar, the Temple is a district of London where two of the Inns of Court are located and where lawyers and law students lease rooms.
2. *Knowing* here denotes smart or chic; a *gig* is a light, two-wheeled carriage, drawn by one horse, and fashionable in the early nineteenth century.
3. Boys began their training for a career in the navy at around the age of twelve by attending the Royal Naval Academy in Portsmouth for three years, as Austen's brother Francis did.

your sons will be brought up to as many pursuits, employments, professions, and trades as Columella's."[4]

"They will be brought up," said he, in a serious accent, "to be as unlike myself as is possible. In feeling, in action, in condition, in every thing."

"Come, come; this is all an effusion of immediate want of spirits, Edward. You are in a melancholy humour, and fancy that any one unlike yourself must be happy. But remember that the pain of parting from friends will be felt by every body at times, whatever be their education or state. Know your own happiness. You want nothing but patience—or give it a more fascinating name, call it hope. Your mother will secure to you, in time, that independence you are so anxious for; it is her duty, and it will, it must ere long become her happiness to prevent your whole youth from being wasted in discontent. How much may not a few months do?"

"I think," replied Edward, "that I may defy many months to produce any good to me."

This desponding turn of mind, though it could not be communicated to Mrs. Dashwood, gave additional pain to them all in the parting, which shortly took place, and left an uncomfortable impression on Elinor's feelings especially, which required some trouble and time to subdue. But as it was her determination to subdue it, and to prevent herself from appearing to suffer more than what all her family suffered on his going away, she did not adopt the method so judiciously employed by Marianne, on a similar occasion, to augment and fix her sorrow, by seeking silence, solitude, and idleness. Their means were as different as their objects, and equally suited to the advancement of each.

Elinor sat down to her drawing-table as soon as he was out of the house, busily employed herself the whole day, neither sought nor avoided the mention of his name, appeared to interest herself almost as much as ever in the general concerns of the family, and if, by this conduct, she did not lessen her own grief, it was at least prevented from unnecessary increase, and her mother and sisters were spared much solicitude on her account.

Such behaviour as this, so exactly the reverse of her own, appeared no more meritorious to Marianne, than her own had seemed faulty to her. The business of self-command she settled very easily; —with strong affections it was impossible, with calm ones it could have no merit. That her sister's affections *were* calm, she dared not

4. As R. W. Chapman observes, this is an allusion to Richard Graves's novel *Columella; or, The Distressed Anchoret* (1779), featuring a father who tries ridiculously to attach his son to a variety of professions ranging from surgery to hops dealing.

deny, though she blushed to acknowledge it; and of the strength of her own, she gave a very striking proof, by still loving and respecting that sister, in spite of this mortifying conviction.

Without shutting herself up from her family, or leaving the house in determined solitude to avoid them, or lieing* awake the whole night to indulge meditation, Elinor found every day afforded her leisure enough to think of Edward, and of Edward's behaviour, in every possible variety which the different state of her spirits at different times could produce;—with tenderness, pity, approbation, censure, and doubt. There were moments in abundance, when, if not by the absence of her mother and sisters, at least by the nature of their employments, conversation was forbidden among them, and every effect of solitude was produced. Her mind was inevitably at liberty; her thoughts could not be chained elsewhere; and the past and the future, on a subject so interesting, must be before her, must force her attention, and engross her memory, her reflection, and her fancy.

From a reverie of this kind, as she sat at her drawing-table, she was roused one morning, soon after Edward's leaving them, by the arrival of company. She happened to be quite alone. The closing of the little gate, at the entrance of the green court in front of the house, drew her eyes to the window, and she saw a large party walking up to the door. Amongst them were Sir John and Lady Middleton and Mrs. Jennings, but there were two others, a gentleman and lady, who were quite unknown to her. She was sitting near the window, and as soon as Sir John perceived her, he left the rest of the party to the ceremony of knocking at the door, and stepping across the turf, obliged her to open the casement to speak to him, though the space was so short between the door and the window, as to make it hardly possible to speak at one without being heard at the other.

"Well," said he, "we have brought you some strangers. How do you like them?"

"Hush! they will hear you."

"Never mind if they do. It is only the Palmers. Charlotte is very pretty, I can tell you. You may see her if you look this way."

As Elinor was certain of seeing her in a couple of minutes, without taking that liberty, she begged to be excused.

"Where is Marianne? Has she run away because we are come? I see her instrument is open."

"She is walking, I believe."

They were now joined by Mrs. Jennings, who had not patience

* lieing] A; laying B.

enough to wait till the door was opened before she told *her* story. She came hallooing to the window, "How do you do, my dear? How does Mrs. Dashwood do? And where are your sisters? What! all alone! you will be glad of a little company to sit with you. I have brought my other son and daughter to see you. Only think of their coming so suddenly! I thought I heard a carriage last night, while we were drinking our tea, but it never entered my head that it could be them. I thought of nothing but whether it might not be Colonel Brandon come back again; so I said to Sir John, I do think I hear a carriage; perhaps it is Colonel Brandon come back again"——

Elinor was obliged to turn from her, in the middle of her story, to receive the rest of the party; Lady Middleton introduced the two strangers; Mrs. Dashwood and Margaret came down stairs at the same time, and they all sat down to look at one another, while Mrs. Jennings continued her story as she walked through the passage into the parlour, attended by Sir John.

Mrs. Palmer was several years younger than Lady Middleton, and totally unlike her in every respect. She was short and plump, had a very pretty face, and the finest expression of good humour in it that could possibly be. Her manners were by no means so elegant as her sister's, but they were much more prepossessing. She came in with a smile, smiled all the time of her visit, except when she laughed, and smiled when she went away. Her husband was a grave looking young man of five or six and twenty, with an air of more fashion and sense than his wife, but of less willingness to please or be pleased. He entered the room with a look of self-consequence, slightly bowed to the ladies, without speaking a word, and, after briefly surveying them and their apartments, took up a newspaper from the table and continued to read it as long as he staid.

Mrs. Palmer, on the contrary, who was strongly endowed by nature with a turn for being uniformly civil and happy, was hardly seated before her admiration of the parlour and every thing in it burst forth.

"Well! what a delightful room this is! I never saw anything so charming! Only think, mama, how it is improved since I was here last! I always thought it such a sweet place, ma'am! (turning to Mrs. Dashwood,) but you have made it so charming! Only look, sister, how delightful every thing is! How I should like such a house for myself! Should not you, Mr. Palmer?"

Mr. Palmer made her no answer, and did not even raise his eyes from the newspaper.

"Mr. Palmer does not hear me," said she, laughing, "he never does sometimes. It is so ridiculous!"

This was quite a new idea to Mrs. Dashwood, she had never been used to find wit in the inattention of any one, and could not help looking with surprise* at them both.

Mrs. Jennings, in the mean time, talked on as loud as she could, and continued her account of their surprise, the evening before, on seeing their friends, without ceasing till every thing was told. Mrs. Palmer laughed heartily at the recollection of their astonishment, and every body agreed, two or three times over, that it had been quite an agreeable surprise.

"You may believe how glad we all were to see them," added Mrs. Jennings, leaning forwards towards Elinor, and speaking in a low voice as if she meant to be heard by no one else, though they were seated on different sides of the room; "but, however, I can't help wishing they had not travelled quite so fast, nor made such a long journey of it, for they came all round by London upon account of some business, for you know (nodding significantly and pointing to her daughter) it was wrong in her situation. I wanted her to stay at home and rest this morning, but she would come with us; she longed so much to see you all!"

Mrs. Palmer laughed, and said it would not do her any harm.

"She expects to be confined[5] in February," continued Mrs. Jennings.

Lady Middleton could no longer endure such a conversation, and therefore exerted herself to ask Mr. Palmer if there was any news in the paper.

"No, none at all," he replied, and read on.

"Here comes Marianne," cried Sir John. "Now, Palmer, you shall see a monstrous pretty girl."

He immediately went into the passage, opened the front door, and ushered her in himself. Mrs. Jennings asked her, as soon as she appeared, if she had not been to Allenham; and Mrs. Palmer laughed so heartily at the question, as to shew she understood it. Mr. Palmer looked up on her entering the room, stared at her some minutes, and then returned to his newspaper. Mrs. Palmer's eye was now caught by the drawings which hung round the room. She got up to examine them.

"Oh! dear, how beautiful these are! Well! how delightful! Do but look, mama, how sweet! I declare they are quite charming; I could look at them for ever." And then sitting down again, she very soon forgot that there were any such things in the room.

When Lady Middleton rose to go away, Mr. Palmer rose also, laid down the newspaper, stretched himself, and looked at them all round.

---

* with surprise] with some surprise A.
5. To be in childbed.

"My love, have you been asleep?" said his wife, laughing.

He made her no answer; and only observed, after again examining the room, that it was very low pitched, and that the ceiling was crooked. He then made his bow and departed with the rest.

Sir John had been very urgent with them all to spend the next day at the park. Mrs. Dashwood, who did not chuse to dine with them oftener than they dined at the cottage, absolutely refused on her own account; her daughters might do as they pleased. But they had no curiosity to see how Mr. and Mrs. Palmer ate their dinner, and no expectation of pleasure from them in any other way. They attempted, therefore, likewise to excuse themselves; the weather was uncertain and not likely to be good. But Sir John would not be satisfied—the carriage should be sent for them and they must come. Lady Middleton too, though she did not press their mother, pressed them. Mrs. Jennings and Mrs. Palmer joined their entreaties, all seemed equally anxious to avoid a family party; and the young ladies were obliged to yield.

"Why should they ask us?" said Marianne, as soon as they were gone. "The rent of this cottage is said to be low; but we have it on very hard terms, if we are to dine at the park whenever any one is staying either with them, or with us."

"They mean no less to be civil and kind to us now," said Elinor, "by these frequent invitations than by those which we received from them a few weeks ago. The alteration is not in them, if their parties are grown tedious and dull. We must look for the change elsewhere."

Chapter XX.

As the Miss Dashwoods entered the drawing-room of the park the next day, at one door, Mrs. Palmer came running in at the other*, looking as good humoured and merry as before. She took them all most affectionately by the hand, and expressed great delight in seeing them again.

"I am so glad to see you!" said she, seating herself between Elinor and Marianne, "for it is so bad a day I was afraid you might not come, which would be a shocking thing, as we go away again to-morrow. We must go, for the Westons come to us next week you know. It was quite a sudden thing our coming at all, and I knew nothing of it till the carriage was coming to the door, and then Mr. Palmer asked me if I would go with him to Barton. He is so droll!

* the other] another A.

He never tells me any thing! I am so sorry we cannot stay longer; however we shall meet again in town very soon, I hope."

They were obliged to put an end to such an expectation.

"Not go to town!" cried Mrs. Palmer, with a laugh, "I shall be quite disappointed if you do not. I could get the nicest house in the world for you, next door to our's, in Hanover-square. You must come, indeed. I am sure I shall be very happy to chaperon you at any time till I am confined, if Mrs. Dashwood should not like to go into public."

They thanked her; but were obliged to resist all her entreaties.

"Oh! my love," cried Mrs. Palmer to her husband, who just then entered the room—"You must help me to persuade* the Miss Dashwoods to go to town this winter."

Her love made no answer; and after slightly bowing to the ladies, began complaining of the weather.

"How horrid all this is!" said he. "Such weather makes every thing and every body disgusting. Dulness is as much produced within doors as without, by rain. It makes one detest all one's acquaintance. What the devil does Sir John mean by not having a billiard room in his house? How few people know what comfort is! Sir John is as stupid as the weather."

The rest of the company soon dropt in.

"I am afraid, Miss Marianne," said Sir John, "you have not been able to take your usual walk to Allenham today."

Marianne looked very grave and said nothing.

"Oh! don't be so sly before us," said Mrs. Palmer; "for we know all about it, I assure you; and I admire your taste very much, for I think he is extremely handsome. We do not live a great way from him in the country, you know. Not above ten miles, I dare say."

"Much nearer thirty," said her husband.

"Ah! well! there is not much difference. I never was at his house; but they say it is a sweet pretty place."

"As vile a spot as I ever saw in my life," said Mr. Palmer.

Marianne remained perfectly silent, though her countenance betrayed her interest in what was said.

"Is it very ugly?" continued Mrs. Palmer—"then it must be some other place that is so pretty I suppose."

When they were seated in the dining room, Sir John observed with regret that they were only eight altogether.**

"My dear," said he to his lady, "it is very provoking that we should be so few. Why did not you ask the Gilberts to come to us to-day?"

---

* to persuade] persuade A.
** altogether.] A; all together. B.

"Did not I tell you, Sir John, when you spoke to me about it before, that it could not be done? They dined with us last."

"You and I, Sir John," said Mrs. Jennings, "should not stand upon such ceremony."

"Then you would be very ill-bred," cried Mr. Palmer.

"My love, you contradict every body,"—said his wife with her usual laugh. "Do you know that you are quite rude?"

"I did not know I contradicted any body in calling your mother ill-bred."

"Aye, you may abuse me as you please," said the good-natured old lady, "you have taken Charlotte off my hands, and cannot give her back again. So there I have the whip hand[1] of you."

Charlotte laughed heartily to think that her husband could not get rid of her; and exultingly said, she did not care how cross he was to her, as they must live together. It was impossible for any one to be more thoroughly good-natured, or more determined to be happy than Mrs. Palmer. The studied indifference, insolence, and discontent of her husband gave her no pain: and when he scolded or abused her, she was highly diverted.

"Mr. Palmer is so droll!" said she, in a whisper, to Elinor. "He is always out of humour."

Elinor was not inclined, after a little observation, to give him credit for being so genuinely and unaffectedly ill-natured or ill-bred as he wished to appear. His temper might perhaps be a little soured by finding, like many others of his sex, that through some unaccountable bias in favour of beauty, he was the husband of a very silly woman,—but she knew that this kind of blunder was too common for any sensible man to be lastingly hurt by it.—It was rather a wish of distinction she believed, which produced his contemptuous treatment of every body, and his general abuse of every thing before him. It was the desire of appearing superior to other people. The motive was too common to be wondered at; but the means, however they might succeed by establishing his superiority in ill-breeding, were not likely to attach any one to him except his wife.

"Oh! my dear Miss Dashwood," said Mrs. Palmer soon afterwards, "I have got such a favour to ask of you and your sister. Will you come and spend some time at Cleveland this Christmas? Now, pray do,—and come while the Westons are with us. You cannot think how happy I shall be! It will be quite delightful!——My love," applying to her husband, "don't you long to have the Miss Dashwoods come to Cleveland?"

---

1. According to the *OED*, the hand in which the whip is held while driving or riding; the driver's or rider's right hand; figuratively, to have the advantage or upper hand, control.

"Certainly,"—he replied with a sneer—"I came into Devonshire with no other view."

"There now"—said his lady, "you see Mr. Palmer expects you; so you cannot refuse to come."

They both eagerly and resolutely declined her invitation.

"But indeed you must and shall come. I am sure you will like it of all things. The Westons will be with us, and it will be quite delightful. You cannot think what a sweet place Cleveland is; and we are so gay now, for Mr. Palmer is always going about the country canvassing against the election;[2] and so many people come to dine with us that I never saw before, it is quite charming! But, poor fellow! it is very fatiguing to him! for he is forced to make every body like him."

Elinor could hardly keep her countenance as she assented to the hardship of such an obligation.

"How charming it will be," said Charlotte, "when he is in Parliament!—won't it? How I shall laugh! It will be so ridiculous to see all his letters directed to him with an M. P.—But do you know, he says, he will never frank[3] for me? He declares he won't. Don't you, Mr. Palmer?"

Mr. Palmer took no notice of her.

"He cannot bear writing, you know," she continued—"he says it is quite shocking."

"No;" said he, "I never said any thing so irrational. Don't palm all your abuses of language upon me."

"There now; you see how droll he is. This is always the way with him! Sometimes he won't speak to me for half a day together, and then he comes out with something so droll—all about any thing in the world."

She surprised Elinor very much as they returned into the drawing-room by asking her whether she did not like Mr. Palmer excessively.

"Certainly;" said Elinor, "he seems very agreeable."

"Well—I am so glad you do. I thought you would, he is so pleasant; and Mr. Palmer is excessively pleased with you and your sisters I can tell you, and you can't think how disappointed he will be if you don't come to Cleveland.—I can't imagine why you should object to it."

Elinor was again obliged to decline her invitation; and by changing the subject, put a stop to her entreaties. She thought it probable

2. Campaigning for the election.
3. Until 1840, Members of Parliament could post letters free by franking—i.e., by signing— the envelope; without such a mark, recipients paid the cost of postage, based on distance and on the number of sheets.

that as they lived in the same county, Mrs. Palmer might be able
to give some more particular account of Willoughby's general character, than could be gathered from the Middletons' partial acquaintance with him; and she was eager to gain from any one, such a
confirmation of his merits as might remove the possibility of fear
for Marianne. She began by inquiring if they saw much of Mr.
Willoughby at Cleveland, and whether they were intimately acquainted with him.

"Oh! dear, yes; I know him extremely well," replied Mrs.
Palmer—"Not that I ever spoke to him indeed; but I have seen him
for ever in town. Somehow or other I never happened to be staying
at Barton while he was at Allenham. Mama saw him here once
before;—but I was with my uncle at Weymouth. However, I dare
say we should have seen a great deal of him in Somersetshire, if it
had not happened very unluckily that we should never have been
in the country together. He is very little at Combe, I believe; but if
he were ever so much there, I do not think Mr. Palmer would visit
him, for he is in the opposition[4] you know, and besides it is such a
way off. I know why you inquire about him, very well; your sister
is to marry him. I am monstrous glad of it, for then I shall have
her for a neighbour you know."

"Upon my word," replied Elinor, "you know much more of the
matter than I do, if you have any reason to expect such a match."

"Don't pretend to deny it, because you know it is what every body
talks of. I assure you I heard of it in my way through town."

"My dear Mrs. Palmer!"

"Upon my honour I did.—I met Colonel Brandon Monday morning in Bond-street,[5] just before we left town, and he told me of it
directly."

"You surprise me very much. Colonel Brandon tell you of it!
Surely you must be mistaken. To give such intelligence to a person
who could not be interested in it, even if it were true, is not what
I should expect Colonel Brandon to do."

"But I do assure you it was so, for all that, and I will tell you how
it happened. When we met him, he turned back and walked with
us; and so we began talking of my brother and sister, and one thing
and another, and I said to him, 'So, Colonel, there is a new family
come to Barton cottage, I hear, and mama sends me word they are
very pretty, and that one of them is going to be married to Mr.

---

4. The party not in power at the moment. Assuming that the action takes place not long
   after 1805, Willoughby might be a Foxite Whig, and Mr. Palmer was certainly a Tory.
   Local politics were often vehement enough to preclude socializing between members of
   opposing parties.
5. A fashionable shopping street in the West End of London.

Willoughby of Combe Magna. Is it true, pray? for of course you must know, as you have been in Devonshire so lately.' "

"And what did the Colonel say?"

"Oh!—he did not say much; but he looked as if he knew it to be true, so from that moment I set it down as certain. It will be quite delightful, I declare! When is it to take place?"

"Mr. Brandon was very well I hope."

"Oh! yes, quite well; and so full of your praises, he did nothing but say fine things of you."

"I am flattered by his commendation. He seems an excellent man; and I think him uncommonly pleasing."

"So do I.—He is such a charming man, that it is quite a pity he should be so grave and so dull. Mama says *he* was in love with your sister too.—I assure you it was a great compliment if he was, for he hardly ever falls in love with any body."

"Is Mr. Willoughby much known in your part of Somersetshire?" said Elinor.

"Oh! yes, extremely well; that is, I do not believe many people are acquainted with him, because Combe Magna is so far off; but they all think him extremely agreeable I assure you. Nobody is more liked than Mr. Willoughby wherever he goes, and so you may tell your sister. She is a monstrous lucky girl to get him, upon my honour; not but that he is much more lucky in getting her, because she is so very handsome and agreeable, that nothing can be good enough for her. However I don't think her hardly at all handsomer than you, I assure you; for I think you both excessively pretty, and so does Mr. Palmer too I am sure, though we could not get him to own it last night."

Mrs. Palmer's information respecting Willoughby was not very material; but any testimony in his favour, however small, was pleasing to her.

"I am so glad we are got acquainted at last," continued Charlotte.—"And now I hope we shall always be great friends. You can't think how much I longed to see you! It is so delightful that you should live at the cottage! Nothing can be like it to be sure! And I am so glad your sister is going to be well married! I hope you will be a great deal at Combe Magna. It is a sweet place by all accounts."

"You have been long acquainted with Colonel Brandon, have not you?"

"Yes, a great while; ever since my sister married.—He was a particular friend of Sir John's. I believe," she added in a low voice, "he would have been very glad to have had me, if he could. Sir John and Lady Middleton wished it very much. But mama did not think the match good enough for me, otherwise Sir John would have mentioned it to the Colonel, and we should have been married immediately."

"Did not Colonel Brandon know of Sir John's proposal to your mother before it was made? Had he never owned his affection to yourself?"

"Oh! no; but if mama had not objected to it, I dare say he would have liked it of all things. He had not seen me then above twice, for it was before I left school. However I am much happier as I am. Mr. Palmer is just the kind of man I like."

Chapter XXI.

The Palmers returned to Cleveland the next day, and the two families at Barton were again left to entertain each other. But this did not last long; Elinor had hardly got their last visitors out of her head, had hardly done wondering at Charlotte's being so happy without a cause, at Mr. Palmer's acting so simply, with good abilities, and at the strange unsuitableness which often existed between husband and wife, before Sir John's and Mrs. Jennings's active zeal in the cause of society, procured her some other new acquaintance to see and observe.

In a morning's excursion to Exeter, they had met with two young ladies, whom Mrs. Jennings had the satisfaction of discovering[1] to be her relations, and this was enough for Sir John to invite them directly to the park, as soon as their present engagements at Exeter were over. Their engagements at Exeter instantly gave way before such an invitation, and Lady Middleton was thrown into no little alarm on the return of Sir John, by hearing that she was very soon to receive a visit from two girls whom she had never seen in her life, and of whose elegance,—whose tolerable gentility even, she could have no proof; for the assurances of her husband and mother on that subject went for nothing at all. Their being her relations too made it so much the worse; and Mrs. Jennings's attempts at consolation were therefore unfortunately founded, when she advised her daughter not to care about their being so fashionable; because they were all cousins and must put up with one another. As it was impossible however now to prevent their coming, Lady Middleton resigned herself to the idea of it, with all the philosophy of a well bred woman, contenting herself with merely giving her husband a gentle reprimand on the subject five or six times every day.

1. Disclosing.

The young ladies arrived, their appearance was by no means ungenteel or unfashionable. Their dress was very smart, their manners very civil, they were delighted with the house, and in raptures with the furniture, and they happened to be so doatingly fond of children that Lady Middleton's good opinion was engaged in their favour before they had been an hour at the Park. She declared them to be very agreeable girls indeed, which for her ladyship was enthusiastic admiration. Sir John's confidence in his own judgment rose with this animated praise, and he set off directly for the cottage to tell the Miss Dashwoods of the Miss Steeles' arrival, and to assure them of their being the sweetest girls in the world. From such commendation as this, however, there was not much to be learned; Elinor well knew that the sweetest girls in the world were to be met with in every part of England, under every possible variation of form, face, temper, and understanding. Sir John wanted the whole family to walk to the Park directly and look at his guests. Benevolent, philanthropic man! It was painful to him even to keep a third cousin to himself.

"Do come now," said he—"pray come—you must come—I declare you shall come.—You can't think how you will like them. Lucy is monstrous pretty, and so good humoured and agreeable! The children are all hanging about her already, as if she was an old acquaintance. And they both long to see you of all things, for they have heard at Exeter that you are the most beautiful creatures in the world; and I have told them it is all very true, and a great deal more. You will be delighted with them I am sure. They have brought the whole coach full of playthings for the children. How can you be so cross as not to come? Why they are your cousins, you know, after a fashion. *You* are my cousins, and they are my wife's, so you must be related."

But Sir John could not prevail. He could only obtain a promise of their calling at the Park within a day or two, and then left them in amazement at their indifference, to walk home and boast anew of their attractions to the Miss Steeles, as he had been already boasting of the Miss Steeles to them.

When their promised visit to the Park and consequent introduction to these young ladies took place, they found in the appearance of the eldest, who was nearly thirty, with a very plain and not a sensible face, nothing to admire; but in the other, who was not more than two or three and twenty, they acknowledged considerable beauty; her features were pretty, and she had a sharp quick eye, and a smartness of air, which though it did not give actual elegance or grace, gave distinction to her person.—Their manners were particularly civil, and Elinor soon allowed them credit for some kind of sense, when she saw with what constant and judicious attentions they were making themselves agreeable to Lady Middleton. With her children they were in continual raptures, extolling their beauty, courting their notice, and humouring all their whims; and such of their time as could be spared from the importunate demands which this politeness made on it, was spent in admiration of whatever her ladyship was doing, if she happened to be doing any thing, or in taking patterns of some elegant new dress, in which her appearance the day before had thrown them into unceasing delight. Fortunately for those who pay their court through such foibles, a fond mother, though, in pursuit of praise for her children, the most rapacious of human beings, is likewise the most credulous; her demands are exorbitant; but she will swallow any thing; and the excessive affection and endurance of the Miss Steeles towards her offspring, were viewed therefore by Lady Middleton without the smallest surprise or distrust. She saw with maternal complacency all the impertitinent incroachments and mischievous tricks to which her cousins submitted. She saw their sashes untied, their hair pulled about their ears, their work-bags[2] searched, and their knives and scissars stolen away, and felt no doubt of its being a reciprocal enjoyment. It suggested no other surprise than that Elinor and Marianne should sit so composedly by, without claiming a share in what was passing.

"John is in such spirits to-day!" said she, on his taking Miss Steele's pocket handkerchief, and throwing it out of window—"He is full of monkey tricks."

And soon afterwards, on the second boy's violently pinching one of the same lady's fingers, she fondly observed, "How playful William is!"

"And here is my sweet little Annamaria," she added, tenderly caressing a little girl of three years old, who had not made a noise for the last two minutes; "And she is always so gentle and quiet—Never was there such a quiet little thing!"

But unfortunately in bestowing these embraces, a pin in her ladyship's head dress slightly scratching the child's neck, produced from this pattern of gentleness, such violent screams, as could hardly be outdone by any creature professedly noisy. The mother's consternation was excessive; but it could not surpass the alarm of the Miss Steeles, and every thing was done by all three, in so critical an emergency, which affection could suggest as likely to assuage the agonies of the little sufferer. She was seated in her mother's lap, covered with kisses, her wound bathed with lavender-water,[3] by one of the Miss Steeles, who was on her knees to attend her, and her mouth stuffed with sugar plums by the other. With such a

2. Bags containing implements for needlework of various kinds.
3. A perfume distilled from lavender flowers, used here to soothe the child's scratch.

reward for her tears, the child was too wise to cease crying. She still screamed and sobbed lustily, kicked her two brothers for offering to touch her, and all their united soothings were ineffectual till Lady Middleton luckily remembering that in a scene of similar distress last week, some apricot marmalade had been successfully applied for a bruised temple, the same remedy was eagerly proposed for this unfortunate scratch, and a slight intermission of screams in the young lady on hearing it, gave them reason to hope that it would not be rejected.—She was carried out of the room therefore in her mother's arms, in quest of this medicine, and as the two boys chose to follow, though earnestly entreated by their mother to stay behind, the four young ladies were left in a quietness which the room had not known for many hours.

"Poor little creature!" said Miss Steele, as soon as they were gone. "It might have been a very sad accident."

"Yet I hardly know how," cried Marianne, "unless it had been under totally different circumstances. But this is the usual way of heightening alarm, where there is nothing to be alarmed at in reality."

"What a sweet woman Lady Middleton is!" said Lucy Steele.

Marianne was silent; it was impossible for her to say what she did not feel, however trivial the occasion; and upon Elinor therefore the whole task of telling lies when politeness required it, always fell. She did her best when thus called on, by speaking of Lady Middleton with more warmth than she felt, though with far less than Miss Lucy.

"And Sir John too," cried the elder sister, "what a charming man he is!"

Here too, Miss Dashwood's commendation, being only simple and just, came in without any eclat. She merely observed that he was perfectly good humoured and friendly.

"And what a charming little family they have! I never saw such fine children in my life.—I declare I quite doat upon them already, and indeed I am always distractedly fond of children."

"I should guess so," said Elinor with a smile, "from what I have witnessed this morning."

"I have a notion," said Lucy, "you think the little Middletons rather too much indulged; perhaps they may be the outside of enough; but it is so natural in Lady Middleton; and for my part, I love to see children full of life and spirits; I cannot bear them if they are tame and quiet."

"I confess," replied Elinor, "that while I am at Barton Park, I never think of tame and quiet children with any abhorrence."

A short pause succeeded this speech, which was first broken by Miss Steele, who seemed very much disposed for conversation, and who now said rather abruptly, "And how do you like Devonshire, Miss Dashwood? I suppose you were very sorry to leave Sussex."

In some surprise at the familiarity of this question, or at least of the manner in which it was spoken, Elinor replied that she was.

"Norland is a prodigious beautiful place, is not it?" added Miss Steele.

"We have heard Sir John admire it excessively," said Lucy, who seemed to think some apology necessary for the freedom of her sister.

"I think every one *must* admire it," replied Elinor, "who ever saw the place; though it is not to be supposed that any one can estimate its beauties as we do."

"And had you a great many smart beaux there? I suppose you have not so many in this part of the world; for my part, I think they are a vast addition always."

"But why should you think," said Lucy, looking ashamed of her sister, "that there are not as many genteel young men in Devonshire as Sussex?"

"Nay, my dear, I'm sure I don't pretend to say that there an't. I'm sure there's a vast many smart beaux in Exeter; but you know, how could I tell what smart beaux there might be about Norland; and I was only afraid the Miss Dashwoods might find it dull at Barton, if they had not so many as they used to have. But perhaps you young ladies may not care about the beaux, and had as lief be without them as with them. For my part, I think they are vastly agreeable, provided they dress smart and behave civil. But I can't bear to see them dirty and nasty. Now there's Mr. Rose at Exeter, a prodigious smart young man, quite a beau, clerk to Mr. Simpson you know, and yet if you do but meet him of a morning, he is not fit to be seen.—I suppose your brother was quite a beau, Miss Dashwood, before he married, as he was so rich?"

"Upon my word," replied Elinor, "I cannot tell you, for I do not perfectly comprehend the meaning of the word. But this I can say, that if he ever was a beau before he married, he is one still, for there is not the smallest alteration in him."

"Oh! dear! one never thinks of married men's being beaux—they have something else to do."

"Lord! Anne," cried her sister, "you can talk of nothing but beaux; —you will make Miss Dashwood believe you think of nothing else." And then to turn the discourse, she began admiring the house and the furniture.

This specimen of the Miss Steeles was enough. The vulgar freedom and folly of the eldest left her no recommendation, and as Elinor was not blinded by the beauty, or the shrewd look of the youngest, to her want of real elegance and artlessness, she left the house without any wish of knowing them better.

Not so, the Miss Steeles.—They came from Exeter, well provided with admiration for the use of Sir John Middleton, his family, and all his relations, and no niggardly proportion was now dealt out to his fair cousins, whom they declared to be the most beautiful, elegant, accomplished and agreeable girls they had ever beheld, and with whom they were particularly anxious to be better acquainted. —And to be better acquainted therefore, Elinor soon found was their inevitable lot, for as Sir John was entirely on the side of the Miss Steeles, their party would be too strong for opposition, and that kind of intimacy must be submitted to, which consists of sitting an hour or two together in the same room almost every day. Sir John could do no more; but he did not know that any more was required; to be together was, in his opinion, to be intimate, and while his continual schemes for their meeting were effectual, he had not a doubt of their being established friends.

To do him justice, he did every thing in his power to promote their unreserve, by making the Miss Steeles acquainted with whatever he knew or supposed of his cousins' situations in the most delicate particulars,—and Elinor had not seen them more than twice, before the eldest of them wished her joy on her sister's having been so lucky as to make a conquest of a very smart beau since she came to Barton.

" 'Twill be a fine thing to have her married so young to be sure," said she, "and I hear he is quite a beau, and prodigious handsome. And I hope you may have as good luck yourself soon,—but perhaps you may have a friend in the corner already."

Elinor could not suppose that Sir John would be more nice in proclaiming his suspicions of her regard for Edward, than he had been with respect to Marianne; indeed it was rather his favourite joke of the two, as being somewhat newer and more conjectural; and since Edward's visit, they had never dined together, without his drinking to her best affections with so much significancy and so many nods and winks, as to excite general attention. The letter F—had been likewise invariably brought forward, and found productive of such countless jokes, that its character as the wittiest letter in the alphabet had been long established with Elinor.

The Miss Steeles, as she expected, had now all the benefit of these jokes, and in the eldest of them they raised a curiosity to know the name of the gentleman alluded to, which, though often impertinently expressed, was perfectly of a piece with her general inquisitiveness into the concerns of their family. But Sir John did not sport long with the curiosity which he delighted to raise, for he had at least as much pleasure in telling the name, as Miss Steele had in hearing it.

"His name is Ferrars," said he, in a very audible whisper; "but pray do not tell it, for it's a great secret."

"Ferrars!" repeated Miss Steele; "Mr. Ferrars is the happy man, is he? What! your sister-in-law's brother, Miss Dashwood? a very agreeable young man to be sure; I know him very well."

"How can you say so, Anne?" cried Lucy, who generally made an amendment to all her sister's assertions. "Though we have seen him once or twice at my uncle's, it is rather too much to pretend to know him very well."

Elinor heard all this with attention and surprise. "And who was this uncle? Where did he live? How came they acquainted?" She wished very much to have the subject continued, though she did not chuse to join in it herself; but nothing more of it was said, and for the first time in her life, she thought Mrs. Jennings deficient either in curiosity after petty information, or in a disposition to communicate it. The manner in which Miss Steele had spoken of Edward, increased her curiosity; for it struck her as being rather ill-natured, and suggested the suspicion of that lady's knowing, or fancying herself to know something to his disadvantage.—But her curiosity was unavailing, for no farther notice was taken of Mr. Ferrars's name by Miss Steele when alluded to, or even openly mentioned by Sir John.

Chapter XXII.

Marianne, who had never much toleration for any thing like impertinence, vulgarity, inferiority of parts,[1] or even difference of taste from herself, was at this time particularly ill-disposed, from the state of her spirits, to be pleased with the Miss Steeles, or to encourage their advances; and to the invariable coldness of her behaviour towards them, which checked every endeavour at intimacy on their side, Elinor principally attributed that preference of herself which soon became evident in the manners of both, but especially of Lucy, who missed no opportunity of engaging her in conversation, or of striving to improve their acquaintance by an easy and frank communication of her sentiments.

Lucy was naturally clever; her remarks were often just and amusing; and as a companion for half an hour Elinor frequently found her agreeable; but her powers had received no aid from education, she was ignorant and illiterate, and her deficiency of all mental

1. Abilities.

improvement, her want of information in the most common particulars, could not be concealed from Miss Dashwood, in spite of her constant endeavour to appear to advantage. Elinor saw, and pitied her for, the neglect of abilities which education might have rendered so respectable; but she saw, with less tenderness of feeling, the thorough want of delicacy, of rectitude, and integrity of mind, which her attentions, her assiduities, her flatteries at the Park betrayed; and she could have no lasting satisfaction in the company of a person who joined insincerity with ignorance; whose want of instruction prevented their meeting in conversation on terms of equality, and whose conduct towards others, made every shew of attention and deference towards herself perfectly valueless.

"You will think my question an odd one, I dare say," said Lucy to her one day as they were walking together from the park to the cottage—"but, pray, are you personally acquainted with your sister-in-law's mother, Mrs. Ferrars?"

Elinor *did* think the question a very odd one, and her countenance expressed it, as she answered that she had never seen Mrs. Ferrars.

"Indeed!" replied Lucy; "I wonder at that, for I thought you must have seen her at Norland sometimes. Then perhaps you cannot tell me what sort of a woman she is?"

"No;" returned Elinor, cautious of giving her real opinion of Edward's mother, and not very desirous of satisfying, what seemed impertinent curiosity—"I know nothing of her."

"I am sure you think me very strange, for inquiring about her in such a way;" said Lucy, eyeing Elinor attentively as she spoke; "but perhaps there may be reasons—I wish I might venture; but however I hope you will do me the justice of believing that I do not mean to be impertinent."

Elinor made her a civil reply, and they walked on for a few minutes in silence. It was broken by Lucy, who renewed the subject again by saying with some hesitation,

"I cannot bear to have you think me impertinently curious. I am sure I would rather do any thing in the world than be thought so by a person whose good opinion is so well worth having as yours. And I am sure I should not have the smallest fear of trusting *you*; indeed I should be very glad of your advice how to manage in such an uncomfortable situation as I am; but however there is no occasion to trouble *you*. I am sorry you do not happen to know Mrs. Ferrars."

"I am sorry I do *not*," said Elinor, in great astonishment, "if it could be of any use to *you* to know my opinion of her. But really, I never understood that you were at all connected with that family, and therefore I am a little surprised, I confess, at so serious an inquiry into her character."

"I dare say you are, and I am sure I do not at all wonder at it. But if I dared tell you all, you would not be so much surprised. Mrs. Ferrars is certainly nothing to me at present,—but the time *may* come—how soon it will come must depend upon herself—when we may be very intimately connected."

She looked down as she said this, amiably bashful, with only one side glance at her companion to observe its effect on her.

"Good heavens!" cried Elinor, "what do you mean? Are you acquainted with Mr. Robert Ferrars? Can you be?" And she did not feel much delighted with the idea of such a sister-in-law.

"No;" replied Lucy, "not to Mr. *Robert* Ferrars—I never saw him in my life; but," fixing her eyes upon Elinor, "to his elder brother."

What felt Elinor at that moment? Astonishment, that would have been as painful as it was strong, had not an immediate disbelief of the assertion attended it. She turned towards Lucy in silent amazement, unable to divine the reason or object of such a declaration, and though her complexion varied, she stood firm in incredulity and felt in no danger of an hysterical fit, or a swoon.

"You may well be surprised," continued Lucy; "for to be sure you could have had no idea of it before; for I dare say he never dropped the smallest hint of it to you or any of your family; because it was always meant to be a great secret, and I am sure has been faithfully kept so by me to this hour. Not a soul of all my relations know of it but Anne, and I never should have mentioned it to you, if I had not felt the greatest dependance in the world upon your secrecy; and I really thought my behaviour in asking so many questions about Mrs. Ferrars, must seem so odd, that it ought to be explained. And I do not think Mr. Ferrars can be displeased, when he knows I have trusted you, because I know he has the highest opinion in the world of all your family, and looks upon yourself and the other Miss Dashwoods, quite as his own sisters."—She paused.

Elinor for a few moments remained silent. Her astonishment at what she heard was at first too great for words; but at length forcing herself to speak, and to speak cautiously, she said with a calmness of manner, which tolerably well concealed her surprise and solicitude—"May I ask if your engagement is of long standing?"

"We have been engaged these four years."

"Four years!"

"Yes."

Elinor, though greatly shocked, still felt unable to believe it.

"I did not know," said she, "that you were even acquainted till the other day."

"Our acquaintance, however, is of many years date. He was under my uncle's care, you know, a considerable while."

"Your uncle!"

"Yes; Mr. Pratt. Did you never hear him talk of Mr. Pratt?"

"I think I have," replied Elinor, with an exertion of spirits, which increased with her increase of emotion.

"He was four years with my uncle, who lives at Longstaple, near Plymouth. It was there our acquaintance begun, for my sister and me was often staying with my uncle, and it was there our engagement was formed, though not till a year after he had quitted as a pupil; but he was almost always with us afterwards. I was very unwilling to enter into it, as you may imagine, without the knowledge and approbation of his mother; but I was too young and loved him too well to be so prudent as I ought to have been.—Though you do not know him so well as me, Miss Dashwood, you must have seen enough of him to be sensible he is very capable of making a woman sincerely attached to him."

"Certainly," answered Elinor, without knowing what she said; but after a moment's reflection, she added with revived security of Edward's honour and love, and her companion's falsehood—"Engaged to Mr. Edward Ferrars!—I confess myself so totally surprised at what you tell me, that really—I beg your pardon; but surely there must be some mistake of person or name. We cannot mean the same Mr. Ferrars."

"We can mean no other," cried Lucy smiling. "Mr. Edward Ferrars, the eldest son of Mrs. Ferrars of Park-street, and brother of your sister-in-law, Mrs. John Dashwood, is the person I mean; you must allow that *I* am not likely to be deceived, as to the name of the man on who all my happiness depends."

"It is strange," replied Elinor in a most painful perplexity, "that I should never have heard him even mention your name."

"No; considering our situation, it was not strange. Our first care has been to keep the matter secret.—You knew nothing of me, or my family, and therefore there could be no *occasion* for ever mentioning my name to you, and as he was always particularly afraid of his sister's suspecting any thing, *that* was reason enough for his not mentioning it."

She was silent.—Elinor's security sunk; but her self-command did not sink with it.

"Four years you have been engaged," said she with a firm voice.

"Yes; and heaven knows how much longer we may have to wait. Poor Edward! It puts him quite out of heart." Then taking a small miniature from her pocket, she added, "To prevent the possibility of mistake,* be so good as to look at this face. It does not do him justice to be sure, but yet I think you cannot be deceived as to the person it was drew for.—I have had it above these three years."

---

* mistake,] a mistake, A.

She put it into her hands as she spoke, and when Elinor saw the painting, whatever other doubts her fear of a too hasty decision, or her wish of detecting falsehood might suffer to linger in her mind, she could have none of its being Edward's face. She returned it almost instantly, acknowledging the likeness.

"I have never been able," continued Lucy, "to give him my picture in return, which I am very much vexed at, for he has been always so anxious to get it! But I am determined to sit* for it the very first opportunity."

"You are quite in the right;" replied Elinor calmly. They then proceeded a few paces in silence. Lucy spoke first.

"I am sure," said she, "I have no doubt in the world of your faithfully keeping this secret, because you must know of what importance it is to us, not to have it reach his mother; for she would never approve of it, I dare say. I shall have no fortune, and I fancy she is an exceeding proud woman."

"I certainly did not seek your confidence," said Elinor; "but you do me no more than justice in imagining that I may be depended on. Your secret is safe with me; but pardon me if I express some surprise at so unnecessary a communication. You must at least have felt that my being acquainted with it could not add to its safety."

As she said this, she looked earnestly at Lucy, hoping to discover something in her countenance; perhaps the falsehood of the greatest part of what she had been saying; but Lucy's countenance suffered no change.

"I was afraid you would think I was taking a great liberty with you," said she, "in telling you all this. I have not known you long to be sure, personally at least, but I have known you and all your family by description a great while; and as soon as I saw you, I felt almost as if you was an old acquaintance. Besides in the present case, I really thought some explanation was due to you after my making such particular inquiries about Edward's mother; and I am so unfortunate, that I have not a creature whose advice I can ask. Anne is the only person that knows of it, and she has no judgment at all; indeed she does me a great deal more harm than good, for I am in constant fear of her betraying me. She does not know how to hold her tongue, as you must perceive, and I am sure I was in the greatest fright in the world t'other day, when Edward's name was mentioned by Sir John, lest she should out with it all. You can't think how much I go through in my mind from it altogether. I only wonder that I am alive after what I have suffered for Edward's sake

---

* sit] set A. A may be right, as Lucy Steele is sometimes provided with inelegant and un-grammatical speech, which the printer may have corrected. On the other hand, distinctions between sit and set are far from stable. See textual note for set on p. 219.

these last four years. Every thing in such suspense and uncertainty; and seeing him so seldom—we can hardly meet above twice a-year. I am sure I wonder my heart is not quite broke." Here she took out her handkerchief; but Elinor did not feel very compassionate.

"Sometimes," continued Lucy, after wiping her eyes, "I think whether it would not be better for us both, to break off the matter entirely." As she said this, she looked directly at her companion. "But then at other times I have not resolution enough for it.—I cannot bear the thoughts of making him so miserable, as I know the very mention of such a thing would do. And on my own account too—so dear as he is to me—I don't think I could be equal to it. What would you advise me to do in such a case, Miss Dashwood? What would you do yourself?"

"Pardon me," replied Elinor, startled by the question; "but I can give you no advice under such circumstances. Your own judgment must direct you."

"To be sure," continued Lucy, after a few minutes silence on both sides, "his mother must provide for him sometime or other; but poor Edward is so cast down about it! Did not you think him dreadful low-spirited when he was at Barton? He was so miserable when he left us at Longstaple, to go to you, that I was afraid you would think him quite ill."

"Did he come from your uncle's then, when he visited us?"

"Oh! yes; he had been staying a fortnight with us. Did you think he came directly from town?"

"No," replied Elinor, most feelingly sensible of every fresh circumstance in favour of Lucy's veracity; "I remember he told us, that he had been staying a fortnight with some friends near Plymouth." She remembered too, her own surprise at the time, at his mentioning nothing farther of those friends, at his total silence with respect even to their names.

"Did not you think him sadly out of spirits?" repeated Lucy.

"We did indeed, particularly so when he first arrived."

"I begged him to exert himself for fear you should suspect what was the matter; but it made him so melancholy, not being able to stay more than a fortnight with us, and seeing me so much affected.—Poor fellow!—I am afraid it is just the same with him now; for he writes in wretched spirits. I heard from him just before I left Exeter;" taking a letter from her pocket and carelessly shewing the direction[2] to Elinor. "You know his hand, I dare say, a charming one it is; but that is not written so well as usual.—He was tired, I

2. Address. By showing Elinor one of Edward's letters, Lucy is in effect presenting proof that she is engaged to him.

dare say, for he had just filled the sheet to me as full as possible."
Elinor saw that it *was* his hand, and she could doubt no longer.
The picture, she had allowed herself to believe, might have been
accidentally obtained; it might not have been Edward's gift; but a
correspondence between them by letter, could subsist only under a
positive engagement, could be authorized by nothing else; for a few
moments, she was almost overcome—her heart sunk within her,
and she could hardly stand; but exertion was indispensably necessary, and she struggled so resolutely against the oppression of her
feelings, that her success was speedy, and for the time complete.

"Writing to each other," said Lucy, returning the letter into her
pocket, "is the only comfort we have in such long separations. Yes,
I have one other comfort in his picture; but poor Edward has not
even *that.* If he had but my picture, he says he should be easy. I
gave him a lock of my hair set in a ring when he was at Longstaple
last, and that was some comfort to him, he said, but not equal to
a picture. Perhaps you might notice the ring when you saw him?"

"I did;" said Elinor, with a composure of voice, under which was
concealed an emotion and distress beyond any thing she had ever
felt before. She was mortified, shocked, confounded.

Fortunately for her, they had now reached the cottage, and the
conversation could be continued no farther. After sitting with them
a few minutes, the Miss Steeles returned to the Park, and Elinor
was then at liberty to think and be wretched.

Volume II

Chapter I.

However small Elinor's* general dependance on Lucy's veracity might be, it was impossible for her on serious reflection to suspect it in the present case, where no temptation could be answerable to the folly of inventing a falsehood of such a description. What Lucy had asserted to be true, therefore, Elinor could not, dared not longer doubt; supported as it was too on every side by such probabilities and proofs, and contradicted by nothing but her own wishes. Their opportunity of acquaintance in the house of Mr. Pratt was a foundation for the rest, at once indisputable and alarming; and Edward's visit near Plymouth, his melancholy state of mind, his dissatisfaction at his own prospects, his uncertain behaviour towards herself, the intimate knowledge of the Miss Steeles as to Norland and their family connections, which had often surprised her, the picture, the letter, the ring, formed altogether such a body of evidence, as overcame every fear of condemning him unfairly, and established as a fact, which no partiality could set aside, his ill-treatment of herself.—Her resentment of such behaviour, her indignation at having been its dupe, for a short time made her feel only for herself; but other ideas, other considerations soon arose. Had Edward been intentionally deceiving her? Had he feigned a regard for her which he did not feel? Was his engagement to Lucy, an engagement of the heart? No; whatever it might once have been, she could not believe it such at present. His affection was all her own. She could not be deceived in that. Her mother, sisters, Fanny, all had been conscious of his regard for her at Norland; it was not an illusion of her own vanity. He certainly loved her. What a softener of the heart was this persuasion! How much could it not tempt her to forgive! He had been blameable, highly blameable, in remaining at Norland after he first felt her influence over him to be more than it ought to be. In that, he could not be defended; but if he had injured her, how much more had he injured himself; if her

---

* Elinor's] her A. Austen emended for clarity, because the referent of her was bound separately in the previous volume.

99

case were pitiable, his was hopeless. His imprudence had made her miserable for a while; but it seemed to have deprived himself of all chance of ever being otherwise. She might in time regain tranquility; but *he*, what had he to look forward to? Could he ever be tolerably happy with Lucy Steele; could he, were his affection for herself out of the question, with his integrity, his delicacy, and well-informed mind, be satisfied with a wife like her—illiterate, artful, and selfish?

The youthful infatuation of nineteen would naturally blind him to every thing but her beauty and good nature; but the four succeeding years—years, which if rationally spent, give such improvement to the understanding, must have opened his eyes to her defects of education, while the same period of time, spent on her side in inferior society and more frivolous pursuits, had perhaps robbed her of that simplicity, which might once have given an interesting character to her beauty.

If in the supposition of his seeking to marry herself, his difficulties from his mother had seemed great, how much greater were they now likely to be, when the object of his engagement was undoubtedly inferior in connections, and probably inferior in fortune to herself. These difficulties, indeed, with an heart so alienated from Lucy, might not press very hard upon his patience; but melancholy was the state of the person, by whom the expectation of family opposition and unkindness, could be felt as a relief!

As these considerations occurred to her in painful succession, she wept for him, more than for herself. Supported by the conviction of having done nothing to merit her present unhappiness, and consoled by the belief that Edward had done nothing to forfeit her esteem, she thought she could even now, under the first smart of the heavy blow, command herself enough to guard every suspicion of the truth from her mother and sisters. And so well was she able to answer her own expectations, that when she joined them at dinner only two hours after she had first suffered the extinction of all her dearest hopes, no one would have supposed from the appearance of the sisters, that Elinor was mourning in secret over obstacles which must divide her for ever from the object of her love, and that Marianne was internally dwelling on the perfections of a man, of whose whole heart she felt thoroughly possessed, and whom she expected to see in every carriage which drove near their house.

The necessity of concealing from her mother and Marianne, what had been entrusted in confidence to herself, though it obliged her to unceasing exertion, was no aggravation of Elinor's distress. On the contrary it was a relief to her, to be spared the communication of what would give such affliction to them, and to be saved likewise from hearing that condemnation of Edward, which would probably flow from the excess of their partial affection for herself, and which was more than she felt equal to support.

From their counsel, or their conversation she knew she could receive no assistance, their tenderness and sorrow must add to her distress, while her self-command would neither receive encouragement from their example nor from their praise. She was stronger alone, and her own good sense so well supported her, that her firmness was as unshaken, her appearance of cheerfulness as invariable, as with regrets so poignant and so fresh, it was possible for them to be.

Much as she had suffered from her first conversation with Lucy on the subject, she soon felt an earnest wish of renewing it; and this for more reasons than one. She wanted to hear many particulars of their engagement repeated again, she wanted more clearly to understand what Lucy really felt for Edward, whether there were any sincerity in her declaration of tender regard for him, and she particularly wanted to convince Lucy, by her readiness to enter on the matter again, and her calmness in conversing on it, that she was no otherwise interested in it than as a friend, which she very much feared her involuntary agitation, in their morning discourse, must have left at least doubtful. That Lucy was disposed to be jealous of her, appeared very probable; it was plain that Edward had always spoken highly in her praise, not merely from Lucy's assertion, but from her venturing to trust her on so short a personal acquaintance, with a secret, so confessedly and evidently important. And even Sir John's joking intelligence must have had some weight. But indeed, while Elinor remained so well assured within herself of being really beloved by Edward, it required no other consideration of probabilities to make it natural that Lucy should be jealous; and that she was so, her very confidence was a proof. What other reason for the disclosure of the affair could there be, but that Elinor might be informed by it of Lucy's superior claims on Edward, and be taught to avoid him in future? She had little difficulty in understanding thus much of her rival's intentions, and while she was firmly resolved to act by her as every principle of honour and honesty directed, to combat her own affection for Edward and to see him as little as possible; she could not deny herself the comfort of endeavouring to convince Lucy that her heart was unwounded. And as she could now have nothing more painful to hear on the subject than had already been told, she did not mistrust her own ability of going through a repetition of particulars with composure.

But it was not immediately that an opportunity of doing so could be commanded, though Lucy was as well disposed as herself to take advantage of any that occurred; for the weather was not often fine enough to allow of their joining in a walk, where they might most easily separate themselves from the others; and though they met at least every other evening either at the park or cottage, and chiefly at the former, they could not be supposed to meet for the sake of conversation. Such a thought would never enter either Sir John or Lady Middleton's head, and therefore very little leisure was ever given for general chat, and none at all for particular discourse. They met for the sake of eating, drinking, and laughing together, playing at cards, or consequences,[1] or any other game that was sufficiently noisy.

One or two meetings of this kind had taken place, without affording Elinor any chance of engaging Lucy in private, when Sir John called at the cottage one morning, to beg in the name of charity, that they would all dine with Lady Middleton that day, as he was obliged to attend the club at Exeter, and she would otherwise be quite alone, except her mother and the two Miss Steeles. Elinor, who foresaw a fairer opening for the point she had in view, in such a party as this was likely to be, more at liberty among themselves under the tranquil and well-bred direction of Lady Middleton than when her husband united them together in one noisy purpose, immediately accepted the invitation; Margaret, with her mother's permission, was equally compliant, and Marianne, though always unwilling to join any of their parties, was persuaded by her mother, who could not bear to have her seclude herself from any chance of amusement, to go likewise.

The young ladies went, and Lady Middleton was happily preserved from the frightful solitude which had threatened her. The insipidity of the meeting was exactly such as Elinor had expected; it produced not one novelty of thought or expression, and nothing could be less interesting than the whole of their discourse both in the dining parlour and drawing room: to the latter, the children accompanied them, and while they remained there, she was too well convinced of the impossibility of engaging Lucy's attention to attempt it. They quitted it only with the removal of the tea-things. The card-table was then placed, and Elinor began to wonder at herself for having ever entertained a hope of finding time for conversation at the park. They all rose up in preparation for a round game.[2]

"I am glad," said Lady Middleton to Lucy, "you are not going to

1. Citing *Sense and Sensibility*, the OED defines *consequences* as a "round game, in which a narrative of the meeting of a lady and a gentleman, their conversation, and the ensuing 'consequences', is concocted by the contribution of a name or fact by each of the players, in ignorance of what has been contributed by the others." Such narrativizing in the absence of certain facts clearly relates to the larger plot of the novel, where characters often invent "consequences" on the basis of information they have assumed.
2. A game, commonly played around a table, in which any number of players can participate. For this reason, Elinor can withdraw from the game without disruption.

finish poor little Annamaria's basket this evening; for I am sure it must hurt your eyes to work fillagree[3] by candlelight. And we will make the dear little love some amends for her disappointment to-morrow, and then I hope she will not much mind it."

This hint was enough, Lucy recollected herself instantly and replied, "Indeed you are very much mistaken, Lady Middleton; I am only waiting to know whether you can make your party without me, or I should have been at my fillagree already. I would not disappoint the little angel for all the world, and if you want me at the card-table now, I am resolved to finish the basket after supper."

"You are very good, I hope it won't hurt your eyes—will you ring the bell for some working candles? My poor little girl would be sadly disappointed, I know, if the basket was not finished to-morrow, for though I told her it certainly would not, I am sure she depends upon having it done."

Lucy directly drew her work table near her and reseated herself with an alacrity and cheerfulness which seemed to infer that she could taste no greater delight than in making a fillagree basket for a spoilt child.

Lady Middleton proposed a rubber of Casino[4] to the others. No one made any objection but Marianne, who, with her usual inattention to the forms of general civility, exclaimed, "Your ladyship will have the goodness to excuse *me*—you know I detest cards. I shall go to the piano-forté; I have not touched it since it was tuned." And without farther ceremony, she turned away and walked to the instrument.

Lady Middleton looked as if she thanked heaven that *she* had never made so rude a speech.

"Marianne can never keep long from that instrument you know, ma'am," said Elinor, endeavouring to smooth away the offence; "and I do not much wonder at it; for it is the very best toned piano-forté I ever heard."

The remaining five were now to draw their cards.

"Perhaps," continued Elinor, "if I should happen to cut out, I may be of some use to Miss Lucy Steele, in rolling her papers for her; and there is so much still to be done to the basket, that it must be impossible I think for her labour singly, to finish it this evening. I should like the work exceedingly, if she would allow me a share in it."

3. Sometimes called rolled paperwork, *fillagree* imitated intricate ornamental metalwork by attaching narrow rolled pieces of paper, often gilded or colored, onto wood, and using them for decoration.
4. Citing this passage, the OED defines *casino* as a card game "in which the ten of diamonds, called great cassino (or *great cass*), counts two points and the two of spades, called little cassino (or *little cass*), counts one; eleven points constituting the game."

"Indeed I shall be very much obliged to you for your help," cried Lucy, "for I find there is more to be done to it than I thought there was; and it would be a shocking thing to disappoint dear Annamaria after all."

"Oh! that would be terrible indeed," said Miss Steele—"Dear little soul, how I do love her!"

"You are very kind," said Lady Middleton to Elinor: "and as you really like the work, perhaps you will be as well pleased not to cut in till another rubber, or will you take your chance now?"

Elinor joyfully profited by the first of these proposals, and thus by a little of that address, which Marianne could never condescend to practise, gained her own end, and pleased Lady Middleton at the same time. Lucy made room for her with ready attention, and the two fair rivals were thus seated side by side at the same table, and with the utmost harmony engaged in forwarding the same work. The piano-forté, at which Marianne, wrapt up in her own music and her own thoughts, had by this time forgotten that any body was in the room besides herself, was luckily so near them that Miss Dashwood now judged, she might safely, under the shelter of its noise, introduce the interesting subject, without any risk of being heard at the card-table.

Chapter II.

In a firm, though cautious tone, Elinor thus began.

"I should be undeserving of the confidence you have honoured me with, if I felt no desire for its continuance, or no farther curiosity on its subject. I will not apologize therefore for bringing it forward again."

"Thank you," cried Lucy warmly, "for breaking the ice; you have set my heart at ease by it; for I was somehow or other afraid I had offended you by what I told you that Monday."

"Offended me! How could you suppose so? Believe me," and Elinor spoke it with the truest sincerity, "nothing could be farther from my intention, than to give you such an idea. Could you have a motive for the trust, that was not honourable and flattering to me?"

"And yet I do assure you," replied Lucy, her little sharp eyes full of meaning, "there seemed to me to be a coldness and displeasure in your manner, that made me quite uncomfortable. I felt sure that you was angry with me; and have been quarrelling with myself ever since, for having took such a liberty as to trouble you with my affairs. But I am very glad to find it was only my own fancy, and that you do not really blame me. If you knew what a consolation it was to me to relieve my heart by speaking to you of what I am always thinking of every moment of my life, your compassion would make you overlook every thing else I am sure."

"Indeed I can easily believe that it was a very great relief to you, to acknowledge your situation to me, and be assured that you shall never have reason to repent it. Your case is a very unfortunate one; you seem to me to be surrounded with difficulties, and you will have need of all your mutual affection to support you under them. Mr. Ferrars, I believe, is entirely dependent on his mother."

"He has only two thousand pounds of his own; it would be madness to marry upon that, though for my own part, I could give up every prospect of more without a sigh. I have been always used to a very small income, and could struggle with any poverty for him; but I love him too well to be the selfish means of robbing him, perhaps, of all that his mother might give him if he married to please her. We must wait, it may be for many years. With almost every other man in the world, it would be an alarming prospect; but Edward's affection and constancy nothing can deprive me of I know."

"That conviction must be every thing to you; and he is undoubtedly supported by the same trust in your's. If the strength of your reciprocal attachment had failed, as between many people and under many circumstances it naturally would during a four years' engagement, your situation would have been pitiable indeed."

Lucy here looked up; but Elinor was careful in guarding her countenance from every expression that could give* her words a suspicious tendency.

"Edward's love for me," said Lucy, "has been pretty well put to the test, by our long, very long absence since we were first engaged, and it has stood the trial so well, that I should be unpardonable to doubt it now. I can safely say that he has never gave me one moment's alarm on that account from the first."

Elinor hardly knew whether to smile or sigh at this assertion.

Lucy went on. "I am rather of a jealous temper too by nature, and from our different situations in life, from his being so much more in the world than me, and our continual separation, I was enough inclined for suspicion, to have found out the truth in an instant, if there had been the slightest alteration in his behaviour to me when we met, or any lowness of spirits that ꞏ could not account for, or if he had talked more of one lady than another, or seemed in any respect less happy at Longstaple than he used to be. I do not mean to say that I am particularly observant or quicksighted in general, but in such a case I am sure I could not be deceived."

---

* give] give to A.

"All this," thought Elinor, "is very pretty; but it can impose upon neither of us."

"But what," said she after a short silence, "are your views? or have you none but that of waiting for Mrs. Ferrars' death, which is a melancholy and shocking extremity?—Is her son determined to submit to this, and to all the tediousness of the many years of suspense in which it may involve you, rather than run the risk of her displeasure for a while by owning the truth?"

"If we could be certain that it would be only for a while! But Mrs. Ferrars is a very headstrong proud woman, and in her first fit of anger upon hearing it, would very likely secure every thing to Robert, and the idea of that, for Edward's sake, frightens away all my inclination for hasty measures."

"And for your own sake too, or you are carrying your disinterestedness beyond reason."

Lucy looked at Elinor again, and was silent.

"Do you know Mr. Robert Ferrars?" asked Elinor.

"Not at all—I never saw him; but I fancy he is very unlike his brother—silly and a great coxcomb."

"A great coxcomb!" repeated Miss Steele, whose ear had caught those words by a sudden pause in Marianne's music.—"Oh! they are talking of their favourite beaux, I dare say."

"No, sister," cried Lucy, "you are mistaken there, our favourite beaux are *not* great coxcombs."

"I can answer for it that Miss Dashwood's is not," said Mrs. Jennings, laughing heartily; "for he is one of the modestest, prettiest behaved young men I ever saw; but as for Lucy, she is such a sly little creature, there is no finding out who *she* likes."

"Oh!" cried Miss Steele, looking significantly round at them, "I dare say Lucy's beau is quite as modest and pretty behaved as Miss Dashwood's."

Elinor blushed in spite of herself. Lucy bit her lip, and looked angrily at her sister. A mutual silence took place for some time. Lucy first put an end to it by saying in a lower tone, though Marianne was then giving them the powerful protection of a very magnificent concerto—

"I will honestly tell you of one scheme which has lately come into my head, for bringing matters to bear; indeed I am bound to let you into the secret, for you are a party concerned. I dare say you have seen enough of Edward to know that he would prefer the church to every other profession; now my plan is that he should take orders as soon as he can, and then through your interest, which I am sure you would be kind enough to use out of friendship for him, and I hope out of some regard to me, your brother might be persuaded to give him Norland living;[1] which I understand is a very good one, and the present incumbent not likely to live a great while. That would be enough for us to marry upon, and we might trust to time and chance for the rest."

"I should be always happy," replied Elinor, "to shew any mark of my esteem and friendship for Mr. Ferrars; but do not you perceive that my interest on such an occasion would be perfectly unnecessary? He is brother to Mrs. John Dashwood—*that* must be recommendation enough to her husband."

"But Mrs. John Dashwood would not much approve of Edward's going into orders."

"Then I rather suspect that my interest would do very little."

They were again silent for many minutes. At length Lucy exclaimed with a deep sigh,

"I believe it would be the wisest way to put an end to the business at once by dissolving the engagement. We seem so beset with difficulties on every side, that though it would make us miserable for a time, we should be happier perhaps in the end. But you will not give me your advice, Miss Dashwood?"

"No;" answered Elinor, with a smile, which concealed very agitated feelings, "on such a subject I certainly will not. You know very well that my opinion would have no weight with you, unless it were on the side of your wishes."

"Indeed you wrong me," replied Lucy with great solemnity; "I know nobody of whose judgment I think so highly as I do of yours; and I do really believe, that if you was to say to me, 'I advise you by all means to put an end to your engagement with Edward Ferrars, it will be more for the happiness of both of you,' I should resolve upon doing it immediately."

Elinor blushed for the insincerity of Edward's future wife, and replied, "this compliment would effectually frighten me from giving any opinion on the subject had I formed one. It raises my influence much too high; the power of dividing two people so tenderly attached is too much for an indifferent person."

" 'Tis because you are an indifferent person," said Lucy, with some pique, and laying a particular stress on those words, "that your judgment might justly have such weight with me. If you could be supposed to be biassed in any respect by your own feelings, your opinion would not be worth having."

Elinor thought it wisest to make no answer to this, lest they might

---

1. A benefice; a tenured ecclesiastical appointment as rector or vicar, providing a livelihood from tithes. In most country churches, the principal landowner had the right to present livings, and often did so to younger sons or to relations.

provoke each other to an unsuitable increase of ease and unreserve; and was even partly determined never to mention the subject again. Another pause therefore of many minutes' duration, succeeded this speech, and Lucy was still the first to end it.

"Shall you be in town this winter, Miss Dashwood?" said she with all her accustomary complacency.

"Certainly not."

"I am sorry for that," returned the other, while her eyes brightened at the information, "it would have gave me such pleasure to meet you there! But I dare say you will go for all that. To be sure, your brother and sister will ask you to come to them."

"It will not be in my power to accept their invitation if they do."

"How unlucky that is! I had quite depended upon meeting you there. Anne and me are to go the latter end of January to some relations who have been wanting us to visit them these several years! But I only go for the sake of seeing Edward. He will be there in February, otherwise London would have no charms for me; I have not spirits for it."

Elinor was soon called to the card-table by the conclusion of the first rubber, and the confidential discourse of the two ladies was therefore at an end, to which both of them submitted without any reluctance, for nothing had been said on either side, to make them dislike each other less than they had done before; and Elinor sat down to the card table with the melancholy persuasion that Edward was not only without affection for the person who was to be his wife; but that he had not even the chance of being tolerably happy in marriage, which sincere affection on *her* side would have given, for self-interest alone could induce a woman to keep a man to an engagement, of which she seemed so thoroughly aware that he was weary.

From this time the subject was never revived by Elinor, and when entered on by Lucy, who seldom missed an opportunity of introducing it, and was particularly careful to inform her confidante, of her happiness whenever she received a letter from Edward, it was treated by the former with calmness and caution, and dismissed as soon as civility would allow; for she felt such conversations to be an indulgence which Lucy did not deserve, and which were dangerous to herself.

The visit of the Miss Steeles at Barton Park was lengthened far beyond what the first invitation implied. Their favour increased, they could not be spared; Sir John would not hear of their going; and in spite of their numerous and long arranged engagements in Exeter, in spite of the absolute necessity of their returning to fulfil them immediately, which was in full force at the end of every week, they were prevailed on to stay nearly two months at the park, and to assist in the due celebration of that festival which requires a more than ordinary share of private balls and large dinners to proclaim its importance.

Chapter III.

Though Mrs. Jennings was in the habit of spending a large portion of the year at the houses of her children and friends, she was not without a settled habitation of her own. Since the death of her husband, who had traded with success in a less elegant part of the town, she had resided every winter in a house in one of the streets near Portman-square. Towards this home, she began on the approach of January to turn her thoughts, and thither she one day abruptly, and very unexpectedly by them, asked the elder Miss Dashwoods to accompany her. Elinor, without observing the varying complexion of her sister, and the animated look which spoke no indifference to the plan, immediately gave a grateful but absolute denial for both, in which she believed herself to be speaking their united inclinations. The reason alledged was their determined resolution of not leaving their mother at that time of the year.* Mrs. Jennings received the refusal with some surprize, and repeated her invitation immediately.

"Oh! Lord, I am sure your mother can spare you very well, and I *do* beg you will favour me with your company, for I've quite set my heart upon it. Don't fancy that you will be any inconvenience to me, for I shan't put myself at all out of my way for you. It will only be sending Betty by the coach,¹ and I hope I can afford *that*. We three shall be able to go very well in my chaise;² and when we are in town, if you do not like to go wherever I do, well and good, you may always go with one of my daughters. I am sure your mother will not object to it; for I have had such good luck in getting my own children off my hands, that she will think me a very fit person to have the charge of you; and if I don't get one of you at least well married before I have done with you, it shall not be my fault. I shall speak a good word for you to all the young men, you may depend upon it."

"I have a notion," said Sir John, "that Miss Marianne would not object to such a scheme, if her elder sister would come into it. It is very hard indeed that she should not have a little pleasure, because Miss Dashwood does not wish it. So I would advise you two,

---

* time of the year.] time of year. A.
1. Here, a stagecoach, a form of public transportation ladies customarily avoided. Because Mrs. Jennings's chaise only accommodates three, she will send her servant by coach.
2. An enclosed carriage seating three.

to set off for town, when you are tired of Barton, without saying a word to Miss Dashwood about it."

"Nay," cried Mrs. Jennings, "I am sure I shall be monstrous glad of Miss Marianne's company, whether Miss Dashwood will go or not, only the more the merrier say I, and I thought it would be more comfortable for them to be together; because if they got tired of me, they might talk to one another, and laugh at my odd ways behind my back. But one or the other, if not both of them, I must have. Lord bless me! how do you think I can live poking by myself, I who have been always used till this winter to have Charlotte with me. Come, Miss Marianne, let us strike hands upon the bargain, and if Miss Dashwood will change her mind by and bye, why so much the better."

"I thank you, ma'am, sincerely thank you," said Marianne, with warmth; "your invitation has insured my gratitude for ever, and it would give me such happiness, yes almost the greatest happiness I am capable of, to be able to accept it. But my mother, my dearest, kindest mother,—I feel the justice of what Elinor has urged, and if she were to be made less happy, less comfortable by our absence—Oh! no, nothing should tempt me to leave her. It should not, must not be a struggle."

Mrs. Jennings repeated her assurance that Mrs. Dashwood could spare them perfectly well; and Elinor, who now understood her sister, and saw to what indifference to almost every thing else, she was carried by her eagerness to be with Willoughby again, made no farther direct opposition to the plan, and merely referred it to her mother's decision, from whom however she scarcely expected to receive any support in her endeavour to prevent a visit, which she could not approve of for Marianne, and which on her own account she had particular reasons to avoid. Whatever Marianne was desirous of, her mother would be eager to promote—she could not expect to influence the latter to cautiousness of conduct in an affair, respecting which she had never been able to inspire her with distrust; and she dared not explain the motive of her own disinclination for going to London. That Marianne, fastidious as she was, thoroughly acquainted with Mrs. Jennings' manners, and invariably disgusted by them, should overlook every inconvenience of that kind, should disregard whatever must be most wounding to her irritable feelings, in her pursuit of one object, was such a proof, so strong, so full of the importance of that object to her, as Elinor, in spite of all that had passed, was not prepared to witness.

On being informed of the invitation, Mrs. Dashwood, persuaded that such an excursion would be productive of much amusement to both her daughters, and perceiving through all her affectionate attention to herself, how much the heart of Marianne was in it, would not hear of their declining the offer upon *her* account; insisted on their both accepting it directly, and then began to foresee with her usual cheerfulness, a variety of advantages that would accrue to them all, from this separation.

"I am delighted with the plan," she cried, "it is exactly what I could wish. Margaret and I shall be as much benefited by it as yourselves. When you and the Middletons are gone, we shall go on so quietly and happily together with our books and our music! You will find Margaret so improved when you come back again! And I have a little plan of alteration for your bedrooms too, which may now be performed without inconvenience to any one. It is very right that you *should* go to town; I would have every young woman of your condition in life, acquainted with the manners and amusements of London. You will be under the care of a motherly good sort of woman, of whose kindness to you I can have no doubt. And in all probability you will see your brother, and whatever may be his faults, or the faults of his wife, when I consider whose son he is, I cannot bear to have you so wholly estranged from each other."

"Though with your usual anxiety for our happiness," said Elinor, "you have been obviating every impediment to the present scheme which occurred to you, there is still one objection which, in my opinion, cannot be so easily removed."

Marianne's countenance sunk.

"And what," said Mrs. Dashwood, "is my dear prudent Elinor going to suggest? What formidable obstacle is she now to bring forward? Do not let me hear a word about the expense of it."

"My objection is this; though I think very well of Mrs. Jennings' heart, she is not a woman whose society can afford us pleasure, or whose protection will give us consequence."

"That is very true," replied her mother; "but of her society, separately from that of other people, you will scarcely have any thing at all, and you will almost always appear in public with Lady Middleton."

"If Elinor is frightened away by her dislike of Mrs. Jennings," said Marianne, "at least it need not prevent *my* accepting her invitation. I have no such scruples, and I am sure, I could put up with every unpleasantness of that kind with very little effort."

Elinor could not help smiling at this display of indifference towards the manners of a person, to whom she had often had difficulty in persuading Marianne to behave with tolerable politeness: and resolved within herself, that if her sister persisted in going, she would go likewise, as she did not think it proper that Marianne should be left to the sole guidance of her own judgment, or that Mrs. Jennings should be abandoned to the mercy of Marianne for all the comfort of her domestic hours. To this determination she was the more easily reconciled, by recollecting, that Edward Ferrars, by Lucy's account, was not to be in town before February; and that their visit, without any unreasonable abridgment, might be previously finished.

"I will have you *both* go," said Mrs. Dashwood; "these objections are nonsensical. You will have much pleasure in being in London, and especially in being together; and if Elinor would ever condescend to anticipate enjoyment, she would foresee it there from a variety of sources; she would perhaps expect some from improving her acquaintance with her sister-in-law's family."

Elinor had often wished for an opportunity of attempting to weaken her mother's dependence on the attachment of Edward and herself, that the shock might be the less when the whole truth were revealed, and now on this attack, though almost hopeless of success, she forced herself to begin her design by saying, as calmly as she could, "I like Edward Ferrars very much, and shall always be glad to see him; but as to the rest of the family, it is a matter of perfect indifference to me, whether I am ever known to them or not."

Mrs. Dashwood smiled and said nothing. Marianne lifted up her eyes in astonishment, and Elinor conjectured that she might as well have held her tongue.

After very little farther discourse, it was finally settled that the invitation should be fully accepted. Mrs. Jennings received the information with a great deal of joy, and many assurances of kindness and care; nor was it a matter of pleasure merely to her. Sir John was delighted; for to a man, whose prevailing anxiety was the dread of being alone, the acquisition of two, to the number of inhabitants in London, was something. Even Lady Middleton took the trouble of being delighted, which was putting herself rather out of her way; and as for the Miss Steeles, especially Lucy, they had never been so happy in their lives as this intelligence made them.

Elinor submitted to the arrangement which counteracted her wishes, with less reluctance than she had expected to feel. With regard to herself, it was now a matter of unconcern whether she went to town or not, and when she saw her mother so thoroughly pleased with the plan, and her sister exhilarated by it in look, voice, and manner, restored to all her usual animation, and elevated to more than her usual gaiety, she could not be dissatisfied with the cause, and would hardly allow herself to distrust the consequence.

Marianne's joy was almost a degree beyond happiness, so great was the perturbation of her spirits and her impatience to be gone. Her unwillingness to quit her mother was her only restorative to calmness; and at the moment of parting, her grief on that score was excessive. Her mother's affliction was hardly less, and Elinor was the only one of the three, who seemed to consider the separation as any thing short of eternal.

Their departure took place in the first week in January. The Middletons were to follow in about a week. The Miss Steeles kept their station at the park, and were to quit it only with the rest of the family.

Chapter IV.

Elinor could not find herself in the carriage with Mrs. Jennings, and beginning a journey to London under her protection, and as her guest, without wondering at her own situation, so short had their acquaintance with that lady been, so wholly unsuited were they in age and disposition, and so many had been her objections against such a measure only a few days before! But these objections had all, with that happy ardour of youth which Marianne and her mother equally shared, been overcome or overlooked; and Elinor, in spite of every occasional doubt of Willoughby's constancy, could not witness the rapture of delightful expectation which filled the whole soul and beamed in the eyes of Marianne, without feeling how blank was her own prospect, how cheerless her own state of mind in the comparison, and how gladly she would engage in the solicitude of Marianne's situation to have the same animating object in view, the same possibility of hope. A short, a very short time however must now decide what Willoughby's intentions were; in all probability he was already in town. Marianne's eagerness to be gone declared her dependance on finding him there; and Elinor was resolved not only upon gaining every new light as to his character which her own observation or the intelligence of others could give her, but likewise upon watching his behaviour to her sister with such zealous attention, as to ascertain what he was and what he meant, before many meetings had taken place. Should the result of her observations be unfavourable, she was determined at all events to open the eyes of her sister; should it be otherwise, her exertions would be of a different nature—she must then learn to avoid every selfish comparison, and banish every regret which might lessen her satisfaction in the happiness of Marianne.

They were three days on their journey, and Marianne's behaviour as they travelled was a happy specimen of what her future complaisance and companionableness to Mrs. Jennings might be expected to be. She sat in silence almost all the way, wrapt in her own meditations, and scarcely ever voluntarily speaking, except when any object of picturesque beauty within their view drew from her an exclamation of delight exclusively addressed to her sister. To

atone for this conduct therefore, Elinor took immediate possession
of the post of civility which she had assigned herself, behaved with
the greatest attention to Mrs. Jennings, talked with her, laughed
with her, and listened to her whenever she could; and Mrs. Jennings
on her side treated them both with all possible kindness, was solicitous on every occasion for their ease and enjoyment, and only disturbed that she could not make them choose their own dinners at
the inn, nor extort a confession of their preferring salmon to cod,
or boiled fowls to veal cutlets. They reached town by three o'clock
the third day, glad to be released, after such a journey, from the
confinement of a carriage, and ready to enjoy all the luxury of a
good fire.

The house was handsome and handsomely fitted up, and the
young ladies were immediately put in possession of a very comfortable apartment. It had formerly been Charlotte's, and over the man-
telpiece still hung a landscape in coloured silks of her performance,
in proof of her having spent seven years at a great school in town
to some effect.

As dinner was not to be ready in less than two hours from their
arrival, Elinor determined to employ the interval in writing to her
mother, and sat down for that purpose. In a few moments Marianne
did the same. "*I* am writing home, Marianne," said Elinor; "had not
you better defer your letter for a day or two?"

"I am *not* going to write to my mother," replied Marianne hastily,
and as if wishing to avoid any farther inquiry. Elinor said no more;
it immediately struck her that she must then be writing to Willoughby, and the conclusion which as instantly followed was, that
however mysteriously they might wish to conduct the affair, they
must be engaged. This conviction, though not entirely satisfactory,
gave her pleasure, and she continued her letter with greater alacrity.
Marianne's was finished in a very few minutes; in length it could
be no more than a note: it was then folded up, sealed and directed
with eager rapidity. Elinor thought she could distinguish a large W.
in the direction, and no sooner was it complete than Marianne,
ringing the bell, requested the footman who answered it, to get that
letter conveyed for her to the two-penny post.[1] This decided the
matter at once.

Her spirits still continued very high, but there was a flutter in
them which prevented their giving much pleasure to her sister, and
this agitation increased as the evening drew on. She could scarcely
eat any dinner, and when they afterwards returned to the draw-

---

1. The local *post* for London, which raised its fee from one to two pennies in 1801, and
hence is one of several general clues as to the dating of the action here. The London
postal system picked up and delivered mail four to eight times daily.

ing room, seemed anxiously listening to the sound of every carriage. It was a great satisfaction to Elinor that Mrs. Jennings, by being much engaged in her own room, could see little of what was passing. The tea things were brought in, and already had Marianne been disappointed more than once by a rap at a neighbouring door, when a loud one was suddenly heard which could not be mistaken for one at any other house. Elinor felt secure of its announcing Willoughby's approach, and Marianne starting up moved towards the door. Every thing was silent; this could not be borne many seconds, she opened the door, advanced a few steps towards the stairs, and after listening half a minute, returned into the room in all the agitation which a conviction of having heard him would naturally produce; in the extasy of her feelings at that instant she could not help exclaiming, "Oh! Elinor, it is Willoughby, indeed it is!" and seemed almost ready to throw herself into his arms, when Colonel Brandon appeared.

It was too great a shock to be borne with calmness, and she immediately left the room. Elinor was disappointed too; but at the same time her regard for Colonel Brandon ensured his welcome with her, and she felt particularly hurt that a man so partial to her sister should perceive that she experienced nothing but grief and disappointment in seeing him. She instantly saw that it was not unnoticed by him, that he even observed Marianne as she quitted the room, with such astonishment and concern, as hardly left him the recollection of what civility demanded towards herself.

"Is your sister ill?" said he.

Elinor answered in some distress that she was, and then talked of head-aches, low spirits, and over fatigues; and of every thing to which she could decently attribute her sister's behaviour.

He heard her with the most earnest attention, but seeming to recollect himself, said no more on the subject, and began directly to speak of his pleasure at seeing them in London, making the usual inquiries about their journey and the friends they had left behind.

In this calm kind of way, with very little interest on either side, they continued to talk, both of them out of spirits, and the thoughts of both engaged elsewhere. Elinor wished very much to ask whether Willoughby were then in town, but she was afraid of giving him pain by any inquiry after his rival; and at length by way of saying something, she asked if he had been in London ever since she had seen him last. "Yes," he replied, with some embarrassment, "almost ever since; I have been once or twice at Delaford for a few days, but it has never been in my power to return to Barton."

This, and the manner in which it was said, immediately brought back to her remembrance, all the circumstances of his quitting that place, with the uneasiness and suspicions they had caused to Mrs.

Jennings, and she was fearful that her question had implied much
more curiosity on the subject than she had ever felt.

Mrs. Jennings soon came in. "Oh! Colonel," said she, with her
usual noisy cheerfulness, "I am monstrous glad to see you—sorry
I could not come before—beg your pardon, but I have been forced
to look about me a little, and settle my matters; for it is a long while
since I have been at home, and you know one has always a world
of little odd things to do after one has been away for any time; and
then I have had Cartwright to settle with—Lord, I have been as
busy as a bee ever since dinner! But pray, Colonel, how came you
to conjure out that I should be in town to-day?"

"I had the pleasure of hearing it at Mr. Palmer's, where I have
been dining."

"Oh! you did; well, and how do they all do at their house? How
does Charlotte do? I warrant you she is a fine size by this time."

"Mrs. Palmer appeared quite well, and I am commissioned to tell
you, that you will certainly see her tomorrow."

"Aye, to be sure, I thought as much. Well, Colonel, I have
brought two young ladies with me, you see—that is, you see but
one of them now, but there is another somewhere. Your friend Miss
Marianne, too—which you will not be sorry to hear. I do not know
what you and Mr. Willoughby will do between you about her. Aye,
it is a fine thing to be young and handsome. Well! I was young
once, but I never was very handsome—worse luck for me. However
I got a very good husband, and I don't know what the greatest
beauty can do more. Ah! poor man! he has been dead these eight
years and better. But Colonel, where have you been to since we
parted? And how does your business go on? Come, come, let's have
no secrets among friends."

He replied with his accustomary mildness to all her inquiries, but
without satisfying her in any. Elinor now began to make the tea,
and Marianne was obliged to appear again.

After her entrance, Colonel Brandon became more thoughtful
and silent than he had been before, and Mrs. Jennings could not
prevail on him to stay long. No other visitor appeared that evening,
and the ladies were unanimous in agreeing to go early to bed.

Marianne rose the next morning with recovered spirits and happy
looks. The disappointment of the evening before seemed forgotten
in the expectation of what was to happen that day. They had not
long finished their breakfast before Mrs. Palmer's barouche stopt
at the door, and in a few minutes she came laughing into the room;
so delighted to see them all, that it was hard to say whether she
received most pleasure from meeting her mother or the Miss Dashwoods again. So surprised at their coming to town, though it was
what she had rather expected all along; so angry at their accepting

her mother's invitation after having declined her own, though at the same time she would never have forgiven them if they had not come!

"Mr. Palmer will be so happy to see you," said she; "what do you think he said when he heard of your coming with mama? I forget what it was now, but it was something so droll!"

After an hour or two spent in what her mother called comfortable chat, or in other words, in every variety of inquiry concerning all their acquaintance on Mrs. Jennings's side, and in laughter without cause on Mrs. Palmer's, it was proposed by the latter that they should all accompany her to some shops where she had business that morning, to which Mrs. Jennings and Elinor readily consented, as having likewise some purchases to make themselves; and Marianne, though declining it at first, was induced to go likewise.

Wherever they went, she was evidently always on the watch. In Bond-street especially, where much of their business lay, her eyes were in constant inquiry; and in whatever shop the party were engaged, her mind was equally abstracted from every thing actually before them, from all that interested and occupied the others. Restless and dissatisfied every where, her sister could never obtain her opinion of any article of purchase, however it might equally concern them both; she received no pleasure from any thing; was only impatient to be at home again, and could with difficulty govern her vexation at the tediousness of Mrs. Palmer, whose eye was caught by every thing pretty, expensive, or new; who was wild to buy all, could determine on none, and dawdled away her time in rapture and indecision.

It was late in the morning before they returned home; and no sooner had they entered the house than Marianne flew eagerly up stairs, and when Elinor followed, she found her turning from the table with a sorrowful countenance, which declared that no Willoughby had been there.

"Has no letter been left here for me since we went out?" said she to the footman who then entered with the parcels. She was answered in the negative. "Are you quite sure of it?" she replied. "Are you certain that no servant, no porter has left any letter or note?"

The man replied that none had.

"How very odd!" said she in a low and disappointed voice, as she turned away to the window.

"How odd indeed!" repeated Elinor within herself, regarding her sister with uneasiness. "If she had not known him to be in town she would not have written to him, as she did; she would have written to Combe Magna; and if he is in town, how odd that he should neither come nor write! Oh! my dear mother, you must be wrong in permitting an engagement between a daughter so young, a man so little known, to be carried on in so doubtful, so mysterious a manner! *I* long to inquire; but how will *my* interference be borne!" She determined after some consideration, that if appearances continued many days longer, as unpleasant as they now were, she would represent in the strongest manner to her mother the necessity of some serious inquiry into the affair.

Mrs. Palmer and two elderly ladies of Mrs. Jennings's intimate acquaintance, whom she had met and invited in the morning, dined with them. The former left them soon after tea to fulfil her evening engagements; and Elinor was obliged to assist in making a whist-table[2] for the others. Marianne was of no use on these occasions, as she would never learn the game, but though her time was therefore at her own disposal, the evening was by no means more productive of pleasure to her than to Elinor, for it was spent in all the anxiety of expectation and the pain of disappointment. She sometimes endeavoured for a few minutes to read; but the book was soon thrown aside, and she returned to the more interesting employment of walking backwards and forwards across the room, pausing for a moment whenever she came to the window, in hopes of distinguishing the long-expected rap.

Chapter V.

"If this open[1] weather holds much longer," said Mrs. Jennings, when they met at breakfast the following morning, "Sir John will not like leaving Barton next week; 'tis a sad thing for sportsmen to lose a day's pleasure. Poor souls! I always pity them when they do; they seem to take it so much to heart."

"That is true," cried Marianne in a cheerful voice, and walking to the window as she spoke, to examine the day.* "I had not thought of *that*. This weather will keep many sportsmen in the country."

It was a lucky recollection, all her good spirits were restored by it. "It is charming weather for *them* indeed," she continued, as she sat down to the breakfast table with a happy countenance. "How much they must enjoy it! But" (with a little return of anxiety) "it cannot be expected to last long. At this time of year, and after such a series of rain, we shall certainly have very little more of it. Frosts will soon set in, and in all probability with severity. In another day or two perhaps; this extreme mildness can hardly last longer—nay, perhaps it may freeze to-night!"

---

2. *Whist* is a card game, a forerunner to bridge, dating from the seventeenth century.
1. Free from frost.
* day.] day, A.

"At any rate," said Elinor, wishing to prevent Mrs. Jennings from seeing her sister's thoughts as clearly as she did, "I dare say we shall have Sir John and Lady Middleton in town by the end of next week."

"Aye, my dear, I'll warrant you we do. Mary always has her own way."

"And now," silently conjectured Elinor, "she will write to Combe by this day's post."

But if she *did*, the letter was written and sent away with a privacy which eluded all her watchfulness to ascertain the fact. Whatever the truth of it might be, and far as Elinor was from feeling thorough contentment about it, yet while she saw Marianne in spirits, she could not be very uncomfortable herself. And Marianne was in spirits; happy in the mildness of the weather, and still happier in her expectation of a frost.

The morning was chiefly spent in leaving cards at the houses of Mrs. Jennings's acquaintance to inform them of her being in town; and Marianne was all the time busy in observing the direction of the wind, watching the variations of the sky and imagining an alteration in the air.

"Don't you find it colder than it was in the morning, Elinor? There seems to me a very decided difference. I can hardly keep my hands warm even in my muff. It was not so yesterday, I think. The clouds seem parting too, the sun will be out in a moment; and we shall have a clear afternoon."

Elinor was alternately diverted and pained; but Marianne persevered, and saw every night in the brightness of the fire, and every morning in the appearance of the atmosphere, the certain symptoms of approaching frost.

The Miss Dashwoods had no greater reason to be dissatisfied with Mrs. Jennings's style of living, and set of acquaintance, than with her behaviour to themselves, which was invariably kind. Every thing in her household arrangements was conducted on the most liberal plan, and excepting a few old city[2] friends, whom, to Lady Middleton's regret, she had never dropped, she visited no one, to whom an introduction could at all discompose the feelings of her young companions. Pleased to find herself more comfortably situated in that particular than she had expected, Elinor was very willing to compound for the want of much real enjoyment from any of their evening parties, which, whether at home or abroad, formed only for cards, could have little to amuse her.

Colonel Brandon, who had a general invitation to the house, was

---

2. The commercial (and hence less fashionable) district of London, where Mrs. Jennings's late husband made his fortune in trade. Mrs. Jennings's loyalty to her City acquaintances embarrasses both her upwardly mobile daughter, Lady Middleton, as well as Elinor, to a lesser extent.

with them almost every day; he came to look at Marianne and talk to Elinor, who often derived more satisfaction from conversing with him than from any other daily occurrence, but who saw at the same time with much concern his continued regard for her sister. She feared it was a strengthening regard. It grieved her to see the earnestness with which he often watched Marianne, and his spirits were certainly worse than when at Barton.

About a week after their arrival it became certain that Willoughby was also arrived. His card was on the table, when they came in from the morning's drive.

"Good God!" cried Marianne, "he has been here while we were out." Elinor, rejoiced to be assured of his being in London, now ventured to say, "depend upon it he will call again to-morrow." But Marianne seemed hardly to hear her, and on Mrs. Jennings's entrance, escaped with the precious card.

This event, while it raised the spirits of Elinor, restored to those of her sister, all, and more than all, their former agitation. From this moment her mind was never quiet; the expectation of seeing him every hour of the day, made her unfit for anything. She insisted on being left behind, the next morning, when the others went out.

Elinor's thoughts were full of what might be passing in Berkeley-street during their absence; but a moment's glance at her sister when they returned was enough to inform her, that Willoughby had paid no second visit there. A note was just then brought in, and laid on the table.

"For me!"* cried Marianne, stepping hastily forward.

"No, ma'am, for my mistress."

But Marianne, not convinced, took it instantly up.

"It is indeed for Mrs. Jennings; how provoking!"

"You are expecting a letter then?" said Elinor, unable to be longer silent.

"Yes, a little—not much."

After a short pause, "you have no confidence in me, Marianne."

"Nay, Elinor, this reproach from *you*—you who have confidence in no one!"

"Me!" returned Elinor in some confusion; "indeed, Marianne, I have nothing to tell."

"Nor I," answered Marianne with energy, "our situations then are alike. We have neither of us any thing to tell; you, because you communicate, and I, because I conceal nothing."

Elinor, distressed by this charge of reserve in herself, which she was not at liberty to do away, knew not how, under such circumstances, to press for greater openness in Marianne.

---

* For me!"] For me?" A.

Mrs. Jennings soon appeared, and the note being given her, she read it aloud. It was from Lady Middleton, announcing their arrival in Conduit-street the night before, and requesting the company of her mother and cousins the following evening. Business on Sir John's part, and a violent cold on her own, prevented their calling in Berkeley-street. The invitation was accepted: but when the hour of appointment drew near, necessary as it was in common civility to Mrs. Jennings, that they should both attend her on such a visit, Elinor had some difficulty in persuading her sister to go, for still she had seen nothing of Willoughby; and therefore was not more indisposed for amusement abroad, than unwilling to run the risk of his calling again in her absence.

Elinor found, when the evening was over, that disposition is not materially altered by a change of abode, for although scarcely settled in town, Sir John had contrived to collect around him, nearly twenty young people, and to amuse them with a ball. This was an affair, however, of which Lady Middleton did not approve. In the country, an unpremeditated dance was very allowable; but in London, where the reputation of elegance was more important and less easily obtained,* it was risking too much for the gratification of a few girls, to have it known that Lady Middleton had given a small dance of eight or nine couple, with two violins, and a mere sideboard collation.[3]

Mr. and Mrs. Palmer were of the party; from the former, whom they had not seen before since their arrival in town, as he was careful to avoid the appearance of any attention to his mother-in-law, and therefore never came near her, they received no mark of recognition on their entrance. He looked at them slightly, without seeming to know who they were, and merely nodded to Mrs. Jennings from the other side of the room. Marianne gave one glance round the apartment as she entered; it was enough, *he* was not there—and she sat down, equally ill-disposed to receive or communicate pleasure. After they had been assembled about an hour, Mr. Palmer sauntered towards the Miss Dashwoods to express his surprise on seeing them in town, though Colonel Brandon had been first informed of their arrival at his house, and he had himself said something very droll on hearing that they were to come.

"I thought you were both in Devonshire," said he.

"Did you?" replied Elinor.

"When do you go back again?"

"I do not know." And thus ended their discourse.

Never had Marianne been so unwilling to dance in her life, as

---

* obtained,] attained, A.
3. Light meal.

she was that evening, and never so much fatigued by the exercise.
She complained of it as they returned to Berkeley-street.

"Aye, aye," said Mrs. Jennings, "we know the reason of all that
very well; if a certain person who shall be nameless, had been there,
you would not have been a bit tired: and to say the truth it was not
very pretty of him not to give you the meeting when he was invited."

"Invited!" cried Marianne.

"So my daughter Middleton told me, for it seems Sir John met
him somewhere in the street this morning." Marianne said no more,
but looked exceedingly hurt. Impatient in this situation to be doing
something that might lead to her sister's relief, Elinor resolved to
write the next morning to her mother, and hoped by awakening her
fears for the health of Marianne, to procure those inquiries which
had been so long delayed; and she was still more eagerly bent on
this measure by perceiving after breakfast on the morrow, that Marianne was again writing to Willoughby, for she could not suppose
it to be to any other person.

About the middle of the day, Mrs. Jennings went out by herself
on business, and Elinor began her letter directly, while Marianne,
too restless for employment, too anxious for conversation, walked
from one window to the other, or sat down by the fire in melancholy
meditation. Elinor was very earnest in her application to her
mother, relating all that had passed, her suspicions of Willoughby's
inconstancy, urging her by every plea of duty and affection to demand from Marianne, an account of her real situation with respect
to him.

Her letter was scarcely finished, when a rap foretold a visitor, and
Colonel Brandon was announced. Marianne, who had seen him
from the window, and who hated company of any kind, left the
room before he entered it. He looked more than usually grave, and
though expressing satisfaction at* finding Miss Dashwood alone, as
if he had somewhat in particular to tell her, sat for some time without saying a word. Elinor, persuaded that he had some communication to make in which her sister was concerned, impatiently
expected its opening. It was not the first time of her feeling the
same kind of conviction; for more than once before, beginning with
the observation of "your sister looks unwell to-day," or "your sister
seems out of spirits," he had appeared on the point, either of disclosing, or of inquiring, something particular about her. After a
pause of several minutes, their silence was broken, by his asking
her in a voice of some agitation, when he was to congratulate her
on the acquisition of a brother? Elinor was not prepared for such
a question, and having no answer ready, was obliged to adopt the

* at] in A.

simple and common expedient, of asking what he meant? He tried to smile as he replied, "your sister's engagement to Mr. Willoughby is very generally known."

"It cannot be generally known," returned Elinor, "for her own family do not know it."

He looked surprised and said, "I beg your pardon, I am afraid my inquiry has been impertinent; but I had not supposed any secrecy intended, as they openly correspond, and their marriage is universally talked of."

"How can that be? By whom can you have heard it mentioned?"

"By many—by some of whom you know nothing, by others with whom you are most intimate, Mrs. Jennings, Mrs. Palmer, and the Middletons. But still I might not have believed it, for where the mind is perhaps rather unwilling to be convinced, it will always find something to support its doubts, if I had not, when the servant let me in to-day, accidentally seen a letter in his hand, directed to Mr. Willoughby in your sister's writing. I came to inquire, but I was convinced before I could ask the question. Is every thing finally settled? Is it impossible to—? But I have no right, and I could have no chance of succeeding. Excuse me, Miss Dashwood. I believe I have been wrong in saying so much, but I hardly know what to do, and on your prudence I have the strongest dependence. Tell me that it is all absolutely resolved on, that any attempt, that in short concealment, if concealment be possible, is all that remains."

These words, which conveyed to Elinor a direct avowal of his love for her sister, affected her very much. She was not immediately able to say anything, and even when her spirits were recovered, she debated for a short time, on the answer it would be most proper to give. The real state of things between Willoughby and her sister was so little known to herself, that in endeavouring to explain it, she might be as liable to say too much as too little. Yet as she was convinced that Marianne's affection for Willoughby, could leave no hope of Colonel Brandon's success, whatever the event of that affection might be, and at the same time wished to shield her conduct from censure, she thought it most prudent and kind, after some consideration, to say more than she really knew or believed. She acknowledged, therefore, that though she had never been informed by themselves of the terms on which they stood with each other, of their mutual affection she had no doubt, and of their correspondence she was not astonished to hear.

He listened to her with silent attention, and on her ceasing to speak, rose directly from his seat, and after saying in a voice of emotion, "to your sister I wish all imaginable happiness; to Willoughby that he may endeavour to deserve her,"—took leave, and went away.

Elinor derived no comfortable feelings from this conversation, to lessen the uneasiness of her mind on other points; she was left, on the contrary, with a melancholy impression of Colonel Brandon's unhappiness, and was prevented even from wishing it removed, by her anxiety for the very event that must confirm it.

Chapter VI.

Nothing occurred during the next three or four days, to make Elinor regret what she had done, in applying to her mother; for Willoughby neither came nor wrote. They were engaged about the end of that time to attend Lady Middleton to a party, from which Mrs. Jennings was kept away by the indisposition of her youngest daughter; and for this party, Marianne, wholly dispirited, careless of her appearance, and seeming equally indifferent whether she went or staid, prepared, without one look of hope, or one expression of pleasure. She sat by the drawing room fire after tea, till the moment of Lady Middleton's arrival, without once stirring from her seat, or altering her attitude, lost in her own thoughts and insensible of her sister's presence; and when at last they were told that Lady Middleton waited for them at the door, she started as if she had forgotten that any one was expected.

They arrived in due time at the place of destination, and as soon as the string of carriages before them would allow, alighted, ascended the stairs, heard their names announced from one landing-place to another in an audible voice, and entered a room splendidly lit up, quite full of company, and insufferably hot. When they had paid their tribute of politeness by curtesying to the lady of the house, they were permitted to mingle in the croud, and take their share of the heat and inconvenience, to which their arrival must necessarily add. After some time spent in saying little and doing less, Lady Middleton sat down to Casino, and as Marianne was not in spirits for moving about, she and Elinor luckily succeeding to chairs, placed themselves at no great distance from the table.

They had not remained in this manner long, before Elinor perceived Willoughby, standing within a few yards of them, in earnest conversation with a very fashionable looking young woman. She soon caught his eye, and he immediately bowed, but without attempting to speak to her, or to approach Marianne, though he could not but see her; and then continued his discourse with the same lady. Elinor turned involuntarily to Marianne, to see whether it could be unobserved by her. At that moment she first perceived him, and her whole countenance glowing with sudden delight, she would have moved towards him instantly, had not her sister caught hold of her.

"Good heavens!" she exclaimed, "he is there—he is there—Oh! why does he not look at me? why cannot I speak to him?"

"Pray, pray be composed," cried Elinor, "and do not betray what you feel to every body present. Perhaps he has not observed you yet."

This however was more than she could believe herself; and to be composed at such a moment was not only beyond the reach of Marianne, it was beyond her wish. She sat in an agony of impatience, which affected every feature.

At last he turned round again, and regarded them both; she started up, and pronouncing his name in a tone of affection, held out her hand to him. He approached, and addressing himself rather to Elinor than Marianne, as if wishing to avoid her eye, and determined not to observe her attitude, inquired in a hurried manner after Mrs. Dashwood, and asked how long they had been in town. Elinor was robbed of all presence of mind by such an address, and was unable to say a word. But the feelings of her sister were instantly expressed. Her face was crimsoned over, and she exclaimed in a voice of the greatest emotion, "Good God! Willoughby, what is the meaning of this? Have you not received my letters? Will you not shake hands with me?"

He could not then avoid it, but her touch seemed painful to him, and he held her hand only for a moment. During all this time he was evidently struggling for composure. Elinor watched his countenance and saw its expression becoming more tranquil. After a moment's pause, he spoke with calmness.

"I did myself the honour of calling in Berkeley-street last Tuesday, and very much regretted that I was not fortunate enough to find yourselves and Mrs. Jennings at home. My card was not lost, I hope."

"But have you not received my notes?" cried Marianne in the wildest anxiety. "Here is some mistake I am sure—some dreadful mistake. What can be the meaning of it? Tell me, Willoughby; for heaven's sake tell me, what is the matter?"

He made no reply; his complexion changed and all his embarrassment returned; but as if, on catching the eye of the young lady with whom he had been previously talking, he felt the necessity of instant exertion, he recovered himself again, and after saying, "Yes, I had the pleasure of receiving the information of your arrival in town, which you were so good as to send me," turned hastily away with a slight bow and joined his friend.

Marianne, now looking dreadfully white, and unable to stand, sunk into her chair, and Elinor, expecting every moment to see her faint, tried to screen her from the observation of others, while reviving her with lavendar water.

"Go to him, Elinor," she cried, as soon as she could speak, "and force him to come to me. Tell him I must see him again—must speak to him instantly.—I cannot rest—I shall not have a moment's peace till this is explained—some dreadful misapprehension or other.—Oh go to him this moment."

"How can that be done? No, my dearest Marianne, you must wait. This is not a place for explanations. Wait only till to-morrow."

With difficulty however could she prevent her from following him herself; and to persuade her to check her agitation, to wait, at least, with the appearance of composure, till she might speak to him with more privacy and more effect, was impossible; for Marianne continued incessantly to give way in a low voice to the misery of her feelings, by exclamations of wretchedness. In a short time Elinor saw Willoughby quit the room by the door towards the staircase, and telling Marianne that he was gone, urged the impossibility of speaking to him again that evening, as a fresh argument for her to be calm. She instantly begged her sister would entreat Lady Middleton to take them home, as she was too miserable to stay a minute longer.

Lady Middleton, though in the middle of a rubber, on being informed that Marianne was unwell, was too polite to object for a moment to her wish of going away, and making over her cards to a friend, they departed as soon as the carriage could be found. Scarcely a word was spoken during their return to Berkeley-street. Marianne was in a silent agony, too much oppressed even for tears; but as Mrs. Jennings was luckily not come home, they could go directly to their own room, where hartshorn[1] restored her a little to herself. She was soon undressed and in bed, and as she seemed desirous of being alone, her sister then left her, and while she waited the return of Mrs. Jennings, had leisure enough for thinking over the past.

That some kind of engagement had subsisted between Willoughby and Marianne she could not doubt; and that Willoughby was weary of it, seemed equally clear; for however Marianne might still feed her own wishes, *she* could not attribute such behaviour to mistake or misapprehension of any kind. Nothing but a thorough change of sentiment could account for it. Her indignation would have been still stronger than it was, had she not witnessed that embarrassment which seemed to speak a consciousness of his own

---

1. A solution of ammonia (sometime derived from the horns of harts or other substances) used as smelling salts.

misconduct, and prevented her from believing him so unprincipled as to have been sporting with the affections of her sister from the first, without any design that would bear investigation. Absence might have weakened his regard, and convenience might have determined him to overcome it, but that such a regard had formerly existed she could not bring herself to doubt.

As for Marianne, on the pangs which so unhappy a meeting must already have given her, and on those still more severe which might await her in its probable consequence, she could not reflect without the deepest concern. Her own situation gained in the comparison; for while she could *esteem* Edward as much as ever, however they might be divided in future, her mind might be always supported. But every circumstance that could embitter such an evil seemed uniting to heighten the misery of Marianne in a final separation from Willoughby—in an immediate and irreconcileable rupture with him.

Chapter VII.

Before the house-maid had lit their fire, the next day, or the sun gained any power over a cold, gloomy, morning in January, Marianne, only half dressed, was kneeling against one of the window-seats for the sake of all the little light she could command from it, and writing as fast as a continual flow of tears would permit her. In this situation, Elinor, roused from sleep by her agitation and sobs, first perceived her; and after observing her for a few moments with silent anxiety, said, in a tone of the most considerate gentleness,

"Marianne, may I ask?"—

"No, Elinor," she replied, "ask nothing; you will soon know all."

The sort of desperate calmness with which this was said, lasted no longer than while she spoke, and was immediately followed by a return of the same excessive affliction. It was some minutes before she could go on with her letter, and the frequent bursts of grief which still obliged her, at intervals, to withhold her pen, were proofs enough of her feeling how more than probable it was that she was writing for the last time to Willoughby.

Elinor paid her every quiet and unobtrusive attention in her power; and she would have tried to soothe and tranquillize her still more, had not Marianne entreated her, with all the eagerness of the most nervous irritability, not to speak to her for the world. In such circumstances, it was better for both that they should not be long together; and the restless state of Marianne's mind not only prevented her from remaining in the room a moment after she was dressed, but requiring at once solitude and continual change of place, made her wander about the house till breakfast time, avoiding the sight of every body.

At breakfast she neither ate, nor attempted to eat any thing; and Elinor's attention was then all employed, not in urging her, not in pitying her, nor in appearing to regard her, but in endeavouring to engage Mrs. Jennings's notice entirely to herself.

As this was a favourite meal with Mrs. Jennings, it lasted a considerable time, and they were just setting themselves, after it, round the common working table, when a letter was delivered to Marianne, which she eagerly caught from the servant, and, turning of a death-like paleness, instantly ran out of the room. Elinor, who saw as plainly by this, as if she had seen the direction, that it must come from Willoughby, felt immediately such a sickness at heart as made her hardly able to hold up her head, and sat in such a general tremour as made her fear it impossible to escape Mrs. Jennings's notice. That good lady, however, saw only that Marianne had received a letter from Willoughby, which appeared to her a very good joke, and which she treated accordingly, by hoping, with a laugh, that she would find it to her liking. Of Elinor's distress, she was too busily employed in measuring lengths of worsted for her rug, to see any thing at all; and calmly continuing her talk, as soon as Marianne disappeared, she said,

"Upon my word I never saw a young woman so desperately in love in my life! *My* girls were nothing to her, and yet they used to be foolish enough; but as for Miss Marianne, she is quite an altered creature. I hope, from the bottom of my heart, he wo'nt keep her waiting much longer, for it is quite grievous to see her look so ill and forlorn. Pray, when are they to be married?"

Elinor, though never less disposed to speak than at that moment, obliged herself to answer such an attack as this, and, therefore, trying to smile, replied, "And have you really, Ma'am, talked yourself into a persuasion of my sister's being engaged to Mr. Willoughby? I thought it had been only a joke, but so serious a question seems to imply more; and I must beg, therefore, that you will not deceive yourself any longer. I do assure you that nothing would surprise me more than to hear of their being going to be married."

"For shame, for shame, Miss Dashwood! how can you talk so! Don't we all know that it must be a match, that they were over head and ears in love with each other from the first moment they met? Did not I see them together in Devonshire every day, and all day long; and did not I know that your sister came to town with me on purpose to buy wedding clothes? Come, come, this wo'nt do. Because you are so sly about it yourself, you think nobody else has any senses; but it is no such thing, I can tell you, for it has been known all over town* this ever so long. I tell every body of it and so does Charlotte."

"Indeed, Ma'am," said Elinor very seriously, "you are mistaken. Indeed, you are doing a very unkind thing in spreading the report, and you will find that you have, though you will not believe me now."

Mrs. Jennings laughed again, but Elinor had not spirits to say more, and eager at all events to know what Willoughby had written, hurried away to their room, where, on opening the door, she saw Marianne stretched on the bed, almost choked by grief, one letter in her hand, and two or three others lying by her. Elinor drew near, but without saying a word; and seating herself on the bed, took her hand, kissed her affectionately several times, and then gave way to a burst of tears, which at first was scarcely less violent than Marianne's. The latter, though unable to speak, seemed to feel all the tenderness of this behaviour, and after some time thus spent in joint affliction, she put all the letters into Elinor's hands; and then covering her face with her handkerchief, almost screamed with agony. Elinor, who knew that such grief, shocking as it was to witness it, must have its course, watched by her till this excess of suffering had somewhat spent itself, and then turning eagerly to Willoughby's letter, read as follows:

Bond Street, January.

My Dear Madam,

   I have just had the honour of receiving your letter, for which I beg to return my sincere acknowledgments. I am much concerned to find there was any thing in my behaviour last night that did not meet your approbation; and though I am quite at a loss to discover in what point I could be so unfortunate as to offend you, I entreat your forgiveness of what I can assure you to have been perfectly unintentional. I shall never reflect on my former acquaintance with your family in Devonshire without the most grateful pleasure, and flatter myself it will not be broken by any mistake or misapprehension of my actions. My esteem for your whole family is very sincere; but if I have been so unfortunate as to give rise to a belief of more than I felt, or meant to express, I shall reproach myself for not having been more guarded in my professions of that esteem. That I should ever have meant more you will allow to be impossible, when you understand that my affections have been long engaged elsewhere, and it will not be many weeks, I believe, before this engagement is fulfilled. It is with great regret that I obey your commands of returning the letters, with which I

---

* all over town] all over the town A.

have been honoured from you, and the lock of hair, which you so obligingly bestowed on me.

I am, dear Madam,
Your most obedient
humble Servant,
JOHN WILLOUGHBY.

With what indignation such a letter as this must be read by Miss Dashwood, may be imagined. Though aware, before she began it, that it must bring a confession of his inconstancy, and confirm their separation for ever, she was not aware that such language could be suffered to announce it!* nor could she have supposed Willoughby capable of departing so far from the appearance of every honourable and delicate feeling—so far from the common decorum of a gentleman, as to send a letter so impudently cruel: a letter which, instead of bringing with his desire of a release any professions of regret, acknowledged no breach of faith, denied all peculiar affection whatever—a letter of which every line was an insult, and which proclaimed its writer to be deep in hardened villany.

She paused over it for some time with indignant astonishment; then read it again and again; but every perusal only served to increase her abhorrence of the man, and so bitter were her feelings against him, that she dared not trust herself to speak, lest she might wound Marianne still deeper by treating their disengagement, not as a loss to her of any possible good but as an escape from the worst and most irremediable of all evils,** a connection, for life, with an unprincipled man, as a deliverance the most real, a blessing the most important.

In her earnest meditations on the contents of the letter, on the depravity of that mind which could dictate it, and, probably, on the very different mind of a very different person, who had no other connection whatever with the affair than what her heart gave him with every thing that passed, Elinor forgot the immediate distress of her sister, forgot that she had three letters on her lap yet unread, and so entirely forgot how long she had been in the room, that when on hearing a carriage drive up to the door, she went to the window to see who could be coming so unreasonably early, she was all astonishment to perceive Mrs. Jennings's chariot,[1] which she knew had not been ordered till one. Determined not to quit Marianne, though hopeless of contributing, at present, to her ease, she hurried away to excuse herself from attending Mrs. Jennings, on

---

* it!] it; A.
** of all evils,] of evils, A.
1. A fancy carriage, fitted with a coach box.

account of her sister being indisposed. Mrs. Jennings, with a thoroughly good-humoured concern for its cause, admitted the excuse most readily, and Elinor, after seeing her safe off, returned to Marianne, whom she found attempting to rise from the bed, and whom she reached just in time to prevent her from falling on the floor, faint and giddy from a long want of proper rest and food; for it was many days since she had any appetite, and many nights since she had really slept; and now, when her mind was no longer supported by the fever of suspense, the consequence of all this was felt in an aching head, a weakened stomach, and a general nervous faintness. A glass of wine, which Elinor procured for her directly, made her more comfortable, and she was at last able to express some sense of her kindness, by saying,

"Poor Elinor! how unhappy I make you!"

"I only wish," replied her sister, "there were any thing I *could* do, which might be of comfort to you."

This, as every thing else would have been, was too much for Marianne, who could only exclaim, in the anguish of her heart, "Oh! Elinor, I am miserable indeed," before her voice was entirely lost in sobs.

Elinor could no longer witness this torrent of unresisted grief in silence.

"Exert yourself, dear Marianne," she cried, "if you would not kill yourself and all who love you. Think of your mother; think of her misery while *you* suffer; for her sake you must exert yourself."

"I cannot, I cannot," cried Marianne; "leave me, leave me, if I distress you; leave me, hate me, forget me!* but do not torture me so. Oh! how easy for those who have no sorrow of their own to talk of exertion! Happy, happy Elinor, *you* cannot have an idea of what I suffer."

"Do you call *me* happy, Marianne? Ah! if you knew!—And can you believe me to be so, while I see you so wretched!"

"Forgive me, forgive me," throwing her arms round her sister's neck; "I know you feel for me; I know what a heart you have; but yet you are—you must be happy; Edward loves you—what, oh! what can do away such happiness as that?"

"Many, many circumstances," said Elinor, solemnly.

"No, no, no," cried Marianne wildly, "he loves you, and only you. You *can* have no grief."

"I can have no pleasure while I see you in this state."

"And you will never see me otherwise. Mine is a misery which nothing can do away."

"You must not talk so, Marianne. Have you no comforts? no

---

* me!] me; A.

friends? Is your loss such as leaves no opening for consolation?
Much as you suffer now, think of what you would have suffered if
the discovery of his character had been delayed to a later period—
if your engagement had been carried on for months and months,
as it might have been, before he chose to put an end to it. Every
additional day of unhappy confidence, on your side, would have
made the blow more dreadful."

"Engagement!" cried Marianne, "there has been no engagement."

"No engagement!"

"No, he is not so unworthy as you believe him. He has broken
no faith with me."

"But he told you that he loved you?"—

"Yes—no—never absolutely. It was every day implied, but never
professedly declared. Sometimes I thought it had been—but it
never was."

"Yet you wrote to him?"—

"Yes—could that be wrong after all that had passed?—But I cannot talk."

Elinor said no more, and turning again to the three letters which
now raised a much stronger curiosity than before, directly ran over
the contents of all. The first, which was what her sister had sent
him on their arrival in town, was to this effect.

Berkeley Street, January.

How surprised you will be, Willoughby, on receiving this; and I
think you will feel something more than surprise, when you know
that I am in town. An opportunity of coming hither, though with
Mrs. Jennings, was a temptation we could not resist. I wish you
may receive this in time to come here to-night, but I will not depend
on it. At any rate I shall expect you to-morrow. For the present,
adieu.

M. D.

Her second note, which had been written on the morning after
the dance at the Middletons', was in these words:—

"I cannot express my disappointment in having missed you the
day before yesterday, nor my astonishment at not having received
any answer to a note which I sent you above a week ago. I have
been expecting to hear from you, and still more to see you, every
hour of the day. Pray call again as soon as possible, and explain the
reason of my having expected this in vain. You had better come
earlier another time, because we are generally out by one. We were
last night at Lady Middleton's, where there was a dance. I have
been told that you were asked to be of the party. But could it be
so? You must be very much altered indeed since we parted, if that

could be the case, and you not there. But I will not suppose this possible, and I hope very soon to receive your personal assurance of its being otherwise."

M. D.

The contents of her last note to him were these:—

"What am I to imagine, Willoughby, by your behaviour last night? Again I demand an explanation of it. I was prepared to meet you with the pleasure which our separation naturally produced, with the familiarity which our intimacy at Barton appeared to me to justify. I was repulsed indeed! I have passed a wretched night in endeavouring to excuse a conduct which can scarcely be called less than insulting; but though I have not yet been able to form any reasonable apology for your behaviour, I am perfectly ready to hear your justification of it. You have perhaps been misinformed, or purposely deceived, in something concerning me, which may have lowered me in your opinion. Tell me what it is, explain the grounds on which you acted, and I shall be satisfied, in being able to satisfy you. It would grieve me indeed to be obliged to think ill of you; but if I am to do it, if I am to learn that you are not what we have hitherto believed you, that your regard for us all was insincere, that your behaviour to me was intended only to deceive, let it be told as soon as possible. My feelings are at present in a state of dreadful indecision; I wish to acquit you, but certainty on either side will be ease to what I now suffer. If your sentiments are no longer what they were, you will return my notes, and the lock of my hair which is in your possession."

M. D.

That such letters, so full of affection and confidence, could have been so answered, Elinor, for Willoughby's sake, would have been unwilling to believe. But her condemnation of him did not blind her to the impropriety of their having been written at all; and she was silently grieving over the imprudence which had hazarded such unsolicited proofs of tenderness, not warranted by anything preceding, and most severely condemned by the event, when Marianne, perceiving that she had finished the letters, observed to her that they contained nothing but what any one would have written in the same situation.

"I felt myself," she added, "to be as solemnly engaged to him, as if the strictest legal covenant had bound us to each other."

"I can believe it," said Elinor; "but unfortunately he did not feel the same."

"He *did* feel the same, Elinor—for weeks and weeks he felt it. I know he did. Whatever may have changed him now, (and nothing but the blackest art employed against me can have done it,) I was once as dear to him as my own soul could wish. This lock of hair, which now he can so readily give up, was begged of me with the most earnest supplication. Had you seen his look, his manner, had you heard his voice at that moment! Have you forgot the last evening of our being together at Barton? The morning that we parted too! When he told me that it might be many weeks before we meet again—his distress—can I ever forget his distress!"

For a moment or two she could say no more; but when this emotion had passed away, she added, in a firmer tone,

"Elinor, I have been cruelly used; but not by Willoughby."

"Dearest Marianne, who but himself? By whom can he have been instigated?"

"By all the world, rather than by his own heart. I could rather believe every creature of my acquaintance leagued together to ruin me in his opinion, than believe his nature capable of such cruelty. This woman of whom he writes—whoever she be—or any one, in short, but your own dear self, mama, and Edward, may have been so barbarous to bely me. Beyond you three, is there a creature in the world whom I would not rather suspect of evil than Willoughby, whose heart I know so well?"

Elinor would not contend, and only replied, "Whoever may have been so detestably your enemy, let them be cheated of their malignant triumph, my dear sister, by seeing how nobly the consciousness of your own innocence and good intentions supports your spirits. It is a reasonable and laudable pride which resists such malevolence."

"No, no," cried Marianne, "misery such as mine has no pride. I care not who knows that I am wretched. The triumph of seeing me so may be open to all the world. Elinor, Elinor, they who suffer little may be proud and independent as they like—may resist insult, or return mortification—but I cannot. I must feel—I must be wretched—and they are welcome to enjoy the consciousness of it that can."

"But for my mother's sake and mine"—

"I would do more than for my own. But to appear happy when I am so miserable—Oh! who can require it?"

Again they were both silent. Elinor was employed in walking thoughtfully from the fire to the window, from the window to the fire, without knowing that she received warmth from one, or discerning* objects through the other; and Marianne, seated at the foot of the bed, with her head leaning against one of its posts, again

---

* discerning] discerned A.

took up Willoughby's letter, and after shuddering over every sentence, exclaimed—

"It is too much! Oh! Willoughby, Willoughby, could this be yours! Cruel, cruel—nothing can acquit you. Elinor, nothing can. Whatever he might have heard against me—ought he not to have suspended his belief? ought he not to have told me of it, to have given me the power of clearing myself? 'The lock of hair, (repeating it from the letter,) which you so obligingly bestowed on me'—That is unpardonable. Willoughby, where was your heart, when you wrote those words? Oh! barbarously insolent!—Elinor, can he be justified?"

"No, Marianne, in no possible way."

"And yet this woman—who knows what her art may have been —how long it may have been premeditated, and how deeply contrived by her!—Who is she?—Who can she be?—Whom did I ever hear him talk of as young and attractive among his female acquaintance?—Oh! no one, no one—he talked to me only of myself."

Another pause ensued; Marianne was greatly agitated, and it ended thus.

"Elinor, I must go home. I must go and comfort mama. Cannot we be gone to-morrow?"

"To-morrow, Marianne!"

"Yes; why should I stay here? I came only for Willoughby's sake —and now who cares for me? Who regards me?"

"It would be impossible to go to-morrow. We owe Mrs. Jennings much more than civility; and civility of the commonest kind must prevent such a hasty removal as that."

"Well then, another day or two perhaps; but I cannot stay here long, I cannot stay to endure the questions and remarks of all these people. The Middletons and Palmers—how am I to bear their pity? The pity of such a woman as Lady Middleton! Oh! what would *he* say to that!"

Elinor advised her to lie down again, and for a moment she did so; but no attitude could give her ease; and in restless pain of mind and body she moved from one posture to another, till growing more and more hysterical, her sister could with difficulty keep her on the bed at all, and for some time was fearful of being constrained to call for assistance. Some lavender drops, however, which she was at length persuaded to take, were of use; and from that time till Mrs. Jennings returned, she continued on the bed quiet and motionless.

Chapter VIII.

Mrs. Jennings came immediately to their room on her return, and without waiting to have her request of admittance answered, opened the door and walked in with a look of real concern.

"How do you do my dear?"—said she in a voice of great compassion to Marianne, who turned away her face without attempting to answer.

"How is she, Miss Dashwood?—Poor thing! she looks very bad. —No wonder. Aye, it is but too true. He is to be married very soon—a good-for-nothing fellow! I have no patience with him. Mrs. Taylor told me of it half an hour ago, and she was told it by a particular friend of Miss Grey herself, else I am sure I should not have believed it; and I was almost ready to sink as it was. Well, said I, all I can say is, that if it is true, he has used a young lady of my acquaintance abominably ill, and I wish with all my soul his wife may plague his heart out. And so I shall always say, my dear, you may depend on it. I have no notion of men's going on in this way: and if ever I meet him again, I will give him such a dressing[1] as he has not had this many a day. But there is one comfort, my dear Miss Marianne; he is not the only young man in the world worth having; and with your pretty face you will never want admirers. Well, poor thing! I won't disturb her any longer, for she had better have her cry out at once and have done with it. The Parrys and Sandersons luckily are coming to-night you know, and that will amuse her."

She then went away, walking on tiptoe out of the room, as if she supposed her young friend's affliction could be increased by noise.

Marianne, to the surprise of her sister, determined on dining with them. Elinor even advised her against it. But "no, she would go down; she could bear it very well, and the bustle about her would be less." Elinor, pleased to have her governed for a moment by such a motive, though believing it hardly possible that she could sit out the dinner, said no more; and adjusting her dress for her as well as she could, while Marianne still remained on the bed, was ready to assist her into the dining room as soon as they were summoned to it.

When there, though looking most wretchedly, she ate more and was calmer than her sister had expected. Had she tried to speak, or had she been conscious of half Mrs. Jennings's well-meant but ill-judged attentions to her, this calmness could not have been maintained; but not a syllable escaped her lips, and the abstraction

---

1. Scolding, chastisement.

of her thoughts preserved her in ignorance of every thing that was passing before her.

Elinor, who did justice to Mrs. Jennings's kindness, though its effusions were often distressing, and sometimes almost ridiculous, made her those acknowledgments, and returned her those civilities, which her sister could not make or return for herself. Their good friend saw that Marianne was unhappy, and felt that every thing was due to her which might make her at all less so. She treated her therefore, with all the indulgent fondness of a parent towards a favourite child on the last day of its holidays. Marianne was to have the best place by the fire, was to be tempted to eat by every delicacy in the house, and to be amused by the relation of all the news of the day. Had not Elinor, in the sad countenance of her sister, seen a check to all mirth, she could have been entertained by Mrs. Jennings's endeavours to cure a disappointment in love, by a variety of sweetmeats and olives, and a good fire. As soon, however, as the consciousness of all this was forced by continual repetition on Marianne, she could stay no longer. With an hasty exclamation of Misery, and a sign to her sister not to follow her, she directly got up and hurried out of the room.

"Poor soul!" cried Mrs. Jennings, as soon as she was gone, "how it grieves me to see her! And I declare if she is not gone away without finishing her wine! And the dried cherries too! Lord! nothing seems to do her any good. I am sure if I knew of any thing she would like, I would send all over the town for it. Well, it is the oddest thing to me, that a man should use such a pretty girl so ill! But when there is plenty of money on one side, and next to none on the other, Lord bless you! they care no more about such things!—"

"The lady then—Miss Grey I think you called her—is very rich?"

"Fifty thousand pounds, my dear. Did you ever see her? a smart, stilish girl they say, but not handsome. I remember her aunt very well, Biddy Henshawe; she married a very wealthy man. But the family are all rich together. Fifty thousand pounds! and by all accounts it wo'nt come before it's wanted; for they say he is all to pieces. No wonder! dashing about with his curricle and hunters! Well, it don't signify talking, but when a young man, be he who he will, comes and makes love to a pretty girl, and promises marriage, he has no business to fly off from his word only because he grows poor, and a richer girl is ready to have him. Why don't he, in such a case, sell his horses, let his house, turn off his servants, and make a thorough reform at once? I warrant you, Miss Marianne would have been ready to wait till matters came round. But that won't do, now-a-days; nothing in the way of pleasure can ever be given up by the young men of this age."

"Do you know what kind of a girl Miss Grey is? Is she said to be amiable?"

"I never heard any harm of her; indeed I hardly ever heard her mentioned; except that Mrs. Taylor did say this morning, that one day Miss Walker hinted to her, that she believed Mr. and Mrs. Ellison would not be sorry to have Miss Grey married, for she and Mrs. Ellison could never agree."—

"And who are the Ellisons?"

"Her guardians, my dear. But now she is of age and may choose for herself; and a pretty choice she has made!—What now," after pausing a moment—"your poor sister is gone to her own room I suppose to moan by herself. Is there nothing one can get to comfort her? Poor dear, it seems quite cruel to let her be alone. Well, by-and-by we shall have a few friends, and that will amuse her a little. What shall we play at? She hates whist I know; but is there no round game she cares for?"

"Dear Ma'am, this kindness is quite unnecessary. Marianne I dare say will not leave her room again this evening. I shall persuade her if I can to go early to bed, for I am sure she wants rest."

"Aye, I believe that will be best for her. Let her name her own supper, and go to bed. Lord! no wonder she has been looking so bad and so cast down this last week or two, for this matter I suppose has been hanging over her head as long as that. And so the letter that came to-day finished it! Poor soul! I am sure if I had had a notion of it, I would not have joked her about it for all my money. But then you know, how should I guess such a thing? I made sure of its being nothing but a common love letter, and you know young people like to be laughed at about them. Lord! how concerned Sir John and my daughters will be when they hear it! If I had had my senses about me I might have called in Conduit-street in my way home, and told them of it. But I shall see them tomorrow."

"It would be unnecessary I am sure, for you to caution Mrs. Palmer and Sir John against ever naming Mr. Willoughby, or making the slightest allusion to what has passed, before my sister. Their own good-nature must point out to them the real cruelty of appearing to know any thing about it when she is present; and the less that may ever be said to myself on the subject, the more my feelings will be spared, as you my dear madam will easily believe."

"Oh! Lord! yes, that I do indeed. It must be terrible for you to hear it talked of; and as for your sister, I am sure I would not mention a word about it to her for the world. You saw I did not all dinner time. No more would Sir John nor my daughters, for they are all very thoughtful and considerate; especially if I give them a hint, as I certainly will. For my part, I think the less that is said about such things, the better, the sooner 'tis blown over and forgot. And what good does talking ever do you know?"

"In this affair it can only do harm; more so perhaps than in many cases of a similar kind, for it has been attended by circumstances which, for the sake of every one concerned in it, make it unfit to become the public conversation. I must do *this* justice to Mr. Willoughby—he has broken no positive engagement with my sister."

"Law, my dear! Don't pretend to defend him. No positive engagement indeed! after taking her all over Allenham House, and fixing on the very rooms they were to live in hereafter!"

Elinor, for her sister's sake, could not press the subject farther, and she hoped it was not required of her for Willoughby's; since, though Marianne might lose much, he could gain very little by the inforcement of the real truth. After a short silence on both sides, Mrs. Jennings, with all her natural hilarity, burst forth again.

"Well, my dear, 'tis a true saying about an ill wind, for it will be all the better for Colonel Brandon. He will have her at last; aye, that he will. Mind me, now, if they an't married by Midsummer.[2] Lord! how he'll chuckle over this news! I hope he will come to-night. It will be all to one a better match for your sister. Two thousand a year without debt or drawback—except the little love-child,[3] indeed; aye, I had forgot her; but she may be 'prenticed out at small cost, and then what does it signify? Delaford is a nice place, I can tell you; exactly what I call a nice old fashioned place, full of comforts and conveniences; quite shut in with great garden walls that are covered with the best fruit-trees in the country: and such a mulberry tree in one corner! Lord! how Charlotte and I did stuff the only time we were there! Then, there is a dove-cote,[4] some delightful stewponds,[5] and a very pretty canal; and every thing, in short, that one could wish for: and, moreover, it is close to the church, and only a quarter of a mile from the turnpike-road, so 'tis never dull, for if you only go and sit up in an old yew arbour behind the house, you may see all the carriages that pass along. Oh! 'tis a nice place! A butcher hard by in the village, and the parsonage-house within a stone's throw. To my fancy, a thousand times prettier than Barton Park, where they are forced to send three miles for their meat, and have not a neighbour nearer than your mother. Well, I shall spirit up the Colonel as soon as I can. One shoulder

2. *Midsummer* Day is June 24; generally, the period of the summer solstice, about June 21.
3. Child born out of wedlock.
4. Roosting house with compartments for doves or pigeons.
5. Fishpond.

of mutton, you know, drives another down.[6] If we *can* but put Willoughby out of her head!"

"Aye, if we can but do *that*, Ma'am," said Elinor, "we shall do very well with or without Colonel Brandon." And then rising, she went away to join Marianne, whom she found, as she expected, in her own room, leaning, in silent misery, over the small remains of a fire, which, till Elinor's entrance, had been her only light.

"You had better leave me," was all the notice that her sister received from her.

"I will leave you," said Elinor, "if you will go to bed." But this, from the momentary perverseness of impatient suffering, she at first refused to do. Her sister's earnest, though gentle persuasion, however, soon softened her to compliance, and Elinor saw her lay her aching head on the pillow, and saw her, as she hoped, in a way to get some quiet rest before she left her.

In the drawing-room, whither she then repaired, she was soon joined by Mrs. Jennings, with a wine-glass, full of something, in her hand.

"My dear," said she, entering, "I have just recollected that I have some of the finest old Constantia wine[7] in the house, that ever was tasted, so I have brought a glass of it for your sister. My poor husband! how fond he was of it! Whenever he had a touch of his old cholicky gout, he said it did him more good than any thing else in the world. Do take it to your sister."

"Dear Ma'am," replied Elinor, smiling at the difference of the complaints for which it was recommended, "how good you are! But I have just left Marianne in bed, and, I hope, almost asleep; and as I think nothing will be of so much service to her as rest, if you will give me leave, I will drink the wine myself."

Mrs. Jennings, though regretting that she had not been five minutes earlier, was satisfied with the compromise; and Elinor, as she swallowed the chief of it, reflected that, though its good effects on a cholicky gout were, at present, of little importance to her, its healing powers on a disappointed heart might be as reasonably tried on herself as on her sister.

Colonel Brandon came in while the party were at tea, and by his manner of looking round the room for Marianne, Elinor immediately fancied that he neither expected, nor wished to see her there, and, in short, that he was already aware of what occasioned her absence. Mrs. Jennings was not struck by the same thought; for, soon after his entrance, she walked across the room to the tea-table

6. R. W. Chapman notes that this is a proverbial expression, an English version of the French *En mangeant, l'appetit vient.*
7. A sweet wine made at Constantia Farm near Cape Town in South Africa, ruled by Great Britain starting in 1795.

where Elinor presided, and whispered—"The Colonel looks as grave as ever you see. He knows nothing of it; do tell him, my dear."

He shortly afterwards drew a chair close to her's, and, with a look which perfectly assured her of his good information, inquired after her sister.

"Marianne is not well," said she. "She has been indisposed all day, and we have persuaded her to go to bed."

"Perhaps, then," he hesitatingly replied, "what I heard this morning may be—there may be more truth in it than I could believe possible at first."

"What did you hear?"

"That a gentleman, whom I had reason to think—in short, that a man, whom I *knew* to be engaged—but how shall I tell you? If you know it already, as surely you must, I may be spared."

"You mean," answered Elinor, with forced calmness, "Mr. Willoughby's marriage with Miss Grey. Yes, we *do* know it all. This seems to have been a day of general elucidation, for this very morning first unfolded it to us. Mr. Willoughby is unfathomable! Where did you hear it?"

"In a stationer's shop in Pall Mall,[8] where I had business. Two ladies were waiting for their carriage, and one of them was giving the other an account of the intended match, in a voice so little attempting concealment, that it was impossible for me not to hear all. The name of Willoughby, John Willoughby, frequently repeated, first caught my attention, and what followed was a positive assertion that every thing was now finally settled respecting his marriage with Miss Grey—it was no longer to be a secret—it would take place even within a few weeks, with many particulars of preparations and other matters. One thing, especially, I remember, because it served to identify the man still more:—as soon as the ceremony was over, they were to go to Combe Magna, his seat in Somersetshire. My astonishment!—but it would be impossible to describe what I felt. The communicative lady I learnt, on inquiry, for I staid in the shop till they were gone, was a Mrs. Ellison, and that, as I have been since informed, is the name of Miss Grey's guardian."

"It is. But have you likewise heard that Miss Grey has fifty thousand pounds? In that, if in any thing, we may find an explanation."

"It may be so; but Willoughby is capable—at least I think"—he stopped a moment; then added in a voice which seemed to distrust itself, "And your sister—how did she—"

"Her sufferings have been very severe. I have only to hope that they may be proportionably short. It has been, it is a most cruel affliction. Till yesterday, I believe, she never doubted his regard;

8. A fashionable street in the West End of London.

and even now, perhaps—but *I* am almost convinced that he never was really attached to her. He has been very deceitful! and, in some points, there seems a hardness of heart about him."

"Ah!" said Colonel Brandon, "there is, indeed! But your sister does not—I think you said so—she does not consider it quite as you do?"

"You know her disposition, and may believe how eagerly she would still justify him if she could."

He made no answer; and soon afterwards, by the removal of the tea-things, and the arrangement of the card parties, the subject was necessarily dropped. Mrs. Jennings, who had watched them with pleasure while they were talking, and who expected to see the effect of Miss Dashwood's communication, in such an instantaneous gaiety on Colonel Brandon's side, as might have become a man in the bloom of youth, of hope and happiness, saw him, with amazement, remain the whole evening more serious and thoughtful than usual.

Chapter IX.

From a night of more sleep than she had expected, Marianne awoke the next morning to the same consciousness of misery in which she had closed her eyes.

Elinor encouraged her as much as possible to talk of what she felt; and before breakfast was ready, they had gone through the subject again and again; with the same steady conviction and affectionate counsel on Elinor's side, the same impetuous feelings and varying opinions on Marianne's, as before. Sometimes she could believe Willoughby to be as unfortunate and as innocent as herself, and at others, lost every consolation in the impossibility of acquitting him. At one moment she was absolutely indifferent to the observation of all the world, at another she would seclude herself from it for ever, and at a third could resist it with energy. In one thing, however, she was uniform, when it came to the point, in avoiding, where it was possible, the presence of Mrs. Jennings, and in a determined silence when obliged to endure it. Her heart was hardened against the belief of Mrs. Jennings's entering into her sorrows with any compassion.

"No, no, no, it cannot be," she cried; "she cannot feel. Her kindness is not sympathy; her good nature is not tenderness. All that she wants is gossip, and she only likes me now because I supply it."

Elinor had not needed this to be assured of the injustice to which her sister was often led in her opinion of others, by the irritable refinement of her own mind, and the too great importance placed by her on the delicacies of a strong sensibility, and the graces of a polished manner. Like half the rest of the world, if more than half there be that are clever and good, Marianne, with excellent abilities and an excellent disposition, was neither reasonable nor candid. She expected from other people the same opinions and feelings as her own, and she judged of their motives by the immediate effect of their actions on herself. Thus a circumstance occurred, while the sisters were together in their own room after breakfast, which sunk the heart of Mrs. Jennings still lower in her estimation; because, through her own weakness, it chanced to prove a source of fresh pain to herself, though Mrs. Jennings was governed in it by an impulse of the utmost good-will.

With a letter in her out-stretched hand, and countenance gaily smiling, from the persuasion of bringing comfort, she entered their room, saying,

"Now, my dear, I bring you something that I am sure will do you good."

Marianne heard enough. In one moment her imagination placed before her a letter from Willoughby, full of tenderness and contrition, explanatory of all that had passed, satisfactory, convincing; and instantly followed by Willoughby himself, rushing eagerly into the room to inforce, at her feet, by the eloquence of his eyes, the assurances of his letter. The work of one moment was destroyed by the next. The hand writing of her mother, never till then unwelcome, was before her; and, in the acuteness of the disappointment which followed such an extasy of more than hope, she felt as if, till that instant, she had never suffered.

The cruelty of Mrs. Jennings no language, within her reach in her moments of happiest eloquence, could have expressed; and now she could reproach her only by the tears which streamed from her eyes with passionate violence—a reproach, however, so entirely lost on its object, that after many expressions of pity, she withdrew, still referring her to the letter for comfort. But the letter, when she was calm enough to read it, brought little comfort. Willoughby filled every page. Her mother, still confident of their engagement, and relying as warmly as ever on his constancy, had only been roused by Elinor's application, to intreat from Marianne greater openness towards them both; and this, with such tenderness towards her, such affection for Willoughby, and such a conviction of their future happiness in each other, that she wept with agony through the whole of it.

All her impatience to be at home again now returned; her mother was dearer to her than ever; dearer through the very excess of her mistaken confidence in Willoughby, and she was wildly urgent to be gone. Elinor, unable herself to determine whether it were better for Marianne to be in London or at Barton, offered no counsel of her own except of patience till their mother's wishes could be known; and at length she obtained her sister's consent to wait for that knowledge.

Mrs. Jennings left them earlier than usual; for she could not be easy till the Middletons and Palmers were able to grieve as much as herself; and positively refusing Elinor's offered attendance, went out alone for the rest of the morning. Elinor, with a very heavy heart, aware of the pain she was going to communicate, and perceiving by Marianne's letter how ill she had succeeded in laying any foundation for it, then sat down to write her mother an account of what had passed, and intreat her directions for the future; while Marianne, who came into the drawing-room on Mrs. Jennings's going away, remained fixed at the table where Elinor wrote, watching the advancement of her pen, grieving over her for the hardship of such a task, and grieving still more fondly over its effect on her mother.

In this manner they had continued about a quarter of an hour, when Marianne, whose nerves could not then bear any sudden noise, was startled by a rap at the door.

"Who can this be?" cried Elinor. "So early too! I thought we *had* been safe."

Marianne moved to the window—

"It is Colonel Brandon!" said she, with vexation. "We are never safe from *him*."

"He will not come in, as Mrs. Jennings is from home."

"I will not trust to *that*," retreating to her own room. "A man who has nothing to do with his own time has no conscience in his intrusion on that of others."

The event proved her conjecture right, though it was founded on injustice and error; for Colonel Brandon *did* come in; and Elinor, who was convinced that solicitude for Marianne brought him thither, and who saw *that* solicitude in his disturbed and melancholy look, and in his anxious though brief inquiry after her, could not forgive her sister for esteeming him so lightly.

"I met Mrs. Jennings in Bond-street," said he, after the first salutation, "and she encouraged me to come on; and I was the more easily encouraged, because I thought it probable that I might find you alone, which I was very desirous of doing. My object—my wish—my sole wish in desiring it—I hope, I believe it is—is to be a means of giving comfort;—no, I must not say comfort—not present comfort—but conviction, lasting conviction to your sister's mind. My regard for her, for yourself, for your mother—will you allow me to prove it, by relating some circumstances, which nothing but a *very* sincere regard—nothing but an earnest desire of being useful———I think I am justified—though where so many hours have been spent in convincing myself that I am right, is there not some reason to fear I may be wrong?' " He stopped. "I understand you," said Elinor. "You have something to tell me of Mr. Willoughby, that will open his character farther. Your telling it will be the greatest act of friendship that can be shewn Marianne. My gratitude will be insured immediately by any information tending to that end, and her's must be gained by it in time. Pray, pray let me hear it."

"You shall; and, to be brief, when I quitted Barton last October —but this will give you no idea—I must go farther back. You will find me a very awkward narrator, Miss Dashwood; I hardly know where to begin. A short account of myself, I believe, will be necessary, and it *shall* be a short one. On such a subject," sighing heavily, "I can have little temptation to be diffuse."

He stopt a moment for recollection, and then, with another sigh, went on.

"You have probably entirely forgotten a conversation—(it is not to be supposed that it could make any impression on you)—a conversation between us one evening at Barton Park—it was the evening of a dance—in which I alluded to a lady I had once known, as resembling, in some measure, your sister Marianne."

"Indeed," answered Elinor, "I have *not* forgotten it." He looked pleased by this remembrance, and added;

"If I am not deceived by the uncertainty, the partiality of tender recollection, there is a very strong resemblance between them, as well in mind as person. The same warmth of heart, the same eagerness of fancy and spirits. This lady was one of my nearest relations, an orphan from her infancy, and under the guardianship of my father. Our ages were nearly the same, and from our earliest years we were playfellows and friends. I cannot remember the time when I did not love Eliza; and my affection for her, as we grew up, was such, as perhaps, judging from my present forlorn and cheerless gravity, you might think me incapable of having ever felt. Her's, for me, was, I believe, fervent as the attachment of your sister to Mr. Willoughby, and it was, though from a different cause, no less unfortunate. At seventeen, she was lost to me for ever. She was married—married against her inclination to my brother. Her fortune was large, and our family estate much encumbered. And this, I fear, is all that can be said for the conduct of one, who was at once her uncle and guardian. My brother did not deserve her; he did not even love her. I had hoped that her regard for me would support her under any difficulty, and for some time it did; but at last the misery of her situation, for she experienced great unkindness, overcame all her resolution, and though she had promised me

that nothing——but how blindly I relate! I have never told you how
this was brought on. We were within a few hours of eloping together
for Scotland.[1] The treachery, or the folly, of my cousin's maid betrayed us. I was banished to the house of a relation far distant, and
she was allowed no liberty, no society, no amusement, till my father's point was gained. I had depended on her fortitude too far,
and the blow was a severe one—but had her marriage been happy,
so young as I then was, a few months must have reconciled me to
it, or at least I should not have now to lament it. This however was
not the case. My brother had no regard for her; his pleasures were
not what they ought to have been, and from the first he treated her
unkindly. The consequence of this, upon a mind so young, so lively,
so inexperienced as Mrs. Brandon's, was but too natural. She resigned herself at first to all the misery of her situation; and happy
had it been if she had not lived to overcome those regrets which
the remembrance of me occasioned. But can we wonder that with
such a husband to provoke inconstancy, and without a friend to
advise or restrain her, (for my father lived only a few months after
their marriage, and I was with my regiment in the East Indies) she
should fall? Had I remained in England, perhaps—but I meant to
promote the happiness of both by removing from her for years, and
for that purpose had procured my exchange.[2] The shock which her
marriage had given me," he continued, in a voice of great agitation,
"was of trifling weight—was nothing—to what I felt when I heard,
about two years afterwards, of her divorce.[3] It was *that* which threw
this gloom,—even now the recollection of what I suffered—"

He could say no more, and rising hastily walked for a few minutes
about the room. Elinor, affected by his relation, and still more by
his distress, could not speak. He saw her concern, and coming to
her, took her hand, pressed it, and kissed it with grateful respect.
A few minutes more of silent exertion enabled him to proceed with
composure.

"It was nearly three years after this unhappy period before I returned to England. My first care, when I *did* arrive, was of course
to seek for her; but the search was as fruitless as it was melancholy.
I could not trace her beyond her first seducer, and there was every
reason to fear that she had removed from him only to sink deeper
in a life of sin. Her legal allowance was not adequate to her fortune,
nor sufficient for her comfortable maintenance, and I learnt from

1. Because the Scottish Presbyterian Church permitted couples to marry without publishing
   banns, couples seeking to marry without a license or parental consent typically crossed
   the border to do so.
2. Arranged to switch from one regiment to another.
3. Divorces were public events, granted by an Act of Parliament and hence quite expensive
   to procure. In this case, it is granted on grounds of adultery.

my brother, that the power of receiving it had been made over some months before to another person. He imagined, and calmly could he imagine it, that her extravagance and consequent distress had obliged her to dispose of it for some immediate relief. At last, however, and after I had been six months in England, I *did* find her. Regard for a former servant of my own, who had since fallen into misfortune, carried me to visit him in a spunging-house,[4] where he was confined for debt; and there, in the same house, under a similar confinement, was my unfortunate sister. So altered—so faded— worn down by acute suffering of every kind! hardly could I believe the melancholy and sickly figure before me, to be the remains of the lovely, blooming, healthful girl, on whom I had once doated. What I endured in so beholding her—but I have no right to wound your feelings by attempting to describe it—I have pained you too much already. That she was, to all appearance, in the last stage of a consumption, was—yes, in such a situation it was my greatest comfort. Life could do nothing for her, beyond giving time for a better preparation for death; and that was given. I saw her placed in comfortable lodgings, and under proper attendants; I visited her every day during the rest of her short life; I was with her in her last moments."

Again he stopped to recover himself; and Elinor spoke her feelings in an exclamation of tender concern, at the fate of his unfortunate friend.

"Your sister, I hope, cannot be offended," said he, "by the resemblance I have fancied between her and my poor disgraced relation. Their fates, their fortunes cannot be the same; and had the natural sweet disposition of the one been guarded by a firmer mind, or an happier marriage, she might have been all that you will live to see the other be. But to what does all this lead? I seem to have been distressing you for nothing. Ah! Miss Dashwood—a subject such as this—untouched for fourteen years—it is dangerous to handle it at all! I *will* be more collected—more concise. She left to my care her only child, a little girl, the offspring of her first guilty connection, who was then about three years old. She loved the child, and had always kept it with her. It was a valued, a precious trust to me; and gladly would I have discharged it in the strictest sense, by watching over her education myself, had the nature of our situations allowed it; but I had no family, no home; and my little Eliza was therefore placed at school. I saw her there whenever I could, and after the death of my brother, (which happened about five years ago, and which left to me the possession of the family

---

4. Defined by the *OED* as a house kept by a bailiff or sheriff's officer, used as a place of preliminary confinement for debtors.

property,) she frequently visited me at Delaford. I called her a distant relation; but I am well aware that I have in general been suspected of a much nearer connection with her. It is now three years ago, (she had just reached her fourteenth year,) that I removed her from school, to place her under the care of a very respectable woman, residing in Dorsetshire, who had the charge of four or five other girls of about the same time of life; and for two years I had every reason to be pleased with her situation. But last February, almost a twelvemonth back, she suddenly disappeared. I had allowed her, (imprudently, as it has since turned out,) at her earnest desire, to go to Bath with one of her young friends, who was attending her father there for his health. I knew him to be a very good sort of man, and I thought well of his daughter—better than she deserved, for, with a most obstinate and ill-judged secrecy, she would tell nothing, would give no clue, though she certainly knew all. He, her father, a well-meaning, but not a quick-sighted man, could really, I believe, give no information; for he had been generally confined to the house, while the girls were ranging over the town and making what acquaintance they chose; and he tried to convince me, as thoroughly as he was convinced himself, of his daughter's being entirely unconcerned in the business. In short, I could learn nothing but that she was gone; all the rest, for eight long months, was left to conjecture. What I thought, what I feared, may be imagined; and what I suffered too."

"Good heavens!" cried Elinor, "could it be—could Willoughby!—"

"The first news that reached me of her," he continued, "came in a letter from herself, last October. It was forwarded to me from Delaford, and I received it on the very morning of our intended party to Whitwell; and this was the reason of my leaving Barton so suddenly, which I am sure must at the time have appeared strange to every body, and which I believe gave offence to some. Little did Mr. Willoughby imagine, I suppose, when his looks censured me for incivility in breaking up the party, that I was called away to the relief of one, whom he had made poor and miserable; but *had* he known it, what would it have availed? Would he have been less gay or less happy in the smiles of your sister? No, he had already done that, which no man who *can* feel for another, would do. He had left the girl whose youth and innocence he had seduced, in a situation of the utmost distress, with no creditable home, no help, no friends, ignorant of his address! He had left her promising to return; he neither returned, nor wrote, nor relieved her."

"This is beyond every thing!" exclaimed Elinor.

"His character is now before you; expensive, dissipated, and worse than both. Knowing all this, as I have now known it many weeks, guess what I must have felt on seeing your sister as fond of him as ever, and on being assured that she was to marry him; guess what I must have felt for all your sakes. When I came to you last week and found you alone, I came determined to know the truth; though irresolute what to do when it *was* known. My behaviour must have seemed strange to you then; but now you will comprehend it. To suffer you all to be so deceived; to see your sister—but what could I do? I had no hope of interfering with success; and sometimes I thought your sister's influence might yet reclaim him. But now, after such dishonourable usage, who can tell what were his designs on her? Whatever they may have been, however, she may now, and hereafter doubtless *will*, turn with gratitude towards her own condition, when she compares it with that of my poor Eliza, when she considers the wretched and hopeless situation of this poor girl, and pictures her to herself, with an affection for him as strong, still as strong as her own, and with a mind tormented by self-reproach, which must attend her through life. Surely this comparison must have its use with her. She will feel her own sufferings to be nothing. They proceed from no misconduct, and can bring no disgrace. On the contrary, every friend must be made still more her friend by them. Concern for her unhappiness, and respect for her fortitude under it, must strengthen every attachment. Use your own discretion, however, in communicating to her what I have told you. You must know best what will be its effect; but had I not seriously, and from my heart believed it might be of service, might lessen her regrets, I would not have suffered myself to trouble you with this account of my family afflictions, with a recital which may seem to have been intended to raise myself at the expense of others."

Elinor's thanks followed this speech with grateful earnestness; attended too with the assurance of her expecting material advantage to Marianne from the communication of what had passed.

"I have been more pained," said she, "by her endeavours to acquit him than by all the rest; for it irritates her mind more than the most perfect conviction of his unworthiness can do. Now, though at first she will suffer much, I am sure she will soon become easier. Have you," she continued, after a short silence, "ever seen Mr. Willoughby since you left him at Barton?"

"Yes," he replied gravely, "once I have. One meeting was unavoidable."

Elinor, startled by his manner, looked at him anxiously, saying, "What? have you met him to—"

"I could meet him in no other way. Eliza had confessed to me, though most reluctantly, the name of her lover; and when he returned to town, which was within a fortnight after myself, we met by appointment,[5] he to defend, I to punish his conduct. We returned unwounded, and the meeting, therefore, never got abroad."

Elinor sighed over the fancied necessity of this; but to a man and a soldier, she presumed not to censure it.

"Such," said Colonel Brandon, after a pause, "has been the unhappy resemblance between the fate of mother and daughter! and so imperfectly have I discharged my trust!"

"Is she still in town?"

"No; as soon as she recovered from her lying-in, for I found her near her delivery, I removed her and her child into the country, and there she remains."

Recollecting, soon afterwards, that he was probably dividing Elinor from her sister, he put an end to his visit, receiving from her again the same grateful acknowledgments, and leaving her full of compassion and esteem for him.

Chapter X.

When the particulars of this conversation were repeated by Miss Dashwood to her sister, as they very soon were, the effect on her was not entirely such as the former had hoped to see. Not that Marianne appeared to distrust the truth of any part of it, for she listened to it all with the most steady and submissive attention, made neither objection nor remark, attempted no vindication of Willoughby, and seemed to shew by her tears that she felt it to be impossible. But though this behaviour assured Elinor that the conviction of his guilt *was* carried home to her mind, though she saw with satisfaction the effect of it, in her no longer avoiding Colonel Brandon when he called, in her speaking to him, even voluntarily speaking, with a kind of compassionate respect, and though she saw her spirits less violently irritated than before, she did not see her less wretched. Her mind did become settled, but it was settled in a gloomy dejection. She felt the loss of Willoughby's character yet more heavily than she had felt the loss of his heart; his seduction and desertion of Miss Williams, the misery of that poor girl, and the doubt of what his designs might *once* have been on herself, preyed altogether so much on her spirits, that she could not bring herself to speak of what she felt even to Elinor; and brooding over her sorrows in silence, gave more pain to her sister than could have been communicated by the most open and most frequent confession of them.

5. Met to duel. Though illegal and widely criticized throughout the eighteenth century, dueling remained the customary means by which gentlemen settled questions of honor.

To give the feelings or the language of Mrs. Dashwood on receiving and answering Elinor's letter, would be only to give a repetition of what her daughters had already felt and said; of a
disappointment hardly less painful than Marianne's, and an indignation even greater that Elinor's. Long letters from her, quickly
succeeding each other, arrived to tell all that she suffered and
thought; to express her anxious solicitude for Marianne, and entreat
she would bear up with fortitude under this misfortune. Bad indeed
must the nature of Marianne's affliction be, when her mother could
talk of fortitude! mortifying and humiliating must be the origin of
those regrets, which *she* could wish her not to indulge!

Against the interest of her own individual comfort, Mrs. Dashwood had determined that it would be better for Marianne to be
anywhere, at that time, than at Barton, where every thing within
her view would be bringing back the past in the strongest and most
afflicting manner, by constantly placing Willoughby before her,
such as she had always seen him there. She recommended it to her
daughters, therefore, by all means not to shorten their visit to Mrs.
Jennings; the length of which, though never exactly fixed, had been
expected by all to comprise at least five or six weeks. A variety of
occupations, of objects, and of company, which could not be procured at Barton, would be inevitable there, and might yet, she
hoped, cheat Marianne, at times, into some interest beyond herself,
and even into some amusement, much as the idea of both might
now be spurned by her.

From all danger of seeing Willoughby again, her mother considered her to be at least equally safe in town as in the country, since
his acquaintance must now be dropped by all who called themselves
her friends. Design could never bring them in each other's way:
negligence could never leave them exposed to a surprise; and
chance had less in its favour in the croud of London than even in
the retirement of Barton, where it might force him before her while
paying that visit at Allenham on his marriage, which Mrs. Dashwood, from foreseeing at first as a probable event, had brought
herself to expect as a certain one.

She had yet another reason for wishing her children to remain
where they were; a letter from her son-in-law had told her that he
and his wife were to be in town before the middle of February, and
she judged it right that they should sometimes see their brother.

Marianne had promised to be guided by her mother's opinion,
and she submitted to it therefore without opposition, though it
proved perfectly different from what she wished and expected,
though she felt it to be entirely wrong, formed on mistaken grounds,
and that by requiring her longer continuance in London it deprived
her of the only possible alleviation of her wretchedness, the per-

sonal sympathy of her mother, and doomed her to such society and such scenes as must prevent her ever knowing a moment's rest.

But it was a matter of great consolation to her, that what brought evil to herself would bring good to her sister; and Elinor, on the other hand, suspecting that it would not be in her power to avoid Edward entirely, comforted herself by thinking, that though their longer stay would therefore militate against her own happiness, it would be better for Marianne than an immediate return into Devonshire.

Her carefulness in guarding her sister from ever hearing Willoughby's name mentioned, was not thrown away. Marianne, though without knowing it herself, reaped all its advantage; for neither Mrs. Jennings, nor Sir John, nor even Mrs. Palmer herself, ever spoke of him before her. Elinor wished that the same forbearance could have extended towards herself, but that was impossible, and she was obliged to listen day after day to the indignation of them all.

Sir John could not have thought it possible. "A man of whom he had always had such reason to think well! Such a good-natured fellow! He did not believe there was a bolder rider in England! It was an unaccountable business. He wished him at the devil with all his heart. He would not speak another word to him, meet him where he might, for all the world! No, not if it were to be by the side of Barton covert, and they were kept waiting for two hours together. Such a scoundrel of a fellow! such a deceitful dog! It was only the last time they met that he had offered him one of Folly's puppies! and this was the end of it!"

Mrs. Palmer, in her way, was equally angry. "She was determined to drop his acquaintance immediately, and she was very thankful that she had never been acquainted with him at all. She wished with all her heart Combe Magna was not so near Cleveland; but it did not signify, for it was a great deal too far off to visit; she hated him so much that she was resolved never to mention his name again, and she should tell everybody she saw, how good-for-nothing he was."

The rest of Mrs. Palmer's sympathy was shewn in procuring all the particulars in her power of the approaching marriage, and communicating them to Elinor. She could soon tell at what coachmaker's the new carriage was building, by what painter Mr. Willoughby's portrait was drawn, and at what warehouse[1] Miss Grey's clothes might be seen.

The calm and polite unconcern of Lady Middleton on the occasion was an happy relief to Elinor's spirits, oppressed as they often

1. During Austen's time, a more dignified term for "shop."

were by the clamorous kindness of the others. It was a great comfort to her, to be sure of exciting no interest in *one* person at least among their circle of friends; a great comfort to know that there was *one* who would meet her without feeling any curiosity after particulars, or any anxiety for her sister's health.

Every qualification is raised at times, by the circumstances of the moment, to more than its real value; and she was sometimes worried down by officious condolence to rate good-breeding as more indispensable to comfort than good-nature.

Lady Middleton expressed her sense of the affair about once every day, or twice, if the subject occured very often, by saying, "It is very shocking indeed!" and by the means of this continual though gentle vent, was able not only to see the Miss Dashwoods from the first without the smallest emotion, but very soon to see them without recollecting a word of the matter; and having thus supported the dignity of her own sex, and spoken her decided censure of what was wrong in the other, she thought herself at liberty to attend to the interest of her own assemblies, and therefore determined (though rather against the opinion of Sir John) that as Mrs. Willoughby would at once be a woman of elegance and fortune, to leave her card with her as soon as she married.

Colonel Brandon's delicate unobtrusive inquiries were never unwelcome to Miss Dashwood. He had abundantly earned the privilege of intimate discussion of her sister's disappointment, by the friendly zeal with which he had endeavoured to soften it, and they always conversed with confidence. His chief reward for the painful exertion of disclosing past sorrows and present humiliations, was given in the pitying eye with which Marianne sometimes observed him, and the gentleness of her voice whenever (though it did not often happen) she was obliged, or could oblige herself to speak to him. *These* assured him that his exertion had produced an increase of good-will towards himself, and *these* gave Elinor hopes of its being farther augmented hereafter; but Mrs. Jennings, who knew nothing of all this, who knew only that the Colonel continued as grave as ever, and that she could neither prevail on him to make the offer himself, nor commission her to make it for him, began, at the end of two days, to think that, instead of Midsummer, they would not be married till Michaelmas,[2] and by the end of a week that it would not be a match at all. The good understanding between the Colonel and Miss Dashwood seemed rather to declare that the honours of the mulberry-tree, the canal, and the yew arbour, would all be made over to *her*; and Mrs. Jennings had for some time ceased to think at all of Mr. Ferrars.

---

2. The feast of St. Michael, September 29; more generally, autumn.

Early in February, within a fortnight from the receipt of Willoughby's letter, Elinor had the painful office of informing her sister that he was married. She had taken care to have the intelligence conveyed to herself, as soon as it was known that the ceremony was over, as she was desirous that Marianne should not receive the first notice of it from the public papers, which she saw her eagerly examining every morning.

She received the news with resolute composure; made no observation on it, and at first shed no tears; but after a short time they would burst out, and for the rest of the day, she was in a state hardly less pitiable than when she first learnt to expect the event.

The Willoughbys left town as soon as they were married; and Elinor now hoped, as there could be no danger of her seeing either of them, to prevail on her sister, who had never yet left the house since the blow first fell, to go out again by degrees as she had done before.

About this time, the two Miss Steeles, lately arrived at their cousin's house in Bartlett's Buildings, Holborn, presented themselves again before their more grand relations in Conduit and Berkeley-street; and were welcomed by them all with great cordiality.

Elinor only was sorry to see them. Their presence always gave her pain, and she hardly knew how to make a very gracious return to the overpowering delight of Lucy in finding her *still* in town.

"I should have been quite disappointed if I had not found you here *still*," said she repeatedly, with a strong emphasis on the word. "But I always thought I *should*. I was almost sure you would not leave London yet awhile; though you *told* me, you know, at Barton, that you should not stay above a *month*. But I thought, at the time, that you would most likely change your mind when it came to the point. It would have been such a great pity to have went away before your brother and sister came. And now to be sure you will be in no *hurry* to be gone. I am amazingly glad you did not keep to *your word*."

Elinor perfectly understood her, and was forced to use all her self-command to make it appear that she did *not*.

"Well, my dear," said Mrs. Jennings, "and how did you travel?"

"Not in the stage, I assure you," replied Miss Steele, with quick exultation; "we came post all the way, and had a very smart beau to attend us. Dr. Davies was coming to town, and so we thought we'd join him in a post-chaise; and he behaved very genteelly, and paid ten or twelve shillings more than we did."

"Oh, oh!" cried Mrs. Jennings; "very pretty, indeed! and the Doctor is a single man, I warrant you."

"There now," said Miss Steele, affectedly simpering, "everybody laughs at me so about the Doctor, and I cannot think why. My cousins say they are sure I have made a conquest; but for my part I declare I never think about him from one hour's end to another. 'Lord! here comes your beau, Nancy,' my cousin said t'other day, when she saw him crossing the street to the house. My beau, indeed! said I—I cannot think who you mean. The Doctor is no beau of mine."

"Aye, aye, that is very pretty talking—but it won't do—the Doctor is the man, I see."

"No, indeed!" replied her cousin, with affected earnestness, "and I beg you will contradict it, if you ever hear it talked of."

Mrs. Jennings directly gave her the gratifying assurance that she certainly would *not*, and Miss Steele was made completely happy.

"I suppose you will go and stay with your brother and sister, Miss Dashwood, when they come to town," said Lucy, returning, after a cessation of hostile hints, to the charge.

"No, I do not think we shall."

"Oh, yes, I dare say you will."

Elinor would not humour her by farther opposition.

"What a charming thing it is that Mrs. Dashwood can spare you both for so long a time together!"

"Long a time, indeed!" interposed Mrs. Jennings. "Why, their visit is but just begun!"

Lucy was silenced.

"I am sorry we cannot see your sister, Miss Dashwood," said Miss Steele. "I am sorry she is not well;" for Marianne had left the room on their arrival.

"You are very good. My sister, will be equally sorry to miss the pleasure of seeing you; but she has been very much plagued lately with nervous head-aches, which make her unfit for company or conversation."

"Oh, dear, that is a great pity! but such old friends as Lucy and me!—I think she might see *us*; and I am sure we would not speak a word."

Elinor, with great civility, declined the proposal. Her sister was perhaps laid down upon the bed, or in her dressing gown, and therefore not able to come to them.

"Oh, if that's all," cried Miss Steele, "we can just as well go and see *her*."

Elinor began to find this impertinence too much for her temper; but she was saved the trouble of checking it, by Lucy's sharp reprimand, which now, as on many occasions, though it did not give much sweetness to the manners of one sister, was of advantage in governing those of the other.

Chapter XI.

After some opposition, Marianne yielded to her sister's entreaties, and consented to go out with her and Mrs. Jennings one morning for half an hour. She expressly conditioned, however, for paying no visits, and would do no more than accompany them to Gray's in Sackville-street,[1] where Elinor was carrying on a negociation for the exchange of a few old-fashioned jewels of her mother.

When they stopped at the door, Mrs. Jennings recollected that there was a lady at the other end of the street, on whom she ought to call; and as she had no business at Gray's, it was resolved, that while her young friends transacted their's, she should pay her visit and return for them.

On ascending the stairs, the Miss Dashwoods found so many people before them in the room, that there was not a person at liberty to attend to their orders; and they were obliged to wait. All that could be done was, to sit down at that end of the counter which seemed to promise the quickest succession; one gentleman only was standing there, and it is probable that Elinor was not without hope[*] of exciting his politeness to a quicker dispatch. But the correctness of his eye, and the delicacy of his taste, proved to be beyond his politeness. He was giving orders for a toothpick-case for himself, and till its size, shape, and ornaments were determined, all of which, after examining and debating for a quarter of an hour over every toothpick-case in the shop, were finally arranged by his own inventive fancy, he had no leisure to bestow any other attention on the two ladies, than what was comprised in three or four very broad stares; a kind of notice which served to imprint on Elinor the remembrance of a person and face, of strong, natural, sterling insignificance, though adorned in the first style of fashion.

Marianne was spared from the troublesome feelings of contempt and resentment, on this impertinent examination of their features, and on the puppyism of his manner in deciding on all the different horrors of the different toothpick-cases presented to his inspection, by remaining unconscious of it all; for she was as well able to collect her thoughts within herself, and be as ignorant of what was passing around her, in Mr. Gray's shop, as in her own bed-room.

At last the affair was decided. The ivory, the gold, and the pearls, all received their appointment, and the gentleman having named the last day on which his existence could be continued without the

---

1. R. W. Chapman points out that the *New Annual Directory of 1800* records a jeweler of this name in Sackville Street in Piccadilly.
* hope] hopes A.

possession of the toothpick-case, drew on his gloves with leisurely care, and bestowing another glance on the Miss Dashwoods, but such a one as seemed rather to demand than express admiration, walked off with an happy air of real conceit and affected indifference.

Elinor lost no time in bringing her business forward, and was on the point of concluding it, when another gentleman presented himself at her side. She turned her eyes towards his face, and found him with some surprise to be her brother.

Their affection and pleasure in meeting, was just enough to make a very creditable appearance in Mr. Gray's shop. John Dashwood was really far from being sorry to see his sisters again; it rather gave them satisfaction; and his inquiries after their mother were respectful and attentive.

Elinor found that he and Fanny had been in town two days.

"I wished very much to call upon you yesterday," said he, "but it was impossible, for we were obliged to take Harry to see the wild beasts at Exeter Exchange:[2] and we spent the rest of the day with Mrs. Ferrars. Harry was vastly pleased. *This* morning I had fully intended to call on you, if I could possibly find a spare half hour, but one has always so much to do on first coming to town. I am come here to bespeak Fanny a seal.[3] But to-morrow I think I shall certainly be able to call in Berkeley-street, and be introduced to your friend Mrs. Jennings. I understand she is a woman of very good fortune. And the Middletons too, you must introduce me to *them*. As my mother-in-law's relations, I shall be happy to shew them every respect. They are excellent neighbours to you in the country, I understand."

"Excellent indeed. Their attention to our comfort, their friendliness in every particular, is more than I can express."

"I am extremely glad to hear it, upon my word; extremely glad indeed. But so it ought to be; they are people of large fortune, they are related to you, and every civility and accommodation that can serve to make your situation pleasant, might be reasonably expected. And so you are most comfortably settled in your little cottage and want for nothing! Edward brought us a most charming account of the place; the most complete thing of its kind, he said, that ever was, and you all seemed to enjoy it beyond any thing. It was a great satisfaction to us to hear it, I assure you."

Elinor did feel a little ashamed of her brother; and was not sorry to be spared the necessity of answering him, by the arrival of Mrs.

---

2. A menagerie located in a building on the north side of the Strand, torn down in 1829.
3. To order a signet ring or other stamping implement, used for sealing letters with wax, at Gray's, the jeweler mentioned above.

Jennings's servant, who came to tell her that his mistress waited for them at the door.

Mr. Dashwood attended them down stairs, was introduced to Mrs. Jennings at the door of her carriage, and repeating his hope of being able to call on them the next day, took leave. His visit was duly paid. He came with a pretence at an apology from their sister-in-law, for not coming too; "but she was so much engaged with her mother, that really she had no leisure for going any where." Mrs. Jennings, however, assured him directly, that she should not stand upon ceremony, for they were all cousins, or something like it, and she should certainly wait on Mrs. John Dashwood very soon, and bring her sisters to see her. His manners to *them*, though calm, were perfectly kind; to Mrs. Jennings most attentively civil; and on Colonel Brandon's coming in soon after himself, he eyed him with a curiosity which seemed to say, that he only wanted to know him to be rich, to be equally civil to *him*.

After staying with them half an hour, he asked Elinor to walk with him to Conduit-street, and introduce him to Sir John and Lady Middleton. The weather was remarkably fine, and she readily consented. As soon as they were out of the house, his enquiries began.

"Who is Colonel Brandon? Is he a man of fortune?"

"Yes; he has very good property in Dorsetshire."

"I am glad of it. He seems a most gentlemanlike man; and I think, Elinor, I may congratulate you on the prospect of a very respectable establishment in life."

"Me, brother! what do you mean?"

"He likes you. I observed him narrowly, and am convinced of it. What is the amount of his fortune?"

"I believe about two thousand a-year."

"Two thousand a-year;" and then working himself up to a pitch of enthusiastic generosity, he added, "Elinor, I wish, with all my heart, it were *twice* as much, for your sake."

"Indeed I believe you," replied Elinor; "but I am very sure that Colonel Brandon has not the smallest wish of marrying *me*."

"You are mistaken, Elinor; you are very much mistaken. A very little trouble on your side secures him. Perhaps just at present he may be undecided; the smallness of your fortune may make him hang back; his friends may all advise him against it. But some of those little attentions and encouragements which ladies can so easily give, will fix him, in spite of himself. And there can be no reason why you should not try for him. It is not to be supposed that any prior attachment on your side—in short, you know as to an attachment of that kind, it is quite out of the question, the objections are insurmountable—you have too much sense not to see all that. Colonel Brandon must be the man; and no civility shall be wanting on my part, to make him pleased with you and your family. It is a match that must give universal satisfaction. In short, it is a kind of thing that"—lowering his voice to an important whisper—"will be exceedingly welcome to *all parties*." Recollecting himself, however, he added, "That is, I mean to say—your friends are all truly anxious to see you well settled; Fanny particularly, for she has your interest very much at heart, I assure you. And her mother too, Mrs. Ferrars, a very good-natured woman, I am sure it would give her great pleasure; she said as much the other day."

Elinor would not vouchsafe any answer.

"It would be something remarkable now," he continued, "something droll, if Fanny should have a brother and I a sister settling at the same time. And yet it is not very unlikely."

"Is Mr. Edward Ferrars," said Elinor, with resolution, "going to be married?"

"It is not actually settled, but there is such a thing in agitation. He has a most excellent mother. Mrs. Ferrars, with the utmost liberality, will come forward, and settle on him a thousand a-year, if the match takes place. The lady is the Hon. Miss Morton, only daughter of the late Lord Morton, with thirty thousand pounds. A very desirable connection on both sides, and I have not a doubt of its taking place in time. A thousand a-year is a great deal for a mother to give away, to make over for ever; but Mrs. Ferrars has a noble spirit. To give you another instance of her liberality:—The other day, as soon as we came to town, aware that money could not be very plenty with us just now, she put bank-notes into Fanny's hands to the amount of two hundred pounds. And extremely acceptable it is, for we must live at a great expense while we are here."

He paused for her assent and compassion; and she forced herself to say,

"Your expenses both in town and country must certainly be considerable, but your income is a large one."

"Not so large, I dare say, as many people suppose. I do not mean to complain, however; it is undoubtedly a comfortable one, and I hope will in time be better. The inclosure⁴ of Norland Common, now carrying on, is a most serious drain. And then I have made a little purchase within this half year; East Kingham Farm, you must remember the place, where old Gibson used to live. The land was so very desirable for me in every respect, so immediately adjoining

---

4. During the eighteenth century and especially later during the Napoleonic Wars, common land—which laborers had previously been able to use for pasturage and for the gathering of wood for use as fuel—was increasingly enclosed in order to create large farms under the ownership of wealthy landowners. The irony here is that John Dashwood is complaining about a phenomenon that is (once again) impoverishing others and enriching himself, for it was small farmers and laborers, rather than major landowners, who lost out as enclosure became more frequent.

my own property, that I felt it my duty to buy it. I could not have answered it to my conscience to let it fall into any other hands. A man must pay for his convenience; and it *has* cost me a vast deal of money."

"More than you think it really and intrinsically worth."

"Why, I hope not that. I might have sold it again the next day, for more than I gave: but with regard to the purchase-money, I might have been very unfortunate indeed; for the stocks were at that time so low, that if I had not happened to have the necessary sum in my banker's hands, I must have sold out to very great loss."

Elinor could only smile.

"Other great and inevitable expenses too we have had on first coming to Norland. Our respected father, as you well know, bequeathed all the Stanhill effects that remained at Norland (and very valuable they were) to your mother. Far be it from me to repine at his doing so; he had an undoubted right to dispose of his own property as he chose. But, in consequence of it, we have been obliged to make large purchases of linen, china, &c. to supply the place of what was taken away. You may guess, after all these expenses, how very far we must be from being rich, and how acceptable Mrs. Ferrars's kindness is."

"Certainly," said Elinor; "and assisted by her liberality, I hope you may yet live to be in easy circumstances."

"Another year or two may do much towards it," he gravely replied; "but however there is still a great deal to be done. There is not a stone laid of Fanny's greenhouse, and nothing but the plan of the flower-garden marked out."

"Where is the green-house to be?"

"Upon the knoll behind the house. The old walnut trees are all come down to make room for it. It will be a very fine object from many parts of the park, and the flower-garden will slope down just before it, and be exceedingly pretty. We have cleared away all the old thorns that grew in patches over the brow."

Elinor kept her concern and her censure to herself; and was very thankful that Marianne was not present, to share the provocation.

Having now said enough to make his poverty clear, and to do away the necessity of buying a pair of ear-rings for each of his sisters, in his next visit at Gray's, his thoughts took a cheerfuller turn, and he began to congratulate Elinor on having such a friend as Mrs. Jennings.

"She seems a most valuable woman indeed.—Her house, her style of living, all bespeak an exceeding good income; and it is an acquaintance that has not only been of great use to you hitherto, but in the end may prove materially advantageous.—Her inviting you to town is certainly a vast thing in your favour; and indeed, it speaks altogether so great a regard for you, that in all probability when she dies you will not be forgotten.—She must have a great deal to leave."

"Nothing at all, I should rather suppose; for she has only her jointure,* which will descend to her children."

"But it is not to be imagined that she lives up to her income. Few people of common prudence will do *that*; and whatever she saves, she will be able to dispose of."

"And do you not think it more likely that she should leave it to her daughters, than to us?"

"Her daughters are both exceedingly well married, and therefore I cannot perceive the necessity of her remembering them farther. Whereas, in my opinion, by her taking so much notice of you, and treating you in this kind of way, she has given you a sort of claim on her future consideration, which a conscientious woman would not disregard. Nothing can be kinder than her behaviour; and she can hardly do all this, without being aware of the expectation she raises."

"But she raises none in those most concerned. Indeed, brother, your anxiety for our welfare and prosperity carries you too far."

"Why to be sure," said he, seeming to recollect himself, "people have little, have very little in their power. But, my dear Elinor, what is the matter with Marianne?—she looks very unwell, has lost her colour, and is grown quite thin. Is she ill?"

"She is not well, she has had a nervous complaint on her for several weeks."

"I am sorry for that. At her time of life, any thing of an illness destroys the bloom for ever! Her's has been a very short one! She was as handsome a girl last September, as any I ever saw; and as likely to attract the men. There was something in her style of beauty, to please them particularly. I remember Fanny used to say that she would marry sooner and better than you did; not but what she is exceedingly fond of *you*, but so it happened to strike her. She will be mistaken, however. I question whether Marianne *now*, will marry a man worth more than five or six hundred a-year, at the utmost, and I am very much deceived if *you* do not do better. Dorsetshire! I know very little of Dorsetshire; but, my dear Elinor, I shall be exceedingly glad to know more of it; and I think I can answer for your having Fanny and myself among the earliest and best pleased of your visitors."

Elinor tried very seriously to convince him that there was no

* jointure,] furniture, A. Mrs. *Jennings is earlier described as having an* ample jointure, *but as that goes to her children after her death, she is not at liberty, as Elinor realizes, to give away her money as she wishes.*

likelihood of her marrying Colonel Brandon; but it was an expectation of too much pleasure to himself to be relinquished, and he
was really resolved on seeking an intimacy with that gentleman, and
promoting the marriage by every possible attention. He had just
compunction enough for having done nothing for his sisters himself, to be exceedingly anxious that everybody else should do a great
deal; and an offer from Colonel Brandon, or a legacy from Mrs.
Jennings, was the easiest means of atoning for his own neglect.

They were lucky enough to find Lady Middleton at home, and
Sir John came in before their visit ended. Abundance of civilities
passed on all sides. Sir John was ready to like anybody, and though
Mr. Dashwood did not seem to know much about horses, he soon
set him down as a very good-natured fellow: while Lady Middleton
saw enough of fashion in his appearance, to think his acquaintance
worth having; and Mr. Dashwood went away delighted with both.

"I shall have a charming account to carry to Fanny," said he, as
he walked back with his sister. "Lady Middleton is really a most
elegant woman! Such a woman as I am sure Fanny will be glad to
know. And Mrs. Jennings too, an exceeding well-behaved woman,
though not so elegant as her daughter. Your sister need not have
any scruple even of visiting *her*, which, to say the truth, has been
a little the case, and very naturally; for we only knew that Mrs.
Jennings was the widow of a man who had got all his money in a
low way; and Fanny and Mrs. Ferrars were both strongly prepos-
sessed that neither she nor her daughters were such kind of women
as Fanny would like to associate with. But now I can carry her a
most satisfactory account of both."

Chapter XII.

Mrs. John Dashwood had so much confidence in her husband's
judgment that she waited the very next day both on Mrs. Jennings
and her daughter; and her confidence was rewarded by finding even
the former, even the woman with whom her sisters were staying,
by no means unworthy her notice; and as for Lady Middleton, she
found her one of the most charming women in the world!

Lady Middleton was equally pleased with Mrs. Dashwood. There
was a kind of cold hearted selfishness on both sides, which mutually
attracted them; and they sympathised with each other in an insipid
propriety of demeanour, and a general want of understanding.

The same manners however, which recommended Mrs. John
Dashwood to the good opinion of Lady Middleton, did not suit the
fancy of Mrs. Jennings, and to *her* she appeared nothing more than
a little proud-looking woman of uncordial address, who met her

husband's sisters without any affection, and almost without having any thing to say to them; for of the quarter of an hour bestowed on Berkeley-street, she sat at least seven minutes and a half in silence.

Elinor wanted very much to know, though she did not chuse to ask, whether Edward was then in town; but nothing would have induced Fanny voluntarily to mention his name before her, till able to tell her that his marriage with Miss Morton was resolved on, or till her husband's expectations on Colonel Brandon were answered; because she believed them still so very much attached to each other, that they could not be too sedulously divided in word and deed on every occasion. The intelligence however, which *she* would not give, soon flowed from another quarter. Lucy came very shortly to claim Elinor's compassion on being unable to see Edward, though he had arrived in town with Mr. and Mrs. Dashwood. He dared not come to Bartlett's Buildings for fear of detection, and though their mutual impatience to meet, was not to be told, they could do nothing at present but write.

Edward assured them himself of his being in town, within a very short time, by twice calling in Berkeley-street. Twice was his card found on the table, when they returned from their morning's engagements. Elinor was pleased that he had called; and still more pleased that she had missed him.

The Dashwoods were so prodigiously delighted with the Middletons, that though not much in the habit of giving any thing, they determined to give them—a dinner; and soon after their acquaintance began, invited them to dine in Harley-street, where they had taken a very good house for three months. Their sisters and Mrs. Jennings were invited likewise, and John Dashwood was careful to secure Colonel Brandon, who, always glad to be where the Miss Dashwoods were, received his eager civilities with some surprise, but much more pleasure. They were to meet Mrs. Ferrars; but Elinor could not learn whether her sons were to be of the party. The expectation of seeing *her*, however, was enough to make her interested in the engagement; for though she could now meet Edward's mother without that strong anxiety which had once promised to attend such an introduction, though she could now see her with perfect indifference as to her opinion of herself, her desire of being in company with Mrs. Ferrars, her curiosity to know what she was like, was as lively as ever.

The interest with which she thus anticipated the party, was soon afterwards increased, more powerfully than pleasantly, by her hearing that the Miss Steeles were also to be at it.

So well had they recommended themselves to Lady Middleton, so agreeable had their assiduities made them to her, that though

Lucy was certainly not* elegant, and her sister not even genteel, she was as ready as Sir John to ask them to spend a week or two in Conduit-street: and it happened to be particularly convenient to the Miss Steeles, as soon as the Dashwoods' invitation was known, that their visit should begin a few days before the party took place.

Their claims to** the notice of Mrs. John Dashwood, as the nieces of the gentleman who for many years had had the care of her brother, might not have done much, however, towards procuring them seats at her table; but as Lady Middleton's guests they must be welcome; and Lucy, who had long wanted to be personally known to the family, to have a nearer view of their characters and her own difficulties, and to have an opportunity of endeavouring to please them, had seldom been happier in her life than she was on receiving Mrs. John Dashwood's card.

On Elinor its effect was very different. She began immediately to determine that Edward who lived with his mother, must be asked as his mother was, to a party given by his sister; and to see him for the first time after all that passed, in the company of Lucy!—she hardly knew how she could bear it!

These apprehensions perhaps were not founded entirely on reason, and certainly not at all on truth. They were relieved however, not by her own recollection but by the good will of Lucy, who believed herself to be inflicting a severe disappointment when she told her that Edward certainly would not be in Harley-street on Tuesday, and even hoped to be carrying the pain still farther by persuading her, that he was kept away by that extreme affection for herself, which he could not conceal when they were together.

The important Tuesday came that was to introduce the two young ladies to this formidable mother-in-law.

"Pity me, dear Miss Dashwood!" said Lucy, as they walked up the stairs together—for the Middletons arrived so directly after Mrs. Jennings, that they all followed the servant at the same time —"There is nobody here but you, that can feel for me.—I declare I can hardly stand. Good gracious!—In a moment I shall see the person that all my happiness depends on—that is to be my mother!"—

Elinor could have given her immediate relief by suggesting the possibility of its being Miss Morton's mother, rather than her own, whom they were about to behold; but instead of doing that, she assured her, and with great sincerity, that she did pity her,—to the utter amazement of Lucy, who, though really uncomfortable herself, hoped at least to be an object of irrepressible envy to Elinor.

---

* certainly not] scarcely A.
** claims to] claims on A.

Mrs. Ferrars was a little, thin woman, upright, even to formality, in her figure, and serious, even to sourness, in her aspect. Her complexion was sallow; and her features small, without beauty, and naturally without expression; but a lucky contraction of the brow had rescued her countenance from the disgrace of insipidity, by giving it the strong characters of pride and ill nature. She was not a woman of many words: for, unlike people in general, she proportioned them to the number of her ideas; and of the few syllables that did escape her, not one fell to the share of Miss Dashwood, whom she eyed with the spirited determination of disliking her at all events.

Elinor could not *now* be made unhappy by this behaviour.—A few months ago it would have hurt her exceedingly; but it was not in Mrs. Ferrars's power to distress her by it now;—and the difference of her manners to the Miss Steeles, a difference which seemed purposely made to humble her more, only amused her. She could not but smile to see the graciousness of both mother and daughter towards the very person—for Lucy was particularly distinguished—whom of all others, had they known as much as she did, they would have been most anxious to mortify; while she herself, who had comparatively no power to wound them, sat pointedly slighted by both. But while she smiled at a graciousness so misapplied, she could not reflect on the mean-spirited folly from which it sprung, nor observe the studied attentions with which the Miss Steeles courted its continuance, without thoroughly despising them all four.

Lucy was all exultation on being so honourably distinguished; and Miss Steele wanted only to be teazed about Dr. Davies to be perfectly happy.

The dinner was a grand one, the servants were numerous, and every thing bespoke the Mistress's inclination for shew, and the Master's ability to support it. In spite of the improvements and additions which were making to the Norland estate, and in spite of its owner having once been within some thousand pounds of being obliged to sell out at a loss, nothing gave any symptom of that indigence which he had tried to infer from it;—no poverty of any kind, except of conversation, appeared—but there, the deficiency was considerable. John Dashwood had not much to say for himself that was worth hearing, and his wife had still less. But there was no peculiar disgrace in this, for it was very much the case with the chief of their visitors, who almost all laboured under one or other of these disqualifications for being agreeable—Want of sense, either natural or improved—want of elegance—want of spirits—or want of temper.

When the ladies withdrew to the drawing-room after dinner, this poverty was particularly evident, for the gentlemen *had* supplied the discourse with some variety—the variety of politics, inclosing land, and breaking horses—but then it was all over; and one subject only engaged the ladies till coffee came in, which was the comparative heights of Harry Dashwood, and Lady Middleton's second son William, who were nearly of the same age.

Had both the children been there, the affair might have been determined too easily by measuring them at once; but as Harry only was present, it was all conjectural assertion on both sides, and every body had a right to be equally positive in their opinion, and to repeat it over and over again as often as they liked.

The parties stood thus:

The two mothers, though each really convinced that her own son was the tallest, politely decided in favour of the other.

The two grandmothers, with not less partiality, but more sincerity, were equally earnest in support of their own descendant.

Lucy, who was hardly less anxious to please one parent than the other, thought the boys were both remarkably tall for their age, and could not conceive that there could be the smallest difference in the world between them; and Miss Steele, with yet greater address gave it, as fast as she could, in favour of each.

Elinor, having once delivered her opinion on William's side, by which she offended Mrs. Ferrars and Fanny still more, did not see the necessity of enforcing it by any farther assertion; and Marianne, when called on for her's, offended them all, by declaring that she had no opinion to give, as she had never thought about it.

Before her removing from Norland, Elinor had painted a very pretty pair of screens[1] for her sister-in-law, which being now just mounted and brought home, ornamented her present drawing room; and these screens, catching the eye of John Dashwood on his following the other gentlemen into the room, were officiously handed by him to Colonel Brandon for his admiration.

"These are done by my eldest sister," said he; "and you, as a man of taste, will, I dare say, be pleased with them. I do not know whether you ever happened to see any of her performances before, but she is in general reckoned to draw extremely well."

The Colonel, though disclaiming all pretensions to connoisseurship, warmly admired the screens, as he would have done any thing painted by Miss Dashwood; and the curiosity of the others being of course excited, they were handed round for general inspection. Mrs. Ferrars, not aware of their being Elinor's work, particularly requested to look at them; and after they had received the gratifying testimony of Lady Middleton's approbation, Fanny presented them

---

1. Firescreens, commonly decorated by ladies and used to shield people from the heat and sparks of the fireplace.

to her mother, considerately informing her at the same time, that they were done by Miss Dashwood.

"Hum"—said Mrs. Ferrars—"very pretty,"—and without regarding them at all, returned them to her daughter.

Perhaps Fanny thought for a moment that her mother had been quite rude enough,—for, colouring a little, she immediately said, "They are very pretty, ma'am—an't they?" But then again, the dread of having been too civil, too encouraging herself, probably came over her, for she presently added, "Do you not think they are something in Miss Morton's style of painting, ma'am?—*She does* paint most delightfully!—How beautifully her last landscape is done!"

"Beautifully indeed! But *she* does every thing well."

Marianne could not bear this.—She was already greatly displeased with Mrs. Ferrars; and such ill-timed praise of another, at Elinor's expense, though she had not any notion of what was principally meant by it, provoked her immediately to say with warmth, "This is admiration of a very particular kind!—what is Miss Morton to us?—who knows, or who cares, for her?—it is Elinor of whom *we* think and speak."

And so saying, she took the screens out of her sister-in-law's hands, to admire them herself as they ought to be admired.

Mrs. Ferrars looked exceedingly angry, and drawing herself up more stiffly than ever, pronounced in retort this bitter phillippic;[2] "Miss Morton is Lord Morton's daughter."

Fanny looked very angry too, and her husband was all in a fright at his sister's audacity. Elinor was much more hurt by Marianne's warmth, than she had been by what produced it; but Colonel Brandon's eyes, as they were fixed on Marianne, declared that he noticed only what was amiable in it, the affectionate heart which could not bear to see a sister slighted in the smallest point.

Marianne's feelings did not stop here. The cold insolence of Mrs. Ferrars's general behaviour to her sister, seemed, to her, to foretel such difficulties and distresses to Elinor, as her own wounded heart taught her to think of with horror; and urged by a strong impulse of affectionate sensibility, she moved, after a moment, to her sister's chair, and putting one arm round her neck, and one cheek close to her's, said in a low, but eager, voice.

"Dear, dear Elinor, don't mind them. Don't let them make *you* unhappy."

She could say no more; her spirits were quite overcome, and hiding her face on Elinor's shoulder, she burst into tears.—Every

---

2. From Demosthenes' orations against Philip, king of Macedon, in defense of Athenian liberty; any diatribe, invective, or denunciation.

body's attention was called, and almost every body was concerned.
—Colonel Brandon rose up and went to them without knowing
what he did.—Mrs. Jennings, with a very intelligent "Ah! poor
dear," immediately gave her, her salts;[3] and Sir John felt so desperately enraged against the author of this nervous distress, that he
instantly changed his seat to one close by Lucy Steele, and gave
her, in a whisper, a brief account of the whole shocking affair.

In a few minutes, however, Marianne was recovered enough to
put an end to the bustle, and sit down among the rest; though her
spirits retained the impression of what had passed, the whole
evening.

"Poor Marianne!" said her brother to Colonel Brandon in a low
voice, as soon as he could secure his attention,—"She has not such
good health as her sister,—she is very nervous,—she has not Elinor's constitution;—and one must allow that there is something
very trying to a young woman who *has been* a beauty, in the loss of
her personal attractions. You would not think it perhaps, but Marianne *was* remarkably handsome a few months ago; quite as handsome as Elinor.—Now you see it is all gone."

Chapter XIII.

Elinor's curiosity to see Mrs. Ferrars was satisfied.—She had found
in her every thing that could tend to make a farther connection
between the families, undesirable.—She had seen enough of her
pride, her meanness, and her determined prejudice against herself,
to comprehend all the difficulties that must have perplexed the engagement, and retarded the marriage, of Edward and herself, had
he been otherwise free;—and she had seen almost enough to be
thankful for her *own* sake, that one greater obstacle preserved her
from suffering under any other of Mrs. Ferrars's creation, preserved
her from all dependence upon her caprice, or any solicitude for her
good opinion. Or at least, if she did not bring herself quite to rejoice
in Edward's being fettered to Lucy, she determined, that had Lucy
been more amiable, she *ought* to have rejoiced.

She wondered that Lucy's spirits could be so very much elevated
by the civility of Mrs. Ferrars;—that her interest and her vanity
should so very much blind her, as to make the attention which
seemed only paid her because she was *not Elinor*, appear a compliment to herself—or to allow her to derive encouragement from
a preference only given her, because her real situation was unknown. But that it was so, had not only been declared by Lucy's

3. Usually an ammonia compound, used to revive those who had swooned.

eyes at the time, but was declared over again the next morning more
openly, for at her particular desire, Lady Middleton set her down
in Berkeley-street on the chance of seeing Elinor alone, to tell her
how happy she was.

The chance proved a lucky one, for a message from Mrs. Palmer
soon after she arrived, carried Mrs. Jennings away.

"My dear friend," cried Lucy as soon as they were by themselves,
"I come to talk to you of my happiness. Could any thing be so
flattering as Mrs. Ferrars's way of treating me yesterday? So exceeding affable as she was!—You know how I dreaded the thoughts
of seeing her;—but the very moment I was introduced, there was
such an affability in her behaviour as really should seem to say, she
had quite took a fancy to me. Now was not it so?—You saw it all;
and was not you quite struck with it?"

"She was certainly very civil to you."

"Civil!—Did you see nothing but only civility?—I saw a vast deal
more. Such kindness as fell to the share of nobody but me!—No
pride, no hauteur, and your sister just the same—all sweetness and
affability!"

Elinor wished to talk of something else, but Lucy still pressed
her to own that she had reason for her happiness; and Elinor was
obliged to go on.—

"Undoubtedly, if they had known your engagement," said she,
"nothing could be more flattering than their treatment of you;—
but as that was not the case"——

"I guessed you would say so"—replied Lucy quickly—"but there
was no reason in the world why Mrs. Ferrars should seem to like
me, if she did not, and her liking me is every thing. You shan't talk
me out of my satisfaction. I am sure it will all end well, and there
will be no difficulties at all, to what I used to think. Mrs. Ferrars
is a charming woman, and so is your sister. They are both delightful
women indeed!—I wonder I should never hear you say how agreeable Mrs. Dashwood was!"

To this, Elinor had no answer to make, and did not attempt any.

"Are you ill, Miss Dashwood?—you seem low—you don't speak;
—sure you an't well."

"I never was in better health."

"I am glad of it with all my heart, but really you did not look it.
I should be so sorry to have *you* ill; you, that have been the greatest
comfort to me in the world!—Heaven knows what I should have
done without your friendship."—

Elinor tried to make a civil answer, though doubting her own
success. But it seemed to satisfy Lucy, for she directly replied,

"Indeed I am perfectly convinced of your regard for me, and next
to Edward's love, it is the greatest comfort I have.—Poor Edward!

—But now, there is one good thing, we shall be able to meet, and meet pretty often, for Lady Middleton's delighted with Mrs. Dash-wood, so we shall be a good deal in Harley-street, I dare say, and Edward spends half his time with his sister—besides, Lady Mid-dleton and Mrs. Ferrars will visit now;—and Mrs. Ferrars and your sister were both so good to say more than once, they should always be glad to see me.—They are such charming women!—I am sure if ever you tell your sister what I think of her, you cannot speak too high."

But Elinor would not give her any encouragement to hope that she *should* tell her sister. Lucy continued.

"I am sure I should have seen it in a moment, if Mrs. Ferrars had took a dislike to me. If she had only made me a formal curtsey, for instance, without saying a word, and never after had took any notice of me, and never looked at me in a pleasant way—you know what I mean,—if I had been treated in that forbidding sort of way, I should have gave it all up in despair. I could not have stood it. For where she *does* dislike, I know it is most violent."

Elinor was prevented from making any reply to this civil triumph, by the door's being thrown open, the servant's announcing Mr. Fer-rars, and Edward's immediately walking in.

It was a very awkward moment; and the countenance of each shewed that it was so. They all looked exceedingly foolish; and Ed-ward seemed to have as great an inclination to walk out of the room again, as to advance farther into it. The very circumstance, in its unpleasantest form, which they would each have been most anxious to avoid, had fallen on them—They were not only all three together, but were together without the relief of any other person. The ladies recovered themselves first. It was not Lucy's business to put herself forward, and the appearance of secrecy must still be kept up. She could therefore only *look* her tenderness, and after slightly address-ing him, said no more.

But Elinor had more to do; and so anxious was she, for his sake and her own, to do it well, that she forced herself, after a moment's recollection, to welcome him, with a look and manner that were almost easy, and almost open; and another struggle, another effort still improved them. She would not allow the presence of Lucy, nor the consciousness of some injustice towards herself, to deter her from saying that she was happy to see him, and that she had very much regretted being from home, when he called before in Berke-ley-street. She would not be frightened from paying him those at-tentions which, as a friend and almost a relation, were his due, by the observant eyes of Lucy, though she soon perceived them to be narrowly watching her.

Her manners gave some re-assurance to Edward, and he had

courage enough to sit down; but his embarrassment still exceeded that of the ladies in a proportion, which the case rendered reasonable, though his sex might make it rare; for his heart had not the indifference of Lucy's, nor could his conscience have quite the ease of Elinor's.

Lucy, with a demure and settled air, seemed determined to make no contribution to the comfort of the others, and would not say a word; and almost every thing that *was* said, proceeded from Elinor, who was obliged to volunteer all the information about her mother's health, their coming to town, &c. which Edward ought to have inquired about, but never did.

Her exertions did not stop here; for she soon afterwards felt herself so heroically disposed as to determine, under pretence of fetching Marianne, to leave the others by themselves: and she really did it, and *that* in the handsomest manner, for she loitered away several minutes on the landing-place, with the most high-minded fortitude, before she went to her sister. When that was once done, however, it was time for the raptures of Edward to cease; for Marianne's joy hurried her into the drawing-room immediately. Her pleasure in seeing him was like every other of her feelings, strong in itself, and strongly spoken. She met him with a hand that would be taken, and a voice that expressed the affection of a sister.

"Dear Edward!" she cried, "this is a moment of great happiness! —This would almost make amends for every thing!"

Edward tried to return her kindness as it deserved, but before such witnesses he dared not say half what he really felt. Again they all sat down, and for a moment or two all were silent; while Marianne was looking with the most speaking tenderness, sometimes at Edward and sometimes at Elinor, regretting only that their delight in each other should be checked by Lucy's unwelcome presence. Edward was the first to speak, and it was to notice Marianne's altered looks, and express his fear of her not finding London agree with her.

"Oh! don't think of me!" she replied, with spirited earnestness, though her eyes were filled with tears as she spoke, "don't think of *my* health. Elinor is well, you see. That must be enough for us both."

This remark was not calculated to make Edward or Elinor more easy, nor to conciliate the good will of Lucy, who looked up at Marianne with no very benignant expression.

"Do you like London?" said Edward, willing to say any thing that might introduce another subject.

"Not at all. I expected much pleasure in it, but I have found none. The sight of you, Edward, is the only comfort it has afforded; and thank Heaven! you are what you always were!"

She paused—no one spoke.

"I think, Elinor," she presently added, "we must employ Edward to take care of us in our return to Barton. In a week or two, I suppose, we shall be going; and, I trust, Edward will not be very unwilling to accept the charge."

Poor Edward muttered something, but what it was, nobody knew, not even himself. But Marianne, who saw his agitation, and could easily trace it to whatever cause best pleased herself, was perfectly satisfied, and soon talked of something else.

"We spent such a day, Edward, in Harley-street yesterday! So dull, so wretchedly dull!—But I have much to say to you on that head, which cannot be said now."

And with this admirable discretion did she defer the assurance of her finding their mutual relatives more disagreeable than ever, and of her being particularly disgusted with his mother, till they were more in private.

"But why were you not there, Edward?—Why did you not come?"

"I was engaged elsewhere."

"Engaged! But what was that, when such friends were to be met?"

"Perhaps, Miss Marianne," cried Lucy, eager to take some revenge on her, "you think young men never stand upon engagements, if they have no mind to keep them, little as well as great."

Elinor was very angry, but Marianne seemed entirely insensible of the sting; for she calmly replied,

"Not so, indeed; for, seriously speaking, I am very sure that conscience only kept Edward from Harley-street. And I really believe he *has* the most delicate conscience in the world; the most scrupulous in performing every engagement however minute, and however it may make against his interest or pleasure. He is the most fearful of giving pain, of wounding expectation, and the most incapable of being selfish, of any body I ever saw. Edward, it is so and I will say it. What! are you never to hear yourself praised!— Then, you must be no friend of mine; for those who will accept of my love and esteem, must submit to my open commendation."

The nature of her commendation, in the present case, however, happened to be particularly ill-suited to the feelings of two thirds of her auditors, and was so very unexhilarating to Edward, that he very soon got up to go away.

"Going so soon!" said Marianne; "my dear Edward this must not be."

And drawing him a little aside, she whispered her persuasion that Lucy could not stay much longer. But even this encouragement failed, for he would go; and Lucy, who would have outstaid him had his visit lasted two hours, soon afterwards went away.

"What can bring her here so often!" said Marianne, on her leav-

ing them. "Could she not see that we wanted her gone!—how teaz-
ing to Edward!"

"Why so?—we were all his friends, and Lucy has been the longest
known to him of any. It is but natural that he should like to see
her as well as ourselves."

Marianne looked at her steadily, and said, "You know, Elinor,
that this is a kind of talking which I cannot bear. If you only hope
to have your assertion contradicted, as I must suppose to be the
case, you ought to recollect that I am the last person in the world
to do it. I cannot descend to be tricked out of assurances, that are
not really wanted."

She then left the room; and Elinor dared not follow her to say
more, for bound as she was by her promise of secrecy to Lucy, she
could give no information that would convince Marianne; and painful as the consequences of her still continuing in an error might
be, she was obliged to submit to it. All that she could hope, was
that Edward would not often expose her or himself to the distress
of hearing Marianne's mistaken warmth, nor to the repetition of
any other part of the pain that had attended their recent meeting
—and this she had every reason to expect.

Chapter XIV.

Within a few days after this meeting, the newspapers announced
to the world, that the Lady of Thomas Palmer, Esq. was safely
delivered of a son and heir; a very interesting and satisfactory paragraph, at least to all those intimate connections who knew it
before.

This event, highly important to Mrs. Jenning's happiness, produced a temporary alteration in the disposal of her time, and influenced, in a like degree, the engagements of her young friends; for
as she wished to be as much as possible with Charlotte, she went
thither every morning as soon as she was dressed and did not return
till late in the evening; and the Miss Dashwoods, at the particular
request of the Middletons, spent the whole of every day in Conduit-
street. For their own comfort, they would much rather have remained, at least all the morning, in Mrs. Jennings's house; but it
was not a thing to be urged against the wishes of everybody. Their
hours were therefore made over to Lady Middleton and the two
Miss Steeles, by whom their company was in fact as little valued,
as it was professedly sought.

They had too much sense to be desirable companions to the former; and by the latter they were considered with a jealous eye, as
intruding on *their* ground, and sharing the kindness which they

wanted to monopolize. Though nothing could be more polite than
Lady Middleton's behaviour to Elinor and Marianne, she did not
really like them at all. Because they neither flattered herself nor
her children, she could not believe them good-natured; and because
they were fond of reading, she fancied them satirical: perhaps without exactly knowing what it was to be satirical; but *that* did not
signify. It was censure in common use, and easily given.

Their presence was a restraint both on her and on Lucy. It
checked the idleness of one, and the business of the other. Lady
Middleton was ashamed of doing nothing before them, and the
flattery which Lucy was proud to think of and administer at other
times, she feared they would despise her for offering. Miss Steele
was the least discomposed of the three, by their presence; and it
was in their power to reconcile her to it entirely. Would either of
them, only have given her a full and minute account of the whole
affair between Marianne and Mr. Willoughby, she would have
thought herself amply rewarded for the sacrifice of the best place
by the fire after dinner, which their arrival occasioned. But this
conciliation was not granted; for though she often threw out expressions of pity for her sister to Elinor, and more than once dropt
a reflection on the inconstancy of beaux before Marianne, no effect
was produced, but a look of indifference from the former, or of
disgust in the latter. An effort even yet lighter might have made her
their friend. Would they only have laughed at her about the Doctor!
But so little were they, any more than the others, inclined to oblige
her, that if Sir John dined from home, she might spend a whole
day without hearing any other raillery on the subject, than what she
was kind enough to bestow on herself.

All these jealousies and discontents, however, were so totally un-
suspected by Mrs. Jennings, that she thought it a delightful thing
for the girls to be together; and generally congratulated her young
friends every night, on having escaped the company of a stupid old
woman so long. She joined them sometimes at Sir John's, and sometimes at her own house; but wherever it was, she always came in
excellent spirits, full of delight and importance, attributing Charlotte's well doing to her own care, and ready to give so exact, so
minute a detail of her situation, as only Miss Steele had curiosity
enough to desire. One thing *did* disturb her; and of that she made
her daily complaint. Mr. Palmer maintained the common, but un-
fatherly opinion among his sex, of all infants being alike; and
though she could plainly perceive at different times, the most striking resemblance between this baby and every one of his relations
on both sides, there was no convincing his father of it; no persuading him to believe that it was not exactly like every other baby of

the same age; nor could he even be brought to acknowledge the simple proposition of its being the finest child in the world.

I come now to the relation of a misfortune, which about this time befell Mrs. John Dashwood. It so happened that while her two sisters with Mrs. Jennings were first calling on her in Harley-street, another of her acquaintance had dropt in—a circumstance in itself not apparently likely to produce evil to her. But while the imaginations of other people will carry them away to form wrong judgments of our conduct, and to decide on it by slight appearances, one's happiness must in some measure be always at the mercy of chance. In the present instance, this last-arrived lady allowed her fancy so far to outrun truth and probability, that on merely hearing the name of the Miss Dashwoods, and understanding them to be Mr. Dashwood's sisters, she immediately concluded them to be staying in Harley-street; and this misconstruction produced within a day or two afterwards, cards of invitation for them as well as for their brother and sister, to a small musical party at her house. The consequence of which was, that Mrs. John Dashwood was obliged to submit not only to the exceedingly great inconvenience of sending her carriage for the Miss Dashwoods; but, what was still worse, must be subject to all the unpleasantness of appearing to treat them with attention: and who could tell that they might not expect to go out with her a second time? The power of disappointing them, it was true, must always be her's. But that was not enough; for when people are determined on a mode of conduct which they know to be wrong, they feel injured by the expectation of any thing better from them.

Marianne had now been brought by degrees, so much into the habit of going out every day, that it was become a matter of indifference to her, whether she went or not: and she prepared quietly and mechanically for every evening's engagement, though without expecting the smallest amusement from any, and very often without knowing till the last moment, where it was to take her.

To her dress and appearance she was grown so perfectly indifferent, as not to bestow half the consideration on it, during the whole of her toilette, which it received from Miss Steele in the first five minutes of their being together, when it was finished. Nothing escaped *her* minute observation and general curiosity; she saw every thing, and asked every thing; was never easy till she knew the price of every part of Marianne's dress; could have guessed the number of her gowns altogether with better judgment than Marianne herself, and was not without hopes of finding out before they parted, how much her washing cost per week, and how much she had every year to spend upon herself. The impertinence of these kind of scrutinies, moreover, was generally concluded with a compliment, which though meant as its douceur,[1] was considered by Marianne as the greatest impertinence of all; for after undergoing an examination into the value and make of her gown, the colour of her shoes, and the arrangement of her hair, she was almost sure of being told that upon "her word she looked vastly smart, and she dared to say would make a great many conquests."

With such encouragement as this, was she dismissed on the present occasion to her brother's carriage; which they were ready to enter five minutes after it stopped at the door, a punctuality not very agreeable to their sister-in-law, who had preceded them to the house of her acquaintance, and was there hoping for some delay on their part that might inconvenience either herself or her coachman.

The events of the evening were not very remarkable. The party, like other musical parties, comprehended a great many people who had real taste for the performance, and a great many more who had none at all; and the performers themselves were, as usual, in their own estimation, and that of their immediate friends, the first[2] private performers in England.

As Elinor was neither musical, nor affecting to be so, she made no scruple of turning away her eyes from the grand pianoforté, whenever it suited her, and unrestrained even by the presence of a harp, and a violon-cello, would fix them at pleasure on any other object in the room. In one of these excursive glances she perceived among a group of young men, the very he, who had given them a lecture on toothpick-cases at Gray's. She perceived him soon afterwards looking at herself, and speaking familiarly to her brother; and had just determined to find out his name from the latter, when they both came towards her, and Mr. Dashwood introduced him to her as Mr. Robert Ferrars.

He addressed her with easy civility, and twisted his head into a bow which assured her as plainly as words could have done, that he was exactly the coxcomb she had heard him described to be by Lucy. Happy had it been for her, if her regard for Edward had depended less on his own merit, than on the merit of his nearest relations! For then his brother's bow must have given the finishing stroke to what the ill-humour of his mother and sister would have begun. But while she wondered at the difference of the two young men, she did not find that the emptiness and conceit of the one, put her at all out of charity with the modesty and worth of the other. Why they *were* different, Robert explained to her himself in

1. A pleasant or conciliatory speech or gesture.
2. Finest.

the course of a quarter of an hour's conversation; for, talking of his brother, and lamenting the extreme *gaucherie*[3] which he really believed kept him from mixing in proper society, he candidly and generously attributed it much less to any natural deficiency, than to the misfortune of a private education; while he himself, though probably without any particular, any material superiority by nature, merely from the advantage of a public school,[4] was as well fitted to mix in the world as any other man.

"Upon my soul," he added, "I believe it is nothing more; and so I often tell my mother, when she is grieving about it. 'My dear Madam,' I always say to her, 'you must make yourself easy. The evil is now irremediable, and it has been entirely your own doing. Why would you be persuaded by my uncle, Sir Robert, against your own judgment, to place Edward under private tuition, at the most critical time of his life? If you had only sent him to Westminster[5] as well as myself, instead of sending him to Mr. Pratt's, all this would have been prevented.' This is the way in which I always consider the matter, and my mother is perfectly convinced of her error."

Elinor would not oppose his opinion, because, whatever might be her general estimation of the advantage of a public school, she could not think of Edward's abode in Mr. Pratt's family, with any satisfaction.

"You reside in Devonshire, I think"—was his next observation, "in a cottage near Dawlish."

Elinor set him right as to its situation, and it seemed rather surprising to him that anybody could live in Devonshire, without living near Dawlish. He bestowed his hearty approbation however on their species of house.

"For my own part," said he, "I am excessively fond of a cottage;[6] there is always so much comfort, so much elegance about them. And I protest, if I had any money to spare, I should buy a little land and build one myself, within a short distance of London, where I might drive myself down at any time, and collect a few friends about

---

3. Awkwardness, lack of tact or address. In keeping with his pretensions to elegance, Robert Ferrars peppers his conversation with French. He sees his brother's preference for a retired life as the absence of polished manners rather than as the presence of moral taste.
4. This section rehearses a longstanding debate about the virtues of "public" schools (i.e., prestigious boarding schools like Eton and Westminster) versus "private" instruction by tutors at home or in a domestic environment. While Robert Ferrars predictably favors the socialization imparted at public schools, Elinor (like Austen) silently prefers the sobriety and sincerity thought to be cultivated by private education.
5. A private boarding school, founded in 1560 by Queen Elizabeth; its famous graduates included Locke, Dryden, and Cowper.
6. During the first decade of the nineteenth century, *cottage ornés*—comfortable and sometimes very elaborate cottages specifically designed for gentlemen—had become popular among the fashionable classes anxious to display their sensitivity to nature as well as their affluence. The kind of cottage Robert Ferrars adores is far removed from the neat but unpretentious abode in which the Dashwood women live.

me, and be happy. I advise every body who is going to build, to build a cottage. My friend Lord Courtland came to me the other day on purpose to ask my advice, and laid before me three different plans of Bonomi's.[7] I was to decide on the best of them. 'My dear Courtland,' said I, immediately throwing them all into the fire, 'do not adopt either of them, but by all means build a cottage.' And that, I fancy, will be the end of it.

"Some people imagine that there can be no accommodations, no space in a cottage; but this is all a mistake. I was last month at my friend Elliott's near Dartford. Lady Elliott wished to give a dance. 'But how can it be done?' said she; 'my dear Ferrars, do tell me how it is to be managed. There is not a room in this cottage that will hold ten couple, and where can the supper be?' *I* immediately saw that there could be no difficulty in it, so I said, 'My dear Lady Elliott, do not be uneasy. The dining parlour will admit eighteen couple with ease; card-tables may be placed in the drawing-room; the library may be open for tea and other refreshments; and let the supper be set out in the saloon.' Lady Elliott was delighted with the thought. We measured the dining-room, and found it would hold exactly eighteen couple, and the affair was arranged precisely after my plan. So that, in fact, you see, if people do but know how to set about it, every comfort may be as well enjoyed in a cottage as in the most spacious dwelling."

Elinor agreed to it all, for she did not think he deserved the compliment of rational opposition.

As John Dashwood had no more pleasure in music than his eldest sister, his mind was equally at liberty to fix on any thing else; and a thought struck him during the evening, which he communicated to his wife, for her approbation, when they got home. The consideration of Mrs. Dennison's mistake, in supposing his sisters their guests, had suggested the propriety of their being really invited to become such, while Mrs. Jennings's engagements kept her from home. The expense would be nothing, the inconvenience not more; and it was altogether an attention, which the delicacy of his conscience pointed out to be requisite to its complete enfranchisement from his promise to his father. Fanny was startled at the proposal.

"I do not see how it can be done," said she, "without affronting Lady Middleton, for they spend every day with her; otherwise I should be exceedingly glad to do it. You know I am always ready to pay them any attention in my power, as my taking them out this evening shews. But they are Lady Middleton's visitors. How can I ask them away from her?"

7. Joseph Bonomi (1739–1808) was a fashionable architect whose work at Eastwell Park near Godmersham and Laverstoke Park near Steventon Austen would surely have known.

Her husband, but with great humility, did not see the force of her objection. "They had already spent a week in this manner in Conduit-street, and Lady Middleton could not be displeased at their giving the same number of days to such near relations."

Fanny paused a moment, and then, with fresh vigour, said, "My love, I would ask them with all my heart, if it was in my power. But I had just settled within myself to ask the Miss Steeles to spend a few days with us. They are very well behaved, good kind of girls; and I think the attention is due to them, as their uncle did so very well by Edward. We can ask your sisters some other year, you know; but the Miss Steeles may not be in town any more. I am sure you will like them; indeed, you *do* like them, you know, very much already, and so does my mother; and they are such favourites with Harry!"

Mr. Dashwood was convinced. He saw the necessity of inviting the Miss Steeles immediately, and his conscience was pacified by the resolution of inviting his sisters another year; at the same time, however, slyly suspecting that another year would make the invitation needless, by bringing Elinor to town as Colonel Brandon's wife, and Marianne as *their* visitor.

Fanny, rejoicing in her escape, and proud of the ready wit that had procured it, wrote the next morning to Lucy, to request her company and her sister's, for some days, in Harley-street, as soon as Lady Middleton could spare them. This was enough to make Lucy really and reasonably happy. Mrs. Dashwood seemed actually working for her, herself; cherishing all her hopes, and promoting all her views! Such an opportunity of being with Edward and his family was, above all things, the most material to her interest, and such an invitation the most gratifying to her feelings! It was an advantage that could not be too gratefully acknowledged, nor too speedily made use of; and the visit to Lady Middleton, which had not before had any precise limits, was instantly discovered to have been always meant to end in two days time.

When the note was shewn to Elinor, as it was within ten minutes after its arrival, it gave her, for the first time, some share in the expectations of Lucy; for such a mark of uncommon kindness, vouchsafed on so short an acquaintance, seemed to declare that the good will towards her arose from something more than merely malice against herself; and might be brought, by time and address, to do every thing that Lucy wished. Her flattery had already subdued the pride of Lady Middleton, and made an entry into the close heart of Mrs. John Dashwood; and these were effects that laid open the probability of greater.

The Miss Steeles removed to Harley-street, and all that reached Elinor of their influence there, strengthened her expectation of the event. Sir John, who called on them more than once, brought home such accounts of the favour* they were in, as must be universally striking. Mrs. Dashwood had never been so much pleased with any young women in her life, as she was with them; had given each of them a needle book, made by some emigrant;[8] called Lucy by her christian name; and did not know whether she should ever be able to part with them.

* favour] favour that A.
8. A needle case, resembling a booklet, evidently made by a genteel Frenchwoman who, having fled the French Revolution, was obliged to work for her subsistence. There were many charitable efforts to raise money on behalf of French emigrants, and purchasing such a needle book would be a small act of charity.

Volume III

Chapter I.

Mrs. Palmer was so well at the end of a fortnight, that her mother felt it no longer necessary to give up the whole of her time to her; and contenting herself with visiting her once or twice a day, returned from that period to her own home, and her own habits, in which she found the Miss Dashwoods very ready to reassume their former share.

About the third or fourth morning after their being thus re-settled in Berkeley-street, Mrs. Jennings, on returning from her ordinary visit to Mrs. Palmer, entered the drawing-room, where Elinor was sitting by herself, with an air of such hurrying importance as prepared her to hear something wonderful; and giving her time only to form that idea, began directly to justify it by saying,

"Lord! my dear Miss Dashwood! have you heard the news!"

"No, ma'am. What is it?"

"Something so strange! But you shall hear it all.—When I got to Mr. Palmer's, I found Charlotte quite in a fuss about the child. She was sure it was very ill—it cried, and fretted, and was all over pimples. So I looked at it directly, and, 'Lord! my dear, says I, 'it is nothing in the world but the red-gum;'[1] and nurse said just the same. But Charlotte, she would not be satisfied, so Mr. Donavan was sent for; and luckily he happened to be just come in from Harley-street, so he stepped over directly, and as soon as ever he saw the child, he said just as we did, that it was nothing in the world but the red-gum, and then Charlotte was easy. And so, just as he was going away again, it came into my head, I am sure I do not know how I happened to think of it, but it came into my head to ask him if there was any news. So upon that, he smirked, and simpered, and looked grave, and seemed to know something or other, and at last he said in a whisper, 'For fear any unpleasant report should reach the young ladies under your care as to their sister's indisposition, I think it advisable to say, that I believe there is no great reason for alarm; I hope Mrs. Dashwood will do very well.' "

1. Citing this passage, the *OED* defines *red-gum* as a teething rash.

"What! is Fanny ill?"

"That is exactly what I said, my dear. 'Lord!' says I, 'is Mrs. Dash-wood ill?' So then it all came out; and the long and the short of the matter, by all I can learn, seems to be this. Mr. Edward Ferrars, the very young man I used to joke with you about (but however, as it turns out, I am monstrous glad there never was any thing in it), Mr. Edward Ferrars, it seems, has been engaged above this twelve-month to my cousin Lucy!—There's for you, my dear!—And not a creature knowing a syllable of the matter except Nancy!—Could you have believed such a thing possible?—There is no great wonder in their liking one another; but that matters should be brought so forward between them, and nobody suspect it! *That* is strange!—I never happened to see them together, or I am sure I should have found it out directly. Well, and so this was kept a great secret, for fear of Mrs. Ferrars, and neither she nor your brother or sister suspected a word of the matter;—till this very morning, poor Nancy, who, you know, is a well-meaning creature, but no con-jurer,[2] popt it all out. 'Lord!' thinks she to herself, 'they are all so fond of Lucy, to be sure they will make no difficulty about it;' and so, away she went to your sister, who was sitting all alone at her carpet-work, little suspecting what was to come—for she had just been saying to your brother, only five minutes before, that she thought to make a match between Edward and some Lord's daugh-ter or other, I forget who. So you may think what a blow it was to all her vanity and pride. She fell into violent hysterics immediately, with such screams as reached your brother's ears, as he was sitting in his own dressing-room down stairs, thinking about writing a let-ter to his steward in the country. So up he flew directly, and a terrible scene took place, for Lucy was come to them by that time, little dreaming* what was going on. Poor soul! I pity *her*. And I must say, I think she was used very hardly; for your sister scolded like any fury, and soon drove her into a fainting fit. Nancy, she fell upon her knees, and cried bitterly; and your brother, he walked about the room, and said he did not know what to do. Mrs. Dash-wood declared they should not stay a minute longer in the house, and your brother was forced to go down upon *his* knees too, to persuade her to let them stay till they had packed up their clothes. *Then* she fell into hysterics again, and he was so frightened that he would send for Mr. Donavan, and Mr. Donavan found the house in all this uproar. The carriage was at the door ready to take my poor cousins away, and they were just stepping in as he came off;

---

2. Johnson's *Dictionary* defines *conjurer* as someone of "shrewd conjecture" and "sagacity."
   * dreaming] dreaming of A.

poor Lucy in such a condition, he says, she could hardly walk; and Nancy, she was almost as bad. I declare, I have no patience with your sister; and I hope, with all my heart, it will be a match in spite of her. Lord! what a taking poor Mr. Edward will be in when he hears of it! To have his love used so scornfully! for they say he is monstrous fond of her, as well he may. I should not wonder, if he was to be in the greatest of a passion!—and Mr. Donavan thinks just the same. He and I had a great deal of talk about it; and the best of all is, that he is gone back again to Harley-street, that he may be within call when Mrs. Ferrars is told of it, for she was sent for as soon as ever my cousins left the house, for your sister was sure *she* would be in hysterics too; and so she may, for what I care. I have no pity for either of them. I have no notion of people's making such a to-do about money and greatness. There is no reason on earth why Mr. Edward and Lucy should not marry; for I am sure Mrs. Ferrars may afford to do very well by her son, and though Lucy has next to nothing herself, she knows better than any body how to make the most of every thing; and I dare say, if Mrs. Ferrars would only allow him five hundred a-year, she would make as good an appearance with it as any body else would with eight. Lord! how snug they might live in such another cottage as yours—or a little bigger—with two maids and two men; and I believe I could help them to a housemaid, for my Betty has a sister out of place, that would fit them exactly."

Here Mrs. Jennings ceased, and as Elinor had had time enough to collect her thoughts, she was able to give such an answer, and make such observations, as the subject might naturally be supposed to produce. Happy to find that she was not suspected of any extraordinary interest in it; that Mrs. Jennings (as she had of late often hoped might be the case) had ceased to imagine her at all attached to Edward; and happy above all the rest, in the absence of Marianne, she felt very well able to speak of the affair without embarrassment, and to give her judgment, as she believed, with impartiality on the conduct of every one concerned in it.

She could hardly determine what her own expectation of its event really was; though she earnestly tried to drive away the notion of its being possible to end otherwise at last, than in the marriage of Edward and Lucy. What Mrs. Ferrars would say and do, though there could not be a doubt of its nature, she was anxious to hear; and still more anxious to know how Edward would conduct himself. For *him* she felt much compassion;—for Lucy very little—and it cost her some pains to procure that little;—for the rest of the party none at all.

As Mrs. Jennings could talk on no other subject, Elinor soon saw the necessity of preparing Marianne for its discussion. No time was to be lost in undeceiving her, in making her acquainted with the real truth, and in endeavouring to bring her to hear it talked of by others, without betraying that she felt any uneasiness for her sister, or any resentment against Edward.

Elinor's office was a painful one.—She was going to remove what she really believed to be her sister's chief consolation,—to give such particulars of Edward, as she feared would ruin him for ever in her good opinion,—and to make Marianne, by a resemblance in their situations, which to *her* fancy would seem strong, feel all her own disappointment over again. But unwelcome as such a task must be, it was necessary to be done, and Elinor therefore hastened to perform it.

She was very far from wishing to dwell on her own feelings, or to represent herself as suffering much, any otherwise than as the self-command she had practised since her first knowledge of Edward's engagement, might suggest a hint of what was practicable to Marianne. Her narration was clear and simple; and though it could not be given without emotion, it was not accompanied by violent agitation, nor impetuous grief.—*That* belonged rather to the hearer, for Marianne listened with horror, and cried excessively. Elinor was to be the comforter of others in her own distresses, no less than in theirs; and all the comfort that could be given by assurances of her own composure of mind, and a very earnest vindication of Edward from every charge but of imprudence, was readily offered.

But Marianne for some time would give credit to neither. Edward seemed a second Willoughby; and acknowledging as Elinor did, that she *had* loved him most sincerely, could she feel less than herself! As for Lucy Steele, she considered her so totally unamiable, so absolutely incapable of attaching a sensible man, that she could not be persuaded at first to believe, and afterwards to pardon, any former affection of Edward for her. She would not even admit it to have been natural; and Elinor left her to be convinced that it was so, by that which only could convince her, a better knowledge of mankind.

Her first communication had reached no farther than to state the fact of the engagement, and the length of time it had existed.—Marianne's feelings had then broken in, and put an end to all regularity of detail; and for some time all that could be done was to soothe her distress, lessen her alarms, and combat her resentment. The first question on her side, which led to farther particulars, was,

"How long has this been known to you, Elinor? has he written to you?"

"I have known it these four months. When Lucy first came to

Barton-park last November, she told me in confidence of her engagement."

At these words, Marianne's eyes expressed the astonishment, which her lips could not utter. After a pause of wonder, she exclaimed,

"Four months!—Have you known of this four months?"— Elinor confirmed it.

"What!—while attending me in all my misery, has this been on your heart?—and I have reproached you for being happy!"—

"It was not fit that you should then know how much I was the reverse."—

"Four months!"—cried Marianne again.—"So calm!—so cheerful!—how have you been supported?"—

"By feeling that I was doing my duty.—My promise to Lucy, obliged me to be secret. I owed it to her, therefore, to avoid giving any hint of the truth; and I owed it to my family and friends, not to create in them a solicitude about me, which it could not be in my power to satisfy."

Marianne seemed much struck.—

"I have very often wished to undeceive yourself and my mother," added Elinor; "and once or twice I have attempted it;—but without betraying my trust, I never could have convinced you."

"Four months!—and yet you loved him!"—

"Yes. But I did not love only him;—and while the comfort of others was dear to me, I was glad to spare them from knowing how much I felt. Now, I can think and speak of it with little emotion. I would not have you suffer on my account; for I assure you I no longer suffer materially myself. I have many things to support me. I am not conscious of having provoked the disappointment by any imprudence of my own, and I have borne it as much as possible without spreading it farther. I acquit Edward of all essential misconduct. I wish him very happy; and I am so sure of his always doing his duty, that though now he may harbour some regret, in the end he must become so. Lucy does not want sense, and that is the foundation on which every thing good may be built.—And after all, Marianne, after all that is bewitching in the idea of a single and constant attachment, and all that can be said of one's happiness depending entirely on any particular person, it is not meant—it is not fit—it is not possible that it should be so.—Edward will marry Lucy; he will marry a woman superior in person and understanding to half her sex; and time and habit will teach him to forget that he ever thought another superior to *her*."—

"If such is your way of thinking," said Marianne, "if the loss of what is most valued is so easily to be made up by something else, your resolution, your self-command, are, perhaps, a little less to be wondered at.—They are brought more within my comprehension."

"I understand you.—You do not suppose that I have ever felt much.—For four months, Marianne, I have had all this hanging on my mind, without being at liberty to speak of it to a single creature; knowing that it would make you and my mother most unhappy whenever it were explained to you, yet unable to prepare you for it in the least.—It was told me,—it was in a manner forced on me by the very person herself, whose prior engagement ruined all my prospects; and told me, as I thought, with triumph.—This person's suspicions, therefore, I have had to oppose, by endeavouring to appear indifferent where I have been most deeply interested;—and it has not been only once;—I have had her hopes and exultation to listen to again and again.—I have known myself to be divided from Edward for ever, without hearing one circumstance that could make me less desire the connection.—Nothing has proved him unworthy; nor has any thing declared him indifferent to me.—I have had to contend against the unkindness of his sister, and the insolence of his mother; and have suffered the punishment of an attachment, without enjoying its advantages.—And all this has been going on at a time, when, as you too well know, it has not been my only unhappiness.—If you can think me capable of ever feeling—surely you may suppose that I have suffered *now*. The composure of mind with which I have brought myself at present to consider the matter, the consolation that I have been willing to admit, have been the effect of constant and painful exertion;—they did not spring up of themselves;—they did not occur to relieve my spirits at first—No, Marianne.—*Then*, if I had not been bound to silence, perhaps nothing could have kept me entirely—not even what I owed to my dearest friends—from openly shewing that I was *very* unhappy."—

Marianne was quite subdued.—

"Oh! Elinor," she cried, "you have made me hate myself for ever.—How barbarous have I been to you!—you, who have been my only comfort, who have borne with me in all my misery, who have seemed to be only suffering for me!—Is this my gratitude!— Is this the only return I can make you?—Because your merit cries out upon myself, I have been trying to do it away."

The tenderest caresses followed this confession. In such a frame of mind as she was now in, Elinor had no difficulty in obtaining from her whatever promise she required; and at her request, Marianne engaged never to speak of the affair to any one with the least appearance of bitterness;—to meet Lucy without betraying the smallest increase of dislike to her;—and even to see Edward himself, if chance should bring them together, without any diminution of her usual cordiality.—These were great concessions;—but where

Marianne felt that she had injured, no reparation could be too much for her to make.

She performed her promise of being discreet, to admiration.—She attended to all that Mrs. Jennings had to say upon the subject, with an unchanging complexion, dissented from her in nothing, and was heard three times to say, "Yes, ma'am."—She listened to her praise of Lucy with only moving from one chair to another, and when Mrs. Jennings talked of Edward's affection, it cost her only a spasm in her throat.—Such advances towards heroism in her sister, made Elinor feel equal to any thing herself.

The next morning brought a farther trial of it, in a visit from their brother, who came with a most serious aspect to talk over the dreadful affair, and bring them news of his wife.

"You have heard, I suppose," said he with great solemnity, as soon as he was seated, "of the very shocking discovery that took place under our roof yesterday."

They all looked their assent; it seemed too awful a moment for speech.

"Your sister," he continued, "has suffered dreadfully. Mrs. Ferrars too—in short it has been a scene of such complicated distress—but I will hope that the storm may be weathered without our being any of us quite overcome. Poor Fanny! she was in hysterics all yesterday. But I would not alarm you too much. Donavan says there is nothing materially to be apprehended; her constitution is a good one, and her resolution equal to any thing. She has borne it all, with the fortitude of an angel! She says she never shall think well of anybody again; and one cannot wonder at it, after being so deceived!—meeting with such ingratitude, where so much kindness had been shewn, so much confidence had been placed! It was quite out of the benevolence of her heart, that she had asked these young women to her house; merely because she thought they deserved some attention, were harmless, well-behaved girls, and would be pleasant companions; for otherwise we both wished very much to have invited you and Marianne to be with us, while your kind friend there, was attending her daughter. And now to be so rewarded! 'I wish with all my heart,' says poor Fanny in her affectionate way, 'that we had asked your sisters instead of them.' "

Here he stopped to be thanked; which being done, he went on.

"What poor Mrs. Ferrars suffered, when first Fanny broke it to her, is not to be described. While she with the truest affection had been planning a most eligible connection for him, was it to be supposed that he could be all the time secretly engaged to another person!—such a suspicion could never have entered her head! If she suspected *any* prepossession elsewhere, it could not be in *that* quarter. 'There, to be sure,' said she, 'I might have thought myself safe.' She was quite in an agony. We consulted together, however, as to what should be done, and at last she determined to send for Edward. He came. But I am sorry to relate what ensued. All that Mrs. Ferrars could say to make him put an end to the engagement, assisted too as you may well suppose by my arguments, and Fanny's entreaties, was of no avail. Duty, affection, every thing was disregarded. I never thought Edward so stubborn, so unfeeling before. His mother explained to him her liberal designs, in case of his marrying Miss Morton; told him* she would settle on him the Norfolk estate, which, clear of land-tax, brings in a good thousand a-year; offered even, when matters grew desperate, to make it twelve hundred; and in opposition to this, if he still persisted in this low connection, represented to him the certain penury that must attend the match. His own two thousand pounds she protested should be his all; she would never see him again; and so far would she be from affording him the smallest assistance, that if he were to enter into any profession with a view of better support, she would do all in her power to prevent his advancing in it."

Here Marianne, in an ecstacy of indignation, clapped her hands together, and cried, "Gracious God! can this be possible!"

"Well may you wonder, Marianne," replied her brother, "at the obstinacy which could resist such arguments as these. Your exclamation is very natural."

Marianne was going to retort, but she remembered her promises, and forbore.

"All this, however," he continued, "was urged in vain. Edward said very little; but what he did say, was in the most determined manner. Nothing should prevail on him to give up his engagement. He would stand to it, cost him what it might."

"Then," cried Mrs. Jennings with blunt sincerity, no longer able to be silent, "he has acted like an honest man! I beg your pardon, Mr. Dashwood, but if he had done otherwise, I should have thought him a rascal. I have some little concern in the business, as well as yourself, for Lucy Steele is my cousin, and I believe there is not a better kind of girl in the world, nor one who more deserves a good husband."

John Dashwood was greatly astonished; but his nature was calm, not open to provocation, and he never wished to offend anybody, especially anybody of good fortune. He therefore replied without any resentment.**

"I would by no means speak disrespectfully of any relation of

---

*   told him] told him that A.
**   resentment.] resentment, A.

your's, madam. Miss Lucy Steele is, I dare say, a very deserving young woman, but in the present case you know, the connection must be impossible. And to have entered into a secret engagement with a young man under her uncle's care, the son of a woman especially of such very large fortune as Mrs. Ferrars, is perhaps altogether a little extraordinary. In short, I do not mean to reflect upon the behaviour of any person whom you have a regard for, Mrs. Jennings. We all wish her extremely happy, and Mrs. Ferrars's conduct throughout the whole, has been such as every conscientious, good mother, in like circumstances, would adopt. It has been dignified and liberal. Edward has drawn his own lot, and I fear it will be a bad one."

Marianne sighed out her similar apprehension; and Elinor's heart wrung for the feelings of Edward, while braving his mother's threats, for a woman who could not reward him.

"Well, sir," said Mrs. Jennings, "and how did it end?"

"I am sorry to say, ma'am, in a most unhappy rupture:—Edward is dismissed for ever from his mother's notice. He left her house yesterday, but where he is gone or whether he is still in town, I do not know; for *we* of course can make no inquiry."

"Poor young man!—and what is to become of him?"

"What, indeed, ma'am! It is a melancholy consideration. Born to the prospect of such affluence! I cannot conceive a situation more deplorable. The interest of two thousand pounds—how can a man live on it!—and when to that is added the recollection, that he might, but for his own folly, within three months have been in the receipt of two thousand, five hundred a-year, (for Miss Morton has thirty thousand pounds,) I cannot picture to myself a more wretched condition. We must all feel for him; and the more so, because it is totally* out of our power to assist him."

"Poor young man!" cried Mrs. Jennings, "I am sure he should be very welcome to bed and board at my house; and so I would tell him if I could see him. It is not fit that he should be living about at his own charge now, at lodgings and taverns."

Elinor's heart thanked her for such kindness towards Edward, though she could not forbear smiling at the form of it.

"If he would only have done as well by himself," said John Dashwood, "as all his friends were disposed to do by him, he might now have been in his proper situation, and would have wanted for nothing. But as it is, it must be out of anybody's power to assist him. And there is one thing more preparing against him, which must be worse than all—his mother has determined, with a very natural kind of spirit, to settle *that* estate upon Robert immediately, which

* totally] so totally A.

might have been Edward's, on proper conditions. I left her this morning with her lawyer, talking over the business."

"Well!" said Mrs. Jennings, "that is *her* revenge. Everybody has a way of their own. But I don't think mine would be, to make one son independent, because another had plagued me."

Marianne got up, and walked about the room.

"Can any thing be more galling to the spirit of a man," continued John, "than to see his younger brother in possession of an estate which might have been his own? Poor Edward! I feel for him sincerely."

A few minutes more spent in the same kind of effusion, concluded his visit; and with repeated assurances to his sisters that he really believed there was no material danger in Fanny's indisposition, and that they need not therefore be very uneasy about it, he went away; leaving the three ladies unanimous in their sentiments on the present occasion, as far at least as it regarded Mrs. Ferrars's conduct, the Dashwoods' and Edward's.

Marianne's indignation burst forth as soon as he quitted the room; and as her vehemence made reserve impossible in Elinor, and unnecessary in Mrs. Jennings, they all joined in a very spirited critique upon the party.

Chapter II.

Mrs. Jennings was very warm in her praise of Edward's conduct, but only Elinor and Marianne understood its true merit. *They* only knew how little he had had to tempt him to be disobedient, and how small was the consolation, beyond the consciousness of doing right, that could remain to him in the loss of friends and fortune. Elinor gloried in his integrity; and Marianne forgave all his offences in compassion for his punishment. But though confidence between them was, by this public discovery, restored to its proper state, it was not a subject on which either of them were fond of dwelling when alone. Elinor avoided it upon principle, as tending to fix still more upon her thoughts, by the too warm, too positive assurances of Marianne, that belief of Edward's continued affection for herself which she rather wished to do away; and Marianne's courage soon failed her, in trying to converse upon a topic which always left her more dissatisfied with herself than ever, by the comparison it necessarily produced between Elinor's conduct and her own.

She felt all the force of that comparison; but not as her sister had hoped, to urge her to exertion now; she felt it with all the pain of continual self-reproach, regretted most bitterly that she had never exerted herself before; but it brought only the torture of penitence, without the hope of amendment. Her mind was so much weakened that she still fancied present exertion impossible, and therefore it only dispirited her more.

Nothing new was heard by them, for a day or two afterwards, of affairs in Harley-street, or Bartlett's Buildings. But though so much of the matter was known to them already, that Mrs. Jennings might have had enough to do in spreading that knowledge farther, without seeking after more, she had resolved from the first to pay a visit of comfort and inquiry to her cousins as soon as she could; and nothing but the hindrance of more visitors than usual, had prevented her going to them within that time.

The third day succeeding their knowledge of the particulars, was so fine, so beautiful a Sunday as to draw many to Kensington Gardens,[1] though it was only the second week in March. Mrs. Jennings and Elinor were of the number; but Marianne, who knew that the Willoughbys were again in town, and had a constant dread of meeting them, chose rather to stay at home, than venture into so public a place.

An intimate acquaintance of Mrs. Jennings joined them soon after they entered the Gardens, and Elinor was not sorry that by her continuing with them, and engaging all Mrs. Jennings's conversation, she was herself left to quiet reflection. She saw nothing of the Willoughbys, nothing of Edward, and for some time nothing of anybody who could by any chance whether grave or gay, be interesting to her. But at last she found herself with some surprise, accosted by Miss Steele, who, though looking rather shy, expressed great satisfaction in meeting them, and on receiving encouragement from the particular kindness of Mrs. Jennings, left her own party for a short time, to join their's. Mrs. Jennings immediately whispered to Elinor,

"Get it all out of her, my dear. She will tell you any thing if you ask. You see I cannot leave Mrs. Clarke."

It was lucky, however, for Mrs. Jennings's curiosity and Elinor's* too, that she would tell any thing *without* being asked, for nothing would otherwise have been learnt.

"I am so glad to meet you;" said Miss Steele, taking her familiarly by the arm—"for I wanted to see you of all things in the world." And then lowering her voice, "I suppose Mrs. Jennings has heard all about it. Is she angry?"

"Not at all, I believe, with you."

"That is a good thing. And Lady Middleton, is *she* angry?"

---

1. The gardens of Kensington Palace, laid out and opened to the public during the eighteenth century.
* curiosity and Elinor's] curiosity, and for Elinor's A.

"I cannot suppose it possible that she should."

"I am monstrous glad of it. Good gracious! I have had such a time of it! I never saw Lucy in such a rage in my life. She vowed at first she would never trim me up a new bonnet, nor do any thing else for me again, so long as she lived; but now she is quite come to, and we are as good friends as ever. Look, she made me this bow to my hat, and put in the feather last night. There now, *you* are going to laugh at me too. But why should not I wear pink ribbons? I do not care if it *is* the Doctor's favourite colour. I am sure, for my part, I should never have known he *did* like it better than any other colour, if he had not happened to say so. My cousins have been so plaguing me!—I declare sometimes I do not know which way to look before them."

She had wandered away to a subject on which Elinor had nothing to say, and therefore soon judged it expedient to find her way back again to the first.

"Well, but Miss Dashwood," speaking triumphantly, "people may say what they chuse about Mr. Ferrars's declaring he would not have Lucy, for it's no such a thing I can tell you; and it's quite a shame for such ill-natured reports to be spread abroad. Whatever Lucy might think about it herself, you know, it was no business of other people to set it down for certain."

"I never heard anything of the kind hinted at before, I assure you," said Elinor.

"Oh! did not you? But it *was* said, I know, very well, and by more than one; for Miss Godby told Miss Sparks, that nobody in their senses could expect Mr. Ferrars to give up a woman like Miss Morton, with thirty thousand pounds to her fortune, for Lucy Steele that had nothing at all; and I had it from Miss Sparks myself. And besides that, my cousin Richard said himself, that when it came to the point, he was afraid Mr. Ferrars would be off; and when Edward did not come near us for three days, I could not tell what to think myself; and I believe in my heart Lucy gave it all up* for lost; for we came away from your brother's Wednesday,** and we saw nothing of him not all Thursday, Friday, and Saturday, and did not know what was become with him. Once Lucy thought to write to him, but then her spirit rose against that. However this morning he came just as we came home from church; and then it all came out, how he had been sent for Wednesday to Harley-street, and been talked to by his mother and all of them, and how he had declared before them all that he loved nobody but Lucy, and nobody but Lucy

---

* gave it all up] A; gave it up all B, *almost certainly an error.*
** Wednesday,] on Wednesday, A.

would he have. And how he had been so worried by what passed, that as soon as he had went away from his mother's house, he had got upon his horse, and rid into the country some where or other; and how he had staid about at an inn all Thursday and Friday, on purpose to get the better of it. And after thinking it all over and over again, he said, it seemed to him as if, now he had no fortune, and no nothing at all, it would be quite unkind to keep her on to the engagement, because it must be for her loss, for he had nothing but two thousand pounds, and no hope of any thing else; and if he was to go into orders,[2] as he had some thoughts, he could get nothing but a curacy,[3] and how was they to live upon that?—He could not bear to think of her doing no better, and so he begged, if she had the least mind for it, to put an end to the matter directly, and leave him to shift for himself. I heard him say all this as plain as could possibly be. And it was entirely for *her* sake, and upon *her* account, that he said a word about being off, and not upon his own. I will take my oath he never dropt a syllable of being tired of her, or of wishing to marry Miss Morton, or anything like it. But, to be sure, Lucy would not give ear to such kind of talking; so she told him directly (with a great deal about sweet and love, you know, and all that—Oh, la! one can't repeat such kind of things you know)— she told him directly, she had not the least mind in the world to be off, for she could live with him upon a trifle, and how little so ever he might have, she should be very glad to have it all, you know, or something of the kind. So then he was monstrous happy, and talked* on some time about what they should do, and they agreed he should take orders directly, and they must wait to be married till he got a living. And just then I could not hear any more, for my cousin called from below to tell me Mrs. Richardson was come in her coach, and would take one of us to Kensington Gardens; so I was forced to go into the room and interrupt them, to ask Lucy if she would like to go, but she did not care to leave Edward; so I just run up stairs and put on a pair of silk stockings, and came off with the Richardsons."

"I do not understand what you mean by interrupting them," said Elinor; "you were all in the same room together, were not you?"

"No, indeed, not us. La! Miss Dashwood, do you think people make love when any body else is by? Oh for shame!—To be sure

2. To become ordained as a priest in the Church of England.
3. A position as assistant to a rector or a vicar. Rectors or vicars who had more than one living, and who benefited from the multiple incomes, frequently employed curates to perform their duties in the parishes where they were not in residence. Without livings of their own and typically very underpaid, curates were often extremely poor.
* and talked] and they talked A. *The difference is significant, for in B Edward is the one doing the talking, while in A Lucy takes part in the discussion.*

you must know better than that. (Laughing affectedly.)—No, no; they were shut up in the drawing-room together, and all I heard was only by listening at the door."

"How!" cried Elinor; "have you been repeating to me what you only learnt yourself by listening at the door? I am sorry I did not know it before; for I certainly would not have suffered you to give me particulars of a conversation which you ought not to have known yourself. How could you behave so unfairly by your sister?"

"Oh, la! there is nothing in *that*. I only stood at the door, and heard what I could. And I am sure Lucy would have done just the same by me; for a year or two back, when Martha Sharpe and I had so many secrets together, she never made any bones of hiding in a closet, or behind a chimney-board,[4] on purpose to hear what we said."

Elinor tried to talk of something else; but Miss Steele could not be kept beyond a couple of minutes, from what was uppermost in her mind.

"Edward talks of going to Oxford soon," said she, "but now he is lodging at No.—, Pall Mall. What an ill-natured woman his mother is, an't she? And your brother and sister were not very kind! However, I shan't say anything against them to *you*; and to be sure they did send us home in their own chariot, which was more than I looked for. And for my part, I was all in a fright for fear your sister should ask us for the huswifes[5] she had gave us a day or two before; but however, nothing was said about them, and I took care to keep mine out of sight. Edward have got some business at Oxford, he says; so he must go there for a time; and after *that*, as soon as he can light upon a Bishop, he will be ordained. I wonder what curacy he will get!—Good gracious! (gigling as she spoke) I'd lay my life I know what my cousins will say, when they hear of it. They will tell me I should write to the Doctor, to get Edward the curacy of his new living. I know they will; but I am sure I would not do such a thing for all the world.—'La!' I shall say directly, 'I wonder how you could think of such a thing. *I* write to the Doctor, indeed!' "

"Well," said Elinor, "it is a comfort to be prepared against the worst. You have got your answer ready."

Miss Steele was going to reply on the same subject, but the approach of her own party made another more necessary.

"Oh, la! here come the Richardsons. I had a vast deal more to say to you, but I must not stay away from them not* any longer. I

---

4. Defined by the *OED* as a board used to close up a fireplace in summer.
5. Cases for threads, pins, needles, scissors, and other sewing implements.
* not] Though A *and* B *both print* not *here, it looks more like a printer's error than like one of Miss Steele's errors or vulgarisms.*

assure you they are very genteel people. He makes a monstrous deal of money, and they keep their own coach. I have not time to speak to Mrs. Jennings about it myself, but pray tell her I am quite happy to hear she is not in anger against us, and Lady Middleton the same; and if any thing should happen to take you and your sister away, and Mrs. Jennings should want company, I am sure we should be very glad to come and stay with her for as long a time as she likes. I suppose Lady Middleton won't ask us any more this bout. Good bye; I am sorry Miss Marianne was not here. Remember me kindly to her. La! if you have not got your best spotted muslin* on!—I wonder you was not afraid of its being torn."

Such was her parting concern; for after this, she had time only to pay her farewell compliments to Mrs. Jennings before her company was claimed by Mrs. Richardson; and Elinor was left in possession of knowledge which might feed her powers of reflection some time, though she had learnt very little more than what had been already foreseen and foreplanned in her own mind. Edward's marriage with Lucy was as firmly determined on, and the time of its taking place remained as absolutely uncertain, as she had concluded it would be;—every thing depended, exactly after her expectation, on his getting that preferment,[6] of which, at present, there seemed not the smallest chance.

As soon as they returned to the carriage, Mrs. Jennings was eager for information; but as Elinor wished to spread as little as possible intelligence that had in the first place been so unfairly obtained, she confined herself to the brief repetition of such simple particulars, as she felt assured that Lucy, for the sake of her own consequence, would chuse to have known. The continuance of their engagement, and the means that were to be taken for promoting its end, was all her communication; and this produced from Mrs. Jennings the following natural remark.

"Wait for his having a living!—aye, we all know how *that* will end;—they will wait a twelvemonth, and finding no good comes of it, will set down upon a curacy of fifty pounds a-year, with the interest of his two thousand pounds, and what little matter Mr. Steele and Mr. Pratt can give her.—Then they will have a child every year! and Lord help 'em! how poor they will be!—I must see what I can give them towards furnishing their house. Two maids and two men indeed!—as I talked of t'other day.—No, no, they must get a stout girl of all works.—Betty's sister would never do for them *now*."

---

* best spotted muslin] A; spotted muslin B. *A is preferable, as Lucy's concern about tearing the dress makes sense only if it is Elinor's "best." Because it comes at the end of the line in A, the typesetter of B probably dropped* best *inadvertently.*
6. A church appointment or promotion bringing financial or social advantage.

The next morning brought Elinor a letter by the two-penny post from Lucy herself. It was as follows:

Bartlett's Buildings, March.

I hope my dear Miss Dashwood will excuse the liberty I take of writing to her; but I know your friendship for me will make you pleased to hear such a good account of myself and my dear Edward, after all the troubles we have went through lately, therefore will make no more apologies, but proceed to say that, thank God! though we have suffered dreadfully, we are both quite well now, and as happy as we must always be in one another's love. We have had great trials, and great persecutions, but however, at the same time, gratefully acknowledge many friends, yourself not the least among them, whose great kindness I shall always thankfully remember, as will Edward too, who I have told of it. I am sure you will be glad to hear, as likewise dear Mrs. Jennings, I spent two happy hours with him yesterday afternoon, he would not hear of our parting, though earnestly did I, as I thought my duty required, urge him to it for prudence sake, and would have parted for ever on the spot, would he consent to it; but he said it should never be, he did not regard his mother's anger, while he could have my affections; our prospects are not very bright, to be sure, but we must wait, and hope for the best; he will be ordained shortly, and should it ever be in your power to recommend him to any body that has a living to bestow, am very sure you will not forget us, and dear Mrs. Jennings too, trust she will speak a good word for us to Sir John, or Mr. Palmer, or any friend that may be able to assist us.—Poor Anne was much to blame for what she did, but she did it for the best, so I say nothing; hope Mrs. Jennings won't think it too much trouble to give us a call, should she come this way any morning, 'twould be a great kindness, and my cousins would be proud to know her. —My paper reminds me to conclude,[7] and begging to be most gratefully and respectfully remembered to her, and to Sir John, and Lady Middleton, and the dear children, when you chance to see them, and love to Miss Marianne,

I am, &c. &c.

As soon as Elinor had finished it, she performed what she concluded to be its writer's real design, by placing it in the hands of Mrs. Jennings, who read it aloud with many comments of satisfaction and praise.

7. Envelopes not being in common use, part of the back side of a sheet of paper had to be left blank so that the address could be written there when the letter was folded and sealed with wax. Like many letter-writing heroines before her, Lucy is saying here that she has to stop writing because she has run out of space.

"Very well indeed!—how prettily she writes!—aye, that was quite proper to let him be off if he would. That was just like Lucy.—Poor soul! I wish I *could* get him a living with all my heart.—She calls me dear Mrs. Jennings, you see. She is a good-hearted girl as ever lived.—Very well upon my word. That sentence is very prettily turned. Yes, yes, I will go and see her, sure enough. How attentive she is, to think of every body!—Thank you, my dear, for shewing it me. It is as pretty a letter as ever I saw, and does Lucy's head and heart great credit."

Chapter III.

The Miss Dashwoods had now been rather more than two months in town, and Marianne's impatience to be gone increased every day. She sighed for the air, the liberty, the quiet of the country; and fancied that if any place could give her ease, Barton must do it. Elinor was hardly less anxious than herself for their removal, and only so much less bent on its being effected immediately, as that she was conscious of the difficulties of so long a journey, which Marianne could not be brought to acknowledge. She began, however, seriously to turn her thoughts towards its accomplishment, and had already mentioned their wishes to their kind hostess, who resisted them with all the eloquence of her good-will, when a plan was suggested, which, though detaining them from home yet a few weeks longer, appeared to Elinor altogether much more eligible than any other. The Palmers were to remove to Cleveland about the end of March, for the Easter holidays; and Mrs. Jennings, with both her friends, received a very warm invitation from Charlotte to go with them. This would not, in itself, have been sufficient for the delicacy of Miss Dashwood;—but it was inforced with so much real politeness by Mr. Palmer himself, as, joined to the very great amendment of his manners towards them since her sister had been known to be unhappy, induced her to accept it with pleasure.

When she told Marianne what she had done, however, her first reply was not very auspicious.

"Cleveland!"—she cried, with great agitation. "No, I cannot go to Cleveland."—

"You forget," said Elinor, gently, "that its situation is not . . . . that it is not in the neighbourhood of . . . ."

"But it is in Somersetshire.—I cannot go into Somersetshire.— There, where I looked forward to going . . . No, Elinor, you cannot expect me to go there."

Elinor would not argue upon the propriety of overcoming such feelings;—she only endeavoured to counteract them by working on others;—and represented it, therefore, as a measure which would fix the time of her returning to that dear mother, whom she so much wished to see, in a more eligible, more comfortable manner, than any other plan could do, and perhaps without any greater delay. From Cleveland, which was within a few miles of Bristol, the distance to Barton was not beyond one day, though a long day's journey; and their mother's servant might easily come there to attend them down; and as there could be no occasion for their staying above a week at Cleveland, they might now be at home in little more than three weeks' time. As Marianne's affection for her mother was sincere, it must triumph, with little difficulty, over the imaginary evils* she had started.

Mrs. Jennings was so far from being weary of her guests, that she pressed them very earnestly to return with her again from Cleveland. Elinor was grateful for the attention, but it could not alter their design; and their mother's concurrence being readily gained, every thing relative to their return was arranged as far as it could be;—and Marianne found some relief in drawing up a statement of the hours, that were yet to divide her from Barton.

"Ah! Colonel, I do not know what you and I shall do without the Miss Dashwoods;"—was Mrs. Jennings's address to him when he first called on her, after their leaving her was settled—"for they are quite resolved upon going home from the Palmers;—and how forlorn we shall be, when I come back!—Lord! we shall sit and gape at one another as dull as two cats."

Perhaps Mrs. Jennings was in hopes, by this vigorous sketch of their future ennui, to provoke him to make that offer, which might give himself an escape from it;—and if so, she had soon afterwards good reason to think her object gained; for, on Elinor's moving to the window to take more expeditiously the dimensions of a print, which she was going to copy for her friend, he followed her to it with a look of particular meaning, and conversed with her there for several minutes. The effect of his discourse on the lady too, could not escape her observation, for though she was too honourable to listen, and had even changed her seat, on purpose that she might *not* hear, to one close by the piano forté on which Marianne was playing, she could not keep herself from seeing that Elinor changed colour, attended with agitation, and was too intent on what he said, to pursue her employment.—Still farther in confirmation of her hopes, in the interval of Marianne's turning from one lesson to another, some words of the Colonel's inevitably reached her ear, in which he seemed to be apologizing for the badness of his house. This set the matter beyond a doubt. She wondered indeed at his

* evils] evil A.

thinking it necessary to do so;—but supposed it to be the proper etiquette. What Elinor said in reply she could not distinguish, but judged from the motion of her lips that she did not think *that* any material objection;—and Mrs. Jennings commended her in her heart for being so honest. They then talked on for a few minutes longer without her catching a syllable, when another lucky stop in Marianne's performance brought her these words in the Colonel's calm voice,

"I am afraid it cannot take place very soon."

Astonished and shocked at so unlover-like a speech, she was almost ready to cry out, "Lord! what should hinder it?"—but checking her desire, confined herself to this silent ejaculation.

"This is very strange!—sure he need not wait to be older."—

This delay on the Colonel's side, however, did not seem to offend or mortify his fair companion in the least, for on their breaking up the conference soon afterwards, and moving different ways, Mrs. Jennings very plainly heard Elinor say, and with a voice which shewed her to feel what she said,

"I shall always think myself very much obliged to you."

Mrs. Jennings was delighted with her gratitude, and only wondered, that after hearing such a sentence, the Colonel should be able to take leave of them, as he immediately did, with the utmost sang-froid, and go away without making her any reply!—She had not thought her old friend could have made so indifferent a suitor.

What had really passed between them was to this effect.

"I have heard," said he, with great compassion, "of the injustice your friend Mr. Ferrars has suffered from his family; for if I understand the matter right, he has been entirely cast off by them for persevering in his engagement with a very deserving young woman—Have I been rightly informed?—Is it so?"—

Elinor told him that it was.

"The cruelty, the impolitic cruelty,"—he replied, with great feeling—"of dividing, or attempting to divide, two young people long attached to each other, is terrible—Mrs. Ferrars does not know what she may be doing—what she may drive her son to. I have seen Mr. Ferrars* two or three times in Harley-street, and am much pleased with him. He is not a young man with whom one can be intimately acquainted in a short time, but I have seen enough of him to wish him well for his own sake, and as a friend of yours, I wish it still more. I understand that he intends to take orders. Will you be so good as to tell him that the living of Delaford, now just vacant, as I am informed by this day's post, is his, if he think it

---

* Mr. Ferrars] Mr. Edward Ferrars A. Austen *evidently did not want to call attention at this point to the possibility of mistaking one Ferrars brother for the other.*

worth his acceptance—but *that*, perhaps, so unfortunately circumstanced as he is now, it may be nonsense to appear to doubt, I only wish it were more valuable.—It is a rectory, but a small one; the late incumbent, I believe, did not make more than 200*l*. per annum, and though it is certainly capable of improvement, I fear, not to such an amount as to afford him a very comfortable income. Such as it is, however, my pleasure in presenting him to it, will be very great. Pray assure him of it."

Elinor's astonishment at this commission could hardly have been greater, had the Colonel been really making her an offer of his hand. The preferment, which only two days before she had considered as hopeless for Edward, was already provided to enable him to marry;—and *she*, of all people in the world, was fixed on to bestow it!—Her emotion was such as Mrs. Jennings had attributed to a very different cause;—but whatever minor feelings less pure, less pleasing, might have a share in that emotion, her esteem for the general benevolence, and her gratitude for the particular friendship, which together prompted Colonel Brandon to this act, were strongly felt, and warmly expressed. She thanked him for it with all her heart, spoke of Edward's principles and disposition with that praise which she knew them to deserve; and promised to undertake the commission with pleasure, if it were really his wish to put off so agreeable an office to another. But at the same time, she could not help thinking that no one could so well perform it as himself. It was an office in short, from which, unwilling to give Edward the pain of receiving an obligation from *her*, she would have been very glad to be spared herself;—but Colonel Brandon, on motives of equal delicacy, declining it likewise, still seemed so desirous of its being given through her means, that she would not on any account make farther opposition. Edward, she believed, was still in town, and fortunately she had heard his address from Miss Steele. She could undertake therefore to inform him of it, in the course of the day. After this had been settled, Colonel Brandon began to talk of his own advantage in securing so respectable and agreeable a neighbour, and *then* it was that he mentioned with regret, that the house was small and indifferent;—an evil which Elinor, as Mrs. Jennings had supposed her to do, made very light of, at least as far as regarded its size.

"The smallness of the house," said she, "I cannot imagine any inconvenience to them, for it will be in proportion to their family and income."

By which the Colonel was surprised to find that *she* was considering Mr. Ferrars's marriage* as the certain consequence of the

---

* Mr. Ferrar's marriage] their marriage A.

presentation; for he did not suppose it possible that Delaford living could supply such an income, as any body in his style* of life would venture to settle on—and he said so.

"This little rectory *can* do no more than make Mr. Ferrars comfortable as a bachelor; it cannot enable him to marry. I am sorry to say that my patronage ends with this; and my interest[1] is hardly more extensive. If, however, by any unforeseen chance it should be in my power to serve him farther, I must think very differently of him from what I now do, if I am not as ready to be useful to him then, as I sincerely wish I could be at present. What I am now doing indeed, seems nothing at all, since it can advance him so little towards what must be his principal, his only object of happiness. His marriage must still be a distant good;—at least, I am afraid it cannot take place very soon.—"

Such was the sentence which, when misunderstood, so justly offended the delicate feelings of Mrs. Jennings; but after this narration of what really passed between Colonel Brandon and Elinor, while they stood at the window, the gratitude expressed by the latter on their parting, may perhaps appear in general, not less reasonably excited, nor less properly worded than if it had arisen from an offer of marriage.

Chapter IV.

"Well, Miss Dashwood," said Mrs. Jennings, sagaciously smiling, as soon as the gentleman had withdrawn, "I do not ask you what the Colonel has been saying to you; for though, upon my honour, I *tried* to keep out of hearing, I could not help catching enough to understand his business. And I assure you I never was better pleased in my life, and I wish you joy of it with all my heart."

"Thank you, ma'am," said Elinor. "It *is* a matter of great joy to me; and I feel the goodness of Colonel Brandon most sensibly. There are not many men who would act as he has done. Few people who have so compassionate an heart! I never was more astonished in my life."

"Lord! my dear, you are very modest! I an't the least astonished at it in the world, for I have often thought of late, there was nothing more likely to happen."

"You judged from your knowledge of the Colonel's general benevolence; but at least you could not foresee that the opportunity would so very soon occur."

---

* his style] their stile A.
1. Influence, patronage.

"Opportunity!" repeated Mrs. Jennings—"Oh! as to that, when a man has once made up his mind to such a thing, somehow or other he will soon find an opportunity. Well, my dear, I wish you joy of it again and again; and if ever there was a happy couple in the world, I think I shall soon know where to look for them."

"You mean to go to Delaford after them I suppose," said Elinor, with a faint smile.

"Aye, my dear, that I do, indeed. And as to the house being a bad one, I do not know what the Colonel would be at, for it is as good a one as ever I saw."

"He spoke of its being out of repair."

"Well, and whose fault is that? why don't he repair it?—who should do it but himself?"

They were interrupted by the servant's coming in, to announce the carriage* being at the door; and Mrs. Jennings immediately preparing to go, said—

"Well, my dear, I must be gone before I have had half my talk out. But, however, we may have it all over in the evening, for we shall be quite alone. I do not ask you to go with me, for I dare say your mind is too full of the matter to care for company; and besides, you must long to tell your sister all about it."

Marianne had left the room before the conversation began.

"Certainly, ma'am, I shall tell Marianne of it; but I shall not mention it at present to any body else."

"Oh! very well," said Mrs. Jennings rather disappointed. "Then you would not have me tell it Lucy, for I think of going as far as Holborn to-day."

"No, ma'am, not even Lucy if you please. One day's delay will not be very material; and till I have written to Mr. Ferrars, I think it ought not to be mentioned to any body else. I shall do *that* directly. It is of importance that no time should be lost with him, for he will of course have much to do relative to his ordination."

This speech at first puzzled Mrs. Jennings exceedingly. Why Mr. Ferrars was to be written to about it in such a hurry, she could not immediately comprehend. A few moments' reflection, however, produced a very happy idea, and she exclaimed;—

"Oh ho!—I understand you. Mr. Ferrars is to be the man. Well, so much the better for him. Aye, to be sure, he must be ordained in readiness; and I am very glad to find things are so forward between you. But, my dear, is not this rather out of character? Should not the Colonel write himself?—sure, he is the proper person."

---

* carriage] chariot A. Earlier, Mrs. Jennings's conveyance is twice described as a chaise and once as a chariot. Carriage for chariot is more likely to be Austen's revision than a printer's error, and it is possible that Austen forgot to revise the earlier instance.

Elinor did not quite understand the beginning of Mrs. Jennings's speech; neither did she think it worth inquiring into; and therefore only replied to its conclusion.

"Colonel Brandon is so delicate a man, that he rather wished any one to announce his intentions to Mr. Ferrars than himself."

"And so *you* are forced to do it. Well, *that* is an odd kind of delicacy! However, I will not disturb you (seeing her preparing to write.) You know your own concerns best. So good bye, my dear. I have not heard of any thing to please me so well since Charlotte was brought to bed."

And away she went; but returning again in a moment,

"I have just been thinking of Betty's sister, my dear. I should be very glad to get her so good a mistress. But whether she would do for a lady's maid, I am sure I can't tell. She is an excellent house-maid, and works very well at her needle. However, you will think of all that at your leisure."

"Certainly, ma'am," replied Elinor, not hearing much of what she said, and more anxious to be alone, than to be mistress of the subject.

How she should begin—how she should express herself in her note to Edward, was now all her concern. The particular circumstances between them made a difficulty of that which to any other person would have been the easiest thing in the world; but she equally feared to say too much or too little, and sat deliberating over her paper, with the pen in her hand, till broken in on by the entrance of Edward himself.

He had met Mrs. Jennings at the door in her way to the carriage, as he came to leave his farewell card; and she, after apologising for not returning herself, had obliged him to enter, by saying that Miss Dashwood was above, and wanted to speak with him on very particular business.

Elinor had just been congratulating herself, in the midst of her perplexity, that however difficult it might be to express herself properly by letter, it was at least preferable to giving the information by word of mouth, when her visitor entered, to force her upon this greatest exertion of all. Her astonishment and confusion were very great on his so sudden appearance. She had not seen him before since his engagement became public, and therefore not since his knowing her to be acquainted with it; which, with the consciousness of what she had been thinking of, and what she had to tell him, made her feel particularly uncomfortable for some minutes. He too was much distressed, and they sat down together in a most promising state of embarrassment.—Whether he had asked her pardon for his intrusion on first coming into the room, he could not recollect; but determining to be on the safe side, he made his apology in form as soon as he could say any thing, after taking a chair. "Mrs. Jennings told me," said he, "that you wished to speak with me, at least I understood her so—or I certainly should not have intruded on you in such a manner; though at the same time, I should have been extremely sorry to leave London without seeing you and your sister; especially as it will most likely be some time— it is not probable that I should soon have the pleasure of meeting you again. I go to Oxford to-morrow."

"You would not have gone, however," said Elinor recovering herself, and determined to get over what she so much dreaded as soon as possible, "without receiving our good wishes, even if we had not been able to give them in person. Mrs. Jennings was quite right in what she said. I have something of consequence to inform you of, which I was on the point of communicating by paper. I am charged with a most agreeable office, (breathing rather faster than usual as she spoke.) Colonel Brandon, who was here only ten minutes ago, has desired me to say that, understanding you mean to take orders, he has great pleasure in offering you the living of Delaford, now just vacant, and only wishes it were more valuable. Allow me to congratulate you on having so respectable and well-judging a friend, and to join in his wish that the living—it is about two hundred a-year—were much more considerable, and such as might better enable you to—as might be more than a temporary accommodation to yourself—such in short, as might establish all your views of happiness."

What Edward felt, as he could not say it himself, it cannot be expected that any one else should say for him.* He *looked* all the astonishment which such unexpected, such** unthought-of information could not fail of exciting; but he said only these two words, "Colonel Brandon!"

"Yes," continued Elinor, gathering more resolution, as some of the worst was over; "Colonel Brandon means it as a testimony of his concern for what has lately passed—for the cruel situation in which the unjustifiable conduct of your family has placed you—a concern which I am sure Marianne, myself, and all your friends must share; and likewise as a proof of his high esteem for your general character, and his particular approbation of your behaviour on the present occasion."

"Colonel Brandon give *me* a living!—Can it be possible?"

"The unkindness of your own relations has made you astonished to find friendship any where."

"No," replied he, with sudden consciousness, "not to find it in

---

* say for him.] say it for him. A.
** such] which such A.

you; for I cannot be ignorant that to you, to your goodness I owe it all.—I feel it—I would express it if I could—but, as you well know, I am no orator."

"You are very much mistaken. I do assure you that you owe it entirely, at least almost entirely, to your own merit, and Colonel Brandon's discernment of it. I have had no hand in it. I did not even know, till I understood his design, that the living was vacant; nor had it ever occurred to me that he might have had such a living in his gift. As a friend of mine, of my family, he may perhaps— indeed I know he *has*, still greater pleasure in bestowing it; but, upon my word, you owe nothing to my solicitation."

Truth obliged her to acknowledge some small share in the action, but she was at the same time so unwilling to appear as the bene-factress of Edward, that she acknowledged it with hesitation; which probably contributed to fix that suspicion in his mind which had recently entered it. For a short time he sat deep in thought, after Elinor had ceased to speak;—at last, and as if it were rather an effort, he said,

"Colonel Brandon seems a man of great worth and respectability. I have always heard him spoken of as such, and your brother I know esteems him highly. He is undoubtedly a sensible man, and in his manners perfectly the gentleman."

"Indeed," replied Elinor, "I believe that you will find him, on farther acquaintance, all that you have heard him to be; and as you will be such very near neighbours, (for I understand the parsonage is almost close to the mansion-house,) it is particularly important that he *should* be all this."

Edward made no answer; but when she had turned away her head, gave her a look so serious, so earnest, so uncheerful, as seemed to say, that he might hereafter wish the distance between the parsonage and the mansion-house much greater.

"Colonel Brandon, I think, lodges in St. James's-street," said he, soon afterwards, rising from his chair.

Elinor told him the number of the house.

"I must hurry away then, to give him those thanks which you will not allow me to give *you*; to assure him that he has made me a very—an exceedingly happy man."

Elinor did not offer to detain him; and they parted, with a very earnest assurance on *her* side of her unceasing good wishes for his happiness in every change of situation that might befal him; on *his*, with rather an attempt to return the same good will, than the power of expressing it.

"When I see him again," said Elinor to herself, as the door shut him out, "I shall see him the husband of Lucy."

And with this pleasing anticipation, she sat down to re-consider the past, recal the words and endeavour to comprehend all the feelings of Edward; and, of course, to reflect on her own with discontent.

When Mrs. Jennings came home, though she returned from seeing people whom she had never seen before, and of whom therefore she must have a great deal to say, her mind was so much more occupied by the important secret in her possession, than by anything else, that she reverted to it again as soon as Elinor appeared.

"Well, my dear," she cried, "I sent you up the young man. Did not I do right?—And I suppose you had no great difficulty—You did not find him very unwilling to accept your proposal?"

"No, ma'am; *that* was not very likely."

"Well, and how soon will he be ready?—For it seems all to depend upon that."

"Really," said Elinor, "I know so little of these kind of forms, that I can hardly even conjecture as to the time, or the preparation necessary; but I suppose two or three months will complete his ordination."

"Two or three months!" cried Mrs. Jennings; "Lord! my dear, how calmly you talk of it; and can the Colonel wait two or three months! Lord bless me!—I am sure it would put *me* quite out of patience! —And though one would be very glad to do a kindness by poor Mr. Ferrars, I do think it is not worth while to wait two or three months for him. Sure, somebody else might be found that would do as well; somebody that is in orders already."

"My dear ma'am," said Elinor "what can you be thinking of?— Why, Colonel Brandon's only object is to be of use to Mr. Ferrars."

"Lord bless you, my dear!—Sure you do not mean to persuade me that the Colonel only marries you for the sake of giving ten guineas to Mr. Ferrars!"

The deception could not continue after this; and an explanation immediately took place, by which both gained considerable amusement for the moment, without any material loss of happiness to either, for Mrs. Jennings only exchanged one form of delight for another, and still without forfeiting her expectation of the first.

"Aye, aye, the parsonage is but a small one," said she, after the first ebullition of surprise and satisfaction was over, "and very likely *may* be out of repair; but to hear a man apologising, as I thought, for a house that to my knowledge has five sitting rooms on the ground-floor, and I think the housekeeper told me, could make up fifteen beds!—and to you too, that had been used to live in Barton cottage!—It seemed quite ridiculous. But, my dear, we must touch up the Colonel to do something to the parsonage, and make it comfortable for them, before Lucy goes to it."

"But Colonel Brandon does not seem to have any idea of the living's being enough to allow them to marry."

"The Colonel is a ninny, my dear; because he has two thousand a-year himself, he thinks that nobody else can marry on less. Take my word for it, that, if I am alive, I shall be paying a visit at Delaford Parsonage before Michaelmas; and I am sure I sha'nt go if Lucy an't there."

Elinor was quite of her opinion, as to the probability of their not waiting for any thing more.

Chapter V.

Edward, having carried his thanks to Colonel Brandon, proceeded with his happiness to Lucy; and such was the excess of it by the time he reached Bartlett's Buildings, that she was able to assure Mrs. Jennings, who called on her again the next day with her congratulations, that she had never seen him in such spirits before in her life.

Her own happiness, and her own spirits, were at least very certain; and she joined Mrs. Jennings most heartily in her expectation of their being all comfortably together in Delaford Parsonage before Michaelmas. So far was she, at the same time, from any backwardness to give Elinor that credit which Edward *would* give her, that she spoke of her friendship for them both with the most grateful warmth, was ready to own all their obligation to her, and openly declared that no exertion for their good on Miss Dashwood's part, either present or future, would ever surprise her, for she believed her capable of doing anything in the world for those she really valued. As for Colonel Brandon, she was not only ready to worship him as a saint, but was moreover truly anxious that he should be treated as one in all worldly concerns; anxious that his tythes[1] should be raised to the utmost; and secretly resolved to avail herself, at Delaford, as far as she possibly could, of his servants, his carriage, his cows, and his poultry.

It was now above a week since John Dashwood had called in Berkeley-street, and as since that time no notice had been taken by them of his wife's indisposition, beyond one verbal inquiry, Elinor began to feel it necessary to pay her a visit.—This was an obligation, however, which not only opposed her own inclination, but which

---

1. The local parish clergyman was entitled to up to one-tenth of each farmer's produce each year. As rector, Edward would be entitled to a full portion of "great" tithes, a considerable benefit.

had not the assistance of any encouragement from her companions. Marianne, not contented with absolutely refusing to go herself, was very urgent to prevent her sister's going at all; and Mrs. Jennings, though her carriage was always at Elinor's service, so very much disliked Mrs. John Dashwood, that not even her curiosity to see how she looked after the late discovery, nor her strong desire to affront her by taking Edward's part, could overcome her unwillingness to be in her company again. The consequence was, that Elinor set out by herself to pay a visit, for which no one could really have less inclination, and to run the risk of a tête-à-tête with a woman, whom neither of the others had so much reason to dislike.

Mrs. Dashwood was denied;[2] but before the carriage could turn from the house, her husband accidentally came out. He expressed great pleasure in meeting Elinor, told her that he had been just going to call in Berkeley-street, and assuring her that Fanny would be very glad to see her, invited her to come in.

They walked up stairs into the drawing-room.—Nobody was there.

"Fanny is in her own room, I suppose," said he;—"I will go to her presently, for I am sure she will not have the least objection in the world to seeing *you*.—Very far from it indeed. *Now* especially there cannot be—but however, you and Marianne were always great favourites.—Why would not Marianne come?"—

Elinor made what excuse she could for her.

"I am not sorry to see you alone," he replied, "for I have a good deal to say to you. This living of Colonel Brandon's—can it be true?—has he really given it to Edward?—I heard it yesterday by chance, and was coming to you on purpose to inquire farther about it."

"It is perfectly true.—Colonel Brandon has given the living of Delaford to Edward."

"Really!—Well, this is very astonishing!—no relationship!—no connection between them!—and now that livings fetch such a price![3]—what was the value of this?"

"About two hundred a-year."

"Very well—and for the next presentation to a living of that value—supposing the late incumbent to have been old and sickly,

2. When gentlemen or ladies of the house did not wish to see the guest who had called to visit, they instructed a servant to inform him or her that they were not at home. This common stratagem of politeness was the subject of considerable controversy in the eighteenth and early nineteenth centuries.

3. See p. 107, n. 1. In most country churches, landowners had the right to present livings to clergymen, and often did so to younger sons or to relations. When they did not patronize relations by giving them a living, they could make money by selling the living. With the narrow-mindedness typical of him, John Dashwood is astonished that Colonel Brandon was not motivated by a desire for personal profit.

and likely to vacate it soon—he might have got I dare say—fourteen hundred pounds. And how came he not to have settled that matter before this person's death?—*Now* indeed it would be too late to sell it, but a man of Colonel Brandon's sense!—I wonder he should be so improvident in a point of such common, such natural, concern!—Well, I am convinced that there is a vast deal of inconsistency in almost every human character. I suppose, however—on recollection—that the case may probably be *this*. Edward is only to hold the living till the person to whom the Colonel has really sold the presentation, is old enough to take it.—Aye, aye, that is the fact, depend upon it."

Elinor contradicted it, however, very positively; and by relating that she had herself been employed in conveying the offer from Colonel Brandon to Edward, and therefore must understand the terms on which it was given, obliged him to submit to her authority.

"It is truly astonishing!"—he cried, after hearing what she said —"what could be the Colonel's motive?"

"A very simple one—to be of use to Mr. Ferrars."

"Well, well; whatever Colonel Brandon may be, Edward is a very lucky man!—You will not mention the matter to Fanny, however, for though I have broke it to her, and she bears it vastly well,—she will not like to hear it much talked of."

Elinor had some difficulty here to refrain from observing, that she thought Fanny might have borne with composure, an acquisition of wealth to her brother, by which neither she nor her child could be possibly impoverished.

"Mrs. Ferrars," added he, lowering his voice to the tone becoming so important a subject, "knows nothing about it at present, and I believe it will be best to keep it entirely concealed from her as long as may be—When the marriage takes place, I fear she must hear of it all."

"But why should such precaution be used?—Though it is not to be supposed that Mrs. Ferrars can have the smallest satisfaction in knowing that her son has money enough to live upon,—for *that* must be quite out of the question; yet why, after her late behaviour, is she supposed to feel at all?—she has done with her son, she has cast him off for ever, and has made all those over whom she had any influence, cast him off likewise. Surely, after doing so, she cannot be imagined liable to any impression of sorrow or of joy on his account—she cannot be interested in any thing that befalls him.— She would not be so weak as to throw away the comfort of a child, and yet retain the anxiety of a parent!"

"Ah! Elinor," said John, "your reasoning is very good, but it is founded on ignorance of human nature. When Edward's unhappy match takes place, depend upon it his mother will feel as much as if she had never discarded him; and therefore every circumstance that may accelerate that dreadful event, must be concealed from her as much as possible. Mrs. Ferrars can never forget that Edward is her son."

"You surprise me; I should think it must nearly have escaped her memory by *this* time."

"You wrong her exceedingly. Mrs. Ferrars is one of the most affectionate mothers in the world."

Elinor was silent.

"We think *now*"—said Mr. Dashwood, after a short pause, "of *Robert's* marrying Miss Morton."

Elinor, smiling at the grave and decisive importance of her brother's tone, calmly replied,

"The lady, I suppose, has no choice in the affair."

"Choice!—how do you mean?"—

"I only mean, that I suppose from your manner of speaking, it must be the same to Miss Morton whether she marry Edward or Robert."

"Certainly, there can be no difference; for Robert will now to all intents and purposes be considered as the eldest son;—and as to any thing else, they are both very agreeable young men, I do not know that one is superior to the other."

Elinor said no more, and John was also for a short time silent.— His reflections ended thus.

"Of *one* thing, my dear sister," kindly taking her hand, and speaking in an awful whisper—"I may assure you;—and I *will* do it, because I know it must gratify you. I have good reason to think— indeed I have it from the best authority, or I should not repeat it, for otherwise it would be very wrong to say any thing about it—but I have it from the very best authority—not that I ever precisely heard Mrs. Ferrars say it herself—but her daughter *did*, and I have it from her—That in short, whatever objections there might be against a certain—a certain connection—you understand me—it would have been far preferable to her, it would not have given her half the vexation that *this* does. I was exceedingly pleased to hear that Mrs. Ferrars considered it in that light—a very gratifying circumstance you know to us all. 'It would have been beyond comparison,' she said, 'the least evil of the two, and she would be glad to compound *now* for nothing worse.' But however, all that is quite out of the question—not to be thought of or mentioned—as to any attachment you know—it never could be—all that is gone by. But I thought I would just tell you of this, because I knew how much it must please you. Not that you have any reason to regret, my dear Elinor. There is no doubt of your doing exceedingly well—quite as well, or better, perhaps, all things considered. Has Colonel Brandon been with you lately?"

Elinor had heard enough, if not to gratify her vanity, and raise her self-importance, to agitate her nerves and fill her mind;—and she was therefore glad to be spared from the necessity of saying much in reply herself, and from the danger of hearing any thing more from her brother, by the entrance of Mr. Robert Ferrars. After a few moments' chat, John Dashwood, recollecting that Fanny was yet uninformed of his sister's being there, quitted the room in quest of her; and Elinor was left to improve her acquaintance with Robert, who, by the gay unconcern, the happy self-complacency of his manner while enjoying so unfair a division of his mother's love and liberality, to the prejudice of his banished brother, earned only by his own dissipated course of life, and that brother's integrity, was confirming her most unfavourable opinion of his head and heart.

They had scarcely been two minutes by themselves, before he began to speak of Edward; for he too had heard of the living, and was very inquisitive on the subject. Elinor repeated the particulars of it, as she had given them to John; and their effect on Robert, though very different, was not less striking than it had been on *him*. He laughed most immoderately. The idea of Edward's being a clergyman, and living in a small parsonage-house, diverted him beyond measure;—and when to that was added the fanciful imagery of Edward reading prayers in a white surplice, and publishing the banns of marriage between John Smith and Mary Brown, he could conceive nothing more ridiculous.

Elinor, while she waited in silence, and immovable gravity, the conclusion of such folly, could not restrain her eyes from being fixed on him with a look that spoke all the contempt it excited. It was a look, however, very well bestowed, for it relieved her own feelings, and gave no intelligence to him. He was recalled from wit to wisdom, not by any reproof of her's, but by his own sensibility.

"We may treat it as a joke," said he at last, recovering from the affected laugh which had considerably lengthened out the genuine gaiety of the moment—"but upon my soul, it is a most serious business. Poor Edward! he is ruined for ever. I am extremely sorry for it—for I know him to be a very good-hearted creature; as well-meaning a fellow perhaps, as any in the world. You must not judge of him, Miss Dashwood, from *your* slight acquaintance.—Poor Edward!——His manners are certainly not the happiest in nature.—But we are not all born, you know, with the same powers—the same address.—Poor fellow!—to see him in a circle of strangers!—to be sure it was pitiable enough!—but, upon my soul, I believe he has as good a heart as any in the kingdom; and I declare and protest to you I never was so shocked in my life, as when it all burst forth. I could not believe it.—My mother was the first person who told me of it, and I, feeling myself called on to act with resolution, immediately said to her, 'My dear madam, I do not know what you may intend to do on the occasion, but as for myself, I must say, that if Edward does marry this young woman, *I* never will see him again.' That was what I said immediately,—I was most uncommonly shocked indeed!—Poor Edward!—he has done for himself completely—shut himself out for ever from all decent society!—but, as I directly said to my mother, I am not in the least surprised at it; from his style of education it was always to be expected. My poor mother was half frantic."

"Have you ever seen the lady?"

"Yes; once, while she was staying in this house, I happened to drop in for ten minutes; and I saw quite enough of her. The merest awkward country girl, without style, or elegance, and almost without beauty—I remember her perfectly. Just the kind of girl I should suppose likely to captivate poor Edward. I offered immediately, as soon as my mother related the affair to me, to talk to him myself, and dissuade him from the match; but it was too late *then*, I found, to do any thing, for unluckily, I was not in the way at first, and knew nothing of it till after the breach had taken place, when it was not for me, you know, to interfere. But had I been informed of it a few hours earlier—I think it is most probable—that something might have been hit on. I certainly should have represented it to Edward in a very strong light. 'My dear fellow,' I should have said, 'consider what you are doing. You are making a most disgraceful connection, and such a one as your family are unanimous in disapproving.' I cannot help thinking, in short, that means might have been found. But now it is all too late. He must be starved, you know;—that is certain; absolutely starved."

He had just settled this point with great composure, when the entrance of Mrs. John Dashwood put an end to the subject. But though *she* never spoke of it out of her own family, Elinor could see its influence on her mind, in the something like confusion of countenance with which she entered, and an attempt at cordiality in her behaviour to herself. She even proceeded so far as to be concerned to find that Elinor and her sister were so soon to leave town, as she had hoped to see more of them;—an exertion in which her husband, who attended her into the room, and hung enamoured over her accents, seemed to distinguish every thing that was most affectionate and graceful.

Chapter VI.

One other short call in Harley-street,* in which Elinor received her brother's congratulations on their travelling so far towards Barton without any expense, and on Colonel Brandon's being to follow them to Cleveland in a day or two, completed the intercourse of the brother and sisters in town;—and a faint invitation from Fanny, to come to Norland whenever it should happen to be in their way, which of all things was the most unlikely to occur, with a more warm, though less public, assurance, from John to Elinor, of the promptitude with which he should come to see her at Delaford, was all that foretold any meeting in the country.

It amused her to observe that all her friends seemed determined to send her to Delaford;—a place, in which, of all others, she would now least chuse to visit, or wish to reside; for not only was it considered as her future home by her brother and Mrs. Jennings, but even Lucy, when they parted, gave her a pressing invitation to visit her there.

Very early in April, and tolerably early in the day, the two parties from Hanover-square and Berkeley-street set out from their respective homes, to meet, by appointment, on the road. For the convenience of Charlotte and her child, they were to be more than two days on their journey, and Mr. Palmer, travelling more expeditiously with Colonel Brandon, was to join them at Cleveland soon after their arrival.

Marianne, few as had been her hours of comfort in London, and eager as she had long been to quit it, could not, when it came to the point, bid adieu to the house in which she had for the last time enjoyed those hopes, and that confidence, in Willoughby, which were now extinguished for ever, without great pain. Nor could she leave the place in which Willoughby remained, busy in new engagements, and new schemes, in which *she* could have no share, without shedding many tears.

Elinor's satisfaction at the moment of removal, was more positive. She had no such object for her lingering thoughts to fix on, she left no creature behind, from whom it would give her a moment's regret to be divided for ever, she was pleased to be free herself from the persecution of Lucy's friendship, she was grateful for bringing her sister away unseen by Willoughby since his marriage, and she looked forward with hope to what a few months of tranquility at

---

* One other short call in Harley-street,] One other call in Harley-street, a short and take-leave call, A.

Barton might do towards restoring Marianne's peace of mind, and confirming her own.

Their journey was safely performed. The second day brought them into the cherished, or the prohibited, county of Somerset, for as such was it dwelt on by turns in Marianne's imagination; and in the forenoon of the third they drove up to Cleveland.

Cleveland was a spacious, modern-built house, situated on a sloping lawn. It had no park,[1] but the pleasure-grounds[2] were tolerably extensive; and like every other place of the same degree of importance, it had its open shrubbery, and closer wood walk, a road of smooth gravel winding round a plantation, led to the front, the lawn was dotted over with timber, the house itself was under the guardianship of the fir, the mountain-ash, and the acacia, and a thick screen of them altogether, interspersed with tall Lombardy poplars, shut out the offices.

Marianne entered the house with an heart swelling with emotion from the consciousness of being only eighty miles from Barton, and not thirty from Combe Magna; and before she had been five minutes within its walls, while the others were busily helping Charlotte shew her child to the house-keeper, she quitted it again, stealing away through the winding shrubberies, now just beginning to be in beauty, to gain a distant eminence; where, from its Grecian temple,[3] her eye, wandering over a wide tract of country to the south-east, could fondly rest on the farthest ridge of hills in the horizon, and fancy that from their summits Combe Magna might be seen.

In such moments of precious, of invaluable misery, she rejoiced in tears of agony to be at Cleveland; and as she returned by a different circuit to the house, feeling all the happy privilege of country liberty, of wandering from place to place in free and luxurious solitude, she resolved to spend almost every hour of every day while she remained with the Palmers, in the indulgence of such solitary rambles.

She returned just in time to join the others as they quitted the house, on an excursion through its more immediate premises; and the rest of the morning was easily whiled away, in lounging round the kitchen garden, examining the bloom upon its walls, and listening to the gardener's lamentations upon blights,—in dawdling through the green-house, where the loss of her favourite plants,

1. A closed-in, often very large landscaped area around a country estate, sometimes with grazing animals such as sheep and deer, maintained for the view it afforded rather than for farming.
2. Defined by the *OED* as "A ground or piece of land laid out or ornamented for purposes of pleasure or amusement, or naturally adapted to such use."
3. Replicas of Greek architecture were a common feature in landscape design during this period.

unwarily exposed, and nipped by the lingering frost, raised the laughter of Charlotte,—and in visiting her poultry-yard, where, in the disappointed hopes of her dairy-maid, by hens forsaking their nests, or being stolen by a fox, or in the rapid decease of a promising young brood, she found fresh sources of merriment.

The morning was fine and dry, and Marianne, in her plan of employment abroad, had not calculated for any change of weather during their stay at Cleveland. With great surprise therefore, did she find herself prevented by a settled rain from going out again after dinner. She had depended on a twilight walk to the Grecian temple, and perhaps all over the grounds, and an evening merely cold or damp would not have deterred her from it; but an heavy and settled rain even *she* could not fancy dry or pleasant weather for walking.

Their party was small, and the hours passed quietly away. Mrs. Palmer had her* child, and Mrs. Jennings her carpet-work; they talked of the friends they had left behind, arranged Lady Middleton's engagements, and wondered whether Mr. Palmer and Colonel Brandon would get farther than Reading that night. Elinor, however little concerned in it, joined in their discourse, and Marianne, who had the knack of finding her way in every house to the library, however it might be avoided by the family in general, soon procured herself a book.

Nothing was wanting on Mrs. Palmer's side that constant and friendly good-humour could do, to make them feel themselves welcome. The openness and heartiness of her manner, more than atoned for that want of recollection and elegance, which made her often deficient in the forms of politeness; her kindness, recommended by so pretty a face, was engaging; her folly, though evident, was not disgusting, because it was not conceited; and Elinor could have forgiven every thing but her laugh.

The two gentlemen arrived the next day to a very late dinner, affording a pleasant enlargement of the party, and a very welcome variety to their conversation, which a long morning of the same continued rain had reduced very low.

Elinor had seen so little of Mr. Palmer, and in that little had seen so much variety in his address to her sister and herself, that she knew not what to expect to find him in his own family. She found him, however, perfectly the gentleman in his behaviour to all his visitors, and only occasionally rude to his wife and her mother; she found him very capable of being a pleasant companion, and only prevented from being so always, by too great an aptitude to fancy himself as much superior to people in general, as he must feel

* her] the A.

himself to be to Mrs. Jennings and Charlotte. For the rest of his character and habits, they were marked, as far as Elinor could perceive, with no traits at all unusual in his sex and time of life. He was nice in his eating, uncertain in his hours; fond of his child, though affecting to slight it; and idled away the mornings at billiards, which ought to have been devoted to business. She liked him, however, upon the whole much better than she had expected, and in her heart was not sorry that she could like him no more;— not sorry to be driven by the observation of his Epicurism, his selfishness, and his conceit, to rest with complacency on the remembrance of Edward's generous temper, simple taste, and diffident feelings.

Of Edward, or at least of some of his concerns, she now received intelligence from Colonel Brandon, who had been into Dorsetshire lately; and who, treating her at once as the disinterested friend of Mr. Ferrars, and the kind confidante of himself, talked to her a great deal of the Parsonage at Delaford, described its deficiencies, and told her what he meant to do himself towards removing them.—His behaviour to her in this, as well as in every other particular, his open pleasure in meeting her after an absence of only ten days, his readiness to converse with her, and his deference for her opinion, might very well justify Mrs. Jennings's persuasion of his attachment, and would have been enough, perhaps, had not Elinor still, as from the first, believed Marianne his real favourite, to make her suspect it herself. But as it was, such a notion had scarcely ever entered her head, except by Mrs. Jennings's suggestion; and she could not help believing herself the nicest observer of the two;—she watched his eyes, while Mrs. Jennings thought only of his behaviour;—and while his looks of anxious solicitude on Marianne's feeling, in her head and throat, the beginning of an heavy cold, because unexpressed by words, entirely escaped the latter lady's observation;—*she* could discover in them the quick feelings, and needless alarm of a lover.

Two delightful twilight walks on the third and fourth evenings of her being there, not merely on the dry gravel of the shrubbery, but all over the grounds, and especially in the most distant parts of them, where there was something more of wildness than in the rest, where the trees were the oldest, and the grass was the longest and wettest, had—assisted by the still greater imprudence of sitting in her wet shoes and stockings—given Marianne a cold so violent, as, though for a day or two trifled with or denied, would force itself by increasing ailments, on the concern of every body, and the notice of herself. Prescriptions poured in from all quarters, and as usual, were all declined. Though heavy and feverish, with a pain in her limbs, a cough, and a sore throat, a good night's rest was to cure her entirely; and it was with difficulty that Elinor prevailed on her, when she went to bed, to try one or two of the simplest of the remedies.

Chapter VII.

Marianne got up the next morning at her usual time; to every inquiry replied that she was better, and tried to prove herself so, by engaging in her accustomary employments. But a day spent in sitting shivering over the fire with a book in her hand, which she was unable to read, or in lying, weary and languid, on a sofa, did not speak much in favour of her amendment; and when, at last, she went early to bed, more and more indisposed, Colonel Brandon was only astonished at her sister's composure, who, though attending and nursing her the whole day, against Marianne's inclination, and forcing proper medicines on her at night, trusted, like Marianne, to the certainty and efficacy of sleep, and felt no real alarm.

A very restless and feverish night, however, disappointed the expectation of both; and when Marianne, after persisting in rising, confessed herself unable to sit up, and returned voluntarily to her bed, Elinor was very ready to adopt Mrs. Jennings's advice, of sending for the Palmers' apothecary.

He came, examined his patient, and though encouraging Miss Dashwood to expect that a very few days would restore her sister to health, yet, by pronouncing her disorder to have a putrid tendency, and allowing the word "infection" to pass his lips, gave instant alarm to Mrs. Palmer on her baby's account. Mrs. Jennings, who had been inclined from the first to think Marianne's complaint more serious than Elinor, now looked very grave on Mr. Harris's report, and confirming Charlotte's fears and caution, urged the necessity of her immediate removal with her infant; and Mr. Palmer, though treating their apprehensions as idle, found the anxiety and importunity of his wife too great to be withstood. Her departure therefore was fixed on; and, within an hour after Mr. Harris's arrival, she set off, with her little boy and his nurse, for the house of a near relation of Mr. Palmer's, who lived a few miles on the other side of Bath; whither her husband promised, at her earnest entreaty, to join her in a day or two; and whither she was almost equally urgent with her mother to accompany her. Mrs. Jennings, however, with a kindness of heart which made Elinor really love her, declared her resolution of not stirring from Cleveland as long as Marianne remained ill, and of endeavouring, by her own attentive care, to supply to her the place of the mother she had taken her from; and Elinor found her on every occasion a most willing and active helpmate, desirous to share in all her fatigues, and often by her better experience in nursing, of material use.

Poor Marianne, languid and low from the nature of her malady, and feeling herself universally ill, could no longer hope that to-morrow would find her recovered; and the idea of what to-morrow would have produced, but for this unlucky illness, made every ailment more severe; for on that day they were to have begun their journey home; and, attended the whole way by a servant of Mrs. Jennings, were to have taken their mother by surprise on the following forenoon. The little that she said, was all in lamentation of this inevitable delay; though Elinor tried to raise her spirits, and make her believe, as she *then* really believed herself, that it would be a very short one.

The next day produced little or no alteration in the state of the patient; she certainly was not better, and except that there was no amendment, did not appear worse. Their party was now farther reduced; for Mr. Palmer, though very unwilling to go, as well from real humanity and good-nature, as from a dislike of appearing to be frightened away by his wife, was persuaded at last by Colonel Brandon to perform his promise of following her; and while he was preparing to go, Colonel Brandon himself, with a much greater exertion, began to talk of going likewise.—Here, however, the kindness of Mrs. Jennings interposed most acceptably; for to send the Colonel away while his love was in so much uneasiness on her sister's account, would be to deprive them both, she thought, of every comfort; and therefore telling him at once that his stay at Cleveland was necessary to herself, that she should want him to play at piquet[1] of an evening, while Miss Dashwood was above with her sister, &c. she urged him so strongly to remain, that he, who was gratifying the first wish of his own heart by a compliance, could not long even affect to demur; especially as Mrs. Jennings's entreaty was warmly seconded by Mr. Palmer, who seemed to feel a relief to himself, in leaving behind him a person so well able to assist or advise Miss Dashwood in any emergency.

Marianne was of course kept in ignorance of all these arrangements. She knew not that she had been the means of sending the owners of Cleveland away, in about seven days from the time of their arrival. It gave her no surprise that she saw nothing of Mrs. Palmer; and as it gave her likewise no concern, she never mentioned her name.

---

1. Defined by the *OED* as a card game played by two persons with a pack of thirty-two cards (the low cards from the two to the six being excluded), in which points are scored on various groups or combinations of cards and on tricks. *Piquet* was among the most popular card games of the time and was often played for money in places of fashion, such as Bath.

Two days passed away from the time of Mr. Palmer's departure, and her situation continued, with little variation, the same. Mr. Harris, who attended her every day, still talked boldly of a speedy recovery, and Miss Dashwood was equally sanguine; but the expectation of the others was by no means so cheerful. Mrs. Jennings had determined very early in the seisure that Marianne would never get over it, and Colonel Brandon, who was chiefly of use in listening to Mrs. Jennings's forebodings, was not in a state of mind to resist their influence. He tried to reason himself out of fears, which the different judgment of the apothecary seemed to render absurd; but the many hours of each day in which he was left entirely alone, were but too favourable for the admission of every melancholy idea, and he could not expel from his mind the persuasion that he should see Marianne no more.

On the morning of the third day however, the gloomy anticipations of both were almost done away; for when Mr. Harris arrived, he declared his patient materially better. Her pulse was much stronger, and every symptom more favourable than on the preceding visit. Elinor, confirmed in every pleasant hope, was all cheerfulness; rejoicing that in her letters to her mother, she had pursued her own judgment rather than her friend's, in making very light of the indisposition which delayed them at Cleveland; and almost fixing on the time when Marianne would be able to travel.

But the day did not close so auspiciously as it began.—Towards the evening, Marianne became ill again, growing more heavy, restless, and uncomfortable than before. Her sister, however, still sanguine, was willing to attribute the change to nothing more than the fatigue of having set* up to have her bed made; and carefully administering the cordials prescribed, saw her with satisfaction sink at last into a slumber, from which she expected the most beneficial effects. Her sleep, though not so quiet as Elinor wished to see it, lasted a considerable time; and anxious to observe the result of it herself, she resolved to sit with her during the whole of it. Mrs. Jennings, knowing nothing of any change in the patient, went unusually early to bed; her maid, who was one of the principal nurses, was recreating[2] herself in the housekeeper's room, and Elinor remained alone with Marianne.

The repose of the latter became more and more disturbed; and her sister, who watched with unremitting attention her continual change of posture, and heard the frequent but inarticulate sounds of complaint which passed her lips, was almost wishing to rouse

---

* set] sat A. Compare the textual note on p. 96. *It is difficult to adjudicate among the usages of Austen, her characters, and the typesetters and proofreaders employed by the printer.*

2. Resting, recovering from work or exhaustion.

her from so painful a slumber, when Marianne, suddenly awakened by some accidental noise in the house, started hastily up, and with feverish wildness, cried out—

"Is mama coming?—"

"Not yet," replied the other, concealing her terror, and assisting Marianne to lie down again, "but she will be here, I hope, before it is long. It is a great way, you know, from hence to Barton."

"But she must not go round by London," cried Marianne, in the same hurried manner, "I shall never see her, if she goes by London."

Elinor perceived with alarm that she was not quite herself, and while attempting to soothe her, eagerly felt her pulse. It was lower and quicker than ever!* and Marianne, still talking wildly of mama, her alarm increased so rapidly, as to determine her on sending instantly for Mr. Harris, and dispatching a messenger to Barton for her mother. To consult with Colonel Brandon on the best means of effecting the latter, was a thought which immediately followed the resolution of its performance; and as soon as she had rung up the maid to take her place by her sister, she hastened down to the drawing-room,** where she knew he was generally to be found at a much later hour than the present.

It was no time for hesitation. Her fears and her difficulties were immediately before him. Her fears,*** he had no courage, no confidence to attempt the removal of;—he listened to them in silent despondence;—but her difficulties were instantly obviated, for with a readiness that seemed to speak the occasion, and the service prearranged in his mind, he offered himself as the messenger who should fetch Mrs. Dashwood. Elinor made no resistance that was not easily overcome. She thanked him with brief, though fervent gratitude, and while he went to hurry off his servant with a message to Mr. Harris, and an order for post-horses[3] directly, she wrote a few lines to her mother.

The comfort of such a friend at that moment as Colonel Brandon—of such a companion for her mother,—how gratefully was it felt!—a companion whose judgment would guide, whose attendance must relieve, and whose friendship might soothe her!—as far as the shock of such a summons *could* be lessened to her, his presence, his manners, his assistance, would lessen it.

He, meanwhile, whatever he might feel, acted with all the firmness of a collected mind, made every necessary arrangement with

---

* ever!] ever; A.
** drawing-room,] dining-room, A. *It makes more sense that Brandon would be waiting in the drawing room.*
*** fears,] fear, A.
3. Horses kept at a post-house or inn which travelers could hire. By arranging for post-horses in advance, Colonel Brandon will be able to change horses quickly at stops, and thus to make his journey as fast as possible.

the utmost dispatch, and calculated with exactness the time in which she might look for his return. Not a moment was lost in delay of any kind. The horses arrived even before they were expected, and Colonel Brandon only pressing her hand with a look of solemnity, and a few words spoken too low to reach her ear, hurried into the carriage. It was then about twelve o'clock, and she returned to her sister's apartment to wait for the arrival of the apothecary, and to watch by her the rest of the night. It was a night of almost equal suffering to both. Hour after hour passed away in sleepless pain and delirium on Marianne's side, and in the most cruel anxiety on Elinor's, before Mr. Harris appeared. Her apprehensions once raised, paid by their excess for all her former security; and the servant who sat up with her, for she would not allow Mrs. Jennings to be called, only tortured her more, by hints of what her mistress had always thought.

Marianne's ideas were still, at intervals, fixed incoherently on her mother, and whenever she mentioned her name, it gave a pang to the heart of poor Elinor, who, reproaching herself for having trifled with so many days of illness, and wretched for some immediate relief, fancied that all relief might soon be in vain, that every thing had been delayed too long, and pictured to herself her suffering mother arriving too late to see this darling child, or to see her rational.

She was on the point of sending again for Mr. Harris, or if *he* could not come, for some other advice, when the former—but not till after five o'clock—arrived. His opinion, however, made some little amends for his delay, for though acknowledging a very unexpected and unpleasant alteration in his patient, he would not allow the danger to be material, and talked of the relief which a fresh mode of treatment must procure, with a confidence which, in a lesser degree, was communicated to Elinor. He promised to call again in the course of three or four hours, and left both the patient and her anxious attendant more composed than he had found them.

With strong concern, and with many reproaches for not being called to their aid, did Mrs. Jennings hear in the morning of what had passed. Her former apprehensions, now with greater reason restored, left her no doubt of the event; and though trying to speak comfort to Elinor, her conviction of her sister's danger would not allow her to offer the comfort of hope. Her heart was really grieved. The rapid decay, the early death of a girl so young, so lovely as Marianne, must have struck a less interested person with concern. On Mrs. Jennings's compassion she had other claims. She had been for three months her companion, was still under her care, and she was known to have been greatly injured, and long unhappy. The distress of her sister too, particularly a favourite, was before her;—

and as for their mother, when Mrs. Jennings considered that Marianne might probably be to *her* what Charlotte was to herself, her sympathy in *her* sufferings was very sincere.

Mr. Harris was punctual in his second visit;—but he came to be disappointed in his hopes of what the last would produce. His medicines had failed;—the fever was unabated; and Marianne only more quiet—not more herself—remained in an heavy stupor. Elinor, catching all, and more than all, his fears* in a moment, proposed to call in farther advice. But he judged it unnecessary; he had still something more to try, some fresh application, of whose success he was almost as confident as the last, and his visit concluded with encouraging assurances which reached the ear, but could not enter the heart, of Miss Dashwood. She was calm, except when she thought of her mother, but she was almost hopeless; and in this state she continued till noon, scarcely stirring** from her sister's bed, her thoughts wandering from one image of grief, one suffering friend to another, and her spirits oppressed to the utmost by the conversation of Mrs. Jennings, who scrupled not to attribute the severity and danger of this attack, to the many weeks of previous indisposition which Marianne's disappointment had brought on. Elinor felt all the reasonableness of the idea, and it gave fresh misery to her reflections.

About noon, however, she began—but with a caution—a dread of disappointment, which for some time kept her silent, even to her friend—to fancy, to hope she could perceive a slight amendment in her sister's pulse;—she waited, watched, and examined it again and again;—and at last, with an agitation more difficult to bury under exterior calmness, than all her foregoing distress, ventured to communicate her hopes. Mrs. Jennings, though forced, on examination, to acknowledge a temporary revival, tried to keep her young friend from indulging a thought of its continuance;—and Elinor, conning over every injunction of distrust, told herself likewise not to hope. But it was too late. Hope had already entered; and feeling all its anxious flutter, she bent over her sister to watch— she hardly knew for what. Half an hour passed away, and the favourable symptom yet blessed her. Others even arose to confirm it. Her breath, her skin, her lips, all flattered Elinor with signs of amendment, and Marianne fixed her eyes on her with a rational, though languid, gaze. Anxiety and hope now oppressed her in equal degrees, and left her no moment of tranquillity till the arrival of Mr. Harris at four o'clock,—when his assurances, his felicitations

---

* fears] A; fear B.
** stirring] stirring an inch A.

on a recovery in her sister even surpassing his expectation, gave her confidence, comfort, and tears of joy.

Marianne was in every respect materially better, and he declared her entirely out of danger. Mrs. Jennings, perhaps satisfied with the partial justification of her forebodings which had been found in their late alarm, allowed herself to trust in his judgment, and admitted with unfeigned joy, and soon with unequivocal cheerfulness, the probability of an entire recovery.

Elinor could not be cheerful. Her joy was of a different kind, and led to anything rather than to gaiety. Marianne restored to life, health, friends, and to her doating mother, was an idea to fill her heart with sensations of exquisite comfort, and expand it in fervent gratitude;—but it led to no outward demonstrations of joy, no words, no smiles. All within Elinor's breast was satisfaction, silent and strong.

She continued by the side of her sister with little intermission the whole afternoon, calming every fear, satisfying every inquiry of her enfeebled spirits, supplying every succour, and watching almost every look and every breath. The possibility of a relapse would of course, in some moments, occur to remind her of what anxiety was—but when she saw, on her frequent and minute examination, that every symptom of recovery continued, and saw Marianne at six o'clock sink into a quiet, steady, and to all appearance comfortable, sleep, she silenced every doubt.

The time was now drawing on, when Colonel Brandon might be expected back. At ten o'clock, she trusted, or at least not much later, her mother would be relieved from the dreadful suspense in which she must now be travelling towards them. The Colonel too! —perhaps scarcely less an object of pity!—Oh!—how slow was the progress of time which yet kept them in ignorance!

At seven o'clock, leaving Marianne still sweetly asleep, she joined Mrs. Jennings in the drawing-room to tea. Of breakfast she had been kept by her fears, and of dinner by their sudden reverse, from eating much;—and the present refreshment, therefore, with such feelings of content as she brought to it, was particularly welcome. Mrs. Jennings would have persuaded her at its conclusion to take some rest before her mother's arrival, and allow *her* to take her place by Marianne; but Elinor had no sense of fatigue, no capability of sleep at that moment about her, and she was not to be kept away from her sister an unnecessary instant. Mrs. Jennings therefore attending her up stairs into the sick chamber, to satisfy herself that all continued right, left her there again to her charge and her thoughts, and retired to her own room to write letters and sleep.

The night was cold and stormy. The wind roared round the

house, and the rain beat against the windows; but Elinor, all happiness within, regarded it not. Marianne slept through every blast, and the travellers—they had a rich reward in store, for every present inconvenience.

The clock struck eight. Had it been ten, Elinor would have been convinced that at that moment she heard a carriage driving up to the house; and so strong was the persuasion that she *did*, in spite of the *almost* impossibility of their being already come, that she moved into the adjoining dressing-closet and opened a window-shutter, to be satisfied of the truth. She instantly saw that her ears had not deceived her. The flaring lamps of a carriage were immediately in view. By their uncertain light she thought she could discern it to be drawn by four horses; and this, while it told the excess of her poor mother's alarm, gave some explanation to such unexpected rapidity.

Never in her life had Elinor found it so difficult to be calm, as at that moment. The knowledge of what her mother must be feeling as the carriage stopt at the door,—of her doubt—her dread—perhaps her despair!—and of what *she* had to tell!—with such knowledge it was impossible to be calm. All that remained to be done, was to be speedy; and therefore staying only till she could leave Mrs. Jennings's maid with her sister, she hurried down stairs.

The bustle in the vestibule, as she passed along an inner lobby, assured her that they were already in the house. She rushed forwards towards the drawing-room,—she entered it,—and saw only Willoughby.

Chapter VIII.

Elinor, starting back with a look of horror at the sight of him, obeyed the first impulse of her heart in turning instantly to quit the room, and her hand was already on the lock, when its action was suspended by his hastily advancing, and saying, in a voice rather of command than supplication,

"Miss Dashwood, for half an hour—for ten minutes—I entreat you to stay."

"No, sir," she replied with firmness, "I shall *not* stay. Your business cannot be with *me*. The servants, I suppose, forgot to tell you that Mr. Palmer was not in the house."

"Had they told me," he cried with vehemence, "that Mr. Palmer and all his relations were at the devil, it would not have turned me from the door. My business is with you, and only you."

"With me!"—in the utmost amazement—"well, sir—be quick—and if you can—less violent."

"Sit down, and I will be both."

She hesitated; she knew not what to do. The possibility of Colonel Brandon's arriving and finding him there, came across her. But she had promised to hear him, and her curiosity no less than her honour was engaged. After a moment's recollection, therefore, concluding that prudence required dispatch, and that her acquiescence would best promote it, she walked silently towards the table, and sat down. He took the opposite chair, and for half a minute not a word was said by either.

"Pray be quick, sir"—said Elinor impatiently—"I have no time to spare."

He was sitting in an attitude of deep meditation, and seemed not to hear her.

"Your sister," said he, with abruptness, a moment afterwards— "is out of danger. I heard it from the servant. God be praised!— But is it true?—is it really true?"

Elinor would not speak. He repeated the inquiry with yet greater eagerness.

"For God's sake tell me, is she out of danger, or is she not?"

"We hope she is."

He rose up, and walked across the room.

"Had I known as much half an hour ago—But since I *am* here" —speaking with a forced vivacity as he returned to his seat—"what does it signify?—For once, Miss Dashwood—it will be the last time, perhaps—let us be cheerful together.—I am in a fine mood for gaiety.—Tell me honestly"—a deeper glow overspreading his cheeks—"do you think me most a knave or a fool?"

Elinor looked at him with greater astonishment than ever. She began to think that he must be in liquor;—the strangeness of such a visit, and of such manners, seemed no otherwise intelligible; and with this impression she immediately rose, saying,

"Mr. Willoughby, I advise you at present to return to Combe.— I am not at leisure to remain with you longer.—Whatever your business may be with me, it will be better recollected and explained to-morrow."

"I understand you," he replied, with an expressive smile, and a voice perfectly calm, "yes, I am very drunk. A pint of porter[1] with my cold beef at Marlborough was enough to over-set me."

"At Marlborough!"—cried Elinor, more and more at a loss to understand what he would be at.

"Yes—I left London this morning at eight o'clock, and the only

---

1. A dark brown beer, chiefly drunk by porters and laborers. It is difficult to imagine how Willoughby could be visibly intoxicated if (as he claims) he had drunk only a pint of porter several hours earlier.

ten minutes I have spent out of my chaise since that time, procured me a nuncheon*[2] at Marlborough."

The steadiness of his manner, and the intelligence of his eye as he spoke, convincing Elinor, that whatever other unpardonable folly might bring him to Cleveland, he was not brought there by intoxication, she said, after a moment's recollection,

"Mr. Willoughby, you *ought* to feel, and I certainly *do*—that after what has passed—your coming here in this manner, and forcing yourself upon my notice, requires a very particular excuse.—What is it, that you mean by it?"—

"I mean"—said he, with serious energy—"if I can, to make you hate me one degree less than you do *now*. I mean to offer some kind of explanation, some kind of apology, for the past; to open my whole heart to you, and by convincing you, that though I have been always a blockhead, I have not been always a rascal, to obtain something like forgiveness from Ma—from your sister."

"Is this the real reason of your coming?"

"Upon my soul it is,"—was his answer, with a warmth which brought all the former Willoughby to her remembrance, and in spite of herself made her think him sincere.

"If that is all, you may be satisfied already,—for Marianne *does* —she has *long* forgiven you."

"Has she!"—he cried, in the same eager tone.—"Then she has forgiven me before she ought to have done it. But she shall forgive me again, and on more reasonable grounds.—*Now* will you listen to me?"

Elinor bowed her assent.

"I do not know," said he, after a pause of expectation on her side, and thoughtfulness on his own,—"how *you* may have accounted for my behaviour to your sister, or what diabolical motive you may have imputed to me.—Perhaps you will hardly think the better of me,— it is worth the trial however, and you shall hear every thing. When I first became intimate in your family, I had no other intention, no other view in the acquaintance than to pass my time pleasantly while I was obliged to remain in Devonshire, more pleasantly than I had ever done before. Your sister's lovely person and interesting manners could not but please me; and her behaviour to me almost from the first, was of a kind—It is astonishing, when I reflect on what it was, and what *she* was, that my heart should have been so insensible!—But at first I must confess, my vanity only was elevated by it. Careless of her happiness, thinking only of my own amuse-

---

* nuncheon] noonchine A. *Citing her letter of June 20, 1808, the OED notes Austen's use of* noonshine, *so A is possibly closer to her own speech.*
2. Defined by Johnson as "A piece of victuals eaten between meals."

ment, giving way to feelings which I had always been too much in the habit of indulging, I endeavoured, by every means in my power, to make myself pleasing to her, without any design of returning her affection."

Miss Dashwood at this point, turning her eyes on him with the most angry contempt, stopped him, by saying,

"It is hardly worth while, Mr. Willoughby, for you to relate, or for me to listen any longer. Such a beginning as this cannot be followed by any thing.—Do not let me be pained by hearing any thing more on the subject."

"I insist on your hearing the whole of it," he replied. "My fortune was never large, and I had always been expensive, always in the habit of associating with people of better income than myself. Every year since my coming of age, or even before, I believe, had added to my debts; and though the death of my old cousin, Mrs. Smith, was to set me free; yet that event being uncertain, and possibly far distant, it had been for some time my intention to re-establish my circumstances by marrying a woman of fortune. To attach myself to your sister, therefore, was not a thing to be thought of;—and with a meanness, selfishness, cruelty—which no indignant, no contemptuous look, even of yours, Miss Dashwood, can ever reprobate too much—I was acting in this manner, trying to engage her regard, without a thought of returning it.—But one thing may be said for me, even in that horrid state of selfish vanity, I did not know the extent of the injury I meditated, because I did not *then* know what it was to love. But have I ever known it?—Well may it be doubted; for, had I really loved, could I have sacrificed my feelings to vanity, to avarice?—or, what is more, could I have sacrificed her's?—But I have done it. To avoid a comparative poverty, which her affection and her society would have deprived of all its horrors, I have, by raising myself to affluence, lost every thing that could make it a blessing."

"You did then," said Elinor, a little softened, "believe yourself at one time attached to her."

"To have resisted such attractions, to have withstood such tenderness!—Is there a man on earth who could have done it!— Yes, I found myself, by insensible degrees, sincerely fond of her; and the happiest hours of my life were what I spent with her when I felt my intentions were strictly honourable, and my feelings blameless. Even *then*, however, when fully determined on paying my addresses to her, I allowed myself most improperly to put off, from day to day, the moment of doing it, from an unwillingness to enter into an engagement while my circumstances were so greatly embarrassed. I will not reason here—nor will I stop for *you* to expatiate on the absurdity, and the worse than absurdity, of scrupling to engage my faith where my honour was already bound. The event has proved, that I was a cunning fool, providing with great circumspection for a possible opportunity of making myself contemptible and wretched for ever. At last, however, my resolution was taken, and I had determined, as soon as I could engage her alone, to justify the attentions I had so invariably paid her, and openly assure her of an affection which I had already taken such pains to display.* But in the interim—in the interim of the very few hours that were to pass, before I could have an opportunity of speaking with her in private—a circumstance occurred—an unlucky circumstance, to ruin all my resolution, and with it all my comfort. A discovery took place,"—here he hesitated and looked down.—"Mrs. Smith had somehow or other been informed, I imagine by some distant relation, whose interest it was to deprive me of her favour, of an affair, a connection—but I need not explain myself farther," he added, looking at her with an heightened colour and an inquiring eye,— "your particular intimacy—you have probably heard the whole story long ago."

"I have," returned Elinor, colouring likewise and hardening her heart anew against any compassion for him, "I have heard it all. And how you will explain away any part of your guilt in that dreadful business, I confess is beyond my comprehension."

"Remember," cried Willoughby, "from whom you received the account. Could it be an impartial one? I acknowledge that her situation and her character ought to have been respected by me. I do not mean to justify myself, but at the same time cannot leave you to suppose that I have nothing to urge—that because she was injured she was irreproachable, and because *I* was a libertine, *she* must be a saint. If the violence of her passions,** the weakness of her understanding—I do not mean, however, to defend myself. Her affection for me deserved better treatment, and I often, with great self-reproach, recal the tenderness which, for a very short time, had the power of creating any return. I wish—I heartily wish it had never been. But I have injured more than herself; and I have injured one, whose affection for me—(may I say it?) was scarcely less warm than her's; and whose mind—Oh! how infinitely superior!"—

"Your indifference, however, towards that unfortunate girl—I must say it, unpleasant to me as the discussion of such a subject may well be—your indifference is no apology for your cruel neglect of her. Do not think yourself excused by any weakness, any natural defect of understanding on her side, in the wanton cruelty so evident on yours. You must have known that while you were enjoying

---

* display.] denote. A.
** passions,] passion. A.

yourself in Devonshire, pursuing fresh schemes, always gay, always happy, she was reduced to the extremest indigence."

"But, upon my soul, I did *not* know it," he warmly replied; "I did not recollect that I had omitted to give her my direction; and common sense might have told her how to find it out."

"Well, sir, and what said Mrs. Smith?"

"She taxed me with the offence at once, and my confusion may be guessed. The purity of her life, the formality of her notions, her ignorance of the world—every thing was against me. The matter itself I could not deny, and vain was every endeavour to soften it. She was previously disposed, I believe, to doubt the morality of my conduct in general, and was moreover discontented with the very little attention, the very little portion of my time that I had bestowed on her, in my present visit. In short, it ended in a total breach. By one measure I might have saved myself. In the height of her morality, good woman! she offered to forgive the past, if I would marry Eliza. That could not be—and I was formally dismissed from her favour and her house. The night following this affair—I was to go the next morning—was spent by me in deliberating on what my future conduct should be. The struggle was great—but it ended too soon. My affection for Marianne, my thorough conviction of her attachment to me—it was all insufficient to outweigh that dread of poverty, or get the better of those false ideas of the necessity of riches, which I was naturally inclined to feel, and expensive society had increased. I had reason to believe myself secure of my present wife, if I chose to address her, and I persuaded myself to think that nothing else in common prudence remained for me to do. An heavy scene however awaited me, before I could leave Devonshire;—I was engaged to dine with you on that very day; some apology was therefore necessary for my breaking the engagement. But whether I should write this apology, or deliver it in person, was a point of long debate. To see Marianne, I felt would be dreadful, and I even doubted whether I could see her again and keep to my resolution. In that point, however, I undervalued my own magnanimity, as the event declared; for I went, I saw her, and saw her miserable, and left her miserable—and left her hoping never to see her again."

"Why did you call, Mr. Willoughby?" said Elinor, reproachfully; "a note would have answered every purpose.—Why was it necessary to call?"

"It was necessary to my own pride. I could not bear to leave the country in a manner that might lead you, or the rest of the neighbourhood, to suspect any part of what had really passed between Mrs. Smith and myself—and I resolved therefore on calling at the cottage, in my way to Honiton. The sight of your dear sister, however, was really dreadful; and to heighten the matter, I found her alone. You were all gone I do not know where. I had left her only the evening before, so fully, so firmly resolved within myself on doing right! A few hours were to have engaged her to me for ever; and I remember how happy, how gay were my spirits, as I walked from the cottage to Allenham, satisfied with myself, delighted with every body! But in this, our last interview of friendship, I approached her with a sense of guilt that almost took from me the power of dissembling. Her sorrow, her disappointment, her deep regret, when I told her that I was obliged to leave Devonshire so immediately—I never shall forget it—united too with such reliance, such confidence in me!—Oh, God!—what an hard-hearted rascal I was!"

They were both silent for a few moments. Elinor first spoke.

"Did you tell her that you should soon return?"

"I do not know what I told her," he replied, impatiently; "less than was due to the past, beyond a doubt, and in all likelihood much more than was justified by the future. I cannot think of it.—It won't do.—Then came your dear mother to torture me farther, with all her kindness and confidence. Thank Heaven! it *did* torture me. I was miserable. Miss Dashwood, you cannot have an idea of the comfort it gives me to look back on my own misery. I owe such a grudge to myself for the stupid, rascally folly of my own heart, that all my past sufferings under it are only triumph and exultation to me now. Well, I went, left all that I loved, and went to those to whom, at best, I was only indifferent. My journey to town—travelling with my own horses, and therefore so tediously—no creature to speak to—my own reflections so cheerful—when I looked forward everything so inviting!—when I looked back at Barton, the picture so soothing!—oh! it was a blessed journey!"

He stopt.

"Well, sir," said Elinor, who, though pitying him, grew impatient for his departure, "and this is all?"

"All!—no,—have you forgot what passed in town?—That infamous letter—Did she shew it you?"

"Yes, I saw every note that passed."

"When the first of her's reached me, (as it immediately did, for I was in town the whole time,) what I felt is—in the common phrase, not to be expressed; in a more simple one—perhaps too simple to raise any emotion—my feelings were very, very painful. —Every line, every word was—in the hackneyed metaphor which their dear writer, were she here, would forbid—a dagger to my heart. To know that Marianne was in town was—in the same language—a thunderbolt.—Thunderbolts and daggers!—what a reproof would she have given me!—her taste, her opinions—I believe they are better known to me than my own,—and I am sure they are dearer."

Elinor's heart, which had undergone many changes in the course of this extraordinary conversation, was now softened again;—yet she felt it her duty to check such ideas in her companion as the last. "This is not right, Mr. Willoughby.—Remember that you are married. Relate only what in your conscience you think necessary for me to hear."

"Marianne's note, by assuring me that I was still as dear to her as in former days, that in spite of the many, many weeks we had been separated, she was as constant in her own feelings, and as full of faith in the constancy of mine as ever, awakened all my remorse. I say awakened, because time and London, business and dissipation, had in some measure quieted it, and I had been growing a fine hardened villain, fancying myself indifferent to her, and chusing to fancy that she too must have become indifferent to me; talking to myself of our past attachment as a mere idle, trifling, business, shrugging up my shoulders in proof of its being so, and silencing every reproach, overcoming every scruple, by secretly saying now and then, 'I shall be heartily glad to hear she is well married.'—But this note made me know myself better. I felt that she was infinitely dearer to me than any other woman in the world, and that I was using her infamously. But everything was then just settled between Miss Grey and me. To retreat was impossible. All that I had to do, was to avoid you both. I sent no answer to Marianne, intending by that means to preserve myself from her farther notice; and for some time I was even determined not to call in Berkeley-street;—but at last, judging it wiser to affect the air of a cool, common acquaintance than anything else, I watched you all safely out of the house one morning, and left my name."

"Watched us out of the house!"

"Even so. You would be surprised to hear how often I watched you, how often I was on the point of falling in with you. I have entered many a shop to avoid your sight, as the carriage drove by. Lodging as I did in Bond-street, there was hardly a day in which I did not catch a glimpse of one or other of you; and nothing but the most constant watchfulness on my side, a most invariably prevailing desire to keep out of your sight, could have separated us so long. I avoided the Middletons as much as possible, as well as everybody else who was likely to prove an acquaintance in common. Not aware of their being in town, however, I blundered on Sir John, I believe, the first day of his coming, and the day after I had called at Mrs. Jennings's. He asked me to a party, a dance at his house in the evening.—Had he *not* told me as an inducement that you and your sister were to be there, I should have felt it too certain a thing, to trust myself near him. The next morning brought another short note from Marianne—still affectionate, open, artless, confiding—everything that could make *my* conduct most hateful. I could not answer it. I tried—but could not frame a sentence. But I thought of her, I believe, every moment of the day. If you *can* pity me, Miss Dashwood, pity my situation as it was *then*. With my head and heart full of your sister, I was forced to play the happy lover to another woman!—Those three or four weeks were worse than all. Well, at last, as I need not tell you, you were forced on me; and what a sweet figure I cut!—what an evening of agony it was!—Marianne, beautiful as an angel on one side, calling me Willoughby in such a tone!—Oh! God!—holding out her hand to me, asking me for an explanation with those bewitching eyes fixed in such speaking solicitude on my face!—and Sophia, jealous as the devil on the other hand, looking all that was—Well, it does not signify; it is over now.—Such an evening!—I ran away from you all as soon as I could; but not before I had seen Marianne's sweet face as white as death.—*That* was the last, last look I ever had of her;—the last manner in which she appeared to me. It was a horrid sight!—Yet when I thought of her to-day as really dying, it was a kind of comfort to me to imagine that I knew exactly how she would appear to those, who saw her last in this world. She was before me, constantly before me, as I travelled, in the same look and hue."

A short pause of mutual thoughtfulness succeeded. Willoughby first rousing himself, broke it thus:

"Well, let me make haste and be gone. Your sister is certainly better, certainly out of danger?"

"We are assured of it."

"Your poor mother too!—doting on Marianne."

"But the letter, Mr. Willoughby, your own letter; have you anything to say about that?"

"Yes, yes, *that* in particular. Your sister wrote to me again, you know, the very next morning. You saw what she said. I was breakfasting at the Ellisons,—and her letter, with some others, was brought to me there from my lodgings. It happened to catch Sophia's eye before it caught mine—and its size, the elegance of the paper, the hand-writing altogether, immediately gave her a suspicion.* Some vague report had reached her before of my attachment to some young lady in Devonshire, and what had passed within her observation the preceding evening had marked who the young lady

---

* suspicion.] suspicion of its nature. A. *The reading from A is plausible, particularly since it straddles a line as well as page break.*

was, and made her more jealous than ever. Affecting that air of playfulness, therefore, which is delightful in a woman one loves, she opened the letter directly, and read its contents. She was well paid for her impudence. She read what made her wretched. Her wretchedness I could have borne, but her passion—her malice—At all events it must be appeased. And in short—what do you think of my wife's style of letter-writing?—delicate—tender—truly feminine—was it not?"

"Your wife!—The letter was in your own hand writing."

"Yes, but I had only the credit of servilely copying such sentences as I was ashamed to put my name to. The original was all her own—her own happy thoughts and gentle diction. But what could I do? —we were engaged, every thing in preparation, the day almost fixed—But I am talking like a fool. Preparation!—day!—In honest words, her money was necessary to me, and in a situation like mine, any thing was to be done to prevent a rupture. And after all, what did it signify to my character in the opinion of Marianne and her friends, in what language my answer was couched?—It must have been only to one end. My business was to declare myself a scoundrel, and whether I did it with a bow or a bluster* was of little importance.—'I am ruined for ever in their opinion—said I to myself—I am shut out for ever from their society, they already think me an unprincipled fellow, this letter will only make them think me a blackguard one.' Such were my reasonings, as, in a sort of desperate carelessness, I copied my wife's words, and parted with the last relics of Marianne. Her three notes—unluckily they were all in my pocket-book, or I should have denied their existence, and hoarded them for ever—I was forced to put them up, and could not even kiss them. And the lock of hair—that too I had always carried about me in the same pocket-book, which was now searched by Madam with the most ingratiating virulence,—the dear lock—all, every memento was torn from me."

"You are very wrong, Mr. Willoughby, very blameable," said Elinor, while her voice, in spite of herself, betrayed her compassionate emotion; "you ought not to speak in this way, either of Mrs. Willoughby or my sister. You have made your own choice. It was not forced on you. Your wife has a claim to your politeness, to your respect, at least. She must be attached to you, or she would not have married you. To treat her with unkindness, to speak of her slightingly is no atonement to Marianne—nor can I suppose it a relief to your own conscience."

"Do not talk to me of my wife," said he with an heavy sigh.—"She does not deserve your compassion.—She knew I had no regard

---

* a bluster] bluster A.

for her when we married.—Well, married we were, and came down to Combe Magna to be happy, and afterwards returned to town to be gay.—And now do you pity me, Miss Dashwood?—or have I said all this to no purpose?—Am I—be it only one degree—am I less guilty in your opinion than I was before?—My intentions were not always wrong. Have I explained away any part of my guilt?"

"Yes, you have certainly removed something—a little.—You have proved yourself, on the whole, less faulty than I had believed you. You have proved your heart less wicked, much less wicked. But I hardly know—the misery that you have inflicted—I hardly know what could have made it worse."

"Will you repeat to your sister when she is recovered, what I have been telling you?—Let me be a little lightened too in her opinion as well as in yours. You tell me that she has forgiven me already. Let me be able to fancy that a better knowledge of my heart, and of my present feelings, will draw from her a more spontaneous, more natural, more gentle, less dignified, forgiveness. Tell her of my misery and my penitence—tell her that my heart was never inconstant to her, and if you will, that at this moment she is dearer to me than ever."

"I will tell her all that is necessary to what may comparatively be called, your justification. But you have not explained to me the particular reason of your coming now, nor how you heard of her illness."

"Last night, in Drury-lane³ lobby, I ran against Sir John Middleton, and when he saw who I was—for the first time these two months—he spoke to me.—That he had cut me ever since my marriage, I had seen without surprise or resentment. Now, however, his good-natured, honest, stupid soul, full of indignation against me, and concern for your sister, could not resist the temptation of telling me what he knew ought to—though probably he did not think it *would*—vex me horridly.——As bluntly as he could speak it, therefore, he told me that Marianne Dashwood was dying of a putrid fever at Cleveland—a letter that morning received from Mrs. Jennings declared her danger most imminent—the Palmers all gone off in a fright, &c.—I was too much shocked to be able to pass myself off as insensible even to the undiscerning Sir John. His heart was softened in seeing mine suffer; and so much of his ill-will was done away, that when we parted, he almost shook me by the hand while he reminded me of an old promise about a pointer puppy. What I felt on hearing that your sister was dying—and dying too, believing me the greatest villain upon earth, scorning, hating me in

3. The Theatre Royal in Drury Lane, London. Many of England's most celebrated actors —such as Garrick, Kean, Kemble, and Mrs. Siddons—acted there.

her latest moments—for how could I tell what horrid projects might not have been imputed? *One* person I was sure would represent me as capable of anything—What I felt was dreadful!—My resolution was soon made, and at eight o'clock this morning I was in my carriage. Now you know all."

Elinor made no answer. Her thoughts were silently fixed on the irreparable injury which too early an independence and its consequent habits of idleness, dissipation, and luxury, had made in the mind, the character, the happiness, of a man who, to every advantage of person and talents, united a disposition naturally open and honest, and a feeling, affectionate temper. The world had made him extravagant and vain—Extravagance and vanity had made him cold-hearted and selfish. Vanity, while seeking its own guilty triumph at the expense of another, had involved him in a real attachment, which extravagance, or at least its offspring, necessity, had required to be sacrificed. Each faulty propensity in leading him to evil, had led him likewise to punishment. The attachment, from which against honour, against feeling, against every better interest he had outwardly torn himself, now, when no longer allowable, governed every thought; and the connection, for the sake of which he had, with little scruple, left her sister to misery, was likely to prove a source of unhappiness to himself of a far more incurable nature. From a reverie of this kind she was recalled at the end of some minutes by Willoughby, who, rousing himself from a reverie at least equally painful, started up in preparation for going, and said,

"There is no use in staying here; I must be off."

"Are you going back to town?"

"No—to Combe Magna. I have business there; from thence to town in a day or two. Good bye."

He held out his hand. She could not refuse to give him her's;—he pressed it with affection.

"And you *do* think something better of me than you did?"—said he, letting it fall, and leaning against the mantle-piece as if forgetting he was to go.

Elinor assured him that she did;—that she forgave, pitied, wished him well—was even interested in his happiness—and added some gentle counsel as to the behaviour most likely to promote it. His answer was not very encouraging.

"As to that," said he, "I must rub through the world as well as I can. Domestic happiness is out of the question. If, however, I am allowed to think that you and yours feel an interest in my fate and actions, it may be the means—it may put me on my guard—at least, it will be something to live for. Marianne to be sure is lost to me for ever. Were I even by any blessed chance at liberty again"—

Elinor stopped him with a reproof.

"Well"—he replied—"once more good bye. I shall now go away and live in dread of one event."

"What do you mean?"

"Your sister's marriage."

"You are very wrong. She can never be more lost to you than she is now."

"But she will be gained by some one else. And if that some one should be the very he whom, of all others, I could least bear—— But I will not stay to rob myself of all your compassionate good-will, by shewing that where I have most injured I can least forgive. Good bye,—God bless you!"

And with these words, he almost ran out of the room.

Chapter IX.

Elinor, for some time after he left her, for some time even after the sound of his carriage had died away, remained too much oppressed by a croud of ideas, widely differing in themselves, but of which sadness was the general result, to think even of her sister.

Willoughby, he, whom only half an hour ago she had abhorred as the most worthless of men, Willoughby, in spite of all his faults, excited a degree of commiseration for the sufferings produced by them, which made her think of him as now separated for ever from her family with a tenderness, a regret, rather in proportion, as she soon acknowledged within herself—to his wishes than to his merits. She felt that his influence over her mind was heightened by circumstances which ought not in reason to have weight; by that person of uncommon attraction, that open, affectionate, and lively manner which it was no merit to possess; and by that still ardent love for Marianne, which it was not even innocent to indulge. But she felt that it was so, long, long before she could feel his influence less.

When at last she returned to the unconscious Marianne, she found her just awaking, refreshed by so long and sweet a sleep to the extent of her hopes. Elinor's heart was full. The past, the present, the future, Willoughby's visit, Marianne's safety, and her mother's expected arrival, threw her altogether into an agitation of spirits which kept off every indication of fatigue, and made her only fearful of betraying herself to her sister. Short was the time, however, in which that fear could affect her, for within half an hour after Willoughby's leaving the house, she was again called down stairs by the sound of another carriage.—Eager to save her mother from every unnecessary moment's horrible suspense, she ran immediately into the hall, and reached the outward door just in time to receive and support her as she entered it.

Mrs. Dashwood, whose terror as they drew near the house had produced almost the conviction of Marianne's being no more, had no voice to inquire after her, no voice even for Elinor; but *she*, waiting neither for salutation nor inquiry, instantly gave the joyful relief;—and her mother, catching it with all her usual warmth, was in a moment as much overcome by her happiness, as she had been before by her fears. She was supported into the drawing-room between her daughter and her friend;—and there, shedding tears of joy, though still unable to speak, embraced Elinor again and again, turning from her at intervals to press Colonel Brandon's hand, with a look which spoke at once her gratitude, and her conviction of his sharing with herself in the bliss of the moment. He shared it, however, in a silence even greater than her own.

As soon as Mrs. Dashwood had recovered herself, to see Marianne was her first desire; and in two minutes she was with her beloved child, rendered dearer to her than ever by absence, unhappiness, and danger. Elinor's delight, as she saw what each felt in the meeting, was only checked by an apprehension of its robbing Marianne of farther sleep;—but Mrs. Dashwood could be calm, could be even prudent, when the life of a child was at stake, and Marianne, satisfied in knowing her mother was near her, and conscious of being too weak for conversation, submitted readily to the silence and quiet prescribed by every nurse around her. Mrs. Dashwood *would* sit up with her all night, and Elinor, in compliance with her mother's entreaty, went to bed. But the rest, which one night entirely sleepless, and many hours of the most wearing anxiety seemed to make requisite, was kept off by irritation of spirits. Willoughby, "poor Willoughby," as she now allowed herself to call him, was constantly in her thoughts; she would not but have heard his vindication for the world, and now blamed, now acquitted herself for having judged him so harshly before. But her promise of relating it to her sister was invariably painful. She dreaded the performance of it, dreaded what its effect on Marianne might be; doubted whether after such an explanation she could ever be happy with another; and for a moment wished Willoughby a widower. Then, remembering Colonel Brandon, reproved herself, felt that to *his* sufferings and *his* constancy far more than to his rival's, the reward of her sister was due, and wished any thing rather than Mrs. Willoughby's death.

The shock of Colonel Brandon's errand at Barton had been much softened to Mrs. Dashwood by her own previous alarm; for so great was her uneasiness about Marianne, that she had already determined to set out for Cleveland on that very day, without waiting for any farther intelligence, and had so far settled her journey before his arrival, that the Careys were then expected every moment to fetch Margaret away, as her mother was unwilling to take her where there might be infection.

Marianne continued to mend every day, and the brilliant cheerfulness of Mrs. Dashwood's looks and spirits proved her to be, as she repeatedly declared herself, one of the happiest women in the world. Elinor could not hear the declaration, nor witness its proofs without sometimes wondering whether her mother ever recollected Edward. But Mrs. Dashwood, trusting to the temperate account of her own disappointment which Elinor had sent her, was led away by the exuberance of her joy to think only of what would increase it. Marianne was restored to her from a danger in which, as she now began to feel, her own mistaken judgment in encouraging the unfortunate attachment to Willoughby, had contributed to place her;—and in her recovery she had yet another source of joy unthought of by Elinor. It was thus imparted to her, as soon as any opportunity of private conference between them occurred.

"At last we are alone. My Elinor, you do not yet know all my happiness. Colonel Brandon loves Marianne. He has told me so himself."

Her daughter, feeling by turns both pleased and pained, surprised and not surprised, was all silent attention.

"You are never like me, dear Elinor, or I should wonder at your composure now. Had I sat down to wish for any possible good to my family, I should have fixed on Colonel Brandon's marrying one of you as the object most desirable. And I believe Marianne will be the most happy with him of the two."

Elinor was half inclined to ask her reason for thinking so, because satisfied that none founded on an impartial consideration of their age, characters, or feelings, could be given;—but her mother must always be carried away by her imagination on any interesting subject, and therefore instead of an inquiry, she passed it off with a smile.

"He opened his whole heart to me yesterday as we travelled. It came out quite unawares, quite undesignedly. I, you may well believe, could talk of nothing but my child;—he could not conceal his distress; I saw that it equalled my own, and he perhaps, thinking that mere friendship, as the world now goes, would not justify so warm a sympathy—or rather not thinking at all, I suppose—giving way to irresistible feelings, made me acquainted with his earnest, tender, constant, affection for Marianne. He has loved her, my Elinor, ever since the first moment of seeing her."

Here, however, Elinor perceived,—not the language, not the professions of Colonel Brandon, but the natural embellishments of her mother's active fancy, which fashioned every thing delightful to her, as it chose.

"His regard for her, infinitely surpassing anything that Willoughby ever felt or feigned, as much more warm, as more sincere or constant—which ever we are to call it—has subsisted through all the knowledge of dear Marianne's unhappy prepossession for that worthless young man!—and without selfishness—without encouraging a hope!—could he have seen her happy with another—Such a noble mind!—such openness, such sincerity!—no one can be deceived in *him*."

"Colonel Brandon's character," said Elinor, "as an excellent man, is well established."

"I know it is"—replied her mother seriously, "or after such a warning, *I* should be the last to encourage such affection, or even to be pleased by it. But his coming for me as he did, with such active, such ready friendship, is enough to prove him one of the worthiest of men."

"His character, however," answered Elinor, "does not rest on *one* act of kindness, to which his affection for Marianne, were humanity out of the case, would have prompted him. To Mrs. Jennings, to the Middletons, he has been long and intimately known; they equally love and respect him; and even my own knowledge of him, though lately acquired, is very considerable; and so highly do *I* value and esteem him, that if Marianne can be happy with him, I shall be as ready as yourself to think our connection the greatest blessing to us in the world. What answer did you give him?—Did you allow him to hope?"

"Oh! my love, I could not then talk of hope to him or to myself. Marianne might at that moment be dying. But he did not ask for hope or encouragement. His was an involuntary confidence, an irrepressible effusion to a soothing friend—not an application to a parent. Yet after a time I *did* say, for at first I was quite overcome—that if she lived, as I trusted she might, my greatest happiness would lie in promoting their marriage; and since our arrival, since our delightful security I have repeated it to him more fully, have given him every encouragement in my power. Time, a very little time, I tell him, will do everything;—Marianne's heart is not to be wasted for ever on such a man as Willoughby.—His own merits must soon secure it."

"To judge from the Colonel's spirits, however, you have not yet made him equally sanguine."

"No.—He thinks Marianne's affection too deeply rooted for any change in it under a great length of time, and even supposing her heart again free, is too diffident of himself to believe, that with such a difference of age and disposition, he could ever attach her. There, however, he is quite mistaken. His age is only so much beyond her's, as to be an advantage, as to make his character and principles fixed; —and his disposition, I am well convinced, is exactly the very one to make your sister happy. And his person, his manners too, are all in his favour. My partiality does not blind me; he certainly is not so handsome as Willoughby—but at the same time, there is something much more pleasing in his countenance.—There was always a something,—if you remember,—in Willoughby's eyes at times, which I did not like."

Elinor could *not* remember it;—but her mother, without waiting for her assent, continued,

"And his manners, the Colonel's manners are not only more pleasing to me than Willoughby's ever were, but they are of a kind I well know to be more solidly attaching to Marianne. Their gentleness, their genuine attention to other people, and their manly unstudied simplicity is much more accordant with her real disposition, than the liveliness—often artificial, and often ill-timed of the other. I am very sure myself, that had Willoughby turned out as really amiable, as he has proved himself the contrary, Marianne would yet never have been so happy with *him*, as she will be with Colonel Brandon."

She paused.—Her daughter could not quite agree with her, but her dissent was not heard, and therefore gave no offence.

"At Delaford, she will be within an easy distance of me," added Mrs. Dashwood, "even if I remain at Barton; and in all probability,—for I hear it is a large village,—indeed there certainly *must* be some small house or cottage close by, that would suit us quite as well as our present situation."

Poor Elinor!—here was a new scheme for getting her to Delaford!—but her spirit was stubborn.

"His fortune too!—for at my time of life you know, everybody cares about *that*;—and though I neither know, nor desire to know, what it really is, I am sure it must be a good one."

Here they were interrupted by the entrance of a third person, and Elinor withdrew to think it all over in private, to wish success to her friend, and yet in wishing it, to feel a pang for Willoughby.

Chapter X.

Marianne's illness, though weakening in its kind, had not been long enough to make her recovery slow; and with youth, natural strength, and her mother's presence in aid, it proceeded so smoothly as to enable her to remove within four days after the arrival of the latter,

into Mrs. Palmer's dressing-room. When there, at her own particular request, for she was impatient to pour forth her thanks to him
for fetching her mother, Colonel Brandon was invited to visit her.

His emotion in entering the room, in seeing her altered looks,
and in receiving the pale hand which she immediately held out to
him, was such, as, in Elinor's conjecture, must arise from something more than his affection for Marianne, or the consciousness
of its being known to others; and she soon discovered in his melancholy eye and varying complexion as he looked at her sister, the
probable recurrence of many past scenes of misery to his mind,
brought back by that resemblance between Marianne and Eliza already acknowledged, and now strengthened by the hollow eye, the
sickly skin, the posture of reclining weakness, and the warm acknowledgment of peculiar obligation.

Mrs. Dashwood, not less watchful of what passed than her
daughter, but with a mind very differently influenced, and therefore
watching to very different effect, saw nothing in the Colonel's behaviour but what arose from the most simple and self-evident sensations, while in the actions and words of Marianne she persuaded
herself to think that something more than gratitude already
dawned.

At the end of another day or two, Marianne growing visibly
stronger every twelve hours, Mrs. Dashwood, urged equally by her
own and her daughter's wishes, began to talk of removing to Barton.
On *her* measures depended those of her two friends; Mrs. Jennings
could not quit Cleveland during the Dashwoods' stay, and Colonel
Brandon was soon brought, by their united request, to consider his
own abode there as equally determinate, if not equally indispensable. At his and Mrs. Jennings's united request in return, Mrs. Dashwood was prevailed on to accept the use of his carriage on her
journey back, for the better accommodation of her sick child; and
the Colonel, at the joint invitation of Mrs. Dashwood and Mrs.
Jennings, whose active good-nature made her friendly and hospi-
table for other people as well as herself, engaged with pleasure to
redeem it by a visit at the cottage, in the course of a few weeks.

The day of separation and departure arrived; and Marianne, after
taking so particular and lengthened a leave of Mrs. Jennings, one
so earnestly grateful, so full of respect and kind wishes as seemed
due to her own heart from a secret acknowledgement of past inattention, and bidding Colonel Brandon farewel with the cordiality
of a friend, was carefully assisted by him into the carriage, of which
he seemed anxious that she should engross at least half. Mrs. Dashwood and Elinor then followed, and the others were left by themselves, to talk of the travellers, and feel their own dulness, till Mrs.
Jennings was summoned to her chaise to take comfort in the gossip

of her maid for the loss of her two young companions; and Colonel Brandon immediately afterwards took his solitary way to Delaford.

The Dashwoods were two days on the road, and Marianne bore her journey on both, without essential fatigue. Every thing that the most zealous affection, the most solicitous care could do to render her comfortable, was the office of each watchful companion, and each found their reward in her bodily ease, and her calmness of spirits. To Elinor, the observation of the latter was particularly grateful. She, who had seen her week after week so constantly suffering, oppressed by anguish of heart which she had neither courage to speak of, nor fortitude to conceal, now saw with a joy, which no other could equally share, an apparent composure of mind, which, in being the result as she trusted of serious reflection, must eventually lead her to contentment and cheerfulness.

As they approached Barton indeed, and entered on scenes, of which every field and every tree brought some peculiar, some painful recollection, she grew silent and thoughtful, and turning away her face from their notice, sat earnestly gazing through the window. But here, Elinor could neither wonder nor blame; and when she saw, as she assisted Marianne from the carriage, that she had been crying, she saw only an emotion too natural in itself to raise anything less tender than pity, and in its unobtrusiveness entitled to praise. In the whole of her subsequent manner, she traced the direction of a mind awakened to reasonable exertion; for no sooner had they entered their common sitting-room, than Marianne turned her eyes around it with a look of resolute firmness, as if determined at once to accustom herself to the sight of every object with which the remembrance of Willoughby could be connected.—She said little, but every sentence aimed at cheerfulness, and though a sigh sometimes escaped her, it never passed away without the atonement of a smile. After dinner she would try her piano-forté. She went to it; but the music on which her eye first rested was an opera, procured for her by Willoughby, containing some of their favourite duets, and bearing on its outward leaf her own name in his hand writing.—That would not do.—She shook her head, put the music aside, and after running over the keys for a minute complained of feebleness in her fingers, and closed the instrument again; declaring however with firmness as she did so, that she should in future practise much.

The next morning produced no abatement in these happy symptoms. On the contrary, with a mind and body alike strengthened by rest, she looked and spoke with more genuine spirit, anticipating the pleasure of Margaret's return, and talking of the dear family party which would then be restored, of their mutual pursuits and cheerful society as the only happiness worth a wish.

"When the weather is settled, and I have recovered my strength," said she, "we will take long walks together every day. We will walk to the farm at the edge of the down, and see how the children go on; we will walk to Sir John's new plantations at Barton-Cross, and the Abbeyland; and we will often go to the old ruins of the Priory, and try to trace its foundations as far as we are told they once reached. I know we shall be happy. I know the summer will pass happily away. I mean never to be later in rising than six, and from that time till dinner I shall divide every moment between music and reading. I have formed my plan, and am determined to enter on a course of serious study. Our own library is too well known to me, to be resorted to for anything beyond mere amusement. But there are many works well worth reading, at the Park; and there are others of more modern production which I know I can borrow of Colonel Brandon. By reading only six hours a-day, I shall gain in the course of a twelvemonth a great deal of instruction which I now feel myself to want."

Elinor honoured her for a plan which originated so nobly as this; though smiling to see the same eager fancy which had been leading her to the extreme of languid indolence and selfish repining, now at work in introducing excess into a scheme of such rational employment and virtuous self-controul. Her smile however changed to a sigh when she remembered that her promise to Willoughby was yet unfulfilled, and feared she had that to communicate which might again unsettle the mind of Marianne, and ruin at least for a time this fair prospect of busy tranquility. Willing therefore to delay the evil hour, she resolved to wait till her sister's health were more secure, before she appointed it. But the resolution was made only to be broken.

Marianne had been two or three days at home, before the weather was fine enough for an invalid like herself to venture out. But at last a soft, genial morning appeared; such as might tempt the daughter's wishes and the mother's confidence; and Marianne, leaning on Elinor's arm, was authorised to walk as long as she could without fatigue, in the lane before the house.

The sisters set out at a pace, slow as the feebleness of Marianne in an exercise hitherto untried since her illness required;—and they had advanced only so far beyond the house as to admit a full view of the hill, the important hill behind, when pausing with her eyes turned towards it, Marianne calmly said,

"There, exactly there"—pointing with one hand, "on that projecting mound,—there I fell; and there I first saw Willoughby."

Her voice sunk with the word, but presently reviving she added,

"I am thankful to find that I can look with so little pain on the spot!—shall we ever talk on that subject, Elinor?"—hesitatingly it was said.—"Or will it be wrong?—I *can* talk of it now, I hope, as I ought to do."—

Elinor tenderly invited her to be open.

"As for regret," said Marianne, "I have done with that, as far as *he* is concerned. I do not mean to talk to you of what my feelings have been for him, but what they are *now*.—At present, if I could be satisfied on one point, if I could be allowed to think that he was not *always* acting a part, not *always* deceiving me;—but above all, if I could be assured that he never was so *very* wicked as my fears have sometimes fancied him, since the story of that unfortunate girl"—

She stopt.—Elinor joyfully treasured her words as she answered, "If you could be assured of that, you think you should be easy."

"Yes. My peace of mind is doubly involved in it;—for not only is it horrible to suspect a person, who has been what *he* has been to *me*, of such designs,—but what must it make me appear to myself?—What in a situation like mine, but a most shamefully un-guarded affection could expose me to"—

"How then," asked her sister, "would you account for his behaviour?"

"I would suppose him,—Oh! how gladly would I suppose him, only fickle, very, very fickle."

Elinor said no more. She was debating within herself on the el-igibility of beginning her story directly, or postponing it till Mari-anne were in stronger health;—and they crept on for a few minutes in silence.

"I am not wishing him too much good," said Marianne at last with a sigh, "when I wish his secret reflections may be no more unpleasant than my own. He will suffer enough in them."

"Do you compare your conduct with his?"

"No. I compare it with what it ought to have been; I compare it with yours."

"Our situations have borne little resemblance."

"They have borne more than our conduct.—Do not, my dearest Elinor, let your kindness defend what I know your judgment must censure. My illness has made me think—It has given me leisure and calmness for serious recollection. Long before I was enough recovered to talk, I was perfectly able to reflect. I considered the past; I saw in my own behaviour since the beginning of our ac-quaintance with him last autumn, nothing but a series of impru-dence towards myself, and want of kindness to others. I saw that my own feelings had prepared my sufferings, and that my want of fortitude under them had almost led me to the grave. My illness, I well knew, had been entirely brought on by myself by such negli-gence of my own health, as I had felt even at the time to be wrong.

Had I died,—it would have been self-destruction.[1] I did not know my danger till the danger was removed; but with such feelings as these reflections gave me, I wonder at my recovery,—wonder that the very eagerness of my desire to live, to have time for atonement to my God, and to you all, did not kill me at once. Had I died,— in what peculiar misery should I have left you, my nurse, my friend, my sister!—You, who had seen all the fretful selfishness of my latter days; who had known all the murmurings of my heart!—How should I have lived in *your* remembrance!—My mother too! How could you have consoled her!—I cannot express my own abhorrence of myself. Whenever I looked towards the past, I saw some duty neglected, or some failing indulged. Every body seemed injured by me. The kindness, the unceasing kindness of Mrs. Jennings, I had repaid with ungrateful contempt. To the Middletons, the Palmers, the Steeles, to every common acquaintance even, I had been insolent and unjust; with an heart hardened against their merits, and a temper irritated by their very attention.—To John, to Fanny,— yes, even to them, little as they deserve, I had given less than their due. But you,—you above all, above my mother, had been wronged by me. I, and only I, knew your heart and its sorrows; yet, to what did it influence me?—not to any compassion that could benefit you or myself.—Your example was before me: but to what avail?—Was I more considerate of you and your comfort? Did I imitate your forbearance, or lessen your restraints, by taking any part in those offices of general complaisance or particular gratitude which you had hitherto been left to discharge alone?—No;—not less when I knew you to be unhappy, than when I had believed you at ease, did I turn away from every exertion of duty or friendship; scarcely allowing sorrow to exist but with me, regretting only *that* heart which had deserted and wronged me, and leaving you, for whom I professed an unbounded affection, to be miserable for my sake."

Here ceased the rapid flow of her self-reproving spirit; and Elinor, impatient to soothe, though too honest to flatter, gave her instantly that praise and support which her frankness and her contrition so well deserved. Marianne pressed her hand and replied,

"You are very good.—The future must be my proof. I have laid down my plan, and if I am capable of adhering to it—my feelings shall be governed and my temper improved. They shall no longer worry others, nor torture myself. I shall now live solely for my family. You, my mother, and Margaret, must henceforth be all the world to me; you will share my affections entirely between you. From you, from my home, I shall never again have the smallest incitement to

1. The subject of suicide, particularly as the result of blighted love, was prominent during this period, in part due to the notoriety of Mary Wollstonecraft's two suicide attempts.

move; and if I do mix in other society it will be only to show that my spirit is humbled, my heart amended, and that I can practise the civilities, the lesser duties of life, with gentleness, and forbearance. As for Willoughby—to say that I shall soon or that I shall ever forget him, would be idle. His remembrance can be overcome by no change of circumstances or opinions. But it shall be regulated, it shall be checked by religion, by reason, by constant employment."

She paused—and added in a lower voice, "If I could but know *his* heart, everything would become easy."

Elinor, who had now been for some time reflecting on the propriety or impropriety of speedily hazarding her narration, without feeling at all nearer decision than at first, heard this; and perceiving that as reflection did nothing, resolution must do all, soon found herself leading to the fact.

She managed the recital, as she hoped, with address; prepared her anxious listener with caution; related simply and honestly the chief points on which Willoughby grounded his apology; did justice to his repentance, and softened only his protestations of present regard. Marianne said not a word.—She trembled, her eyes were fixed on the ground, and her lips became whiter than even sickness had left them. A thousand inquiries sprung up from her heart, but she dared not urge one. She caught every syllable with panting eagerness; her hand, unknowingly to herself, closely pressed her sister's, and tears covered her cheeks.

Elinor, dreading her being tired, led her towards home; and till they reached the door of the cottage, easily conjecturing what her curiosity must be though no question was suffered to speak it, talked of nothing but Willoughby, and their conversation together; and was* carefully minute in every particular of speech and look, where minuteness could be safely indulged. As soon as they entered the house, Marianne with a kiss of gratitude and these two words just articulate through her tears, "Tell mama," withdrew from her sister and walked slowly up stairs. Elinor would not attempt to disturb a solitude so reasonable as what she now sought; and with a mind anxiously pre-arranging its result, and a resolution of reviving the subject again, should Marianne fail to do it, she turned into the parlour to fulfil her parting injunction.

---

* and was] was A.

Chapter XI.

Mrs. Dashwood did not hear unmoved the vindication of her former favourite. She rejoiced in his being cleared from some part of his imputed guilt;—she was sorry for him;—she wished him happy. But the feelings of the past could not be recalled.—Nothing could restore him with a faith unbroken—a character unblemished, to Marianne. Nothing could do away the knowledge of what the latter had suffered through his means, nor remove the guilt of his conduct towards Eliza. Nothing could replace him, therefore, in her former esteem, nor injure the interests* of Colonel Brandon.

Had Mrs. Dashwood, like her daughter, heard Willoughby's story from himself—had she witnessed his distress, and been under the influence of his countenance and his manner, it is probable that her compassion would have been greater. But it was neither in Elinor's power, nor in her wish, to rouse such feelings in another, by her retailed¹ explanation, as had at first been called forth in herself. Reflection had given calmness to her judgment, and sobered her own opinion of Willoughby's deserts;—she wished, therefore, to declare only the simple truth, and lay open such facts as were really due to his character, without any embellishment of tenderness to lead the fancy astray.

In the evening, when they were all three** together, Marianne began voluntarily to speak of him again;—but that it was not without an effort, the restless, unquiet thoughtfulness in which she had been for some time previously sitting—her rising colour, as she spoke—and her unsteady voice, plainly shewed.

"I wish to assure you both," said she, "that I see every thing—as you can desire me to do."

Mrs. Dashwood would have interrupted her instantly with soothing tenderness, had not Elinor, who really wished to hear her sister's unbiassed opinion, by an eager sign, engaged her silence. Marianne slowly continued—

"It is a great relief to me—what Elinor told me this morning—I have now heard exactly what I wished to hear."—For some moments her voice was lost; but recovering herself, she added, and with greater calmness than before—"I am now perfectly satisfied, I wish for no change. I never could have been happy with him, after knowing, as sooner or later I must have known, all this.—I should

---

* interests] interest A.
1. Recounted, repeated to others.
** three] there A.

have had no confidence, no esteem. Nothing could have done it away to my feelings."

"I know it—I know it," cried her mother. "Happy with a man of libertine practices!—With one who had so injured the peace of the dearest of our friends, and the best of men!—No—my Marianne has not a heart to be made happy with such a man!—Her conscience, her sensitive conscience, would have felt all that the conscience of her husband ought to have felt."

Marianne sighed, and repeated—"I wish for no change."

"You consider the matter," said Elinor, "exactly as a good mind and a sound understanding must consider it; and I dare say, you perceive, as well as myself, not only in this, but in many other circumstances, reason enough to be convinced that your marriage must have involved you in many certain troubles and disappointments, in which you would have been poorly supported by an affection, on his side, much less certain. Had you married, you must have been always poor. His expensiveness is acknowledged even by himself, and his whole conduct declares that self-denial is a word hardly understood by him. His demands and your inexperience together on a small, very small income, must have brought on distresses which would not be the *less* grievous to you, from having been entirely unknown and unthought of before. *Your* sense of honour and honesty would have led you, I know, when aware of your situation, to attempt all the economy that would appear to you possible; and perhaps, as long as your frugality retrenched only on your own comfort, you might have been suffered to practise it, but beyond that—and how little could the utmost of your single management do to stop the ruin which had begun before your marriage? —Beyond *that*, had you endeavoured, however reasonably, to abridge *his* enjoyments, is it not to be feared, that instead of prevailing on feelings so selfish to consent to it, you would have lessened your own influence on his heart, and made him regret the connection which had involved him in such difficulties?"

Marianne's lips quivered, and she repeated the word "Selfish?" in a tone that implied—"do you really think him selfish?"

"The whole of his behaviour," replied Elinor, "from the beginning to the end of the affair, has been grounded on selfishness. It was selfishness which first made him sport with your affections; which afterwards, when his own were engaged, made him delay the confession of it, and which finally carried him from Barton. His own enjoyment, or his own ease, was, in every particular, his ruling principle."

"It is very true. *My* happiness never was his object."

"At present," continued Elinor, "he regrets what he has done. And why does he regret it?—Because he finds it has not answered towards himself. It has not made him happy. His circumstances are now unembarrassed—he suffers from no evil of that kind; and he thinks only that he has married a woman of a less amiable temper than yourself. But does it thence follow that had he married you, he would have been happy?—The inconveniencies would have been different. He would then have suffered under the pecuniary distresses which, because they are removed, he now reckons as nothing. He would have had a wife of whose temper he could make no complaint, but he would have been always necessitous—always poor; and probably would soon have learnt to rank the innumerable comforts of a clear estate and good income as of far more importance, even to domestic happiness, than the mere temper of a wife."

"I have not a doubt of it," said Marianne; "and I have nothing to regret—nothing but my own folly."

"Rather say your mother's imprudence, my child," said Mrs. Dashwood; "*she* must be answerable."

Marianne would not let her proceed;—and Elinor, satisfied that each felt their own error, wished to avoid any survey of the past that might weaken her sister's spirits; she therefore, pursuing the first subject, immediately continued,

"*One* observation may, I think, be fairly drawn from the whole of the story—that all Willoughby's difficulties have arisen from the first offence against virtue, in his behaviour to Eliza Williams. That crime has been the origin of every lesser one, and of all his present discontents."

Marianne assented most feelingly to the remark; and her mother was led by it to an enumeration of Colonel Brandon's injuries and merits, warm as friendship and design could unitedly dictate. Her daughter did not look, however, as if much of it were heard by her.

Elinor, according to her expectation, saw on the two or three following days, that Marianne did not continue to gain strength as she had done; but while her resolution was unsubdued, and she still tried to appear cheerful and easy, her sister could safely trust to the effect of time upon her health.

Margaret returned, and the family were again all restored to each other, again quietly settled at the cottage, and if not pursuing their usual studies with quite so much vigour as when they first came to Barton, at least planning a vigorous prosecution of them in future.

Elinor grew impatient for some tidings of Edward. She had heard nothing of him since her leaving London, nothing new of his plans, nothing certain even of his present abode. Some letters had passed between her and her brother, in consequence of Marianne's illness; and in the first of John's, there had been this sentence:—"We know nothing of our unfortunate Edward, and can make no inquiries on so prohibited a subject, but conclude him to be still at Oxford;"

which was all the intelligence of Edward afforded her by the correspondence, for his name was not even mentioned in any of the succeeding letters. She was not doomed, however, to be long in ignorance of his measures.

Their man-servant had been sent one morning to Exeter on business; and when, as he waited at table, he had satisfied the inquiries of his mistress as to the event of his errand, this was his voluntary communication—

"I suppose you know, ma'am, that Mr. Ferrars is married."

Marianne gave a violent start, fixed her eyes upon Elinor, saw her turning pale, and fell back in her chair in hysterics. Mrs. Dashwood, whose eyes, as she answered the servant's inquiry, had intuitively taken the same direction, was shocked to perceive by Elinor's countenance how much she really suffered, and in a moment afterwards, alike distressed by Marianne's situation, knew not on which child to bestow her principal attention.

The servant, who saw only that Miss Marianne was taken ill, had sense enough to call one of the maids, who, with Mrs. Dashwood's assistance, supported her into the other room. By that time, Marianne was rather better, and her mother leaving her to the care of Margaret and the maid, returned to Elinor, who, though still much disordered, had so far recovered the use of her reason and voice as to be just beginning an inquiry of Thomas, as to the source of his intelligence. Mrs. Dashwood immediately took all that trouble on herself; and Elinor had the benefit of the information without the exertion of seeking it.

"Who told you that Mr. Ferrars was married, Thomas?"

"I see Mr. Ferrars myself, ma'am, this morning in Exeter, and his lady too, Miss Steele as was. They was stopping in a chaise at the door of the New London Inn, as I went there with a message from Sally at the Park to her brother, who is one of the post-boys. I happened to look up as I went by the chaise, and so I see directly it was the youngest Miss Steele; so I took off my hat, and she knew me and called to me, and inquired after you, ma'am, and the young ladies, especially Miss Marianne, and bid me I should give her compliments and Mr. Ferrars's, their best compliments and service, and how sorry they was they had not time to come on and see you, but they was in a great hurry to go forwards, for they was going further down for a little while, but howsever, when they come back, they'd make sure to come and see you."

"But did she tell you she was married, Thomas?"

"Yes, ma'am. She smiled, and said how she had changed her name since she was in these parts. She was always a very affable and free-spoken young lady, and very civil behaved. So, I made free to wish her joy."

"Was Mr. Ferrars in the carriage with her?"

"Yes, ma'am, I just see him leaning back in it, but he did not look up;—he never was a gentleman much for talking."

Elinor's heart could easily account for his not putting himself forward; and Mrs. Dashwood probably found the same explanation.

"Was there no one else in the carriage?"

"No, ma'am, only they two."

"Do you know where they came from?"

"They come straight from town, as Miss Lucy—Mrs. Ferrars told me."

"And are going farther westward?"

"Yes, ma'am—but not to bide long. They will soon be back again, and then they'd be sure and call here."

Mrs. Dashwood now looked at her daughter; but Elinor knew better than to expect them. She recognised the whole of Lucy in the message, and was very confident that Edward would never come near them. She observed, in a low voice, to her mother, that they were probably going down to Mr. Pratt's, near Plymouth.

Thomas's intelligence seemed over. Elinor looked as if she wished to hear more.

"Did you see them off, before you came away?"

"No, ma'am—the horses was just coming out, but I could not bide any longer; I was afraid of being late."

"Did Mrs. Ferrars look well?"

"Yes, ma'am, she said how she was very well; and to my mind she was always a very handsome young lady—and she seemed vastly contented."

Mrs. Dashwood could think of no other question, and Thomas and the table-cloth, now alike needless, were soon afterwards dismissed. Marianne had already sent to say that she should eat nothing more. Mrs. Dashwood's and Elinor's appetites were equally lost, and Margaret might think herself very well off, that with so much uneasiness as both her sisters had lately experienced, so much reason as they had often had to be careless of their meals, she had never been obliged to go without her dinner before.

When the dessert and the wine were arranged, and Mrs. Dashwood and Elinor were left by themselves, they remained long together in a similarity of thoughtfulness and silence. Mrs. Dashwood feared to hazard any remark, and ventured not to offer consolation. She now found that she had erred in relying on Elinor's representation of herself; and justly concluded that every thing had been expressly softened at the time, to spare her from an increase of unhappiness, suffering as she then had suffered for Marianne. She found that she had been misled by the careful, the considerate attention of her daughter, to think the attachment, which once she

had so well understood, much slighter in reality, than she had been
wont to believe, or than it was now proved to be. She feared that
under this persuasion she had been unjust, inattentive, nay, almost
unkind, to her Elinor;—that Marianne's affliction, because more
acknowledged, more immediately before her, had too much engrossed her tenderness, and led her away to forget that in Elinor
she might have a daughter suffering almost as much, certainly with
less self-provocation, and greater fortitude.

Chapter XII.

Elinor now found the difference between the expectation of an unpleasant event, however certain the mind may be told to consider
it, and certainty itself. She now found, that in spite of herself, she
had always admitted a hope, while Edward remained single, that
something would occur to prevent his marrying Lucy; that some
resolution of his own, some mediation of friends, or some more
eligible opportunity of establishment for the lady, would arise to
assist the happiness of all. But he was now married, and she condemned her heart for the lurking flattery, which so much heightened the pain of the intelligence.

That he should be married so soon, before (as she imagined) he
could be in orders, and consequently before he could be in possession of the living, surprised her a little at first. But she soon saw
how likely it was that Lucy, in her self-provident care, in her haste
to secure him, should overlook every thing but the risk of delay.
They were married, married in town, and now hastening down to
her uncle's. What had Edward felt on being within four miles of
Barton, on seeing her mother's servant, on hearing Lucy's message!

They would soon, she supposed, be settled at Delaford.—
Delaford,—that place in which so much conspired to give her an
interest; which she wished to be acquainted with, and yet desired
to avoid. She saw them in an instant in their parsonage-house; saw
in Lucy, the active, contriving manager, uniting at once a desire of
smart appearance, with the utmost frugality, and ashamed to be
suspected of half her economical practices;—pursuing her own interest in every thought, courting the favour of Colonel Brandon, of
Mrs. Jennings, and of every wealthy friend. In Edward,—she knew
not what she saw, nor what she wished to see;—happy or
unhappy,—nothing pleased her; she turned away her head from
every sketch of him.

Elinor flattered herself that some one of their connections in
London would write to them to announce the event, and give farther particulars,—but day after day passed off, and brought no let-

ter, no tidings. Though uncertain that any one were to blame, she found fault with every absent friend. They were all thoughtless or indolent.

"When do you write to Colonel Brandon, ma'am?" was an inquiry which sprung from the impatience of her mind to have something going on.

"I wrote to him, my love, last week, and rather expect to see, than to hear from him again. I earnestly pressed his coming to us, and should not be surprised to see him walk in to-day or to-morrow, or any day."

This was gaining something, some thing to look forward to. Colonel Brandon *must* have some information to give.

Scarcely had she so determined it, when the figure of a man on horseback drew her eyes to the window. He stopt at their gate. It was a gentleman, it was Colonel Brandon himself. Now she should hear more; and she trembled in expectation of it. But—it was *not* Colonel Brandon—neither his air—nor his height. Were it possible, she should say it must be Edward. She looked again. He had just dismounted;—she could not be mistaken;—it *was* Edward. She moved away and sat down. "He comes from Mr. Pratt's purposely to see us. I *will* be calm; I *will* be mistress of myself."

In a moment she perceived that the others were likewise aware of the mistake. She saw her mother and Marianne change colour; saw them look at herself, and whisper a few sentences to each other. She would have given the world to be able to speak—and to make them understand that she hoped no coolness, no slight, would appear in their behaviour to him;—but she had no utterance, and was obliged to leave all to their own discretion.

Not a syllable passed aloud. They all waited in silence for the appearance of their visitor. His footsteps were heard along the gravel path; in a moment he was in the passage; and in another, he was before them.

His countenance, as he entered the room, was not too happy, even for Elinor. His complexion was white with agitation, and he looked as if fearful of his reception, and conscious that he merited no kind one. Mrs. Dashwood, however, conforming, as she trusted, to the wishes of that daughter, by whom she then meant in the warmth of her heart to be guided in everything, met him with a look of forced complacency, gave him her hand, and wished him joy.

He coloured, and stammered out an unintelligible reply. Elinor's lips had moved with her mother's, and when the moment of action was over, she wished that she had shaken hands with him too. But it was then too late, and with a countenance meaning to be open, she sat down again and talked of the weather.

Marianne had retreated as much as possible out of sight, to conceal her distress; and Margaret, understanding some part, but not the whole, of the case, thought it incumbent on her to be dignified, and therefore took a seat as far from him as she could, and maintained a strict silence.

When Elinor had ceased to rejoice in the dryness of the season, a very awful pause took place. It was put an end to by Mrs. Dashwood, who felt obliged to hope that he had left Mrs. Ferrars very well. In an hurried manner, he replied in the affirmative.

Another pause.

Elinor, resolving to exert herself, though fearing the sound of her own voice, now said,

"Is Mrs. Ferrars at Longstaple?"

"At Longstaple!" he replied, with an air of surprise—"No, my mother is in town."

"I meant," said Elinor, taking up some work from the table, "to inquire after Mrs. *Edward* Ferrars."

She dared not look up;—but her mother and Marianne both turned their eyes on him. He coloured, seemed perplexed, looked doubtingly, and after some hesitation, said,

"Perhaps you mean—my brother—you mean Mrs.—Mrs. *Robert* Ferrars."

"Mrs. Robert Ferrars!"—was repeated by Marianne and her mother, in an accent of the utmost amazement;—and though Elinor could not speak, even *her* eyes were fixed on him with the same impatient wonder. He rose from his seat and walked to the window, apparently from not knowing what to do; took up a pair of scissars that lay there, and while spoiling both them and their sheath by cutting the latter to pieces as he spoke, said, in an hurried voice,

"Perhaps you do not know—you may not have heard that my brother is lately married to—to the youngest—to Miss Lucy Steele."

His words were echoed with unspeakable astonishment by all but Elinor, who sat with her head leaning over her work, in a state of such agitation as made her hardly know where she was.

"Yes," said he, "they were married last week, and are now at Dawlish."

Elinor could sit it no longer. She almost ran out of the room, and as soon as the door was closed, burst into tears of joy, which at first she thought would never cease. Edward, who had till then looked any where, rather than at her, saw her hurry away, and perhaps saw—or even heard, her emotion; for immediately afterwards he fell into a reverie, which no remarks, no inquiries, no affectionate address of Mrs. Dashwood could penetrate, and at last, without saying a word, quitted the room, and walked out towards the village—leaving the others in the greatest astonishment and perplexity on a change in his situation, so wonderful and so sudden; —a perplexity which they had no means of lessening but by their own conjectures.

Chapter XIII.

Unaccountable, however, as the circumstances of his release might appear to the whole family, it was certain that Edward was free: and to what purpose that freedom would be employed was easily pre-determined by all;—for after experiencing the blessings of *one* imprudent engagement, contracted without his mother's consent, as he had already done for more than four years, nothing less could be expected of him in the failure of *that*, than the immediate contraction of another.

His errand at Barton, in fact, was a simple one. It was only to ask Elinor to marry him;—and considering that he was not altogether inexperienced in such a question, it might be strange that he should feel so uncomfortable in the present case as he really did, so much in need of encouragement and fresh air.

How soon he had walked himself into the proper resolution, however, how soon an opportunity of exercising it occurred, in what manner he expressed himself, and how he was received, need not be particularly told. This only need be said;—that when they all sat down to table at four o'clock, about three hours after his arrival, he had secured his lady, engaged her mother's consent, and was not only in the rapturous profession of the lover, but in the reality of reason and truth, one of the happiest of men. His situation indeed was more than commonly joyful. He had more than the ordinary triumph of accepted love to swell his heart, and raise his spirits. He was released without any reproach to himself, from an entanglement which had long formed his misery, from a woman whom he had long ceased to love;—and elevated at once to that security with another, which he must have thought of almost with despair, as soon as he had learnt to consider it with desire. He was brought, not from doubt or suspense, but from misery to happiness;—and the change was openly spoken in such a genuine, flowing, grateful cheerfulness, as his friends had never witnessed in him before.

His heart was now open to Elinor, all its weaknesses, all its errors confessed, and his first boyish attachment to Lucy treated with all the philosophic dignity of twenty-four.

"It was a foolish, idle inclination on my side," said he, "the consequence of ignorance of the world—and want of employment. Had my mother given me some active profession when I was removed at eighteen from the care of Mr. Pratt, I think—nay, I am sure, it would never have happened; for though I left Longstaple with what I thought, at the time, a most unconquerable preference for his niece, yet had I then had any pursuit, any object to engage my time and keep me at a distance from her for a few months, I should very soon have outgrown the fancied attachment, especially by mixing more with the world, as in such a case I must have done. But instead of having anything to do, instead of having any profession chosen for me, or being allowed to chuse any myself, I returned home to be completely idle; and for the first twelvemonth afterwards, I had not even the nominal employment, which belonging to the university would have given me, for I was not entered at Oxford till I was nineteen. I had therefore nothing in the world to do, but to fancy myself in love; and as my mother did not make my home in every respect comfortable, as I had no friend, no companion in my brother, and disliked new acquaintance, it was not unnatural for me to be very often at Longstaple, where I always felt myself at home, and was always sure of a welcome; and accordingly I spent the greatest part of my time there from eighteen to nineteen: Lucy appeared every thing that was amiable and obliging. She was pretty too—at least I thought so *then*, and I had seen so little of other women, that I could make no comparisons, and see no defects. Considering everything, therefore, I hope, foolish as our engagement was, foolish as it has since in every way been proved, it was not at the time an unnatural, or an inexcusable piece of folly."

The change which a few hours had wrought in the minds and the happiness of the Dashwoods, was such—so great—as promised them all, the satisfaction of a sleepless night. Mrs. Dashwood, too happy to be comfortable, knew not how to love Edward, nor praise Elinor enough, how to be enough thankful for his release without wounding his delicacy, nor how at once to give them leisure for unrestrained conversation together, and yet enjoy, as she wished, the sight and society of both.

Marianne could speak *her* happiness only by tears. Comparisons would occur—regrets would arise;—and her joy, though sincere as her love for her sister, was of a kind to give her neither spirits nor language.

But Elinor—How are *her* feelings to be described?—From the moment of learning that Lucy was married to another, that Edward was free, to the moment of his justifying the hopes which had so instantly followed, she was everything by turns but tranquil. But when the second moment had passed, when she found every doubt, every solicitude removed, compared her situation with what so lately it had been,—saw him honourably released from his former engagement, saw him instantly profiting by the release, to address herself and declare an affection as tender, as constant as she had ever supposed it to be,—she was oppressed, she was overcome by her own felicity;—and happily disposed as is the human mind to be easily familiarized with any change for the better, it required several hours to give sedateness to her spirits, or any degree of tranquility to her heart.

Edward was now fixed at the cottage at least for a week;—for whatever other claims might be made on him, it was impossible that less than a week should be given up to the enjoyment of Elinor's company, or suffice to say half that was to be said of the past, the present, and the future;—for though a very few hours spent in the hard labour of incessant talking will dispatch more subjects than can really be in common between any two rational creatures, yet with lovers it is different. Between *them* no subject is finished, no communication is even made, till it has been made at least twenty times over.

Lucy's marriage, the unceasing and reasonable wonder among them all, formed of course one of the earliest discussions of the lovers;—and Elinor's particular knowledge of each party made it appear to her in every view, as one of the most extraordinary and unaccountable circumstances she had ever heard. How they could be thrown together, and by what attraction Robert could be drawn on to marry a girl, of whose beauty she had herself heard him speak without any admiration,—a girl too already engaged to his brother, and on whose account that brother had been thrown off by his family—it was beyond her comprehension to make out. To her own heart it was a delightful affair, to her imagination it was even a ridiculous one, but to her reason, her judgment, it was completely a puzzle.

Edward could only attempt an explanation by supposing, that perhaps at first accidentally meeting, the vanity of the one had been so worked on by the flattery of the other, as to lead by degrees to all the rest. Elinor remembered what Robert had told her in Harley-street, of his opinion of what his own mediation in his brother's affairs might have done, if applied to in time. She repeated it to Edward.

"*That* was exactly like Robert,"—was his immediate observation.—"And *that*," he presently added, "might perhaps be in *his* head when the acquaintance between them first began. And Lucy perhaps at first might think only of procuring his good offices in my favour. Other designs might afterwards arise."

How long it had been carrying on between them, however, he was equally at a loss with herself to make out; for at Oxford, where he had remained by choice ever since his quitting London, he had had no means of hearing of her but from herself, and her letters to the very last were neither less frequent, nor less affectionate than usual. Not the smallest suspicion, therefore, had ever occurred to prepare him for what followed;—and when at last it burst on him in a letter from Lucy herself, he had been for some time, he believed, half stupified between the wonder, the horror, and the joy of such a deliverance. He put the letter into Elinor's hands.

"DEAR SIR,

BEING very sure I have long lost your affections, I have thought myself at liberty to bestow my own on another, and have no doubt of being as happy with him as I once used to think I might be with you; but I scorn to accept a hand while the heart was another's. Sincerely wish you happy in your choice, and it shall not be my fault if we are not always good friends, as our near relationship now makes proper.* I can safely say I owe you no ill-will, and am sure you will be too generous to do us any ill offices. Your brother has gained my affections entirely, and as we could not live without one another, we are just returned from the altar, and are now on our way to Dawlish for a few weeks, which place your dear brother has great curiosity to see, but thought I would first trouble you with these few lines, and shall always remain,
Your sincere well-wisher, friend, and sister,   LUCY FERRARS.

I have burnt all your letters, and will return your picture the first opportunity. Please to destroy my scrawls—but the ring with my hair you are very welcome to keep."

Elinor read and returned it without any comment.
"I will not ask your opinion of it as a composition," said Edward.—"For worlds would not I have had a letter of her's seen by *you* in former days.—In a sister it is bad enough, but in a wife!—how I have blushed over the pages of her writing!—and I believe I may say that since the first half year of our foolish—business—this is the only letter I ever received from her, of which the substance made me any amends for the defect of the style."
"However it may have come about," said Elinor, after a pause—"they are certainly married. And your mother has brought on herself a most appropriate punishment. The independence she settled on Robert, through resentment against you, has put it in his power to make his own choice; and she has actually been bribing one son with a thousand a-year, to do the very deed which she disinherited the other for intending to do. She will hardly be less hurt, I suppose,

---

* proper.] proper, A.

by Robert's marrying Lucy, than she would have been by your marrying her."

"She will be more hurt by it, for Robert always was her favourite.—She will be more hurt by it, and on the same principle will forgive him much sooner."

In what state the affair stood at present between them, Edward knew not, for no communication with any of his family had yet been attempted by him. He had quitted Oxford within four and twenty hours after Lucy's letter arrived, and with only one object before him, the nearest road to Barton, had had no leisure to form any scheme of conduct, with which that road did not hold the most intimate connection. He could do nothing till he were assured of his fate with Miss Dashwood; and by his rapidity in seeking *that* fate, it is to be supposed, in spite of the jealousy with which he had once thought of Colonel Brandon, in spite of the modesty with which he rated his own deserts, and the politeness with which he talked of his doubts, he did not, upon the whole, expect a very cruel reception. It was his business, however, to say that he *did*, and he said it very prettily. What he might say on the subject a twelvemonth after, must be referred to the imagination of husbands and wives.

That Lucy had certainly meant to deceive, to go off with a flourish of malice against him in her message by Thomas, was perfectly clear to Elinor; and Edward himself, now thoroughly enlightened on her character, had no scruple in believing her capable of the utmost meanness of wanton ill-nature. Though his eyes had been long opened, even before his acquaintance with Elinor began, to her ignorance and a want of liberality in some of her opinions—they had been equally imputed, by him, to her want of education; and till her last letter reached him, he had always believed her to be a well-disposed, good-hearted girl, and thoroughly attached to himself. Nothing but such a persuasion could have prevented his putting an end to an engagement, which, long before the discovery of it laid him open to his mother's anger, had been a continual source of disquiet and regret to him.

"I thought it my duty," said he, "independent of my feelings, to give her the option of continuing the engagement or not, when I was renounced by my mother, and stood to all appearance without a friend in the world to assist me. In such a situation as that, where there seemed nothing to tempt the avarice or the vanity of any living creature, how could I suppose, when she so earnestly, so warmly insisted on sharing my fate, whatever it might be, that any thing but the most disinterested affection was her inducement? And even now, I cannot comprehend on what motive she acted, or what fancied advantage it could be to her, to be fettered to a man for whom she had not the smallest regard, and who had only two thousand pounds in the world. She could not foresee that Colonel Brandon would give me a living."

"No, but she might suppose that something would occur in your favour; that your own family might in time relent. And at any rate, she lost nothing by continuing the engagement, for she has proved that it fettered neither her inclination nor her actions. The connection was certainly a respectable one, and probably gained her consideration among her friends; and, if nothing more advantageous occurred, it would be better for her to marry *you* than be single."

Edward was of course immediately convinced that nothing could have been more natural than Lucy's conduct, nor more self-evident than the motive of it.

Elinor scolded him, harshly as ladies always scold the imprudence which compliments themselves, for having spent so much time with them at Norland, when he must have felt his own inconstancy.

"Your behaviour was certainly very wrong," said she, "because— to say nothing of my own conviction, our relations were all led away by it to fancy and expect *what*, as you were *then* situated, could never be."

He could only plead an ignorance of his own heart, and a mistaken confidence in the force of his engagement.

"I was simple enough to think, that because my *faith* was plighted to another, there could be no danger in my being with you; and that the consciousness of my engagement was to keep my heart as safe and sacred as my honour. I felt that I admired you, but I told myself it was only friendship; and till I began to make comparisons between yourself and Lucy, I did not know how far I was got. After that, I suppose, I *was* wrong in remaining so much in Sussex, and the arguments with which I reconciled myself to the expediency of it, were no better than these:—The danger is my own; I am doing no injury to anybody but myself."

Elinor smiled, and shook her head.

Edward heard with pleasure of Colonel Brandon's being expected at the Cottage, as he really wished not only to be better acquainted with him, but to have an opportunity of convincing him that he no longer resented his giving him the living of Delaford—"Which, at present," said he, "after thanks so ungraciously delivered as mine were on the occasion, he must think I have never forgiven him for offering."

Now he felt astonished himself that he had never yet been to the place. But so little interest had he taken in the matter that he owed all his knowledge of the house, garden, and glebe, extent of the

parish, condition of the land, and rate of the tythes, to Elinor herself, who had heard so much of it from Colonel Brandon, and heard
it with so much attention, as to be entirely mistress of the subject.
One question after this only remained undecided between them,
one difficulty only was to be overcome. They were brought together
by mutual affection, with the warmest approbation of their real
friends, their intimate knowledge of each other seemed to make
their happiness certain—and they only wanted something to live
upon. Edward had two thousand pounds, and Elinor one, which,
with Delaford living, was all that they could call their own; for it
was impossible that Mrs. Dashwood should advance anything, and
they were neither of them quite enough in love to think that three
hundred and fifty pounds a-year would supply them with the comforts of life.[1]

Edward was not entirely without hopes of some favourable
change in his mother towards him; and on *that* he rested for the
residue of their income. But Elinor had no such dependance; for
since Edward would still be unable to marry Miss Morton, and his
chusing herself had been spoken of in Mrs. Ferrar's flattering language as only a lesser evil than his chusing Lucy Steele, she feared
that Robert's offence would serve no other purpose than to enrich
Fanny.

About four days after Edward's arrival Colonel Brandon appeared,
to complete Mrs. Dashwood's satisfaction, and to give her the dignity of having, for the first time since her living at Barton, more
company with her than her house would hold. Edward was allowed
to retain the privilege of first comer, and Colonel Brandon therefore
walked every night to his old quarters at the Park; from whence he
usually returned in the morning, early enough to interrupt the lovers' first tête-à-tête before breakfast.

A three weeks' residence at Delaford, where, in his evening hours
at least, he had little to do but to calculate the disproportion between thirty-six and seventeen, brought him to Barton in a temper
of mind which needed all the improvement in Marianne's looks, all
the kindness of her welcome, and all the encouragement of her
mother's language, to make it cheerful. Among such friends, however, and such flattery, he did revive. No rumour of Lucy's marriage
had yet reached him;—he knew nothing of what had passed; and
the first hours of his visit were consequently spent in hearing and
in wondering. Every thing was explained to him by Mrs. Dashwood,
and he found fresh reason to rejoice in what he had done for Mr.
Ferrars, since eventually it promoted the interest of Elinor.

1. See p. 21, n. 1.

It would be needless to say, that the gentlemen advanced in the good opinion of each other, as they advanced in each other's acquaintance, for it could not be otherwise. Their resemblance in good principles and good sense, in disposition and manner of thinking, would probably have been sufficient to unite them in friendship, without any other attraction; but their being in love with two sisters, and two sisters fond of each other, made that mutual regard inevitable and immediate, which might otherwise have waited the effect of time and judgment.

The letters from town, which a few days before would have made every nerve in Elinor's body thrill with transport, now arrived to be read with less emotion than mirth. Mrs. Jennings wrote to tell the wonderful tale, to vent her honest indignation against the jilting girl, and pour forth her compassion towards poor Mr. Edward, who, she was sure, had quite doted upon the worthless hussey, and was now, by all accounts, almost broken-hearted, at Oxford.—"I do think," she continued, "nothing was ever carried on so sly; for it was but two days before Lucy called and sat a couple of hours with me. Not a soul suspected anything of the matter, not even Nancy, who, poor soul! came crying to me the day after, in a great fright for fear of Mrs. Ferrars, as well as not knowing how to get to Plymouth; for Lucy it seems borrowed all her money before she went off to be married, on purpose we suppose to make a shew with, and poor Nancy had not seven shillings in the world;—so I was very glad to give her five guineas to take her down to Exeter, where she thinks of staying three or four weeks with Mrs. Burgess, in hopes, as I tell her, to fall in with the Doctor again. And I must say that Lucy's crossness not to take her along with them in the chaise is worse than all. Poor Mr. Edward! I cannot get him out of my head, but you must send for him to Barton, and Miss Marianne must try to comfort him."

Mr. Dashwood's strains were more solemn. Mrs. Ferrars was the most unfortunate of women—poor Fanny had suffered agonies of sensibility—and he considered the existence of each, under such a blow, with grateful wonder. Robert's offence was unpardonable, but Lucy's was infinitely worse. Neither of them was ever again to be mentioned to Mrs. Ferrars; and even, if she might hereafter be induced to forgive her son, his wife should never be acknowledged as her daughter, nor be permitted to appear in her presence. The secrecy with which every thing had been carried on between them, was rationally treated as enormously heightening the crime, because, had any suspicion of it occurred to the others, proper measures would have been taken to prevent the marriage; and he called on Elinor to join with him in regretting that Lucy's engagement with Edward had not rather been fulfilled, than that she should thus be the means of spreading misery farther in the family.—He thus continued:

"Mrs. Ferrars has never yet mentioned Edward's name, which does not surprise us; but to our great astonishment, not a line has been received from him on the occasion. Perhaps, however, he is kept silent by his fear of offending, and I shall, therefore, give him a hint, by a line to Oxford, that his sister and I both think a letter of proper submission from him addressed perhaps to Fanny, and by her shewn to her mother, might not be taken amiss; for we all know the tenderness of Mrs. Ferrars's heart, and that she wishes for nothing so much as to be on good terms with her children."

This paragraph was of some importance to the prospects and conduct of Edward. It determined him to attempt a reconciliation, though not exactly in the manner pointed out by their brother and sister.

"A letter of proper submission!" repeated he; "would they have me beg my mother's pardon for Robert's ingratitude to *her*, and breach of honour to *me*?—I can make no submission—I am grown neither humble nor penitent by what has passed.—I am grown very happy, but that would not interest.—I know of no submission that *is* proper for me to make."

"You may certainly ask to be forgiven," said Elinor, "because you have offended;—and I should think you might *now* venture so far as to profess some concern for having ever formed the engagement which drew on you your mother's anger."

He agreed that he might.

"And when she has forgiven you, perhaps a little humility may be convenient while acknowledging a second engagement, almost as imprudent in *her* eyes, as the first."

He had nothing to urge against it, but still resisted the idea of a letter of proper submission; and therefore, to make it easier to him, as he declared a much greater willingness to make mean concessions by word of mouth than on paper, it was resolved that, instead of writing to Fanny, he should go to London, and personally intreat her good offices in his favour.—"And if they really *do* interest themselves," said Marianne, in her new character of candour, "in bringing about a reconciliation, I shall think that even John and Fanny are not entirely without merit."

After a visit on Colonel Brandon's side of only three or four days, the two gentlemen quitted Barton together.—They were to go immediately to Delaford, that Edward might have some personal knowledge of his future home, and assist his patron and friend in deciding on what improvements were needed to it; and from thence, after staying there a couple of nights, he was to proceed on his journey to town.

Chapter XIV.

After a proper resistance on the part of Mrs. Ferrars, just so violent and so steady as to preserve her from that reproach which she always seemed fearful of incurring, the reproach of being too amiable, Edward was admitted to her presence, and pronounced to be again her son.

Her family had of late been exceedingly fluctuating. For many years of her life she had had two sons; but the crime and annihilation of Edward a few weeks ago, had robbed her of one; the similar annihilation of Robert had left her for a fortnight without any; and now, by the resuscitation of Edward, she had one again.

In spite of his being allowed once more to live, however, he did not feel the continuance of his existence secure, till he had revealed his present engagement; for the publication of that circumstance, he feared, might give a sudden turn to his constitution, and carry him off as rapidly as before. With apprehensive caution therefore it was revealed, and he was listened to with unexpected calmness. Mrs. Ferrars at first reasonably endeavoured to dissuade him from marrying Miss Dashwood, by every argument in her power;—told him, that in Miss Morton he would have a woman of higher rank and larger fortune;—and enforced the assertion, by observing that Miss Morton was the daughter of a nobleman with thirty thousand pounds, while Miss Dashwood was only the daughter of a private gentleman, with no more than *three*; but when she found that, though perfectly admitting the truth of her representation, he was by no means inclined to be guided by it, she judged it wisest, from the experience of the past, to submit—and therefore, after such an ungracious delay as she owed to her own dignity, and as served to prevent every suspicion of good-will, she issued her decree of consent to the marriage of Edward and Elinor.

What she would engage to do towards augmenting their income, was next to be considered; and here it plainly appeared, that though Edward was now her only son, he was by no means her eldest; for while Robert was inevitably endowed with a thousand pounds a-year, not the smallest objection was made against Edward's taking orders for the sake of two hundred and fifty at the utmost; nor was any thing promised either for the present or in future, beyond the ten thousand pounds, which had been given with Fanny.

It was as much, however, as was desired, and more than was expected by Edward and Elinor; and Mrs. Ferrars herself, by her shuffling excuses, seemed the only person surprised at her not giving more.

With an income quite sufficient to their wants thus secured to them, they had nothing to wait for after Edward was in possession of the living, but the readiness of the house, to which Colonel Brandon, with an eager desire for the accommodation of Elinor, was making considerable improvements; and after waiting some time for their completion, after experiencing, as usual, a thousand disappointments and delays, from the unaccountable dilatoriness of the workmen, Elinor, as usual, broke through the first positive resolution of not marrying till every thing was ready, and the ceremony took place in Barton church early in the autumn.

The first month after their marriage was spent with their friend at the Mansion-house, from whence they could superintend the progress of the Parsonage, and direct every thing as they liked on the spot;—could chuse papers,[1] project shrubberies, and invent a sweep.[2] Mrs. Jennings's prophecies, though rather jumbled together, were chiefly fulfilled; for she was able to visit Edward and his wife in their Parsonage by Michaelmas, and she found in Elinor and her husband, as she really believed, one of the happiest couple in the world. They had in fact nothing to wish for, but the marriage of Colonel Brandon and Marianne, and rather better pasturage for their cows.

They were visited on their first settling by almost all their relations and friends. Mrs. Ferrars came to inspect the happiness which she was almost ashamed of having authorised; and even the Dashwoods were at the expense of a journey from Sussex to do them honour.

"I will not say that I am disappointed, my dear sister," said John, as they were walking together one morning before the gates of Delaford House, "*that* would be saying too much, for certainly you have been one of the most fortunate young women in the world, as it is. But, I confess, it would give me great pleasure to call Colonel Brandon brother. His property here, his place, his house, every thing in such respectable and excellent condition!—and his woods!—I have not seen such timber any where in Dorsetshire, as there is now standing in Delaford Hanger![3]—And though, perhaps, Marianne may not seem exactly the person to attract him—yet I think it would altogether be adviseable for you to have them now frequently staying with you, for as Colonel Brandon seems a great deal at home, nobody can tell what may happen—for, when people are much thrown together, and see little of anybody else—and it will always be in your power to set her off to advantage, and so forth;—in short, you may as well give her a chance—You understand me."—

1. Wallpaper.
2. Citing this passage, the *OED* defines *sweep* as a curved carriage drive leading to a house.
3. Woods on the side of a steep hill or bank.

But though Mrs. Ferrars *did* come to see them, and always treated them with the make-believe of decent affection, they were never insulted by her real favour and preference. *That* was due to the folly of Robert, and the cunning of his wife; and it was earned by them before many months had passed away. The selfish sagacity of the latter, which had at first drawn Robert into the scrape, was the principal instrument of his deliverance from it; for her respectful humility, assiduous attentions, and endless flatteries, as soon as the smallest opening was given for their exercise, reconciled Mrs. Ferrars to his choice, and re-established him completely in her favour.

The whole of Lucy's behaviour in the affair, and the prosperity which crowned it, therefore, may be held forth as a most encouraging instance of what an earnest, an unceasing attention to self-interest, however its progress may be apparently obstructed, will do in securing every advantage of fortune, with no other sacrifice than that of time and conscience. When Robert first sought her acquaintance, and privately visited her in Bartlett's Buildings, it was only with the view imputed to him by his brother. He merely meant to persuade her to give up the engagement; and as there could be nothing to overcome but the affection of both, he naturally expected that one or two interviews would settle the matter. In that point, however, and that only, he erred;—for though Lucy soon gave him hopes that his eloquence would convince her in *time*, another visit, another conversation, was always wanted to produce this conviction. Some doubts always lingered in her mind when they parted, which could only be removed by another half hour's discourse with himself. His attendance was by this means secured, and the rest followed in course. Instead of talking of Edward, they came gradually to talk only of Robert,—a subject on which he had always more to say than on any other, and in which she soon betrayed an interest even equal to his own; and in short, it became speedily evident to both, that he had entirely supplanted his brother. He was proud of his conquest, proud of tricking Edward, and very proud of marrying privately without his mother's consent. What immediately followed is known. They passed some months in great happiness at Dawlish; for she had many relations and old acquaintance to cut— and he drew several plans for magnificent cottages;—and from thence returning to town, procured the forgiveness of Mrs. Ferrars, by the simple expedient of asking it, which, at Lucy's instigation, was adopted. The forgiveness at first, indeed, as was reasonable, comprehended only Robert; and Lucy, who had owed his mother no duty, and therefore could have transgressed none, still remained some weeks longer unpardoned. But perseverance in humility of conduct and messages, in self-condemnation for Robert's offence, and gratitude for the unkindness she was treated with, procured her in time the haughty notice which overcame her by its graciousness, and led soon afterwards, by rapid degrees, to the highest state of affection and influence. Lucy became as necessary to Mrs. Ferrars, as either Robert or Fanny; and while Edward was never cordially forgiven for having once intended to marry her, and Elinor, though superior to her in fortune and birth, was spoken of as an intruder, *she* was in every thing considered, and always openly acknowledged, to be a favourite child. They settled in town, received very liberal assistance from Mrs. Ferrars, were on the best terms imaginable with the Dashwoods; and setting aside the jealousies and ill-will continually subsisting between Fanny and Lucy, in which their husbands of course took a part, as well as the frequent domestic disagreements between Robert and Lucy themselves, nothing could exceed the harmony in which they all lived together.

What Edward had done to forfeit the right of eldest son, might have puzzled many people to find out; and what Robert had done to succeed to it, might have puzzled them still more. It was an arrangement, however, justified in its effects, if not in its cause; for nothing ever appeared in Robert's style of living or of talking, to give a suspicion of his regretting the extent of his income, as either leaving his brother too little, or bringing himself too much;—and if Edward might be judged from the ready discharge of his duties in every particular, from an increasing attachment to his wife and his home, and from the regular cheerfulness of his spirits, he might be supposed no less contented with his lot, no less free from every wish of an exchange.

Elinor's marriage divided her as little from her family as could well be contrived, without rendering the cottage at Barton entirely useless, for her mother and sisters spent much more than half their time with her. Mrs. Dashwood was acting on motives of policy as well as pleasure in the frequency of her visits at Delaford; for her wish of bringing Marianne and Colonel Brandon together was hardly less earnest, though rather more liberal than what John had expressed. It was now her darling object. Precious as was the company of her daughter to her, she desired nothing so much as to give up its constant enjoyment to her valued friend; and to see Marianne settled at the mansion-house was equally the wish of Edward and Elinor. They each felt his sorrows, and their own obligations, and Marianne, by general consent, was to be the reward of all.

With such a confederacy against her—with a knowledge so intimate of his goodness—with a conviction of his fond attachment to herself, which at last, though long after it was observable to everybody else—burst on her—what could she do?

Marianne Dashwood was born to an extraordinary fate. She was born to discover the falsehood of her own opinions, and to counteract, by her conduct, her most favourite maxims. She was born to overcome an affection formed so late in life as at seventeen, and with no sentiment superior to strong esteem and lively friendship, voluntarily to give her hand to another!—and *that* other, a man who had suffered no less than herself under the event of a former attachment, whom, two years before, she had considered too old to be married,—and who still sought the constitutional safeguard of a flannel waistcoat!

But so it was. Instead of falling a sacrifice to an irresistible passion, as once she had fondly flattered herself with expecting,—instead of remaining even for ever with her mother, and finding her only pleasures in retirement and study, as afterwards in her more calm and sober judgment she had determined on,—she found herself at nineteen, submitting to new attachments, entering on new duties, placed in a new home, a wife, the mistress of a family, and the patroness of a village.

Colonel Brandon was now as happy, as all those who best loved him, believed he deserved to be;—in Marianne he was consoled for every past affliction;—her regard and her society restored his mind to animation, and his spirits to cheerfulness; and that Marianne found her own happiness in forming his, was equally the persuasion and delight of each observing friend. Marianne could never love by halves; and her whole heart became, in time, as much devoted to her husband, as it had once been to Willoughby.

Willoughby could not hear of her marriage without a pang; and his punishment was soon afterwards complete in the voluntary forgiveness of Mrs. Smith, who, by stating his marriage with a woman of character, as the source of her clemency, gave him reason for believing that had he behaved with honour towards Marianne, he might at once have been happy and rich. That his repentance of misconduct, which thus brought its own punishment, was sincere, need not be doubted;—nor that he long thought of Colonel Brandon with envy, and of Marianne with regret. But that he was for ever inconsolable, that he fled from society, or contracted an habitual gloom of temper, or died of a broken heart, must not be depended on—for he did neither. He lived to exert, and frequently to enjoy himself. His wife was not always out of humour, nor his home always uncomfortable; and in his breed of horses and dogs, and in sporting of every kind, he found no inconsiderable degree of domestic felicity.

For Marianne, however—in spite of his incivility in surviving her loss—he always retained that decided regard which interested him in everything that befell her, and made her his secret standard of perfection in woman;—and many a rising beauty would be slighted by him in after-days as bearing no comparison with Mrs. Brandon. Mrs. Dashwood was prudent enough to remain at the cottage, without attempting a removal to Delaford; and fortunately for Sir John and Mrs. Jennings, when Marianne was taken from them, Margaret had reached an age highly suitable for dancing, and not very ineligible for being supposed to have a lover.

Between Barton and Delaford, there was that constant communication which strong family affection would naturally dictate;— and among the merits and the happiness of Elinor and Marianne, let it not be ranked as the least considerable, that though sisters, and living almost within sight of each other, they could live without disagreement between themselves, or producing coolness between their husbands.

FINIS.

CONTEXTS

ADAM SMITH

From Theory of Moral Sentiments (1759)†

Part III. Of the Foundation of Our Judgments Concerning Our Own Sentiments and Conduct, and of the Sense of Duty.

CHAP. I. OF THE PRINCIPLE OF SELF-APPROBATION, AND OF SELF-DISAPPROBATION.

In the two foregoing parts of this discourse, I have chiefly considered the origin and foundation of our judgments concerning the sentiments and conduct of others. I come now to consider more particularly the origin of those concerning our own.

The principle by which we naturally either approve or disapprove of our own conduct, seems to be altogether the same with that by which we exercise the like judgments concerning the conduct of other people. We either approve or disapprove of the conduct of another man, according as we feel that, when we bring his case home to ourselves, we either can or cannot entirely sympathize with the sentiments and motives which directed it. And, in the same manner, we either approve or disapprove of our own conduct, according as we feel that, when we place ourselves in the situation of another man, and view it, as it were, with his eyes, and from his station, we either can or cannot entirely enter into and sympathize with the sentiments and motives which influenced it. We can never survey our own sentiments and motives, we can never form any judgment concerning them, unless we remove ourselves, as it were, from our own natural station, and endeavour to view them as at a certain distance from us. But we can do this in no other way than by endeavouring to view them with the eyes of other people, or as other people are likely to view them. Whatever judgment we can form concerning them, accordingly, must always bear some secret reference, either to what are, or to what, upon a certain condition, would be, or to what, we imagine, ought to be the judgment of others. We endeavour to examine our own conduct as we imagine any other fair and impartial spectator would examine it. If, upon

† Adam Smith (1723–1790) was a prominent Scottish moral philosopher and economist. A leading theorist of sympathy, Smith holds that moral behavior results both from our capacity to reconstruct and share in the experiences of others and from our sensitivity to the approval or disapproval of onlookers we imagine to be impartially observing us. As the excerpts presented here indicate, exertion and self-control also play large roles in the sentimental theory he develops. As such, his theory may be considered more appropriately in relation to Elinor than to Marianne.

placing ourselves in his situation, we thoroughly enter into all the passions and motives which influenced it, we approve of it, by sympathy with the approbation of this supposed equitable judge. If otherwise, we enter into his disapprobation, and condemn it.

Were it possible that a human creature could grow up to manhood in some solitary place, without any communication with his own species, he could no more think of his own character, of the propriety or demerit of his own sentiments and conduct, of the beauty or deformity of his own mind, than of the beauty or deformity of his own face. All these are objects which he cannot easily see, which naturally he does not look at, and with regard to which he is provided with no mirror which can present them to his view. Bring him into society, and he is immediately provided with the mirror which he wanted before. It is placed in the countenance and behaviour of those he lives with, which always mark when they enter into, and when they disapprove of his sentiments. * * *

* * *

Part VII. Of Systems of Moral Philosophy

SECTION II, CHAP. I. OF THOSE SYSTEMS WHICH MAKE VIRTUE
CONSIST IN PROPRIETY

* * *

The plan and system which nature has sketched out for our conduct, seems to be altogether different from that of the Stoical philosophy.

By nature, the events which immediately affect that little department in which we ourselves have some little management and direction, which immediately affect ourselves, our friends, our country, are the events which interest us the most, and which chiefly excite our desires and aversions, our hopes and fears, our joys and sorrows. Should those passions be, what they are very apt to be, too vehement, nature has provided a proper remedy and correction. The real, or even the imaginary presence of the impartial spectator, the authority of the man within the breast, is always at hand to overawe them into the proper tone and temper of moderation.

If, notwithstanding our most faithful exertions, all the events which can affect this little department should turn out the most unfortunate and disastrous, nature has by no means left us without consolation. That consolation may be drawn, not only from the complete approbation of the man within the breast, but, if possible, from a still nobler and more generous principle, from firm reliance upon, and a reverential submission to, that benevolent wisdom

which directs all the events of human life, and which, we may be
assured, would never have suffered those misfortunes to happen,
had they not been indispensably necessary for the good of the
whole.

* * *

SAMUEL JOHNSON

Rambler†

No. 32. Saturday, July 7, 1750.

Οσσα τε δαιμονιητι τυχαις βροτοι αλγε εχουσιν,
'Ων αν μοιραν εχης, πραως, φερε, μηδ' αγανακλει
'Ιασθαι δε πρεπει καθοσον δυνη.
PYTHAGORAS.

Of all the woes that load the mortal state,
Whate'er thy portion, mildly meet thy fate;
But ease it as thou can'st—
ELPHINSTON.

So large a part of human life passes in a state contrary to our natural desires, that one of the principal topicks of moral instruction
is the art of bearing calamities, and such is the certainty of evil,
that it is the duty of every man to furnish his mind with those
principles that may enable him to act under it with decency and
propriety.

The sect of ancient philosophers, that boasted to have carried
this necessary science to the highest perfection, were the Stoicks,
or scholars of Zeno, whose wild enthusiastick virtue pretended to
an exemption from the sensibilities of unenlightened mortals, and
who proclaimed themselves exalted, by the doctrines of their sect,
above the reach of those miseries which embitter life to the rest of
the world. They therefore removed pain, poverty, loss of friends,
exile, and violent death, from the catalogue of evils; and passed, in
their haughty style, a kind of irreversible decree, by which they
forbad them to be counted any longer among the objects of terror

† Samuel Johnson (1709–1784) was the most celebrated and authoritative literary person-
age of his day, and one of Austen's favorite prose writers. In the periodical essays reprinted here, from the *Rambler* and the *Idler*, Johnson dismisses stoic ideals of rational
detachment and indifference and, granting the prominence of desire in human life, discusses the importance of struggling to maintain a nonobsessive, well-regulated mind. As
such, these two essays indicate that the sort of lucidity and patience Elinor values has
a background that extends beyond debates about gender.

or anxiety, or to give any disturbance to the tranquillity of a wise man.

This edict was, I think, not universally observed; for though one of the most resolute, when he was tortured by a violent disease, cried out, that let pain harass him to his utmost power, it should never force him to consider it as other than indifferent and neutral; yet all had not stubbornness to hold out against their senses; for a weaker pupil of Zeno is recorded to have confessed in the anguish of the gout, that *he now found pain to be an evil.*

It may, however, be questioned, whether these philosophers can be very properly numbered among the teachers of patience; for if pain be not an evil, there seems no instruction requisite how it may be borne; and, therefore, when they endeavour to arm their followers with arguments against it, they may be thought to have given up their first position. But such inconsistencies are to be expected from the greatest understandings, when they endeavour to grow eminent by singularity, and employ their strength in establishing opinions opposite to nature.

The controversy about the reality of external evils is now at an end. That life has many miseries, and that those miseries are sometimes, at least, equal to all the powers of fortitude, is now universally confessed; and therefore it is useful to consider not only how we may escape them, but by what means those, which either the accidents of affairs, or the infirmities of nature, must bring upon us, may be mitigated and lightened, and how we may make those hours less wretched, which the condition of our present existence will not allow to be very happy.

The cure for the greatest part of human miseries is not radical, but palliative. Infelicity is involved in corporeal nature, and interwoven with our being; all attempts therefore to decline it wholly are useless and vain: the armies of pain send their arrows against us on every side, the choice is only between those which are more or less sharp, or tinged with poison of greater or less malignity; and the strongest armour which reason can supply, will only blunt their points, but cannot repel them.

The great remedy which Heaven has put in our hands is patience, by which, though we cannot lessen the torments of the body, we can in a great measure preserve the peace of the mind, and shall suffer only the natural and genuine force of an evil, without heightening its acrimony, or prolonging its effects.

There is indeed nothing more unsuitable to the nature of man in any calamity than rage and turbulence, which, without examining whether they are not sometimes impious, are at least always offensive, and incline others rather to hate and despise than to pity and assist us. If what we suffer has been brought upon us by ourselves, it is observed by an ancient poet, that patience is eminently our duty, since no one should be angry at feeling that which he has deserved.

Leniter ex merito quicquid patiare ferendum est.
Let pain deserv'd without complaint be borne.

And surely, if we are conscious that we have not contributed to our own sufferings, if punishment falls upon innocence, or disappointment happens to industry and prudence, patience, whether more necessary or not, is much easier, since our pain is then without aggravation, and we have not the bitterness of remorse to add to the asperity of misfortune.

In those evils which are allotted us by Providence, such as deformity, privation of any of the senses, or old age, it is always to be remembered, that impatience can have no present effect, but to deprive us of the consolations which our condition admits, by driving away from us those by whose conversation or advice we might be amused or helped; and that, with regard to futurity, it is yet less to be justified, since without lessening the pain, it cuts off the hope of that reward which he, by whom it is inflicted, will confer upon them that bear it well.

In all evils which admit a remedy, impatience is to be avoided, because it wastes that time and attention in complaints, that, if properly applied, might remove the cause. Turenne,[1] among the acknowledgments which he used to pay in conversation to the memory of those by whom he had been instructed in the art of war, mentioned one with honour, who taught him not to spend his time in regretting any mistake which he had made, but to set himself immediately and vigorously to repair it.

Patience and submission are very carefully to be distinguished from cowardice and indolence. We are not to repine, but we may lawfully struggle; for the calamities of life, like the necessities of nature, are calls to labour and exercises of diligence. When we feel any pressure of distress, we are not to conclude that we can only obey the will of Heaven by languishing under it, any more than when we perceive the pain of water, we are to imagine that water is prohibited. Of misfortune it never can be certainly known whether, as proceeding from the hand of God, it is an act of favour, or of punishment: but since all the ordinary dispensations of Providence are to be interpreted according to the general analogy of things, we may conclude that we have a right to remove one inconvenience as well as another; that we are only to take care lest we purchase ease with guilt; and that our Maker's purpose, whether of

1. A French military leader during the reign of Louis XIV.

reward or severity, will be answered by the labours which he lays us under the necessity of performing. This duty is not more difficult in any state than in diseases intensely painful, which may indeed suffer such exacerbations as seem to strain the powers of life to the utmost stretch, and leave very little of the attention vacant to precept or reproof. In this state the nature of man requires some indulgence, and every extravagance but impiety may be easily forgiven him. Yet, lest we should think ourselves too soon entitled to the mournful privileges of irresistible misery, it is proper to reflect, that the utmost anguish which human wit can contrive, or human malice can inflict, has been borne with constancy; and that if the pains of disease be, as I believe they are, sometimes greater than those of artificial torture, they are therefore in their own nature shorter; the vital frame is quickly broken, or the union between soul and body is for a time suspended by insensibility, and we soon cease to feel our maladies when they once become too violent to be borne. I think there is some reason for questioning whether the body and mind are not so proportioned, that the one can bear all that can be inflicted on the other, whether virtue cannot stand its ground as long as life, and whether a soul well principled will not be separated sooner than subdued.

In calamities which operate chiefly on our passions, such as diminution of fortune, loss of friends, or declension of character, the chief danger of impatience is upon the first attack, and many expedients have been contrived, by which the blow may be broken. Of these the most general principle is, not to take pleasure in any thing, of which it is not in our power to secure the possession to ourselves. This counsel, when we consider the enjoyment of any terrestrial advantage as opposite to a constant and habitual solicitude for future felicity, is undoubtedly just, and delivered by that authority which cannot be disputed; but in any other sense, it is not like advice, not to walk lest we should stumble, or not to see lest our eyes should light upon deformity? It seems to me reasonable to enjoy blessings with confidence as well as to resign them with submission, and to hope for the continuance of good which we possess without insolence or voluptuousness, as for the restitution of that which we lose without despondency or murmurs.

The chief security against the fruitless anguish of impatience, must arise from frequent reflection on the wisdom and goodness of the GOD of nature, in whose hands are riches and poverty, honour and disgrace, pleasure and pain, and life and death. A settled conviction of the tendency of every thing to our good, and of the possibility of turning miseries into happiness, by receiving them rightly, will incline us to bless the name of the LORD whether he gives or takes away.

SAMUEL JOHNSON

Idler

No. 72. Saturday, September 1, 1759.

Men complain of nothing more frequently than of deficient memory; and, indeed, every one finds that many of the ideas which he desired to retain have slipped irretrievably away; that the acquisitions of the mind are sometimes equally fugitive with the gifts of fortune; and that a short intermission of attention more certainly lessens knowledge than impairs an estate.

To assist this weakness of our nature, many methods have been proposed, all of which may be justly suspected of being ineffectual; for no art of memory, however its effects have been boasted or admired, has been ever adopted into general use, nor have those who possessed it appeared to excel others in readiness of recollection or multiplicity of attainments.

There is another art of which all have felt the want, though *Themistocles*[1] only confessed it. We suffer equal pain from the pertinacious adhesion of unwelcome images, as from the evanescence of those which are pleasing and useful; and it may be doubted whether we should be more benefited by the art of memory or the art of forgetfulness.

Forgetfulness is necessary to remembrance. Ideas are retained by renovation of that impression which time is always wearing away, and which new images are striving to obliterate. If useless thoughts could be expelled from the mind, all the valuable parts of our knowledge would more frequently recur, and every recurrence would reinstate them in their former place.

It is impossible to consider, without some regret, how much might have been learned, or how much might have been invented by a rational and vigorous application of time, uselessly or painfully passed in the revocation of events which have left neither good nor evil behind them, in grief for misfortunes either repaired or irreparable, in resentment of injuries known only to ourselves, of which death has put the authors beyond our power.

Philosophy has accumulated precept upon precept, to warn us against the anticipation of future calamities. All useless misery is certainly folly, and he that feels evils before they come may be deservedly censured; yet surely to dread the future is more reasonable than to lament the past. The business of life is to go forwards:

---

1. Athenian politician and naval strategist (c. 524 B.C.E.–460 B.C.E.).

he who sees evil in prospect meets it in his way; but he who catches it by retrospection turns back to find it. That which is feared may sometimes be avoided, but that which is regretted to-day may be regretted again to-morrow.

Regret is indeed useful and virtuous, and not only allowable but necessary, when it tends to the amendment of life, or to admonition of error which we may be again in danger of committing. But a very small part of the moments spent in meditation on the past, produce any reasonable caution or salutary sorrow. Most of the mortifications that we have suffered, arose from the concurrence of local and temporary circumstances, which can never meet again; and most of our disappointments have succeeded those expectations, which life allows not to be formed a second time.

It would add much to human happiness, if an art could be taught of forgetting all of which the remembrance is at once useless and afflictive, if that pain which never can end in pleasure could be driven totally away, that the mind might perform its functions without incumbrance, and the past might no longer encroach upon the present.

Little can be done well to which the whole mind is not applied; the business of every day calls for the day to which it is assigned; and he will have no leisure to regret yesterday's vexations who resolves not to have a new subject of regret to-morrow.

But to forget or to remember at pleasure, are equally beyond the power of man. Yet as memory may be assisted by method, and the decays of knowledge repaired by stated times of recollection, so the power of forgetting is capable of improvement. Reason will, by a resolute contest, prevail over imagination, and the power may be obtained of transferring the attention as judgment shall direct.

The incursions of troublesome thoughts are often violent and importunate; and it is not easy to a mind accustomed to their inroads to expel them immediately by putting better images into motion; but this enemy of quiet is above all others weakened by every defeat; the reflexion which has been once overpowered and ejected, seldom returns with any formidable vehemence.

Employment is the great instrument of intellectual dominion. The mind cannot retire from its enemy into total vacancy, or turn aside from one object but by passing to another. The gloomy and the resentful are always found among those who have nothing to do, or who do nothing. We must be busy about good or evil, and he to whom the present offers nothing will often be looking backward on the past.

EDMUND BURKE

From Reflections on the Revolution in France (1790)†

* * *

You will observe, that from Magna Charta to the Declaration of Right, it has been the uniform policy of our constitution to claim and assert our liberties, as an *entailed inheritance* derived to us from our forefathers, and to be transmitted to our posterity; as an estate specially belonging to the people of this kingdom without any reference whatever to any other more general or prior right. By this means our constitution preserves an unity in so great a diversity of its parts. We have an inheritable crown; an inheritable peerage; and an house of commons and a people inheriting privileges, franchises, and liberties, from a long line of ancestors.

This policy appears to me to be the result of profound reflection; or rather the happy effect of following nature, which is wisdom without reflection, and above it. A spirit of innovation is generally the result of a selfish temper and confined views. People will not look forward to posterity, who never look backward to their ancestors. Besides, the people of England well know, that the idea of inheritance furnishes a sure principle of conservation, and a sure principle of transmission; without at all excluding a principle of improvement. It leaves acquisition free; but it secures what it acquires. Whatever advantages are obtained by a state proceeding on these maxims, are locked fast as in a sort of family settlement; grasped as in a kind of mortmain for ever. By a constitutional policy, working after the pattern of nature, we receive, we hold, we transmit our government and our privileges, in the same manner in which we enjoy and transmit our property and our lives. The institutions of policy, the goods of fortune, the gifts of Providence, are handed down, to us and from us, in the same course and order. Our political system is placed in a just correspondence and symmetry with the order of the world, and with the mode of existence decreed to a permanent body composed of transitory parts; wherein, by the disposition of a stupendous wisdom, moulding together the

---

† Edmund Burke (1729–1797) was a statesman, orator, and man of letters. Burke supported such causes as the independence of the American colonies, the emancipation of Ireland, and the impeachment of Warren Hastings (a friend of the Austen family), and his vehement opposition to the French Revolution struck many contemporaries as inconsistent. In the excerpts presented here, Burke celebrates the continuities of family, property, inheritance, and the landed life that some readers believe are cherished in Austen's novels as well. The text reprinted here is from the tenth edition of 1790.

great mysterious incorporation of the human race, the whole, at one time, is never old, or middle-aged, or young, but in a condition of unchangeable constancy, moves on through the varied tenour of perpetual decay, fall, renovation, and progression. Thus, by preserving the method of nature in the conduct of the state, in what we improve we are never wholly new; in what we retain we are never wholly obsolete. By adhering in this manner and on those principles to our forefathers, we are guided not by the superstition of antiquarians, but by the spirit of philosophic analogy, in this choice of inheritance we have given to our frame of polity the image of a relation in blood; binding up the constitution of our country with our dearest domestic ties; adopting our fundamental laws into the bosom of our family affections; keeping inseparable, and cherishing with the warmth of all their combined and mutually reflected charities, our state, our hearths, our sepulchres, and our altars.

Through the same plan of a conformity to nature in our artificial institutions, and by calling in the aid of her unerring and powerful instincts, to fortify the fallible and feeble contrivances of our reason, we have derived several other, and those no small benefits, from considering our liberties in the light of an inheritance. Always acting as if in the presence of canonized forefathers, the spirit of freedom, leading in itself to misrule and excess, is tempered with an awful gravity. This idea of a liberal descent inspires us with a sense of habitual native dignity, which prevents that upstart insolence almost inevitably adhering to and disgracing those who are the first acquirers of any distinction. By this means our liberty becomes a noble freedom. It carries an imposing and majestic aspect. It has a pedigree and illustrating ancestors. It has its bearings and its ensigns armorial. It has its gallery of portraits; its monumental inscriptions; its records, evidences, and titles. We procure reverence to our civil institutions on the principle upon which nature teaches us to revere individual men; on account of their age; and on account of those from whom they are descended. All your sophisters cannot produce any thing better adapted to preserve a rational and manly freedom than the course that we have pursued, who have chosen our nature rather than our speculations, our breasts rather than our inventions, for the great conservatories and magazines of our rights and privileges.

* * *

The power of perpetuating our property in our families is one of the most valuable and interesting circumstances belonging to it, and that which tends the most to the perpetuation of society itself. It makes our weakness subservient to our virtue; it grafts benevolence even upon avarice. The possessors of family wealth, and of the distinction which attends hereditary possession (as most concerned in it) are the natural securities for this transmission. With us, the house of peers is formed upon this principle. It is wholly composed of hereditary property and hereditary distinction; and made therefore the third of the legislature; and in the last event, the sole judge of all property in all its subdivisions. The house of commons too, though not necessarily, yet in fact, is always so composed in the far greater part. Let those large proprietors be what they will, and they have their chance of being amongst the best, they are at the very worst, the ballast in the vessel of the commonwealth. For though hereditary wealth, and the rank which goes with it, are too much idolized by creeping sycophants, and the blind abject admirers of power, they are too rashly slighted in shallow speculations of the petulant, assuming, short-sighted coxcombs of philosophy. Some decent regulated pre-eminence, some preference (not exclusive appropriation) given to birth, is neither unnatural, nor unjust, nor impolitic.

* * *

THOMAS PAINE

From Rights of Man (1791)†

* * *

That, then, which is called aristocracy in some countries, and nobility in others, arose out of the governments founded upon conquest. It was originally a military order, for the purpose of supporting military government, (for such were all governments founded in conquest); and to keep up a succession of this order for the purpose for which it was established, all the younger branches of those families were disinherited, and the law of *primogeniture-ship* set up.

The nature and character of aristocracy shews itself to us in this law. It is a law against every law of nature, and Nature herself calls for its destruction. Establish family justice, and aristocracy falls. By the aristocratical law of primogenitureship, in a family of six children, five are exposed. Aristocracy has never more than *one* child.

† Thomas Paine (1737–1809) was an Anglo-American political radical who wrote on behalf of American independence as well as the French Revolution. The *Rights of Man* (part I, 1791; part 2, 1792) is one of the most famous rebuttals of Burke's *Reflections on the Revolution in France*. The excerpt presented here attacks the notion of primogeniture as a principal of political and family virtue, a notion Paine finds at the heart of Burke's conservatism. It is offered here as an instance of how the family, along with debates over wills and inheritance, was understood to be freighted with broad significance. The text is reprinted from the sixth edition of 1791.

The rest are begotten to be devoured. They are thrown to the cannibal for prey, and the natural parent prepares the unnatural repast.

As every thing which is out of nature in man, affects, more or less, the interest of society, so does this. All the children which the aristocracy disowns (which are all, except the eldest) are, in general, cast like orphans on a parish, to be provided for by the public, but at a greater charge.—Unnecessary offices and places in governments and courts are created at the expence of the public, to maintain them.

With what kind of parental reflections can the father or mother contemplate their younger offspring. By nature they are children, and by marriage they are heirs; but by aristocracy they are bastards and orphans. They are the flesh and blood of their parents in one line, and nothing akin to them in the other. To restore, therefore, parents to their children, and children to their parents—relations to each other, and man to society—and to exterminate the monster Aristocracy, root and branch—the French constitution has destroyed the law of PRIMOGENITURESHIP. Here then lies the monster; and Mr. Burke, if he pleases, may write its epitaph.

* * *

MARY WOLLSTONECRAFT

From A Vindication of the Rights of Woman (1792)†

From *Chapter IV. Observations on the State of Degradation to which Woman Is Reduced by Various Causes*

* * *

Novels, music, poetry, and gallantry, all tend to make women the creatures of sensation, and their character is thus formed in the mould of folly during the time they are acquiring accomplishments, the only improvement they are excited, by their station in society, to acquire. This overstretched sensibility naturally relaxes the other powers of the mind, and prevents intellect from attaining that sovereignty which it ought to attain to render a rational creature useful

† Mary Wollstonecraft (1759–1797) was a novelist and polemicist on behalf of radical causes. Her most famous work, *A Vindication of the Rights of Woman* (1792), was among other things a tract on the education of women, and before Wollstonecraft became a popularly anathematized figure—with the increasing reaction against the Revolution in France, and with disclosures about her unconventional personal life—it was well received, expressing views about the duties of rationality, sobriety, and self-control with which many writers agreed. The selections presented here denounce the fad of female sensibility and address the vulnerability of unprovisioned widows and daughters. The text and notes are reprinted from the Norton Critical Edition of *A Vindication of the Rights of Woman*, 2nd ed., Carol Poston, editor.

to others, and content with its own station: for the exercise of the understanding, as life advances, is the only method pointed out by nature to calm the passions.

Satiety has a very different effect, and I have often been forcibly struck by an emphatical description of damnation:—when the spirit is represented as continually hovering with abortive eagerness round the defiled body, unable to enjoy any thing without the organs of sense. Yet, to their senses, are women made slaves, because it is by their sensibility that they obtain present power.

And will moralists pretend to assert, that this is the condition in which one half of the human race should be encouraged to remain with listless inactivity and stupid acquiescence? Kind instructors! what were we created for? To remain, it may be said, innocent; they mean in a state of childhood.—We might as well never have been born, unless it were necessary that we should be created to enable man to acquire the noble privilege of reason, the power of discerning good from evil, whilst we lie down in the dust from whence we were taken, never to rise again.—

It would be an endless task to trace the variety of meannesses, cares, and sorrows, into which women are plunged by the prevailing opinion, that they were created rather to feel than reason, and that all the power they obtain, must be obtained by their charms and weakness:

'Fine by defect, and amiably weak!'[1]

And, made by this amiable weakness entirely dependent, excepting what they gain by illicit sway, on man, not only for protection, but advice, is it surprising that, neglecting the duties that reason alone points out, and shrinking from trials calculated to strengthen their minds, they only exert themselves to give their defects a graceful covering, which may serve to heighten their charms in the eye of the voluptuary, though it sink them below the scale of moral excellence?

Fragile in every sense of the word, they are obliged to look up to man for every comfort. In the most trifling dangers they cling to their support, with parasitical tenacity, piteously demanding succour; and their *natural* protector extends his arm, or lifts up his voice, to guard the lovely trembler—from what? Perhaps the frown of an old cow, or the jump of a mouse; a rat, would be a serious danger. In the name of reason, and even common sense, what can save such beings from contempt; even though they be soft and fair?

These fears, when not affected, may produce some pretty attitudes; but they shew a degree of imbecility which degrades a ra-

1. A misquotation of Pope, *Moral Essays* II.44: "Fine by defect, and delicately weak."

tional creature in a way women are not aware of—for love and esteem are very distinct things.

I am fully persuaded that we should hear of none of these infantine airs, if girls were allowed to take sufficient exercise, and not confined in close rooms till their muscles are relaxed, and their powers of digestion destroyed. To carry the remark still further, if fear in girls, instead of being cherished, perhaps, created, were treated in the same manner as cowardice in boys, we should quickly see women with more dignified aspects. It is true, they could not then with equal propriety be termed the sweet flowers that smile in the walk of man; but they would be more respectable members of society, and discharge the important duties of life by the light of their own reason. 'Educate women like men,' says Rousseau, 'and the more they resemble our sex the less power will they have over us.'[2] This is the very point I aim at. I do not wish them to have power over men; but over themselves.

In the same strain have I heard men argue against instructing the poor; for many are the forms that aristocracy assumes. 'Teach them to read and write,' say they, 'and you take them out of the station assigned them by nature.' An eloquent Frenchman has answered them, I will borrow his sentiments. But they know not, when they make man a brute, that they may expect every instant to see him transformed into a ferocious beast.[3] Without knowledge there can be no mortality!

Ignorance is a frail base for virtue! Yet, that it is the condition for which woman was organized, has been insisted upon by the writers who have most vehemently argued in favour of the superiority of man; a superiority not in degree, but essence; though, to soften the argument, they have laboured to prove, with chivalrous generosity, that the sexes ought not to be compared; man was made to reason, woman to feel: and that together, flesh and spirit, they make the most perfect whole, by blending happily reason and sensibility into one character.

And what is sensibility? 'Quickness of sensation; quickness of perception; delicacy.' Thus is it defined by Dr. Johnson;[4] and the definition gives me no other idea than of the most exquisitely polished instinct. I discern not a trace of the image of God in either

---

2. *Emile.* Rousseau, of course, is not advocating equal education: he has made the point that women have sexual power over men. If women were educated, they would lose their sway, presumably an undesirable state of affairs for them.

3. Since Wollstonecraft was deeply absorbed in the French political cause at this time, she could possibly be referring to the great French statesman Mirabeau's remark to Abbé Siéyès, who had just met with discourtesy on the floor of the Constituent Assembly in 1790. Mirabeau is supposed to have chided him by saying, "My dear abbé, you have loosed the bull: do you expect he is not to make use of his horns?"

4. Samuel Johnson's *Dictionary* of 1755, the first of its kind in English, was the arbiter of linguistic correctness.

sensation or matter. Refined seventy times seven,[5] they are still material; intellect dwells not there; nor will fire ever make lead gold!

I come round to my old argument; if woman be allowed to have an immortal soul, she must have, as the employment of life, an understanding to improve. And when, to render the present state more complete, though every thing proves it to be but a fraction of a mighty sum, she is incited by present gratification to forget her grand destination, nature is counteracted, or she was born only to procreate and rot. Or, granting brutes, of every description, a soul, though not a reasonable one, the exercise of instinct and sensibility may be the step, which they are to take, in this life, towards the attainment of reason in the next; so that through all eternity they will lag behind man, who, why we cannot tell, had the power given him of attaining reason in his first mode of existence.

When I treat of the peculiar duties of women, as I should treat of the peculiar duties of a citizen or father, it will be found that I do not mean to insinuate that they should be taken out of their families, speaking of the majority. 'He that hath wife and children,' says Lord Bacon, 'hath given hostages to fortune; for they are impediments to great enterprises, either of virtue or mischief. Certainly the best works, and of greatest merit for the public, have proceeded from the unmarried or childless men.'[6] I say the same of women. But, the welfare of society is not built on extraordinary exertions; and were it more reasonably organized, there would be still less need of great abilities, or heroic virtues.

In the regulation of a family, in the education of children, understanding, in an unsophisticated sense, is particularly required: strength both of body and mind; yet the men who, by their writings, have most earnestly laboured to domesticate women, have endeavoured, by arguments dictated by a gross appetite, which satiety had rendered fastidious, to weaken their bodies and cramp their minds. But, if even by these sinister methods they really *persuaded* women, by working on their feelings, to stay at home, and fulfil the duties of a mother and mistress of a family, I should cautiously oppose opinions that led women to right conduct, by prevailing on them to make the discharge of such important duties the main business of life, though reason were insulted. Yet, and I appeal to experience, if by neglecting the understanding they be as much, may, more detached from these domestic employments, than they could be by the most serious intellectual pursuit, though it may be observed, that the mass of mankind will never vigorously pursue an

---

5. Matthew 18.22: "Jesus saith unto him, I say not unto thee, Until seven times: but, Until seventy times seven."
6. Francis Bacon, Essay VIII, "Of Marriage and the Single Life."

intellectual object,[7] I may be allowed to infer that reason is absolutely necessary to enable a woman to perform any duty properly, and I must again repeat, that sensibility is not reason.

The comparison with the rich still occurs to me; for, when men neglect the duties of humanity, women will follow their example; a common stream hurries them both along with thoughtless celerity. Riches and honours prevent a man from enlarging his understanding, and enervate all his powers by reversing the order of nature, which has ever made true pleasure the reward of labour. Pleasure —enervating pleasure is, likewise, within women's reach without earning it. But, till hereditary possessions are spread abroad, how can we expect men to be proud of virtue? And, till they are, women will govern them by the most direct means, neglecting their dull domestic duties to catch the pleasure that sits lightly on the wing of time.

'The power of the woman,' says some author, 'is her sensibility;'[8] and men, not aware of the consequence, do all they can to make this power swallow up every other. Those who constantly employ their sensibility will have most: for example; poets, painters, and composers.[9] Yet, when the sensibility is thus increased at the expence of reason, and even the imagination, why do philosophical men complain of their fickleness? The sexual attention of man particularly acts on female sensibility, and this sympathy has been exercised from their youth up. A husband cannot long pay those attentions with the passion necessary to excite lively emotions, and the heart, accustomed to lively emotions, turns to a new lover, or pines in secret, the prey of virtue or prudence. I mean when the heart has really been rendered susceptible, and the taste formed; for I am apt to conclude, from what I have seen in fashionable life, that vanity is oftener fostered than sensibility by the mode of education, and the intercourse between the sexes, which I have reprobated; and that coquetry more frequently proceeds from vanity than from that inconstancy, which overstrained sensibility naturally produces.

Another argument that has had great weight with me, must, I think, have some force with every considerate benevolent heart. Girls who have been thus weakly educated, are often cruelly left by

7. The mass of mankind are rather the slaves of their appetites than of their passions [*Wollstonecraft's note*].
8. The sentiment is a commonplace, but Wollstonecraft may be referring to Edmund Burke's phrase: "The beauty of women is considerably owing to their weakness, or delicacy . . ." (Edmund Burke, *A Philosophical Enquiry into the Origin of Our Ideas of the Sublime and Beautiful* [London, 1759 (repr. The Scolar Press, 1970)], p. 219).
9. Men of these descriptions pour it into their compositions, to amalgamate the gross materials; and, moulding them with passion, give to the inert body a soul; but, in woman's imagination, love alone concentrates these ethereal beams [*Wollstonecraft's note*].

their parents without any provision; and, of course, are dependent on, not only the reason, but the bounty of their brothers. These brothers are, to view the fairest side of the question, good sort of men, and give as a favour, what children of the same parents had an equal right to. In this equivocal humiliating situation, a docile female may remain some time, with a tolerable degree of comfort. But, when the brother marries, a probable circumstance, from being considered as the mistress of the family, she is viewed with averted looks as an intruder, an unnecessary burden on the benevolence of the master of the house, and his new partner.[1]

Who can recount the misery, which many unfortunate beings, whose minds and bodies are equally weak, suffer in such situations—unable to work, and ashamed to beg? The wife, a cold-hearted, narrow-minded, woman, and this is not an unfair supposition; for the present mode of education does not tend to enlarge the heart any more than the understanding, is jealous of the little kindness which her husband shews to his relations; and her sensibility not rising to humanity, she is displeased at seeing the property of *her* children lavished on an helpless sister.

These are matters of fact, which have come under my eye again and again. The consequence is obvious, the wife has recourse to cunning to undermine the habitual affection, which she is afraid openly to oppose; and neither tears nor caresses are spared till the spy is worked out of her home, and thrown on the world, unprepared for its difficulties; or sent, as a great effort of generosity, or from some regard to propriety, with a small stipend, and an uncultivated mind, into joyless solitude.

These two women may be much upon a par, with respect to reason and humanity; and changing situations, might have acted just the same selfish part; but had they been differently educated, the case would also have been very different. The wife would not have had that sensibility, of which self is the centre, and reason might have taught her not to expect, and not even to be flattered by, the affection of her husband, if it led him to violate prior duties. She would wish not to love him merely because he loved her, but on account of his virtues; and the sister might have been able to struggle for herself instead of eating the bitter bread of dependence.

* * *

1. Wollstonecraft may have in mind the situation of her sister Everina, who, before Mary Wollstonecraft helped to make her independent, had been living off their brother Edward.

From *Chapter XIII. Some Instances of the Folly which the Ignorance of Women Generates*

SECT. IV

Women are supposed to possess more sensibility, and even humanity, than men, and their strong attachments and instantaneous emotions of compassion are given as proofs; but the clinging affection of ignorance has seldom any thing noble in it, and may mostly be resolved into selfishness, as well as the affection of children and brutes. I have known many weak women whose sensibility was entirely engrossed by their husbands; and as for their humanity, it was very faint indeed, or rather it was only a transient emotion of compassion. Humanity does not consist 'in a squeamish ear,' says an eminent orator. 'It belongs to the mind as well as the nerves.'

But this kind of exclusive affection, though it degrades the individual, should not be brought forward as a proof of the inferiority of the sex, because it is the natural consequence of confined views: for even women of superior sense, having their attention turned to little employments, and private plans, rarely rise to heroism, unless when spurred on by love! and love, as an heroic passion, like genius, appears but once in an age. I therefore agree with the moralist who asserts, 'that women have seldom so much generosity as men;'[2] and that their narrow affections, to which justice and humanity are often sacrificed, render the sex apparently inferior, especially, as they are commonly inspired by men; but I contend that the heart would expand as the understanding gained strength, if women were not depressed from their cradles.

I know that a little sensibility, and great weakness, will produce a strong sexual attachment, and that reason must cement friendship; consequently, I allow that more friendship is to be found in the male than the female world, and that men have a higher sense of justice. The exclusive affections of women seem indeed to resemble Cato's most unjust love for his country.[3] He wished to crush Carthage, not to save Rome, but to promote its vain-glory; and, in general, it is to similar principles that humanity is sacrificed, for genuine duties support each other.

Besides, how can women be just or generous, when they are the slaves of injustice?

---

2. Adam Smith, *Theory of Moral Sentiments*: "Humanity is the virtue of a woman, generosity of a man. The fair sex, who have commonly much more tenderness than ours, have seldom so much generosity."
3. Marcus Porcius Cato (234–149 B.C.E.), once he learned of the civilization of Carthage, felt it must be razed if Rome were to survive. His unceasing message was "Delenda est Carthago"—"Carthage must be destroyed."

HANNAH MORE

From Sensibility: An Epistle to the Honourable Mrs.
Boscawen (1782)†

* * *

Let not the vulgar read this pensive strain,
Their jests the tender anguish wou'd prophane.   130
Yet these some deem the happiest of their kind,
Whose low enjoyments never reach'd the mind,
Who ne'er a pain but for themselves have known,
Who ne'er have felt a sorrow but their own:
Who deem romantic ev'ry finer thought
Conceiv'd by pity, or by friendship wrought;
Whose insulated souls ne'er feel the pow'r
Of gen'rous sympathy's extatic hour;
Whose disconnected hearts ne'er taste the bliss
Extracted from another's happiness;   140
Who ne'er the high heroic duty know,
For public good the private to forego.
    Then wherefore happy? Where's the kindred mind?
Where the large soul which takes in human kind?
Yes—tis the untold sorrow to explain,
To mitigate the but suspected pain;
The rule of holy sympathy to keep,
Joy for the joyful, tears for them that weep
To these the virtuous half their pleasures owe,
Pleasures, the selfish are not born to know;   150
They never know, in all their coarser bliss,
The sacred rapture of a pain like this.
Then take ye happy vulgar, take your part
Of sordid joy which never touch'd the heart.
    Benevolence, which seldom stays to chuse,
Lest pausing prudence tempt her to refuse;
Friendship, which once determin'd never swerves,
Weighs ere it trusts, but weighs not ere it serves;
And soft ey'd pity, and forgiveness bland,

---

† Hannah More (1745–1833), an eminent bluestocking, was a poet, playwright, novelist,
and author of religious and political tracts of a conservative, counterrevolutionary tendency. Because it was a hotly contested term, writers of the period typically broke "sensibility" down into "true" and "false" sorts. The 1782 poem printed here exemplifies the
positive case commonly made on behalf of the virtues and charms of true sensibility,
although More is careful to denounce the dangers of affected, irreligious, and sensual
sorts as well. The text here is printed from *The Works of Hannah More*, 8 vols. (London,
1801), vol. I.

And melting *charity with open hand*;   160
And artless love, believing and believ'd,
And honest confidence which ne'er deceiv'd;
And mercy, stretching out ere want can speak,
To wipe the tear which stains affliction's cheek;
These ye have never known—then take your part
Of sordid joy which never touch'd the heart.
   You who have melted in bright glory's flame,
Or felt the grateful breath of well-earn'd fame;
Or you, the chosen agents from above,
Whose bounty vindicates Almighty love;   170
You, who subdue the vain desire of show,
Not to accumulate but to bestow;
You, who the dreary haunts of sorrow seek,
Raise the sunk heart, and flush the fading cheek;
You, who divide the joys and share the pains,
When merit triumphs, or oppress'd complains;
You, who with pensive Petrarch,[1] love to mourn,
Or weave the garland for Tibullus[2] urn;
You, whose touch'd hearts with real sorrows swell,
Or feel, when genius paints those sorrows well,   180
Wou'd you renounce such energies as those
For vulgar pleasures or for selfish ease?
Wou'd you, to 'scape the pain, the joy forego,
And miss the transport to avoid the woe?
Wou'd you the sense of actual pity lose,
Or cease to share the mournings of the mufe?

                         *   *   *

   Yet while we claim the Sympathy divine,
Which makes, O man, the woes of others thine;   220
While her fair triumphs swell the modish page,
She drives the sterner virtues from the stage:
While FEELING boasts her ever tearful eye,
Fair Truth, firm Faith, and manly justice fly:
Justice, prime good! from whose prolific law,
All worth, all virtue, their strong essence draw;
Justice, a grace quite obsolete we hold,
The feign'd Astrea of an age of gold:
The sterling attribùte we scarcely own,
While spurious Candour fills the vacant throne.   230
   Sweet SENSIBILITY! Thou secret pow'r
Who shed'st thy gifts upon the natal hour,
Like fairy favours; art can never seize,

---

1. Fourteenth-century Italian poet whose sonnets address Laura, his idealized beloved.
2. Roman elegiac poet of the first century B.C.E.

Nor affection catch thy pow'r to please:
Thy subtile essence still eludes the chains
Of definition, and defeats her pains.
Sweet SENSIBILITY! thou keen delight!
Unprompted moral! Sudden sense of right!
Perception exquisite! fair virtue's feed!
Thou quick precursor of the lib'ral deed!   240
Thou hastly conscience! reason's blushing morn!
Instinctive kindness e'er reflexion's born!
Prompt sense of equity! to thee belongs
The swift redress of unexamin'd wrongs!
Eager to serve, the cause perhaps unified,
But always apt to chuse the suff'ring side!
To those who know thee not no words can paint,
And those who know thee, know all words are faint!
  She does not feel thy pow'r who boasts thy flame,
And rounds her every period with thy name;   250
Nor she who vents her disproportion'd sighs
With pining *Lesbia* when her sparrow dies:
Nor she who melts when hapless *Shore* expires,
While real mis'ry unreliev'd retires!
Who thinks feign'd sorrows all her tears deserve,
And weeps o'er WERTER³ while her children starve.
  As words are but th' external marks to tell
The fair ideas in the mind that dwell;
And only are of things the outward sign,
And not the things themselves they but define;   260
So exclamations, tender tones, fond tears,
And all the graceful drapery FEELING wears;
These are her garb, not her, they but express
Her form, her semblance, her appropriate dress;
And these fair marks, reluctant I relate,
Those lovely symbols may be counterfeit.
There are, who fill with brilliant plaints the page,
If a poor linnet meet the gunner's rage;
There are, who for a dying fawn deplore,
As if friend, parent, country, were no more;   270
  Who boast quick rapture trembling in their eye,
If from the spider's snare they snatch a fly;
There are, whose well sung plaints each breast inflame,
And break all hearts—but his from whom they came!
He, scorning life's low duties to attend,
Writes odes on friendship, while he cheats his friend.
Of jails and punishments he grieves to hear,

---

3. Sensitive and melancholy hero of Goethe's novel *The Sorrows of Young Werther* (1774),
which was much imitated throughout England and Europe.

And pensions 'prison'd virtue with a tear;
While unpaid bills his creditor presents,
And ruin'd innocence his crime laments.   280
Not so the tender moralist of Tweed,
His gen'rous *man of feeling* feels indeed.
  O LOVE DIVINE! sole source of Charity!
More dear one genuine deed perform'd for thee,
Than all the periods FEELING e'er cou'd turn,
Than all thy touching page, perverted STERNE![4]
Not that by deeds alone this love's express'd,
If so the affluent only were the bless'd;
One silent wish, one pray'r, one soothing word,
The page of mercy shall, well pleas'd, record;   290
One soul-felt sigh by pow'rless pity given,
Accepted incense! Shall ascend to heav'n!
  Since trifles make the sum of human things,
And half our misery from our foibles springs;
Since life's best joys consift in peace and ease,
And tho' but few can serve, yet all may please;
O let th' ungentle spirit learn from hence,
A small unkindness is a great offence,
To spread large bounties, tho' we wish in vain,
Yet all may shun the guilt of giving pain: 300
To bless mankind with tides of flowing wealth,
With rank to grace them, or to crown with health,
Our little lot denies; yet lib'ral still,
Heav'n gives its counterpoise to ev'ry ill;
Nor let us murmur at our stinted pow'rs,
When kindness, love, and concord, may be ours.
The gift of ministring to other's ease,
To all her sons impartial she decrees;
The gentle offices of patient love,
Beyond all flattery, and all price above;   310
The mild forbearance at a brother's fault,
The angry word suppress'd, the taunting thought;
Subduing and subdu'd, the petty strife,
Which clouds the colour of domestic life;
The sober comfort, all the peace which springs,
From the large aggregate of little things;
On these small cares of daughter, wife, or friend,
The almost sacred joys of *Home* depend:
There, SENSIBILITY, thou best may'st reign,

---

4. Laurence Sterne, English novelist (1713–1768), author of *Tristram Shandy* (1759–67)
   and *Sentimental Journey* (1768), which was associated with the sentimental excesses
   More deplores.

HOME is thy true legitimate domain. 320
A folitary bliss thou ne'er couldst find,
Thy joys with those thou lov'st are intertwin'd;
And he whose helpful tenderness removes
The rankling thorn which wounds the breast he loves,
Smooths not another's rugged path alone,
But clears th' obstruction which impedes his own.
 The hint malevolent, the look oblique,
The obvious satire, or implied dislike;
The sneer equivocal, the harsh reply,
And all the cruel language of the eye; 330
The artful injury, whose venom'd dart,
Scarce wounds the hearing, while it stabs the heart;
The guarded phrase, whose meaning kills, yet told
The list'ner wonders, how you thought it cold;
Small slights, neglect, unmix'd perhaps with hate,
Make up in number what they want in weight.
These, and a thousand griefs minute as these,
Corrode our comfort and destroy our ease.
 As FEELING tends to good or leans to ill,
It gives fresh force to vice or principle 340
'Tis nor a gift peculiar to the good,
'Tis often but the virtue of the blood:
And what wou'd seem compassion's moral flow,
Is but a circulation swift or slow:
But to divert it to its proper course,
There wisdom's pow'r appears, there reason's force:
If ill-directed it pursue the wrong,
It adds new strength to what before was strong;
Breaks out in wild irregular desires,
Disorder'd passions, and illicit fires; 350
Without, deforms the man, depraves within,
And makes the work of GOD the slave of sin.
But if RELIGION's bias rule the foul,
Then SENSIBILITY exalts the whole;
Sheds its sweet sunshine on the moral part,
Nor wastes on fancy what shou'd warm the heart.
Cold and inert the mental pow'rs wou'd lie,
Without this quick'ning spark of deity.
To melt the rich materials from the mine,
To bid the mass of intellect refine, 360
To bend the firm, to animate the cold,
And heav'n's own image stamp on nature's gold;
To give immortal MIND its finest tone,
Oh, SENSIBILITY! is all; thy own.

HANNAH MORE

From Strictures on the Modern System of Female Education (1799)†

Chapter XVI.

ON THE DANGER OF AN ILL-DIRECTED SENSIBILITY.

* * *

In forming the female character, it is of importance that those on whom the task devolves should possess so much penetration as accurately to discern the degree of sensibility, and so much judgment as to accommodate the treatment to the individual character. By constantly stimulating and extolling feelings naturally quick, those feelings will be rendered too acute and irritable. On the other hand, a calm and equable temper will become obtuse by the total want of excitement: the former treatment converts the feelings into a source of error, agitation, and calamity; the latter starves their native energy, deadens the affections, and produces a cold, dull, selfish spirit; for the human mind is an instrument which will lose its sweetness if strained too high, and will be deprived of its tone and strength if not sufficiently raised.

It is cruel to chill the precious sensibility of an ingenuous soul, by treating with supercilious coldness and unfeeling ridicule every indication of a warm, tender, disinterested, and enthusiastic spirit, as if it exhibited symptoms of a deficiency in understanding or in prudence. How many are apt to intimate, with a smile of mingled pity and contempt, in considering such a character, that when she knows the world, that is, in other words, when she shall be grown cunning, selfish, and suspicious, she will be ashamed of her present glow of honest warmth, and of her lovely susceptibility of heart. May she never know the world, if the knowledge of it must be acquired at such an expense! But to sensible hearts, every indication of genuine feeling will be dear, for they well know, that it is this temper which, by the guidance of the divine Spirit, may make her one day become more enamored of the beauty of holiness; which, with the cooperation of principle, and under its direction, will ren-

† Hannah More's *Strictures on the Modern System of Female Education* (1799) was a phenomenal commercial success, going through thirteen editions and selling nine thousand copies. Although acknowledging some of the charms of sensibility, the *Strictures* severely exhorts parents to cultivate sober and dutiful dispositions in their daughters. The chapter excerpted here demonstrates the prominence of female sensibility as a subject for public debate. The text here is printed from *The Works of Hannah More*, 8 vols. (London, 1801).

der her the lively agent of Providence in diminishing the misery that is in the world; into which misery this temper will give her a quicker intuition than colder characters possess. It is this temper which, when it is touched and purified by a "live coal from the altar,"[1] will give her a keener taste for the spirit of religion, and a quicker zeal in discharging its duties. But let it be remembered likewise, that as there is no quality in the female character which more raises its tone, so there is none which will be so likely to endanger the peace, and to expose the virtue, of the possessor; none which requires to have its luxuriances more carefully watched, and its wild shoots more closely lopped.

For young women of affections naturally warm, but not carefully disciplined, are in danger of incurring an unnatural irritability; and while their happiness falls a victim to the excess of uncontrolled feelings, they are liable at the same time to indulge a vanity of all others the most preposterous, that of being vain of their very defect. They have heard sensibility highly commended, without having heard any thing of those bounds and fences which were intended to confine it, and without having been imbued with that principle which would have given it a beneficial direction. Conscious that they possess the quality itself in the extreme, and not aware that they want all that makes that quality safe and delightful, they plunge headlong into those sins and miseries from which they conceitedly and ignorantly imagine, that not principle, but coldness, has preserved the more sober-minded and well-instructed of their sex.

* * *

Women of this cast of mind are less careful to avoid the charge of unbounded extremes, than to escape at all events the imputation of insensibility. They are little alarmed at the danger of exceeding, though terrified at the suspicion of coming short, of what they take to be the extreme point of feeling. They will even resolve to prove the warmth of their sensibility, though at the expense of their judgment, and sometimes also of their justice. Even when they earnestly desire to be and to do good, they are apt to employ the wrong instrument to accomplish the right end. They employ the passions to do the work of the judgment; forgetting, or not knowing, that the passions were not given us to be used in the search and discovery of truth, which is the office of a cooler and more discriminating faculty, but to animate to warmer zeal in the pursuit and practice of truth, when the judgment shall have pointed out what is truth.

1. Isaiah vi.6 [*More's note*].

Through this natural warmth, which they have been justly told is so pleasing, but which, perhaps, they have not been told will be continually exposing them to peril and to suffering, their joys and sorrows are excessive. Of this extreme irritability, as was before remarked, the ill-educated learn to boast, as if it were a decided indication of superiority of soul, instead of laboring to restrain it, as the excess of a temper which ceases to be amiable when it is no longer under the control of the governing faculty. It is misfortune enough to be born more liable to suffer and to sin, from this conformation of mind; it is too much to nourish the evil by unrestrained indulgence; it is still worse to be proud of so misleading a quality.

Flippancy, impetuosity, resentment, and violence of spirit, grow out of this disposition, which will be rather promoted than corrected by the system of education on which we have been animadverting; in which system, emotions are too early and too much excited, and tastes and feelings are considered as too exclusively making up the whole of the female character; in which the judgment is little exercised, the reasoning powers are seldom brought into action, and self-knowledge and self-denial scarcely included.

* * *

On such a mind as we have been describing, novelty also will operate with peculiar force, and in nothing more than in the article of charity. Old established institutions, whose continued existence must depend on the continued bounty of that affluence to which they owed their origin, will be sometimes neglected, as presenting no variety to the imagination, as having by their uniformity ceased to be interesting: there is now a total failure of those springs of mere sensitive feeling which set the charity a-going, and those sudden emotions of tenderness and gusts of pity, which once were felt, must now be excited by newer forms of distress. As age comes on, that charity which has been the effect of mere feeling, grows cold and rigid; this hardness is also increased by the frequent disappointments charity has experienced in its too high expectations of the gratitude and subsequent merit of those it has relieved; and by withdrawing its bounty, because some of its objects have been undeserving, it gives clear proof that what it bestowed was for its own gratification; and now finding that self-complacency at an end, it bestows no longer. Probably, too, the cause of so much disappointment may have been, that ill choice of the objects to which feeling, rather than a discriminating judgment, has led. The summer showers of mere sensibility soon dry up, while the living spring of Christian charity flows alike in all seasons.

* * *

Those young women in whom feeling is indulged to the exclusion of reason and examination, are peculiarly liable to be the dupes of prejudice, rash decisions, and false judgment. The understanding having but little power over the will, their affections are not well poised, and their minds are kept in a state ready to be acted upon by the fluctuations of alternate impulses, by sudden and varying impressions, by casual and contradictory circumstances, and by emotions excited by every accident. Instead of being guided by the broad views of general truth—instead of having one fixed principle—they are driven on by the impetuosity of the moment. And this impetuosity blinds the judgment as much as it misleads the conduct; so that, for want of a habit of cool investigation and inquiry, they meet every want without any previously-formed opinion or settled rule of action. And as they do not accustom themselves to appreciate the real value of things, their attention is as likely to be led away by the under parts of a subject, as to seize on the leading feature. The same eagerness of mind which hinders the operation of the discriminating faculty, leads also to the error of determining on the rectitude of an action by its success, and to that of making the event of an undertaking decide on its justice or propriety: it also leads to that superficial and erroneous way of judging, which fastens on exceptions, if they make in our own favor, as grounds of reasoning, while they lead us to overlook received and general rules which tend to establish a doctrine contrary to our wishes.

* * *

THE LADY'S MAGAZINE

The Enthusiasm of Sentiment; a Fragment (1798)†

———"Yes," said Maria, kneeling with fervent ardour, "I will indulge in the enthusiasm of my heart,—I will cherish the sensibility of my nature. Retired within myself, I hear not the confused noise of the jarring world, I heed not its follies, I escape the contagion of its vices. I cultivate that benevolence, that charity which endureth and pardoneth all things. My heart was once fixed on the gay, but, I fear, the deluding Florio. If all that rumour alleges be true, that heart must be torn from him, though it bleed to death at the

† *The Lady's Magazine* was a prominent sixpenny monthly periodical for women that ran from 1770 to 1832. In addition to giving away sheet music and embroidery patterns, *The Lady's Magazine* published poetry and stories by women, and book reviews. The "Fragment," which ran in December 1798 and is printed here in its entirety, indicates how commonly the hyperbole of female sensibility was parodied.

separation. Yet amidst the pangs of my sufferings I shall feel a con-
soling sentiment arising from conscious integrity, which deceit and
vice cannot know. Time may perhaps heal my wound; I may at
length become capable of reflecting with calmness on the worth-
lessness of the object of which I was enamoured. The face of nature
again shall smile as it was wont, and my mind resume its former
chearfulness and emotions of delight. Yet, should the worst be true,
I will cherish that sensibility to which I owe my pain: exquisite has
been the delight it has afforded, and I cannot consent to purchase
even exemption from misery at the price of becoming torpid and
unfeeling."

A shower of tears here relieved the swelling heart of the fair
enthusiast; but she was soon after more effectually relieved by
learning that all that rumour had insinuated against her lover had
been merely the invention of venemous slander; and her melancholy and fears were succeeded by the liveliest emotions of rapturous joy.

MARIA EDGEWORTH

From Mademoiselle Panache (1796)†

Part I.

Mrs. Temple had two daughters, Emma and Helen; she had taken
great care of their education, and they were very fond of their
mother, and particularly happy whenever she had leisure to converse with them: they used to tell her everything that they thought
and felt; so that she had it in her power early to correct, or rather
to teach them to correct any little faults in their disposition, and to
rectify those errors of judgment to which young people, from want
of experience, are so liable.

Mrs. Temple lived in the country, and her society was composed
of a few intimate friends; she wished, especially during the educa-

---

† Author of novels, stories, and educational tracts, Maria Edgeworth (1768–1849) was one
of the most distinguished writers of the period, and one whom Austen much admired.
"Mademoiselle Panache" was first published in *Parent's Assistant* (1796), a collection of
stories that is as instructive to parents as it is to children themselves. Like Jane West's
A Gossip's Story (1799), Ann Radcliffe's *Sicilian Romance* (1790), and Edgeworth's *Patronage* (1814), among many others, it is structured around a contrast between the ju-
diciousness of one sister and the impetuosity of another. Although Edgeworth's story has
the heroine duped by the coldness and amorality of a female friend rather than by a
male admirer, it explores issues of candor, doubt, ardor, and emotional conduct. More
didactic than Austen's novel, "Mademoiselle Panache" pointedly recommends the virtues
of restraint and good judgment without subjecting them to the sorts of challenges that
baffle Elinor Dashwood. The text here is printed from *Parent's Assistant; or, Stories for
Children* (London, 1858).

tion of her children, to avoid the numerous inconveniences of what is called an extensive acquaintance. However, as her children grew older, it was necessary that they should be accustomed to see a variety of characters, and still more necessary that they should learn to judge of them. There was little danger of Emma's being hurt by the first impressions of new facts and new ideas; but Helen, of a more vivacious temper, had not yet acquired her sister's good sense. We must observe that Helen was a little disposed to be fond of novelty, and sometimes formed a prodigiously high opinion of persons whom she had seen but for a few hours. "Not to admire," was an art which she had to learn.

When Helen was between eleven and twelve years old Lady S * * * returned from abroad, and came to reside at her country-seat, which was very near Mrs. Temple's. The lady had a daughter, Lady Augusta, who was a little older than Helen. One morning a fine carriage drove to the door, and Lady S * * * and her daughter were announced.—We shall not say anything at present of either of the ladies, except that Helen was much delighted with them, and talked of nothing else to her sister all the rest of the day.

The next morning, as these two sisters were sitting at work in their mother's dressing-room, the following conversation began:—

"Sister, do you like pink or blue the best?" said Helen.

"I don't know; blue, I think."

"Oh blue, to be sure. Mamma, which do you like best?"

"Why 'tis a question of such importance, I must have time to deliberate; I am afraid I like pink the best."

"Pink! dear, that's very odd!—But, Mamma, did'nt you think yesterday that Lady Augusta's sash was a remarkably pretty pale blue?"

"Yes; I thought it was very pretty; but as I have seen a great many such sashes, I did not think it was anything very remarkable."

"Well, perhaps it was not remarkably pretty; but you'll allow, Mamma, that it was very well put on."

"It was put on as other sashes are, as well as I remember."

"I like Lady Augusta exceedingly, Mamma."

"What! because she has a blue sash?"

"No, I'm not quite so silly as that," said Helen, laughing; "not because she has a blue sash."

"Why then did you like her?—because it was well put on?"

"Oh! no, no."

"Why then?"

"Why! Mamma, why do you ask why?—I can't tell why—you know one often likes and dislikes people at first without exactly knowing why."

"One! whom do you mean by one?"

"Myself, and everybody."

"You, perhaps, but not everybody; for only silly people like and dislike without any reason."

"But I hope I'm not one of the silly people; I only meant that I had no thought about it: I dare say, if I were to think about it, I should be able to give you a great many reasons."

"I shall be contented with one good one, Helen."

"Well then, Mamma, in the first place I liked her because she was so good-humoured."

"You saw her but for one half hour. Are you sure that she is good-humoured?"

"No, Mamma! but I'm sure she looked very good-humoured."

"That's another affair; however, I acknowledge it is reasonable, to feel disposed to like any one who has a good-humoured countenance, because the temper has, I believe, a very strong influence upon certain muscles of the face; and, Helen, though you are no great physiognomist, we will take it for granted that you are not mistaken; now I did not think Lady Augusta had a remarkably good-tempered countenance, but I hope that I am mistaken. Was this your only reason for liking her exceedingly?"

"No, not my only reason; I liked her——because——because——indeed, Mamma," said Helen, growing a little impatient at finding herself unable to arrange her own ideas—"indeed, Mamma, I don't just remember anything in particular, but I know I thought her very agreeable altogether."

"Saying that you think a person very agreeable *altogether*, may be a common mode of expression; but I am obliged to inform you, that it is no reason, nor do I exactly comprehend what it means, unless it means, in other words, that you don't choose to be at the trouble of thinking. I am sadly afraid, Helen, that you must be content at last to be ranked among the silly ones, who like and dislike without knowing why.—Hey, Helen?"

"Oh no indeed, Mamma," said Helen, putting down her work.

"My dear, I am sorry to distress you; but what are become of the *great many* good reasons?"

"Oh! I have them still; but then I'm afraid to tell them, because Emma will laugh at me."

"No, indeed, I won't laugh," said Emma; "besides, if you please, I can go away."

"No, no, sit still; I will tell them directly.—Why, Mamma, you know, before we saw Lady Augusta, everybody told us how pretty, and accomplished, and agreeable she was."

"Everybody!—nobody that I remember," said Emma, "but Mrs. H. and Miss K."

"Oh! indeed, sister, and Lady M. too."

"Well, and Lady M., that makes three."

"But are three people everybody?"

"No, to be sure," said Helen, a little disconcerted; "but you promised not to laugh at me, Emma.—However, Mamma, without joking, I am sure Lady Augusta is very accomplished at least. Do you know, Mamma, she has a French governess? But I forget her name."

"Never mind her name, it is little to the purpose."

"Oh! but I recollect it now: Mademoiselle Panache."

"Why, undoubtedly, Lady Augusta's having a French governess, and her name being Mademoiselle Panache, are incontrovertible proofs of the excellence of her education. But I think you said you were sure that she was very accomplished; what do you mean by accomplished?"

"Why, that she dances extremely well, and that she speaks French and Italian, and that she draws exceedingly well indeed: takes likenesses, Mamma! likenesses in miniature, Mamma!"

"You saw them, I suppose?"

"Saw them! No, I did not see them, but I heard of them."

"That's a singular method of judging of pictures."

"But, however, she certainly plays extremely well upon the pianoforte, and understands music perfectly. I have a particular reason for knowing this, however."

"You did not hear her play?"

"No; but I saw an Italian song written in her own hand, and she told me she set it to music herself."

"You saw her music, and heard of her drawings;—excellent proofs!—Well, but her dancing?"

"Why, she told me the name of her dancing-master, and it sounded like a foreign name."

"So, I suppose, he must be a good one," said Emma, laughing.

"But, seriously, I do believe she is sensible."

"Well: your cause of belief?"

"Why, I asked her if she had read much history, and she answered 'a little;' but I saw by her look, she meant a great deal. Nay, Emma, you are laughing now; I saw you smile."

"Forgive her, Helen, indeed it was very difficult to help it!" said Mrs. Temple.

"Well, Mamma," said Helen, "I believe I have been a little hasty in my judgment, and all my good reasons are reduced to nothing: I dare say all this time Lady Augusta is very ignorant, and very ill-natured."

"Nay, now, you are going into the opposite extreme; it is possible she may have all the accomplishments and good qualities which you first imagined her to have; I only meant to show you that you had no proofs of them hitherto."

"But surely, Mamma, it would be but good-natured to believe a stranger to be amiable and sensible, when we know nothing to the contrary. Strangers may be as good as the people we have known all our lives; so it would be very hard upon them, and very silly in us, too, if we were to take it for granted they were everything that was bad, merely because they were strangers."

"You do not yet reason with perfect accuracy, Helen: is there no difference between thinking people every thing that is good and amiable, and taking it for granted they are everything that is bad?"

"But then, Mamma, what can one do?—To be always doubting, and doubting, is very disagreeable; and at first, when one knows nothing of a person, how can we judge?"

"There is no necessity, that I can perceive, for your judging of people's characters the very instant they come into a room, which I suppose is what you mean by 'at first.' And thought it be disagreeable to be always 'doubting and doubting,' yet it is what we must submit to patiently, Helen, unless we would submit to the consequences of deciding ill; which, let me assure you, my little daughter, are infinitely more disagreeable."

"Then," said Helen, "I had better doubt and doubt a little longer, Mamma, about Lady Augusta."

Here the conversation ended. A few days afterwards, Lady Augusta came with her mother to dine at Mrs. Temple's. For the first hour, Helen kept her resolution, and, with some difficulty, maintained her mind in the painful philosophic state of doubt; but the second hour, Helen thought that it would be unjust to doubt any longer; especially as Lady Augusta had just shown her a French pocket-fan, and at the very same time observed to Emma, that her sister's hair was a true auburn colour.

In the evening, after they had returned from a walk, they went into Mrs. Temple's dressing-room, to look at a certain black japanned cabinet, in which Helen kept some dried specimens of plants, and other curious things. Half the drawers in this cabinet were hers, and the other half her sister's. Now Emma, though she was sufficiently obliging and polite towards her new acquaintance, was by no means enchanted with her; nor did she feel the least disposition suddenly to contract a friendship, with a person she had seen but a few hours. This reserve, Helen thought, showed some want of feeling, and seemed determined to make amends for it, by the warmth and frankness of her own manners. She opened all the drawers of the cabinet; and whilst Lady Augusta looked and admired, Helen watched her eye, as Aboulcasem, in the Persian Tales, watched the eye of the stranger, to whom he was displaying his treasures. Helen, it seems, had read the story, which had left a deep impression upon her imagination; and she had long determined, on the first convenient opportunity, to imitate the conduct of the "generous Persian." Immediately, therefore, upon observing that anything struck her guest's fancy, she withdrew it, and secretly set it apart for her, as Aboulcasem set apart the slave, and the cup, and the peacock. At night, when Lady Augusta was preparing to depart, Helen slipped out of the room, packed up the things, and as Aboulcasem wrote a scroll with his presents, she thought it necessary to accompany hers with a billet. All this being accomplished, with much celerity, and some trepidation, she hurried down stairs, gave her packet to one of the servants, and saw it lodged in Lady S * * * 's carriage.

When the visit was ended, and Helen and Emma had retired to their own room at night, they began to talk instead of going to sleep.—"Well, sister," said Helen, "and what did you give to Lady Augusta?"

"I! nothing."

"Nothing!" repeated Helen, in a triumphant tone: "then she will not think you very generous."

"I do not want her to think me very generous," said Emma, laughing;—"neither do I think that making presents to strangers is always a proof of generosity."

"Strangers or no strangers, that makes no difference; for surely a person's giving away anything that they like themselves is a pretty certain proof, Emma, of their generosity."

"Not quite so certain," replied Emma; "at least I mean as far as I can judge of my own mind; I know I have sometimes given things away that I liked myself, merely because I was ashamed to refuse; now I should not call that, generosity, but weakness; and besides, I think it does make a great deal of difference, Helen, whether you mean to speak of strangers or friends. I am sure, at this instant, if there is anything of mine in that black cabinet that you wish for, Helen, I'll give it you with the greatest pleasure."

"And not to Lady Augusta?"

"No; I could not do both: and do you think I would make no distinction between a person I have lived with and loved for years, and a stranger whom I know and care very little about?"

Helen was touched by this speech, especially as she entirely believed her sister; for Emma was not one who made sentimental speeches.

* * *

MARIA EDGEWORTH

From Belinda (1801)†

From *Chapter XIX. A Wedding*

"Nobody more likely to do a generous action than Mr. Hervey," repeated Belinda, in rather a low tone. She could now praise Clarence Hervey without blushing, and she could think even of his generosity without partiality, though not without pleasure. By strength of mind, and timely exertion, she had prevented her prepossession from growing into a passion that might have made her miserable. Proud of this conquest over herself, she was now disposed to treat Mr. Vincent with more favour than usual. Self-complacency generally puts us in good-humour with our friends.

After spending some pleasant hours in Lord C——'s beautiful grounds, where the children explored to their satisfaction every dingle and bushy dell, they returned home in the cool of the evening. Mr. Vincent thought it the most delightful evening he had ever felt.

"What! as charming as a West Indian evening?" said Mr. Percival. "This is more than I expected ever to hear you acknowledge in favour of England. Do you remember how you used to rave of the climate and of the prospects of Jamaica?"

"Yes, but my taste has quite changed."

"I remember the time," said Mr. Percival, "when you thought it impossible that your taste should ever change; when you told me that taste, whether for the beauties of animate or inanimate nature, was immutable."

"You and Miss Portman have taught me better sense. First loves are generally silly things," added he, colouring a little. Belinda coloured also.

"First loves," continued Mr. Percival, "are not necessarily more foolish than others; but the chances are certainly against them. From poetry or romance, young people usually form their earlier

---

† *Belinda* (1801) was Edgeworth's first full-length novel, and Austen singled it out for special commendation in *Northanger Abbey*. In the excerpt presented here, Edgeworth dramatizes a conversation about first attachments, a subject discussed at length in *Sense and Sensibility* and much debated during the period. Like writers such as Wollstonecraft and Macaulay, Edgeworth criticizes standards of female worth holding that a woman's first love must ideally be her only true love. It is worth noting, however, that though Belinda shows her rationality by being willing to love Mr. Vincent rather than her first love, Clarence Hervey, the novel finally lets her have it both ways, disclosing Mr. Vincent's tarnished character and bringing Belinda and Hervey together at the end. The text here is printed from *The Tales and Novels of Maria Edgeworth*, 10 vols. (London, 1870), vol. III.

ideas of love, before they have actually felt the passion; and the image which they have in their own minds of the *beau ideal*[1] is cast upon the first objects they afterward behold. This, if I may be allowed the expression, is Cupid's Fata Morgana.[2] Deluded mortals are in ecstacy whilst the illusion lasts, and in despair when it vanishes."

Mr. Percival appeared to be unconscious that what he was saying was any way applicable to Belinda. He addressed himself to Mr. Vincent solely, and she listened at her ease.

"But," said she, "do not you think that this prejudice, as I am willing to allow it to be, in favour of first loves, may *in our sex* be advantageous? Even when a woman may be convinced that she ought not to indulge a *first* love, should she not be prevented by delicacy from thinking of a second?"

"Delicacy, my dear Miss Portman, is a charming word, and a still more charming thing, and Mrs. Freke has probably increased our affection for it; but even delicacy, like all other virtues, must be judged of by the test of utility. We should run into romance, and error, and misery, if we did not constantly refer to this standard. Our reasonings as to the conduct of life, as far as moral prudence is concerned, must depend ultimately upon facts. Now, of the numbers of people in this world, how many do you think have married their *first loves*? Probably not one out of ten. Then, would you have nine out of ten pine all their lives in celibacy, or fret in matrimony, because they cannot have the persons who first struck their *fancy*?"

"I acknowledge this would not add to the happiness of society," said Belinda.

"Nor to its virtue," said Mr. Percival. "I scarcely know an idea more dangerous to domestic happiness than this belief in the unextinguishable nature of a first flame. There are people who would persuade us that, though it may be smothered for years, it must break out at last, and blaze with destructive fury. Pernicious doctrine! false as it is pernicious!—The struggles between duty and passion may be the charm of romance, but must be the misery of real life. The woman who marries one man, and loves another, who, in spite of all that an amiable and estimable husband can do to win her confidence and affection, nourishes in secret a *fatal* prepossession for her first love, may perhaps, by the eloquence of a fine writer, be made an interesting heroine;—but would any man of sense or feeling choose to be troubled with such a wife?—Would not even the idea that women admired such conduct necessarily

1. Perfect beauty (French).
2. Mirage.

tend to diminish our confidence, if not in their virtue, at least in their sincerity? And would not this suspicion destroy our happiness? Husbands may sometimes have delicate feelings as well as their wives, though they are seldom allowed to have any by these unjust novel writers. Now, could a husband who has any delicacy be content to possess the person without the mind?—the duty without the love?—Could he be perfectly happy, if, in the fondest moments, he might doubt whether he were an object of disgust or affection?—whether the smiles of apparent joy were only the efforts of a suffering martyr?—Thank Heaven! I am not married to one of these charming martyrs. Let those live with them who admire them. For my part, I admire and love the wife, who not only seems but is happy—as I," added Mr. Percival smiling, "have the fond credulity to believe. If I have spoken too long or too warmly upon the chapter of *first loves*, I have at least been a perfectly disinterested declaimer; for I can assure you, Miss Portman, that I do not suspect Lady Anne Percival of sighing in secret for some vision of perfection, any more than she suspects me of pining for the charming Lady Delacour, who, perhaps, you may have heard was my *first love*. In these days, however, so few people marry with even the pretence to love of any sort, that you will think I might have spared this tirade. No; there are ingenuous minds which will never be enslaved by fashion or interest, though they may be exposed to be deceived by romance, or by the *delicacy* of their own imaginations."

"I hear," said Belinda, smiling, "I hear and understand the emphasis with which you pronounce that word *delicacy*. I see you have not forgotten that I used it improperly half an hour ago, as you have convinced me."

"Happy they," said Mr. Percival, "who can be convinced in half an hour! There are some people who cannot be convinced in a whole life, and who end where they began, with saying—'This is my opinion—I always thought so, and always shall.' "

Mr. Vincent at all times loved Mr. Percival; but he never felt so much affection for him as he did this evening, and his arguments appeared to him unanswerable. Though Belinda had never mentioned to Mr. Vincent the name of Clarence Hervey till this day, and though he did not in the least suspect from her manner that this gentleman ever possessed any interest in her heart; yet, with her accustomed sincerity, she had confessed to him that an impression had been made upon her mind before she came to Oaklypark.

After this conversation with Mr. Percival, Mr. Vincent perceived that he gained ground more rapidly in her favour; and his company grew every day more agreeable to her taste: he was convinced that, as he possessed her esteem, he should in time secure her affections.

"In time," repeated Lady Anne Percival: "you must allow her time, or you will spoil all."

It was with some difficulty that Mr. Vincent restrained his impatience, even though he was persuaded of the prudence of his friend's advice. Things went on in this happy, but as he thought slow, state of progression till towards the latter end of September.

* * *

CRITICISM

Early Views

CRITICAL REVIEW

From Unsigned Review (February 1812)†

The lovers of novel reading can have but a very faint idea of the difficulty which we reviewers experience in varying the language with which we are to give our judgment on this species of writing. The numerous novels which are continually presenting themselves to our notice, are in substance, style, and size, so much alike, that after reading the three first pages, we may with very little difficulty not only know how they will end, but may give a shrewd guess of the various incidents which are to occur, the difficulties and dangers which must accrue, with all the vexations, aukward rencounters, &c. &c. which are so highly necessary to make up a fashionable novel.

We are no enemies to novels or novel writers, but we regret, that in the multiplicity of them, there are so few worthy of any particular commendation. A genteel, well-written novel is as agreeable a lounge as a genteel comedy, from which both amusement and instruction may be derived. 'Sense and Sensibility' is one amongst the few, which can claim this fair praise. It is well written; the characters are in genteel life, naturally drawn, and judiciously supported. The incidents are probable, and highly pleasing, and interesting; the conclusion such as the reader must wish it should be, and the whole is just long enough to interest without fatiguing. It reflects honour on the writer, who displays much knowledge of character, and very happily blends a great deal of good sense with the lighter matter of the piece.

The story may be thought trifling by the readers of novels, who are insatiable after *something new*. But the excellent lesson which

† This unsigned review of *Sense and Sensibility* consists mostly of plot summary and lengthy excerpts. It appeared in *Critical Review*, 4th series, vol. I, no. ii (February 1812): 149–57.

it holds up to view, and the useful moral which may be derived from the perusal, are such essential requisites, that the want of *newness* may in this instance be readily overlooked. The characters of Ellen [sic] and Marianne are very nicely contrasted; the former possessing great good sense, with a *proper quantity of sensibility*, the latter an equal share of the sense which renders her sister so estimable, but blending it at the same time with an *immoderate* degree of sensibility which renders her unhappy on every trifling occasion, and annoys every one around her. The wary prudence of John Dashwood and the good nature of Sir John Middleton, the volatile dissipation of Willoughby, and the steady feeling of Colonel Brandon, are all equally well conceived and well executed.

* * *

Mrs. Dashwood, the mother of these daughters, possessed an eagerness of mind, which would have hurried her into indiscretions, had it not been somewhat checked by her good disposition and affectionate heart. Elinor, the eldest daughter, has a strong understanding and cool judgment, an amiable temper, with strong feelings, which she knew how to govern. Marianne's abilities are equal to Elinor's; she is sensible and clever, but so terribly impetuous in all her joys and all her sorrows as to know no moderation. She is generous, amiable, interesting, and every thing but prudent. Her *sensibilities* are all in the extreme.

* * *

The *sensibility* of Marianne is without bounds. She is rendered miserable, and in her peculiar temperament, this misery is extravagantly cherished, whilst Elinor, who has her own love-difficulties to encounter and her own *sensibilities* to subdue, has the painful task of endeavouring to alleviate her sister's grief, which preys upon her health so much, that she is soon reduced to the brink of the grave. The patience and tenderness of Elinor during the long illness of her sister, and the knowledge of her bearing up in so exemplary a manner against the disappointments and mortifications which she has had to endure, sink deep into the mind of Marianne. Her confinement produces reflection, and her good sense at length prevails over her *sensibility*. After a time, she marries a most amiable man, who had long loved her, and whom, in the height of her delirium of sensibility, she could not bear even to think on for the very wise reason, that he was *five* and *thirty*, and consequently in Marianne's ideas of love, had *out-lived* every *sensation* of *that kind*. In her notions, at that period, a man, at the advanced age of *five and thirty*, could not have any thing to do with matrimony. Marianne sees the fallacy of all this nonsense, and becomes a good wife to this *old gentleman* of thirty-five, even though he declares it was necessary for him to wear a flannel waistcoat to prevent a rheumatic affection in one of his shoulders.

* * *

BRITISH CRITIC

Unsigned Review (May 1812)†

We think so favourably of this performance that it is with some reluctance we decline inserting it among our principal articles, but the productions of the press are so continually multiplied, that it requires all our exertions to keep tolerable pace with them.

The object of the work is to represent the effects on the conduct of life, of discreet quiet good sense on the one hand, and an over-refined and excessive susceptibility on the other. The characters are happily delineated and admirably sustained. Two sisters are placed before the reader, similarly circumstanced in point of education and accomplishments, exposed to similar trials, but the one by a sober exertion of prudence and judgment sustains with fortitude, and overcomes with success, what plunges the other into an abyss of vexation, sorrow, and disappointment. An intimate knowledge of life and of the female character is exemplified in the various personages and incidents which are introduced, and nothing can be more happily pourtrayed than the picture of the elder brother, who required by his dying father, to assist his mother and sisters, first, resolves to give the sisters a thousand pounds a-piece, but after a certain deliberation with himself, and dialogue with his *amiable* wife, persuades himself that a little fish and game occasionally sent, will fulfil the real intentions of his father, and satisfy every obligation of duty. Not less excellent is the picture of the young lady of over exquisite sensibility, who falls immediately and violently in love with a male coquet, without listening to the judicious expostulations of her sensible sister, and believing it impossible for man to be fickle, false, and treacherous. We will, however, detain our female friends no longer than to assure them, that they may peruse these volumes not only with satisfaction but with real benefits, for they may learn from them, if they please, many sober and salutary maxims for the conduct of life, exemplified in a very pleasing and entertaining narrative. There is a little perplexity in the genealogy of the first chapter, and the reader is somewhat bewildered among half-sisters,

---

† This unsigned review of *Sense and Sensibility* is from *British Critic*, vol. 39 (May 1812): 527, and is reprinted in its entirety.

cousins, and so forth; perhaps, too, the good humoured Baronet, who is never happy but with his house full of people, is rather overcharged, but for these trifling defects there is ample compensation.

W. F. POLLOCK

From British Novelists (1860)†

* * *

Sense and Sensibility was the first published of Miss Austen's novels. It has perhaps more of movement than its successors, and in no other is there a character of so much passionate tenderness as belongs to Marianne. It is not, however, as a whole, equal to her later works; yet it may be as often resorted to with advantage as any of them, and it is full of its author's genius. How well the littleness and respectable selfishness of Mr. John Dashwood are brought out. How naturally his generous intentions to provide for his sisters dwindle down from a splendid three thousand pounds to half that amount—then to an annuity—then to an occasional present of fifty pounds—and lastly to vague promises of kindness and assistance. The charming but not too judicious mother of Elinor and Marianne Dashwood has always been one of our greatest favourites among Miss Austen's ladies. The sensible, considerate, and self-denying Elinor is a beautiful character, and is well contrasted with the enthusiastic and delightful, but somewhat unreasonable, Marianne. So is the delicate, well-informed, and high-minded Edward Ferrars, with his coxcomb brother Robert, and the agreeable but selfish Willoughby. The youngest sister, Margaret, must not be forgotten, though she seldom appears; for the object of her existence is amply justified by her utterance of the famous wish 'that somebody would give us all a large fortune a-piece,' even if she were not wanted to live with Mrs. Dashwood after her sisters are married. Then there is the good-humoured and friendly Sir John Middleton, who never came to the cottage without either inviting them to dine at the Park the next day or to drink tea that evening. We like Mrs. Jennings, with her good nature and gossip, and her notion that poor Marianne, in the first agonies of disappointed love, could be consoled by sweetmeats, constantia, and playing at her favourite round game. Mr. Palmer, a gentleman when he pleases, but spoiled by living

† From "British Novelists," *Fraser's Magazine* 61 (January 1860): 30–35. W. F. Pollock (1815–1888) was a barrister and a man of letters. Pollock's is an early example of what would become the customary view of *Sense and Sensibility*.

with people inferior to himself, and discontented, even to rudeness, with his silly wife, is brought out with much humour. We properly feel how objectionable are the Miss Steeles, with their vulgar cunning and admiration for smart beaux. We despise and shrink from the elder Mrs. Ferrars, with her pride, ill-nature, and narrow mind. We cordially respect and like the excellent Colonel Brandon, who though suffering under the advanced age and infirmities of thirty-six, is at length accepted by the youthful and once scornful Marianne. We are personally glad when Edward is released from his odious engagement to the artful Lucy Steele, and when his marriage with Elinor is rendered possible. Finally, we acquiesce in the sober and natural sentences with which the characters are dismissed from appearance. No poetical justice dogs those who have behaved wrongly and foolishly, to make them miserable to the end of time. We are invited to think of Willoughby as enjoying some share of domestic felicity with the wife whom he married for money and without love. Robert Ferrars, who actually marries the very woman for refusing to give up whom his brother was disinherited in his favour, regains his mother's goodwill—the two low natures suiting each other too well to be long separated—and is tolerably happy with his underbred wife. This is as it all would be in real life, and so Miss Austen, abjuring her undoubted right to inflict retribution, chooses it to be in that transcript of an imagined portion of it which she has selected for consideration in the tale called *Sense and Sensibility*.

* * *

ANONYMOUS

From Miss Austen (1866)†

* * *

In *Sense and Sensibility*, the first work she published, we find a great advance in every respect. Greater breadth, greater variety of character and incident, more interest. In some respects we think it unsurpassed by any of her works. She never drew a more humorous character than Mrs. Jennings, nor a more interesting one than Marianne Dashwood. All the characters are several hair's breadths broader than in any other of her books. The book, however, to our

† From "Miss Austen," *The Englishwoman's Domestic Magazine* (July, August 1866), 3rd series, no. ii, 238–39, 278–82. This unsigned discussion is extracted from a pair of articles devoted to Austen. It is notable for the acuteness of its appreciation of satiric characterization as well as for a preference of sensibility over sense which it assumes the novel does not intend.

mind fails in its intention by making sensibility more attractive than sense. Ellinor [sic] is too good; one feels inclined to pat her on the back and say, "Good girl," but all sympathy is with the unfortunate Marianne. But for all that, the contrast between the two temperaments, which was, perhaps, the principal aim of the book, is complete, and at the same time subtle and not too violent. The character of Willoughby is one of the best of her male impersonations. But the prevailing merit of *Sense and Sensibility* is the excellent treatment of the subordinate characters, and in their excellence in themselves. As we have given one illustration of her art from her poorest work, we will give another from one of her most insignificant characters.

To gain effect by appearance of broad treatment, and to obtain amusing foils to the more distinguished persons of the drama, it is a great temptation to an artist to render the subordinate characters more interesting and effective by exaggeration, and skill is never more shown than in producing such necessary relief without sacrifice to truth. Others, again, from want of patience or true artistic feeling, are apt to treat such secondary figures with something like contempt, using them as necessary evils, careless of drawing and finish, bestowing all their labour on the principal groups. Miss Austen, the most patient and conscientious of artists, never falls into these errors. If she exaggerates even in appearance, it is only as in the cases where, as we have just shown, her characters are more typical than usual; if she sketches slightly, it is because the character itself is a slight one, not from any want of patience. It is, indeed, in these very slightest characters that her art becomes most obvious on a close examination. They do not obtrude themselves into the centre of the composition, they hold their duly subordinate position, but if we look into them we find each touch laid on with the same regard for truth and the same firm hand. No labour has been spared on account of their comparative insignificance in the general effect. Nor is this labour thrown away by an artist, though the public have not, perhaps, the discernment to appreciate it fully. The effect desired is produced, and the labour has its result in the increased delight of the reader, although be may be quite unconscious of the cause of his additional pleasure. And what is more, such good and thorough work will last, in spite of this want of ready appreciation, when the glamour of false effect has long lost its charm. Those who only write to create excitement sink into oblivion as soon as that excitement is over, but writers who, like Miss Austen, work with a reverence for art in itself, and a disregard of immediate popularity as an aim, and are content to labour in the mine of human nature for their material, cannot fail to find the good ore, and to work it into lasting monuments. Mrs. Radcliffe, a woman of considerable ability, now scarcely affords amusement to the lowest class; but Miss Austen, though she may not be much read by the general public, is, perhaps, more completely appreciated than ever by minds of the highest culture.

Lady Middleton is a good example of those inferior characters on which she has expanded so much skill, if not labour—characters of the very slightest structure—mere elementary forms, of which most writers, if they had not disdained to use them, would have made but dreary personifications of abstract stupidity, but which in her hands become lifelike studies of our friends.

Who does not know Lady Middleton? perhaps the veriest nobody that ever was drawn. She is the wife of a baronet (Miss Austen never gets higher than baronets), is handsome, of tall and striking figure and graceful address, but from her first visit it is plain to the Dashwoods, who have settled near the seat of Sir John and Lady Middleton, that, though perfectly well-bred, she is reserved, cold, and has nothing to say for herself beyond the most commonplace inquiry or remark. Having read so much, the reader imagines that the character is not one which will interest him much, and does not care to hear much more of her. Miss Austen knew this, and does not introduce her often, and when introduced she seldom speaks; but, nevertheless, the woman lives in the mind of the reader, and, in spite of her insipid character, affords him some amusement. When she goes out visiting she takes a child with her, to afford a subject of interest, if not of conversation. Her only resource is the humouring of her children. She piques herself on the elegance of her table and of all her domestic arrangements, and from this kind of vanity derives her greatest enjoyment in any of her parties, which are very numerous, as her husband, Sir John, delights in collecting around him more young people than his house will hold. According to her mother, she need to play on the piano extremely well, and was very fond of it, but she has given up music since her marriage. All these, and many other apparently insignificant traits in an inaignificant character, yet produce a substantial effect in bringing the lady before the reader. They are all of a piece, and at the end of the book the memory has put them together like the bits of a puzzle, and a complete though faint effect is produced, for they all fit. No incident that is recorded of her but is in perfect keeping. She is not silly, she is not exactly inane—what she is it is difficult to say, but her character would take up a large stock of negatives before you exhausted her deficiencies.

* * *

ALICE MEYNELL

From The Classic Novelist (1894)†

Jane Austen seldom begins a novel without a deliberate chapter —generally a family chapter. A masterly consciousness of her own authority gives her the right of control over her reader's impatience or slovenliness. The order of things is hers, not his, and he must wait her time for wit. Hers are what Jeremy Taylor,[1] even at his prayers, calls 'measures of address'. Her openings imply a firmer hold upon narrative than later novelists, with their verbless first sentences, their 'he' and 'she' for persons to be named later, thought to grasp at. The moderns would be much depressed were they required to open thus: 'The family of Dashwood had long been settled in Sussex. Their estate was large, and their residence was at Norland Park, in the centre of their property, where, for many generations, they had lived in so respectable a manner as to engage the general good opinion of their surrounding acquaintance.' We consent to read the dismal opening; we endure the pother of the unmusical words; we tolerate it all because we know that in a page or two the respectable Dashwoods will be deprived of some of the general good opinion of their surrounding acquaintance. We know that Miss Austen will make of her personages good sport for her reader, her sense of derision being equal to that of her own kin, the original Philistines. * * *

That Jane works upon very small matters is hardly worth saying, and certainly not worth complaining of. Things are not trivial merely because they are small; but that which makes life, art, and work trivial is a triviality of relations. Mankind lives by vital relations; and if these are mean, so is the life, so is the art that expresses them because it can express no more. With Miss Austen love, vengeance, devotion, duty, maternity, sacrifice, are infinitely trivial. There is also a constant relation of watchfulness, of prudence. As the people in her stories watch one another so does Miss Austen seem to be watching them, and her curiosity is intense indeed; she realizes their colds—her female characters take a great many colds—so that one seems to hear her narrate the matter in a muf-

---

† From the *Pall Mall Gazette* (February 16, 1894). This unsigned article is by Alice Meynell (1847–1922), a poet and novelist. Ending with the not unperceptive observation that Austen's is "an unheavenly world," Meynell's article blends acute observation with an antipathy for the irony pervasive in *Sense and Sensibility*. Reprinted in *The Second Person Singular* (London: Oxford UP, 1922), pp. 62–67.

1. Anglican clergyman (1613–1667), famous for his devotional handbooks, *The Rule and Exercises of Holy Living* (1650) and *The Rule and Exercises of Holy Dying* (1651).

fled voice, but not precisely because of her sympathy. That such close observation can work on without tenderness must be a proof of this author's exceeding cynicism. Triviality of relations among Miss Austen's personages does not prevent a certain kind of intensity. Lying and spite among her women work at close quarters.

*   *   *

Miss Austen's art and her matter are made for one another. Miss Austen's art is not of the highest quality; it is of an admirable secondary quality. Her gentle spinsterly manner prevents us from perceiving at first how much of her derision—for she is mistress of derision rather than of wit or humour—is caricature of a rather gross sort. 'Lady Middleton resigned herself to the idea with all the philosophy of a well-bred woman, contenting herself with merely giving her husband a gentle reprimand on the subject five or six times every day.' *   *   *

Her irony is now and then exquisitely bitter. 'Who could tell'— Miss Austen is presenting the thoughts of Mrs. John Dashwood in regard to her unwelcome sisters-in-law—'that they might not expect to go out with her a second time? The power of disappointing them, it was true, must always be hers. But that was not enough.' About the following little sentence there is something of the wit of surprise. It describes the joys of a young woman of the less admirable sort, lately married: 'They passed some months in great happiness at Dawlish; for she had many relations and old acquaintances to cut.' Miss Austen has a word in dismissing the inconstant Mr. Willoughby: 'His wife was not always out of humour; and in his breed of horses and dogs, and in sporting of every kind, he found no inconsiderable degree of domestic felicity.'

The lack of tenderness and of spirit is manifest in Miss Austen's indifference to children. They hardly appear in her stories except to illustrate the folly of their mothers. They are not her subjects as children; they are her subjects as spoilt children, and as children through whom a mother may receive flattery from her designing acquaintance, and may inflict annoyance on her sensible friends. The novelist even spends some of her irony upon a little girl of three. She sharpens her pen over the work. The passage is too long to quote, but the reader may refer to *Sense and Sensibility*. In this coldness or dislike Miss Austen resembles Charlotte Brontë.

REGINALD FARRER

From Jane Austen (1917)†

* * *

Wars may be raging to their end as the background of 'Persuasion,' or social miseries strike a new facet of 'Emma'; otherwise all the vast anguish of her time is non-existent to Jane Austen, when once she has got pen in hand, to make us a new kingdom of refuge from the toils and frets of life. Her kingdoms are hermetically sealed, in fact, and here lies the strength of their impregnable immortality; it is not without hope or comfort for us nowadays, to remember that 'Mansfield Park' appeared the year before Waterloo, and 'Emma' the year after. For Jane Austen is always concerned only with the universal, and not with the particular. And it is according as they invest their souls in the former or the latter that authors eternally survive or rapidly pass away. Fashions change, fads and fancies come and go, tyrannies and empires erupt and collapse; those who make events and contemporary ideas the matter of their work have their reward in instant appreciation of their topical value. And with their topical value they die. Art is a mysterious entity, outside and beyond daily life, whether its manifestation be by painting or sculpture or literature. If it use outside events at all, it must subdue them to its medium, and become their master, not their mere vehicle. So a hundred thousand novels come and go; but Jane Austen can never be out of date, because she never was in any particular date (that is to say, never imprisoned in any), but is co-extensive with human nature.

Talk of her 'limitations' is vain, and based on a misapprehension. When we speak of her as our greatest artist in English fiction we do not mean that she has the loudest mastery of any particular mood, the most clamant voice, the widest gamut of subjects; we mean that she stands supreme and alone among English writers in possession of the secret which so many French ones possess—that is, a most perfect mastery of her weapons, a most faultless and precise adjustment of means to end. She is, in English fiction, as Milton in English poetry, the one completely conscious and almost unerring artist. This is to take only the technical side of her work; her scale and scope are different matters. There is, in some quar-

---

† From *Quarterly Review* (July 1917). Reginald Farrer (1880–1920) was a botanist as well as a man of letters. His essay on Jane Austen, which places the centenary of her death against the backdrop of the close of World War I, remains one of the most vigorous discussions of her artistry, its affects, and its effects.

ters, a tendency to quarrel with Jane Austen because in her books there is nothing that she never intended to be there, no heroic hectorings, no Brontesque ebulliencies, no mountain or moor or 'bonny beck' (to use Charlotte Brontë's own phrase)—surely one of the monumental ineptitudes of criticism, seeing that the most elementary axiom of art is the artist's initial right to choose his own medium. We have no more right, in fact, to cavil at Jane Austen for not writing 'The Duchess of Malfi' than at Webster for not writing 'Northanger Abbey.'

* * *

The secret of her immortality is to be found in that underlying something which is the woman herself; for, of all writers, she it is who pursues truth with most utter and undeviable devotion. The real thing is her only object always. She declines to write of scenes and circumstances that she does not know at first hand; she refuses recognition, and even condonement, to all thought or emotion that conflicts with truth, or burkes[1] it, or fails to prove pure diamond to the solvent of her acid. She is, in fact, the most merciless, though calmest, of iconoclasts; only her calm has obscured from her critics the steely quality the inexorable rigour of her judgment. Even Butler,[2] her nearest descendant in this generation, never seems really to have recognised his affinity. For Jane Austen has no passion, preaches no gospel, grinds no axe; standing aloof from the world, she sees it, on the whole, as silly. She has no animosity for it; but she has no affection. She does not want to better fools, or to abuse them; she simply sets herself to glean pleasure from their folly. Nothing but the first-rate in life is good enough for her tolerance; remember Anne Elliot's definition of 'good company,' and her cousin's rejoinder, 'That is not good company; that is the best.' Everything false and feeble, in fact, withers in the demure greyness of her gaze; in 'follies and nonsense, whims and inconsistencies,' she finds nothing but diversion, dispassionate but pitiless. For, while no novelist is more sympathetic to real values and sincere emotion, none also is so keen on detecting false currency, or so relentless in exposing it.

* * *

With 'Sense and Sensibility' we approach the maturing Jane Austen. But it has the almost inevitable frigidity of a reconstruction, besides an equally inevitable uncertainty in the author's use of her

---

1. Smothers; hushes up.
2. Iconoclastic English essayist and novelist (1835–1902), author of *Erewhon* (1872) and *The Way of All Flesh* (1903).

weapons. There are *longueurs*[3] and clumsinesses; its conviction lacks fire; its development lacks movement; its major figures are rather incarnate qualities than qualified incarnations. Never again does the writer introduce a character so entirely irrelevant as Margaret Dashwood, or marry a heroine to a man so remote in the story as Colonel Brandon. This is not, however, to say that 'Sense and Sensibility,' standing sole, would not be itself enough to establish an author's reputation. The opening dialogue, for instance, between John and Fanny Dashwood—obviously belonging to the second version of the story—ranks among the finest bits of revelation that even Jane Austen has given us; and criticism stands blissfully silent before Sir John Middleton, Mrs Jennings, and the juxtaposition of Lady Middleton and Fanny Dashwood, 'who sympathised with each other in an insipid propriety of demeanour and a general want of understanding.' But its tremendous successors set up a standard beside which. 'Sense and Sensibility' is bound to appear grey and cool; nobody will choose this as his favourite Jane Austen, whereas each one of the others has its fanatics who prefer it above all the rest.

*   *   *

3. Lengthy or tedious passages.

Modern Views

JAN FERGUS

First Publication: Thomas Egerton, *Sense and Sensibility*, and *Pride and Prejudice*†

Most biographers infer that Austen attempted to publish *Sense and Sensibility* at this time [1810], rather than *Pride and Prejudice* because the latter had been rejected sight unseen by Cadell and Davies. *Sense and Sensibility*, however, had been completed later than *Pride and Prejudice* and may have required less revision. I suspect too that Austen's exasperating experience with Crosby and Company caused her to prefer *Sense and Sensibility*. Despite an unconventional focus upon a community of women, its emphasis upon the importance as well as the costs of self-command made it her most orthodox novel both aesthetically and morally. *Susan* or *Northanger Abbey* constituted a bold experiment in burlesque over which Crosby had clearly vacillated, thinking it a profitable speculation at first and then a poor risk. *Pride and Prejudice* contained an extremely unorthodox heroine, and Austen may have feared either similar vacillation from another publisher, if she succeeded in selling the copyright, or a more ambivalent reception from reviewers and the reading public than *Sense and Sensibility* was likely to obtain. Mary Russell Mitford wrote to a friend in December 1814, for instance, deploring 'the entire want of taste which could produce so pert, so worldly a heroine as the beloved of such a man as Darcy'[1]

Sense and Sensibility was a safer choice—almost too much so, as Austen jokingly feared when it was in the press. Mary Brunton's improving novel *Self-Control: a Novel* had appeared early in 1811, and Austen wrote in April:

† From *Jane Austen: A Literary Life* (New York: St. Martin's Press, 1991), pp. 129–36, 141. Copyright © Jan Fergus. Reprinted by permission of St. Martin's Press, LLC, and Macmillan Ltd. Quotations of Austen's novels are from Chapman's editions.
1. A. G. L'Estrange, *The Life of Mary Russell Mitford* (London: Richard Bentley, 1870), 1:300.

We have tried to get Self-controu!, but in vain.—I *should* like to know what her Estimate is—but am always half afraid of finding a clever novel *too clever*—& of finding my own story and my own people all forestalled.

(*Letters*, 30 Apr. 1811)

This statement interestingly implies that, for Austen, self-control *was* a theme central to *Sense and Sensibility*. Brunton's novel, however, certainly did not 'forestall' Austen's. Two years later, Austen re-read *Self-Control* with much amusement:

I am looking over Self Control again, & my opinion is confirmed of its being an excellently-meant, elegantly-written Work, without anything of Nature or Probability in it. I declare I do not know whether Laura's passage down the American River, is not the most natural, possible, everyday thing she ever does.

(*Letters*, 11 Oct. 1813)

Austen may have approached the publisher Thomas Egerton through Henry, perhaps using his agent Seymour again. Egerton, after all, had sold James's and Henry's *The Loiterer* in his Whitehall shop more than 20 years earlier. We do not know what made Egerton prepared to produce *Sense and Sensibility* on commission. He was not known for bringing out novels, nor did publishing on commission ever prove very remunerative to the publisher. He must have liked the novel well enough to feel that he would gain prestige by being associated with it, and perhaps more important, he must have felt that he could trust Henry Austen, at this time a banker, to settle the bill for costs. Possibly he insisted, unlike some other publishers, on being paid for paper and printing in advance. Certainly Austen herself supposed so (*Letters*, 3 Nov. 1813).

Once Egerton had agreed to publish the novel, he sent it to the printer Charles Roworth, of Bell Yard, Temple Bar, perhaps in February or March 1811. Roworth was in fact the most frequently employed printer for Austen's works, producing at least 14 of the 27 volumes that were issued through December 1817. Their first association was disappointing to Austen:

M^rs K[night] regrets in the most flattering manner that she must wait *till* May [for *Sense and Sensibility*], but I have scarcely a hope of its being out in June—Henry does not neglect it; he *has* hurried the Printer. . . .

(*Letters*, 25 Apr. 1811)

The delay was much worse than Austen anticipated; the novel was not advertised until the end of October. She experienced some delay from printers on every novel that she published for herself, though none was as lengthy as this. By contrast, Egerton was able to issue *Pride and Prejudice* within a few months of purchasing it,[2] doubtless because his own profit was at stake. He would earn less than £36 by publishing *Sense and Sensibility* on commission in an edition of 750 copies, by my calculations, whereas Austen herself made £140, as she wrote to her brother Frank (*Letters*, 3 July 1813). It was not worth Egerton's while to hurry the printers. Although he stood to gain little by agreeing to publish *Sense and Sensibility* on commission, Egerton ran no risk; only the author did. Austen was 'so persuaded . . . that its sale would not repay the expense of publication, that she actually made a reserve from her very moderate income to meet the expected loss' (*Northanger Abbey* 6). At this time, the expenses of publishing 750 copies of the novel would come to about £155, and advertisements would ordinarily take another £24 or so.[3] The novel retailed at 15s, but the books were accounted for to the author at the trade price, about a third less than the retail price. If every copy were sold at the trade price of 9s6d, receipts would be over £356,[4] leaving a maximum profit of

2. JA wrote to Martha Lloyd on 29 Nov. 1812, that Egerton had paid £110 for the copyright; she writes as if the event were fairly recent (*Letters*). He issued PP at the end of Jan. 1813. Egerton allowed Roworth to print the first volume, but employed G. Sidney for the other two, which are 'more carelessly printed', perhaps because he was demanding speed (Gilson, p. 22).
3. I have arrived at these figures by examining the Archives of the House of Longman, microfilmed by Chadwyck-Healey (Cambridge), hereafter cited as Longman. Because my conclusions about JA's early costs, editions and profits differ significantly from other accounts, these notes will document my calculations in detail. The Longman records usefully supplement those of JA's publisher John Murray, which offer no specific information about publishing costs and sales for *any* novels before Dec. 1815, when they begin to record such information for MP (2nd edn), E, NA and P. For very different estimates of JA's editions and profits, see (among others) Jane Aiken Hodge, 'JA and her Publishers', in John Halperin (ed.), *JA: Bicentenary Essays* (Cambridge University Press, 1975), pp. 75–85.
   Longman brought out 750 copies of a Mrs Hurst's three-volume novel, *She Thinks for Herself*, in Jan. 1813, at a cost for paper and printing of £161.9.3. (Longman reel 1, I/2/230; the novel was published anonymously, but the author's name is given in Longman Letter Books, transcribed by Michael Bott, I/97/377). The cost for printing 750 copies of JA's SS over a year earlier is very unlikely to be higher: both required about the same quantity of paper; both were printed in duodecimo, 23 lines to the page; but JA's novel used slightly larger type, which means that composing costs might have been less. Bibliographical analysis shows that *She Thinks for Herself* required about 37 printed sheets; Gilson's analysis of SS indicates that it required slightly more, about 38 sheets. Using the best available figures for a printing in 1811, JA's novel may have cost about 31s per ream for the 57 reams of paper needed, and probably about 35s per sheet to print, yielding costs of £155. Exactly £24.9.2 was spent advertising Maria Benson's novel *The Wife. A Novel*, issued in Feb. 1810; I am assuming about the same for JA's novel (Longman reel 1, I/2/156). See David Gilson, *A Bibliography of Jane Austen* (Oxford: Clarendon Press, 1982).
4. The trade price to booksellers for a novel expected to retail at 15s would be 9s6d according to Longman's formula as expressed to Mrs Hughes, the author of *She Thinks for Herself*: 'If your work be sold retail at 4/6 Pr. Volume the trade sale price will be 2/ 10 *in sheets*; and if the price be higher or lower, the trade price will be more or less nearly in that proportion' (Longman Letter Books, I/97/381; 26 Nov. 1812). A volume that retailed at 5s would thus be sold to the trade in sheets at 3s2d or 9s6d for 3 vols. Booksellers purchased copies at this discounted price and themselves added cardboard

about £140 after deducting expenses of £179 and Egerton's ten per cent commission on the sales.

Austen was risking, then, about £180 on the chance of earning £140. In fact, however, her risk was substantially less. The buyer's market for novels was small, but sales to circulating libraries were fairly certain. Even the small circulating library at Alton purchased *Sense and Sensibility*, Anna Austen Lefroy's daughter amusingly recalled:

> It was in searching this Library that my mother came across a copy of *Sense & Sensibility* which she threw aside with careless contempt, little imagining who had written it, exclaiming to the great amusement of her Aunts who stood by 'Oh that must be rubbish I am sure from the title'.[5]

A novel normally would have to sell between one half and two-thirds of an edition to become profitable. For example, within five months of being issued in February 1810, Maria Benson's *The Wife. A Novel* had sold 275 of the 500 copies printed, and in two more years another 49, realising £7.6.4 to split with Longman, who had agreed to share profits with the author. By June 1812, however, sales had stalled. No more copies were sold until the work was remaindered in April 1813, when 151 were taken at 1s6d each, yielding another £10.11.10 to be split between the author and her publisher. Benson made about £9 finally, as did her publisher, who risked more than £155 to do so.[6]

We can presume that the 275 copies of *The Wife* that were taken right away, however, represent the number that just about any new novel might expect to dispose of on the market. The figure is probably uninflated by sales to family and friends, for Benson took 25 copies for herself to supply that market. (In fact, the copy in the British Library was presented to the Rev. J. Jamison by 'his friend the Author'.) If only 275 copies of *Sense and Sensibility* had sold, Austen would have had £130, less Egerton's ten per cent, to offset her expenses of £179; that is, she would have owed about £62. If the other 475 copies had been remaindered at the same price as Benson's novel, Austen would have received another £32 or so. At worst, then, her loss was unlikely to be more than £30. Although she probably was unable to 'reserve' such a sum from her own 'mod-

---

covers ('boards') before selling them. If 750 copies of SS were sold at the trade price, receipts would be £356.5.0, and Egerton's 10 per cent commission would come to £35.12.0. Author's copies, if any, would be deducted from the total sold; for every copy JA took, she would lose 9s6d of possible gain. She would pay no commission on such copies, however.

5. Quoted in Jane Austen: *A Family Record*, rev. and enl. by Deirdre Le Faye (London: The British Library, 1989), pp. 170–1.
6. Longman reel 1, I/2/156.

erate income', to use Henry's words—for most of her life, her dress allowance had been £20 a year[7]—she could perhaps set aside about half. And every additional copy of her novel that was sold at the full trade price of 9s6d would reduce this possible debt. She would break even once 419 copies were sold, even allowing for Egerton's commission.

In other words, if Austen had been more aware of the economics of publishing for herself, if she had known that even at worst her losses were likely to be manageable, she might have published sooner—perhaps when she inherited £50 in 1807. The women whom she would have considered models, however, Frances Burney, Charlotte Smith, Anne Radcliffe and later Maria Edgeworth, published by selling the copyright of their works. Perhaps because these respected women novelists sold copyright and because doing so entailed no risk to herself, Austen evidently preferred that option until 1811, for otherwise she would not have accepted the offer of £10 for the copyright of *Susan* in 1803. Fortunately, by 1811 Austen was prepared to invest money in herself, in her own authorship.[8]

Austen saw her own words in print for the first time in April 1811—an exciting experience for any writer—when she was in London and had received the first two 'sheets' of *Sense and Sensibility* to correct. Like almost all novels at this time, it appeared in 'duodecimo': each printed sheet was folded so as to produce 12 leaves or one 'gathering' of 24 pages to the sheet. Printing was charged by the sheet, and one ream of paper was required to print 500 copies of one sheet. The first volume of *Sense and Sensibility* took more than 13 gatherings or sheets. Austen thus replied to Cassandra's query as to the progress of the novel through the press: 'I have had two sheets to correct, but the last only brings us to W[illoughby']s first appearance' (*Letters*, 25 Apr. 1811). She had actually received four gatherings to correct,[9] taking the novel

7. JA and her sister seem to have received £5 a quarter during their father's lifetime, and the sum is unlikely to have been increased after his death (*Letters*, 24 Dec. 1798; *Letters*, 28 Dec. 1798).
8. Had JA offered her novels to the House of Longman, she might well have begun her publishing career earlier, for they almost certainly would have offered to share profits with her. A curious reference to JA's work survives in a letter dated 11 Oct. 1813 from one of the Longman partners to Amelia Opie: 'we are particularly interested for the success of the Austen and we sincerely regret that her works have not met with the encouragement we could wish' (Longman Letter Books I/98/75). If this reference has been accurately transcribed, it suggests that JA's authorship was indeed widely known, as she acknowledged in a letter of 25 Sep. 1813 (*Letters*). It also suggests that the House of Longman was not impressed by the small editions of her works that Egerton had issued. Second editions of both SS and PP, however, were to be advertised in a few weeks, on 29 Oct. 1813.
9. The discrepancy can be easily accounted for: the printer might be using larger sheets of paper so as to print two gatherings per 'sheet', a common enough practice in duodecimo printing. Two sheets would thus equal four gatherings of 24 pp. each. Standard printing prices would take this practice into consideration.

through 96 pages of the first volume and ending with these words in Chapter 9:

> A gentleman carrying a gun, with two pointers playing round him, was passing up the hill and within a few yards of Marianne, when her accident happened. He put down his gun and ran to her assistance. She . . .
>
> (42)

It must have been tantalising to Austen to read so far and no further, especially since she strongly doubted the printer Roworth's reliability.

Although in her works Austen employs similes and metaphors sparingly, in her references to her novels she uses them much more freely. She notoriously referred several times to her novels as her children—but only once she had begun to see them in print. She responds thus to Cassandra's enquiry:

> No indeed, I am never too busy to think of S & S. I can no more forget it, than a mother can forget her sucking child; & I am much obliged to you for your enquiries.
>
> (*Letters*, 25 Apr. 1811)

She then mentions having the two sheets to correct. Her analogy here is very powerful. Her own mother had suckled eight children, and she herself had recently lived with a mother and her sucking child at Southampton. She knew very well the degree of intense absorption that she was evoking to describe the impossibility of forgetting her first novel. The comparison suggests that, at 35, Austen was happy and proud to feel that she had produced and was nurturing or mothering a book. This maternal pride is evident in the rest of the passage, culminating in the reference to her character as 'my Elinor'. Similar tenderness and pride appear later, when Austen refers to *Pride and Prejudice* as 'my own darling child' (*Letters*, 29 Jan. 1813) and sends a copy of *Emma* to her niece Anna, whose newborn daughter Austen has not yet seen: 'As I wish very much to see *your* Jemima, I am sure you will like to see *my* Emma, & have therefore great pleasure in sending it for your perusal' (*Letters*, Dec. 1815). Austen even permits herself comparable references to her characters, as in *Mansfield Park*: 'My Fanny indeed at this very time, I have the satisfaction of knowing, must have been happy in spite of every thing' (461).

This tendency to refer to books (or characters) as one's offspring should not be regarded too simply as revealing a spinster's wish to be a mother. Had Austen strongly desired children, she would have married Bigg-Wither. Her mature attitudes to actual pregnancy and mothering express a sense of the burdens of these states rather than

anything else. And in fact, a maternal metaphor for one's relationship to a book is conventional.[1]

Sense and Sensibility received two favourable reviews, a lengthy
one with many long quotations in the *Critical*, and a short one in
the *British Critic*. One contemporary comment has been recorded:
in a letter postmarked 24 November 1811, Henrietta, Countess of
Bessborough, wrote to Lord Granville Leveson Gower, 'Have you
read "Sense and Sensibility"? It is a clever novel. They were full of
it at Althorp, and tho' it ends stupidly I was much amus'd by it'.[2]
(The stupid ending might have been Marianne's marriage.) Althorp
in Northamptonshire was the seat of Lady Bessborough's father
Lord Spencer; someone in the family had evidently purchased the
novel early in November, as soon as it was advertised.

Two good reviews and a steady sale must have been exhilarating
to Austen. Her family's immediate response to her publication has
not been recorded, but certainly they shared her delight. She visited
her brother James and his family at Steventon in November 1811,
shortly after the novel came out; possibly the family read it among
themselves then. If any of the children were present at such a reading, Austen's authorship was kept a secret, not revealed until a few
years later. When he finally learned that his aunt had written two
novels, James Edward Austen-Leigh was inspired to versify his
amazement:

> That you made the Middletons, Dashwoods, and all,
> And that you (not young Ferrars) found out that a ball
> May be given in cottages, never so small. . .[3]

No family member or friend seems to have preferred *Sense and
Sensibility* to the other novels. James Edward's half sister Anna did
like it better than *Mansfield Park* and *Pride and Prejudice*, in that
order, but she thought *Emma* equally good (*Minor Works*, 431,
438). Only four other 'Opinions' of *Mansfield Park* and *Emma* actually mention *Sense and Sensibility* at all by name or implication,
and none rank it clearly in relation to the others, perhaps because
it was not fresh enough in anyone's mind. It had been published

1. Maria Benson, for instance, used the metaphor in her preface to *The Wife. A Novel*
   (London: Longman *et al.*, 1810), p. 4. Even a man could employ it, as did the author
   and bookseller Robert Dodsley 50 years earlier, when he begged William Shenstone to
   supply copy for the fifth and sixth volumes of Dodsley's *Collection of Poems by Several
   Hands*: 'Ah, dear Mr. Shenstone! consider what a sad situation I am in—big with *twins*,
   at my *full time*, and no hopes of your assistance to *deliver* me! Was ever *man* in such a
   situation before?', James E. Tierney (ed.), *The Correspondence of Robert Dodsley 1733–
   1764* [Cambridge University Press, 1988], pp 331–2).
2. Quoted by Gilson, p. 9. [For the *Critical Review* and *British Critic* reviews, see above,
   pp. 313–16—*Editor*.]
3. Quoted in *Jane Austen: A Family Record*, p. 180; Le Faye conjectures that the lines were
   written on a visit to Chawton in the summer of 1813.

nearly three years before Austen began to collect opinions—no sooner than May 1814.

Egerton had almost certainly accepted *Sense and Sensibility* by February 1811.[4] This acceptance made Austen optimistic enough about the possibilities of publication to begin her most ambitious novel to date, *Mansfield Park.* According to Cassandra's memorandum, this novel was begun 'somewhere about Feb[y] 1811—Finished soon after June 1813' (*Minor Works*, facing p. 242).[5] No other novel took Austen so long to write. Probably part of the time was spent revising *Pride and Prejudice,* perhaps taken up when she discovered that *Sense and Sensibility* had sold well enough to break even; this point was quite likely to be reached within six months of issue, in May 1812. By the following November, Austen had completed her revisions, made a fair copy and sold the manuscript to Egerton for £110, as she wrote to Martha Lloyd: 'It's being sold will I hope be a great saving of Trouble to Henry, & therefore must be welcome to me.—The Money is to be paid at the end of the twelvemonth' (*Letters*, 29 Nov. 1812). Austen's unfortunate decision to part with the copyright of *Pride and Prejudice* for less than the £150 she had wished for was made before she could predict that the first edition of *Sense and Sensibility* would sell out and bring her £140. Again, most novels sold best immediately after being published. Egerton is likely to have advised Austen, quite accurately, that publishing a second novel would assist sales of the first. Her acceptance of Egerton's offer may have been influenced by this consideration, not simply by her wish to save Henry the trouble he had evidently undergone in supervising the printing of *Sense and Sensibility* between April and October 1811.

* * *

The success of *Pride and Prejudice* certainly increased the demand for *Sense and Sensibility,* which was sold out by 3 July 1813, according to a letter written on that date to Frank (*Letters*). It had taken about 20 months to clear the edition. By contrast, *Pride and Prejudice* was probably sold out before the second edition appeared on 29 October, nine months after its first appearance. Egerton may have ordered the reprint of *Pride and Prejudice* before the first edition was exhausted because a clever publisher who owned the copyright of a work generally did not allow it to go out of print while there was still a decent demand. To do otherwise was to damage

---

4. JA's presence in London to read proofs in March along with her hope to see the book before the end of April suggests that Egerton sent SS to the printer in late January.

5. I cannot accept Deirdre Le Faye's conjecture that JA could not have begun *MP* at this time because she was busy correcting proofs of SS and planning revisions to PP; see *Jane Austen: A Family Record*, p. 176.

the value of the copyright.[6] He advised Austen to reprint *Sense and Sensibility* at the same time as he was reprinting *Pride and Prejudice*: Austen wrote as a postscript to Frank on 25 September 1813 that 'There is to be a 2 ᵈ Edition of S. & S. Egerton advises it' (*Letters*) and both works were advertised together on 29 October. Egerton may not have suggested an immediate reprint of *Sense and Sensibility* in July because he judged that a joint publication would stimulate the sale of both works, or because he calculated that they could be advertised together (at a slight saving to both). He was also unconcerned with preserving the value of a copyright that he did not own. On the whole, however, his advice to Austen was sound enough. She never lost money by publishing with Egerton, although she had to wait until 1816 before receiving profits on the second edition of *Sense and Sensibility*.[7]

RAYMOND WILLIAMS

Sensibility†

Sensibility became a very important word in English between mC18 and mC20, but in recent years this importance has quite sharply declined. It is a very difficult word, both in its senses and variations within this historical period, and in its relations within the very complicated group of words centred on *sense*. We have only to remember that **sensibility** is not a general noun for the condition of being *sensible* to realize how difficult this group can be. Some of the interrelations of the group have been analysed by William Empson in *The Structure of Complex Words*, 250–310; 1951.

The earliest uses of **sensibility**, fw *sensibilitas*, L, followed the earliest uses of **sensible**, fw *sensible*, F, *sensibilis*, lL—felt, perceived, through the (physical) *senses*. This use of **sensible**, from C14, underlay **sensibility** as physical feeling or sense perception from C15. But it was not a word often used. The significant development in *sense* was the extension from a process to a particular kind of product: *sense* as good sense, good judgment, from which

---

6. The publishing house of Longman wrote to Robert Cruttwell, who owned the copyright of *Cruttwell's Gazetteer*, that 'We consider it justice to the proprietor of the Copyright to inform you that we have but 54 copies remaining, & that if a new edition be not immediately proceeded with the property will suffer most materially' (Longman Letter Books, I/98/123; 27 Jan. 1814).

7. See JA's note of 'Profits of my Novels', reproduced in facsimile in *Plan of a Novel* (Oxford: Clarendon Press, 1926).

† From Raymond Williams, *Keywords: A Vocabulary of Culture and Society*, rev. ed. (New York: Oxford UP, 1983), pp. 280–83. Reprinted by permission of Oxford University Press and HarperCollins Publishers Ltd.

the predominant modern meaning of **sensible** was to be derived. (*Common sense* has followed this track, ending in a blunt assertion of the obvious—what everybody knows, or knows to be practical—after its earlier and more active reference to a *sense* achieved by common process; the variations of COMMON. * * * But before sensible was specialized to this limited use, it had moved, temporarily, in another direction, towards 'tender' or 'fine' feeling, from C16. This just survives in **sensible of** (cf. the special use of *touched*); *sense* of has a wider actual range, including neutrality. It was from **sensible** in this particular use that the important C18 use of **sensibility** was derived. It was more than *sensitivity*, which can describe a physical or an emotional condition. It was, essentially, a social generalization of certain personal qualities, or, to put it another way, a personal appropriation of certain social qualities. It thus belongs in an important formation which includes TASTE, *cultivation* and *discrimination*, and, at a different level, CRITICISM, and CULTURE in one of its uses, derived from *cultivated* and *cultivation*. All describe very general human processes, but in such a way as to specialize them; the negative effects of the actual exclusions that are so often implied can best be picked up in *discrimination*, which has survived both as the process of fine or informed judgment and as the process of treating certain groups unfairly. *Taste* and *cultivation* make little sense unless we are able to contrast their presence with their absence, in ways that depend on generalization and indeed on CONSENSUS. **Sensibility** in its C18 uses ranged from a use much like that of modern *awareness* (not only *consciousness* but *conscience*) to a strong form of what the word appears literally to mean, the ability to feel: 'dear Sensibility! source . . . unexhausted of all that's precious in our joys, or costly in our sorrows' (Sterne, 1768).

It was at this point that its relation to *sentimental* became important. Sentiment, from fw *sentimentum*, mL, rw *sentire*, L—to feel, had ranged from C14 uses for physical feeling, and feeling of one's own, to C17 uses for both opinion and emotion. In mC18 *sentimental* was widely used: '*sentimental*, so much in vogue among the polite . . . Everything clever and agreeable is comprehended in that word . . . a *sentimental* man . . . a *sentimental* party . . . a *sentimental* walk' (Lady Bradshaugh, 1749). The association with **sensibility** was then close: a conscious openness to feelings, and also a conscious consumption of feelings. The latter use made *sentimental* vulnerable, and in C19 this was, often crudely, pushed home: 'that rosepink vapour of Sentimentalism, Philanthropy and Feasts of Morals' (Carlyle, 1837); 'Sentimental Radicalism' (Bagehot on Dickens, 1858). Much that was moral or radical, in intention and in effect, was washed with the same brush that was used to depict self-conscious or self-indulgent displays of *sentiment*. Southey, in his conservative phase, brought the words together: 'the sentimental classes, persons of ardent or morbid sensibility' (1823). This complaint is against people who feel 'too much' as well as against those who 'indulge their emotions'. This confusion has permanently damaged *sentimental* (though limited positive uses survive, typically in *sentimental value*) and wholly determined *sentimentality*.

Sensibility escaped this. It maintained its C18 range, and became important in one special area, in relation to AESTHETIC feeling. (Jane Austen, of course, in *Sense and Sensibility*, had explored the variable qualities which the specialized terms appeared to define. In *Emma* she may have picked up one tendency in 'more acute sensibility to fine sounds than to my feelings' (II, vi; 1815).) Ruskin wrote of 'sensibility to colour' (1843). The word seems to have been increasingly used to distinguish a particular area of interest and response which could be distinguished not only from RATIONALITY or *intellectuality* but also (by contrast with one of its C18 associations) from *morality*. By eC20 **sensibility** was a key word to describe the human area in which artists worked and to which they appealed. In the subsequent development of a CRITICISM (q.v.) based on distinctions between *reason* and *emotion*, **sensibility** was a preferred general word for an area of human response and judgment which could not be reduced to the *emotional* or *emotive*. What T. S. Eliot, in the 1920s, called the **dissociation of sensibility** was a supposed disjunction between 'thought' and 'feeling'. **Sensibility** became the apparently unifying word, and on the whole was transferred from kinds of response to a use equivalent to the formation of a particular mind: a whole activity, a whole way of perceiving and responding, not to be reduced to either 'thought' or 'feeling'. EXPERIENCE, in its available senses of something active and something formed, took on the same generality. For an important period, **sensibility** was that from which art proceeded and through which it was received. In the latter use, *taste* and *cultivation*, which had been important associates in the original formation, were generally replaced by *discrimination* and *criticism*. But for all the interest of this phase, which was dominant to c. 1960, the key terms were still predominantly social generalizations of personal qualities or, as became increasingly apparent, personal appropriations of social qualities. **Sensibility** as an apparently neutral term in discussion of the sources of art, without the difficult overtones of *mind* or the specializations of *thought* and *feeling*, proved more durable than as a term of appeal or ratification for any particular response. But, as in the C18 emergence, the abstraction and generalization of an active personal quality, as if it were an evident social fact or process, depended on a consensus of particular valuations, and as these broke down or were rejected **sensibility** came to seem too deeply coloured by them to be available for general use. The word faded from active discussion, but it is significant that in its actual range (which is what is fundamentally at issue) no adequate replacement has been found.

MARILYN BUTLER

Sensibility and the Worship of Self†

* * *

It is the role of Marianne Dashwood, who begins with the wrong ideology, to learn the right one. After her illness she applies her naturally strong feelings to objects outside herself, and her intelligence to thorough self-criticism in the Christian spirit. In what for her is the crisis of the book, her confession of her errors to Elinor,[1] Marianne resembles Jane Austen's other heroines Catherine, Elizabeth, and Emma, all of whom arrive at the same realization that (in the words of Jane Austen's prayer) 'pride' and 'vanity' have blinded them in relation both to themselves and to external reality.

It is quite false to assume that merely because Marianne is treated with relative gentleness, Jane Austen has no more than a qualified belief in the evils of sensibility. She spares Marianne, the individual, in order to have her recant from sensibility, the system. Even this is possible only because Marianne, with her naturally affectionate disposition and her intelligence, is never from the start a typical adherent of the doctrine of self: youth and impetuosity for a time blinded her, so that she acted against the real grain of her nature.[2] Because Marianne is not representative, other characters are needed, especially in the second half of the novel, to show the system of self in full-blooded action. Jane Austen provides them in the group of characters who fawn upon and virtually worship that false idol compounded of materialism, status-seeking and self-interest, Mrs. Ferrars.

---

† From *Jane Austen and the War of Ideas* (Oxford: Clarendon P, 1975), pp. 192–94. © Oxford University Press 1975. Reprinted by permission of the publisher. Quotations from *Sense and Sensibility* are from the Chapman edition.

1. *Sense and Sensibility*, pp. 345 ff.

2. Marianne's intelligence is of a kind which gives her moral stature within Jane Austen's system of belief. Although she begins the novel professing an erroneous system, it is always clear that she has the capacity for the searching self-analysis of the Christian. Simple, good characters like Mrs. Jennings are valued by Jane Austen, but she never leaves any doubt that individuals with active moral intelligence are a higher breed.

The leading characters who take over from Marianne the role of illustrating what worship of the self really means are Lucy Steele and Fanny Dashwood. It is clear, of course, that neither Lucy nor Fanny is a 'feeling' person at all. Both are motivated by ruthless self-interest, Lucy in grimly keeping Edward to his engagement, Fanny in consistently working for her immediate family's financial advantage. But both Lucy and Fanny, though in reality as hard-headed as they could well be, clothe their mercenariness decently in the garments of sensibility. Lucy flatters Lady Middleton by pretending to love her children. She acts the lovelorn damsel to Elinor. Her letters are filled with professions of sensibility. Similarly, in the successive shocks inflicted by Lucy's insinuation of herself into the family, 'poor Fanny had suffered agonies of sensibility'.[3] It is no accident that at the end the marriages of the two model couples, Elinor and Marianne and their two diffident, withdrawing husbands, are contrasted with the establishments, far more glorious in worldly terms, of Lucy and Fanny and their complacent, mercenary husbands.[4] Lucy and Fanny may quarrel, but it is suitable that they should end the novel together, the joint favourites of old Mrs. Ferrars, and forever in one another's orbit. However it begins, the novel ends by comparing the moral ideal represented by Sense with a new interpretation of 'individualism'. The intellectual position, originally held in good faith by Marianne, is abandoned; what takes its place is selfishness with merely a fashionable cover of idealism—and, particularly, the pursuit of self-interest in the economic sense. Willoughby's crime proves after all not to have been rank villainy, but expensive self-indulgence so habitual that he must sacrifice everything, including domestic happiness, to it. Lucy's behaviour is equally consistent, and it, too, is crowned with wordly success:

> The whole of Lucy's behaviour in the affair, and the prosperity which crowned it, therefore, may be held forth as a most encouraging instance of what an earnest, an unceasing attention to self-interest . . . will do in securing every advantage of fortune, with no other sacrifice than that of time and conscience.[5]

Jane Austen's version of 'sensibility'—that is, individualism, or the worship of self, in various familiar guises—is as harshly dealt with here as anywhere in the anti-jacobin tradition. Even without

---

3. *Sense and Sensibility*, p. 371.
4. Some critics have called Elinor's marriage 'romantic', Lucy's 'prudent', and the end another instance between sense and sensibility. (Cf. Andrew Wright, *Jane Austen's Novels*, p. 92.) But this shows a continued misunderstanding of JA's interpretation of her two terms: her 'sense' approximates to the traditional Christian personal and social ethic, her 'sensibility' to a modern individualist ethic in two different manifestations, Marianne's and Lucy's.
5. *Sense and Sensibility*, p. 376.

the melodramatic political subplot of many anti-jacobin novels, Mrs. Ferrars's London is recognizably a sketch of the anarchy that follows the loss of all values but self-indulgence. In the opening chapters especially, where Marianne is the target of criticism, 'sensibility' means sentimental (or revolutionary) idealism, which Elinor counters with her sceptical or pessimistic view of man's nature. Where the issue is the choice of a husband, Jane Austen's criteria prove to be much the same as Mrs. West's: both advocate dispassionate assessment of a future husband's qualities, discounting both physical attractiveness, and the *rapport* that comes from shared tastes, while stressing objective evidence. Both reiterate the common conservative theme of the day, that a second attachment is likely to be more reliable than a first.[6] By all these characteristic tests, *Sense and Sensibility* is an anti-jacobin novel just as surely as is *A Gossip's Story* [by Jane West].

* * *

MARY POOVEY

Ideological Contradictions and the Consolations of Form: *Sense and Sensibility*†

* * *

Sense and Sensibility is a much darker novel than any of the juvenilia or the parodic *Northanger Abbey* (1818),[1] and we might speculate that one origin of its somber tone and the eruptions of anarchic feeling that punctuate it lies in the anxiety with which Austen viewed individualism's challenge to paternalism. For in *Sense and Sensibility*, as, in a slightly different way, in *Lady Susan* and *Northanger Abbey*, the most fundamental conflict is between

6. Marianne, Colonel Brandon, Edward Ferrars, the late Mr. Dashwood, and even perhaps Lucy Steele are better matched in their second choice than in their first.
† From *The Proper Lady and the Woman Writer: Ideology as Style in the Works of Mary Wollstonecraft, Mary Shelley, and Jane Austen* (Chicago: U of Chicago P, 1984), pp. 183–94. Reprinted by permission of the publisher. Quotations of *Sense and Sensibility* are from the Chapman edition.
1. The precise order in which Austen composed her major works is unknown, but B. C. Southam, having consulted Cassandra's original memorandum and the surviving manuscripts, argues persuasively for the following chronology: *Elinor and Marianne*—completed before 1796; *First Impressions*—October 1796–August 1797; *Sense and Sensibility*, the revision of *Elinor and Marianne*—begun November 1797, revised again at Chawton 1809–10; *Northanger Abbey*, originally entitled *Susan*—c. 1798–99, never substantially revised; *Pride and Prejudice*, the revision of *First Impressions*—conducted in 1809–10 and 1812; *Mansfield Park*—February 1811–June 1813; *Emma*—21 January 1814–29 March 1815; *Persuasion*—8 August 1815–6 August 1816 (Southam, *Jane Austen's Literary Manuscripts*, pp. 52–58). The dates given in parentheses in my text are the publication dates.

Austen's own imaginative engagement with her self-assertive characters and the moral code necessary to control their anarchic desires.

In the greater part of *Sense and Sensibility*, Austen's aesthetic strategies endorse the traditional values associated with her "sensible" heroine, Elinor Dashwood. One of these strategies consists in measuring all of the characters (including Elinor) against an implicit, but presumably authoritative, moral norm. As early as the second chapter, in that free, indirect discourse that is the hallmark of her mature style, Austen shadows the opinion of a single fallible character with this implicit moral standard.[2] Irony in *Sense and Sensibility* arises for the most part from the novel's action; the dialogue between Mr. and Mrs. John Dashwood points up as surely as any overt narrative commentary the parsimony behind their dwindling good will. But our response to this dialogue is initially shaped by such sentences as the following: "To take three thousand pounds from the fortune of their dear little boy, would be impoverishing him to the most dreadful degree"; "How could he answer it to himself to rob his child, and his only child too, of so large a sum?"[3] The hyperbole expressed in the words "impoverishing," "dreadful," and "rob" conveys both the strategy of Mrs. Dashwood's rhetoric and its absurdity, and the repeated use of the word "child" suggests how effective she is in manipulating John Dashwood's generosity. Because these sentences belong to the narrative and not to direct dialogue, they mimetically convey the tone of the conversation and simultaneously judge it by reference to an implicit system of more humane values—the undeniably Christian values that one should love one's neighbor as one's self and that the man who hoards treasures in this world (or the woman who encourages him to do so) will never get into the kingdom of heaven.

But despite this ground of Christian principles, nearly everything in the plot of *Sense and Sensibility* undermines the complacent assumption that they are principles generally held or practically effective. Almost every action in the novel suggests that, more often than not, individual will triumphs over principle and individual desire proves more compelling than moral law. Even the narrator, the apparent voice of these absolute values, reveals that moral principles are qualified in practice. The narrator's prefatory evaluation of John Dashwood, for example—"he was not an ill-disposed young man, unless to be rather cold hearted, and rather selfish, is to be ill-disposed" (p. 5)—directs our attention most specifically to the

2. For a discussion of Austen's "free, indirect speech," see Norman Page, *The Language of Jane Austen* (New York: Barnes & Noble, 1972), pp. 123 ff.
3. *Sense and Sensibility*, in *The Works of Jane Austen*, 1:8.

way in which what should, in theory, be moral absolutes can, and
in practice do, shade off into infinite gradations and convenient
exceptions. Is it always morally wrong to be "rather" selfish, especially in a society in which such selfishness is the necessary basis
for material prosperity? What efficacy will moral absolutes have in
such a society? How could Elinor's patient, principled fidelity win
the passive, principled Edward if it were not, finally, for Lucy
Steele's avarice?

A second strategy that is apparently designed to forestall such
questions by aligning the reader's sympathies with Elinor's "sense"
involves the juxtaposition of Elinor and her sister Marianne at
nearly every critical juncture in the novel. Consistently, Elinor
makes the prudent choice, even when doing so is painful; almost
as consistently, Marianne's decisions are self-indulgent and harm-
ful, either to herself or to someone else. But this neat design is less
stable than an absolute and authoritative moral system would seem
to require. Many readers have found Marianne's "spirit" more appealing than Elinor's cautious, prim, and even repressive reserve,
and they have found Marianne's passionate romance with Willoughby more attractive than the prolonged frustration to which
Elinor submits. That such preferences may be in keeping with at
least one countercurrent of the novel is suggested by the fact that
whenever Austen herself explicitly compares the two putative
heroes—Colonel Brandon and Edward Ferrars—with the less
moral, more passionate Willoughby, it is Willoughby who is appealing. On two occasions when Willoughby is expected but one of
the more subdued lovers appears instead, the disappointment is
unmistakable; and when the reverse situation occurs, in the cli-
mactic final encounter between Elinor and Willoughby, Elinor is
aroused to a pitch of complex emotion we never see Edward inspire
in anyone. Moreover, Willoughby repeatedly bursts into the narrative with "manly beauty and more than common gracefulness," but
Edward and Brandon seem inert fixtures of the plot, incapable of
energetic galantry and attractive only to the most generous observer.
The initial description of each of them is dominated by negative
constructions and qualifying phrases, and even Elinor cannot un-
reservedly praise the man she wants to marry. "At first sight," she
admits, "his address is certainly not striking; and his person can
hardly be called handsome, till the expression of his eyes, which
are uncommonly good, and the general sweetness of his countenance, is perceived. At present, I know him so well, that I think
him really handsome; or, at least, almost so" (p. 20). Colonel Brandon, "neither very young nor very gay," is "silent and grave" much
of the time (p. 34), and his "oppression of spirits," like Edward's
chronic depression, can scarcely compete with Willoughby's charm.

The most telling dramatization of the contest between the potentially anarchic power of feeling and the restraint that moral principles require takes the form of a conflict within Elinor herself. This scene, in the final volume, owes much to conventional eighteenth-century didactic novels, but Austen's placing it at a moment when the generally self-disciplined Elinor is unusually susceptible to emotion gives it a particularly complicated effect. Colonel Brandon has presented a living to Edward Ferrars, and Elinor is finally, but sadly, reconciled to the fact that her lover will marry someone else. In the midst of this personal disappointment, she is also particularly sensitive to her sister's condition, for Marianne, whose own romantic disappointment had sent her into a dangerous decline, has just been declared out of danger. Elinor's "fervent gratitude" for this news is especially great because of the joy and relief it will bring to her mother, whose arrival is expected at any moment. It is this hectic peace—as Marianne sleeps quietly upstairs and a violent storm assaults the house—that Willoughby invades when he melodramatically steps into the drawing-room.

Elinor's first response is "horror" at his audacious intrusion; but before she can leave the room, Willoughby appeals to something even more powerful than Elinor's "honour": her curiosity. Elinor is momentarily captivated by Willoughby's "serious energy" and "warmth," and she listens "in spite of herself" to the story he unfolds—the chronicle of his passions, both honorable and base. At the end of his dramatic recital, Willoughby asks Elinor for pity, and, even though she feels it is her "duty" to check his outburst, she cannot repress her "compassionate emotion." It is this emotion that governs her judgment of Willoughby—a judgment that verges disconcertingly on rationalization:

> Elinor made no answer. Her thoughts were silently fixed on the irreparable injury which too early an independence and its consequent habits of idleness, dissipation, and luxury, had made in the mind, the character, the happiness, of a man who, to every advantage of person and talents, united a disposition naturally open and honest, and a feeling, affectionate temper. The world had made him extravagant and vain—Extravagance and vanity had made him cold-hearted and selfish. [P. 331]

When Willoughby departs, he leaves Elinor in an even greater "agitation" of spirits, "too much oppressed by a croud of ideas . . . to think even of her sister."

> Willoughby, in spite of all his faults, excited a degree of commiseration for the sufferings produced by them, which made her think of him as now separated for ever from her family with a tenderness, a regret, rather in proportion, as she soon

acknowledged within herself—to his wishes than to his merits. She felt that his influence over her mind was heightened by circumstances which ought not in reason to have weight; by that person of uncommon attraction, that open, affectionate, and lively manner which it was no merit to possess; and by that still ardent love for Marianne, which it was not even innocent to indulge. But she felt that it was so, long, long before she could feel his influence less. [P. 333]

One purpose of this episode is clearly to dramatize the odds against which Elinor's "sense," or reason, ultimately triumphs and therefore to increase, not undermine, our admiration for that faculty. But a second effect of the passage is to subject the reader to the same temptation that assails Elinor. Because the presentation is dramatic and because, for a moment at least, the character whose judgment has thus far directed our own hesitates in her moral evaluation, the reader is invited to judge Willoughby not by reference to an objective standard but by his immediate appeal to our imaginative, sympathetic engagement. As Elinor temporizes, the moral principle for which she otherwise speaks seems dangerously susceptible to circumstances, to the appeal of "lively manners," and to the special pleading of aroused female emotion.

Jane Austen seems anxious to control the moral anarchy that strong appeals to feeling can unleash; yet, significantly, she does not exclude passion from the novel, nor does she so completely qualify it as to undermine its power. Instead, Austen attempts to bend the imaginative engagement it elicits in the reader to the service of moral education. To do so, she restricts the reader's access to the romantic plot by conveying its details and its emotional affect only through indirect narration. At the beginning of the novel, for example, the incident in which Willoughby rescues Marianne is summarized by the dispassionate narrative persona, who supplies sentimental clichés but *not* Marianne's response to her rescue: "The gentleman offered his services, and perceiving that her modesty declined what her situation rendered necessary, took her up in his arms without farther delay" (p. 42). Similarly, the episode in which Willoughby cuts and kisses a lock of Marianne's hair is given to Margaret to relate (p. 60), and the emotional specifics of Willoughby's farewell at Barton Cottage can be deduced only from their aftermath (p. 82). Most of Marianne's outbursts of passion to Willoughby are confined to letters, which are concealed from the reader until after Willoughby has snubbed Marianne. In fact, the only emotionally charged encounter between the lovers that Austen presents dramatically is their final meeting at the London ball, and there Marianne's passion is transmuted by Willoughby's silence into the terrible muffled scream that both voices and symbolizes her thwarted love. So careful is Austen to keep the reader on the outside of such "dangerous" material that she embeds the most passionate episodes within other, less emotionally volatile stories. Thus the story of the two Elizas—related, as we will see, by a character whose relationship to the tale immediately activates our judgment—is contained within the story of Marianne's passion for Willoughby—a relationship whose emotional content is conveyed to the reader more by innuendo, summary, and indirection than by dramatic presentation. And this second story, in turn, is contained within the story of the relationship that opens and closes the novel—Elinor's considerably less demonstrative affection for Edward. By embedding these stories in this way, Austen seeks to defuse their imaginative affect and increase their power to educate the reader: from the fates of the two Elizas we learn to be wary of Marianne's quick feelings, and from the consequences of Marianne's self-indulgent passion we learn to value Elinor's reserve.

Instead of being allowed to identify with Marianne, then, for most of the novel we are restricted to Elinor's emotional struggles. This enables Austen to dramatize the complexities of what might otherwise seem an unattractive and unyielding obsession with propriety; it also permits her to filter the two stories of illicit passion through a character whose judgment generally masters emotion. That the passion bleeds from the narrators of these two tales into Elinor's "sense" attests to the power of this force and to the dangerous susceptibility that, without proper control, might undermine the judgment of even the most rational reader.

Austen also attempts to control the allure of Marianne's romantic desires by refusing to consider seriously either their social origin or their philosophical implications. As Tony Tanner has pointed out, Austen really avoids the systematic examination of "sensibility" that the novel seems to promise.[4] The novel begins like a novel of social realism. In the first paragraphs the narrator sounds like a lawyer or a banker; family alliances, the estate that is the heart of paternalistic society, even the deaths of loved ones, are all ruthlessly subordinated to the economic facts. Given this introduction, the reader has every reason to believe that the most important fact—that Mrs. Dashwood will have only five hundred pounds a year with which to raise and dower her daughters—will govern the futures of Elinor, Marianne, and Margaret. And given this probable development, the reader can understand why romantic fantasies are appealing. It is no wonder that Marianne—facing a life of poverty, the spiritual

---

4. Tony Tanner, Introduction to the Penguin edition of *Sense and Sensibility* (Harmondsworth, Eng., 1969), p. 32.

banality of relatives like the John Dashwoods, and the superficial urbanities of a neighborhood composed only of the Middletons and Mrs. Jennings—turns to Cowper for imaginative compensation; nor is it surprising that she fancies (in accordance with the promises of romantic novels) that her beauty will win the heart and hand of an errant knight. Beneath Marianne's effusions on nature and her passionate yearning for a hero lies the same "hunger of imagination" that Mary Wollstonecraft tried and failed to analyze in *Maria*. But to take Marianne's passions and longings seriously on their own terms would be to call into question the basis of Christian moral authority, the social order that ideally institutionalizes that authority, and, finally, the capacity of orthodox religion or society to gratify imaginative desires.[5] Elinor's sense, despite its admirable capacity to discipline and protect the self, cannot begin to satisfy this appetite, and no other social institution in the novel does any better. Instead of taking this implicit criticism to its logical conclusion, as Wollstonecraft tried to do, Jane Austen defuses its threat by directing our judgment away from bourgeois society and toward the self-indulgent individual. Austen caricatures just enough of Marianne's responses to nature and love to make her seem intermittently ridiculous, and, when her desires finally explode all social conventions, Austen stifles her with an illness that is not only a result but also a purgation of her passion. At the end of the novel, Austen ushers Marianne into Brandon's world of diminished desires in such a way as to make Marianne herself negate everything she has previously wanted to have and to be.

* * *

CLAUDIA L. JOHNSON

Sense and Sensibility: Opinions Too Common and Too Dangerous†

* * *

If conservative novelists held that the patriarchal family regulated and improved the passions, in *Sense and Sensibility* the family tends to be the locus of venal and idle habits. When we read the novel exclusively as a discussion of female propriety, a quasi-allegorical representation of "sense" and "sensibility," we overlook just how

5. See Tanner, ibid., p. 30.
† From *Jane Austen: Women, Politics, and the Novel* (Chicago: U of Chicago P, 1988), pp. 55–58. Reprinted by permission of the publisher. Quotations of *Sense and Sensibility* are from the Chapman edition.

much material it devotes to the manners of men of family. In fact, *Sense and Sensibility* methodically examines the sexual relations gentlemen pursue, either to strengthen patriarchal interests or to relieve the tedium of their existences, which are doomed to dependency and ennui until the death of a near relation will supply the money and liberty they crave. The stories of the two Elizas dramatize each of these possibilities.

The depiction of illicit sexual behavior was a possibility always open to Austen. The refusal to center her fiction on problematic sexual passion distinguishes Austen from her contemporaries, conservative and progressive alike. Seduced and abandoned women are the stuff of many a prerevolutionary English novel, preeminently *Clarissa*, but they positively crowd the pages of the political novel, in conservative fiction attesting to the vulnerability of the nation's decent families to rootless marauders, and in progressive fiction attesting to the abuses of established power. For Austen, however, to have foregrounded the tales of the Elizas would have entailed earmarking a progressive stance, which she evidently did not want to do. Their stories, while stopping decidedly short of pardoning failures of female chastity, nevertheless divulge the callousness of the ruling class, and they would not be out place beside such unequivocally radical novels as Hays's *Victim of Prejudice* (1799) and Inchbald's Rousseauvian *Nature and Art* (1796). As if to defuse the sensitivity of the subject matter, Austen distances herself from the story of the two Elizas by tucking it safely within the center of *Sense and Sensibility* and delegating its narration to the safe Colonel Brandon. But if this inset tale is never permitted to become central, it nevertheless is linked to the larger story in *Sense and Sensibility* through the use of common thematic and descriptive details. In fact, the part-to-whole relationship here functions in much the same way gothic fiction does in *Northanger Abbey*. In both cases, worst-case scenarios with highly conventionalized contours are invoked in order to illuminate what is "too common and too dangerous" about the "ordinary" experiences of her heroines.

In *Sense and Sensibility*, the age of seventeen is the turning point for unprotected females. It is at this age that the first Eliza, a rich orphan, is forced by her uncle, Brandon's father, to marry his eldest son specifically in order to fill the family coffers: "Her fortune was large, and our family estate much encumbered" (SS 205). No pains are spared to heighten Eliza's persecution. Her longstanding and mutual love for Brandon is brutally prohibited, and after an attempted elopement, she is locked up until she submits to her uncle's demand: "She was allowed no liberty, no society, no amusement, till my father's point was gained" (SS 206). Miseries of an evidently unspeakable sort follow her in her married life.

Brandon is too gentlemanly to detail a brother's depravities to a young lady like Elinor, but he intimates them with tantalizing indirection: "His pleasures were not what they ought to have been, and from the first he treated her unkindly" (SS 206). Brandon does everything possible to exonerate Eliza, short of pardoning her adultery outright: "Can we wonder that with such a husband to provoke inconstancy, and without a friend to advise or restrain her . . . she should fall?" (SS 206). Cheated out of her own patrimony, Eliza is not given a "legal allowance . . . adequate to her fortune, nor sufficient for her comfortable maintenance" (SS 207), and is thus left after her divorce "to sink deeper in a life of sin" (SS 207), melancholia, and mortal illness. Eliza's fate testifies to the failures of conservative ideology. As an orphan and an heiress, Eliza is a creature so vulnerable that she ought to melt the honorable breast of a Burkean man of feeling. But Eliza's uncle is not in the least susceptible to the melting sensations of solicitude and protectiveness. Rather than feel for the helplessness of his dependent, he looks only to keep up his country estate, while her dissolute husband no sooner possesses a wife's fortune than he abuses the wife herself. Far from being a cautionary tale about the duty of fidelity, Eliza's story, like so much of the central matter in *Sense and Sensibility*, indicts the license to coercion, corruption, and avarice available to grasping patriarchs and their eldest sons.

When the second Eliza is seventeen, she too, in the absence of responsible paternal protection, falls victim to unscrupulous male designs. Unlike Wickham, a propertyless upstart, and unlike the roving seducers in anti-Jacobin fiction, Willoughby is a landed gentleman, in straitened circumstances, but respectable nonetheless. His faults are explicitly related to the corrupt social practices of which he is himself in some senses the victim. While he awaits "the death of [his] old cousin . . . to set [him] free" (SS 320), Willoughby has nothing better to do than accumulate debts and prey on women. The only women available for his dark purposes are the unsheltered and unprotected—like Eliza Williams, and later Marianne Dashwood. Indeed, if Willoughby sports with Marianne only to gratify his vanity, "careless of her happiness, thinking only of [his] own amusement" (SS 320), his intentions for Eliza were always even less honorable. Willoughby is strikingly unrepentant about debauching Eliza and abandoning her and his child by her, and he even appears to consider the fact that he "did not recollect" (SS 322) to give her his address an adequate defense for his negligence. Willoughby's failures as a gentleman and a father are attributed to a deficiency of sensibility. As Colonel Brandon puts it, "[Willoughby] had already done that, which no man who *can* feel for another, would do" (SS 209). Not unlike Brandon's father and brother, Willoughby is governed by the need for money to support the habits of his class: "it had been for some time my intention to re-establish my circumstances by marrying a woman of fortune" (SS 320). Thus while Eliza's seduction is born of anomie, her abandonment is born of avarice, for when Willoughby's aunt vows to disinherit him unless he marries the girl, Willoughby simply states, "That could not be" (SS 323). The "dread of poverty" (SS 323) precludes this even more surely than it does a marriage to Marianne.

The most striking thing about the tales of the two Elizas is their insistent redundancy. One Eliza would have sufficed as far as the immediate narrative purpose is concerned, which is to discredit Willoughby with a prior attachment. But the presence of two unfortunate heroines points to crimes beyond Willoughby's doing, and their common name opens the sinister possibility that plights such as theirs proliferate throughout the kingdom. This redundancy has a generalizing effect, for it invites us to consider how much male behavior in Sense and Sensibility redoubles with what is depicted in their tales. The parallels between the Eliza stories and Marianne's experiences are overt. The bearing of the Eliza stories on Edward's treatment of Elinor and Lucy Steele, on the other hand, is, though submerged, more disturbing, because Edward is often regarded as the positive foil to Willoughby: modest, retiring, indifferent to dead leaves. But Edward too forms an early attachment out of the idleness endemic to landed gentlemen as presented in Sense and Sensibility. Although Edward, unlike Willoughby, is still under a parent's thumb, he too is holding out for an inheritance that will give him the money and the independence he needs to sustain, not an extravagant, but still a rather aimless life as a private gentleman. In the meantime, he expresses no interest in the energetic management of a country estate and discloses no enthusiasm or talent for a profession, not even the Church. Edward himself describes his relationship with Lucy Steele as a "fancied attachment" (SS 362), and as such it is not different from Willoughby's early feelings about Eliza, whose tenderness towards him "for a very short time, had the power of creating [a] return" (SS 322). But gentlemen in Sense and Sensibility are uncommitted sorts. They move on, more or less encumbered by human wreckage from the past. No sooner does Edward, like Willoughby, bind himself to one woman than he proceeds to engage the heart of another. Elinor moralizes upon Willoughby's faults. But not so quick to "scold the imprudence which compliments" herself (SS 368), she is not inclined to worry about Edward's similar, though less glaring, defects. When Elinor chides him for being inconstant to Lucy, Edward tepidly replies:

"I was simple enough to think, that because my *faith* was plighted to another, there could be no danger in my being with you; and that the consciousness of my engagement was to keep my heart as safe and sacred as my honour. I felt that I admired you, but I told myself it was only friendship . . . [that] I am doing no injury to anybody but myself." (SS 368)

Elinor chalks up all of Willoughby's "behaviour . . . from the beginning to the end" to "selfishness" (SS 351), but she appears not to notice that Edward's self-defense is animated solely by self-concern. While Willoughby at least admits to having amused himself with Marianne "without any design of returning her affection" (SS 320), Edward never hints at any consciousness that he may carelessly have created an attachment in Elinor that he had no intention of reciprocating. As different as Edward and Willoughby are individually, as English gentlemen many of their failures are identical. In marked contrast to the Darcys and Knightleys of this world, they are weak, duplicitous, and selfish, entirely lacking in that rectitude and forthrightness with which Austen is capable of endowing exemplary gentlemen when she wishes. In *Sense and Sensibility*, as in *Persuasion*, these faults are described as the effects of established and accepted social practices for men of family, not as aberrations from them. It is their commonplace lapses towards women that render female manners so desperately important and so impossibly problematic.

* * *

GENE RUOFF

Wills†

Sense and Sensibility is a darker, more serious and more troubled novel than Austen's other two mature works begun in the 1790s. But its peculiar kind of darkness, so often given a psychological reading, is starkly social in nature. Take its opening movement, as stunning a public advent of a new writer as we have ever witnessed. The first two chapters of *Sense and Sensibility* are in the purest sense expository. They introduce the family on which the novel will centre, provide brief descriptions of central characters, create a physical and socio-economic setting, and in general give the nec-

---

† From *Jane Austen's "Sense and Sensibility"* (Hemel Hempstead: Harvester Wheatsheaf, 1992), pp. 35–48. Reprinted by permission of the publisher. Complete bibliographical information regarding the critics alluded to parenthetically is available in the Selected Bibliography at the end of this volume. Quotations of *Sense and Sensibility* are from the Chapman edition.

essary background for the action to come, which might be said, since the novel bases its plot on the physical movement of characters, to begin with the removal of the surviving family of Henry Dashwood from the family seat at Norland Park in Sussex to Barton Cottage in Devonshire. But neither Marianne, Elinor, nor Mrs Dashwood appears in a scene, and none of the young ladies' love interests is mentioned. Marianne and Elinor first appear in a scene, and are first given dialogue, in Chapter III. From all indications provided by its first two chapters, the novel will not be about romantic entanglements but about inheritance. This appearance is not wholly misleading.

The first two chapters of *Sense and Sensibility* are fictively excessive. To the degree that their narrative function is to get two young ladies on the road so that they can get about their educations, nothing like the amount of detail we are given on family history, family finances or inheritance practices is necessary. The excess functions thematically rather than narratively, as it pertains to the social matrix in which the characters find themselves rather than the development of their individual characters. For many readers, who have minimised Austen's social and political vision, the chapters are just intrusive, if maddeningly, brilliantly, so. Both contemporary reviewers recognised their power, and the notice in the *Critical Review* closed by reprinting extensive selections from Chapter II.

Austen is precise about the succession of the Norland Park estate. The family of Henry Dashwood—including himself, his second wife and three daughters—has lived with his uncle, the current bachelor owner of Norland, for the ten years following the death of his sister. Since Henry Dashwood is described as both the 'legal inheritor' of Norland and the person to whom his uncle 'intended to bequeath it' (3), we can only conclude that the estate lies within the uncle's unrestricted gift. It is not, in the language of the day, under 'strict settlement' during the uncle's lifetime. Were he to die intestate, by common law it would legally pass to Henry Dashwood without restrictions.

That succession is disrupted by the will of the 'old Gentleman' (4), which entails the estate through three generations: providing life tenancies for Henry Dashwood, then for Henry's son John by his first marriage, with the actual inheritor to be on his father's death John's four-year-old son, 'poor little Harry' (8), as his mother is wont to call him. The value of the estate, we are able to compute later, is about £80,000 (its £4,000 annual income multiplied by twenty). One current estimate would make the inherited fortune approximately 16 million in today's US dollars (Julia P. Brown 7–8; Gaull 379). 'Not to be unkind, however, and as a mark of his affection for the three girls [who have attended him for ten years], he left them a thousand pounds a-piece' (4). Although the equivalent of two hundred thousand dollars is hardly a small amount, the income it would generate— £50 per year—would not permit any of the girls individually to move easily within the class of the gentry to which they were born: 'borderline gentlemen and their families lived on about £700 to £1,000 a year' (Julia P. Brown 7). One is tempted in this context to recall the generously sentimental grandfather of Austen's adolescent romp, *Love and Freindship*, who miraculously encounters for the first time four grandchildren in the space of five minutes at a Scottish inn. After describing their places on the family tree, with careful attention to birth order ('Philander the son of my Laurina's 3d Girl the amiable Bertha') he hands each of them a fifty-pound note and takes his leave, saying 'remember I have done the Duty of a Grandfather' (31–2).

It should be noted that estates of the magnitude of Norland Park were seldom conveyed by wills, because the current owner would then remain free until his death to change the terms of the settlement of the estate. Normally estates were conveyed by deed upon such an occasion as the coming of age or the marriage of the heir in tail. At such times the life tenant and heir in tail joined to break the existing settlement and resettle the estate. The heir was normally given his independence through an annuity made at this time—a strong inducement for him to agree to restrict his future absolute hold on the property by joining with his father in the resettlement—and suitable provisions could be made for a jointure for the current life-incumbent's widow and portions for the other surviving children (English and Saville 132–40). The will in *Sense and Sensibility* is entirely of the uncle's devising, and Austen chooses for him the mode of conveyance that leaves the Dashwood women most precariously exposed.

Henry Dashwood survives his uncle by only a year, leaving an estate of ten thousand pounds, 'including the late legacies . . . for his widow and daughters' (4). All he can do on his deathbed is call for his son and recommend 'with all the strength and urgency which illness could command, the interest of his mother-in-law and sisters' (5). Though lacking 'the strong feelings of the rest of the family' (5), John Dashwood is still moved by his father's request and promises 'to do everything in his power to make them comfortable' (5). What lies within his 'power' becomes the issue.

From some perspectives that power might seem substantial. He received half the fortune of his mother, described only as 'large' (3), upon his coming of age. His marriage soon thereafter 'added to his wealth' (3). Austen sets up John's fulfilment of his filial obligation beautifully:

When he gave his promise to his father, he meditated within himself to increase the fortunes of his sisters by the present of a thousand pounds a-piece. He then really thought himself equal to it. The prospect of four thousand a-year, in addition to his present income, besides the remaining half of his own mother's fortune, warmed his heart and made him feel capable of generosity.—'Yes, he would give them three thousand pounds: it would be liberal and handsome! It would be enough to make them completely easy. Three thousand pounds! he could spare so considerable a sum with little inconvenience.' —He thought of it all day long, and for many days successively, and he did not repent. (5)

We are led to conceive of his father's eighty thousand pounds as an 'addition' to the son's wealth, by no means the bulk of it. By inference, John Dashwood commands a fortune close to that which we will see later in Darcy of *Pride and Prejudice*, perhaps ten thousand a year from holdings of, say, two hundred thousand pounds. Although our figures do not have to be exact to understand how three thousand might be spared 'with little inconvenience', it requires a bit of a stretch to accept his description of his intention as 'liberal and handsome!' (5). And we can only conclude that Austen's ironic treatment of the wealthy gentry's fantasies about its benevolence is mercilessly broad and direct. John and Fanny Dashwood are near to being fabulously wealthy—only 300 to 400 families in England had incomes of over £10,000 a year (Julia P. Brown 7)—yet they manage to justify giving the Dashwood women not even a crumb.

John's 'repentance', formulated as a recognition of the stern demands of stewardship which entailment entails, begins in Chapter II under the guidance of his wife Fanny:

> Mrs. John Dashwood did not at all approve of what her husband intended to do for his sisters. To take three thousand pounds from the fortune of their dear little boy, would be impoverishing him to the most dreadful degree. She begged him to think again on the subject. How could he answer it to himself to rob his child, and his only child too, of so large a sum? And what possible claim could the Miss Dashwoods, who were related to him only by half blood, which she considered as no relationship at all, have on his generosity to so large an amount. It was very well known that no affection was ever supposed to exist between the children of any man by different marriages; and why was he to ruin himself, and their poor little Harry, by giving away all his money to his half sisters? (8)

Robbery, impoverishment, half-blood (the precise relationship, if my genetic understanding is good, of a father to his son). John protests, 'It was my father's last request to me', but steadily, in a sequence of enormous power, his intention is whittled to five hundred pounds apiece, then to a life annuity only for the mother of a hundred pounds a year, then to 'a present of fifty pounds now and then' (11), and finally to occasional 'presents of fish and game' (12). As Fanny verbally impoverishes her husband, herself and poor little Harry, she enriches Mrs Dashwood and her daughters:

> 'Do but consider, my dear Mr. Dashwood, how excessively comfortable your mother-in-law and her daughters may live on the interest of seven thousand pounds, besides the thousand pounds belonging to each of the girls, which brings them in fifty pounds a-year a-piece, and, of course, they will pay their mother for their board out of it. Altogether, they will have five hundred a-year amongst them, and what on earth can four women want for more than that?— They will live so cheap! Their housekeeping will be nothing at all. They will have no carriage, no horses, and hardly any servants; they will keep no company, and can have no expences of any kind! Only conceive how comfortable they will be! Five hundred a-year! I am sure I cannot imagine how they will spend half of it; and as to your giving them more, it is quite absurd to think of it. They will be much more able to give you something.'

Fanny ends in some resentment of the quality of the china and linen Mrs Dashwood will retain: '. . . the set of breakfast china is twice as handsome as what belongs to this house. A great deal too handsome, in my opinion, for any place *they* can ever afford to live. But, however, so it is. Your father thought only of *them*' (13).

A few observations: by the end of Chapter II Austen has broadened the term *will* from a simple legal document into a weapon of family and class warfare. Notice its thudding repetition as an auxiliary verb in Fanny's diatribe: 'they *will* have . . . they *will* pay . . . they *will* live so cheap . . . they *will* have no carriage . . . they *will* keep no company' (12). Wills become purely wilful, simple, arbitrary exercises of power. As Johnson observes (51–2), that surely is the point of Austen's not having placed Norland Park under a tradition of entail in the male line, consequently turning the principle of entailment itself into what Edmund Burke might call an 'innovation'. Further, the chapter is an exercise in perverse hermeneutics, as John and Fanny struggle to understand what John's father could possibly have meant: 'He did not know what he was talking of, I dare say: ten to one he was light-headed at the time. Had he been in his right senses, he could not have thought of such a thing as begging you to give away half your fortune from your own child' (9). 'I am convinced within myself that your father had no idea of your giving them any money at all' (12).

But aside from a thoroughgoing demonstration that John is not a generous son or brother, and that his wife is worse, what is the point of all this? Even Mary Poovey, who is nothing if not attentive to the cultural constructions of women's narratives, finds in the episode little more than a setting of John's and Fanny's actions against an 'implicit system' of 'undeniably Christian values' (*Proper Lady* 184). I would offer, in agreement with Johnson and Margaret Doody, that the values under examination are considerably more specific and local than such a formulation would suggest.

In an essay isolating the features of the Romantic novel, including the work of Austen, Joseph Kestner insisted some years ago that its 'great symbolic subject in both the matter and the method is the *entail*, a legal conception whose essence is restriction and limitation, and whose decisive element is the restriction of choice' ('Jane Austen' 305). He suggested how focus on the entail enabled such writers as Austen, Maria Edgeworth, Susan Ferrier, John Galt and Sir Walter Scott to explore their twinned themes of law and education, but he offered no historical explanation for the prevalence of the theme. Situated as we now are, both after pioneering feminist studies of Austen by such critics as Doody, Johnson, Poovey, Sandra M. Gilbert and Susan Gubar, Margaret Kirkham and Alison Sulloway, and after new historicist analyses of other writers and of the period generally, we may be able to fit out the foundations and sketch a structure for Kestner's observation.

As Austen assures us, wills, inheritance and inheritance laws have always been the subject of as much private discontent as joy. The emergence of inheritance as a central subject of public political discourse, however, is most easily traced to Edmund Burke's *Reflections on the Revolution in France* (1790), a work whose widespread influence is at last again being taken for granted. Burke's treatise sold 30,000 copies in its first few years and generated no fewer than seventy printed responses by 1793. One of these, Thomas Paine's *Rights of Man* (1791), was reprinted in massive numbers: its circulation has been estimated as having been up to 1.5 million copies (Chandler 17–18).

Burke's premise is familiar, and it has been used to bolster conservative interpretations of Austen's social thought from Avrom Fleishman's *A Reading of Mansfield Park* (1967) and Alistair M. Duckworth's *The Improvement of the Estate* (1971) through the studies of Marilyn Butler to the present. The government of England must be considered as a family. Englishmen 'claim and assert' their liberties 'as an *entailed inheritance* derived to us from our forefathers, and to be transmitted to our posterity' (45). According to Burke, 'the idea of inheritance furnishes a sure principle of conservation, and a sure principle of transmission; without at all excluding a principle of improvement. Whatever advantages are obtained by a state proceeding on these maxims, are locked fast as in a sort of family settlement; grasped as in a kind of mortmain for ever' (45). 'In this choice of inheritance', he continues,

> we have given to our frame of polity the image of a relation in blood, binding up the constitution of our country with our dearest domestic ties; adopting our fundamental laws into the bosom of our family affections; keeping inseparable, and cherishing with the warmth of all their combined and mutually reflected charities, our states, our hearths, our sepulchres, and our altars. (46)[1]

Burke places his security in the linear family: 'People will not look forward to posterity, who never look backward to their ancestors' (45). Indeed, the linear family serves as a check upon what we might call the lateral family, metaphorically the society living in a given generation, the shallow and selfish discontents of which can lead to dangerous acts of innovation.

Burke further claims that the principle of inheritance is the nursemaid of public as well as private morality:

> The power of perpetuating our property in our families is one of the most valuable and interesting circumstances belonging to it, and that which tends the most to the perpetuation of society itself. It makes our weakness subservient to our virtue; it grafts benevolence even upon avarice. The possessors of family wealth, and of the distinction which attends hereditary possession (as most concerned in it) are the natural securities for this transmission. (64)

As an experienced member of Parliament, Burke would have known that his argument was playing fast and loose with history. Between 1500 and 1660 current owners of estates had been relatively free to dispose of their properties as they chose (Stone 166), and eighteenth-century entailments were strengthened by relatively new laws and practices. In effect, the viability of strict settlements depended on their being broken and resettled every generation or two. Much of the business of the parliaments in which Burke sat consisted of considering private acts to change the terms of settlements: an average of twenty to thirty such acts per year were executed

---

1. Edmund Burke, *Reflections on the Revolution in France* (Garden City: Doubleday, 1973), p. 46. Subsequent citations from Burke will be noted parenthetically. Selections from Burke's *Reflections* are also reprinted in this volume [*Editor*].

throughout the eighteenth and the first half of the nineteenth centuries (English and Saville 80). But the point of Burke's hyperbolic identification of family virtue and civic virtue, with inheritance as its governing trope, is not lost on radical writers of the 1790s. Mary Wollstonecraft, in *A Vindication of the Rights of Woman* (1792), provides a brief sketch noted by Doody (xv) that foresees the situation of the Dashwood women. She imagines girls who are 'weakly educated'—for Wollstonecraft these would be girls not educated for independence—'cruelly left by their parents without any provision'. They become dependent, then, 'not only on the reason, but the bounty of their brothers. These brothers are, to view the fairest side of the question, good sort of men, and give as a favour what children of the same parents had an equal right to.' But when the brother marries, she goes on to observe, the following occurs:

> The wife, a cold-hearted, narrow-minded, woman, and this is not an unfair supposition, for the present mode of education does not tend to enlarge the heart any more than the understanding—is jealous of the little kindness which her husband shows to his relations; and her sensibility not rising to humanity, she is displeased at seeing the property of *her* children lavished on an helpless sister. (157)

Austen's language in describing John and Fanny Dashwood echoes Wollstonecraft's, though with an even harder ironic edge:

> He was not an ill-disposed young man, unless to be rather cold hearted, and rather selfish, is to be ill-disposed: but he was, in general, well respected; for he conducted himself with propriety in the discharge of his ordinary duties. Had he married a more amiable woman, he might have been made still more respectable than he was:—he might even have been made amiable himself; for he was very young when he married, and very fond of his wife. But Mrs. John Dashwood was a strong caricature of himself;—more narrow-minded and selfish. (5)

Austen softens the economic situation of the Dashwood women, who have an adequate if less than lavish provision, and she complicates the family situation by making them half-sisters. But she also exonerates the father, who is powerless to change the transmission of the estate, shifting the problem of equity squarely on to the shoulders of the inheriting son and his wife. Whereas Wollstonecraft sees a solution for such situations in improved education for women, which would both enable discarded sisters to become economically independent and enlarge the social vision of selfish and narrow-minded wives, Austen provides the materials for a structural critique of the system of inheritance. In this she is closer to Paine.

The Rights of Man argues that social justice in England is poi-
soned at its source, Burke's governing idea of family inheritance, as
Paine provides a scathing account of 'the law of *primogenitureship*'
(320). He says:

> The nature and character of aristocracy shows itself to us in
> this law. It is a law against every law of nature, and nature
> itself calls for its destruction. Establish family justice, and ar-
> istocracy falls. By the aristocratical law of primogenitureship,
> in a family of six children, five are exposed. Aristocracy has
> never more than *one* child. The rest are begotten to be de-
> voured. They are thrown to the cannibal for prey, and the nat-
> ural parent prepares the unnatural repast.
>
> With what kind of parental reflections can the father or
> mother contemplate their younger offspring? By nature they
> are children, and by marriage they are heirs; but by aristocracy
> they are bastards and orphans. They are flesh and blood of
> their parents in one line, and nothing akin to them in the other.
> To restore, then, parents to their children, and children to their
> parents—relations to each other, and man to society—and to
> exterminate the monster, aristocracy, root and branch, the
> French Constitution has destroyed the law of *Primogeniture-
> ship*. (320–1)

Paine further argues that

> there is an unusual unfitness in an aristocracy to be legislators
> for a nation. Their ideas of *distributive justice* are corrupted at
> the very source. They begin life by trampling on all their
> younger brothers and sisters, and relations of every kind, and
> are taught and educated to do so. With what ideas of justice
> or honor can that man enter a house of legislation, who ab-
> sorbs in his own person the inheritance of a whole family of
> children, or doles out to them some pitiful portion with the
> insolence of a gift? (321)

Like Burke, Paine would probably have known that his depiction
of the near-abandonment of younger children had little basis in the
facts of estate settlement; he is responding to Burke's fiction of
inter-generational continuity with a counter-fiction of intra-gener-
ational savagery.

Such are the broad political implications of the discourse of inheritance in the 1790s, a discourse widely enough understood to
have been assumed as a given by writers otherwise as far removed
from one another as William Wordsworth (in 'Michael') and Maria
Edgeworth (in *Castle Rackrent*), both published in 1800 (see Ruoff,
'1800' *passim*). Without attempting to demonstrate the indemon-
strable, we may safely assume Austen's awareness of it. Her rep-

resentation of inheritance in *Sense and Sensibility* more closely reflects its polemical role in the debate over political principles than any concrete observation of actual inheritance practices. A discourse that at both political extremes posits the wholesale convertibility of domestic and civic virtue places the emergence of the domestic novel in England in a rather different light than that in which it used to be routinely depicted. Arguably, family history has become political history.

If we set the first two chapters of *Sense of Sensibility* against appropriate passages from Burke and Paine, it is clear, again as Johnson (53) and Doody (xlii–xlv) observe, that they constitute a powerful critique of Burkean claims. Naked self-interest shines through Fanny's concerns for poor dear Harry and the future, even as she rhetorically effaces all concern for herself or the present. Her whining arguments about the tiresomeness of paying annuities to superannuated servants effectively puncture claims that the privileges of the gentry beget a spirit of benevolence, or even a willingness to meet contractual obligations that have been undertaken as a condition of inheritance. It is revealing that at one point John woundedly remarks of his father's request, 'Perhaps it would have been as well if he had left it wholly to myself. He could hardly suppose I should neglect them' (9)—as he then proceeds to do. It is as though John has internalised Burke's assertion of the natural, hereditarily-generated benevolence of his class, and is resentful of an effort to compel him to perform acts of generosity which should come unbidden, even when they will not. John's and Fanny's actions seem inevitably to confirm Paine's critique of hereditary principle: that it provides a schooling in self-interest which blinds its adherents to notions of distributive justice.

What remains to be determined is whether Austen's opening representation of abusive practices suggests a gentry which must clean up its act—reform itself in genuine alignment with Burkean principles—or a gentry which is so far past amendment as to call for other principles for establishing social justice. By definition, apologists display and account for abuses in systems which are under attack, and reformist and radical critiques often share points of affinity. For this reason novelists give us books, not just scenes. Whatever else, we find no relief in John and Fanny Dashwood, whose every reappearance provides evidence of thoughtless arrogance: fresh instances of lavish expenditures coupled with fresh protestations of impoverishment. Nor are they to be written off as upstarts, newer gentry with no understanding of tradition: the Dashwood family 'had long been settled in Sussex' and had been respectable 'for many generations' (3). John may reach his apex of venality, and simultaneously his strongest advocacy of Burkean principles of stewardship, in his reflections on his wife's brother, Edward Ferrars, another victim of parental will.

Edward, who allows himself to fall in love with Elinor despite his secret engagement to Lucy Steele, is an eldest son. His mother controls him by withholding his independence, as his current portion lies in her gift rather than having (like John Dashwood's) descended upon his coming of age. His family wishes to see him take a profession, but not for any potential service to society. Edward is described in this way:

> His understanding was good, and his education had given it solid improvement. But he was neither fitted by abilities nor disposition to answer the wishes of his mother and sister, who longed to see him distinguished—as—they hardly knew what. They wanted him to make a fine figure in the world in some manner or other. His mother wished to interest him in political concerns, to get him into parliament, or to see him connected with some of the great men of the day. Mrs. John Dashwood wished it likewise; but in the mean while, till one of these superior blessings could be attained, it would have quieted her ambition to see him driving a barouche. But Edward had no turn for great men or barouches. All his wishes centered in domestic comfort and the quiet of private life. Fortunately he had a younger brother who was more promising. (15–16)

Elinor is forced time and again to account for abrupt changes in Edward's mood and behaviour. In general she attributes his gloomy and withdrawn periods to the 'inevitable necessity of temporising with his mother. The old, well-established grievance of duty against will, parent against child, was the cause of all' (102). Austen splits radically the Burkean formula: instead of the will generating in the privileged property-holder a sense of duty, the will becomes an oppressive force which compels the duty of the subject child. Both Austen's presentation and Elinor's analysis of Edward's situation recall, if indirectly, the observations of Wollstonecraft:

> Parental affection is, perhaps, the blindest modification of self-love. . . . Parents often love their children in the most brutal manner, and sacrifice every relative duty to promote their advancement in the world. To promote, such is the perversity of unprincipled prejudices, the future welfare of the very beings whose present existence they imbitter by the most despotic stretch of power. (*Vindication* 150)

Mrs Dashwood echoes Elinor's internal language when she attempts to reassure Edward: 'Your mother will secure to you, in time, that independence you are so anxious for; it is her duty, and it will, it must ere long become her happiness to prevent your whole youth from being wasted in discontent' (103). Mrs Dashwood's words are darkly and ironically prophetic, because Edward's literal independence follows his figurative death.

When Edward's engagement to Lucy Steele becomes known, he is disinherited, 'dismissed for ever from his mother's notice' (268). When his 'more promising' younger brother Robert, given his economic independence in a fit of retributive pique by Mrs Ferrars, later marries the same objectionable young lady, he too is disowned and dismissed. Austen's description of Mrs Ferrars's situation is delicious:

> Her family of late had been exceedingly fluctuating. For many years of her life she had had two sons; but the crime and annihilation of Edward a few weeks ago, had robbed her of one. The similar annihilation of Robert had left her for a fortnight without any; and now, by the resuscitation of Edward, she had one again.
>
> In spite of his being allowed once more to live, however, he did not feel the continuance of his existence secure, till he had revealed his present engagement [to Elinor]; for the publication of that circumstance, he feared, might give a sudden turn to his constitution, and carry him off as rapidly as before. (373)

The linear family, secured by the firm principle of inheritance, seems a shaky cornerstone for the English nation, and Austen's ironic adaptation of Paine's rhetoric of family savagery has more than comic effects. Mrs Ferrars is given to capital punishment, in both its senses. To literalise Burke's term, her hold on her sons is a mortmain indeed.

PATRICIA MEYER SPACKS

The Novel's Wisdom: *Sense and Sensibility*†

* * *

Like all of Austen's novels, *Sense and Sensibility*, with its vivid narrative voice, makes its readers conscious of the obvious but often forgotten fact that causality in fiction is a narrative construction. One can say * * * that important things happen in *Sense and Sen-*

† From *Desire and Truth: Functions of Plot in Eighteenth-Century English Novels* (Chicago: U of Chicago P, 1990), pp. 214–18. Reprinted by permission of the publisher and the author. Footnotes have been omitted. Complete bibliographical information regarding the critics alluded to parenthetically is available in the Selected Bibliography at the end of this volume. Quotations of *Sense and Sensibility* are from the Chapman edition.

sibility because of male desire or impulse. Such narrative arrangements, however, also participate in the dialectic pattern through which Austen's narrator enforces distinctions that clarify the novel's moral universe. Important things happen in the novel in order to reveal the difference between false appearance and the reality it parodies.

The minor figure of Mr. Palmer illustrates characteristic complexities of causality. Elinor, possessed of considerable discriminatory power, finds herself initially at a loss to understand why he appears so oddly intent on being disagreeable. "Sir John is as stupid as the weather," he remarks of his father-in-law. "As vile a spot as I ever saw in my life," he observes of the estate at Allenham that Willoughby will inherit (111). When he scolds or abuses his wife, she is "highly diverted." " 'Mr. Palmer is so droll!' said she, in a whisper, to Elinor. 'He is always out of humour' " (112).

This marital relationship parodies the novel's typical situation in which women choose and act but men possess determinative power. Mrs. Palmer interprets her husband with utter disregard for what he says. If he sneers at the idea of inviting the Miss Dashwoods to his home, " 'There now"—said his lady, 'you see Mr. Palmer expects you; so you cannot refuse to come' " (113). She proceeds blithely on her foolish and good-humored course, in her comments transforming her husband's bad temper to good. On the other hand, he decides where they will go and when. Her resources, only verbal, make nothing happen.

But what *he* says also proves nugatory. His utterances typically bear only a devious relation to his intent. They may convey accurately his contempt for his wife's verbal folly, but they rarely mean what they say. Elinor quickly figures out Mr. Palmer's operations. "It was the desire of appearing superior to other people," she deduces, that governs his speech. Much later, she finds "him very capable of being a pleasant companion. . . . For the rest of his character and habits, they were marked, as far as Elinor could perceive, with no traits at all unusual in his sex and time of life" (304). This last generalization turns out to mean that the man is lazy, selfish, and conceited.

Mr. Palmer has little function in the novel's plot. His effort to make himself opaque, however, mirrors the conduct of those more fully responsible for the web of feeling and action that structures the narrative. Colonel Brandon conceals his relation to the two Elizas and his consequent duel with Willoughby; Willoughby conceals his financial calculations and, for a time, his engagement to another woman; Edward conceals his alliance with Lucy. Nor do the women—even apparently artless Marianne—prove more transparent to the novel's other characters. Marianne conceals the lack of formal commitment between her and Willoughby; Elinor conceals her putative lover's commitment elsewhere. Moreover, the major characters often remain opaque even to themselves. Marianne of course stays unaware of the selfishness masked by her claims of freedom and expressiveness, but even self-analyzing Elinor has moments of blindness: when, for instance, she explains Edward's ambiguous behavior as the product of his mother's cruelty or understands his ring set with hair as a covert acknowledgement of his love for her. Her judgment of Mr. Palmer as possessing the characteristic traits of his age and gender turns out to derive from her desire to assert Edward's superiority, although Edward, as far as she knows, will soon marry another woman. Desire always deceives, this novel suggests.

Given its pattern of intentional and unintentional deception, the novel's action necessarily concentrates on disentangling. Elinor and Marianne must make urgent discriminations (like Waverley's, in a sense *generic* discriminations): between true and false intimacy, language, love, interpretation. The false intimacy claimed by Lucy and her sister, by Lady Middleton's bland social behavior, by Mrs. John Dashwood's invitation to the Steele sisters, contrasts with the saving closeness between Elinor and Marianne. The inauthentic language of Lady Middleton, of the Misses Steele, of Marianne and Willoughby at their worst throws into sharp relief the genuineness of Willoughby's confession, of Elinor's revelation of suffering, of Colonel Brandon's concern for Marianne. Specious interpretations yield to accurate ones, false love gives place to true.

All of which makes *Sense and Sensibility* sound cheerily conventional. In fact, its cheer does not extend far. Although the firm control of the narrator's tone assures the reader that nothing will go permanently wrong in this fictional universe, the novel makes it apparent that only the freedoms of fictionality ensure happy outcomes. The concealments indulged in by virtually every character come to an end. Truth manifests itself, often through operations of self-interest, but it possesses no salvationary force. To know that Edward is engaged to someone else explains his actions and his psychic state to Elinor without providing any help for her own emotional dilemma. To hear that Colonel Brandon has fought a duel attests to his orthodox manliness ("Elinor sighed over the fancied necessity of this; but to a man and a soldier, she presumed not to censure it" [211]), but the knowledge helps no one. Discriminating between actuality and appearance is a praiseworthy activity. Elinor's capacity for fine discrimination marks her moral and intellectual excellence, but it makes no difference to her fate. More emphatically than any of Austen's other novels, *Sense and Sensibility* suggests life's essential unfairness.

That unfairness manifests itself particularly in the distribution of power. Not only do men, as we have seen, possess a kind of power unavailable to women. Women too, given sufficient unscrupulousness or moral blindness, can make others do their will. Edward Ferrars's mother, a bully by virtue of her money, provides one case in point, Lucy Steele another. Mary Poovey points out that "Willoughby's aunt, who is empowered by money and age, is even more tyrannical; and Sophia Grey, Willoughby's fiancée, enacts her passion and her will when she commands Willoughby to copy her cruel letter for Marianne" (189). By relentless manipulation in the service of her ends, Lucy Steele gets what she wants in life: a wealthy and foolish husband. "The whole of Lucy's behaviour in the affair," the narrator comments,

> and the prosperity which crowned it, . . . may be held forth as a most encouraging instance of what an earnest, an unceasing attention to self-interest, however its progress may be apparently obstructed, will do in securing every advantage of fortune, with no other sacrifice than that of time and conscience. (376)

Neither sacrifice matters to Lucy. The narrator's irony at her expense affirms the moral order assumed in the novel's tone, but it does not obviate the probability that dislocations of that order will occur as men and women seek and find power that can make life a misery for others.

Sense and Sensibility resembles *Waverley* in the relative helplessness of its protagonists. Lacking the concerted will to self-aggrandizement that motivates such as Lucy, the Dashwood sisters, like Edward Waverley, must depend on others to give their lives ultimate direction. Benign outcomes will develop, within the world of fiction, but the presence of such characters as Lucy and Donald Bean (in *Waverley*) reminds the reader of other possibilities implicit in the presence of powerful plotters. The plots of these fictions deprive figures enveloped in their own romantic dreams (Marianne and Waverley) of romantic outcomes. Scott grants romantic Fergus romantic fulfillment—but only in death. Scott presents a rather chaotic plot, Austen offers an ostentatiously neat one, in which, as Marilyn Butler points out, "the same things happen to two girls in each of two volumes" ("Disregarded Designs" 58). Scott's novel and Austen's, both written in their authors' youth, conform to long-established convention in resolving their characters' problems through marriage, but both also hint that marriage may not after all settle every difficulty. Neatness may prove illusory. Scott's cavalier plotting and Austen's partly ironic control make the same point.

To recur to familiar terms: marriage in these novels does not

altogether reconcile "masculine" and "feminine" principles. Both
novels give the "feminine" apparent preeminence. Austen depicts
an almost completely feminized world, Scott stresses Waverley's re-
pudiation of conflict and his desire for domesticity. But Scott also
reminds us insistently of "history," and he knows, if Waverley does
not, its danger: the unpredictable pressure of public facts on private
lives. Austen's novel invites the reader to contemplate ominous possibilities of what Edward may say to his wife a twelvemonth after
his marriage, ominous implications of Colonel Brandon's unques-
tioning assumption of authority over women. It may be true, as
Tony Tanner says, that Marianne "is married off to Brandon to
complete a pattern, to satisfy that instinct for harmonious arranging
which is part of the structure both of that society and of the book
itself" (*Jane Austen* 100). But the anomalies of male-female relations in *Sense and Sensibility* raise questions about the nature of
society's (and books') harmonious arrangements. Although a
wealthy woman like Mrs. Ferrars or Sophia Grey may exercise
power, female hegemony remains essentially impossible. "Feminine" consciousness typically find themselves power's victims. The
best that can be hoped for the possessors of such consciousness is
that they may not mind the role.

* * *

ISOBEL ARMSTRONG

Taste: Gourmets and Ascetics†

The female Dashwoods appear to occupy themselves with the traditional accomplishments of the women of the leisured classes.
They are pictured reading, drawing and making music. Elinor's
painted screens, of course, occasion the deliberate insults of Mrs
Ferrars at the Dashwood dinner. Marianne's passion for Cowper is
apparent from one of her earliest conversations, when she describes
Edward's dull and unexpressive reading of his poetry: 'I could hardly
keep my seat. To hear those beautiful lines which have frequently
almost driven me wild, pronounced with such impenetrable calmness, such dreadful indifference!' (Chapter 3, p. 51). There is a
distribution of aptitude which, we shall see, is significant. Elinor
paints and draws, and Marianne sings, plays and reads poetry. But
what must be stressed, and what is the most important aspect of

† From *Jane Austen: "Sense and Sensibility": Penguin Critical Studies* (Harmondsworth:
Penguin Books, 1994), pp. 41–50. Reprinted by permission of the author. Quotations
of *Sense and Sensibility* are from the Chapman edition.

their aesthetic occupations, is the intense seriousness with which these pursuits are regarded. This seriousness differentiates the Dashwood women as a family from everyone else in the novel; for them, the new bourgeois category of the aesthetic is of the utmost importance. It is a form of *knowledge*. Lady Middleton packed in her music the moment she married. Fanny has a new greenhouse built especially for her, but that is the end of her aesthetic interests. Charlotte Palmer and the Steeles have no intellectual interests. The Dashwood dinner betrays 'no poverty of any kind, except of conversation . . .' (Chapter 34, p. 239). 'Politics, inclosing land, and breaking horses', is all that the gentlemen supply, though this is preferable to the incessant talk about children.

In a typically muted aside, Jane Austen lets us know the grounds of Lady Middleton's dislike of the Dashwood girls. They do not flatter her or her children as the Steeles do. But, more important, they have 'too much sense to be desirable companions' (Chapter 36, p. 250). Again, Elinor and Marianne are *both* associated with sense here, just as they are both associated with sensibility at other times in the novel. What disqualifies them for Lady Middleton, it is made clear, is that they are intellectual women. In a blind and prejudiced way she thinks of them as bluestockings, intelligent and critical women, who 'because they were fond of reading, she fancied them satirical: perhaps without exactly knowing what it was to be satirical; but *that* did not signify. It was censure in common use, and easily given' (Chapter 36, p. 250).

Jane Austen is implicitly allying the Dashwood sisters with the famous eighteenth-century Blue Stocking Circle, an association which included women intellectuals who gathered together for conversation, and who made a very considerable impact on high society and intellectual life in the metropolis.[1] As intellectual women, the Dashwoods put Lady Middleton on the defensive. She is thoroughly suspicious of them. And they, in their turn, are only too aware of her limitations. It is clear that their confidence and belief in themselves stem from their commitment to aesthetic and intellectual pursuits and the capacity for detachment and critique which this allows. This seriousness gives dignity to their poverty. It makes Marianne arrogant on occasion. Their pursuits are not mere accomplishments but genuine intellectual and aesthetic projects; real work. (Think how Marianne vows to undertake a massive programme of music and reading when she returns to Barton Cottage after the Willoughby crisis.) 'What a happy day for booksellers, mu-

---

1. See, for an account of the Bluestocking Circle, Sylvia Harcstark Myers, *The Bluestocking Circle: Women, Friendship, and the Life of the Mind in Eighteenth-Century England*, Oxford, 1990. Also, for the Bluestockings' problematical relations to family, see Gary Kelly, *Women, Writing, and Revolution 1790–1827*, Oxford, 1993, 150–51.

sicsellers, and print-shops!', Edward says, when he imagines what the Dashwoods would do were they to come into unexpected fortunes (Chapter 17, p. 118). The Dashwood women—for Mrs. Dashwood is included in the education of the mind—are distinctive, and perhaps distinctive not simply in this text but among Jane Austen's women figures, in being deliberately presented as thinking, articulate, and intellectually aware. Aesthetic practices give them a sense of autonomy and identity. It is therefore not surprising that some of the crucial contemporary debates around aesthetics and taste should enter naturally into their conversation. Indeed, at times the text is dense with allusion to current discussions of the principles of art and conducts a highly self-conscious exploration of the nature of the aesthetic and aesthetic experience. Because they subscribe to the view (itself a political view) that 'taste' belongs to the moral and social virtues which transcend wealth and class, legitimizing their poverty and exclusion, the *politics* of the aesthetic are crucial for both girls. The extent to which the aesthetic confirms the social order or enables a critique of it is at issue in their debates.

There are three important discussions near the beginning of the novel. The first is an ongoing debate on taste between Marianne and Mrs Dashwood and Marianne and Elinor, covering the end of Chapter 3 and the beginning of Chapter 4. The second is a tripartite discussion with Edward, Elinor and Marianne on landscape (Chapter 16) and the third is effectively an extension of this discussion, continuing with a debate on the picturesque (Chapter 18). These discussions are all instigated, directly or indirectly, by Edward. But aesthetic judgements are implicity made in Willoughby's case also. The difference between them is considerable. It is the difference between an ethical and a psychological aesthetic, a social and an individualist understanding of taste. The qualities of sense and sensibility perhaps relate more appositely to these two male figures than to the sisters. Jane Austen is fascinated by an affective masculinity which is deeply attractive but socially ruthless. She continues an exploration of this aestheticized male consciousness into *Mansfield Park* (1814) with Henry Crawford. In just the same way as in *Sense and Sensibility*, civic and sexual issues are disclosed in the exploration of matters of art. In *Mansfield Park* these questions are explored through Humphry Repton's theories of landscape gardening. In *Sense and Sensibility* the intertextual reference is to different accounts of the picturesque, a relatively new and much disputed category of taste, in the work of William Gilpin, Uvedale Price and William Payne Knight. These are works which continued to preoccupy Jane Austen in *Pride and Prejudice* (1813). Thus *Sense and Sensibility* initiates an important exploration, which continues in the mature novels. Before we see how aesthetics are thematized in this novel, however, the environment in which the Dashwoods come to debate some of the central aesthetic texts of their culture needs to be further understood. To retire to a cottage in a rural environment was a familiar eighteenth-century literary convention. The trope of retirement would have been recognizable in the Dashwoods' move to Devon. 'Retirement' (1782) is the title of a poem by Marianne's favourite poet, Cowper. Columella, the central figure in Richard Graves's satirical novel of the same name, which is mentioned by Mrs Dashwood in conversation with Edward, is in part an enquiry into the virtues of rural retirement.[2] Henry Mackenzie's novel, *The Man of Feeling* (1771), another text which is a presence in Jane Austen's novel, as we shall see, contains episodes which move from the rural tranquility and decent poverty of the country scene to London and back. But there are substantial and important variations on these tropes. For one thing, the Dashwood poverty is involuntary. There is no element of choice about their move. For another, they take up the convention of retirement, which is a male choice and prerogative, as a community of *women*. The change of gender radically alters this literary convention in two ways. The women are disempowered by poverty rather than enabled by it. But on the other hand, they enter the masculine preserve of thought and meditation in retirement and occupy its ground as women forced to be autonomous figures. Elinor is sharply aware of their subordination and of the way lack of money constricts their lives. She counters Marianne's romantic disdain and lack of realism about money—'money can only give happiness where there is nothing else to give it'—with hard materialist argument: 'Your competence and *my* wealth are very much alike' (Chapter 17, p. 117). Yet the small, contracted, vulnerable group of Dashwood women do have independence of a kind. It enables Marianne to challenge Sir John's cheerful assumption that every girl is looking for a 'conquest', for instance. How little this unconventional independence is understood is disclosed in the supremely uncomprehending reply.

> Sir John did not much understand this reproof; but he laughed as heartily as if he did, and then replied,
> 'Aye, you will make conquests enough, I dare say.' (Chapter 9, p. 77)

To live at Barton Cottage is to see experience from the perspective of the less privileged vision. For the cottage is a trope within the

---

2. *Columella, or the Distressed Anchoret* (1776), 2 vols, London, 1779, II, 66. Richard Graves also satirizes a number of contemporary affectations including picturesque landscape. The toothpick case ordered by Robert Ferrars might derive from Grave's attack on affluence (II, 245).

trope of retirement, and Jane Austen's almost stylized allusion to it testifies to the self-consciousness and originality with which she makes literary devices work for her. For the cottage, normally a *part* of the picturesque landscape the viewer in search of aesthetic scenes would comprehend in his (and it is usually his) gaze, is the place where the Dashwoods see experience, including landscape, *from*. This literally gives them a different perspective on the landscape and aesthetic of the picturesque.

Everybody else looks *at* the cottage, not *from* it. Mrs Palmer exclaims at its prettiness; Willoughby, in an extravagant moment of sentimentality which earns some costive responses from Elinor, says that he would pull down Combe Magna if he could and rebuild a replica of Barton Cottage there, a kind of reverse 'improvement'; Robert Ferrars describes the fashionable cottage of the aristocrat playing at rural solitude. He is oblivious of the functional nature of a cottage to the poor agricultural day labourer of the times, and his advice to Lord Courtland reflects only an acquisitive pleasure in luxury and consumption: 'I advise everybody who is going to build, to build a cottage' (Chapter 36, p. 255). Jane Austen satirizes the sentimentalizing tendency among aristocrats (the Marie Antoinette factor) and even of the Dashwood family itself: as a house, she writes, their dwelling was perfectly satisfactory. As a cottage, 'it was defective, for the building was regular, the roof was tiled, the window shutters were not painted green, nor were the walls covered with honeysuckles' (Chapter 6, p. 61). In other words, this is not the idyllic English thatched cottage which, with its labouring occupants, was the subject of literary discussion and debate, mystified and demystified, from Goldsmith and Crabbe right through to the Romantic poets, either praised for its signs of agrarian contentment and simple virtue among the labouring classes or vilified as a wretched hovel, occupied by the exploited and degenerate poor.[3] Southey, Jane Austen's contemporary, nostalgically celebrated the thatched cottage a few years after the publication of *Sense and Sensibility*. The 'rose bushes beside the door' indicated an 'innocent and healthful employment', he wrote, a description which was sharply questioned by Macauley, who saw the conservative vision of an England of 'Rosebushes and poor rates' as evidence of a blind and retrograde politics.[4]

---

3. Goldsmith's *The Deserted Village* (1770) idealizes rural life and laments the depopulation of the rural village. Crabbe's *The Village* (1783) is an anti-pastoral poem attacking the idyll of country life and work described by Goldsmith. For the representation of the rural in England see *The English Rural Community: Image and Analysis*, Brian Short, ed., Cambridge, 1992.
4. Robert Southey, *Sir Thomas More: or Colloquies*, 2 vols, London, 1829, I, 174. Thomas Macaulay replied in a review of 1830, reprinted in *Works of Thomas Macaulay*, London, 1897, V, 342.

The glancing satirical remark about the cottage 'defective' in honeysuckle shows Jane Austen to be well aware of the simmering beginnings of the cottage controversy and its ideological issues as well as of the false sentiment of bourgeois-aristocratic 'retirement' conventions. While the rich built cottages the dwellings of the poor decayed in direct consequence of the French wars, as is suggested by Wordworth's 'The Ruined Cottage' (begun in 1797 and included in *The Excursion* [1814]). Margaret, another husbandless woman, lapses into despair and indifference when her husband disappears after enlisting for the French wars. The decaying cottage signifies her psychological disintegration and the decay of the social fabric: unpruned, 'The honeysuckle, crowding round the porch' (1, 715), is the first sinister sign of trouble to the visitor.[5] Jane Austen could not have known Wordsworth's poem, yet she was sharply aware of the bad faith engendered by false sentimentality about cottages and those forced to live in them. The privilege of a tiled roof is not to be taken lightly and bad fortune is always relative.

There are other intertextual hints which satirize the convention of rural idyll in poverty. 'To what purpose do we cultivate an exquisite taste and delicacy of sentiment, that only serves to make us miserable?', asks Hortensius, one of the characters in Richard Graves's *Columella*, in a discussion of the actual boredom of 'the pleasures of retirement, and a rural life'. Columella, whose nickname betokens classical pastoral, instances the gentleman who retires, but whose 'whole happiness' is in 'visiting and cards', or looking out for people travelling along the public road, almost as if anticipating Sir John's restlessness and Mrs Jennings's curiosity. *Columella* too debates the question of what constitutes a '*competence*' in retirement. In an area of upper-class luxury and the increasing tendency of the landed elite to see property as investment this is an important question because, as Elinor also sees, the idea of the competence has been relativized: of this new, aggressive seeking out of profit, a character in Graves's novel remarks, 'It shocks me to observe, how small a part of mankind are able to set bounds to their avaricious desires'.[6] Retirement cannot escape from the money society.

What kind of socially sustaining experience can be gained from the life of retirement and aesthetic contemplation? Do their values betray a truly civic or civil life, marking a turn from a public understanding of civil society to the politics of privacy? What are the responsibilities of sensibility? To see how Jane Austen takes up

---

5. *The Poetical Works of Wordsworth* (1904, Oxford Standard Authors), Ernest De Selincourt, ed., rev. edn, London, New York and Toronto, 1950, 599.
6. *Columella*, II, 77; 229.

these questions it is necessary to look more closely at the ethics and economics of landscape appreciation in the novel, and to the dialogue between Elinor and Marianne about it.

The location of the new dwelling is very carefully described. Since it is rare to find Jane Austen describing scenery, it is worth pausing on her description. The West Country landscape of Barton Valley 'was a pleasant fertile spot, well wooded, and rich in pasture. After winding along it for more than a mile, they reached their own house' (Chapter 6, p. 61). The 'situation' of the house, which was 'good', is further described.

> High hills rose immediately behind, and at no great distance on each side; some of which were open downs, the others cultivated and woody. The village of Barton was chiefly on one of these hills, and formed a pleasant view from the cottage windows. The prospect in front was more extensive; it commanded the whole of the valley, and reached into the country beyond. The hills which surrounded the cottage terminated the valley in that direction; under another name, and in another course, it branched out again between two of the steepest of them. (Chapter 6, pp. 61–2)

With delicate topographical precision the landscape comes into being. It is a mixed agrarian landscape of timber, pasture (for cattle and sheep) and crops (signified by the designation 'cultivated'). It is enclosed by hills and subordinated to the village (as also to the country seat, Barton Park), which is above it, at the back. Yet it opens out on to an expansive prospect at the front. In its valleys and wooded hills, declivities and rising ground, it is subtly expressive of feminine symbols. At the same time it is scrupulously attentive to the social. The 'views' from the cottage are split. Behind it is the village, in front of it is the expansive natural landscape stretching far into the distance. One view looks to community and hierarchy, the other celebrates the privacy of the individual eye which 'commanded' a view of the whole valley. There is a hint of a will to power and control over space and territory as the gaze attempts to encompass an expansive scene. Marianne experiences a similar split vision, though one of a far more schizophrenic kind, when she describes the illicit visit to Allenham made with Willoughby on the event of the cancelled excursion occasioned by Colonel Brandon's sudden departure. She speaks of one 'remarkably pretty sitting room' (Chapter 13, p. 98):

> It is a corner room, and has windows on two sides. On one side you look across the bowling-green, behind the house, to a beautiful hanging wood, and on the other you have a view of

the church and village, and, beyond them, of those fine bold hills we have so often admired. (p. 98)

The pleasure ground and the hanging wood on one side, bespeaking the private pleasures of the rich, the church and the village on the other, bespeaking the symbols of community and religious authority, disclose a more extreme division than that expressed by the topography of the cottage, but it is structurally the same. Marianne implies an ownership of village, church *and* the expansive prospect, as she considers the view from the Allenham window. The topographical ordering round the cottage is less aggrandizing, and in this sense more realistic. It does not presuppose that the Dashwoods are in control of their environment.

Through these exquisitely scrupulous visual details the text seeks to explore the ethical and political significance of the aesthetics of retirement. The Dashwoods have not chosen the split vision induced by the situation of the cottage ground, but they can choose to intensify the split between the social and the individual, as Marianne's experience suggests, or they can choose to mitigate it, as Elinor's experience will show. But neither choice is simple. And, to use a term overdetermined in the novel, the 'connection' between the social and individual, public and private, seems to have been lost.

The complexity of the Dashwood choices is mediated through allusion to a popular writer on the picturesque landscape, William Gilpin. At first it even seems as if Jane Austen's description is mimicking the language of his many tours through England in the late-eighteenth century. Gilpin's *Observations on the Western Parts of England* (1798) includes a critical account of a view near Exeter, a view which Jane Austen's prose seems almost labouring to correct, making ideal what Gilpin had seen as deficient.

> From Exeter to Honiton we passed through a rich country, yet somewhat flatter than we met with on the western side of Exeter. We found, however, here and there, an eminence, which gave us a view of the distances around. At Fair-Mile-hill, particularly, a very *extensive* view opened before us; but nothing can make it pleasing, as it is *bounded* by a *hard edge*. A distance should either melt into the sky, or terminate in a soft and varied mountain line.[7]

The landscape of the novel indeed 'terminated' in a line of hills, as the valley branches under another name.

This artful correction draws attention to the strangeness of Gilpin's position. For while he insists that the beauty and variety of

---

7. William Gilpin, *Observations on the Western Parts of England*, London, 1798, 255.

the natural scene can never be rivalled by art, his criteria for the 'good', picturesque landscape are precisely those kinds of beauty 'which *would look well in a picture*'.[8] In making the landscape into that which looks well in a novel Jane Austen is reminding us that experience, far from being unmediated as Gilpin suggests, is perpetually reconstructed by the perceiver. Gilpin is perfectly happy to think of the artist as adding to or subtracting from a scene to give it more 'consequence', as he put it in his *Observations on the River Wye* (1770).[9] But for him the artist and viewer are exactly alike in their ability to select and order experience at will, seeking out what is pleasurable to the eye. Mediation is unimportant to Gilpin because his stress is on aesthetic *experience*, which can be gained either directly or through pictures. Pictorial elements might provide the criteria for pleasurable order but the status of both experiences is the same even if the actual, first-hand experience of landscape is preferable to art. To gain *actual* picturesque experience Gilpin will seek out the 'eminence' or vantage point which will best enable him to control and organize the visual elements he requires. The power of the eye—'command'—as Jane Austen knowingly puts it, is all-important. Gilpin complains of overbuilding in Devon, for instance, and selects out human habitation from the prospect. The selective eye censors as it views. So that near Taunton, the view from 'high grounds is very grand'. He thinks of the prospect as direct, unmediated experience, but it is not:

> composed on one side of Barnstaple-bay, and on the other of an extensive vale; the vale of Taunton carrying the eye far and wide into its rich and ample bosom. It is one of those views which is too great a subject for painting. (*Observations on the Western Parts of England*, 175)

Viewing the picturesque is actually about power. John Barrell has argued that the controlling eye betokens ownership of the wide expanse of enclosed land.[1] The view or prospect is seen from a fixed position and the eye sweeps immediately from horizon to foreground and back. This is a way of controlling nature and subjecting it to civilized order. Nature, for the Whig and mercantile elements of eighteenth-century society in particular, was there to be conquered and to yield up riches. One can add to this that in Gilpin's description the eye becomes sexualized as it is carried into the

8. Gilpin, *Observations on the Western Parts of England*, 328.
9. Gilpin, *Observations on the River Wye*, London, 1770, 14.
1. John Barrell, *The Idea of Landscape and the Sense of Place 1730–1840: An Approach to the Poetry of John Clare*, London, 1972. Barrell argues throughout that the picturesque is the aesthetic of ownership, where the eye is at 'ease in landscape which had been enclosed' (32), that is, in landscape which betokens uninterrupted ownership of the land viewed.

bosom of the vale. Strikingly, however, it is impossible for the Dashwood women to establish this perspective. Divided though their vision might be between community and privacy, the appropriating,
individualistic gaze is not available to them in the form Gilpin prefers. The 'prospect' is not seen from an 'eminence' or from 'high
grounds', and it is not 'extensive', only 'more extensive' than the view
behind. The 'prospect' is actually seen from below, seen from a
restricted perspective, not from the wide expanse of enclosed land
indicative of unimpeded possession. And it is the prospect, the syntax allows, not the eye, which commands space. Landscape is independent of the self. In fact Jane Austen's passage challenges
Gilpin's picturesque perspective and its values of control and command. If the women take over the masculine prerogative of retirement and aesthetic speculation, they do so, if not to create a
feminized picturesque, at least from another position altogether, a
position which relinquishes the assumption of control. It is also a
position which recognizes selection and mediation as inevitable.
Thus it recognizes that the response to landscape is ideological.

It appears to be easier for Elinor to recognize the Barton perspective than for Marianne. It is not simply that she is aware of
social obligations and dependencies in a way that Marianne refuses.
Marianne struggles to regain the lost high ground, though rather
to transcend her powerlessness than to regain power. She is described as possessing 'a life, a spirit, an eagerness, which could
hardly be seen without delight' (Chapter 10, p. 78), and it is this
energy which impels her, for instance, to challenge a rainy day and
to seek the fresh air on the high downs surrounding the cottage on
the day of the fatal fall down the hill. The iconography of this episode is crucial to Jane Austen's critique of picturesque experience.
Marianne's favourite Cowper speaks of the customary move to high
ground:

> Now roves the eye;
> And, posted on this speculative height,
> Exults in its command.
> (*The Task*, Book I, 'The Sofa', 288–90)[2]

In like fashion, the girls ascend the hill 'rejoicing' (Chapter 9, p.
74), but Marianne never reaches the 'command' of the summit.
Warning against impetuosity, Cowper writes, 'Descending now (but
cautious, lest too fast) / A sudden steep . . . We mount again' (I,
266–7, 271). The text fails to accept Cowper's admonition and
stages the fall he warns against. This fall from the overview, from

---

2. *The Poetical Works of William Cowper* (1905, Oxford Standard Authors), H. S. Milford,
   ed., 4th ed., London, New York and Toronto, 1934, 135.

control and power, can also be staged as a moral and sexual fall, for after all, Marianne falls into Willoughby's arms. But its significance is wider. Marianne is quite literally precipitate, 'too fast' in many senses, perhaps. Her fall dislodges her not only from a 'command' of experience but also from a fixed position. Unlike the self-stabilizing and self-protective Cowper, her volatile energy disrupts the order of the picturesque even while she feels that it is with the picturesque that she belongs emotionally. The novel mounts a double critique. The omniscient, possessive, exploitative power of the overview is unacceptable to it. At the same time, the uncentred emotions of the perspective from below lead to incoherence, fragmentation. Fragmentation is constantly Marianne's problem, created by the very spirit of life which makes her so attractive.

* * *

MARY FAVRET

Sense and Sensibility: The Letter, Post Factum†

Having wrestled with epistolary form in *Lady Susan* and in the subsequent, lost novels, *Elinor and Marianne* (1796) and *First Impressions* (1797), Austen spent over a decade—until 1810—waiting, revising and strengthening her skills.[1] With the publication of *Sense and Sensibility* in 1811, she announced her victory over the constraints of the letter. *Sense and Sensibility* initiates a trend in Austen's writing to establish a "new privacy" in the novel.[2] With the character of Elinor Dashwood Austen creates an interiority which remains intact and independent through the mediation of a narrative *style indirect libre*.[3] Elinor is an anti-epistolary heroine: the inner world of her thoughts and feelings finds no direct expression in the novel, although her point of view controls the story. She is bound both by a promise of secrecy and a sense of integrity and

---

† From *Romantic Correspondence: Women, Politics, and the Fiction of Letters* (Cambridge: Cambridge UP, 1993), pp. 145–54. Reprinted by permission of the publisher. Quotations of *Sense and Sensibility* are from the Chapman edition.

1. B. C. Southam, *Jane Austen's Literary Manuscripts* (London: Oxford UP, 1964), pp. 52–62.
2. Susan Pepper Robbins, "The Included Letter in Jane Austen's Fiction," unpublished Ph.D. thesis, University of Virginia, 1976, p. 30, writes that in *Sense and Sensibility*, "the letter [serves] as a model of shattered relationships and the new privacy that results."
3. Dorrit Cohn, in *Transparent Minds: Narrative Modes for Presenting Consciousness in Fiction* (Princeton: Princeton UP, 1978), locates Austen as "one of the first" to use *style indirect libre*, or what he calls "the narrated [interior] monologue," "frequently and extensively" in fiction (p. 113). For a brief account of the differences between epistolary style and Austen's use of *style indirect libre*, see David Lodge, "Jane Austen's Novels: Form and Structure," in J. David Grey, ed., *Jane Austen Companion* (New York: Macmillan, 1986), pp. 175–7.

self-protection. Marianne Dashwood, by contrast, insists on making explicit her innermost thoughts; she "demands that outward forms exactly project or portray inner feelings."[4] But Marianne's *style direct*, epitomized by her letters to Willoughby, exposes her to the harsh judgment of "the World." Throughout the novel, Austen manipulates the device of the letter, setting it against Elinor's interiority and using it to emphasize Marianne's vulnerability.

In *Sense and Sensibility*, the novelist deliberately maneuvers against the very structure which fascinated and challenged her in *Lady Susan*. Here the letter's effectiveness as a story-telling vehicle is exposed as impotent and unnatural; the letter becomes a relic of a romance that never was. Although *Sense and Sensibility* rewrites the epistolary *Elinor and Marianne*, it retains enough letters (twenty-one) to make the author's point: the letter no longer represents or expresses (safely) the interior freedom which her heroines seek. It threatens to kill the sentimental heroine more by its impersonality than by its emotive force. Austen wants to recontextualize the letter and place it under the light of a new realism, a realism coincident with an expanding sense of "society" and "the World." In such a society, the lesson which Marianne must learn and the novel must enact, is that a letter's content is nothing, its appearance is all.

If we look carefully at one specific scene, we can begin to understand how and why Austen de-activates the content of letters in this novel. In the central portion of *Sense and Sensibility*, Austen connects the dangerous power of the letter to Marianne's romance with Willoughby: both prove false. Before we may examine the lovers' abortive correspondence, however, the narrator gives us instruction on how to read. Halfway through the novel, upon their arrival in London, we watch the two sisters sit down to write—letters, of course:

> Elinor determined to employ the interval [before dinner] in writing to her mother, and sat down for that purpose. In a few moments, Marianne did the same. "I am writing home, Marianne," said Elinor; "had not you better defer your letter a day or two?"
>
> "I am *not* going to write my mother," replied Marianne hastily, as if wishing to avoid any further inquiry. Elinor said no more; it immediately struck her that she must then be writing to Willoughby, and the conclusion which instantly followed was, that however mysteriously they might wish to conduct the affair, they must be engaged. This conviction, though not entirely satisfactory, gave her pleasure, and she continued her

4. Tony Tanner, *Jane Austen* (Cambridge: Harvard UP, 1986), p. 84.

letter with greater alacrity. Marianne's was finished in a very few minutes; in length it could be no more than a note: it was then folded up, sealed and directed with great rapidity. Elinor thought she could distinguish a large W. in the direction, and no sooner was it complete than Marianne, ringing the bell, requested the footman to get that letter conveyed for her to the two-penny post. This decided the matter at once.[5]

Of course, the simple opposition between the dutiful letter of the "sensible" sister and the vaguely illicit letter of the "sensitive" sister is clear. But more complex narrative oppositions cloud the picture. In this passage, we participate in the workings of Elinor's mind, we follow her eyes as they survey her sister. By contrast, we "see" Marianne's letter, but her thoughts remain inaccessible. We and Elinor are left to speculate. In fact, this scene initiates Marianne's turn from open-hearted honesty to a covert behavior which, if not deceptive, hints of dissimulation. Only a page before, Elinor had "read" her sister like an open book: she saw "the rapture of a delightful expectation which filled the whole soul and beamed in the eyes of Marianne" (S&S, p. 159). This letter, however, marks a break between the interior and exterior; it separates Marianne's "soul" from Elinor's "eyes." With no recourse to her sister's thoughts, Elinor must draw her conclusions from the letter itself: imagining the missive's affective content, Elinor is misled into assuming a secret engagement. Yet her close attention to the physical details of the note almost eclipses any interest in the writer herself. And the sensible sister's thought turns to a social arrangement (engagement), rather than to any unlicensed feeling. If Marianne's inner state is now unavailable, it becomes immaterial: the letter alone speaks. Marianne's letter concretizes the tradition of epistolary fiction for Jane Austen. This letter gathers all the lawlessness of "Love and Friendship" into a single piece of paper, marked with a tell-tale "W," and places it under a scrutinizing eye.

Austen emphasizes the quiddity of the letter here, stressing its everyday, practical existence: if I write home now, shouldn't you wait? In epistolary fiction, such concerns rarely emerge; yet here we see a letter written, sealed and sent off to the London two-penny post. This concentration on the pragmatics of letter-writing remains a constant in all of Austen's fiction, and signals an obstacle to the "inner life" of her characters. On the farcical side, the heroine of "Amelia Webster" consistently points out that her "paper" limits her discourse: "I have a thousand things to tell you, but my paper will only permit me to add that I am your affectionate friend"; and "I have many things to inform you of besides, but my paper reminds

---

5. *Sense and Sensibility*, in *Works*, vol. I, pp. 160–1. Hereafter cited as S&S.

me of concluding."[6] Such insistent materialism deflates the mystique of correspondence.

As in Austen's own correspondence, the surface of the fictionalized letters in her early novels is significant, and significantly opaque. In *Pride and Prejudice*, for example, we witness a debate over the letter-writing skills of Messrs. Darcy and Bingley, which is actually a discussion of orthography. This debate opens the door to Elizabeth's remarks about "reading character"—remarks which point out the prejudice of superficial "first impressions."[7] This sharp focus on the scripted word also appears in *Mansfield Park*. Fanny lingers over a scribbled fragment of a note from Edmund, its negligible contents outweighed by the mere fact of its appearance:

> Never were such characters cut by any other human being, as Edmund's commonest handwriting gave! This specimen, written in haste, had not a fault, and there was a felicity in the first four words, in the arrangement of "My dear Fanny," which she could have looked at forever. (*MP*, p. 265)

Austen tells us that Fanny reads more into the form and the handwriting of a note than we, her readers, ever could; and not surprisingly, since for us all letters in the novel are selectively represented and have uniform print and format. A barrier exists: we cannot even "see" the telling script without the narrator's help.

The markings, shown to us indirectly, hardly reveal any truth or provide any real connection. If anything, these markings close off direct correspondence with and within the text. Elinor, like us, remains in the dark about her sister's liaison. (So does Marianne, but we only learn this later.) Not for Austen alone, but for her contemporaries as well, affective communication through letters gives way to a sort of hieroglyphic art, the meaning and dynamic of which is lost without a skilled translator. A similar instance of epistolary hieroglyphics occurs in Walter Scott's *The Heart of Midlothian* (1820), when Jeanie Deans refuses to write a letter for precisely these reasons:

> We must try by all means . . . but writing winna do it. A letter canna look and pray and beg and beseech, as the human voice can do to the human heart. A letter's like the music that the ladies have for their spinets—naething but black scores.[8]

6. "Amelia Webster," in *Works*, vol. VI, p. 48.
7. *Pride and Prejudice*, vol. II, in *Works*, pp. 47–50. Hereafter cited as *P&P*. Other notable examples of the "look" of letters include Frank Churchill's "handsome" correspondence in *Emma*, and Lucy Steele's note, which Mrs Jennings proclaims "as pretty a letter as I ever saw, and does Lucy's head and heart great credit" (*S&S*, p. 277).
8. Walter Scott, *The Heart of Midlothian* (London: J. M. Dent & Sons, Ltd., 1978), pp. 290–1.

The letter, which once offered a flexible, "natural" or "realistic" frame for human experience, has been reduced to a stubborn, solid object. The who, what, when, where and why of correspondence only go as far as the surface—if that far.

As a physical artifact, Austen's version of the letter serves as a misleading guide to the human heart which, in the best instances, is always changing and adapting. This view clearly separates her from her admired predecessor, Samuel Richardson, and from his letter-master, Lovelace. Correspondence, Lovelace maintains (disingenuously), "[is] writing from the heart . . . not the heart only; the *soul* [is] in it. Nothing of the body . . . when friend writes to friend."[9] For the earlier novelist, the letter was not yet solidified: like the characters it represented, it was still in process, changeable and adaptive. Epistolary writing, writing "to the moment," according to Richardson, provides "the minutiae" wherein "lie often the unfoldings of a Story, as well as of the heart . . . an action undecided."[1] The example of Marianne's letter, among others, places Austen more in agreement with recent critics of epistolary form. John Preston, for example, claims that "the medium (the written word and the narrative letter) is its own story: it is opaque, it attests to nothing but itself . . . What happens to the words on the page . . . [to] letters rather than people."[2] When applied to Richardson's work, Preston's opinion of the letter is possibly anachronistic; perhaps the medium was not as opaque to eighteenth-century readers as we might assume. Indeed, the careful markings and pointing fingers in *Clarissa's* letters, especially the typographical disorder of Clarissa's "mad" letters, transposed by Lovelace, suggest that Richardson's readers demanded such "markings" and read through what Jeanie Deans would call "black scores." Such historical changes in the way readers perceive and interpret the written word are to be expected, as the work of Svetlana Alpers and Robert Darnton indicates.[3]

9. Samuel Richardson, *Clarissa*, ed. John Butt, 4 vols. (New York: E. P. Dutton, 1962), vol. IV, p. 431.

1. Samuel Richardson, *Selected Letters*, ed. John Carroll (Oxford: Clarendon Press, 1964), p. 289.

2. John Preston, *The Created Self: The Reader's Role in Eighteenth Century Fiction* (New York: Barnes and Noble, Inc., 1970), pp. 63, 66. Preston suggests that epistolary writing, by its very nature, represents an "estrangement and alienation." The "tragedy" of its form, depicted in Richardson's *Clarissa*, lies in the fact that it "affirms the reality of what it must exclude," i.e. "the whole experience of love"—or union (pp. 80–1, 86). For further discussion of the letter as artifact in *Clarissa*, see Terry Castle, *Clarissa's Ciphers* (Ithaca: Cornell UP, 1982), pp. 119–23; and Robert Paulson, *Emblem and Expression* (Cambridge: Harvard UP, 1975), p. 51.

3. See Robert Darnton, "Readers Respond to Rousseau," in *The Great Cat Massacre and Other Episodes in French Cultural History* (New York: Vintage Books, 1985), pp. 215–55; and "Five Steps Toward a History of Reading," in *The Kiss of Lamourette: Reflections on Cultural History* (New York: W. W. Norton, Inc. 1990), pp. 154–87; and Svetlana Alpers, *The Art of Describing: Dutch Art in the Seventeenth Century* (Chicago: University of Chicago Press, 1984), pp. 192–207.

Twentieth-century critics and readers are likely to evaluate epistolary "opacity" in the light of later narrative developments—those of
Jane Austen, for example.

The movement from the "personality" of the familiar letter toward
an impersonal, constrained letter is already apparent in the letters
of Helen Maria Williams. * * * In her early novels, Austen elabo-
rates this transformation, objectifying the letter as an emblem of
empty convention, the "letter of the law" cited by Frederica in *Lady
Susan. Sense, and Sensibility, Pride and Prejudice,* and *Northanger
Abbey* all testify to—and escape from—the formal limitations and
dictations of the letter. Even Darcy's epistle, which disrupts both
Elizabeth's pride and her prejudice, is less a confession (it offers
little insight into the "personality" Elizabeth will learn to love) than
a legal defense.[4] The changing character of the letter, from Richardson to Austen, seems less a matter of aesthetic distancing (Austen's rejection of an obsolete form) than a reaction to actual
changes in the ways and means of letter-writing.

The ability of a letter to "unfold" a story was, therefore, nearly
defunct. Instead, the letter in fiction had the capacity to bolster
social institutions and duties—as we see when Elinor sends a
prompt note home to her mother. The effort is almost *pro forma*:
as Mrs. Dashwood's reply indicates, she barely attends to the content of her daughter's missives. Elsewhere, Elinor finds it necessary
to exchange letters with her officious brother. She takes the occasion to ask him for information about Edward, but her brother responds that he can "make no inquiries on so prohibited a subject"
(S&S, p. 353). As an avenue to the personal realm, correspondence
fails. Once again, Elinor must gather intelligence from sources outside the letter.

The letter's tendency to defend propriety against the claims of
feeling leads Elinor (and later, Colonel Brandon) to presume Marianne and Willoughby officially engaged. Lucy Steele exploits this
same connection when she boldly displays to her rival Edward's
letters to herself.

> Elinor saw that it *was* his hand, and she could doubt [an en-
> gagement between Lucy and Edward] no longer . . . a corre-
> spondence between them by letter could subsist only under a
> positive engagement, could be authorized by nothing else; for
> a few moments, she was almost overcome—her heart sank
> within her. (S&S, pp. 134–5).

---

4. Darcy's letter begins by explaining that the reputation of his "character required it to be
written and read." Elizabeth "must, therefore, pardon the freedom with which I demand
your attention; your feelings, I know, will bestow it unwillingly, but I demand it of your
justice." The letter proceeds to refute "two offences" which Elizabeth had "laid to the
charge" of Mr. Darcy (P&P, p. 196).

In both cases, the appearance of letters "authorizes" the fiction of a social engagement which later proves null and void. Lucy's letters, like Marianne's, point to nothing substantial. Their only power lies in representing vacant social obligations at the expense of human feeling. They are a travesty of epistolary romance.

The final travesty arrives, of course, with Willoughby's letter. It is written in his hand, but dictated with horrifying composure by his fiancée. Personal feeling surrenders to social formulae: as Marianne perceives, that letter is written "by all the World, rather than by his own heart" (S&S, p. 189). The letter ultimately speaks its own betrayal. The only letter in *Sense and Sensibility* whose "substance" makes "amends for the defect of its style," is Lucy Steele's, announcing her marriage to Robert Ferrars: poetic justice weds vanity to vanity, and seals the match with letters.

In general, *Sense and Sensibility* uses the letter to clarify not only the break between inner meaning and outer form, between the personal and the institutional, but also between human beings. It is significant that the lovers who correspond never unite. Moreover, the letters themselves do not "connect." They travel by indirection and are subject to mass inspection. We hardly ever see a letter read by a person to whom it is nominally sent.[5] The amount of interference provoked by letters accumulates in the course of the novel. From the outset, Sir Thomas Middleton proclaims himself the embodiment of the Royal Mail, meddling with his tenants' messages: "He insisted on conveying all their letters to and from the post for them" (S&S, p. 30). Postal supervisors multiply: not only does Elinor watch Marianne writing (on three occasions), but Colonel Brandon also oversees the tell-tale "W" in the hands of the footman. Later, we learn that Willoughby's fiancée, Sophia, has surveyed and read Marianne's letter as well (S&S, p. 321). In all, Marianne's letters to Willoughby are reported as seen four times in the novel; her loss of privacy grows proportionately. Col. Brandon remarks that "as they [Marianne and Willoughby] openly correspond . . . their marriage is *universally* talked of," and mentioned "by many— by some of whom you know nothing, by others with whom you are most intimate" (S&S, p. 173). The "whole World," it seems, knows the significance of the letters, without even reading them. And those letters that *are* read are *over*-read, the link between correspondents constantly interrupted or mediated.

Rather than a connected story, the letters in Austen's novels portray *faits accomplis*, leaving little room for question or conjecture: "this decided the matter at once," "she could doubt no longer," "it must . . . confirm their separation forever," etc. Lucy's announce-

5. Robbins, "The Included Letter," p. 25.

ment of marriage is only the luckiest and most ironic of these *fails accomplis*. For with all the supervision given to letter-writing, the notes themselves have lost the power to connect events or activate the plot: the epistolary "agent" disappears. Often, the letters simply block or divert narrative progression; like Lady Susan juggling to maintain a status quo, they circulate in order to combat structural change or individual desire.

Austen verifies this sense of inertia in the novel's belated presentation of Marianne's three letters and the single reply from Willoughby. With Elinor, we read the letters all together: Willoughby's harsh announcement followed by her sister's love letters. Perhaps, if we had seen them at the time of writing, in the order of writing, Marianne's sincere expressions would have encouraged our faith in the romance. Assembled now in this collection, *post factum*, her letters mock their own sincerity and generosity. Willoughby's letter defuses all the rest, robbing them of any potency they may once have had. This collection is dead in time. Having denied the validity of past feeling, it negates the possibility for any future movement. Austen brilliantly frames the presentation of these letters with Marianne's final burst of emotion—a near-scream of agony—and her acknowledgment of exposure: "I must feel—I must be wretched—and they are welcome to enjoy the consciousness of it that can" (S&S, pp. 189–90). The collection of love letters depicts the very death of connection and story, and they threaten the death of Marianne.[6]

Unlike her fictional predecessors, however, the letter-writing Marianne does not die; instead, the threat of the letter is continually revealed and overcome in the novel. Although the institutionalizing power of letters does temporarily silence and debilitate both Marianne and Elinor, Austen's narrative technique rescues them both, weaning both them and her readers away from a tragic epistolary closure. We recognize in Austen's scrutiny of the letter the tactics of Williams' *Letters from France*. By delineating the contours of an epistle, Williams sought to free herself from scrutiny. Austen gives the revision one more turn: she objectifies the letter, but not at the expense of closing off all interiority or personal feeling, as Williams did. If we return to our initial scene of letter-writing, we notice that even as Marianne's letter introduces dissimulation and signals her betrayal, Elinor's silent thoughts and feelings remain unrestrained and open to view. In that scene, through the use of free indirect discourse, Austen produces the "unreserved participation in the inner lives of fictional characters" which was once

---

6. Tanner discusses Marianne's reaction to this impasse quite eloquently, although he does not link the episode to the history of epistolary fiction (*Jane Austen*, pp. 75–102).

reserved for the epistolary novel.[7] Elinor's letters, we notice, never enter the novel—they disappear, uninspected. Instead, Austen's reading lesson persuades us to accept the intervention of the narrator, in order to protect the interests of her heroines.

The lesson does not, however, suggest that Elinor's "sense" should negate Marianne's "sensibility": Elinor has plenty of sensibility of her own. Rather, *Sense and Sensibility* creates a new arena for personal feeling in the novel: more inward, more distant from formal restrictions. For all her self-restraint, Elinor has a "mind . . . inevitably at liberty; her thoughts could not be chained elsewhere; and the past and the future . . . must be before her" (*S&S*, p. 105). Austen shows us Elinor's "reveries," which echo the liberating "reveries" described by Wollstonecraft in her *Letters*. Elinor, however, is protected from self-disclosure and public censure. Austen converts Elinor's reserve into fortifying "reserves" and self-possession: we sense she would survive Edward's marriage to Lucy. Similarly, Marianne must learn to convert her indiscriminate confidences into self-confidence and composure. Indeed, Marianne's recovery attests to the newly forged integrity of her feelings: "I could never have been happy with [Willoughby]," she admits, though shakily. "I should have had no confidence, no esteem. Nothing could have done it away to my feelings" (*S&S*, p. 350).

This "new privacy" has a cost, nonetheless. Although Austen replaces the interiority of the epistolary novel with a "safer," less constraining mode of narration, she cannot replace the social connection, the personal correspondence which the letter once promised. In its hour of glory, the letter in fiction created an interpenetration of consciousness between readers and writers which has rarely, if ever, been repeated. Individual independence, on the other hand, brings with it isolation. This retreat is whispered in Marianne's words: what was once "confidence" between sisters, or lovers, has withdrawn to an insular, protective self-confidence. Similarly, Elinor's integrity—the appeal of a unique consciousness, which Austen produces—owes much to its incompatibility with the world around it. Her mind is free to wander, her feelings are granted intensity, but that license is resolutely circumscribed by her awareness of "the World," of social forms, of definite structures. The interiority of Elinor Dashwood's world maintains its place in *Sense and Sensibility*, but it cannot replace that outer world.[8]

Austen's narrative intervention presupposes the impotence of individual feeling to "realize" anything in a world of exteriors and

7. Ian Watt, *The Rise of the Novel* (Berkeley: University of California Press, 1964), p. 208.
8. In this I cannot agree with Robbins, who maintains that Elinor's view does replace the view of the "World." Robbins, "The Included Letter," p. 19.

materials.⁹ This is the new "realism" she brings to the novel. Georg
Lukács defines this distinction between the nineteenth-century
novel and earlier works as

> the elevation of interiority to the status of a completely inde-
> pendent world [which] is not only a psychological fact but also
> a decisive value judgement on reality; this self-sufficiency of
> the subjective self is its most desperate self-defence.¹

In self-defense, the inner self runs from the reign of the letter. In
the process, the letter becomes more solid, material, "real."

DEIDRE SHAUNA LYNCH

The Personal and the Pro Forma†

Austen's comfort with the paradoxes that attend the mechanical
reproducibility of personal effects shapes not only her novels' comedy but also their concern with the cultivation of feeling. To get a
sense of that comfort, one might start by recognizing how the Dashwood sisters' enthusiastic participation in commercialized print culture contributes toward *Sense and Sensibility*'s creation of "a new
arena for personal feeling in the novel."¹ Margaret, the youngest
Dashwood, engages her elders in a game of speculation when,
"striking out a novel thought," she wonders aloud what they would
do " 'if somebody [gave them] all a large fortune apiece.' " In response Edward Ferrars predicts that the Dashwoods would shop:
" 'What magnificent orders would travel from this family to London
. . . in such an event! What a happy day for booksellers, music-
sellers and print-shops!' " (79). Edward's suggestion that the sisters'

9. Tanner, *Jane Austen*, p. 84.
1. Georg Lukács, *The Historical Novel*, trans. Hannah and Stanley Mitchell (London: Mer-
lin Press, 1965), pp. 300–22.
† From *The Economy of Character: Novels, Market Culture, and the Business of Inner
Meaning* (Chicago: U of Chicago P, 1998), pp. 228–33, 233–35, 236–37. Reprinted by
permission of the publisher. Quotations of *Sense and Sensibility* are from the Chapman
edition.
1. Favret, *Romantic Correspondence*, 152–53. For guidance in thinking about Austen's capacity to be comfortable and to comfort readers, I am indebted to Clifford Siskin's discussion of Austen's canonization and what it can tell us about the history of the category
of literature. Siskin focuses on the ways her novels respond to worries about the prolif-
eration of writing. "The discomforting question is whether we become what we read.
Austen's answer—an answer that I would argue signals a change in writing's status from
a worrisome new technology to a more trusted tool—is 'Yes and no, but don't worry.'
Catherine Morland does, at times, behave somewhat like the gothic heroines she reads
about but she is neither 'born' . . . to be such a heroine or doomed to become one. The
linkage is too complex to be predictable" ("Jane Austen and the Engendering of Disci-
plinarity," in *Jane Austen and the Discourses of Feminism*, ed. Devoney J. Looser [New
York: St. Martin's, 1995], 60–61).

shopping spree would encompass the sister arts—literature, music, and graphic art—indexes the degree to which Austen identifies both Marianne and Elinor with the project of "taste." Both are committed to developing their aesthetic sensibilities. When he continues, however, Edward lingers on the mixed motives that would inform Marianne's particular share in this shopping: " 'Thomson, Cowper, Scott—[Marianne] would buy them all over and over again; she would buy up every copy, I believe, to prevent their falling into unworthy hands' " (79). Marianne, Edward suggests, would not only buy for pleasure, but would also buy to make poetry into a controlled substance, property reserved for those few who could consume it appropriately. The desire Edward attributes to Marianne— for a property of a rigorously personalized kind—seems to motivate the dissatisfaction she expresses later with the codes of picturesque description: "It is very true . . . that admiration of landscape scenery is become a mere jargon. Every body pretends to feel and tries to describe with the taste and elegance of him who first defined what picturesque beauty was. I detest jargon of every kind, and sometimes I have kept my feelings to myself, because I could find no language to describe them in but what was worn and hackneyed out of all sense and meaning" (83). Unlike Anne Elliot, who, as I have noted, is a quoting heroine and who in this capacity *does* repeat what others have uttered, Marianne, uncomfortable with being numbered among "every body" and being a face in the crowd, wants language to herself. " 'I abhor every common-place phrase' " (38). The fact that language circulates, and the possibility that words— like coins traveling from hand to hand—may be "worn" in their passage from mouth to mouth, bother her.[2] Marianne takes pride in how her self-fashioned ethical program gives preference to the authentic over the imitative, real feelings over pretended feelings, and self-expression over conformity to " 'common-place notions' " (45). But here this scheme leads Marianne into a logical quandary. To describe her rapturous feelings about the countryside around Barton Cottage involves, simultaneously, expressing herself *and* immersing herself in the conventional and commonplace: Marianne is almost tempted therefore to conform to what she identifies as Elinor's overcautious self-restraint and so fall silent.

Despite her best intentions, Marianne copies. In this instance, she is almost tempted to copy her sister's silence. Austen arranges

2. Literally, a hackneyed language is a language hired out by others—as the OED's definition has it, "worn out like a hired horse by indiscriminate or vulgar use." In eighteenth-century usage, the word *hackney* is also freighted with suggestions of prostitution. Marianne's complaint about the hackneyed language of books thus points to the connections that commentators who were worried about female reading and writing often made as they linked automatic, indiscriminate reading to automatic, indiscriminate sexuality.

for repetition and for convention to prove crucial to Marianne's
fate. For instance, that complaint about the hackneyed jargon of
the picturesque echoes any number of literary reviews that, in
equally programmatic ways, lamented the repetitive propensities of
the travelers who published accounts of their journeys in quest
of the picturesque. "Next to novels," the most "fashionable kind of
reading," according to one rather jaded reviewer, the descriptive
tour, another reviewer observed, soon makes us "sensible of that
disgust, which attends the frequent repetition of the same remarks."
These tours, it was said, could place the reader "in an unvaried
reverie, like that produced by the constant and uniform repetition
of any heavy sound."[3] Willoughby, who at the start of the novel
devotedly copies out pieces of piano music for Marianne (72), goes
on to betray her with copying in the novel's second volume. The
insulting letter he sends to her in London turns out in some sense
not to be his own: " '[he] had only the credit of servilely copying' "
what his fiancée dictated to him (288). Noting the resemblances
that affiliate Marianne with Colonel Brandon's two Elizas, other
readers have speculated that, in creating Marianne, Austen gave
herself a means of examining her genre's sentimental investment in
repeating the stereotypes of female suffering.[4] Marianne is a new
edition of a half-century's worth of betrayed heroines. The fact that
she's taken a page (or more) from sentimental fiction's book alters
how we assess her claim to posses an inner uniqueness that would
be compromised by association with other people's commonplaces.
In her cultivation of individuality (*because* of her cultivation of individuality), Marianne may be recognized as a type—a victim of
convention in more than one sense.

If Austen slyly arranges for Marianne, the sister with sensibility,
to be read like a book, it does not follow that she wants the inner
life of the sister with sense to be identified in any simple way with
notions of deep meanings too personal to be articulated. When Elinor Dashwood describes personal responses—even so personal a

3. *Monthly Review* 1:419; *Critical Review* 32:144; *Edinburgh Review* 4:208: all quoted in
      Richard G. Swartz, "Dorothy Wordsworth, Local Tourism, and the Anxiety (or Semiotics)
      of Description," *Prose Studies*, forthcoming.
4. Claudia L. Johnson, "A 'Sweet Face as White as Death': Jane Austen and the Politics of
      Female Sensibility," *Novel: A Forum on Fiction* 22 (1989): 159–74; cf. Deborah Kaplan,
      "Achieving Authority: Jane Austen's First Published Novel," in *Jane Austen: Modern Crit-
      ical Views*, ed. Harold Bloom (New York: Chelsea, 1986), 203–18.
      According to Colonel Brandon, Marianne resembles his first love, Eliza Williams, in
      body and mind; she likewise resembles Eliza's namesake and illegitimate daughter in
      being the second victim of Willoughby's charms. Johnson aligns the Elizas in their turn
      with a long list of heroines that extends from Clarissa to Charlotte Temple; Nicola J.
      Watson, concentrating on anti-Jacobin tales of seduction that flourished in the 1790s,
      also locates them within a crowd of fictional predecessors (*Revolution and the Form of
      the British Novel, 1790–1825: Intercepted Letters, Interrupted Seductions* [Oxford: Clar-
      endon, 1994], 89 n. 28).

response as her attraction to Edward Ferrars—her language is at
once impersonal *and* self-betraying. This is the language that Elinor
uses to Marianne at the moment when she does not " 'attempt to
deny . . . that [she thinks] very highly of [Edward]—that [she]
greatly esteem[s], that [she] like[s] him' " (17):

> Of his sense and his goodness, . . . no one can, I think, be in
> doubt, who has seen him often enough to engage him in un-
> reserved conversation. . . . upon the whole, I venture to pro-
> nounce that his mind is well-informed, his enjoyment of books
> exceedingly great, his imagination lively, his observation just
> and correct, and his taste delicate and pure. His abilities in
> every respect improve as much upon acquaintance as his man-
> ners and person. At first sight, his address is certainly not strik-
> ing; and his person can hardly be called handsome, till the
> expression of his eyes, which are uncommonly good, and the
> general sweetness of his countenance, is perceived. (16–17)

Barbara M. Benedict has called attention to the "mannered paral-
lelisms, abstract diction and passive phrasing" that make this little
speech curiously evocative of the moral essays that Mary Bennet in
Pride and Prejudice parrots and copies into her commonplace book.
Benedict proposes that what we are hearing from Elinor is a version
of the dispassionate language of a third-person narrator, a version
of novels' language of communal judgment and social authority.
Indeed, the description of Edward that Elinor offers could be one
that such a narrator would use to introduce a heroine, a character
whose worth, in conformity to the program of the period, could not
be judged at "first sight." Oddly, the phrasing that allies Elinor with
the faceless narrator of *Sense and Sensibility* also characterizes and
personalizes her. For all its stilted formality and impersonality, this
passage of description tells us more about Elinor's caution than it
does about Edward's worth. It suggests Elinor's curiously distanced
relation to her own feelings: how Elinor's resolve is not so much *to*
judge objectively as it is *not to* let desire sway her.[5]
    That the passage points in two directions invites us to think fur-
ther about how, with Elinor, the language of private feeling, which
gives readers an inside view, is articulated with the language of
commonplaces and crowd portraits. Austen's handling of point of
view and use of free indirect discourse, I have suggested, render
the real story of *Sense and Sensibility* the story of Elinor's inner
experience. Yet Austen makes us work if we want straightforwardly
to correlate psychological effects with individuality or to correlate
what is most private with what is most personal. In talking of her

5. Benedict, "Politics of Point of View," 458.

love, Elinor places herself in a crowd and re-cites what everyone says and feels. (" 'No one' " can doubt Edward's abilities; the sweetness of his face " 'is perceived,' " perhaps by all the world, certainly not by Elinor in particular.) In *Emma*, Jane Fairfax (at least when she is seen in company in Highbury) adopts a similar habit of speech. The transcript of Emma's attempts to pump Jane for information about Frank Churchill, with whom Jane was ostensibly "a little acquainted" at Weymouth, reads like this: " 'Was he handsome?'—'She believed he was reckoned a very fine young man.' . . . 'Did he appear a sensible young man; a young man of information?'—'At a watering-place, or in a common London acquaintance, it was difficult to decide on such points. Manners were all that could be safely judged of. . . . She believed every body found his manners pleasing' " (151). The conversations that engage Highbury socialites (like the shopping excursions in *Camilla*) seem to have encouraged recent readers, whenever they talk about character, to mobilize an opposition between self and society and an opposition between what separates individuals and what connects them. Civility for Austen, accounts of her "conservatism" have proposed, exacts a heavy but necessary toll from the self because it demands a perfect conformity between personal and public opinion: the conventions of drawing-room culture have the power to make Austen's most adamant individualists fall into line.[6] This seems a simplification. Manipulating such demands that the personal be aligned with the public, Jane Fairfax echoes what "every body" thinks of Frank's looks and manners in ways that safeguard her personal opinions and her private life (including her private life as the woman to whom Frank is secretly engaged). If we were to draw our conclusions from her responses to Emma, it would appear that for Jane the voice of the world is protective of feeling—affording a kind of camouflage—as much as it is restrictive.

This may also be true for Elinor Dashwood: Elinor's distinction from Marianne, and from the heroines of the Burney school of novelists, lies with the fact that she never occupies a victim position vis-à-vis a censorious, gossiping world. After Willoughby rejects her, Marianne's feelings *are* exposed as material for the world's rumor mill, a consequence of the value she placed on sincerity and openness from the very start of her acquaintance with him. That exposure compounds her wretchedness. Elinor's situation is different. As early as the first volume of *Sense and Sensibility* Elinor's vexation when Sir John and Mrs. Jennings tease her about the beau she must

---

6. For one of the most adept examples of such a reading see Casey Finch and Peter Bowen, "The Tittle-Tattle of Highbury': Gossip and the Free Indirect Style in *Emma*," *Representations* 31 (1990): 1–18.

have left behind her in Sussex is not so acute that Marianne, who "felt for her most sincerely," cannot augment it, doing "more harm than good to the cause, by speaking . . . in an angry manner" (53); "Elinor was much more hurt by Marianne's warmth than she had been by what produced it" (206). Here it is not the collective consciousness of the world (that abstract entity that recognizable vulgarians such as Sir John and Mrs. Jennings incarnate) that poses a problem for the self but instead one's intimates, not public exposure but what transpires in the apparently safe zone of semiprivacy. Daniel Cottom's nod toward Marianne as he examines love's "commonness" in the Austen novel suggests one way to assess what Austen might value about Elinor's—or for that matter her readers'—relation to the impersonal: "[T]he only persons liable to be ruined by love are those who are ashamed of how essentially impersonal and insignificant it is and who therefore try to exaggerate it into some realm of sublime transcendence."[7]

Extrapolating from Barbara Benedict's account of Elinor's language, one could conjecture that by virtue of her alliance with the narrator of *Sense and Sensibility* Elinor avoids being the lead character in a novel about being ruined by love. One way Austen makes her characters deep is by reworking what her contemporaries did in juxtaposing a self-effacing heroine with her over-dressed foil. In Austen's novels, relations between women—the relations between Marianne and Elinor; between Jane and Elizabeth Bennet; between Fanny Price and Mary Crawford; between Jane Fairfax and Harriet Smith, on the one hand, and Emma Woodhouse, on the other; or even between the Misses Musgrove and Anne Elliot—also involve two sorts of characters. These relations involve secondary characters who lead their romantic lives in public—who are "out," who "can act," who, like Jane Bennet, "are the only handsome girl[s] in the room" (9), or whose appearance, like Harriet Smith's in *Emma* or Clara Brereton's in *Sanditon*, which I quote, suggests "the most perfect representation of [a] Heroine" (346)—and they involve heroines to whom these statements will scarcely apply.[8] "No one who had ever seen Catherine Morland in her infancy, would have supposed her born to be an heroine" (1), the narrator of *Northanger Abbey* declares as she bemoans her fate in being saddled with such unpropitious material. Within the Austen canon, Catherine has a lot of company. Austen does more, however, than comply with the

---

7. Daniel Cottom, *The Civilized Imagination* (Cambridge: Cambridge UP), p. 91.
8. Emma is the exception, perhaps, since she is, as Miss Bates inadvertently discloses, a topic for Highbury's gossip. She looks like a heroine to them. But Emma's conviction that the incentives women usually have for marrying do not apply to her make her much readier to identify other people's desires than she is to identify her own: she does, however deludedly, consider herself Harriet Smith's foil.

fictional convention that locates authentic subjectivity with the woman who is *not* favored by the public voice; she also casts her protagonists as the silent and sympathetic observers of other people's stories and the repositories of their secrets.

Their participation in situations of spectatorship and secret-sharing endows Anne Elliot and Elinor Dashwood, in particular, with the qualities that novel readers in Austen's lifetime were learning to associate with third-person narrators; likewise the capacity that each has for a self-possession that seems to numb her sense of self-interest. Anne and Elinor each partake of something like a narrator's invisibility, omniscience, and capacity to enter into others' feelings and coordinate and harmonize others' perspectives.[9] * * * It is in Elinor's consciousness that the subplots of *Sense and Sensibility* come together.

The suspension of individuality that Elinor's performance of this quasi-institutional office entails is also a requisite part of being a sister to Marianne: it is part of acting as Marianne's stand-in in conversations with Colonel Brandon (who in volume 2 comes almost daily to Mrs. Jennings's "to look at Marianne and talk to Elinor" [145]) and with Willoughby and, in the episode in which she tells Marianne about Edward's engagement to Lucy, part of acting as "the comforter of others in her own distresses, no less than in theirs" (227). Arguments for recognizing *Sense and Sensibility*'s centrality in the history of the novel often proceed by applauding Austen's use of free indirect discourse and her reworking of the form of the epistolary novel and by suggesting that the language of inward experience these innovations produce is capable of conveying what is most authentically individual about the individual. These ways of valuing the characterization of Elinor, I would suggest, need to be qualified along the lines of the formulation that Eve Sedgwick offers when, adopting the language of codependency that is mobilized in late-twentieth-century family analysis, she highlights Elinor's self-forgetting attentiveness to her oblivious sister: "As far as this novel is concerned, the co-dependent subjectivity simply is *subjectivity*."[1]

The content of the rich inner life Austen grants to Elinor is a mindfulness of others. The strategy Barbara Benedict pursues to demonstrate the distinction between the impersonal language that Elinor adopts in speaking of her own feelings—the language of a narrator's general moral lessons—and the internal language that

---

9. I draw here on the discussion of narrative omniscience in Elizabeth Ermarth, *Realism and Consensus* (Princeton: Princeton UP, 1983).
1. Eve Sedgwick, "Jane Austen and the Masturbating Girl," *Critical Inquiry* 17 (1991): 830. A germinal account of the technical innovations in *Sense and Sensibility* is Butler, *Jane Austen and the War of Ideas*.

presents Elinor as a "heroine" is illuminating in this regard. To supply a contrast to the passage in which Elinor gives her opinion of Edward Ferrars by giving everybody's opinion, Benedict chooses a passage from the third volume of *Sense and Sensibility* in which the narrative "employs the punctuation and syntax of sentimental impressionism: exclamation points, fragmented sentences, italicized words."[2] The passage of free indirect discourse that Benedict describes unfolds as Elinor awaits the arrival of her mother, who, with Colonel Brandon, is rushing the eighty miles from Barton Cottage to Cleveland in order to be, as she thinks, beside Marianne's deathbed. (Mrs. Dashwood does not yet know that Marianne's sickness has suddenly abated.)

> Never in her life had Elinor found it so difficult to be calm, as at that moment. The knowledge of what her mother must be feeling as the carriage stopt at the door,—of her doubt— her dread—perhaps her despair!—and of what *she* had to tell!—with such knowledge it was impossible to be calm. All that remained to be done, was to be speedy; and therefore staying only till she could leave Mrs. Jennings's maid with her sister, she hurried down stairs.
>
> The bustle in the vestibule, as she passed along an inner lobby, assured her that they were already in the house. She rushed forwards towards the drawing-room,—she entered it,— and saw only Willoughby. (277)

The energies of this passage derive from Elinor's capacity for sympathy—for feeling in another's place. And, tellingly, it is succeeded immediately by a conversation between Elinor and Willoughby that offers the sole example in the novel of an intimate tête-à-tête between a woman and a man, in which Willoughby " 'open[s] [his] whole heart' " (279) and in which, accordingly, Elinor again plays the role of confidante.[3] As the passage and its sequel suggest, what transpires in the interior space that the text hollows out for Elinor is the vicarious experience of another's feelings.

What transpires in that space is also, however, the unceasing mental activity involved in acting as Marianne's minister of the exterior, smoothing her run-of-the-mill transactions with the outside world. The exercise of covering up Marianne's failures to "tell lies when politeness required it" (105) and of giving social countenance

---

2. Benedict, "Politics of Point of View," 464.
3. In a strange way, the story that Willoughby recounts to Elinor to explain his conduct toward Marianne becomes Elinor's property—a personal effect. Austen emphasizes the "heightened" degree of "influence" Willoughby exercises "over [Elinor's] mind" (292). She also has Elinor first withhold the story and then retell it with "address," first to Marianne, and then to Mrs. Dashwood, doling it out selectively and to a slight degree begrudgingly: "it was neither in Elinor's power, *nor in her wish*, to raise such feelings in another . . . as had at first been called forth in herself" (305, 307; emphasis mine).

to Marianne's wool-gathering and her gift for becoming "insensible" of others' presence make Elinor a mistress of the pro forma. Devoted to making the "usual inquiries" about other people's health or the usual compliments to one's host, and so reiterating the customary phrases that pass from mouth to mouth in polite circles, Elinor's language is often language on automatic pilot. On a visit to Barton Park, she reiterates (in only a slightly different key) the politely fatuous exclamations of the Misses Steele over Sir John, Lady Middleton, and the little Middletons' "charm" (105). On arriving in London, Elinor writes the letters home that are the currency of filial duty and, as such, contentless—we know without getting the chance to read them the little they will say. (As if to point the contrast, Marianne, for her part, writes at the same time her sister does, but those letters to Willoughby are feeling-filled *cris de coeur*.)[4] The language of inward experience that makes Elinor a mind-full heroine is articulated with language that, "worn and hackneyed out of all sense and meaning," brings to view an Elinor mindful of maintaining the forms of common courtesy. By such means, the heroine's interior monologues are set off by the noise of automated communications.

*   *   *

After all, Austen too is a mistress of the pro forma. Her forte is in part her ability to play with the compulsoriness of forms: her capacity to take the overcoded, or overcrowded, conditions of modern novel writing in her stride. Take, for instance, her ways of winding up her novels' marriage plots. Austen's endings tend to call attention to the tension between the forms for expression and the creative imagination that uses those forms. When Edward Ferrars, providentially jilted by Lucy Steele, can at last honorably declare himself to Elinor, the narrator of *Sense and Sensibility* deals with his declaration by resorting to the impersonal language of the crowd portrait: "[In] what manner he expressed himself, and how he was received, need not be particularly told. This only need be said;— that when they all sat down to table at four o'clock, about three hours after his arrival, he had secured his lady, engaged her mother's consent, and was not only in the rapturous profession of the lover, but in the reality of reason and truth, one of the happiest of men" (317). Austen can be delightfully perfunctory when she gestures in this manner toward satisfying run-of-the-mill demands for closure—when, as here, she echoes what other novels in the circulating-library swarm talk about ("the happiest of men"), and when she arranges for her characters to be subjected to the com-

---

4. See Favret, *Romantic Correspondence*, 146–52.

mon fate and lost in the crowd. (Thus this passage with its generic terms reveals Elinor as a lover's "lady," much as in the proposal scene of *Emma* "all that need be said" about the dawning of our heroine's nuptial bliss is that, in her response to Knightley's proposal, "[Emma] spoke, on being so entreated.—What did she say? —Just what she ought, of course. A lady always does" [391].) When in this knowing manner Austen hints that her pen is hardwired with the novel-writing engines that obsessed romantic reviewers, she is both catering to our pleasure as convention-spotters in being *knowing* ourselves, and encouraging us to apprehend this recourse to the pro forma as the very sign of a meaningfulness that resists formalization.[5]

* * *

EVE KOSOFSKY SEDGWICK

Jane Austen and the Masturbating Girl†

* * *

Bedroom scenes are not so commonplace in Jane Austen's novels that readers get jaded with the chiaroscuro of sleep and passion, wan light, damp linen, physical abandon, naked dependency, and the imperfectly clothed body. *Sense and Sensibility* has a particularly devastating bedroom scene, which begins:

> Before the house-maid had lit their fire the next day, or the sun gained any power over a cold, gloomy morning in January, Marianne, only half-dressed, was kneeling against one of the window-seats for the sake of all the little light she could command from it, and writing as fast as a continual flow of tears would permit her. In this situation, Elinor, roused from sleep by her agitation and sobs, first perceived her; and after observing her for a few moments with silent anxiety, said, in a tone of the most considerate gentleness,
> "Marianne, may I ask?—"
> "No, Elinor," she replied, "ask nothing; you will soon know all."
> The sort of desperate calmness with which this was said, lasted no longer than while she spoke, and was immediately followed by a return of the same excessive affliction. It was some minutes before she could go on with her letter, and the

5. For a good discussion of Austen's endings, see Cotton, *Civilized Imagination*.
† From *Tendencies* (Durham: Duke UP, 1993) 113–26. Reprinted by permission of the author. Quotations of *Sense and Sensibility* are from the 1967 Penguin Edition, edited by Tony Tanner.

frequent bursts of grief which still obliged her, at intervals, to withhold her pen, were proofs enough of her feeling how more than probable it was that she was writing for the last time to Willoughby.[1]

We know well enough who is in this *bedroom:* two women. They are Elinor and Marianne Dashwood, they are sisters, and the passion and perturbation of their love for each other is, at the very least, the backbone of this powerful novel. But who is in this *bedroom scene?* And, to put it vulgarly, what's their scene? It is the naming of a man, the absent Willoughby, that both marks this as an unmistakably sexual scene, and by the same gesture seems to displace its "sexuality" from the depicted bedroom space of same-sex tenderness, secrecy, longing, and frustration. Is this, then, a hetero- or a homoerotic novel (or moment in a novel)? No doubt it must be said to be both, if love is vectored toward an object and Elinor's here flies toward Marianne, Marianne's in turn toward Willoughby. But what, if love is defined only by its gender of object-choice, are we to make of Marianne's terrible isolation in this scene; of her unstanchable emission, convulsive and intransitive; and of the writing activity with which it wrenchingly alternates?

Even before this, of course, the homo/hetero question is problematical for its anachronism: homosexual identities, and certainly female ones, are supposed not to have had a broad discursive circulation until later in the nineteenth century, so in what sense could heterosexual identities as against them?[2] And for that matter, if we are to trust Foucault, the conceptual amalgam represented in the very term "sexual identity," the cementing of every issue of individuality, filiation, truth, and utterance *to* some representational metonymy of the genital, was a process not supposed to have been perfected for another half-century or three-quarters of a century after Austen; so that the genital implication in either "homosexual" *or* "heterosexual," to the degree that it differs from a plot of the procreative or dynastic (as each woman's desire seems at least for

1. Jane Austen, *Sense and Sensibility* (Harmondsworth, Middlesex: Penguin Books, 1967), p. 193. Further citations from this edition are incorporated in the text.
2. This is (in relation to women) the argument of, most influentially, Lilian Faderman in *Surpassing the Love of Men: Romantic Friendship and Love between Women from the Renaissance to the Present* (New York: William Morrow, 1981), and Carroll Smith-Rosenberg in "The Female World of Love and Ritual," in *Disorderly Conduct: Visions of Gender in Victorian America* (New York: Oxford University Press, 1985). A recently discovered journal, published as *I Know My Own Heart: The Diaries of Anne Lister (1791–1840),* ed. Helena Whitbread (London: Virago, 1988), suggests that revisions of this narrative may, however, be necessary. It is the diary (for 1817–23) of a young, cultured, religious, socially conservative, self-aware, land-owning rural Englishwoman— an almost archetypal Jane Austen heroine—who formed her sense of self around the pursuit and enjoyment of genital contact and short- and long-term intimacies with other women of various classes.

the moment to do), may mark also the possibility of an anachronistic gap.[3]

* * *

One "sexual identity" that did exist as such in Austen's time, already bringing a specific genital practice into dense compaction with issues of consciousness, truth, pedagogy, and confession, was that of the onanist. Among the sexual dimensions overridden within the past century by the world-historical homo/hetero cleavage is the one that discriminates, in the first place, the autoerotic and the alloerotic. Its history has been illuminated by recent researches of a number of scholars.[4] According to their accounts, the European phobia over masturbation came early in the "sexualizing" process described by Foucault, beginning around 1700 with publication of *Onania*, and spreading virulently after the 1750s. Although originally applied with a relative impartiality to both sexes, antionanist discourse seems to have bifurcated in the nineteenth century, and the systems of surveillance and the rhetorics of "confession" for the two genders contributed to the emergence of disparate regulatory categories and techniques, even regulatory worlds. According to Ed Cohen, for example, anxiety about boys' masturbation motivated mechanisms of school discipline and surveillance that were to contribute so much to the late-nineteenth-century emergence of a widespread, class-inflected male homosexual identity and hence to the modern crisis of male homo/heterosexual definition. On the other hand, anxiety about girls' and women's masturbation contributed more to the emergence of gynecology, through an accumulated expertise in and demand for genital surgery; of such identities as that of the hysteric; and of such confession-inducing disciplinary discourses as psychoanalysis.

3. Michel Foucault, *The History of Sexuality: An Introduction*, trans. Robert Hurley (New York: Pantheon Books, 1978), p.1.
4. Useful historical work touching on masturbation and masturbation phobia includes G. J. Barker-Benfield, *The Horrors of the Half-Known Life: Male Attitudes Toward Women and Sexuality in Nineteenth-Century America* (New York: Harper and Row, 1976); Ed Cohen, *Talk on the Wilde Side* (New York: Routledge, 1993); John D'Emilio and Estelle B. Freedman, *Intimate Matters: A History of Sexuality in America* (New York: Harper and Row, 1988); E. H. Hare, "Masturbatory Insanity: The History of an Idea," *Journal of the Mental Sciences* 108 (1962):1–25; Robert H. MacDonald, "The Frightful Consequences of Onanism: Notes on the History of a Delusion," *Journal of the History of Ideas* 28(1967): 423–31; John Money, *The Destroying Angel: Sex, Fitness and Food in the Legacy of Degeneracy Theory, Graham Crackers, Kellogg's Corn Flakes and the American Health History* (Buffalo, N.Y.: Prometheus, 1985); George L. Mosse, *Nationalism and Sexuality: Respectability and Abnormal Sexuality in Modern Europe* (New York: Fertig, 1985); Robert P. Neuman, "Masturbation, Madness, and the Modern Concept of Childhood and Adolescence," *Journal of Social History* 8 (1975): 1–22; Elaine Showalter, *The Female Malady: Women, Madness, and English Culture, 1830–1980* (New York: Pantheon Books, 1985); Smith-Rosenberg, *Disorderly Conduct*; and Jean Stengers and Anne van Neck, *Histoire d'une grande peur: la masturbation* (Brussels: Editions de l'Université de Bruxelles, 1984).

Far from there persisting a minority identity of "the masturbator" today, of course, autoeroticism per se in the twentieth century has been conclusively subsumed under that normalizing developmental model, differently but perhaps equally demeaning, according to which it represents a relatively innocuous way station on the road to a "full," i.e., alloerotic, adult genitality defined almost exclusively by gender of object choice. As Foucault and others have noted, a lush plurality of (proscribed and regulated) sexual identities had developed by the end of the nineteenth century: even the most canonical late-Victorian art and literature are full of sadomasochistic, pederastic and pedophilic, necrophilic, as well as autoerotic images and preoccupations; while Foucault mentions the hysterical woman and the masturbating child along with "entomologized" sexological categories such as zoophiles, zooerasts, automonosexualists, and gynecomasts, as typifying the new sexual taxonomies, the sexual *"specification of individuals,"* that he sees as inaugurating the twentieth-century regime of sexuality.[5] Although Foucault is concerned to demonstrate our own continuity with nineteenth-century sexual discourse, however (appealing to his readers as "we 'Other Victorians' "),[6] it makes a yet-to-be-explored difference that the Victorian multiplication of sexual species has today all but boiled down to a single, bare—and moreover fiercely invidious—dichotomy. Most of us now correctly understand a question about our "sexual orientation" to be a demand that we classify ourselves as a heterosexual or a homosexual, regardless of whether we may or may not individually be able or willing to perform that blank, binarized act of category assignment. We also understand that the two available categories are not symmetrically but hierarchically constituted in relation to each other. The identity of the masturbator was only one of the sexual identities subsumed, erased, or overridden in this triumph of the heterosexist homo/hetero calculus. But I want to argue here that the status of the masturbator among these many identities was uniquely formative. I would suggest that as one of the very earliest embodiments of "sexual identity" in the period of the progressive epistemological overloading of sexuality, the masturbator may have been at the cynosural center of a remapping of individual identity, will, attention, and privacy along modern lines that the reign of "sexuality," and its generic concomitant in the novel and in novelistic point of view, now lead us to take for granted. It is of more than chronological import if the (lost) identity of the masturbator was the proto-form of modern sexual identity itself.

Thus it seems likely that in our reimaginings of the history of

5. Foucault, *History of Sexuality*, 1:105, 43.
6. Ibid., 1:1.

sexuality "as" (we vainly imagine) "we know it," through readings of classic texts, the dropping out of sight of the autoerotic term is also part of what falsely naturalizes the heterosexist imposition of these books, disguising both the rich, conflictual erotic complication of a homoerotic matrix not yet crystallized in terms of "sexual identity" and the violence of heterosexist definition finally carved out of these plots. I am taking *Sense and Sensibility* as my example here because of its odd position, at once germinal and abjected, in the Austen canon and hence in "the history of the novel"; and because its erotic axis is most obviously the unwavering but difficult love of a woman, Elinor Dashwood, for a woman, Marianne Dashwood. I don't think we can bring this desire into clear focus until we also see how Marianne's erotic identity, in turn, is not in the first place exactly either a same-sex-loving one or a cross-sex-loving one (though she loves both women and men), but rather the one that today no longer exists *as* an identity: that of the masturbating girl.

Reading the bedroom scenes of *Sense and Sensibility*, I find I have lodged in my mind a bedroom scene from another document, a narrative structured as a case history of "Onanism and Nervous Disorders in Two Little Girls" and dated "1881":

> Sometimes [X. . . .'s] face is flushed and she has a roving eye; at others she is pale and listless. Often she cannot keep still, pacing up and down the bedroom, or balancing on one foot after the other. . . . During these bouts X . . . is incapable of anything: reading, conversation, games, are equally odious. All at once her expression becomes cynical, her excitement mounts. X . . . is overcome by the desire to do it, she tries not to or someone tries to stop her. Her only dominating thought is to succeed. Her eyes dart in all directions, her lips never stop twitching, her nostrils flare! Later, she calms down and is herself again. "If only I had never been born," she says to her little sister, "we would not have been a disgrace to the family!" And Y . . . replies: "Why did you teach me all these horrors then?" Upset by the reproach, X . . . says: "If someone would only kill me! What joy. I could die without committing suicide."[7]

If what defines "sexual identity" is the impaction of epistemological issues around the core of a particular genital possibility, then

7. Démétrius Zambaco, "Onanism and Nervous Disorders in Two Little Girls," trans. Catherine Duncan, *Semiotext(e)* 4 ("Polysexuality") (1981): 30; further citations are incorporated in the text as DZ. The letters standing in place of the girls' names are followed by ellipses in the original; other ellipses are mine. In quoting from this piece I have silently corrected some obvious typographical errors; since this issue of *Semiotext(e)* is printed entirely in capital letters, and with commas and periods of indistinguishable shape, I have also had to make some guesses about sentence division and punctuation.

the compulsive attention paid by antionanist discourse to disorders *of* attention makes it a suitable point of inauguration for modern sexuality. Marianne Dashwood, though highly intelligent, exhibits the classic consciousness symptoms noted by Tissot in 1758, including "the impairment of memory and the senses," "inability to confine the attention," and "an air of distraction, embarrassment and stupidity."[8] A surprising amount of the narrative tension of *Sense and Sensibility* comes from the bent bow of the absentation of Marianne's attention from wherever she is. "Great," at one characteristic moment, "was the perturbation of her spirits and her impatience to be gone" (p. 174); once out on the urban scene, on the other hand, "her eyes were in constant inquiry; and in whatever shop the party were engaged, her mind was equally abstracted from every thing actually before them, from all that interested and occupied the others. Restless and dissatisfied every where . . . she received no pleasure from any thing; was only impatient to be at home again . . ." (p. 180). Yet when at home, her "agitation increased as the evening drew on. She could scarcely eat any dinner, and when they afterwards returned to the drawing room, seemed anxiously listening to the sound of every carriage" (p. 177).

Marianne incarnates physical as well as perceptual irritability, to both pleasurable and painful effect. Addicted to "rapidity" (p. 75) and "requiring at once solitude and continual change of place" (p. 193), she responds to anything more sedentary with the characteristic ejaculation: "I could hardly keep my seat" (p. 51). Sitting is the most painful and exciting thing for her. Her impatience keeps her "moving from one chair to another" (p. 266) or "[getting] up, and walk[ing] about the room" (p. 269). At the happiest moments, she frankly pursues the locomotor pleasures of her own body, "running with all possible speed down the steep side of the hill" (p. 74) (and spraining her ankle in a tumble), eager for "the delight of a gallop" when Willoughby offers her a horse (p. 88).

* * *

As undisciplined as Marianne Dashwood's "abstracted" attention is, the farouche, absent presence of this figure compellingly reorganizes the attention of others: Elinor's rapt attention to her, to begin with, but also, through Elinor's, the reader's. *Sense and Sensibility* is unusual among Austen novels not for the (fair but unrigorous) consistency with which its narrative point of view is routed through a single character, Elinor; but rather for the undeviating consistency with which Elinor's regard in turn is vectored in the direction of her beloved. Elinor's self-imposed obligation to offer

8. Quoted and discussed in Cohen, *Talk on the Wilde Side*, pp. 89–90.

social countenance to the restless, insulting, magnetic, and dangerous abstraction of her sister constitutes most of the plot of the novel.

It constitutes more than plot, in fact; it creates both the consciousness and the privacy of the novel. The projectile of surveillance, epistemological demand, and remediation that both desire and "responsibility" constrain Elinor to level at Marianne, immobilized or turned back on herself by the always-newly-summoned-up delicacy of her refusal to press Marianne toward confession, make an internal space—internal, that is, to Elinor, hence to the reader hovering somewhere behind her eyes—from which there is no escape but more silent watching. About the engagement she is said to assume to exist between Marianne and Willoughby, for example, her "wonder"

> was engrossed by the extraordinary silence of her sister and Willoughby on the subject. . . . Why they should not openly acknowledge to her mother and herself, what their constant behaviour to each other declared to have taken place, Elinor could not imagine.
> . . . For this strange kind of secrecy maintained by them relative to their engagement, which in fact concealed nothing at all, she could not account; and it was so wholly contradictory to their general opinions and practice, that a doubt sometimes entered her mind of their being really engaged, and this doubt was enough to prevent her making any enquiry of Marianne.
> (p. 100)

To Marianne, on the other hand, the question of an engagement seems simply not to have arisen.

The insulation of Marianne from Elinor's own unhappiness, when Elinor is unhappy; the buffering of Marianne's impulsiveness, and the absorption or, where that is impossible, coverture of her terrible sufferings; the constant, reparative concealment of Marianne's elopements of attention from their present company: these activities hollow out a subjectivity for Elinor and the novel that might best be described in the 1980s jargon of codependency, were not the pathologizing stigma of that term belied by the fact that, at least as far as this novel is concerned, the codependent subjectivity simply is subjectivity. Even Elinor's heterosexual plot with Edward Ferrars merely divides her remedial solicitude (that distinctive amalgam of "tenderness, pity, approbation, censure, and doubt" [p. 129]) between the sister who remains her first concern, and a second sufferer from mauvaise honte, the telltale "embarrassment," "settled" "absence of mind" (p. 123), unsocializable shyness, "want of spirits, of openness, and of consistency," "the same fettered inclination, the same inevitable necessity of temporizing with his mother" (p. 126), and a "desponding turn of mind" (p. 128), all consequent on his own servitude to an erotic habit formed in the idleness and isolation of an improperly supervised youth.

The codependency model is the less anachronistic as Marianne's and Edward's disorders share with the pre-twentieth-century version of masturbation the property of being structured as addictions. (Here, of course, I'm inviting a meditation on the history of the term "self-abuse," which referred to masturbation from the eighteenth century until very recently—when it's come, perhaps by analogy to "child abuse," to refer to battering or mutilation of oneself. Where that older sense of "abuse" has resurfaced, on the other hand, is in the also very recent coinage, "substance abuse.") Back to 1881:

> The afternoon of the 14th of September X . . . is in a terribly overexcited state. She walks about restlessly, grinding her teeth. . . . There is foam on her lips, she gasps, repeating, "I don't want to, I don't want to, I can't stop myself, I must do it! Stop me, hold my hands, tie my feet!" A few moments later she falls into a state of prostration, becomes sweet and gentle, begging to be given another chance. "I know I'm killing myself," she says. "Save me." (DZ, p. 30)

Although *the addict*, as a medicalized personal identity, was (as Virginia Berridge and Griffith Edwards demonstrate in *Opium and the People*) another product of the latter nineteenth century, the hypostatization of the notion of "will" that would soon give rise to the "addict" identity, and that by the late twentieth century would leave no issue of voluntarity untinged by the concept of addiction, is already in place in *Sense and Sensibility*.[9] A concept of addiction involves understanding something called "the will" as a muscle that can strengthen with exercise or atrophy with disuse; the particular muscle on which "will" is modeled in this novel is a sphincter, which, when properly toned, defines an internal space of private identity by holding some kinds of material inside, even while guarding against the admission of others. Marianne's unpracticed muscle lets her privacy dribble away, giving her "neither courage to speak of, nor fortitude to conceal" (p. 333) the anguish she experiences. By contrast, in the moment of Elinor's profoundest happiness, when Marianne is restored from a grave illness, Elinor's well-exercised muscle guarantees that what expands with her joy is the private space that, constituting her self, constitutes it also as the space of narrative self-reflection (not to say hoarding):

9. Virginia Berridge and Griffith Edwards, *Opium and the People: Opiate Use in Nineteenth-Century England*, 2d ed. (New Haven, Conn.: Yale University Press, 1987).

Elinor could not be cheerful. Her joy was of a different kind, and led to anything rather than to gaiety. Marianne restored to life, health, friends, and to her doating mother, was an idea to fill her heart with sensations of exquisite comfort, and expand it in fervent gratitude;—but it led to no outward demonstrations of joy, no words, no smiles. All within Elinor's breast was satisfaction, silent and strong. (p. 310)

Such an apparently generalizable ideal of individual integrity, the unitary self-containment of the strong, silent type, can never be stable, of course. Elinor has constructed herself in this way around an original lack: the absentation of her sister, and perhaps in the first place the withholding from herself of the love of their mother, whom she then compulsively unites with Marianne, the favorite, in the love-drenched tableaux of her imagination. In the inappropriately pathologizing but descriptively acute language of self-help, Marianne's addiction has mobilized in her sister a discipline that, posed as against addiction, nonetheless also is one. Elinor's pupils, those less tractable sphincters of the soul, won't close against the hapless hemorrhaging of her visual attention flow toward Marianne; it is this, indeed, that renders her consciousness, in turn, habitable, inviting, and formative to readers as "point of view."

But that hypostatization of "will" had always anyway contained the potential for the infinite regress enacted in the uncircumscribable twentieth-century epidemic of addiction attribution: the degenerative problem of where, if not in some further compulsion, one looks for the will *to* will. As when Marianne, comparing herself with the more continent Elinor,

felt all the force of that comparison, but not as her sister had hoped, to urge her to exertion now; she felt it with all the pain of continual self-reproach, regretted most bitterly that she had never exerted herself before; but it brought only the torture of penitence, without the hope of amendment. Her mind was so much weakened that she still fancied present exertion impossible, and therefore it only dispirited her the more. (p. 270)

In addition, the concept of addiction involves a degenerative perceptual narrative of progressively deadened receptiveness to a stimulus that therefore requires to be steadily increased—as when Marianne's and her mother's "agony of grief" over the death of the father, at first overpowering, was then "voluntarily renewed, was sought for, was created again and again" (p. 42). Paradoxically afflicted, as Marianne is, by both hyperesthesia and an emboldening and addiction-producing absent-mindedness ("an heart hardened against [her friends'] merits, and a temper irritated by their very attention" [p. 337]), the species of the masturbating girl was described by Augustus Kinsley Gardner in 1860 as one

> in whom the least impression is redoubled like that of a "tamtam," [yet who seeks] for emotions still more violent and more varied. It is this necessity which nothing can appease, which took the Roman women to the spectacles where men were devoured by ferocious beasts. . . . It is the emptiness of an unquiet and sombre soul seeking some activity, which clings to the slightest incident of life, to elicit from it some emotion which forever escapes; in short, it is the deception and disgust of existence[1]

The subjectivity hollowed out by *Sense and Sensibility*, then, and made available *as* subjectivity for heterosexual expropriation, is not Marianne's but Elinor's; the novel's achievement of a modern psychological interiority fit for the heterosexual romance plot is created for Elinor through her completely one-directional visual fixation on her sister's specularized, desired, envied, and punished autoeroticism. This also offers, however, a useful model for the chains of reader relations constructed by the punishing, girl-centered moral pedagogy and erotics of Austen's novels more generally. Austen criticism is notable mostly, not just for its timidity and banality, but for its unresting exaction of the spectacle of a Girl Being Taught a Lesson—for the vengefulness it vents on the heroines whom it purports to love, and whom, perhaps, it does. Thus Tony Tanner, the ultimate normal and normalizing reader of Austen, structures sentence after sentence: "Emma . . . *has to be tutored.* . . into correct vision and responsible speech. Anne Elliot *has to move,* painfully, from an excessive prudence."[2] "Some Jane Austen heroines *have to learn* their true 'duties.' They all *have to find* their proper homes" (TT, p. 33). Catherine "quite literally is in danger of perverting reality, and one of the things she *has to learn* is to break out of quotations" (TT, pp. 44–45); she "*has to be disabused* of her naive and foolish 'Gothic' expectations" (TT, p. 48). [Elizabeth and Darcy] *have to learn to see* that their novel is more properly called . . ." (TT, p. 105). A lot of Austen criticism sounds hilariously like the leering school prospectuses or governess manifestoes brandished like so many birch rods in Victorian S-M pornography. Thus Jane Nardin:

---

1. Augustus Kinsley Gardner, "Physical Decline of American Women" (1860), quoted in Barker-Benfield, *Horrors of the Half-Known Life*, pp. 273–74.
2. Tony Tanner, *Jane Austen* (Cambridge, Mass.: Harvard University Press, 1986), p. 6; page numbers of remaining quotations cited in the text with TT; emphasis, in each case, added.

The discipline that helps create the moral adult need not necessarily be administered in early childhood. Frequently, as we have seen, it is not—for its absence is useful in helping to create the problems with which the novel deals. But if adequate discipline is lacking in childhood, it must be supplied later, and this happens only when the character learns "the lessons of affliction" (*Mansfield Park*, p. 459). Only after immaturity, selfishness, and excessive self-confidence have produced error, trouble, and real suffering, can the adult begin to teach himself or herself the habits of criticism and self-control which should have been inculcated in childhood.[3]

How can it have taken this long to see that when Colonel Brandon and Marianne finally get together, their first granddaughter will be Lesbia Brandon?

Even readings of Austen that are not so frankly repressive have tended to be structured by what Foucault calls "the repressive hypothesis"—especially so, indeed, to the degree that their project is avowedly *anti*repressive. And these antirepressive readings have their own way of re-creating the spectacle of the girl being taught a lesson. Call her, in this case, "Jane Austen." The sight to be relished here is, as in psychoanalysis, the forcible exaction from her manifest text of what can only be the barest confession of a self-pleasuring sexuality, a disorder or subversion, seeping out at the edges of a policial conservatism always presumed and therefore always available for violation. That virginal figure "Jane Austen," in these narratives, is herself the punishable girl who "has to learn," "has to be tutored"—in truths with which, though derived from a reading of Austen, the figure of "Jane Austen" can no more be credited than can, for their lessons, the figures "Marianne," "Emma," or, shall we say, "Dora" or "Anna O."

It is partly to interrupt this seemingly interminable scene of punitive/pedagogical reading, interminably structured as it is by the concept of repression, that I want to make available the sense of an alternative, passionate sexual ecology—one fully available to Austen for her exciting, productive, and deliberate use, in a way it no longer is to us.

* * *

3. She is remarkably unworried about any possible excess of severity: "In this group of characters [in *Mansfield Park*], lack of discipline has the expected effect, while excessive discipline, though it causes suffering and creates some problems for Fanny and Susan Price, does indeed make them into hard-working, extremely conscientious women. The timidity and self-doubt which characterize Fanny, and which are a response to continual censure, seem a reasonable price to pay for the strong conscience that even the unfair discipline she received has nurtured in her." Jane Nardin, "Children and Their Families," *Jane Austen: New Perspectives*, ed. Janet Todd, *Women and Literature*, New Series, vol. 3 (New York: Holmes and Meier, 1983), pp. 73–87; both passages quoted are from p. 83.

DEBORAH KAPLAN

Mass Marketing Jane Austen: Men, Women, and Courtship in Two Film Adaptations†

Some years ago I was given the "tip sheet"—guidelines for prospective writers—distributed by a well-known publishing house of mass-market contemporary romances.[1] Prescriptions for the characterization of the hero immediately caught my eye: "The hero is 8 to 12 years older than the heroine. He is self-assured, masterful, hot-tempered, capable of violence, passion, and tenderness. He is often mysteriously moody. Heathcliff (*Wuthering Heights*) is a rougher version; Darcy (*Pride and Prejudice*) a more refined one."

The tip sheet thus makes explicit that Jane Austen's *Pride and Prejudice* is one of the models for the late twentieth-century's mass-market romance. To be sure, some of the guidelines have little connection to the world of Austen's novel. The aspiring romance writer is advised that the heroine should have little interest in alcohol and cigarettes and that love scenes should be described sensuously and in detail. Nudity is acceptable, indeed welcome, as long as it is not presented too graphically—"references to pain and blood," the would-be writer is told emphatically, "are out." Nevertheless, if suggestions for the hero's characterization do not give admirers of *Pride and Prejudice* a sense of déjà vu, the tip sheet's plot outline will:

> the action should explore the relationship between the lovers. . . . The story usually begins with a clash between the hero and the heroine. Often this has to do with misapprehensions each has about the other. Sometimes the heroine has heard a great deal about the hero and has some reason to resent him before they actually meet, or they meet under inauspicious circumstances and the heroine is put off by the hero's ruthless, domineering, and arrogant manner. Or the hero has formed an opinion of the heroine before he meets her. [Silhoutte tip sheet]

† From *Jane Austen in Hollywood*, eds. Linda Troost and Sayre Greenfield (Lexington: UP of Kentucky, 1998), pp. 77–186. Reprinted by permission of the publisher. Quotations of *Sense and Sensibility* are from the Chapman edition. Complete bibliographical information regarding the critics alluded to parenthetically is available in the Selected Bibliography at the end of the volume.
1. Dated 1980, the tip sheet outlines novels for Silhouette Romances, which at the time was a Simon & Schuster line. In 1984 Harlequin Enterprises, owned by Toronto's Torstar Corporation, purchased Silhouette. In 1997, Torstar was the world's largest publisher of mass-market paperback romances, offering three lines: Harlequin, Silhouette, and Mira.

Jane Austen as one of the mothers of the Harlequin or Silhouette novel? This genealogy should amuse many of Austen's admirers, who know her novels to be much more culturally and linguistically complex than the mass-market romance. And yet, recent popular representations reveal a distinct trend: the harlequinization of Jane Austen's novels. If Austen is one of the ancestors of the paperback romance, recent films of her work are now the heirs of this popular form. The two most explicit descendants in this romance genealogy are the films of *Sense and Sensibility*, adapted by Emma Thompson and directed by Ang Lee, and *Emma*, adapted and directed by Douglas McGrath.

By *harlequinization* I mean that, like the mass-market romance, the focus is on a hero and heroine's courtship at the expense of other characters and other experiences, which are sketchily represented. As the tip sheet suggests, the hero and heroine's plot should begin in the first chapter—no wasting time even with matters as extraneous as the heroine's life before she first encounters the hero. Harlequinization does not require a plot closely patterned on *Pride and Prejudice*. But it does necessitate an unswerving attention to the hero's and heroine's desires for one another and a tendency to represent those desires in unsurprising, even clichéd ways (Radway 122).[2] The mass-market romance suggests that familiarity breeds content. The pleasures of this form are to be found not only in the unfolding of desire and the achievement of gratification but also in the comfortable knowledge of what is to come and how it is to occur.[3] Finally, harlequinization is typified by attention to physical appearances, the result of the subtle and not-so-subtle commodification of persons in this intensely commercial form. Hero and heroine should be both good-looking and sexy. And since much of selfhood is loaded into and expressed by appearance, love at first sight is understandable and appropriate. Clothes, too, are of interest, not only as a means of bringing attention to the bodies of the hero and the heroine but as objects of desire in their own right—another reminder of this highly commercial form.

Since I am going to be critical of some of the films' divergences from the novels, I want to say at the outset that I do not think the medium itself is the culprit. Granted, film inevitably transforms novels. To take an obvious and important example, although Austen's ironic narrators are central to the reader's encounter with her

---

2. Radway's well-known study of readers and the mass-market romance confirms the central trait of these novels: "the most striking characteristic of the ideal romance [is] its resolute focus on a single, developing relationship between heroine and hero" (122).

3. Moffat argues that genres in general provide their readers with the satisfaction of being able to predict a work's outcome (48). "Formula fictions," such as mass-market romances, may be said to intensify the satisfactions of predicting a fiction's conclusion.

books, most filmmakers wisely reject the amount of voice-over that would be necessary to reproduce the experience of a narrator. Moreover, the transfer to film of a work written in an earlier period also makes film versions radically different. Even had all those involved in making the Austen films worked at rendering the novels as exactly and authentically as possible—and they did not—their efforts would still have been heavily mediated by late twentieth-century minds and bodies. The films were made by writers and directors and for audiences with inescapably modern mental lives. And actors, however good their period-style technique, have been physically shaped by late twentieth-century food, medical treatments, skin and hair care products, sneakers, soft sofas, and weight machines.

A film of a book will always be different from the book itself, but let us also acknowledge that film has the power to show us aspects of Jane Austen's novels in new and revitalizing ways. For example, Ang Lee captures the emotional tension in Barton Cottage after Willoughby leaves for good and the personality differences among the inhabitants in a scene of breathtaking visual beauty, shot looking down a staircase at the three bedroom doors and the landing connecting them. Elinor has pursued her mother up to the landing from below, where they had been arguing about the meaning of Willoughby's sudden departure. Mrs. Dashwood goes into her bedroom weeping and shuts the door. Margaret, who has been trying in vain to get Marianne to open her bedroom door in order to hand her a cup of tea, passes the cup and saucer to Elinor, goes into her bedroom, bursts into tears, and shuts *her* door. Elinor, out on the landing, hears weeping coming from behind all the doors. Sitting down carefully on the stairs, she drinks the tea, an activity evocative of custom and propriety. Emphasizing the solitude of her calm, quiet misery, the scene dramatizes the difference between Elinor and the rest of her family. Moreover, by placing the camera outside the bedroom doors and behind Elinor, the film aligns the audience with Elinor's viewpoint and way of coping.

I am critical then not of film alterations per se—but of alterations made in the service, I presume, of broad commercial appeal. *Sense and Sensibility* cost $15.5 million to make (Gunther 128). While substantially less than the $70-million budget for the 1996 summer blockbuster *Independence Day*, this is still an expenditure necessitating, as cultural critic Louis Menand recently put it, "the maximally profitable economic niche" (Gunther 4). McGrath's *Emma* cost considerably less to make—only $7 million[4]—and is consid-

---

4. Bob Fenster, "History of Frugal 'Emma' Quite Hectic," *Arizona Republic*, 11 Aug. 1996, F8.

ered a specialized "boutique film" (Menand 6). Nevertheless, it too has been in search of a profitable market share. Both films have been hyped aggressively, through magazine and television interviews with the films' stars and those seemingly endless, insipid newspaper articles on the making of these films and the reasons for the rash of Jane Austen movies. *Sense and Sensibility*, as of July 1996, had grossed $43 million, and *Emma*, as of early October 1996, had grossed $20 million ("Film")[5] These are only *domestic* earnings, however. Between February and June 1996, *Sense and Sensibility* opened in ten other countries, including Australia, Brazil, Mexico, and Japan. It has grossed over $125 million worldwide (Gunther 128). Like modern romance paperbacks, the films are mass-market products, and this accounts for their similarities. The conventions of romance have sold well in Harlequin and Silhouette novels, and they have made box-office successes out of mainstream American films.

The medium of film itself may be neutral, but American-produced popular films generally are not. To put Austen novels on film by means of corporations (Columbia Pictures and Miramax) that produce what is now a global popular culture informed by American tastes is to enter a medium shaped by powerful generic conventions of romance. But the films' romantic emphasis also functions as a critique of Austen's writing. Told by a third-person narrator intimate with the consciousness of the female characters and usually at a distance from the mental lives and daily activities of men, Austen's novels, so the films suggest, underrepresent men. The films redress that imbalance by amplifying and glamorizing Austen's heroes, but, as I shall show, doing so prevents them from capturing the nuances of Austen's male characters as well as the teasing ambiguities of the novelist's representations of women and courtship.

The casting of the films' heroes was instrumental in achieving the onscreen romancification of Austen's work. * * * The actors playing Edward Ferrars (Hugh Grant) and Colonel Brandon (Alan Rickman) are also too physically appealing. Austen's *Sense and Sensibility* emphatically denies these characters striking appearances. "Edward Ferrars," explains the narrator, "was not recommended to their [Mrs. Dashwood and her daughters'] good opinion by any peculiar graces of person or address. He was not handsome, and his manners required intimacy to make them pleasing" (*Sense* 15). Similarly, Colonel Brandon's "face was not handsome" (*Sense* 34). To be sure, both men have gentlemanly behavior, affectionate hearts, and other admirable qualities. But they are made plain in part to contribute to the novel's antiromance argument. The one male

5. "Film Box Office Report," *Daily Variety*, 2 July 1996 and 1 Oct. 1996.

character in the novel who is endowed with the dashing looks of a romantic hero, Mr. Willoughby, proves to be not only immoral but also mercenary (a quality at odds with the romantic sensibility).

Judgments of personal attractiveness are, of course, highly subjective, but the stage and film careers of Jeremy Northam, Hugh Grant, and Alan Rickman indicate that all have been widely understood to have at least as much romantic appeal as Greg Wise, who plays the role of Willoughby in the film. Moreover, those prior roles inevitably mediate at least some audience members' perceptions of their characters in the Austen films. Referring to the intertextuality that affects the reception of plays but could apply just as well to films, theater historian Marvin Carlson has noted "that every specific production is composed in large part of elements already encountered elsewhere, that often bring with them as a necessary and inevitable part of reception certain ghosts of these previous encounters".[6] I have already suggested that the mass-market romance is a very important "ghost" affecting the scripting and direction of the films. But some of the actors' past roles also "haunt" their characters in these films. * * * Colonel Brandon, for some of the audience, would not have escaped the aura of Alan Rickman's charming and charismatic villains, such as the terrorist in *Die Hard* and the Sheriff of Nottingham in *Robin Hood: Prince of Thieves*, or his poignant dead lover in *Truly, Madly, Deeply*. The nervous charm and amorousness of Hugh Grant's character in the film *Four Weddings and a Funeral* may have affected some filmgoers' experience of his Edward Ferrars. (For some viewers, however, that impact was superseded by another memory: Grant's Beverly Hills sex scandal, which occurred in June 1995, while the filming of *Sense and Sensibility* was still in progress but after his scenes had been completed. Incidents in the private lives of public persons may also become ghosts that haunt a particular production.)

The film versions of Austen's men provide sustained dramatizations of their love for the heroines. Colonel Brandon's intense response to Marianne, particularly when she becomes gravely ill, is inflected, according to the novel, by his tragic history with his father's ward, the first Eliza. There is much more than déjà vu, however, in Alan Rickman's interpretation of the character. Like "a man thawing out after having been in a fridge for twenty years" is the way he described his role (quoted in Thompson 251), but he moves rapidly in the part of Brandon from thaw to burn. In the book,

6. Marvin Carlson, "The Haunted Stage: Recycling and Reception in the Theatre," *Theatre Survey* 35.1 (May 1994): 5–18.

Brandon embarks on the journey to bring Mrs. Dashwood to her severely ill daughter, after being requested to do so by Elinor. In the film, she finds him pacing outside Marianne's bedroom in one of his most fetching outfits. He does wear a flannel waistcoat, and for Marianne that article of clothing has symbolized his age and infirmity. But because it is combined with boots, tight breeches, a white shirt with long flowing sleeves, and a thin black scarf draped carelessly around his neck, the romanticism he has quietly repressed in the novel is vividly displayed on his body in the film. His plea to be assigned a useful task—"Give me an occupation, Miss Dashwood, or I shall run mad" (Thompson 181)—combines the conduct-book virtue of industriousness with emotional excess and suggests the hilariously contradictory Laura of Austen's youthful masterpiece *Love and Friendship*. The next scene prolongs this romantic vision of the Colonel, showing him mounting his horse in dashing hat and riding coat, taking a last look toward Marianne's bedroom window, and racing off alone in quest of Mrs. Dashwood.

The affection that Hugh Grant's Edward Ferrars shows toward Elinor in the film also substantially embellishes the novel. Austen's narrator refers to but does not dramatize their "growing attachment" (*Sense* 15). The novelist did not indulge in depictions of hero and heroine falling in love for crucial reasons. First, Austen presents the relationship of Elinor and Edward as one which, however strong their feelings, is conducted with a quiet decorum that surprises her mother and sister and is not, if we can be guided by their reactions, evocative for onlookers. Second, as Edward is already engaged, his affection for Elinor is tinged with guilt and the knowledge that his feelings are hopeless. In the early scenes at Norland Park and during his visit to Barton Cottage (not presented in the film), Austen prefers to focus on his consequent bouts of dejection, perhaps as a way of dealing with the dubious moral stance of a suitor already promised to someone else. The film compensates for Edward's shaky morality by showing him to be sympathetic not only to a family of grieving women, particularly the youngest, Margaret, but to the plight of genteel women in general. That portrait enables the film's indulgence in conventional scenes of courtship, dramatizing Edward's pleasure in looking at Elinor and feeling her gaze upon him, the intimacy of their conversations, and the moments of subtle physical contact, as when he retrieves the end of her shawl and places it around her again.

*   *   *

Consistent with their focus on the romantic couple, the films of *Sense and Sensibility* and *Emma* thin out and underpopulate the social world. Sir John Middleton is made a childless widower in Thompson's screenplay. The vulgar Lucy Steele no longer has an even more vulgar sister. * * * Austen's works have engaged successive generations of readers because of their interpretive richness. None is reducible to a single, simple portrait of courtship (whether or not it is harlequinized). Indeed, many critics have argued that Jane Austen's representations of women challenge the dominance and centrality of the courtship plot. * * * Feminist and nonfeminist critics alike have been known to applaud Marianne's passionate vitality and independence, preferring it to Elinor's self-suppression. Marianne's champions have generally charged her creator with "betraying" her by marrying her off to the drab Colonel Brandon at the novel's conclusion.[7]

Critics have also argued that, in several of the novels, the friendships of the women characters with one another are at least as important as their relationships with male characters. * * * Some critics have also maintained that the strength of Marianne and Elinor's attachment to one another sometimes seems to overshadow *Sense and Sensibility*'s courtship plot.

In finding profoundly rendered relationships among women in Austen's novels, critics such as Susan Lanser and Ruth Perry have suggested that Austen was not genuinely committed to the courtship plots that structure her novels.[8] My own book, *Jane Austen among Women,* suggests that Austen's attitude toward and treatment of the courtship plot was more equivocal. It shows the basis in the author's life for her fictional representations of women's loving ties, maintaining that without the support of her sister, Cassandra, and a handful of other female kin and friends, Jane Austen could not have become a novelist. But it suggests that Austen was also sincerely attached to the larger culture of the gentry and specifically to its high valuation of marriage and family life. Hence, *Jane Austen among Women* argues that Austen's novels both endorse and subtly challenge the courtship plot's emphasis on heterosexual romance. Indeed, at least in part it is because they are equivocal that so many diverse interpretations have been and will continue to be generated about the six novels.

Neither of the recent films suggests that female friendships are sufficient to sustain an alternative emotional life for heroines without men. Emma's intense focus on and feelings for Harriet Smith are not given much weight in the film. She and Harriet are "girl-

---

7. See, for example, Kirkham (87) and Tanner (100–2).
8. Numerous critics have argued that Austen treats the conventions of the courtship plot ironically and wants her reader, in effect, to read against the grain. See for example, Booth, "Emma."

friends" in a modern, trivialized sense, talking about boys or playing with puppies. The film also considerably reduces representations of not only her contacts with but also her thoughts about Jane Fairfax. The presentation of women's relationships is more complex in *Sense and Sensibility*. The filmmakers were concerned that the film not seem to be about "a couple of women waiting around for men,"[9] and so they did emphasize the relationship between Elinor and Marianne.

An early scene in Barton Cottage, invented for the film, illustrates both the discomforts of the Dashwoods' new home and the daily, ongoing intimacy of the sisters. The scene shows Elinor laying another blanket on the bed with Marianne in their small room. She then wraps a shawl around her nightgown, blows out the candle, and seeks the warmth of the bedcovers and Marianne's body heat —only to be greeted by Marianne's complaint that her feet are cold. Elinor jumps out of bed, grabs some stockings, and returns to put them on. The intensity of their bond is also dramatized. At the height of Marianne's illness, Elinor leans over her unconscious sister, runs a hand slowly up the sheet covering her left leg and, in tears, pleads with her: "I cannot do without you. Oh, please, I have tried to bear everything else—I will try—but please, dearest, beloved Marianne, do not leave me alone" (Thompson 184). Although such scenes convey the importance of this relationship, they compete with and are ultimately trumped by other invented scenes between Marianne and Colonel Brandon, His day-to-day presence in Marianne's life is embellished by scenes such as that in which he offers her a knife with which to cut reeds, and her growing love for him is established in one of the film's last scenes, in which he reads to her on the lawn in front of Barton Cottage. Readers who have felt that in marrying Marianne off to the Colonel, Austen was "betraying" her character must surely be placated by this scene and by Rickman's interpretation of this suitor in general. The films of both *Sense and Sensibility* and *Emma* assert not just the appropriateness but also the romantic pleasure of their heroines' marriages.

The recent films of Jane Austen's novels have increased sales of her books. But those who read as well as buy are going to discover that her books are not harlequinized. When they encounter Edward Ferrars's silent despondency and Mr. Knightley's cool sternness, the constant noisy intrusiveness of the Dashwoods' social circle and the loneliness and solitude threatening Emma, and always the self-discipline required for the good manners Jane Austen advocates—

9. Lindsay Dovan, "Introduction" to Emma Thompson, *The Sense and Sensibility Screenplay and Diaries*, rev. ed. (New York: Newmarket, 1996), p. 14.

will they continue to be enthusiastic about the novelist? We can hope that if some new readers are first escorted to the novels by Jeremy Northam and Alan Rickman, they will stay to appreciate the encounters the books stage between wishes and deeds, glorious dreams and mundane material constraints, and, most of all, simple certainties and interpretive ambiguity.

Jane Austen: A Chronology†

1775	Jane Austen born, December 16, at Steventon, Hampshire, the seventh of eight children of the Rev. George Austen. George III is on the throne of England.
1784	Formal education ends at age 9, at school in Reading.
1789–91	Between the ages of 14 and 16, she writes a novel called "Love and Friendship," a "History of England," and stories called "Lesley Castle" and "A Collection of Letters."
1793–96	Writes "Lady Susan" and "Elinor and Marianne," the earliest version of *Sense and Sensibility*.
1797	Writes "First Impressions," the earliest version of *Pride and Prejudice*.
1797–98	Rewrites "Elinor and Marianne" as *Sense and Sensibility* (which remains unpublished until 1811).
1798–99	Writes *Susan* (an early version of *Northanger Abbey*).
1801	Austen family moves to Bath.
1803	Sells *Susan* to Crosby of London for publication.
1804	Writes *The Watsons*.
1805	Her father dies. The following year, Jane, Cassandra, and their mother move to Southhampton.
1809	They move to Chawton Cottage in Hampshire. Austen resumes interest in publication.
1810–11	Begins revising "Elinor and Marianne" into *Sense and Sensibility*, and "First Impressions" into *Pride and Prejudice*.
1811–20	The Regency: George, Prince of Wales—who would become an admirer of Austen's novels—takes over the powers of George III, who lives on until 1820.
1813	*Pride and Prejudice* published.
1814	Writes *Emma* and publishes *Mansfield Park*.
1815	Writes *Persuasion*.
1816	*Emma* published, dedicated to Prince Regent. Buys back *Susan* and revises as *Northanger Abbey*.

† From Jane Austen, *Persuasion: A Norton Critical Edition*, edited by Patricia Meyer Spacks (New York: Norton, 1995). Reprinted by permission of Patricia Meyer Spacks and W. W. Norton & Company, Inc.

1817   Jane Austen dies at the age of 42 in Winchester, of Addison's disease, leaving "Sanditon," an unfinished novel.

1818   *Northanger Abbey* and *Persuasion* published, again anonymously.

Selected Bibliography

JANE AUSTEN'S WRITINGS

The Novels of Jane Austen. Ed. R. W. Chapman. 5 vols. 3rd ed. London: Oxford UP, 1932–34.
Minor Works. Ed. R. W. Chapman. Vol. 6 of *The Novels of Jane Austen.* London: Oxford UP, 1954.
Jane Austen's Letters. 3rd ed. Ed. Deirdre Le Faye. Oxford: Oxford UP, 1995.
Sense and Sensibility. Ed. and with an introduction by Tony Tanner. Harmondsworth: Penguin, 1969.
Sense and Sensibility. Ed. and with an introduction by Margaret Doody. Oxford: Oxford World Classics, 1990.

BIOGRAPHICAL AND CRITICAL STUDIES

• indicates works included or excerpted in this Norton Critical Edition.

Austen-Leigh, J. E. *A Memoir of Jane Austen.* London, 1870.
Austen-Leigh, W., and R. A. *Jane Austen: A Family Record.* Rev. and enl. by Deirdre Le Faye. London: The British Library, 1989.
Amis, Kingsley. "What Became of Jane Austen?" *Spectator* 199 (1957): 439–40.
• Armstrong, Isobel. *Jane Austen: "Sense and Sensibility."* Harmondsworth: Penguin, 1993.
Armstrong, Nancy. *Desire and Domestic Fiction: A Political History of the Novel.* New York and London: Oxford UP, 1987.
Benedict, Barbara M. "Jane Austen's *Sense and Sensibility*: The Politics of Point of View." *Philological Quarterly* 69.4 (Fall 1990): 453–70.
Boyd, Zelda. "The Language of Supposing: Modal Auxilliaries in *Sense and Sensibility.*" *Women and Literature* 3 (1983): 142–54.
Bradbrook, Frank W. *Jane Austen and Her Predecessors.* Cambridge: Cambridge UP, 1966.
Brissenden, R. F. "The Task of Telling Lies: Candor and Deception in *Sense and Sensibility.*" In Paul J. Korshin and Robert R. Allen, eds., *Greene Centennial Studies: Essays Presented to Donald Greene in the Centennial Year of the University of Southern California.* Charlottesville: UP of Virginia, 1984. 442–57.
Brown, Julia Prewitt. *Jane Austen's Novels: Social Change and Literary Form.* Cambridge: Harvard UP, 1979.
———. *A Reader's Guide to the Nineteenth-Century English Novel.* London: Macmillan, 1985.
Brown, Lloyd. *Bits of Ivory: Narrative Techniques in Jane Austen's Fiction.* Baton Rouge: Louisiana State UP, 1973.
Burrows, J. F. *Computation into Criticism: A Study of Jane Austen's Novels and an Experiment in Method.* Oxford: Clarendon, 1987.
• Butler, Marilyn. *Jane Austen and the War of Ideas.* Oxford: Clarendon, 1975. Rpt. with new introduction, 1990.
———. *Romantics, Rebels, and Reactionaries: English Literature and Its Backgrounds, 1760–1830.* Oxford: Oxford UP, 1981.
———. "Disregarded Designs: Jane Austen's Sense of the Volume." In David Monaghan, ed., *Jane Austen in a Social Context.* Totowa, NJ: Barnes & Noble, 1981. 49–65.
Chandler, James K. *Wordsworth's Second Nature: A Study of Poetry and Politics.* Chicago: U of Chicago P, 1984.
Clark, Robert, ed. *"Sense and Sensibility" and "Pride and Prejudice."* Jane Austen, New Casebooks. New York: St. Martin's, 1994.

Conger, Syndy McMillen. "Austen's Sense and Radcliffe's Sensibility." *Gothic* 2 (1987): 16–24.

Copeland, Edward. *Women Writing about Money: Women's Fiction in England, 1790–1820.* Cambridge: Cambridge UP, 1995.

———, and Juliet McMaster, eds. *The Cambridge Companion to Jane Austen.* Cambridge: Cambridge UP, 1997.

Devlin, David. *Jane Austen and Education.* Totowa, NJ: Barnes & Noble, 1975.

Duckworth, Alistair M. *The Improvement of the Estate: A Study of Jane Austen's Novels.* Baltimore, MD: Johns Hopkins UP, 1971.

Easton, Celia A. "*Sense and Sensibility* and the Joke of Substitution." *Journal of Narrative Technique* 23.2 (Spring 1993): 114–26.

Empson, William. *Structure of Complex Words.* New York: New Directions, 1951.

English Barbara, and Saville, John. *Strict Settlement: A Guide for Historians.* Hull: U of Hull P, 1983.

Evans, Mary. *Jane Austen and the State.* London: Tavistock Publications, 1987.

• Farrar, Reginald. "Jane Austen." *Quarterly Review* (July 1917).

• Favret, Mary. *Romantic Correspondence: Women, Politics, and the Fiction of Letters.* Cambridge: Cambridge UP, 1993.

• Fergus, Jan S. *Jane Austen: A Literary Life.* London: Macmillan; New York: St. Martin's, 1991.

———. *Jane Austen and the Didactic Novel: "Northanger Abbey," "Sense and Sensibility," and "Pride and Prejudice".* London: Macmillan; Totowa, NJ: Barnes & Noble, 1983.

Gaull, Marilyn. *English Romanticism.* New York: Norton, 1988.

Gard, Roger. *Jane Austen's Novels: The Art of Clarity.* New Haven, CT: Yale UP, 1992.

Gilbert, Sandra M., and Susan Gubar. *The Madwoman in the Attic: The Woman Writer and the Nineteenth-Century Literary Imagination.* New Haven, CT: Yale UP, 1979.

Gilson, David. *A Bibliography of Jane Austen.* Oxford: Clarendon P, 1948.

Grey, J. David, ed. *The Jane Austen Companion.* New York: Macmillan, 1986.

Gunther, Mark. "Alas, Poor Son." *Fortune* 30 Sept. 1996: 128–34.

Haggerty, George E. "The Sacrifice of Privacy in *Sense and Sensibility.*" *Tulsa Studies in Women's Literature* 7.2 (Fall 1988): 221–37.

Halperin, John, ed. *Jane Austen: Bicentenary Essays.* Cambridge: Cambridge UP, 1975.

Harding, D. W. "Regulated Hatred: An Aspect of the Work of Jane Austen." *Scrutiny* 8 (1940): 346–62.

Hardwick, Michael. *A Guide to Jane Austen/The Osprey Guide to Jane Austen.* New York: Scribner, 1973.

Hardy, Barbara Nathan. *A Reading of Jane Austen.* London: Owen, 1975.

Harris, Jocelyn. *Jane Austen's Art of Memory.* Cambridge: Cambridge UP, 1989.

Heath, William, ed. *Discussions of Jane Austen.* Boston: Heath, 1961.

Heldman, James. "How Wealthy Is Mr. Darcy—Really? Pounds and Dollars in the World of *Pride and Prejudice.*" *Persuasions: Journal of the Jane Austen Society of North America* (Dec. 1990): 38–49.

Honan, Park. *Jane Austen: Her Life.* London: Weidenfeld and Nicholson, 1987.

Jenkins, Elizabeth. *Jane Austen: A Biography.* London: Gollancz, 1939.

• Johnson, Claudia L. *Jane Austen: Women, Politics, and the Novel.* Chicago: U of Chicago P, 1988.

———. "A 'Sweet Face as White as Death': Jane Austen and the Politics of Female Sensibility." *Novel: A Forum on Fiction* 22.2 (Winter 1989): 159–74.

———. *Equivocal Beings: Politics, Gender, and Sentimentality in the 1790s: Wollstonecraft, Radcliffe, Burney, Austen.* Chicago: U of Chicago P, 1995.

Kaplan, Deborah. *Jane Austen among Women.* Baltimore, MD: Johns Hopkins UP, 1992.

Kaplan, Laurie, and Richard S. Kaplan. "What Is Wrong with Marianne? Medicine and Disease in Jane Austen's England." *Persuasions: Journal of the Jane Austen Society of North America* (Dec. 1990): 117–30.

Kestner, Joseph. "Jane Austen: The Tradition of the English Romantic Novel, 1800–1832." *Wordsworth Circle* 7 (1976): 297–311.

Kirkham, Margaret. *Jane Austen, Feminism and Fiction.* Totowa, NJ: Barnes & Noble, 1983.

Koppel, Gene. *The Religious Dimension of Jane Austen's Novels.* Ann Arbor, MI: UMI Research P, 1988. Lascelles, Mary. *Jane Austen and Her Art.* Oxford: Oxford UP, 1939.

Kaufmann, David. "Law and Propriety, *Sense and Sensibility*: Austen on the Cusp of Modernity." *ELH* 59.2 (Summer 1992): 385–408.

Kent, Christopher. "Learning History with, and from, Jane Austen." In J. David Grey, ed., *Jane Austen's Beginnings: The Juvenilia and "Lady Susan."* Ann Arbor, MI: UMI Research P, 1989.

Kroeber, Karl. *Styles in Fictional Structures: The Art of Jane Austen, Charlotte Brontë, and George Eliot.* Princeton, NJ: Princeton UP, 1971.

———. "Jane Austen as an Historical Novelist: *Sense and Sensibility*." *Persuasions: Journal of the Jane Austen Society of North America* (Dec. 1990): 10–18.
Leighton, Angela. "Sense and Silences: Reading Jane Austen Again." *Women and Literature* (1983): 128–41.
Litz, A. Walton. *Jane Austen: A Study of Her Artistic Development*. New York: Oxford UP, 1965.
Looser, Devoney, ed. *Jane Austen and Discourses of Feminism*. New York: St. Martin's, 1995.
• Lynch, Deidre Shauna. *The Economy of Character: Novels, Market Culture, and the Business of Inner Meaning*. Chicago: U of Chicago P, 1998.
MacDonagh, Oliver. *Jane Austen: Real and Imagined Worlds*. New Haven, CT: Yale UP, 1991.
McGann, Jerome J. *The Romantic Ideology*. Chicago: U of Chicago P, 1983.
McMaster, Juliet. *Jane Austen on Love*. Victoria: U of Victoria P, 1978.
Menand, Louis. "Hollywood's Trap." *New York Review of Books* 19 Sept. 1996: 4–6.
———. *Jane Austen the Novelist*. New York: St. Martin's, 1996.
———, ed. *Jane Austen's Achievement*. London: Macmillan, 1973.
———, and Bruce Stovel, eds. *Jane Austen's Business: Her World and Her Profession*. London: Macmillan, 1996.
• Meynell, Alice. "The Classic Novelist." In *The Second Person Singular*. London: Oxford UP, 1922. 62–67.
Miller, D. A. *Narrative and Its Discontents: Problems of Closure in the Traditional Novel*. Princeton, NJ: Princeton UP, 1981.
———. "The Late Jane Austen." *Raritan: A Quarterly Review* 10.1 (Summer 1990): 55–79.
———. "Austen's attitude." *Yale Journal of Criticism* 8 (Spring 1995): 1–5.
Moffat, Wendy. "Identifying with Emma: Some Problems for the Feminist Reader." *College English* 53 (1991): 45–59.
Moler, Kenneth L. *Jane Austen's Art of Allusion*. Lincoln: U of Nebraska P, 1968.
Mooneyham, Laura. *Romance, Language and Education in Jane Austen's Novels*. London: Macmillan; Totowa: Barnes & Noble, 1988.
Monaghan, David, ed. *Jane Austen in a Social Context*. London: Macmillan; Totowa, NJ: Barnes & Noble, 1981.
———. *Jane Austen, Structure and Social Vision*. London: Macmillan, 1980.
Morgan, Susan. *In the Meantime: Character and Perception in Jane Austen's Fiction*. Chicago: U of Chicago P, 1980.
Mudrick, Marvin. *Jane Austen: Irony as Defense and Discovery*. Princeton: Princeton UP, 1952.
Nardin, Jane. *Those Elegant Decorums: The Concept of Propriety in Jane Austen's Novels*. Albany: State U of New York P, 1973.
Page, Norman. *The Language of Jane Austen*. Oxford: Blackwell, 1972.
Perkins, Moreland. *Reshaping the Sexes in "Sense and Sensibility."* Charlottesville: UP of Virginia, 1998.
Phillips, K. C. *Jane Austen's English*. London: André Deutsch, 1970.
• Poovey, Mary. *The Proper Lady and the Woman Writer: Ideology as Style in the Works of Mary Wollstonecraft, Mary Shelley, and Jane Austen*. Chicago: U of Chicago P, 1984.
Radway, Janice. *Reading the Romance: Women, Patriarchy, and Popular Literature*. Chapel Hill: U of North Carolina P, 1984.
Roth, Barry. *An Annotated Bibliography of Jane Austen Studies, 1973–83*. Charlottesville: UP of Virginia, 1985.
———. *An Annotated Bibliography of Jane Austen Studies, 1984–94*. Athens: Ohio UP, 1996.
———, and Joel Weinsheimer. *An Annotated Bibliography of Jane Austen Studies, 1952–1972*. Charlottesville: UP of Virginia, 1973.
• Ruoff, Gene W. *Jane Austen's "Sense and Sensibility."* New York: St. Martin's; London: Harvester Wheatsheaf, 1992.
———. "1800 and the Future of the Novel: William Wordsworth, Maria Edgeworth, and the Vagaries of Literary History." In *The Age of William Wordsworth: Critical Essays on the Romantic Tradition*. Ed. Kenneth R. Johnston and Gene W. Ruoff. New Brunswick: Rutgers UP, 1987. 291–314.
Saisselin, Remy G. "The Man of Taste as Social Model, or, *Sense and Sensibility*." In Carré, Jacques, ed. *The Crisis of Courtesy: Studies in the Conduct-Book in Britain, 1600–1900*. New York: Brill, 1994.
• Sedgwick, Eve Kosofsky. "Jane Austen and the Masturbating Girl." In *Tendencies*. Durham, NC: Duke UP, 1993. 113–26.
Southam, B. C. *Jane Austen's Literary Manuscripts*. London: Oxford UP, 1964.
———, ed. *Critical Essays on Jane Austen*. London: Routledge, 1968.

———, ed. *Jane Austen: The Critical Heritage*. Vol. 1. London: Routledge, 1968.

———, ed. *Jane Austen: "Sense and Sensibility," "Pride and Prejudice," and "Mansfield Park": A Casebook*. London: Macmillan, 1976.

———, ed. *Jane Austen: The Critical Heritage: 1870–1940*. Vol. 2. London and New York: Routledge, 1987.

• Spacks, Patricia Meyer. *Desire and Truth: Functions of Plot in Eighteenth-Century English Novels*. Chicago: U of Chicago P, 1990.

Spring, David. "Interpreters of Jane Austen's Social World: Literary Critics and Historians." *Women and Literature* (1983): 53–72.

Stewart, Brian. "The Picturesque Ideal." In *The Smith Brothers of Chichester*. Chichester: The Pallant House Gallery Exhibition Catalogue, 1986, 49–553.

———, and Mervyn Cutten. *The Shayer Family of Painters*. London: F. Lewis, 1982.

Stewart, Maaja. *Domestic Realities and Imperial Fictions: Jane Austen's Novels in Eighteenth-Century Contexts*. Athens: U of Georgia P, 1993.

Stone, Lawrence. *The Family, Sex and Marriage in England, 1500–1800*. Abr. ed. New York: Harper & Row, 1979.

Sulloway, Alison. *Jane Austen and the Province of Womanhood*. Philadelphia: U of Pennsylvania P, 1989.

Tanner, Tony. *Jane Austen*. Cambridge: Harvard UP, 1986.

Tave, Stuart. *Some Words of Jane Austen*. Chicago: U of Chicago P, 1973.

Thompson, James. *Between Self and World: The Novels of Jane Austen*. University Park: Pennsylvania State UP, 1988.

Todd, Janet, ed. *Jane Austen: New Perspectives. Women & Literature*. N.s. no. 3. New York: Holmes & Meier, 1983.

———. "Jane Austen, Politics and Sensibility." In Susan Sellers, Linda Hutcheon, and Paul Perron, eds., *Feminist Criticism: Theory and Practice*. Toronto: U of Toronto P, 1991. 71–87.

• Troost, Linda, and Sayre Greenfield, eds. *Jane Austen in Hollywood*. Lexington: UP of Kentucky, 1998.

Tucker, George Holbert. *A Goodly Heritage: A History of Jane Austen's Family*. Manchester: Carcanet New Press, 1983.

———. *Jane Austen: The Woman: Some Biographical Insights*. New York: St. Martin's, 1994.

Wallace, Tara Ghoshal. *Jane Austen and Narrative Authority*. New York: St. Martin's, 1995.

Watt, Ian, ed. *Jane Austen: A Collection of Critical Essays*. Englewood Cliffs, NJ: Prentice-Hall, 1963.

Wiesenfarth, John. *The Errand of Form*. New York: Fordham UP, 1967.

• Williams, Raymond. *Keywords: A Vocabulary of Culture and Society*. Rev. ed. New York: Oxford UP, 1983.

Wilson, Edmund. "A Long Talk about Jane Austen." In *Classics and Commercials*. New York: Farrar, 1950. 196–203.

Wiltshire, John. *Jane Austen and the Body: "The Picture of Health."* Cambridge: Cambridge UP, 1992.